International Business Strategy

Verbeke provides a new perspective on international business strategy by combining analytical rigour and true managerial insight on the functioning of large multinational enterprises (MNEs). With unique commentary on forty-eight seminal articles published in the *Harvard Business Review*, *Sloan Management Review* and *California Management Review* over the past three decades, Verbeke shows how these can be applied to real businesses engaged in international expansion programmes, especially as they venture into high-distance markets. The second edition has been thoroughly updated and features greater coverage of emerging markets with a new chapter and seven new cases. Suited for advanced undergraduates and graduate courses, students will benefit from updated case studies and improved learning features including 'management takeaways', key lessons that can be applied to MNEs and a wide range of online resources.

'Two things make Alain Verbeke's book stand out from other textbooks. First, it incorporates the latest theoretical insights and helps students to understand the complexities of international business in the real world. Second, it is truly integrative, presenting a framework in the first half of the book that is consistently used in all subsequent chapters and applications.'

Sjoerd Beugelsdijk, Professor of International Business, University of Groningen, The Netherlands

'This is a most impressive textbook which effortlessly blends analytical depth, strategic problem-solving skills and vivid engagement with the most challenging international contexts. Having long searched in vain for such a three-dimensional textbook, I believe it is one of a kind. Alain Verbeke has pulled off one of the hardest feats in management education.'

Manuel Hensman, Professor of Strategic Management, Solvay Brussels School of Economics and Management, Belgium

From 1st edition: 'Alain Verbeke draws on his unmatched knowledge of international business research and provides a fresh and insightful, integrated perspective for rethinking the foundations of international strategy. This highly readable text supported by excellent cases should appeal to students whose managerial careers will span an increasingly global economy. International strategy faculty will find that the text easily lends itself to customizing the course to their particular needs. This book deepens our understanding of the global economy and the evolving role of the multinational enterprise.'

Arie Y. Lewin, Professor of Strategy and Sociology, The Fuqua School of Business, Duke University, and Editor-in-Chief of the *Journal of International Business Studies* (2002–7)

'Being the first of its kind, this insightful textbook not only describes the main academic insights relevant to international business strategy, but also rigorously scrutinizes and reinterprets them using an overarching yet simple framework composed of country, firm, and individual-level concepts. By taking this reflective and integrative approach, Verbeke offers an unprecedented learning experience to both students and practitioners by greatly enhancing their understanding of successful international strategy formulation and implementation.'

Arjen Slangen, Associate Professor of International Business, Rotterdam School of Management, The Netherlands

International Business Strategy

Rethinking the Foundations of Global Corporate Success

Second Edition

ALAIN VERBEKE

CAMBRIDGE UNIVERSITY PRESS
Cambridge, New York, Melbourne, Madrid, Cape Town,
Singapore, São Paulo, Delhi, Mexico City

Cambridge University Press
The Edinburgh Building, Cambridge CB2 8RU, UK

Published in the United States of America by Cambridge University Press, New York

www.cambridge.org
Information on this title: www.cambridge.org/9781107683099

First published 2013

Printed and bound in the United Kingdom by the MPG Books Group

A catalogue record for this publication is available from the British Library

Library of Congress Cataloguing in Publication data
Verbeke, Alain, author.
International business strategy : rethinking the foundations of global corporate
success / Alain Verbeke. – Second edition.
    pages   cm
ISBN 978-1-107-68309-9 (pbk.)
1. International business enterprises – Management.   2. International business
enterprises – Management – Case studies.   3. Strategic planning.   4. Strategic planning – Case
studies.   I. Title.
HD62.4.V466   2013
658.4′092–dc23   2012033810

ISBN 978-1-107-02789-3 Hardback
ISBN 978-1-107-68309-9 Paperback

Additional resources for this publication at www.cambridge.org/verbeke

Contents

Figures

Case studies

About the author

Dr Alain Verbeke is an Elected Fellow of the Academy of International Business and former Editor of the *Journal of International Business Studies* (Area Multinational Enterprise Theory and International Strategy). He is an Academic Associate of the Centre for International Business and Management, Judge Business School, University of Cambridge (UK).

Dr Verbeke holds the McCaig Research Chair in Management at the Haskayne School of Business, University of Calgary (Canada). He was previously the Director of the MBA programme, Solvay Business School, University of Brussels (VUB, Belgium). He has also been a Visiting Professor at Dalhousie University (Canada), the University of Toronto (Canada) and the Université Catholique de Louvain (Belgium), as well as an Associate Fellow of Templeton College, University of Oxford (UK).

Dr Verbeke has consulted widely for a variety of firms and public agencies, evaluating large-scale, strategic investment projects and restructuring programmes. His research and advisory work has involved numerous large multinational enterprises from Europe, North America and Asia. He has particular expertise in the linkages between multinational enterprise corporate headquarters and foreign affiliates.

Foreword

Too many international business strategy textbooks slavishly adhere to mainstream conceptual models. The publication of those models in prestigious practitioner journals such as the *Harvard Business Review* seems to shelter them from scholarly criticism. The problem is that the policy recommendations derived from these models, while sometimes insightful, are all too often based on implicit and restrictive assumptions. They are frequently oversimplified and seldom based on a rigorous analytical framework that assesses the opportunity costs of following the recommended paths, that is the costs of foregoing alternative strategies.

In this textbook of unusual depth and scope, Alain Verbeke provides a critical reassessment of Theodore Levitt's famous edicts on global marketing, Michael Porter's diamond, Prahalad and Hamel's core competence, Bartlett and Ghoshal's transnational solution, and many other conceptual models that have until now been treated as almost sacrosanct. These mainstream views are not analysed in isolation, but systematically within the context of a simple but insightful conceptual framework, which synthesizes several decades of scholarly research on multinational enterprise strategy.

In addition to solid conceptual foundations, this book provides a rich empirical background. Every concept is illustrated with examples drawn from actual managerial practice. The tight link between theory and practice makes for a powerful intellectual toolkit, which can be directly used by senior managers as they weigh alternative global strategies.

As a scholar engaged in the comparative institutional analysis of multinational enterprises, I am struck by the ad hoc quality of much of the advice offered to senior managers. Too often such advice makes short shrift of the considerable body of theoretical insights and empirical evidence that has been amassed by international business researchers over the last decades. Not so with this book which shows, once again, that 'nothing is more practical than a good theory'.

Jean-François Hennart
Fellow of the Academy of International Business
Professor of International Management
Tilburg University
The Netherlands

Acknowledgements

It has been a privilege to work on the second edition of this book with Paula Parish, Editor and Josephine Lane, Assistant Editor at Cambridge University Press. I would not have been able to complete the work without the extraordinary help of Jenny Hillemann.

I am pleased to acknowledge the generous financial support of the McCaig family in Calgary, Canada. Their leadership in funding the McCaig Research Chair in Management allowed me to write this textbook. I have also received valuable financial support from the Social Sciences and Humanities Research Council (SSHRC) in Canada and, earlier, from the Geconcerteerde Onderzoeksactie (GOA) at the University of Brussels (VUB), Belgium.

Denise Larsen, Jill Thorlacius and Amin Zargarzadeh provided fine research assistance for this second edition. Intellectual exchanges with Sjoerd Beugelsdijk, Markus Nordberg, Christos Pitelis, Bob Schulz, Paul Beamish, John Cantwell, Shih-Fen Chen, Anthony Goerzen, Birgitte Grøgaard, Liena Kano, Ans Kolk, Sarianna Lundan, Anoop Madhok, Hemant Merchant, Ravi Ramamurti, Peter Sherer, Steven Tallman, Ilan Vertinsky, Bernard Wolf, Bernard Yeung and George Yip helped me refine various components of the manuscript.

With pride, I acknowledge my former student and friend, Wenlong Yuan, whose assistance has been invaluable. He co-drafted most of the cases in the book's first edition, and provided substantive comments on the manuscript throughout the writing process.

Sjoerd Beugelsdijk, a well-known business scholar, developed a substantial body of excellent online materials while using the book at the University of Groningen in the Netherlands. I am very grateful to him for making these available to other instructors adopting the book.

With abiding gratitude, I acknowledge my colleagues in international business, whose ideas have inspired the concepts developed throughout the text. First, my friend and mentor, Alan Rugman, with whom I have worked for twenty-five years. Second, the late John Dunning, Peter Buckley, Mark Casson, Jean-François Hennart, Julian Birkinshaw and the late Sumantra Ghoshal, whose brilliant conceptual ideas have greatly influenced my own thinking and writing on international business strategy. Third, my colleagues, Jean Boddewyn, Lorraine Eden, Arie Lewin, Klaus Macharzina and Daniel Van Den Bulcke, from whom I have learned much about collegiality, inclusion and institution building in the field of international business.

I should also like to acknowledge the hundreds of senior managers from around the globe who shared with me their insight and dreams of international growth for the companies they cherish.

Finally, I thank my wife and our children for their patient support. In particular, I am grateful to Sophie-Charlotte for her eager solidarity. When drafting the book's initial version, she sat shoulder to shoulder with me watching *Dora, the Explorer*. Embarked on separate adventures, we happily travelled together.

Calgary

Abbreviations

3M	Minnesota Mining and Manufacturing Company
AB	Anheuser Busch
A&C	Automation and control
AAFLI	Asian-American Free Labor Institute
AAU	American Asiatic Underwriters
ACLA	Acer Computec Latino America
AIA	American International Assurance
AIG	American International Group
Ambev	Companhia de bebidas das Américas
APEAL	Automotive performance, execution and layout
ARIS	Architecture of integrated information systems
ASAs	Alliance-specific advantages
ATM	Automated teller machines
BEF	Brightness enhancement film
BFW	Bayerische Flugzeugwcrke
BLMC	British Leyland Motor Corporation
BMW	Bayerische Motoren Werke
BP	Best position, best practice, and best performance
BP	British Petroleum
BPI	Beauté Prestige International
BRIC	Brazil, Russia, India and China
BSN	Boussois-Souchon-Neuvesel
C&C	Computers and communications
CAD	Computer-aided design
CAM	Computer-aided manufacturing
CCC	China customer centre
CD	Compact disk
CEO	Chief executive officer
CMD	Committee of Managing Directors
CMR	*California Management Review*
CNOOC	China National Offshore Oil Corporation
CNPC	China National Petroleum Company
CSR	Corporate social responsibility
CT	Corporate technology

CTO	Chief technology officer
CVCC	Controlled vortex combustion chamber
DEC	Digital Equipment Corporation
DGC	Data General Corp.
DM	Deutsche Mark
EBC	European business centre
EDC	European distribution centres
EDLP	Every day low price
EMNEs	Emerging economy multinational enterprises
EMS	Electronics manufacturing service
ERP	Enterprise resource planning
FAA	Federal Aviation Administration
FDI	Foreign direct investment
FLA	Fair Labor Association
FMS	Flexible manufacturing systems
FSA	Firm-specific advantage
GCI	Global competitiveness index
GDP	Gross domestic product
GE	General Electric
GM	General Motors
GMS	Global manufacturing system
GNPOC	Greater Nile Petroleum Operating Company
GOS	Government of Sudan
GTF	Global technology fields
H&C	Harrisons & Crosfields
HAM	Honda of America manufacturing
HBR	*Harvard Business Review*
HBS	Harvard Business School
HP	Hewlett-Packard
HPs	High potentials
HR	Human resources
HTML	Hyper text mock-up language
HTTP	Hyper text transfer protocol
I&C	Information and communication
IBM	International Business Machines
ICJ	International Court of Justice
ICT	Information communication technology
IE	Instrumentation Engineering, Inc.
IPO	Initial public offering
IPR	Intellectual property rights
IT	Information technology

JIT	Just-in-time
JV	Joint venture
KFC	Kentucky Fried Chicken
LA	Location advantages
LB	Location-bound
LCD	Liquid crystal display
LNG	Liquefied natural gas
LSID	Lake Stevens Instrument Division
LVMH	Moët Hennessy Louis Vuitton
M&As	Mergers and acquisitions
MBA	Master of Business Administration
MCM	Multi-chip module
MFA	Multifiber Arrangement
MIC	Market information centre
MIT	Massachusetts Institute of Technology
MNE	Multinational enterprise
NAFTA	North-American Free Trade Agreement
NAO	North American operations
NASDAQ	National Association of Securities Dealers Automated Quotations
NCR	National Cash Register
NDG	Nippon Data General Corporation
NEC	Nippon Electric Company
NGO	Non-governmental organization
NIOC	National Iranian Oil Company
NLB	Non-location-bound
NMC	Nippon Mini Computer Corporation
NPPC	Nestlé Purina PetCare
NUMMI	New United Motor Manufacturing Inc.
NYSE	New York Stock Exchange
ODM	Original design manufacturing
OEM	Original equipment manufacturing
OMR	Organizational and management review
P&G	Procter & Gamble
PC	Personal computer
PCB	Printed circuit boards
PCBA	Printed circuit board assemblies
PICC	People's Insurance Company of China
PTH	Pin-through-hole
R&D	Research and development
RMB	Renminbi
RTUs	Remote terminal units

SAPREF	Shell African Petroleum Refinery
SBC	Sony Broadcast Limited
SBU	Strategic business unit
SCGP	Shell coal gasification process
SCR	Siemens Corporate Research
SINOPEC	China Petroleum and Chemical Corporation
SISL	Siemens Information Systems Limited
SMI	Societa Metallurgica Italiana
SMR	*Sloan Management Review*
SMT	Surface mount technology
SONAM	Sony Corporation of America
SOSA	Sony Overseas S.A.
SPDC	Shell Petroleum Development Company
SPLM	Sudanese People's Liberation Movement
SRI	Stanford Research Institute
SSAs	Subsidiary-specific advantages
SSI	Strategic sourcing initiative
SUV	Sport utility vehicle
TBT	Technical barriers to trade
TCS	Tata Consultancy Services
TKS	Time-keeping system
TPS	Toyota production system
TQM	Total quality management
TSX	Toronto Stock Exchange
TTB	Technology-to-business
UNCTAD	United Nations Conference on Trade and Development
UNCTC	United Nations Centre on Transnational Corporations
VET	Vocational education and training
VLSI	Very large scale integration
VUB	University of Brussels

(Compiled by: Charles A. Backman)

Chapter 1

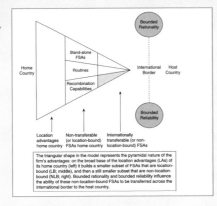

The triangular shape in the model represents the pyramidal nature of the firm's advantages: on the broad base of the location advantages (LAs) of its home country (left) it builds a smaller subset of FSAs that are location-bound (LB; middle), and then a still smaller subset that are non-location-bound (NLB; right). Bounded rationality and bounded reliability influence the ability of these non-location-bound FSAs to be transferred across the international border to the host country.

International Business Strategy presents, interprets and critiques 48 seminal articles from the *Harvard Business Review, Sloan Management Review* and *California Management Review*. It synthesizes the practical knowledge contained in these articles into a unifying framework of seven key concepts for successful global business. These concepts are analysed in detail in Chapter 1.

Case examples

Case example In 1996, Kao was Japan's largest consur the shampoo market, three quarters of the bleach marke market.

One of the main reasons for Kao's dominant dome comprehensive distribution system within Japan. Kao own which distributed only Kao's products. As a result, Kao was also prevent outsiders from entering the market. More privileged information on consumers' shopping habits. F Kao has failed to build the comprehensive distribution sys around 20 per cent of Kao's sales came from overseas m foreign sales had risen to nearly 30 per cent, in ascendin America, Europe and Asia/Oceania. Kao has not been able abroad.[30] ∎

Case example The immobility of domestic networks lenges to many foreign retail banks in Japan, such as Citiban position in the US retail banking industry and a large netv found it difficult to access Japanese customers when it decic 1984. It took Citi-Japan a full ten years to break into the Jap "[R]etail banking . . . is like the petrol-station business: you'

Chapter 1 includes a wide range of short case examples featuring high-profile multinational firms. The case examples illustrate aspects of each of the seven key concepts of successful business strategy in practice.

Management Insight

ve see that Prahalad and Hamel's to the higher-order FSA concept, ation capabilities. Recombination nd Hamel, but, as they correctly or to deconstruct. These FSAs are : or heritage that has evolved over gredients are similar to the ones *ttitude* of senior corporate-level) identifying and pursuing new *ces that are not yet fully utilized* 1 *organizational ability* to meld

iscussed in Chapter 1, the authors gure 1.7 in Chapter 1), with core ountry (guided by corporate-level :st of the firm. Here, the firm has cross product lines and units, but abroad. The authors assume that ffective than Asian companies in ernationally transferable FSAs are eir exploitation is, unfortunately, across the company. The authors

MANAGEMENT
INSIGHTS

A rigorous and in-depth analysis of articles drawn from the leading practitioner journals. Their content is fully explored in terms of the key concepts in international business strategy, as well as recent real-world examples.

Thirty 'half-length' case studies are spread throughout the text to relate the concepts discussed to real-life examples in global business. These provide up-to-date coverage of leading firms and offer valuable material for independent or classroom study.

Case studies

Case 1.1 Honda's 'answers' to the seven basic questions in international strategy formation CASE

For the Japanese car manufacture Honda, the domestic and international environments in the early 1970s brought tremendous challenges to its export strategy, previously based on mass production in Japan. Honda wanted to develop extensive international production capabilities in overseas markets, especially the US market. However, Honda doubted its foreign manufacturing facilities could attain the quality level characteristic of its Japanese-built cars. Furthermore, Honda also wondered whether its foreign manufacturing facilities could achieve Japanese cost levels.

The environment in the early 1970s

Internationally, Honda faced three major environmental changes in the early 1970s: the rising value of the yen against the US dollar, new US regulations of tailpipe emissions and the first oil crisis. Although the rising yen threatened Honda's traditional export strategy, the other two changes – together with the success of its small, fuel-efficient Civic model in Japan and the US – provided a window of opportunity for Honda to expand in the US.

Specifically, the rising value of the yen in 1971 increased the costs of exporting cars to the US, Honda's largest overseas market. The first oil crisis of 1973 negatively affected Honda's domestic operations, as rising oil prices significantly increased Honda's manufacturing costs. At the same time, however, the public demanded more fuel-efficient cars to reduce the costs brought by the roaring oil prices.

In 1970, the US Congress passed the Clean Air Act, imposing stricter requirements on tailpipe emissions. However, the US automakers had not been able to reach a consensus regarding the appropriate technology to meet such requirements. Both the first oil crisis and the Clean Air Act pushed the demand for fuel-efficient cars, which became the market niche US automakers had not been able to occupy. Clearly, Honda viewed the US regulations as a welcome opportunity for it to catch up, as reflected in the words of Honda's President Soichiro Honda: "(T)his allows latecomers like us to line up at the same starting line as our rivals".[107]

In 1972, Honda brought to the Japanese market its Civic model with the CVCC (Controlled Vortex Combustion Chamber) engine, which met the US emissions standards. The CVCC engine permitted the regulated burning of a very lean mixture without the catalytic converter or exhaust-gas recirculation required by most other engines. In Japan, the Civic model won the Car of the Year Award for three consecutive years as of 1973; in the US, it beat all other competitors in a fuel-economy test for four consecutive years as of 1974.

Questions at the end of each case study test and reinforce the reader's knowledge and understanding of the main ideas discussed in the case.

Case questions

QUESTIONS

1. What was Four Seasons' distinct resource base, including elements of its administrative heritage, that provided internationally transferrable FSAs?
2. Which value-added activities in which foreign location(s) permitted Four Seasons to exploit and augment its distinct resource base to the fullest?
3. What were the expected costs and difficulties Four Seasons faced when transferring this distinct resource base?
4. What specific resource recombination (associated with each alternative foreign entry and operating mode) was required so as to make the proposed international value-added activities successful?
5. Did Four Seasons have the required resource recombination capability in-house?
6. What were the costs and benefits of using complementary resources of external actors to fill resource gaps?
7. What were the main bounded rationality and bounded reliability problems Four Seasons faced when extending the geographic scope of the firm's activities, given the changed boundaries of the firm, the changed linkages with outside stakeholders and the changes in its internal functioning?

Web materials

For students:

- Links to articles in *Fortune, FT*, etc., with cases that can be applied to the framework developed in the book. This set will be updated and will grow over time.
- Links to useful databases and other electronic sources of useful information relevant to international business strategy.

For lecturers:

- The answers to the case study questions (password protected).
- Downloadable PowerPoint slides for every chapter and all figures.
- Multiple choice questions to test student understanding.

Introduction and overview of the book's framework

Senior managers in multinational enterprises (MNEs) have a healthy appetite for knowledge that will improve their firm's performance. They want to know which models from the international business strategy literature can actually be applied in their own firm.

Rethinking the classics in international business strategy

Many MNE senior managers hold (or pursue) MBA or executive MBA degrees, and they certainly read whatever is of use in publications such as the *Financial Times*, the *Wall Street Journal*, *The Economist*, *Business Week* and *Fortune*. When these managers seek practical advice on improving multinational operations, however, one publication stands out: the *Harvard Business Review* (*HBR*).

For at least the past 30 years, *HBR* has published the frontier knowledge on everything that really matters to senior MNE managers. This explains why so many classroom readers include reprints of *HBR* articles, and why so many international management teachers use *HBR* articles in their classes. Apart from the *Harvard Business Review*, two other academic publications are highly relevant to managers: the *MIT Sloan Management Review* (*SMR*), published by the Massachusetts Institute of Technology (MIT), and the *California Management Review* (*CMR*), published by the Haas School of Business at the University of California at Berkeley.

The first articles on globalization and its impact on MNE strategy appeared in the early 1980s. The growing economic interdependence between nations – especially the rise of the Triad of the US, Europe and Japan (replacing post-World War II US hegemony) – drove much of this work. Since the early 1980s, *HBR* has published several outstanding and now classic research papers on how to improve MNE strategy. The two other key journals, *SMR* and *CMR*, have often published useful, complementary perspectives on the same international business subjects. Senior managers like these articles because they are well written, insightful and practical: they lead directly to improved managerial practice.[1]

Although I have used these articles with great success in my MBA and Executive MBA classes, both students and MNE senior managers have told me that they would like a general, unifying framework that managers can use to synthesize the valuable, practical knowledge that the articles contain. This book tries to provide such a framework; it is a synthesis of the best **practitioner-oriented** work in international business.[2]

Such a synthesis might seem to be an impossible task, as there are as many views on international business strategy as there are people writing about it.[3] Nevertheless, I think that most of international business strategy can be captured by just a few simple concepts. Differences among authors are usually just variations on these central themes.

The structure of the book is as follows. In Chapter 1, I lay out the main building blocks of the unifying framework used throughout the book. This framework should allow MNE senior managers to grasp the essence, in strategy terms, of what happens in a complex international business setting.

In addition to describing managers' possible strategies, the framework of Chapter 1 also makes normative suggestions about which strategies are most effective. Most notably, the framework suggests how to improve MNE performance in two areas: value creation and satisfying stakeholder goals across borders. This normative approach is warranted because many MNEs can learn substantially in the short run from best practices adopted by other companies, and in the long run only firms adopting such best practices will survive. As much as possible, I try to specify the preconditions that must be fulfilled for these specific normative suggestions to be valid, often informed by my own research and consulting experience with senior MNE managers. Insufficient specification of when particular normative suggestions will actually improve performance, and when they will not, is probably the most common criticism voiced against articles published in *HBR*, *SMR* and *CMR*. This is a trap I try to avoid in the present book.

In Chapters 2 to 16, I discuss what I consider to be the best international business articles published in *HBR*, *SMR* and *CMR* since the early 1980s, and I systematically apply the unifying framework. After starting each chapter by discussing an *HBR* article, I then extend the analysis by describing the additional insights gained from articles published in *SMR* and *CMR*. I also include in each chapter one or two short case studies (for a total of 30 in the entire book), which illustrate the main concepts developed in that chapter. Finally, I add at the end of the book, in a short appendix, a small number of references from the more academically oriented literature that I consider particularly relevant to senior managers.

I believe that this extensive use of practitioner-oriented journal articles has produced a book that is more practitioner-friendly than most of the existing books on international business strategy.

The book is divided into three parts: core concepts (Chapters 1 to 5), functional issues (Chapters 6 to 10), and the dynamics of international strategy (Chapters 11 to 16). Chapter 16 has two distinct parts. Both parts address the broader responsibilities of MNEs, beyond satisfying the demands of their three main stakeholder groups (shareholders, customers and employees). Part A addresses corporate social responsibility. Part B discusses MNE environmental sustainability. In the book's Conclusion, I briefly address a few key implications of the book's analysis for MNE managers to help them respond better to both the challenges and unprecedented opportunities of managing international operations.

This book does not limit itself to a specific country or industry context. Such context is obviously important, as suggested by the many examples from practice and the 30 case studies included in the book, but managers should be able to apply the key concepts developed in this book to a wide variety of country and industry settings.

I assume that the reader has a basic understanding of strategic management concepts as developed for domestic contexts. My purpose, however, is not simply to add an incremental 'international dimension' to the discussion of a set of conventional strategy problems. My goal is to explain what lies at the heart of a successful international business strategy, through rethinking a large number of classic articles in international management, and thereby the foundations of global corporate success.

Changes in the second edition

I have made a number of changes to the book while preparing this second edition, based on the suggestions made by senior scholars who have adopted it in their courses at leading business schools. Five changes are critical. *First*, and most importantly, I have added a *new Chapter 15* on MNEs from emerging economies, as well as five new case studies on emerging economy MNEs. *Second*, all the *case studies* from the first edition have been *updated* where relevant, and there are now *thirty cases* (up from twenty-three in the first edition). *Third*, in order to improve the book's pedagogical quality, I have added a set of *learning objectives* at the beginning of each chapter, as well as a set of *management takeaways* after each section with managerial insights. *Fourth*, the *textboxes* explaining the various figures are now included in *larger font*, thereby making these figures easier to read and to understand when shown as slides on a screen. *Fifth*, *exam materials* in the form of *multiple choice questions* will be made available to the instructors adopting the book, thereby making it easy to set up a midterm or final exam to test the class participants' knowledge of the book's materials.

Definition of international business strategy

International business strategy means effectively and efficiently matching an MNE's internal strengths (relative to competitors) with the opportunities and challenges found in geographically dispersed environments that cross international borders. Such matching is a precondition to creating value and satisfying stakeholder goals, both domestically and internationally.

The above definition focuses on the MNE, a firm with economic operations located in at least two countries. This book will also note some of the special opportunities and challenges that arise when doing business across regions, such as those created by the European Union (EU) and the North-American Free Trade Agreement (NAFTA). 'Matching' does not mean that this book proposes a set of easy how-to-do-it prescriptions. Rather, this book intends to educate and further sharpen the intuition of MNE senior managers, when faced with strategic opportunities and challenges in international environments. As regards the relevant stakeholders, I consider satisfying the requirements of the firm's shareholders, its customers and its employees (including managers) as equally important, though there may obviously be conflicts among the goals of each stakeholder group, and within each stakeholder group – especially between domestic and foreign stakeholders. Many stakeholder groups other than shareholders, customers and employees may be relevant in terms of their potential impact on value creation, but I consider them secondary as compared to the three main groups. Shareholders and employees provide the inputs most critical to the MNE's functioning, and success can ultimately only be achieved if customers purchase the firm's products.

The seven concepts of the unifying framework – a brief overview

Most complex issues in international business strategy revolve around just seven concepts (Figure I.1). Differences among authors are usually just variations on these central themes. These seven concepts form a unifying framework that constitutes the essence of international business strategy, and reflects the foundations of global corporate success:

1. Internationally transferable (or non-location-bound) firm-specific advantages (FSAs)
2. Non-transferable (or location-bound) FSAs
3. Location advantages
4. Investment in – and value creation through – recombination

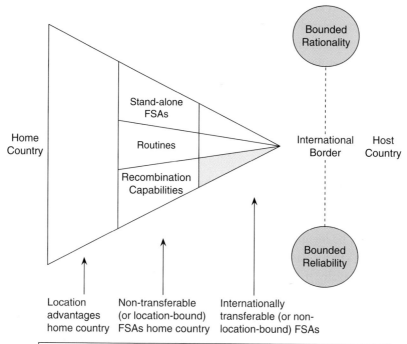

Figure I.1
Core concepts

The triangular shape in the model represents the pyramidal nature of the firm's advantages: on the broad base of the location advantages (LAs) of its home country (left) it builds a smaller subset of FSAs that are location-bound (LB; middle), and then a still smaller subset that are non-location-bound (NLB; right). Bounded rationality and bounded reliability influence the ability of these non-location-bound FSAs to be transferred across the international border to the host country.

5. Complementary resources of external actors (not shown explicitly in figure)
6. Bounded rationality
7. Bounded reliability

The *first three concepts* above (*internationally transferable FSAs, non-transferable FSAs* and *location advantages*), as a set, reflect the distinct resource base available to the firm, critical to achieving success in the marketplace. In this book, the firm is viewed as essentially a bundle of resources under common governance.[4]

Expressed in practical, managerial terms, this resource base has various components, either owned by – or accessible to – the firm:

1. Physical resources, including natural resources, buildings, plant equipment, etc.
2. Financial resources, including access to equity and loan capital
3. Human resources, including both individuals and teams. These individuals and teams have both entrepreneurial and operational (or efficiency-related) skills

4. Upstream knowledge, including sourcing knowledge, as well as product- and process-related technological knowledge
5. Downstream knowledge, critical to the interface with customers, and related to marketing, sales, distribution and after-sales service activities
6. Administrative (governance-related) knowledge regarding the functioning of the organizational structure, organizational culture and organizational systems
7. Reputational resources, including brand names, a good reputation for honest business dealings, etc.

A firm can have FSAs – i.e., strengths relative to rival companies – in each of the above resource areas. The nature, level and contestability of these strengths vis-à-vis rivals is not always fully understood by outsiders, but these strengths should, in principle, be identifiable through a properly conducted benchmarking exercise. The firm's particular location may contribute significantly to this distinct resource base, especially if this location provides privileged access to specific resources external to the firm itself. Thus, FSAs and location advantages can be intimately related. For example, FSAs such as patents in the upstream knowledge area, or brand names in the reputational resource area, confer value only if supported by a favourable property rights regime (patent laws, trademark protection, etc.) that protects proprietary knowledge. The specifics of the property rights regime are different in each nation, and can thus represent a location advantage for firms with substantial proprietary knowledge and operating in countries with a favourable regime, in this case institutionalized through government intervention.

Routines reflect the distinct ability to combine further the above resources, in unique ways valued by the firm's stakeholders. Routines are stable patterns of decisions and actions that coordinate the productive use of resources, and thereby generate value, whether domestically or internationally. The combination ability expressed in routines is a higher-order FSA, because routines are more complex than an FSA derived from distinct but stand-alone resources. Therefore, rival companies face more difficulties imitating or otherwise acquiring it.

Case example Consider the example of Federal Express' mail delivery system. Frederick W. Smith founded Federal Express in 1971, based on his innovation of the 'hub-and-spoke' approach to mail delivery. In a change from the traditional direct shipping from origin to destination, Federal Express developed a new routine: it first gathered all mail in its hub in Memphis, Tennessee, sorted the mail there, and then shipped it from the hub to a variety of final destinations. Using this hub-and-spoke routine, the company was able to provide overnight delivery services with fewer trucks and planes.

Building upon this simple hub-and-spoke concept, Federal Express created multiple business processes, such as a sophisticated tracking and tracing system to monitor the routing of each item, a customized weather forecasting system to aid in flight scheduling, fleet management systems for its planes and trucks and a distinct management approach to its network of distributors. Although many competitors tried to copy these routines in the 1980s, Federal Express remained the industry leader.[5] It is important to understand that early entrepreneurial judgement was critical here. Mr Smith invented the hub-and-spoke model in an undergraduate essay he wrote at Yale University, and the idea of combining fleets of aircraft and trucks to create seamless logistics chains came from his service with the US Marines, which combined air and ground equipment in their military operations.[6]

Federal Express also applied the above routines when expanding internationally. For example, when Federal Express entered China, it rolled out its key routines, covering the entire upstream and downstream areas of the firm's value chain. It transferred its prevailing management systems, bought its own planes for this market, acquired its own air routes, and tried to establish its own network of distributors. As noted by T. Michael Glenn, executive vice president for marketing at FedEx's parent, FDX Corp, "We've got a pretty good formula for attacking any market . . . Whether it's China or Japan or Germany, it really doesn't make any difference."[7]

Compared with an FSA derived from a single, stand-alone resource, a capability to combine resources may be more flexible and durable, because it often involves substituting one resource (such as a high-quality human resource or a type of equipment) for another, similar, one without loss of long-term productive value. The combination capability may also guarantee the continued control over distinct, stand-alone resources, such as human resources, when it allows both higher productivity benefiting the firm and higher rewards to these distinct resources than they could earn outside of the firm.

Transferring and exploiting a routine across borders may pose problems, however, if the routine is not fully understood by either the source in the home country or the recipient in the host country, even if has been deployed frequently and reliably in the home country. Failure to fully understand a routine typically occurs if the routine has a 'cultural' component. In such cases, the routine relies on a distinct, national cultural characteristic which may not be present in host country environments. ◾

Case example Cisco, headquartered in the US, is the world's largest networking equipment manufacturer. In 1994, it began the implementation of an enterprise resource planning (ERP) system and by 1998 was poised to focus its attention on the Chinese market. Cisco had garnered first-mover advantages and continued to maintain a considerable reputation with a single system image on a completely Web-based platform throughout the world.[8]

However, the local management in China identified a number of issues of local adaptation that could threaten the effective adoption of the common system platform and damage Cisco's market reputation (for example, a need for Chinese character-based financial statements). Cisco listened to the advice of its local representatives and ultimately adapted successfully to the idiosyncratic requirements of the local Chinese workplace by, among other things, producing Chinese character-based financial statements. ◾

The simple point made by this last example is that knowledge management systems themselves, though at the heart of knowledge transfer within MNEs, may face a variety of problems when diffused throughout the MNE network. Importantly, the failure to transfer these types of routines effectively may have broader spillover effects on the MNE as a whole.

International transfer difficulties in part reflect the presence of generic differences, including cultural differences, between home and host countries (these differences require adaptation and a recombination capability, as explained below). In addition, another common transfer difficulty is that those supposed to implement a practice abroad lack a crucial piece of experiential knowledge. This problem is sometimes compounded by the lack of sufficient attention to the routine's tacit knowledge attributes by those supposed to transfer the practice from the source country.

The *fourth concept, recombination*, constitutes the heart of international business strategy: international corporate success requires more than just routines, whether internationally transferable or location-bound ones, that allow for stable and predictable patterns in combining resources. The highest-order FSA is the ability, not just to combine reliably the MNE's existing resources, but to recombine its resources in novel ways, usually including newly accessed resources, whether in a limited geographic space (in which case the firm engages in domestic product diversification or innovation) or internationally. In the international context, MNEs must engage in the artful orchestration of resources, especially knowledge bundles, as a response to differences between national and foreign environments, and to satisfy new stakeholder demands in these foreign environments. In practical terms, entrepreneurial judgement is at the heart of the MNE's recombination capability: individuals inside the MNE act as entrepreneurs and craft new ways of combining and deploying the resources under their control as a response to perceived business opportunities. It is important to understand that recombination does not just mean adding new resources and managerial practices to existing ones: recombination means by definition foregoing at least some standard resources and standard practices before a new business opportunity can successfully be acted upon. A resource recombination capability is thus a precondition to value creation and satisfying stakeholder needs when operating in complex international settings.

The *fifth concept, complementary resources of external actors*, represents the additional resources, provided by external actors but accessible to the MNE, which may be necessary to fill resource gaps and achieve success in the marketplace. This book will focus solely on the complementary resources provided by external actors that are critical to international success.

Finally, the *sixth* and *seventh concepts, bounded rationality* and *bounded reliability*, reflect the behavioural characteristics (of both senior MNE managers and other relevant economic actors) that may impede international success. Bounded rationality implies limits to the capacity of individuals to absorb, process and act upon complex and often incomplete information, Bounded reliability implies insufficient effort to deliver on promised behaviour or performance. As this book will demonstrate, acute problems of bounded rationality and bounded reliability characterize many international business decisions and actions.

This book discusses in much more detail the complexities associated with each of these seven concepts, as well as the sometimes subtle linkages among them.

Notes

1. In my own advisory and research work, I have interviewed many hundreds of MNE senior managers, and it has become abundantly clear to me that most academic research on international business strategy, by contrast, simply does not appeal to these practitioners.

2. I have studied international business strategy as a researcher and practitioner since the early 1980s and have written books and journal articles to conceptualize what I have observed. Together with my colleague, Professor Alan Rugman (Reading University), I published the book *Analysis of Multinational Strategic Management*, which includes 25 of our best academic papers. The papers contain substantive contributions to five key sub-areas: (1) the theory of multinational strategic management; (2) new analysis of multinational strategic management; (3) location and multinational strategic management; (4) environmental regulations and multinational strategic management; and (5) public policy and multinational strategic management. Those academic papers provide the intellectual foundations of the framework developed in the present book. See Alan M. Rugman and Alain Verbeke, *Analysis of Multinational Strategic Management* (Cheltenham: Edward Elgar, 2005).

3. In the textbook sphere, I have used three outstanding books in my MBA and Executive MBA classes. The first is Chris Bartlett and Sumantra Ghoshal's *Managing Across Borders: The Transnational Solution* (Boston: Harvard Business School Press, 1989). It provides a good description of various MNE types and their historical development over time. The second is the late John Dunning's *Multinational Enterprises and the Global Economy* (Reading, Mass.: Addison-Wesley, 1992). This book provides an impressive overview of the entire economics and economic-policy-based literature on the MNE, including its wide variety of impacts on home and host country stakeholders. By the time the first edition of the present book was published, an excellent new edition of Dunning's book, co-authored with Sarianna Lundan was in print. The third is Julian Birkinshaw's book *Entrepreneurship in the Global Firm* (London: Sage, 2000). This short volume provides a superb subsidiary perspective on the challenges and opportunities facing managers in the international environment. For instructors teaching undergraduates, and wishing to provide a rich, historical perspective on the evolution of the multinational enterprise, I recommend the well-written work by Geoffrey Jones, *Multinationals and Global Capitalism* (Oxford: Oxford University Press, 2005).

4. This reflects a view of the firm inspired by Edith Penrose's magnum opus, *The Theory of the Growth of the Firm*, 1st edition (Oxford: Basil Blackwell, 1959). For a discussion on the importance of Edith Penrose's work and the relevance of her work for multinational growth, see Christos Pitelis (ed.), *The Growth of the Firm: the Legacy of Edith Penrose* (Oxford: Oxford University Press, 2002), Alan M. Rugman and Alain Verbeke, 'Edith Penrose's contribution to the resource-based view of strategic management', *Strategic Management Journal* 23 (2002), 769–80, and Alan M. Rugman and Alain Verbeke, 'A final word on Edith Penrose', *Journal of Management Studies* 41 (2004), 205–17.

5. 'Federal Express spreads its wings: an interview with CEO Frederick W. Smith', *The Journal of Business Strategy* 9 (1988), 15–20.

6. Justin Baer and Francesco Guerrera, 'The man who reinvented the wheel', *Financial Times* (3 December 2007),

7. Douglas A. Blackmon and Diane Brady, 'Orient Express: just how hard should a U.S. company woo a big foreign market? – In China, FedEx and UPS compete in contrasts; a risk-vs.-reward issue – planes at the Forbidden City', *Wall Street Journal (Eastern Edition)* (6 April, 1998), A.1.

8. A. Hartman, J. Sifonis and J. Kador, *Net ready: Cisco's Rules for Success in the E-economy* (Toronto, ON: McGraw-Hill Ryerson, 1999).

PART I

CORE CONCEPTS

1

Conceptual foundations of international business strategy

Five learning objectives

1. To develop an understanding of the seven concepts of this book's unifying framework.
2. To link specific types of transfers of firm-specific advantages (FSAs) across borders with the four corresponding MNE archetypes of administrative heritage.
3. To describe the various motivations for foreign direct investment (FDI) and to explain the linkages among non-location-bound (or internationally transferable) FSAs, location-bound (or non-transferable) FSAs and location advantages within each of the four MNE archetypes.
4. To define the ten often-observed patterns of FSA development and resource recombination in international business.
5. To explain the need for complementary resources of external actors and the potential reasons for bounded rationality and bounded reliability when doing international business.

In this chapter, we will look in greater detail at each of the seven concepts of this book's unifying framework. The reader will recall the seven concepts, shown again in Figure 1.1:

1. Non-location-bound firm-specific advantages (FSAs). We will use the words 'internationally transferable' FSAs interchangeably with 'non-location-bound' FSAs, but it should be clear that when using the former, we also assume that the internationally transferred FSAs can be effectively deployed and profitably exploited in foreign locations. In other words, 'international transferability' in this book involves more than the mere technical transfer across borders of knowledge and other company strengths.
2. Location-bound FSAs. Here, we will use the words 'non-transferable' FSAs as synonymous with 'location-bound' FSAs, thereby **not** simply referring to

Figure 1.1
Core concepts

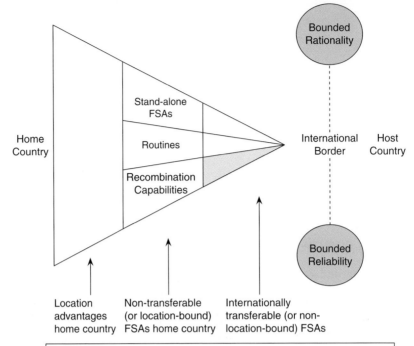

The triangular shape in the model represents the pyramidal nature of the firm's advantages: on the broad base of the location advantages (LAs) of its home country (left) it builds a smaller subset of FSAs that are location-bound (LB; middle), and then a still smaller subset that are non-location-bound (NLB; right). Bounded rationality and bounded reliability influence the ability of these non-location-bound FSAs to be transferred across the international border to the host country.

technical transfer difficulties, but to the totality of challenges facing the company in the realm of technical transfer, effective deployment and profitable exploitation of FSAs abroad.

3. Location advantages.
4. Investment in – and value creation through – recombination. Recombining resources is not the same as combining resources. Recombination means that some resources used in an initial combination need to be dropped. For example, recombination could refer to something as simple as changing the packaging of products and as complex as completely reconfiguring a firm's logistics system to meet the requirements of foreign customers.
5. Complementary resources of external actors (not shown explicitly in figure).
6. Bounded rationality.
7. Bounded reliability.

Let us start by discussing internationally transferable FSAs, which constitute the heart of conducting international business transactions.

Internationally transferable FSAs and the four MNE archetypes

The MNE creates value and satisfies stakeholder needs by operating across national borders. When crossing its home country border to create value in a host country, the MNE is, almost by definition, at a disadvantage as compared to firms from the host country, because these firms possess a knowledge base that is more appropriately matched to local stakeholder requirements. The MNE incurs additional costs of doing business abroad, resulting from cultural, economic, institutional and spatial distance between home and host country environments. MNE managers often find it particularly difficult to anticipate the liability of foreignness resulting from the cultural and institutional differences with their home country environments, even though these may be reduced over time as the firm learns and gains increased legitimacy in the host country.[1]

In order to overcome these additional costs of doing business abroad, the MNE must have proprietary internal strengths, such as technological, marketing or administrative (governance-related) knowledge. This set of MNE internal strengths, the availability of which both allows and constrains the scope of the firm's expansion across borders, is called the ***non-location-bound FSAs***. These FSAs do not stop creating value when the border is crossed between the home and the host country, though their precise value may be somewhat different in the two countries.[2] In principle, the MNE can transfer, deploy and exploit these FSAs successfully across borders. Non-location-bound FSAs can be embodied in final products, for example when the MNE exports goods and services that are valued highly by host country customers. Think of an automobile such as a Toyota car, exported from Japan to the US. The exported vehicle itself embodies the outstanding production quality, characteristic of Toyota products, that results from superior manufacturing processes and quality control systems.

Alternatively, when faced with natural or government-imposed trade barriers, the MNE may transfer some FSAs abroad directly, as 'intermediate' products. In the Toyota case, the FSAs in manufacturing and quality control will then be deployed and exploited abroad through an affiliate in the host country, which will produce and market the automobiles itself, building upon the knowledge bundles it receives from the parent company. The exploitation of FSAs transferred abroad can also be done by external actors (such as licensees), or by network partners (such as joint venture partners or distributors), who may add their own complementary resources to the foreign operation and thereby strengthen the MNE's position in the foreign marketplace by filling resource gaps.[3]

The paradox of an internationally transferable FSA is the following: if the FSA consists of easily codifiable knowledge (i.e., if it can be articulated explicitly, as in a handbook or blueprint), then it can be cheaply transferred, and effectively deployed and exploited abroad, but it can also be easily imitated by other firms. In other words, the costs of FSA transfer, deployment and exploitation may be relatively low, but the potential value that can be derived from actually deploying and exploiting the FSA may also be relatively low, namely if competitors can easily imitate what the MNE is best at.

In contrast, MNEs face great difficulty transferring, deploying and exploiting FSAs that consist of tacit knowledge. Tacit knowledge is difficult to transfer, deploy and exploit abroad because it cannot be fully replicated through simple communication channels (e.g., technical manuals). Employing tacit knowledge requires person-to-person communication, and is necessarily associated with sending human resources abroad, building up experience over time, learning by doing, etc. If the tacit knowledge is collective knowledge, embedded in a team of individuals rather than a single person, it may be necessary to re-embed this knowledge in a foreign team. Though it is expensive and time-consuming to transfer, deploy and exploit tacit knowledge across borders, the benefit to the MNE is that this knowledge is also difficult to imitate. Therefore, tacit knowledge is often a key source of competitive advantage when doing business abroad.

Perhaps the most important bundle of tacit knowledge is contained in the MNE's administrative heritage: the key routines developed by the firm since its inception. These are often determined by the vision of the founder and the firm's particular set of external circumstances ('this is the way we do things in this company'). At a general level, and when looking at the early history of large numbers of MNEs, we can distinguish among four archetypes of administrative heritage, each associated with a specific routine of international FSA transfer.[4]

First, the ***centralized exporter***: this home-country-managed firm builds upon a tradition of selling products internationally, out of a limited number of (scale-efficient) facilities in the home country, and with only minor, usually customer-oriented, value-creating activities abroad. ***Standardized products manufactured at home embody the firm's FSAs (themselves developed on the basis of a favourable home country environment, including local clustering) and make the exporting firm successful in international markets***. The foreign subsidiaries act largely as facilitators of efficient home country production. Multinational activities occur primarily in the downstream end of the value chain, and are related to marketing, distribution and related logistics operations. Many large Japanese MNEs have this type of heritage. They became serious about international expansion in the 1960s, in an era of declining trade barriers, communication and transport costs. For example, the introduction of the container as a cargo unit in maritime transport in the mid 1960s greatly facilitated international trade in manufactured goods.[5]

Case example An example of a centralized exporter is Nippon Electric Limited Partnership (NEC), established in 1899. In 1929, NEC developed the A-type switching system, the first of this type of radio communication systems, and supplied it to Japan's Ministry of Communications. In 1939, NEC established a full-fledged research laboratory, leading to successful new product development, including the first crossbar switching system adopted in Japan.

NEC's international expansion was characterized by the export of products that had already been successful domestically. As early as 1934, NEC provided the Chinese Xinjing station with a radio broadcasting system. However, extensive international expansion only started in the 1960s, when sales subsidiaries such as NEC de Mexico, NEC do Brasil, NEC Australia and NEC Electronics (Europe) were established. At that stage, NEC also exported satellite communication systems to the US, Switzerland, China, etc. NEC started to open foreign plants during the so-called 'C&C' era. C&C refers to the integration of computers and communications technologies from 1978 to 1989. This expansion included a telephone systems plant in the US and a VLSI (Very Large Scale Integration) plant in the UK, capable of placing hundreds of thousands of electronic components on a single chip. In 2012, manufacturing is geographically dispersed: NEC has 54 plants in Japan, including 5 plants in or near Tokyo, and 58 manufacturing plants overseas, meaning that NEC is no longer a 'pure' centralized exporter.[6]

In spite of its extensive international operations, NEC still functions with strongly centralized domestic R&D capabilities. In 2012, NEC had domestic R&D laboratories in four locations. In addition, five international laboratories were located in Heidelberg (Germany), Acton (United Kingdom), Beijing (China), Princeton and Silicon Valley (United States). NEC operates in four R&D domains, specializing in service platform technologies, IT/Network system platform technologies, green technologies, and C&C (Computer and Communication) innovation. Despite its global R&D facilities, NEC has central laboratories and innovation centres for all four R&D domains located in Japan. The domestic facilities employ more than 80 per cent of NEC's global R&D workforce and are the source for most of NEC's new products.[7] The domestic concentration of formal new knowledge development suggests the continued relevance of the firm's longstanding administrative heritage as a centralized exporter. ■

Case example Motion picture studios are typical centralized exporters, and thus their final products incorporate all of the companies' FSAs. Motion pictures are typically exported from the place where they are created. Warner Bros. Pictures, a major US motion picture studio, has done very well in attracting foreign customers. Through its international offices in more than 30 countries, the company distributes films to more than 120 territories outside of North America. In 2011, its worldwide box office revenues reached US $4.7 billion, with US $2.87 billion coming from overseas. As one typical example of the importance of foreign markets, in the debut weekend of its 2011 film *Harry Potter and the Deathly Hallows – Part 2*, the company grossed US $168.6 million in North America versus US $307 million in 59 countries abroad.[8] ■

The second archetype of administrative heritage is the ***international projector***: this firm builds upon a tradition of transferring its proprietary knowledge developed in the home country to foreign subsidiaries, which are essentially clones of the home operations. Many American MNEs fit this model, as they expand internationally based upon a large and sophisticated home country market, as well as proprietary technology and unique management practices. *Knowledge-based FSAs developed in the home country are transferred to subsidiaries in host countries. The international projector MNE seeks international expansion by projecting its home country success recipes abroad*. To the extent that international projection requires the systematic and continuous transfer of tacit knowledge to multiple locations (particularly when the product offering contains a large service component), this firm relies on an extensive cadre of professional managers who can act as expatriates or repositories/transfer agents of the home country success recipes.

Case example The American automobile manufacturer Ford is a well-known example of a firm with an administrative heritage dominated by international projection. Ford, established in 1903, rapidly started to export cars to Canada and Europe through export agents.

In Canada, for example, Ford essentially cloned its American operations. In 1904, Gordon McGregor, a Canadian from Walkerville, Ontario, suggested the creation of a new company to manufacture the Model A in Canada. The anticipated significant tariff savings and new capability of rapid response to Canadian demand, as well as local financing possibilities, motivated Ford to sign the agreement that established Ford Canada. Ford agreed to "furnish it with patents, plans, drawings, and specifications needed to build automobiles",[9] but Ford United States would retain control of Canadian operations, with 51 per cent of equity.

As a latecomer in internationalization as compared to the Olds Motor Company and the Cadillac Automobile Company, Ford benefited from strengths in the extensive use of machine tools as compared with the European automakers, but also faced the challenge of widespread prejudice against American cars sold in Europe.

At first, Ford exported to Great Britain through agents. Ford did not bear any duties on automobiles exported to Britain, and its low prices helped its expansion into the British market. However, other European countries imposed protective import duties, and this complicated business. The rising sales in Britain, especially with the introduction of the Model T, made it attractive to establish an assembly plant in Britain, in order to reduce shipping and other transaction costs associated with exports. The Ford Motor Company Ltd (England) was established in March 1911. The manufacturing plant in Manchester followed the American production pattern almost exactly, with obvious exceptions such as right-hand drive: "Variations at the factory were rare", and "in production and purchasing techniques the resemblance between Manchester and Detroit was also close".[10]

By 1921, Ford had opened plants in France, Denmark, Ireland and Argentina. All these affiliates operated as branch plants, receiving "the same general letters of instruction, the same communications about accounting, sales, production, and purchasing". Marketing was also done according to 'the Ford Bible' emanating from Detroit.[11] ■

Case example Disney opened Disneyland, its first theme park, in Anaheim, California (US), in 1955. The park's success helped the company to open a second theme park, Walt Disney World, in Orlando, Florida (US), in 1971. It then opened Tokyo Disneyland (Japan) in 1983, and Disneyland Paris (France) in 1992. Hong Kong Disneyland opened in 2005. The opening of Shanghai Disney Resort is scheduled for late 2015.

Disney is an international projector, and Tokyo Disneyland, Disneyland Paris and Hong Kong Disneyland cloned the original park in Anaheim. For example, except for some subtle local adaptations, Hong Kong Disneyland mirrored the Anaheim park, "from Main Street, USA to the Space Mountain roller coaster to Sleeping Beauty's castle".[12] As noted by Wing Chao, Vice-Chairman for the Asia Pacific development of Disney parks: "(T)he Disney American spirit is in the architecture and the whole ambiance . . . We're bringing Disney America . . . to Hong Kong."[13] All the face characters in these international parks are played by "white actors who speak only English".[14]

However, planting the US approach in Hong Kong without an in-depth understanding of the Hong Kong situation "left Mickey Mouse looking like Cinderella's stepmother".[15] Nasty headlines clouded the opening period. In addition to labour relations problems, a Disney official prevented government food inspectors from entering Disney until they removed their caps and badges to be indistinguishable from other visitors; Hong Kong pop stars filming promotional videos for the park for free were enraged by impolite treatment.

Disney's unfamiliarity with the local culture was exemplified by Disney's failure to host unanticipated larger numbers of visitors during the Chinese New Year holidays in late January and early February 2006. Disney sold discounted and undated one-day tickets, which allowed holders to visit Disney any time in the next six months except special days designated by Disney. Hong Kong had a four-day public holiday for the Chinese New Year, but mainland China had a one-week holiday. Disney designated only the Hong Kong public holidays as special days, and failed to anticipate the large number of mainlanders who were brought by Chinese tour agencies. Faced with swelling visitors beyond its size to host, Disney turned away thousands of visitors who had bought tickets. Ultimately, Disney's enragement of its visitors led the Hong Kong government to ask the firm to improve its ticketing.

In September 2006, Hong Kong Disneyland celebrated its first anniversary. Attendance exceeded 5 million, poorer than the expected 5.6 million visitors. After a sharp decline of attendance in the second year, visitor numbers again increased over time reaching similar attendance as in the opening year. Hong Kong Disneyland clearly needed time to understand fully customers from Hong Kong and mainland China.[16] ∎

The third archetype of administrative heritage is the ***international coordinator***: this centrally managed firm's international success does not build primarily on home country FSAs embodied in products exported internationally (as was the case with the centralized exporter), nor does it simply transfer FSAs to foreign subsidiaries to replicate home country success (as was the case with the international projector). The international coordinator builds upon a tradition of managing international operations, both upstream and downstream, through a tightly controlled but still flexible logistics function. *International operations are specialized in specific value-added activities and form vertical value chains across borders. The MNE's key FSAs are in efficiently linking these geographically dispersed operations through seamless logistics*. Many large MNEs in natural resources industries fit this archetype. They search for relevant resources internationally, manufacture in the most cost-efficient locations, and sell their products wherever there is demand for them.

Case example BP (British Petroleum Ltd) was established as the Anglo-Persian Oil Company in 1909, to develop the oilfield in southwest Persia. Anglo-Persian soon constructed a refinery at Abadan on the Shatt-al-Arab waterway in 1913 and started to sell fuel oil to the British navy. In 1914, the British Government bought a controlling interest in order to ensure an oil supply for the British navy. In these early days, the expertise of Anglo-Persian was its ability to link its oil supply in Persia with its customers in Britain. After World War I, however, Anglo-Persian expanded into new markets, building refineries around the world. By 1938, its products were sold in Europe, Africa, the Middle East, India and Australia. However, prior to World War II, Anglo-Iranian (renamed as such in 1935) still had only two major sources for oil: Iraq and Iran.

Over time, BP (renamed The British Petroleum Company in 1954) diversified its sources of oil, finding oil in the UK (the North Sea), the US (Alaska), Abu Dhabi, Australia, Colombia, Kuwait, Norway, Papua New Guinea and Qatar. Today, BP's businesses include a wide variety of activities in exploration and production of crude oil and natural gas; refining and marketing oil and gas; and manufacturing and marketing petrochemicals. Almost all of the company's activities rely on trans-border coordination.

For example, because of the long distances between natural gas fields and many major markets such as the US, UK, Japan and South Korea, BP's liquefied natural gas (LNG) business operates its own vessels as a 'mobile pipeline' to serve its customers. In BP's words: "LNG bridges the gap: gas is lifted from underground, chilled to liquid, transported on ships from one part of the world to another, and then warmed back into gas to fuel a power plant, factory or home." Further, BP also manages long-term, point-to-point contracts to integrate supply coming from specific production sites with demand in specific markets. For example, in Guangdong, China, BP operates an LNG import facility, which is supplied from the North West Shelf project in Australia.[17] ∎

Case example Logitech, a firm with a Swiss heritage and the world leading mouse manufacturer, is another international coordinator that has been very effective in coordinating its various operations dispersed around the globe. The company has one manufacturing site in Suzhou (China), many distribution centres in Europe, North America and Asia, and nine engineering centres, specializing in different technologies, located in Romanel-sur-Morges (Switzerland), California (US), Texas (US), Utah (US), Chennai (India), Hsinchu (Taiwan), Vancouver (Canada), Mississauga (Canada) and Munich (Germany).[18]

To a large extent, Logitech's success depends on the international coordination of its activities. For example, its Swiss engineering centre develops new products in cooperation with several external design partners such as Design Partners, located in Ireland. Designs are sent to Fremont, California (Logitech's operating headquarters), for approval, after which the Hsinchu engineering centre in Taiwan performs pilot runs to check for any potential manufacturing problems. Finally, the products are moved to Suzhou, China, for high-volume manufacturing, and transported to distributors and large retailers around the world. The distribution centres also perform product localization functions, such as adding local language manuals and software CDs. Similarly, most new products designed at other R&D centres are tested in Hsinchu, Taiwan, manufactured in Suzhou, China, and subsequently shipped to distributors, retailers and consumers.[19] ■

The fourth and final archetype of administrative heritage is the **multi-centred MNE**: this firm's international success does not build primarily on knowledge-based FSAs developed in the home country. *The multi-centred MNE consists of a set of entrepreneurial subsidiaries abroad, which are key to knowledge-based FSA development. National responsiveness is the foundation of the international strategy. The non-location-bound FSAs that hold these firms together are minimal: common financial governance and the identity and specific business interests of the founders or main owners (typically entrepreneurial families or financial investors).* Ultimately, the multi-centred MNE should be viewed as a portfolio of largely independent businesses. Many older European MNEs fit this mould. Unlike many of the large Japanese MNEs, these European MNEs expanded internationally before the second half of the twentieth century, in an era of trade, transport and communication barriers. They operated with highly independent local production facilities to satisfy local market needs, and wealthy financial investors provided the required financial resources in an environment of poorly functioning financial markets.

Case example In 1891, the two Philips brothers, Gerard and Anton, established the Philips company in order to manufacture incandescent light bulbs in the Netherlands. The small size of the home country soon forced Philips to export its products to foreign countries. In 1921, Philips started to establish sales affiliates in the US, Canada, France, etc.

However, after World War I, rising trade protectionism also forced Philips to establish factories in countries where it wished to sell. In Europe, most nations imposed import duties and quotas, aiming to protect domestic industry. As a result, Philips expanded its manufacturing operations in Czechoslovakia, Yugoslavia, Romania, Hungary and Poland during this period. Philips ran its affiliates as semi-autonomous organizations because high cultural differences among the host countries acted as a major barrier to a more centralized or coordinated approach.

After World War II, the "daughter companies had become [even] more independent",[20] mainly because the affiliates had continued to operate without much contact between the headquarters and the affiliates during the war. Consequently, Philips had to decide "whether to revert to the pre-war system, or to continue on the road which the separate parts had already taken".[21] It decided to stick with the newly established, decentralized course.

In the 1950s, Philips continued to set up new plants as a result of both trade barriers and the need to adapt its products to local conditions. At that stage, it manufactured in more than 50 countries and sold in more than 70. Yet, it did not even have any specific department to monitor overseas operations, but only coordinators at the headquarters to maintain connections with the foreign affiliates. The management board was informed about overseas conditions through both direct reporting from its affiliates and personal travelling by board members all over the world. In 1954, Philips established the International Concern Council, consisting of all the principal managers from around the world and the management board, to review the past year, plan for the future, provide opportunities for personal contacts, arrange promotions, etc. ■

Case example Lafarge Group, a firm with French roots and one of the largest manufacturers of building materials, has largely adopted a multi-centred approach, while also encouraging knowledge sharing within the company.

The company's official goals are: "first, to ensure total cohesion within a major multi-national Group present in 75 different countries; and second, to encourage the exchange of best practices, yet leave operating units with a high degree of autonomy".[22]

To meet these goals, Lafarge is organized into three levels, as a 'multi-local' organization: the corporate level, the divisional level and the business unit level. "The Corporate level defines the Group's long-term strategies and ensures they are implemented", "[t]he Divisions are responsible for enhancing performance and for the long-term success of their respective business segment" and "[the business unit] most often corresponds to a Division's business segment or to a business segment in a given country or geographical area".[23] Examples of business units include: Lafarge Gypsum Korea, the Business Unit of the Gypsum Division in South Korea; Fabrica Nacional de Cementos, the Business unit of the Cement Division in Venezuela; Lafarge Bétons, the concrete Business Unit in France; Lafarge Aggregates, the Aggregates Business Unit in the United Kingdom; and Lafarge Dachsysteme, the Roofing Business Unit in Germany.[24]

Lafarge provides the following rationale for its decentralized organization: "Each of our businesses is primarily a local business: our products cannot economically be transported over significant distances, construction markets have strong local characteristics, proximity is important to our customers, relationships with local communities are key, and much of our know-how originates from local experience."[25] ■

Is the above set of four MNE archetypes a complete set, given the large variety of MNE governance forms in practice? No: although the four archetypes probably describe the bulk of most large MNEs, especially the *Fortune 500* ones, there are other types. ***However, the commonality among all these types is the transfer of at least some FSAs across borders***.

A *first example* from the late nineteenth century, not included in the above archetypes, is that of freestanding companies: companies that were set up abroad – mainly by British and Dutch investors – often in their home country's colonies, without a prior domestic production base. Harrisons & Crosfield, the Hong Kong and Shanghai Bank and Rio Tinto Zinc were all established in this way.[26] These cases went beyond the simple financing of foreign operations (in fact, simple financing, in the sense of portfolio investment, often appeared impossible, given the inefficiency of the capital markets at that time). Here, entrepreneurial judgement and sound (though rather basic) governance were deployed internationally. The prior (macro-level) institutional linking of home and host countries through colonial relationships greatly facilitated this micro-level process. In other words, public policy and institutional convergence greatly reduced the additional costs of doing business abroad, and provided home country entrepreneurs with more direct access to the location advantages of the host countries involved. The coordination skills of the home country entrepreneurs thereby allowed for the establishment of easy linkages between abundant financial resources and project-management skills in the colonial power and abundant raw materials or cheap labour in the host country. The focus on coordination suggests at least some similarity with the international coordinator archetype, discussed above. To the extent that freestanding companies were actually part of larger business networks, the value of entrepreneurial coordination skills and other managerial services (in addition to the obvious value of substituting for imperfect capital markets) was even more apparent.

A *second example* of firms that may not fit the above archetypes includes many emerging economy MNEs (EMNEs). These firms typically do not derive their strengths primarily from advanced technology, brand names or a sophisticated logistics apparatus. Rather, building upon generally available resources in their home country such as low-cost labour and various forms of government support (e.g., access to capital; usage of the government international trade and investment apparatus, etc.), these firms thrive on recombining whatever FSAs they may possess with resources accessed abroad. Many of these firms' initial FSAs when crossing borders revolve around – or result from – entrepreneurial judgement, knowledge borrowed from advanced economy MNEs, and disciplined execution of a firm-level strategy. Even when supported by cheap home country resources and an activist home nation government with deep pockets, international success will only materialize if the EMNE can effectively link new knowledge and other assets sourced abroad, with a set of internal strengths.

EMNE FSAs identified in the literature and facilitating international expansion in early stages include:[27]

- Entrepreneurial quality of management (e.g., in the Taiwanese company Acer);
- Management capabilities in effective strategy execution (e.g., in the Mexican cement company Cemex);
- Learned technologies, resulting from a role as licensee or subcontractor for technology-rich MNEs from developed economies, as in the context of outsourcing strategies in offshore locations (e.g., Indian software development companies in the ICT business);

- Learned knowledge from early alliance formation with other MNEs, whereby the EMNE may have provided strengths in government relations or access to local resources to the alliance (e.g., the Chinese company Haier with various partners);
- Privileged access to home country resources (e.g., Venezuelan resource companies);
- Cost innovations/operational excellence, sometimes as the result of functioning in adverse environmental circumstances and ill-functioning external markets (valid for most EMNEs);
- Ability to adapt technology/products to emerging economy needs (e.g., as suggested by the Tata Group's Nano car).

Whatever archetype an MNE falls under, history suggests that the MNE will usually overestimate the international transferability from a mere technical standpoint, the potential for foreign deployment and the profitable exploitation of its FSAs. Even when knowledge transfer across borders is achieved rather easily, contextual variables change: first, the forces that reflect extended rivalry (relevant competitors, suppliers, customers, potential entrants and substitutes); second, government regulation and other non-market forces, such as environmental pressure groups; and third, the other relevant stakeholders in the broader business and economic environment. What may constitute an FSA in the home country – whether a set of distinct stand-alone resources, a routine or even a recombination capability – does not necessarily confer the same value in a foreign context. Whereas upstream resource bundles – such as a superior sourcing system or unique product technology – may have universal, transferable appeal, this usually does not hold for more downstream strengths, where the interface with the customer is key to successful sales and profit performance. Here, substantial investments may be required to allow the deployment and profitable exploitation of the firm's existing FSAs, which may have limited international exploitation potential without such investments. More specifically, if many FSAs developed at home are really location-bound, the MNE's challenge is to develop a new set of location-bound FSAs in host countries that permit successful operations there.[28]

Non-transferable (or location-bound) firm-specific advantages

Let us turn now to the second concept of this book's unifying framework: location-bound or non-transferable firm-specific advantages. These FSAs cannot be easily transferred, deployed and exploited in foreign markets. There are four main types of location-bound FSAs. *First*, stand-alone resources linked to location advantages, such as a network of privileged retail locations leading to a dominant market share in the home market (as often found in retail banking), are immobile, and therefore inherently non-transferable. The immobility of domestic networks is a key reason why Japan-based Kao has had only little success in penetrating foreign markets.

Case example In 1996, Kao was Japan's largest consumer goods company, with a quarter of the shampoo market, three quarters of the bleach market and half of the laundry detergent market.

One of the main reasons for Kao's dominant domestic position was its control of a comprehensive distribution system within Japan. Kao owned Hansha, a wholesale distributor, which distributed only Kao's products. As a result, Kao was able to supply small shops easily and also prevent outsiders from entering the market. Moreover, Hansha allowed Kao to gain privileged information on consumers' shopping habits. However, "[I]n Europe and America Kao has failed to build the comprehensive distribution system that it has in Japan".[29] In 1996, around 20 per cent of Kao's sales came from overseas markets; by 2011, the percentage of foreign sales had risen to nearly 30 per cent, in ascending order of proportion from North America, Europe and Asia/Oceania. Kao has not been able to replicate fully its domestic success abroad.[30] ■

Case example The immobility of domestic networks has also brought tremendous challenges to many foreign retail banks in Japan, such as Citibank (now Citigroup). Despite its leading position in the US retail banking industry and a large network of branches in the US, Citibank found it difficult to access Japanese customers when it decided to target individual consumers in 1984. It took Citi-Japan a full ten years to break into the Japanese market. According to Citibank, "[R]etail banking . . . is like the petrol-station business: you've got to have your pumps in all the right locations. In Japan, the best spots are hard to get."[31] In Japan, land prices were extremely high, and building a profitable retail network required large-scale investments and substantial time to establish the network. Moreover, Japanese consumers tended to view foreign banks as less trustworthy than local banks.

By 1990, Citibank was "the last of 83 foreign banks in Japan still interested in retail banking".[32] The number of its retail branches in Japan had grown from 6 in 1985 to 19 in 1993, but it was still a minor player: the smallest Japanese retail bank had 41 branches in 1985.[33]

However, things changed in the mid 1990s, as a result of both Japan's financial turmoil and Citibank's new strategies. In the early 1990s, Citibank hired Masamoto Yashiro from Exxon to head Citi-Japan. With his extensive knowledge of Exxon's retail gas stations, Yashiro saw the need for a large local distribution channel in Japan. Rather than building branches or purchasing a local retailing bank, Yashiro came up with the idea of linking Citi-Japan's financial network with the ATMs of Japanese commercial banks. Although this idea did not come to fruition, Japanese regulators did allow Citi-Japan to affiliate with the Japanese Postal System in 1999. In this way, Citi-Japan gained access to more than 20,000 branches of the Post Office and its ATMs. In return, the Post Office was provided the opportunity to learn about Citi-Japan's funds management capability. This learning was viewed as particularly useful, because the Japanese Post Office was expanding into the banking and insurance business.[34]

When many Japanese banks then encountered severe financial problems, Japanese consumers stopped viewing Citigroup as inferior to Japanese banks. Its affiliation with the Post Office even created the perception that Citigroup was more trustworthy, as the Post Office was widely viewed as the safest institution for deposits in Japan.

Not having a large and wholly fowned, dedicated network of retail outlets as in the United States, i.e., a location-bound FSA, but thanks to the above partnership, Citi-Japan ultimately became a significant competitor for Japanese banking giants. In 2012, the bank operated 32 retail branches throughout the country. Citigroup's deposits in Japan rose to Yen 3,510 billion (approximately US $44 billion) as of March 2012. In that financial year, Citi-Japan's profits reached Yen 5,847 million (around US $74 million). After the financial crisis, Citi-Japan has focused on financial security and ranks today among the leading Japanese banks in terms of capital adequacy ratios.[35] ■

The *second* kind of non-transferable FSA: other resources such as local marketing knowledge and reputational resources (e.g., brand names), may not have the same value across borders, either because they are not applicable to a host country context, or because they are simply not valued to the same extent by foreign stakeholders.

Case example We can illustrate the importance of reputational resources with the example of the Polo Ralph Lauren Company, a leading company in so-called 'opulent lifestyle products'. In North America, its brands – such as Polo by Ralph Lauren, Ralph Lauren Purple Label and Black Label – have long been viewed as reflecting a 'classic American gentry style'. In Europe, by contrast, Ralph Lauren has built up a reputation as a high-quality sportswear manufacturer, known for high-quality sports shirts and golf jackets with the distinct Polo logo.

When the company decided it wanted to expand more rapidly in Europe in 2002, especially by pushing its Purple label brand, representative of its upper-class American style, the difference between its European and American reputational resources became very apparent. According to one leading men's fashion news magazine, "Europeans see [Ralph] Lauren as classic sportswear – the epitome being his polo shirt. This typecast won't be easy to overcome."[36] ■

Third, local best practices (i.e., routines considered highly effective and efficient in one country, such as incentive systems for highly skilled workers or buyer–supplier relations) may not be considered as such abroad by a variety of stakeholders, and may even be deemed illegal.

Case example A typical example is the assessment of service quality in the hotel industry in locations such as Hong Kong versus the US. Hong Kong-based hotel groups such as the Peninsula have developed a high quality of services, partially because of Hong Kong's location characteristics as a regional business centre and travelling site. This quality of services is manifested by a high ratio of employees to rooms, among other factors.

However, when these firms bought US hotels in the late 1980s, such practices were not appropriate, simply because labour in the US is more expensive than in Hong Kong. Therefore, maintaining the same high ratio of employees to rooms, though viewed as a best practice in Hong Kong luxury hotels, was inefficient in US luxury hotels. As a result, the Hong Kong hotel groups had to rely more on other methods to assess and improve the quality of services in their US subsidiaries, such as a focus on more in-house training and the recruiting of more enthusiastic and younger staff.[37] ■

The *fourth* kind of non-transferable FSA: even the firm's domestic recombination capability, which may have led to a dominant market share and superior expansion rate in the home country market, as the firm engaged in product diversification or innovation, and thereby increased its geographic market coverage domestically, may not be adept enough to confront the additional complexities of foreign markets.

Case example Office Depot, the leading office supply retailer in the US, entered the Japanese market in 1997. Trying to follow its American retailing style, Office Depot found it hard to attract Japanese customers. Office Depot opened stores in Japan following the American format: more than 20,000 square feet in size, wide aisles, signs in English, etc. In other words, the firm's initial focus was on transferring its domestic routines rather than its recombination capabilities.

However, such an American format not only significantly increased the operating costs of the stores, but also failed to meet the habits of Japanese customers.[38] On the one hand, both the personnel costs and the rents in Japan were significantly higher than in the US, resulting in excessive operating costs. On the other hand, Japanese customers did not value the American format: the large size gave them an unfavourable warehouse impression, as they were used to narrow aisles. In addition, the English signs confused them. On top of these problems, Office Depot needed to provide Japanese-style office products, different from American ones, which it had to purchase from local suppliers, who did not necessarily offer them the best possible prices.

More recently, the company has tried to use its recombination ability to adapt to the idiosyncrasies of the Japanese market. For example, it started to operate both large and small stores, and strengthened its delivery capabilities. However, the company has only achieved limited success. "Following a strategic review of the business in late 2008", Office Depot closed all its retail operations in Japan in 2009 and has continued to participate in this market solely through licensing agreements.[39] ■

One of the most interesting aspects of all four of these kinds of location-bound FSAs (immobile resources linked to location advantages, local marketing knowledge and reputational resources, local best practices in the form of routines and a domestic recombination ability) is that the corresponding FSA in each host country will need to be created or acquired from third parties operating in these foreign markets. Linking investments (such as Citigroup's affiliation with the

Japanese Post Office, above) may be required to allow the matching of the MNE's internationally transferable FSAs with the relevant characteristics in host countries and regions. These linking investments can be viewed as investments in host country or host region responsiveness.[40]

Case example The Taiwanese computer manufacturer Acer Inc. engaged in such linking investments when it entered Mexico in 1989. An experienced original equipment manufacturer for IBM and other top international PC companies, Acer did not have a distribution network in Mexico, nor did it benefit from strong brand recognition. Acer therefore contracted out its distribution and marketing activities to Computec de Mexico, a local Mexican distributor, and, in 1992, formed Acer Computec Latino America (ACLA), a joint venture between Acer and Computec. Acer manufactured the PCs, but Computec (and later ACLA) was given high autonomy at the downstream end of the value chain in Mexico. They focused on small businesses and home PCs, and continued to invest in TV advertisements and other marketing media even during the 1994 peso collapse.

   This strategy paid off: by 1992, Acer's linking investments had made it the dominant brand in Mexico.[41] After having been listed on the Mexican Stock Exchange for a period of four years, in 2000 ACLA was privatized as "part of Acer's group-wide re-engineering effort that seeks to increase synergy between the group companies and the Taiwanese parent".[42] ∎

Location advantages

Having discussed transferable and non-transferable FSAs, *let us turn now to the third concept of the unifying framework: location advantages*. The MNE's economic success does not occur in a spatially homogeneous environment: location matters. Specifically, many firms are successful internationally because they take advantage of a favourable local environment. Location advantages represent the entire set of strengths characterizing a specific location, and useable by firms operating in that location.[43] These strengths should always be assessed relative to the useable strengths of other locations. Such strengths are really stocks of resources accessible to firms operating locally, and not accessible, or less so, to firms lacking local operations. Location advantages are often instrumental to the type of FSAs that can be developed by locally operating firms relative to firms operating elsewhere.

   For example, abundant natural resources may help the creation of successful firms in the natural resource industry.

Case example Consider the example of natural resources in Canada. Domestic firms have been able to leverage domestic natural endowments to compete successfully in the resource industry. Ranking fourth in the world in terms of natural resources reserves (subsoil assets and timber resources) behind only Saudi Arabia, Norway and Venezuela, Canada has significant reserves of wood, water, natural gas, oil, gold, coal, copper, iron ore, nickel, potash, uranium and zinc. In 2012, the Toronto Stock Exchange (TSX) and TSX Venture Exchange had over 1,600 mining companies listed, ranging from emerging explorers to world-class producers, and valued at over US $479 billion. As of 2012, major Canadian mining companies included: Alcan Aluminum Ltd., acquired by Anglo-Australian Rio-Tinto in 2007 and now the largest aluminum producer in the world; Inco Limited, purchased by Vale in 2006 and the second largest producer of nickel; Barrick Gold Corporation, the largest gold mining company in the world; Noranda, one of the world's largest producers of zinc and now part of the global mining company Xstrata; and PotashCorp, the world's largest producer of potash.[44] ■

A superior educational system – another location advantage – will support firms that build upon sophisticated human resource skills.

Case example In Germany, the dual system for vocational education and training (VET) has historically provided a stable source of highly skilled workers for German firms, and has helped these firms build a reputation for high product quality. VET covers several hundred occupations and focuses on the majority of young Germans who will not pursue university-level studies. The responsibility for training is shared by both public training schools and private companies. Such VET programmes, specialized in printing, optics, automotive assembly, hydraulics, etc., have historically led to "highly skilled, technologically competent graduates who are thoroughly familiar with the flexible manufacturing systems typical of today's industry".[45] VET programmes have thereby played an important role in helping a large number of German firms (Siemens, BASF, Volkswagen, etc.) retain their competitiveness in product performance and quality. ■

For similar reasons, the presence of a demanding and sophisticated local market for specific products will likely foster local innovation in the relevant industry.

Case example Consider the history of the Japanese home appliances industry. With limited natural resources and a large population, Japan has long been characterized by high energy costs, high living expenses and small dwellings, mainly apartments.

Customer needs regarding home appliances have reflected these housing conditions. Air conditioners, washing machines, etc., need to be compact, convenient, quiet and energy-efficient, in order to fit into small apartments and use minimal energy. Such requirements have historically led Japanese firms to respond in innovative ways. For example, in the 1980s, "[W]hen market surveys revealed that workers living in apartments tend to do their laundry early in the morning or late at night – and that the sound irritated their neighbours – Japanese washing-machine makers came up with high-tech solutions. Their steel suppliers came up with noise-absorbent sheets – a layer of resin or polymer sandwiched between two thin steel plates. The new technique, also used to quiet noisy refrigerators, has led to a buying boom in two markets which had experienced virtually zero growth for several years."[46] ■

Location advantages do not confer an equal strength to all locally operating firms vis-à-vis firms operating elsewhere. Rather, the more effective and efficient use of location advantages by some firms – usually the combination of these location advantages with specific proprietary resources – may confer to them an additional FSA over other locally operating firms. This may explain why only a few firms from world-renowned domestic industries, such as the French perfume industry, have been able to grow internationally.

Case example In France, almost half of the perfume business has historically been concentrated in and around Grasse, a small town in southern France with "the largest concentration on earth of the most fragrant species of flowers".[47] Such unique natural resources and three centuries of experience in the perfume business have helped French firms develop world-class processing capabilities and craft skills in perfume development.

However, only a handful of French perfume firms have grown into large-scale MNEs. These firms, such as Moët Hennessy Louis Vuitton (LVMH), were best able to combine generally available, localized knowledge with modern product development processes. Traditionally, perfume firms relied on a 'nose' – a fragrance expert – to determine the right combination of fragrances to be included in a new perfume. However, most successful perfume developers – such as LVMH – now develop products 'backwards': they start with a concept, then design an ad campaign, and finally focus on the actual perfume to be produced.[48] ∎

Location advantages can vary widely in their geographical scope. In some cases, a location advantage accrues to all firms operating in a particular country, for example if the government has created a favourable tax regime for specific economic activities, or general business incentives for skill upgrading of human resources.

Case example Consider India's location advantages. The impressive recent growth of India has been attributed to a series of country-specific factors after the economic reforms in 1991, including the abolishment of barriers to international trade and investment, tax reforms, deregulation, and the promotion of privatization. In addition, India offers a large supply of skilled workers with university degrees and proficiency in English. Despite the recent financial crisis, all these factors boost the Indian economy and cause India's GDP growth rate to be one of the highest in the world.

More emerging and underdeveloped economies from Asia might want to follow the Indian formula for success, but this will not be easy, as it is almost impossible to replicate the trajectory over time of the entire portfolio of parameters that led to India's success at the macro-level. ∎

In some cases, location advantages accrue only to firms operating in part of a country. Economic clusters, for example, are usually located in only part of a country. The physical locations of the firms that constitute the heart of the cluster determine the cluster boundaries.

Case example The US, the leading country for biotechnology innovation, has nine established and seven emerging biotechnology clusters – small, distinct regions that have been called "self-perpetuating centres of innovation and, hopefully, profit".[49] According to a recent study by Jones Lang LaSalle, based upon qualitative and quantitative data such as the amount of venture capital funding and the availability of local infrastructure, the Greater Boston cluster is ranked first, followed by clusters in the region of New York/New Jersey, the San Francisco Bay Area, Los Angeles, and finally Washington DC.[50] These five clusters received about 66 per cent of all venture capital funding disbursed to the 16 US life sciences clusters in 2010.[51]

A successful biotech cluster requires four pillars: at least one large, non-profit research university with a strong biomedical curriculum; venture capitalists who provide funding to biotech companies; local governmental support in creating a favourable environment for biotech firms; and a few publicly traded biotech companies.[52]

Firms tend to invest in established clusters to get close to the research environment there. One high-profile example is the shift of the command centre for global research at Novartis AG from Switzerland to the campus of the Massachusetts Institute of Technology, to be close to "the centre of genetic research in the US",[53] and "to parlay the knowledge gleaned from gene hunting into the next generation of innovation treatments".[54] As noted by CEO Daniel Vasella, "[B]asing its research headquarters alongside the Boston area's booming biotechnology industry, academic institutions and their pools of scientific talent will play a critical role in discovering those drugs".[55]

Before this shift, Novartis had already established its US base in New Jersey, and had sited the Novartis Institute for Functional Genomics in La Jolla, California. The new command centre is close to the Greater Boston cluster, the operation in New Jersey is close to the New York/New Jersey/Connecticut 'Pharm Country', and the institute in California is close to the San Diego cluster. ■

In other cases, location advantages reach across country borders. The creation of cross-border location advantages is one of the key purposes of most regional trading and investment agreements, intended at least partly to confer a location advantage to insiders at the expense of outsiders.

Case example The North American Free Trade Agreement (NAFTA) has changed the distribution of trade. The sharp increase of trade among the NAFTA countries suggests trade diversion: "the NAFTA may have deflected trade internally that would otherwise have taken place between individual North American countries and [the rest of the world] (the NAFTA dealt Mexico and Canada a price advantage over other countries and produced incentives for US customers not only to shift from domestic goods to imports, but to substitute imports from Mexico and Canada for imports from elsewhere)".[56] ■

Another way to classify location advantages, as opposed to classifying by geographical scope (which may extend to a narrow cluster, a broader region within a country, a country or a region spanning more than a country), is to classify them by what motivates a firm to conduct economic activity in that location. Because most of the book's examples to this point concerned **home country** location advantages (e.g., Canada's abundant natural resources conferring an advantage to domestic resource-based industries), the following discussion and classification of a firm's motivations will, for balance, focus on **host country** location advantages.

Why would an MNE want to engage in foreign direct investment in a host country? First of all, a key definition: **foreign direct investment** (FDI) is the allocation of resource bundles (combinations of physical, financial, human, knowledge and reputational resources) by an MNE in a host country, with the purpose of performing business activities over which the MNE retains strategic control in that country. The answer is that an MNE should engage in FDI only if the host country confers a location advantage relative to the home country. In each case, the value proposition of the foreign activity must be more attractive than alternative value propositions at home. We can distinguish among four motivations to perform activities in a host country rather than at home.[57]

The first motivation, **natural resource seeking**, entails the search for physical, financial or human resources in host countries. These resources are in principle not proprietary, and their availability in host countries (which constitutes the location advantage of those countries) means that investment abroad leads to higher value creation than investment at home. A precondition to such investment is that the host country institutional environment actually allows foreign MNEs to access these resources.

Case example Faced with the continuing growth in the demand for energy, oil companies like ExxonMobil are striving to replenish their reserves by developing or buying new oil fields around the world. ExxonMobil, the largest refiner and one of the largest publicly traded companies by market capitalization in the world, has been expanding its access to new reserves through various forms of FDI in the past several years.

For example, in 2012, the Nigerian subsidiaries of ExxonMobil, Total SA, Chevron Petroleum and Nexen Petroleum formed a joint venture for oil exploration in deep water, 2,400 feet under water and 62 miles from the coast of Nigeria.[58]

In 2011, ExxonMobil signed an agreement with the leading Russian petroleum company Rosneft to develop projects in the Russian Federation. Besides a planned exploration programme of US $3.2 billion for Kara Sea and Black Sea, they agreed to establish a joint Arctic R&D centre for offshore developments and to exploit oil resources in Western Siberia.[59] ∎

The second motivation, **market seeking**, reflects the search for customers in host countries. Firms are market seeking when they conclude that deploying productive activities and selling in the foreign market confers higher value to the firm than engaging in alternative investment projects at home. The host country location advantage is the presence of customers willing and able to purchase the firm's products. Note that market seeking is not the same as mere exporting: market seeking involves business activities in the host country, based on resource bundles transferred there over which the MNE retains strategic control.

Case example With a population of 1.3 billion and a continuously growing middle class, China has become an attractive market for many US food services brands, including Kentucky Fried Chicken (KFC), McDonald's, Dairy Queen and Pizza Hut.

KFC was the first US food services company to invest in China, opening the first unit in Beijing in 1987. "From the opening day the Beijing unit has served an average of 9,000 customers a day. Its astounding popularity has broken all the company's world sales records."[60] Individual restaurants had sales as high as US $4 million per year, and the margins in China were more than twice the US average.[61]

Another early success story has been McDonald's. As early as 1994, its huge 700-seat outlet in Beijing was reportedly serving "20,000 McDonald's customers a day, and as many as 50,000 on holidays".[62] ■

The third motivation for an MNE to invest abroad, *strategic resource seeking*, is the desire to gain access to advanced resources in the sphere of upstream knowledge, downstream knowledge, administrative knowledge or reputational resources. These resources, which constitute the host country location advantages, are in principle not generally accessible, in contrast to the resources sought with natural resource seeking and market seeking. Therefore, this type of FDI typically involves taking over other companies, engaging in alliance activity or becoming an insider in foreign knowledge clusters. The underlying reasons to engage in strategic resource seeking typically include the goal to become an established industry player in a set of strategically important knowledge development centres or output markets.

Case example The Korean firm Samsung Electronics is now viewed as one of the world's leading companies in consumer electronics and has made up for the years of trying to catch up with foreign technologies in consumer electronics.

From the early 1970s to the early 1990s, Samsung was able to reduce to less than one year its new product development gap behind the leading MNEs from the US and Japan. However, it realized it still needed additional access to advanced foreign technologies. To accomplish this, Samsung strengthened its in-house R&D and acquired/invested in high-tech companies such as LUX, a Japanese producer of high-end audio systems, and the US firm AST Research. Access to the latter firm's technical know-how and patented technology allowed Samsung to reduce its technology sourcing and licensing dependence on IBM and other large firms. ■

Finally, *efficiency seeking* is a firm's desire to capitalize on environmental changes that make specific locations in the MNE's international network of operations more attractive than before for the consolidation or concentration of specific activities. Such environmental changes may include technological break-throughs allowing greater scale economies; an increased industry focus on innovation, triggering higher required R&D investments; customer-induced, shorter product cycles; and the reduction of trade and investment barriers through regional agreements such as NAFTA and the EU. Here, the location advantages of the various relevant countries may change relative to each other, making one more attractive than another and therefore more likely to receive new FDI.[63]

Case example Logitech, the world's leading mouse manufacturer, established its first manufacturing plant in Switzerland in 1981. It then established three foreign plants in the US, Ireland and Taiwan, to serve US and European PC manufacturers who wanted their suppliers to be nearby, and to benefit from lower costs and manufacturing design capabilities in Taiwan. After establishing its Irish plant, Logitech closed its Swiss plant.

However, in the first half of the 1990s, Logitech suffered from inefficient manufacturing and an unclear customer focus. In order to remain competitive in an environment focused on cost cutting, it engaged in efficiency seeking FDI, and started production in 1994 at a plant in Suzhou, China. It simultaneously closed its Irish and US factories, and retained only a small production line for pilot runs in Taiwan.

Logitech reinforced its manufacturing base in China by launching a new factory in 2005. It currently manufactures half of its products at its Suzhou plant, with the other half outsourced to suppliers in Mexico, Hungary, Thailand and China.[64] ∎

Now that location advantages have been discussed, all the pieces are in place for us to show a pictorial representation of the essence of international business strategy.

Figure 1.2 shows the basic linkages among internationally transferable FSAs, location-bound FSAs and location advantages. On the left-hand side of Figure 1.2, as noted above, location-bound FSAs in the home country often result from privileged access to location advantages, or from a more efficient and effective use thereof as compared to other companies. The location advantages themselves may in principle be generally available to all firms operating in a specific location, and therefore only reflect an advantage vis-à-vis firms operating elsewhere. In general, a domestically operating firm may have both routines and even recombination capabilities that lead to great business success domestically, but are only partially useable in an international context.

Why is there a shaded area on the right-hand side of Figure 1.2? A firm's success abroad depends on its ability to link its internationally transferable FSAs with location advantages (whether valuable inputs or attractive market conditions) in host countries, which are the reasons why the MNE expanded there in the first place. This linking process often requires developing new, location-bound FSAs in the host country. As a result, the existing base of internationally transferable FSAs is extended with a location-bound component, thereby improving its exploitation potential in the host country. This is a common resource

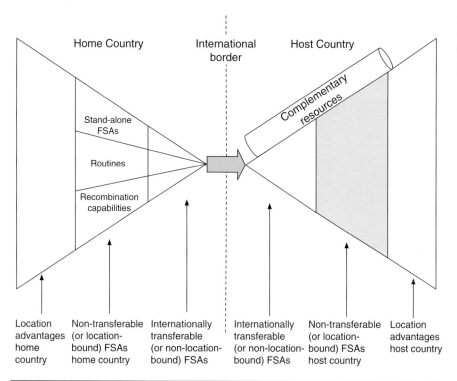

Figure 1.2
The essence of
international
business strategy

| Location advantages home country | Non-transferable (or location-bound) FSAs home country | Internationally transferable (or non-location-bound) FSAs | Internationally transferable (or non-location-bound) FSAs | Non-transferable (or location-bound) FSAs host country | Location advantages host country |

The shading of the middle of the host country triangle emphasizes the importance of developing new, LB FSAs in the host country. These LB FSAs complement the FSAs the firm has transferred from the home country, and are critical to achieve the firm's goals, in terms of accessing and benefiting from the location advantages (LAs) of the host country. If the firm commands insufficient FSAs internally to access and benefit from these LAs, it may draw upon complementary resources of external economic actors to achieve its goals in the host country.

recombination activity performed by the MNE. In other words, the new location-bound FSA bundle improves access to the location advantages of the host country. However, such national responsiveness is often difficult to achieve and may require substantial investments. These location-bound FSAs are shown as a shaded area on the right-hand side of Figure 1.2. Here, we should emphasize again that recombining resources entails more than just 'adding' new location-bound FSAs to a set of internationally transferable ones. Recombination also requires 'letting go' of existing assets and capabilities that could be effectively deployed and profitably exploited in the home country, but less so in the host country.

Figures 1.3, 1.4, 1.5 and 1.6 take the basic template of Figure 1.2 and visualize how a **centralized exporter**, an **international projector**, an **international co-ordinator** and a **multi-centred MNE** typically address the problem of partial rather than full usability at an international level of its routines and recombination capabilities. In each case, the shaded area on the right-hand side (host country),

Figure 1.3
Centralized
exporter

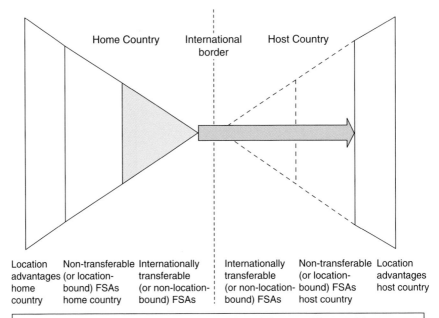

Location advantages home country	Non-transferable (or location-bound) FSAs home country	Internationally transferable (or non-location-bound) FSAs	Internationally transferable (or non-location-bound) FSAs	Non-transferable (or location-bound) FSAs host country	Location advantages host country

The arrow cutting through dotted areas represents the direct link between home country NLB FSAs, and the host country's LAs (i.e., the foreign market), without development of new, LB FSAs in the host country, or formal transfer of existing NLB FSAs to the host country (the NLB FSAs are embodied in the centralized exporter's products).

Figure 1.4
International
projector

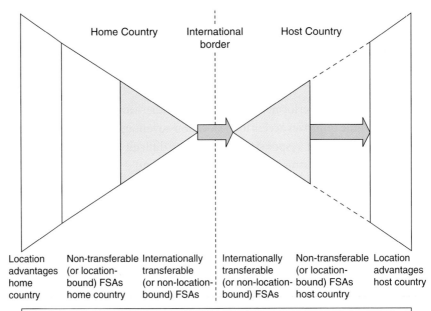

Location advantages home country	Non-transferable (or location-bound) FSAs home country	Internationally transferable (or non-location-bound) FSAs	Internationally transferable (or non-location-bound) FSAs	Non-transferable (or location-bound) FSAs host country	Location advantages host country

The dotted area of LB FSAs in the middle of the host country triangle reflects the international projector's lack of development of LB FSAs in the host country, where operations simply clone those prevailing in the home country. Extant NLB FSAs suffice to access and benefit from host country LAs.

International
border
Home
Country
LAs
LB
FSAs
NLB
FSAs
Host
Country A
Host
Country B
Host
Country C
The different sizes of the shaded areas in the various host countries reflect the different types and levels of home country NLB FSAs to be transferred to different host environments in function of the LAs the firm wishes to access. The circle linking the various countries reflects the international coordinator's strengths in putting together a value chain based upon access to the coveted LAs of each country where the firm operates.

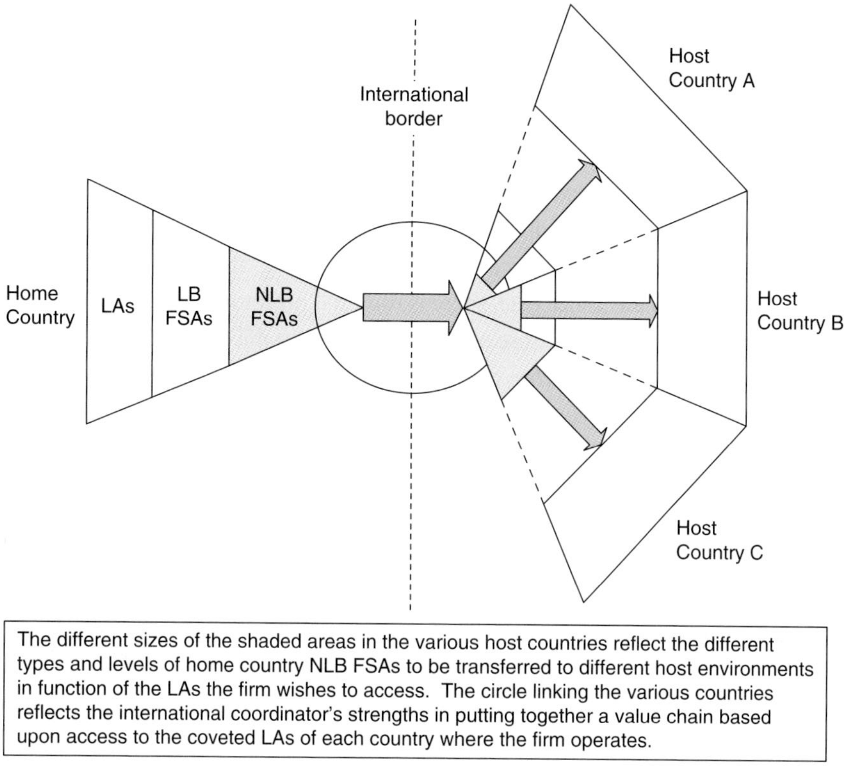

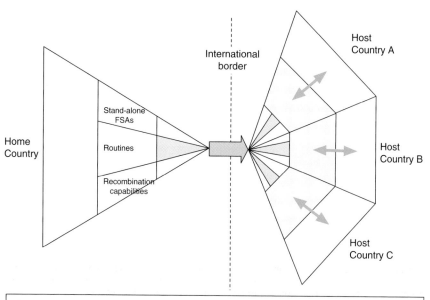

Figure 1.5 International coordinator

International
border
Home
Country
Stand-alone
FSAs
Routines
Recombination
capabilities
Host
Country A
Host
Country B
Host
Country C
The multi-centred MNE transfers only key routines from the home country to host countries. The large, shaded middle areas in the host countries represent the necessity to build new, LB FSAs in each host country. The double-headed arrows reflect the close alignment the host country operations must develop between their own LB FSAs and the host's LAs.

Figure 1.6 Multi-centred MNE

if any, identifies the most critical linkages required with the shaded area on the left-hand side. The shaded area on the left-hand side represents the relevant bundle of internationally transferable FSAs in the home country, whether embodied in a centralized exporter's final products or, in the case of the other archetypes, transferred as intermediate goods.

The *centralized exporter* is essentially a market seeker: its internationally transferable FSAs are embodied in its final products, and the host country location advantage is simply the presence of customers willing and able to purchase the firm's products. In the 'ideal' case, there is minimal need to develop location-bound FSAs in the host country, because of the products' desirability in host environments.

The *international projector* clones its home operations in the host country, replicating its internationally transferable FSAs. In the 'ideal' case, the host country operations directly access the local customers, without much need to develop new location-bound knowledge, again because of the desirability of the MNE's products.

The *international coordinator's* main transferable FSA is its ability to coordinate the location advantages accessed in multiple host countries. In some host countries, it may still be necessary to transfer substantial resource bundles to the host country operations, so as to gain access to the host's location advantages (e.g., production capacity to access abundant natural resources). In other countries there may be little need for this, namely if inputs can be accessed largely through third parties, such as the owners of natural resources or integrated logistics services providers. The actual coordination may occur largely in the home country or may be shared by a variety of locations.

The decentralized *multi-centred MNE*, recognizing that each host country operation needs to build upon its own distinct location-bound FSAs, transfers only core routines (e.g., in the area of financial management and administrative best practices) to each host country operation.

Value creation through recombination

Having discussed transferable FSAs, non-transferable FSAs and location advantages – as well as the corresponding four archetypes of MNEs – *let us turn now to the fourth concept of the unifying framework: value creation through recombination*. Value creation through recombination means that the firm is able to grow by innovating and diversifying. This means combining in novel ways existing resources, often in conjunction with newly accessed resources. In this process, managers find new profitable ways – in this case across borders – to use excess resources at a relatively low marginal cost and to meld these with newly accessed resources. Resource recombination is both a key driver and a key constraint of firm growth.

In any organization, resource recombination requires three things: *first*, entrepreneurial skills possessed by managers and other employees that can be deployed in the face of new productive opportunities; *second*, slack or unused productive resources, beyond those needed for the efficient functioning of current operations; *third*, the willingness and capacity to let go of some resources embedded in extant FSAs, and to replace these by resources with higher value creating potential in host environments. Here, the newly accessed resources in each host environment should be melded with existing resources.

Resource recombination in general – and knowledge recombination in particular – is critical to creating value and satisfying customer demand, because all MNEs, even the largest firms included in the *Fortune Global 500* list, have rivals who are trying to capture market share. Continuous innovation and effective exploitation of innovation is required to stay ahead of the competition.

Case example Carrefour, the world's second largest and most internationalized retailer, has been challenged by competitors both at home and abroad.

In its French home market, Carrefour has lost market share to Aldi and Lidl, two German chains that have competed successfully based on their private label products and low prices. Carrefour has not been able to match these rivals' lower prices, as French regulations limit the extent to which retailers can reduce prices for branded products.

In Japan, Carrefour has had difficulties in purchasing land suited for new stores and in understanding Japanese consumers' needs. In 2005, it decided to leave Japan by selling its eight stores to Aeon Co., a local Japanese retailer. In the same year, it sold its Mexican operations, which failed to gain a sufficient market share after ten years of operation.[65]

Thus, Carrefour has faced severe challenges when applying its recombination capabilities to either maintain home market share or penetrate overseas markets. ■

When faced with competition, the MNE's most important strengths are usually not its physical, financial or human resources as stand-alone items. Instead, the MNE's key strengths are its valuable, often proprietary knowledge, particularly its routines and recombination capabilities. Here, competitiveness results from the combination of stand-alone resources into bundles of location-bound and non-location-bound FSAs in technology, marketing and reputation, and from the capability to recombine these knowledge bundles with newly accessed resources to produce goods and services that meet stakeholder needs internationally. Because the MNE is to a large extent a repository of knowledge bundles that can be deployed and recombined across borders, the firm's recombination capability can itself become the MNE's most important strength. Recombination, especially critical when satisfying stakeholder needs abroad, requires more than stand-alone knowledge bundles or existing routines. The MNE's recombination capability leads to processes and products that embody 'integrated bundles' of knowledge, meaning melded bundles of old and newly accessed knowledge.

The recombination capability is the MNE's highest-order FSA. This capability means the firm can not only transfer abroad its existing set of FSAs, but also create new knowledge, integrate it with the existing knowledge base and exploit the resulting, new knowledge bundles across geographic space, in ways that satisfy stakeholder needs.

Effective recombination requires more than simply superior technology on the upstream side, market research skills on the downstream side, recognized brand names at the reputational side, the competent administration of current operations, etc. Instead, it requires entrepreneurial skills, because recombination cannot be easily planned beforehand, but requires the capability to adapt to new circumstances, especially when setting up a new business in a host country. It also requires unused or slack resources that can be deployed to develop new knowledge and perform the actual recombination. Finally, in host environments, it usually entails melding selectively existing resources with newly accessed resources so as to overcome the 'distance' between existing operations and the host environment. One paradox needs to be noted here: strong routines, though a critical component of the MNE's FSAs, can sometimes be detrimental to recombination, and thus to the MNE's recombination capability. There is a fine line between routines being helpful to international business strategy, by contributing to economies of scope (sharing of knowledge across borders), and these same routines becoming detrimental to further resource recombination, thereby impeding national responsiveness or even the creation of new, non-location-bound FSAs.

Figure 1.7 shows ten common patterns of FSA development and resource recombination in international business. The horizontal axis shows the two generic FSA types: FSAs are either internationally transferable (whereby we refer to the possibility of technical transfer, effective deployment and profitable exploitation abroad of these FSAs) or location-bound. The vertical axis identifies the three possible geographic sources of an FSA: an FSA can be developed in a home country operation, in a host country operation or by a network of MNE units.

The resulting matrix allows the identification of ten different patterns of FSA development, nine of which involve recombination and only one of which (Pattern I) does not involve recombination. The MNE's ability to carry out these patterns in real-world situations defines its recombination capability. Note that firms can – and usually do – carry out more than one pattern of FSA development at any given time.

Pattern I An internationally transferable FSA is developed in the home country and can be utilized across borders without any need for adaptation. This pattern is typical for stand-alone, advanced technical knowledge, which is valuable across borders (because it satisfies the objectives of shareholders, customers and employees), and is not affected much by international differences in property rights regimes.

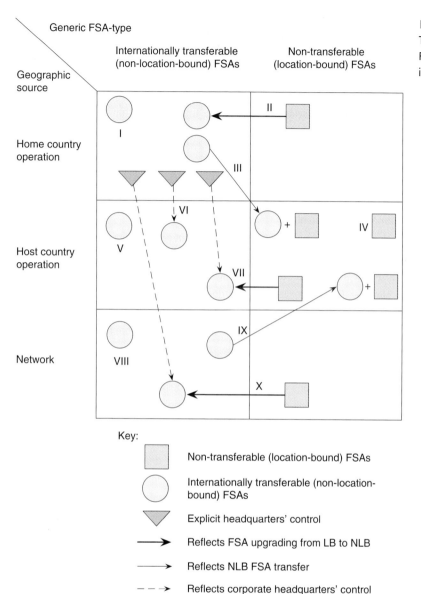

Figure 1.7
Ten patterns of
FSA development
in MNEs

As this FSA development pattern does not require recombination, it will not be discussed in detail, but it lies at the heart of FSA transfer in the **centralized exporter**, **international projector** and **international coordinator** archetypes.

Pattern II A location-bound FSA is developed domestically, in the home country, and is then upgraded so as to become internationally transferable. The upgrading draws on the firm's recombination capability, which may be helped by favourable location advantages at home.

Such an FSA upgrading pattern may occur at both the upstream and downstream ends of the value chain, as shown by respectively the development of new, proprietary drugs at Ranbaxy, and the development of a firm-specific sensitivity to local tastes at Jollibee. As noted earlier, recombination implies both 'adding' and 'letting go'. It does not suffice simply to add resources to an existing 'recipe'; the challenge is also to eliminate the 'ingredients' that will not lead to successful resources deployment and exploitation.

Case example Ranbaxy, India's largest pharmaceutical MNE, was incorporated in 1961. It quickly developed as a low-cost medicine manufacturer by leveraging the Indian intellectual property rights regime from the early 1970s to 2005, a regime that recognized process patents, but not product patents.

Using reverse engineering, Ranbaxy figured out how to duplicate existing molecules using its own innovative processes. As long as it used its own newly discovered manufacturing processes, it could legally manufacture and sell existing drugs that were still 'on patent' elsewhere in the world.

However, Ranbaxy realized that this domestic haven of loose intellectual property restrictions would not last forever. Furthermore, the firm realized that its reverse-engineering skills were not an internationally deployable FSA: those skills would not suffice for international expansion into markets with stronger intellectual property rights protection, such as the US. In 1994, its new research centre at Gurgaon (near Delhi, India) started to extend its knowledge base from mere reverse engineering and copying towards developing new, proprietary drugs. This centre was staffed by both domestic researchers and Indian-origin researchers who were "poached from [US] and European companies".[66] (By 1999, 20 of the 85 members in the new drug development team were such Indian-origin researchers, reflecting a reverse brain drain towards India.) In 1996, Ranbaxy launched 15 of its own branded generic drugs in the US, building upon its newly developed upstream transferable FSAs back in India. In 1999, "it sold to Bayer AG an advanced formulation of one of the German company's most profitable drugs, ciprofloxacin . . . The tablet conceived by Ranbaxy enable[d] patients to take only one dose a day, instead of several, by discharging the drug over a prolonged period of time."[67] ■

Case example More at the downstream end of the value chain, Jollibee, the largest food chain in the Philippines and known as "the company that beat McDonald's",[68] has upgraded its recombination skills to conform to local tastes in host markets around the world. This firm, incorporated in 1978, had only a few burger kitchens when McDonald's opened its first outlet in Manila in 1981.

From the outset, the company's founder, Tony Tan Caktiong, combined the US fast-food approach with a high sensitivity to local tastes. Jollibee had in-store playgrounds with costumed characters, as did McDonald's. At Jollibee, burgers were sweet and juicy, and spaghetti was saccharine. To most Filipinos, the food at Jollibee tasted better than that at McDonald's. Further, Jollibee's marketing reflected its local roots. For example, its advertising campaign in 1998 was linked to the country's centennial. By 2010, Jollibee had captured 65 per cent of local fast food sales, about twice of McDonald's sales.

The expansion to overseas markets targeted Filipinos abroad. To succeed, the company had to upgrade its non-transferable FSA – sensitivity to Filipino tastes in the Philippines – into a transferable FSA: sensitivity to Filipino tastes in each host country. As explained by a former general manager of Jollibee's international division: "[W]e have come up with dishes that are popular in the country we're in, and we make the burgers suitable to their palate".[69] For instance, Jollibee makes a spicy and sweet Heavyweight Champ hamburger in Guam, a distinctive chicken curry in Indonesia and a special spicy chicken dish in China.[70] By 2012, Jollibee also operated outlets in Brunei, Hong Kong, Vietnam, Qatar, Saudi Arabia and the US. ■

This last example demonstrates that learning at home may create an internationally transferable FSA, in this case built around a high sensitivity to Filipino tastes in each host country. Such recombination capability may make it easier to understand what location-bound FSAs must be developed or otherwise accessed abroad (e.g., leading to the Heavyweight Champ hamburger that Jollibee sells in Guam) and to use those in conjunction with the company's other non-location-bound FSAs when penetrating foreign markets. The next pattern explicitly focuses on this creation of location-bound FSAs in host countries.

Pattern III An internationally transferable FSA is developed at home, but, in order to exploit it profitably in host countries, location-bound knowledge must be added to it, in the various host countries where the MNE operates. This is an expression of the philosophy 'think globally, act locally'. In this case, investments in location-bound FSAs complement the extant, internationally transferable FSAs, thereby allowing national responsiveness. When using Pattern III, the MNE is trying to achieve simultaneously both the benefits of integration and the benefits of national responsiveness. Similar to Pattern II, Pattern III may relate to either upstream or downstream activities, as observed respectively in the implementation of diversity management at Alcatel-Lucent and the adaptation of host country marketing strategies at Whirlpool. Again, the process of 'adding' new knowledge, typically also implies 'discarding' extant knowledge that worked well in the home country but less so across borders.

Case example France-based Alcatel-Lucent, a major telecommunications company, believes that "the most effective diversity initiatives arise from the company's grass roots".[71] The corporate headquarters provides subsidiaries with a corporate-wide diversity message, as well as diversity tools and templates, but each subsidiary is responsible for the design and implementation of its own diversity management practices.

For example, a three-day training programme from corporate headquarters initiated the early diversity management practices at the Hilversum plant in the Netherlands. In response, a small group of R&D managers at the plant modified the programme to better address issues with local relevance, including "fostering a climate open to new ideas, improving operational efficiency, raising managers' awareness of their cultural assumptions, and reducing conflicts between American and Dutch managerial styles".[72] ■

Case example Whirlpool Corporation, the world's leading manufacturer and marketer of major home appliances, successfully recombined its internationally transferable design and marketing skills with location-bound knowledge of consumer preferences in India.

Indian customers have a comparative preference for white garments, associated with purity and hygiene. However, frequent machine-washing in local water often discolours white fabrics. After learning about local preferences, Whirlpool designed washing machines that are particularly effective on white fabrics.[73]

In addition to appropriate product design, Whirlpool also produced a supporting TV commercial that appealed to Indian customers. It shows the daydream of a mother, in which her daughter dressed as Snow White wins a beauty contest against other contestants dressed in grey. At the end of the commercial, the mother awakes and "glances proudly at her Whirlpool White Magic washing machine".[74]

From 2005 to 2011, Whirlpool's sales in India nearly tripled, and it became the leading brand in India for fully automatic washing machines. ■

Pattern IV Location-bound FSAs are developed in each host country where the MNE operates, and these FSAs are exploited locally, usually by autonomous affiliates. Does this involve recombination? Yes, it will almost always involve some recombination, as by definition the foreign affiliate can develop the new FSA only by recombining prior knowledge (for which the MNE as a whole acts as repository) with local knowledge. Why? Any foreign subsidiary exists only because of prior FDI and related transfer of resource bundles. When the foreign subsidiary starts developing its own FSAs, there must, by definition, be recombination. While this is particularly the case with greenfield FDI (i.e., direct investment in new facilities or the expansion of existing facilities), it will even be the case when the host country operation is acquired through a merger or acquisition, because the acquisition presumably makes sense only if the MNE feels that it can usefully combine its own knowledge with that of the merger partner or acquired company in the host country. This would typically entail replacing the accounting systems, ICT tools and a variety of governance mechanisms that prevailed in the formerly independent firm, even if the content of strategic decision making such as choices in the realm of new product development and branding are left to the new unit's management.

If the new affiliate is indeed an existing company acquired by the MNE so as to achieve national responsiveness in the host market, the resistance to any imposed resources recombination in the realm of strategy content can be intense. This is a typical pattern for technological knowledge development in *multi-centred MNEs*.

This pattern is manifested in the cases of US-based Parke-Davis and the Dutch MNE Philips. The degree to which the FSAs were location-bound is evident by the immense resistance each company met when it tried to recombine the company's resources by integrating the autonomous subsidiaries.

Case example In 1970, the pharmaceutical company Warner-Lambert (since purchased by Pfizer) purchased US-based Parke-Davis in order to expand its international market coverage. At the time of acquisition, Parke-Davis operated manufacturing plants in the UK, France, Italy, Spain, Germany, Belgium and Ireland. Responsible for blending and packaging to meet local needs, these national subsidiaries "had historically enjoyed considerable autonomy and had developed substantial competences".[75]

The Parke-Davis administrative heritage of autonomous subsidiaries and location-bound FSAs became obvious in the mid 1980s when, faced with the single European market, Warner-Lambert tried to restructure its operations by closing some plants and specializing the others along non-geographic lines. "Fearful of losing power, and convinced that the parent was overestimating the impact of globalization, subsidiary managers fought back."[76] Only after three years of intense debate did rationalization finally occur. ■

Case example Philips relied on the extant capabilities of its national subsidiaries when the management board at Philips decided to reorganize the firm after World War II.

This autonomy facilitated flexible responses needed for each host environment, leading to specific technical skills developed at the national subsidiary level. For example, the firm's UK subsidiary developed the world's first teletext TV, its Canadian subsidiary designed the company's first colour TV and its Australian subsidiary built the world's first stereo TV. In each case, the FSA was driven by local opportunities, often in the form of sophisticated local demand that did not exist elsewhere at the same time.

By the 1960s, however, such separate capabilities struck senior management as inadequate to meet the challenges brought by the development of the European common market. For Philips, the multi-centred administrative heritage was so ingrained that the reorganization efforts to gain control over its national subsidiaries spanned more than two decades. ■

Pattern V An internationally transferable FSA is developed autonomously in a host country affiliate and then diffused internationally, either as an intermediate good, or embodied in finished products. Though this pattern looks similar to Pattern I, there are two key differences. First, the FSA is developed in the host country rather than the home country. Second, as discussed immediately above with regard to Pattern IV, Pattern V will almost always involve recombination, namely when the transfer of resource bundles overseas requires cooperation with other affiliates in the MNE that will have their say in the development or marketing of the product. Pattern V thus usually describes only part of a broader capability development process.

The European affiliate of US-based Goodyear and the Canadian affiliate of US-based Hewlett-Packard (HP) developed such internationally transferable FSAs in response to their local environments. At Goodyear, the design knowledge was transferred from the European affiliate to the US design centre; at HP, the product was developed in the Canadian affiliate but sold to customers around the world.

Case example In the mid 1960s, the French tyre manufacturer Michelin expanded to the US with its radial tyre, which "lasted far longer and provided better gas mileage than conventional bias-ply tires".[77] Goodyear, a major US tyre manufacturer, still produced conventional tyres, and was not able to compete in its home market.

As a response, Goodyear's European affiliate developed its own radials, after observing Michelin's success in Europe. The engineers at the European technical centre "took work done [in Europe] on radials and built on that base in the US".[78] That base included "tire-building machines and rubber compounds, which are different for radials than for bias-ply tires, and expertise in making steel-wire belts, which aren't used at all in conventional tires".[79] ■

In 1984, the two technical centres coordinated to design a new radial truck tyre, the first time the two centres worked together.

Whereas the Goodyear case involved the transfer of design knowledge, the HP case included the development of a product.

Case example In 1985, Johann Stich, the HP district sales manager in Calgary (Canada) identified the need for remote terminal units (RTUs) among some of his customers in the oil and gas industry. As one of the world's major centres for the oil and gas industry, Calgary hosts many oil and gas firms that need to monitor wells dispersed across a variety of remote environments.

With support from the Canadian executive group, Stich established his RTU team in 1986. By mid 1988 the team started to test some components of the product at the site of a local customer. At the same time, the Calgary team won the charter from HP's corporate level against an internal competitor, as the product in Calgary was close to completion and Shell Oil had committed to buy the product.

The product sold well in Canada and, by 1990, also sold well in Europe. In 1993, the Calgary team, as well as the product, became part of HP's Lake Stevens Instrument Division (LSID), based near Seattle.[80] ■

Pattern VI As with the previous pattern, the foreign affiliate develops an internationally transferable FSA, but in this case guided by corporate headquarters in the home country. The recombination capability is co-located in the home and the host country.

In the following, both Data General Corp. (DGC) and Honeywell successfully guided the development path of their subsidiaries.

Case example DGC, an American manufacturer of small mainframes, expanded into Japan by licensing its products to Nippon Mini Computer Corporation (NMC) as early as 1971. In the 1970s, its Japanese affiliate mainly focused on adapting products to Japanese consumers' needs. After becoming NMC's largest shareholder in 1979, DGC renamed NMC as Nippon Data General Corporation (NDG).

At that point, DGC decided to allocate more responsibilities to NDG in product development, especially to leverage the local capability in compact design. NDG's involvement greatly helped the success of the first portable computer with a bigger screen, which incorporated several key technologies from NDG. For example, the liquid crystal display screen came from Japan's digital-watch industry. Applying the surface mounting technique developed in Japan's consumer electronics industry, NDG's engineers were able to save more space on the baseboard, thereby allowing more components to be mounted.[81] ∎

Case example A second example involves Honeywell Homes Canada's upgrading of its manufacturing charter. Established in 1930, Honeywell Homes Canada developed from a distributor to an autonomous subsidiary of US-based conglomerate Honeywell, with a full range of value-chain activities by the early 1980s. Its Scarborough (Canada) plant manufactured products mainly for the Canadian market. These products were also produced at the Minneapolis plant in the US.

Around 1985, increased price competition and overcapacity among branch plants pushed senior management in the US to consider rationalizing plants in North America.

In this context, Honeywell Homes Canada proposed a plan to produce the Zone Valves and Fan & Limit products for the entire North American market, and to move its other ten products to the Minneapolis plant. This plan won the buy-in from the divisional general manager in the US, though small changes were made to the proposal on the division of labour between the Minneapolis plant and the Scarborough plant. The shift in product lines was implemented in 1987 and 1988, with the Scarborough plant specializing in the Zone Valves and the Fan & Limit products. All the other products previously produced in the Scarborough plant were moved to the US. Thus, both sites had to give up on manufacturing some products and focused on a more limited product mix, resulting in improved efficiency. ∎

Pattern VII In this case, a foreign affiliate first develops a location-bound FSA, typically to cater to the host country market requirements for national responsiveness, as in Pattern IV, but then upgrades this FSA to make it internationally transferable, again guided by the home country corporate headquarters. The recombination capability is co-located in the home and the host country, as in Pattern VI.

Such a pattern can be found in the cases of 3M Canada and Citibank (now the retail and corporate banking arm of Citigroup, the largest financial services company in the world). 3M Canada developed distinct marketing strategies, which eventually led to earning a North American mandate; Citibank honed its capability to respond to financial crises during the Latin American crisis and the Mexican peso crisis and later transferred this locally created knowledge to its Asian operations, allowing it to more effectively address the Asian crisis.

Case example Established in the US in 1981, the animal health care business at 3M expanded to Canada in 1984, to market a flea-control insecticide to Canadian customers.

In the US, the product was sold through distributors. However, the Canadian business manager preferred direct sales to veterinarians through 3M representatives, believing that such a channel choice "would provide greater control and a better understanding of the market".[82]

Through the late 1980s and early 1990s, the insecticide product held around 50 per cent market share in Canada, but only about 10 per cent in the US. This discrepancy "was felt to be a function of the different distribution systems".[83]

The 1993 reorganization of the animal health care business established a distinct insecticides division. When the US and Canadian managers joined the business team of this new insecticides division, both the team leader and the marketing representative were Canadians. This shifted the business management and marketing activities of the insecticides division largely to Canada, allowing the division to change its distribution system across North America. ■

Case example US-based Citibank suffered losses as a result of the Latin American debt crisis of the 1980s and the Mexican peso crisis of 1994/1995. As a result of these crises, both the corporate executives at the headquarters and senior managers in Latin America learned to take preventive measures in the face of potential financial crises: techniques included removing weak customers, applying stricter accounting standards and shunning certain business sectors.

When Mexico experienced severe financial problems in 1994, Citibank, like many other investors, started to investigate whether such a crisis could occur in Asia. Two weeks after the Mexican peso crisis in 1994, Citibank sent Alex Erskine, an economist in Citibank Australia, to Asia to find out which Asian countries were economically similar to Mexico. In 1996, Citibank Vice Chairman William Rhodes chaired a conference to evaluate the firm's risk, followed in 1997 by two similar conferences on its Asian operations.

Citibank made sure that many of its senior Asian personnel had first-hand experience of the Latin American crisis. The corporate banking unit for all emerging markets, emerging market retail banking, the North Asia division and the South Asia division were all headed by veterans of the Latin American crisis, who had been relocated to these positions in the early 1990s. Also, many senior executives in Thailand, Indonesia, South Korea and the Philippines had lived through the Latin American crisis. For example, Dennis Martin, an Argentine and head of corporate banking for all emerging markets, spent 17 years with Citibank in Latin America; Michael Contreras, who led the Southeast Asia Division in 1996, had spent 20 years with Citibank in its Central American Division.

As a result, Citibank was able to interpret correctly the early signs of the Asian crisis in 1997/1998. Even before the Asian crisis emerged, Citibank took several preventive measures. By mid 1996, when the first signs of a crisis materialized in Asian financial markets, its senior executives deployed strategies they had learned in Latin America. For example, Michael Contreras started to cut Citibank's lending volume in Thailand and Indonesia by about half; Citibank in Asian countries also strengthened its scrutiny when lending money to conglomerates by investigating the health of the entire company rather than just that of the division receiving the money. Ultimately, the knowledge transfers, embedded in the managers operating in Asia, helped Citibank not only to avoid disastrous losses in Asia but even to achieve some earnings growth in 1997.[84] ■

Pattern VIII Several affiliates, located in different countries, develop an internationally transferable FSA together. Some may contribute upstream knowledge (e.g., in the technological sphere), whereas others may contribute downstream knowledge (e.g., in the marketing and distribution sphere). In this case, the recombination capability is co-located in all the participating affiliates, without central guidance from home country corporate headquarters.

Case example The development of a so-called 'technology transfer toolbox' at HP involved engineers, scientists and managers working in several countries. An HP scientist, dissatisfied with the impact of the main research centres on HP businesses, took the initiative to build a project toolbox for scientists and project managers, recruiting team members in research centres in England, the US and Italy. These team members then in turn identified key new members. Ultimately, the team consisted of scientists, engineers and managers who continued to work in their separate countries.

Lacking a common vision, the project did not start well, but after the team members held a two-day face-to-face discussion on the project's objectives it proceeded smoothly, with team members communicating by email, video or telephone.

The team's work resulted in the 'technology transfer toolbox', based on Internet technologies and packaged in a process reference documentation template. By 2003, this template was considered "a de facto standard internal to HP for capturing best practices".[85] ▪

Pattern IX Again, a set of affiliates develops an internationally transferable FSA, as in Pattern VIII. In this case, however, location-bound knowledge is added in the various countries involved, thereby allowing national responsiveness, similar to Pattern III.

This pattern is reflected in the organization of Citibank in the late 1980s and early 1990s, as well as in the development of the cleansing cloth at Procter & Gamble (P&G).

Case example From the very beginning of its international expansion, Citibank operated through autonomous national subsidiaries. In the 1980s and 1990s, however, it slowly changed its decentralized structure in Europe into a network-based structure.

In 1985, Citibank's European regional management started 'the European Bank' initiative. This initiative created informal regional product and customer units. Normally, an executive from a large affiliate would head each unit, and would be responsible for identifying opportunities and challenges facing the subsidiaries in the region. However, the regional units did not actually develop any specific strategic responses, and national subsidiaries kept their autonomy to respond as they deemed fit in each market.

Further regional coordination continued with 'the Unique European Bank' initiative, announced in 1988, and a global reorganization in 1990. Still retaining its geography-based national structure, Citibank structured linkages "across affiliates to leverage dispersed resources"[86] through specialized product- and customer-focused units. Thus, the specialized units and the local affiliates became jointly responsible for local activities, through "shared management"[87] of these activities.

Citibank in Europe continued to pursue such regional integration strategies in the early 1990s. By 1994, it had transitioned to a truly network-based structure. ■

Case example In the late 1990s, consumer researchers at US-based consumer goods MNE Procter & Gamble (P&G) found that women in the US, Europe and Japan were not satisfied with their facial cleansing products. In the US, bar soaps left the skin dry; in Europe, cleansing milk did not clean the skin very well; and in Japan, foaming facial cleansers did not leave the skin sufficiently moisturized.

In response, P&G set up a technology team in Cincinnati (US) to apply technologies from all over the world to design a product suitable to satisfy consumers' needs internationally. For example, the team drew on Japanese technologists for their knowledge of cleansing processes. Using input from experts around the world, the team developed a cleansing cloth truly effective at both cleaning and moisturizing the skin.

This impregnated cloth technology became the 'chassis', based upon which subsidiaries engaged in further adaptations, adding location-bound knowledge specific to their own geographic markets. For example, a Japanese technology team impregnated the cleansing cloth with a cleanser specific to the Japanese market.

At the same time, a US marketing team developed the one-step routine concept for the US market, and a marketing team in Japan emphasized the cloth's ability to increase skin circulation "through a massage while bossing skin clarity due to the micro fibers' ability to clean pores and trap dirt".[88]

Thus, "[I]n the end, each market ended up with a distinct product built on a common technology platform".[89] ■

Pattern X As with the previous pattern, a set of affiliates works together. Here, they first jointly develop a location-bound FSA geared towards one specific host country market. When successful, this FSA is then upgraded into an internationally transferable FSA, under the guidance of the MNE corporate headquarters. This pattern is often observed in strategic management consulting, whereby international expert teams provide solutions to specific problems in a specific country and, if particularly successful, then turn their approach into a company best practice with wide geographic application potential. The case of TRW Automotive illustrates this pattern.

Case example TRW Automotive (purchased by the Blackstone group in 2002) is one of the world's largest suppliers of automobile components. In 1993, Nissan, one of TRW's customers, complained about the high defect rate and high cost structure of the steering assemblies manufactured by TRW-UK. An internal investigation at TRW-UK found that employees responsible for engineering, product design and process design had poor communications with each other and were also particularly weak at execution.

To solve this problem, TRW established the Nissan Global Team. For each of the three regions (the US, Japan and the UK), TRW chose the individuals considered the best engineer and best customer support professional. These six members together "represented TRW's best capabilities in lean principles as they applied to product and process engineering and design, manufacturing, shop floor issues, and customer service".[90] Within less than two years, TRW-UK became one of the most efficient and high-quality operations inside TRW.

TRW did not stop there. As of 1996, the Nissan Global Team was still in operation, applying what it had learned to other parts of TRW's operations.[91] ∎

The ten above patterns of FSA development may not be an exhaustive set, but each can be observed regularly in international business practice. An MNE's overall recombination capability can be described, roughly, as its mastering a variety of FSA development patterns. The firm's recombination capability will evolve over time, particularly as foreign affiliates develop their own recombination strengths.

Complementary resources of external actors

Having discussed value creation through recombination, *let us turn now to the fifth concept of the unifying framework: complementary resources of external actors*. In many cases, MNEs need complementary resources of external actors (technology providers, licensees, local distributors, joint venture partners, etc.) to be successful abroad. The firm's domestically successful stand-alone FSAs, its routines and even its recombination capabilities may be insufficient or inappropriate to operate successfully in host countries and regions, because of the cultural, economic, institutional and spatial 'distance' from the home country or home region. In other words, some success ingredients may be missing, and these can then be provided by external actors, if at least two conditions are fulfilled. First, internal development of the required strengths is expected to bring a lower net value than relying upon external actors. Second, the need to rely on external actors can be satisfied in practice, and does not jeopardize the specific expansion project considered.

Case example   The experience of Montedison in the US helps to illuminate the importance of complementary resources of external actors. Montedison, an Italian chemical company, tried to re-enter the US in the early 1980s, a few years after it failed in that same market with a wholly owned subsidiary.

Montedison held about 17 per cent of the European capacity in polypropylene production, but it was weak in the US. Although it had experienced success in Europe and had even developed an advanced new processing technology for the production of polypropylene, venturing into the unfamiliar US market on its own appeared too risky, especially given its earlier failure.

Montedison decided to team up with Hercules, the leading polypropylene producer in the US market. Hercules had FSAs in marketing and product applications, but was weak in process technology. Thus, the two companies felt they could achieve synergies through collaboration.

In 1983, the two companies established a fifty-fifty equity joint venture, incorporating the successful marketing strategies from Hercules and the process technologies from Montedison. This joint venture grew into the world leader in polypropylene.[92] ■

Case example EnCana, Canada's largest natural gas producer, and ConocoPhillips, the US oil major, agreed in October 2006 to form a joint venture and to invest more than US $10 billion over the next decade to expand the joint venture's production. The joint venture would include two new companies, one in upstream activities and one in downstream activities. The upstream company would own two EnCana oil sands projects at Foster Creek and Christina Lake in Alberta, Canada. The downstream company would own two ConocoPhillips refineries in Roxana, Illinois, and Borger, Texas, both in the US. Today, as part of a split transaction in 2009, EnCana's joint operations have been transferred to Cenovus Energy, EnCana's integrated oil company.

EnCana contributed unique strengths in underground oil sands operations. EnCana CEO Randy Eresman told reporters at a news conference in Calgary, Alberta, in 2006 that EnCana, compared with other players in the oil sands business, had been particularly effective in extracting oil from oil sands. However, EnCana did not have sufficient expertise in above-ground processes, such as processing the heavy tar extracted from rock and sand. Moreover, building a refinery in Alberta was not perceived as a cost-effective solution. Construction costs in Alberta had soared because oil sands development had created a labour and materials shortage.

For its part, ConocoPhillips contributed expertise in heavy oil refining. However, strong competition had made it difficult for ConocoPhillips to access stable and secure oil supplies. With crude output from Alberta's oil sands expected to triple to three million barrels a day by 2015, ConocoPhillips was eager to become a significant player in the oil sands game.

Thus, the partnership had something to offer to both companies. It strengthened ConocoPhillips's presence in North America by "repositioning 10 per cent of its US downstream business to access a large upstream resource base".[93] EnCana immediately became involved in the North American refining industry and had the opportunity for future upgrader development.[94] ■

Bounded rationality

Having discussed value creation through complementary resources, *let us turn now to the sixth concept of the unifying framework: bounded rationality*. Bounded rationality reflects 'scarcity of mind', meaning that the managers responsible for making decisions and engaging in purposive action in the firm always face information problems.[95]

Access to information sufficient in quality and quantity to guide decision making and managerial action is the first problem. However, even in the presence of all required information, managers have a second problem as well: a limited capability to process complex information bundles. Let us look at these information problems in more detail.

The first problem: any information about the environment relevant to the MNE's functioning and performance, especially about the future state of the environment, is necessarily partial and incomplete, given the complexity and uncertainty characterizing the environment and its evolution.

Incomplete information about environmental complexity may impede successful international expansion, as documented by hundreds of international business case studies, and as observed on an almost daily basis in the media. However, we should also recognize, paradoxically, that newly acquired foreign market knowledge may in some cases alleviate bounded rationality constraints at home.

Case example In 1997, the US-based ice cream company Häagen-Dazs launched the 'dulce de leche' flavour – a flavour similar to caramel – in Argentina, as the company realized that this flavour of ice cream accounted for about 30 per cent of the Argentinian market. This locally developed product proved to be a big hit in Argentina.

At training seminars, "North American executives who had tried dulce de leche at a brand conference in 1997 realized it might fit with the company's recent move to target Latinos in the US."[96] The dulce de leche flavour ice cream was introduced in the US in 1998, at first only in heavily Hispanic areas. The product did better than expected: sales in the US grew by about 27 per cent per month in 1998, and by 2001 it became the company's sixth-best-selling flavour in the US (out of 34 flavours).[97] "It's remarkable and unusual to have a new flavour do so well", said Vivian P. Godfrey, former Häagen-Dazs vice-president for North America.[98] The product's success in Argentina had given the company information relevant to its home market. ∎

The second problem: even if critical information is abundant and rather accurate, senior MNE management faces a problem of processing this information, especially in determining its relevance to the firm and its implications for strategy.

Case example Consider the use of newspaper inserts by Wal-Mart, the world's largest retailer, in Japan in 2004 and 2005: "[Wal-Mart] has made several changes in its use of newspapers' inserts, for instance, first eliminating them, then bringing them back when sales suffered. But it still hasn't made the inserts attractive enough ... [During 2005, Wal-Mart planned to] make more use of the inserts to highlight products centered on traditional Japanese holidays and events such as cherry blossom viewing."[99]

Newspaper inserts may be viewed as a minor, almost trivial managerial issue, but even for this seemingly trivial matter, it is interesting to observe that mighty Wal-Mart – with an experienced management team and a great deal of information about the Japanese consumer – could not easily and rapidly process this information to find the optimal insert template for Japan. ∎

These two bounded rationality problems – incomplete information and difficulty with processing information – are compounded when operating in multiple geographic environments simultaneously, each with different levels of complexity and uncertainty, and therefore different implications for international business strategy.

Let us look at an example of bounded rationality that is particularly relevant to senior managers in MNEs. When contemplating international expansion, and reflecting on transferring FSAs abroad, senior management in MNEs try to choose the optimal entry mode: for example FDI (whereby FSAs covering the entire value chain are transferred to foreign affiliates) versus licensing (whereby typically technology-based and manufacturing FSAs are transferred to a foreign licensee) versus original equipment manufacturing (OEM, whereby typically only technology-based FSAs are transferred, to be combined with the manufacturing capability of a foreign producer). Which entry mode will likely lead to the highest value creation and the greatest satisfaction of stakeholder needs? Four problems arise in this enormously complex decision. The first problem is one of property rights: if outside actors such as licensees and OEM suppliers can capture the MNE's FSAs, even within the realm of what is legally permitted, this may reduce the value of these FSAs to the MNE. Second, outside contracting partners may not fully respect the quality standards normally upheld by the MNE; these actors may thereby create negative spillover effects for the MNE, such as negative responses by customers and shareholders. Third, in the case of FDI, the MNE has to cope with a new institutional regime and usually foreign employees and work practices. Here, the question arises whether the MNE will be able to reach home country or preset productivity standards, and perhaps more generally, whether home country routines in the workplace and established best practices can actually be deployed successfully. Even past experience abroad, in a number of foreign environments that has led to new routines on how to operate in host markets, may be of little use in new host environments that are 'distant' from the originally penetrated markets. Finally, to the extent that international expansion implies recombination of resources, the use of outside actors versus complete internalization will have an impact on the development trajectory of the MNE's recombination capability.

Case example The unique benefits attainable through global alliance formation, and the substantial costs involved in the establishment of their own worldwide service networks, pushed many intercontinental passenger carriers to offer global services through international alliances, even when they had free access to host countries without institutional restrictions. In this case, the bounded rationality problem consisted of figuring out how to combine extant intercontinental services with local services in a multitude of host countries, and also how to combine these extant intercontinental services with other intercontinental services so as to achieve a seamless, worldwide network service. No single airline in the world has figured out how to achieve this on its own. In 2009, the three global alliances, namely Oneworld, Skyteam and Star Alliance, accounted for more than 70 per cent of realized revenue passenger kilometres in scheduled traffic.[100]

From a customer perspective, a fully integrated service across regions is more convenient than separate offerings from a number of independently operating airlines. For example, suppose that a passenger needs to travel from a spoke station (e.g., Pittsburgh) in the US to a spoke station (e.g., Lyon) in Europe. Without a global alliance, the passenger has to buy three flights from three airlines separately: a flight from the US spoke to a US hub (e.g., New York), a second flight from the US hub to a European hub (e.g., Paris), and a third flight from the European hub to the European spoke. With a global alliance, by contrast, the passenger only has to buy flight services from a single airline. Through this type of seamless service, a global alliance may provide more convenience and better coordination of schedules than independent, non-allied airlines.

Global alliances offer cost advantages to the member carriers. It is expensive (and institutionally perhaps impossible) for carriers to establish an independent marketing base and obtain strategic landing slots in host countries; it is usually cheaper to provide such services via alliance partners. For example: as of 2003, 15 EU members allowed US carriers to fly from the US to any of these member countries and then to another country with open skies, yet most US carriers chose to offer global services through their alliance instead, with only Northwest and Delta operating such routes.

In addition to cost savings, global airline alliance groupings also give their members increased traffic volumes across the combined networks, operational bases, brand names, computer reservation systems and FSAs in external relations. For example, a member carrier increases its foreign partners' existing market through extra traffic generated by the feed to the foreign partners, and it also expands its own market through extra traffic by the feed from foreign partners; joint advertising across markets increases demand and the number of passengers in the global alliance group; and frequent flyer programmes allow passengers to collect air miles even if they fly with a partner airline, and to spend air-mile points on flights of all member carriers, thereby offering more opportunities for passengers to earn air-mile points and use rewards.[101] ■

A second noteworthy example of bounded rationality, commonly encountered by senior managers of MNEs, is the phenomenon that senior managers in the home country and senior managers in the host country may adopt different decision-making approaches. Senior managers in the home country, especially those at the corporate level, and managers in foreign subsidiaries may select different information facets as relevant to strategy, given the multifacetedness of the relevant information. Multifaceted information is not the same as complex information; rather, multifacetedness refers to the variety of types of accessible information, and to the phenomenon that decision makers will select only some of these types as relevant to strategic decisions, based upon elements such as personal or institutional experience. Furthermore, even if corporate and subsidiary managers agree that the same information facets are relevant, the two groups of managers may interpret those facets differently in terms of their implications for strategy. Such divergence in judgement, which leads to alternative predictions of the future in a context of high uncertainty, again results from elements such as differences in experience between the corporate level and the firm's subsidiaries.

Why would subsidiary managers view opportunities for value creation differently from corporate-level management in the home country? First, subsidiary managers receive information directly from the local, external environment (local clients, suppliers, newspapers, etc.): this information is typically optimistic and framed in the form of very broad opportunities (new customer demands, supplier suggestions, macro-economic trends, etc.). Second, acting on this information, the subsidiary managers then engage in their own framing efforts: they reconstruct the outside information in the form of demand forecasts, growth scenarios and so on. Such reconstruction leads to the creation of an 'inside view'. The inside view is typically an optimistic perspective on the future. This optimism is grounded in three forms of subsidiary manager confidence: confidence in the subsidiary unit as the source of success, confidence in the probable state of the future environment, especially the local environment, and confidence in the subsidiary's ability to control events. By contrast, projected scenarios that come from home country managers are typically more pessimistic and conservative.

Case example Such a divergence of judgement occurred at Xerox when its Japanese affiliate, Fuji Xerox, wanted to develop compact copiers. As an insider in the Japanese market, Fuji Xerox viewed this as a good business opportunity, while the Xerox group in the US thought differently.

Fuji Xerox was established in 1962 as a joint venture between the American document management company Xerox and the Japanese photographic company Fuji Photo. Fuji Xerox gradually expanded its mandate from merely marketing xerographic products to developing its own products, as well as modifying Xerox designs to local demands. In the late 1960s and early 1970s, some Japanese competitors (e.g., Ricoh) started to produce high-quality, low-cost copiers. Competing with these local Japanese rivals, Fuji Xerox experienced these market changes intimately and foresaw increasing demand for compact, high-quality copiers.

However, at the same time, the central management at Xerox was more concerned with IBM and Eastman Kodak entering the copier industry in the US. These two new entrants targeted the mid- and high-volume segments of the market in the US, which were the key businesses and lucrative market segments for Xerox. From the Xerox perspective, the low-volume segment was a minor part of its business.

Fuji Xerox in Japan and Xerox in the US had very different perceptions about future market development, and they also assessed the technical knowledge at Fuji Xerox quite differently. By the late 1960s, Fuji Xerox had already developed experimental inexpensive compact copiers. However, from Xerox's perspective, such technical capabilities were not comparable to those of IBM or Kodak, and Fuji Xerox was perceived as little more than a faraway unit in a tiny market.

Fuji Xerox tried to convince Xerox to develop compact machines, but different perceptions between Fuji Xerox and Xerox on future market developments made this task very difficult. As explained by Tony Kobayashi, the former president of Fuji Xerox, "(W)e had been insisting that the Xerox Group needed to develop small copiers as an integral part of its worldwide strategy. However, Xerox's attitude was that the low end of the market was not a priority . . . On the other hand, we were seeing rising demand for small copiers in Japan."[102]

The senior managers at Fuji Xerox persisted and successfully developed small copiers for the Japanese market. Later, in 1979, Fuji Xerox even started to export such compact copiers to Xerox in the US, and Fuji Xerox literally rescued Xerox when Xerox failed to mount an effective response to the rise of Japanese competitors, which took away Xerox's market in the US.[103] ∎

Bounded reliability

Having discussed bounded rationality, *let us turn now to the seventh and final concept of the unifying framework: bounded reliability*. Bounded reliability reflects the 'scarcity of effort to make good on open-ended promises': agents do not always carry through on their expressed intentions to try to achieve a particular outcome or performance level. This is why firms introduce safeguards or enforcement mechanisms to heighten detection of, and provide punishment for, reneging.

A *first source* of bounded reliability is opportunism, which involves ex ante false promises and/or ex post reneging on promises, either by external contracting parties or by employees inside the firm. Opportunism is self-interest-seeking behaviour with guile. Here, an intentional effort to cheat/shirk prevails, which benefits the cheating/shirking party.[104]

A *second source* of bounded reliability is benevolent preference reversal, in which an actor's initial promise is made in good faith, but the actor's preferences then change over time, though not with the intent to harm the party to which the promise was made. For senior managers in MNEs, there are two key types of benevolent preference reversal: 'good faith local prioritization' and 'scaling back on over-commitments'.

In the realm of reprioritization, a common case involves overseas actors initially making a promise in good faith but, over time, diverting their effort (and resources under their control) to the pursuit of local preferences, at the expense of organizational/global preferences. For example, at the level of foreign affiliates, the subsidiary manager may typically promise to try to carry out specific investment projects determined by corporate headquarters, and commit to specific performance requirements. However, the manager may change his/her preferences for several reasons, including: a substantial distance in time from any punishment for non-achievement; a substantial distance in space from the headquarters' monitoring apparatus; and the relative proximity and intrinsic satisfaction derived from focusing on autonomous, locally driven investment opportunities that give immediate local rewards to the subsidiary (such as an improvement of relationships with local stakeholders).

Scaling back on over-commitment typically implies that the actor who made an initial promise was overconfident in his/her capacity to deliver. This overestimation may have various sources, including: a dysfunctional impulsivity when making a promise; fallacious planning, meaning the consideration from past experience of only 'best case' rather than 'average case' implementation scenarios; excessive discounting of known risks; exaggerating the extent to which the environment can be controlled, etc.

These bounded reliability problems cannot be simply reduced to bounded rationality issues, because they are not caused by a lack of information or an inability to process information. In the case of opportunism, the individual may possess all the relevant information, and in fact may process it perfectly. The problem with opportunism lies with the individual's self-centred desires and effort. In the case of benevolent preference reversal, the problem is not with the individual's assessment of how the world is or will be. It is about making the same mistakes over and over again, even if the outcomes of these mistakes are predictable. Bounded reliability does not only occur at the subsidiary level, but can also be characteristic of head office behaviour, e.g., when specific promises for resource allocation are made to particular affiliates and then reversed at a later stage. *Bounded rationality is about the imperfect assessment of a present or future state of affairs, thereby leading to incorrect beliefs; bounded reliability is about imperfect effort towards pre-specified goal achievement, thereby leading to incomplete fulfilment of promises*.

A single individual can engage in both benevolent preference reversal and opportunism. For example, suppose that an individual has engaged in good faith local prioritization: good faith promises were made to corporate headquarters, but efforts to make good on those promises have been replaced by the pursuit of local goals. As the time for performance appraisal approaches, this individual may wilfully and opportunistically engage in incomplete and inaccurate reporting of the performance gap.

It is also worth pointing out that individuals can perform as expected in the short term, yet also have underlying tendencies towards good faith local prioritization – tendencies that have not yet affected their behaviour (perhaps they are 'doing the right things for the wrong reasons'). Such individuals may produce long-term conflicts between the subsidiary and corporate headquarters (and perhaps the remainder of the MNE network).

It is important to recognize that bounded reliability at the level of the individual may translate into behaviour of teams, entire units within the MNE, and even the MNE as a whole. When transactions are conducted with external actors, bounded reliability challenges emanating from both the MNE and from these external actors should be assessed. Irrespective of the sources of bounded reliability, it should be emphasized that a particular level of unreliability in the MNE can be eliminated by a number of governance mechanisms. These include, *inter alia*: (1) contractual safeguards (such as sufficient monitoring and proper incentives) to align interests, thereby curbing opportunism; (2) joint goal development, goal segmentation (setting milestones) and frequent communication to align expectations and to sustain cognitive proximity, thereby reducing reprioritization; (3) routines such as multi-level and multi-stage decision-making processes to reduce the impact of individual evaluation biases and impulsivity, thereby reducing the occurrence of over-commitments and the subsequent need to scale back on such over-commitments.[105]

Implications of international business strategy for MNE performance

MNE managers can use the seven core elements of the international business framework described in this chapter, at various levels: the level of a single expansion project, the level of a divisional/business unit's growth strategy or the level of the firm's overall international business strategy. It is critical for managers to reflect on the MNE's strengths (relative to rival companies) and its ability to match its distinct resource base with the challenges and opportunities found in the international environment, thereby creating value and satisfying shareholder needs.

The question then arises whether an international expansion programme is likely to improve MNE performance. A vast international business literature attempts to answer the question whether international expansion and the related increase of international diversification (e.g., the share of foreign investment to total investment, foreign sales to total sales or foreign production to total pro-duction) is likely to have positive effects on the MNE's return and risk. The answer is: it depends on several factors.

First, at the project level, the MNE should compare the expected net present value per invested monetary unit in foreign expansion with that of domestic expansion, taking into account a variety of risk factors. MNEs should undertake foreign expansion projects only if these make more economic sense than domestic projects. MNEs should expand internationally until, at the margin, the next domestic and foreign expansion projects are equally attractive.

Second, the international transfer of FSAs, whether embodied in final products (leading to scale economies), intermediate products such as R&D and marketing knowledge (leading to scope economies, as benefits are gained from transferring and sharing valuable knowledge across borders) or coordinating skills (leading to benefits of exploiting national differences), is not costless. In most cases, even internationally transferable FSAs need to be complemented by additional, location-bound FSAs in host countries. In more general terms, even with a strong recombination capability (entailing entrepreneurial dynamism, available excess resources and access to new resources in host environments) international success requires substantial investments, learning and legitimacy creation over time.

Third, even if the necessary investments in location-bound knowledge have been made, and both learning and legitimacy-building have occurred in host nations, the MNE's growth will not necessarily lead to improved economic performance. Substantial adaptation to host country environments will increase the costs of internal governance. Central headquarters, faced with increased bounded rationality and bounded reliability problems, will find it more difficult to select particular investment trajectories and to choose among alternative international expansion patterns, each favouring specific subunits in the organization located in different countries.

The framework outlined in Figure 1.1 and Figure 1.2 suggests that expanding internationally may have important effects on the firm in terms of where and how it creates value. However, the keys to successful international business strategy – and thus the MNE's performance – are its FSAs relative to rivals, and its effectiveness and efficiency in deploying and augmenting these FSAs across borders.[106]

Takeaway messages for managers: The seven key questions in international business strategy

The above analysis suggests that managers should answer the following seven basic questions in international strategy formation:

1. What is our distinct resource base, including elements of our administrative heritage, that provides internationally transferable FSAs?
2. Which value-added activities in which foreign location(s) will permit us to exploit and augment to the fullest our distinct resource base?
3. What are the expected costs and difficulties we will face when transferring this distinct resource base?
4. What specific resource recombination (associated with each alternative foreign entry and operating mode) will be required so as to make the proposed international value-added activities successful?
5. Do we have the required resource recombination capability in-house?
6. What are the costs and benefits of using complementary resources of external actors to fill resource gaps?
7. What are the main bounded rationality and bounded reliability problems we will face when extending the geographic scope of our firm's activities, given the changed boundaries of the firm, the changed linkages with outside stakeholders and the changes in our internal functioning?

The following two case studies (Honda and Four Seasons Hotels) illustrate how answering these questions can be useful to managerial practice in MNE.

Case 1.1 Honda's 'answers' to the seven basic questions in international strategy formation

For the Japanese car manufacturer Honda, the domestic and international environments in the early 1970s brought tremendous challenges to its export strategy, previously based on mass production in Japan. Honda wanted to develop extensive international production capabilities in overseas markets, especially the US market. However, Honda doubted its foreign facilities could attain the quality level characteristic of its Japanese-built cars. Furthermore, Honda also wondered whether its foreign manufacturing facilities could achieve Japanese cost levels.

The environment in the early 1970s

Internationally, Honda faced three major environmental changes in the early 1970s: the rising value of the yen against the US dollar, new US regulations of tailpipe emissions and the first oil crisis. Although the rising yen threatened Honda's traditional export strategy, the other two changes – together with the success of its small, fuel-efficient Civic model in Japan and the US – provided a window of opportunity for Honda to expand in the US.

Specifically, the rising value of the yen in 1971 increased the costs of exporting cars to the US, Honda's largest overseas market. The first oil crisis of 1973 negatively affected Honda's domestic operations, as rising oil prices significantly increased Honda's manufacturing costs. At the same time, however, the public demanded more fuel-efficient cars to reduce the costs brought by the roaring oil prices.

In 1970, the US Congress passed the Clean Air Act, imposing stricter requirements on tailpipe emissions. However, the US automakers had not been able to reach a consensus regarding the appropriate technology to meet such requirements. Both the first oil crisis and the Clean Air Act pushed the demand for fuel-efficient cars, which became the market niche US automakers had not been able to occupy. Clearly, Honda viewed the US regulations as a welcome opportunity for it to catch up, as reflected in the words of Honda's President Soichiro Honda: "(T)his allows latecomers like us to line up at the same starting line as our rivals".[107]

In 1972, Honda brought to the Japanese market its Civic model with the CVCC (Controlled Vortex Combustion Chamber) engine, which met the US emissions standards. The CVCC engine permitted the regulated burning of a very lean mixture without the catalytic converter or exhaust-gas recirculation required by most other engines. In Japan, the Civic model won the Car of the Year Award for three consecutive years as of 1973; in the US, it beat all other competitors in a fuel-economy test for four consecutive years as of 1974.

Initial puzzle

The popularity of the Civic model in the US suggested an increase in car imports to the US, but such an increase might have provoked the US government to impose import restrictions. This fear, together with the rising yen and the first oil crisis, led Honda to consider establishing a motorcycle manufacturing operation in the US. For this purpose, Kiyoshi Kawashima, Honda's President, requested a feasibility study in 1974. This study expressed doubts about the feasibility of achieving the required quality levels in US-based motorcycle production. Further, the study suggested a Honda factory would not be profitable if it manufactured only motorcycles. For those reasons, Kawashima decided not to build a manufacturing base in the US at that time.

However, the concept of a manufacturing base in the US resurfaced with the high demand for the Civic model in Japan and the US. To satisfy this demand, Honda's Suzuka and Saitama factories had been operating at full capacity. Expecting further growth in market share, Honda had the option to expand its domestic factories, but Kiyoshi insisted on putting that plan on hold. He said, "[s]ince it [Honda's auto business] is a budding business, we shouldn't assume we're ready to charge into competition with the other Japanese manufacturers, either in terms of sales or capital. So, rather than compete domestically to no avail, I would like to use this opportunity to take a chance in America, the world's largest market. I would like to build a motorcycle factory and eventually an automobile factory in the United States."[108] Masami Suzuki, the managing director in charge of overseas manufacturing, was assigned the responsibility for a new feasibility study. With this mission, Suzuki left for the US in January 1976.

The second feasibility study

Suzuki first discussed the plan with the American managers at American Honda Motor Co. These managers expressed scepticism about achieving comparable quality standards by manufacturing in the US. They based their scepticism on their own experiences with what they saw as the intrinsic quality problems of contemporary American-made cars. For Suzuki, these discussions still left the quality issue unanswered.

In the spring of 1976, Lee Iacocca, President of Ford, gave Suzuki the chance to investigate the American way of auto manufacturing. Because Suzuki was negotiating selling CVCC engines to Ford, Iacocca gave Suzuki permission to tour the most highly rated plant at Ford. The tour gave Suzuki a detailed look at the knockdown system characteristic of American auto manufacturing. With the knockdown system, the main car assemblies were shipped via railroad from Detroit, Michigan, to the Ford plant, where multiple-variety and small-volume production methods were used to manufacture cars. Compared with the American system, Honda's manufacturing system used much less presswork, more integrated welding processes, and delivered better real cost-performance.

Suzuki came out of the tour convinced that car quality depended primarily on the management system, and that Honda would be able to produce high-quality cars in the US by applying its existing management principles. At that stage, Honda started to search for an appropriate US location for its plant. Honda wanted a site of 100 to 200 acres, with easy access to railroad transport and a pool of highly skilled labour.

In 1976, Honda commissioned an American consulting firm to search for an optimal location, and in 1977 it hired a research institute to analyse labour-market conditions. Based on these two research results, Suzuki and his colleagues visited more than fifty sites in Ohio without finding the right site.

Just before giving up on an Ohio location, Suzuki visited the state governor and the chief of Ohio's Economic Development Bureau in July 1977, leading to the selection of a location in Marysville, Ohio.

Employees and suppliers required to manufacture motorcycles

Honda of America Manufacturing (HAM) was established in 1978. It planned to manufacture motorcycles first, and cars later once it had built up sufficient manufacturing experience. HAM's top priority, to manufacture high-quality products, was deemed to depend on two key elements: capable employees who would make the cars, and reliable suppliers who would provide the parts and raw materials.

The first challenge: selecting and training employees. To do this, a selection committee, led by HAM's Executive Vice-President and Manager of General Affairs, chose 50 people out of more than 3,000 applicants. Interestingly, they were hired not because of their experience or knowledge in motorcycle manufacturing, but because of their passion for their work. Honda believed it would be easier to transfer Honda's work philosophy to this type of employee.

In 1979, Japanese engineers started to train the workers at HAM, and HAM's American managers were sent to Japan to learn about Honda's manufacturing processes. In September 1979, HAM started to manufacture the CR250R, a motocross bike. After the workers gained sufficient experience, the production of the Gold Wing GL1000, a more sophisticated model, was transferred to HAM in April 1980.

The second challenge: developing a lean supplier network in the US. In Japan, Honda had its supplier groups, but only a few of them agreed to follow Honda and build plants in the US. To supplement those suppliers, Honda had to develop a supplier network from three sources: suppliers of motorcycle parts (who had to be willing to eventually make auto parts); other small suppliers in Ohio and surrounding states, which had to learn Honda's requirements of quality, cost and timely delivery; and large suppliers which also serviced other automakers, especially the US Big Three (General Motors, Ford and Chrysler).

Honda decided to focus on the first two groups, as it felt managerial attitudes were more important than technical expertise per se. The first two groups appeared more willing to respond to Honda's needs, despite facing challenges in terms of technical and organizational skills. The third group, with superior capabilities, was not as responsive to Honda's requirements as the other two.

To upgrade the expertise of the selected suppliers, Honda became actively involved in their operations, from examining manufacturing processes, to developing quality circles, to hiring new managers. The core of such supplier development activities later became a programme called 'BP', which stood for Best Position, Best Practice, Best Process and Best Performance. With the BP programme, Honda sent out teams of specialists to its suppliers, to help them improve to the required performance level.

HAM expanded its supplier network from a handful of local suppliers in the early 1980s to 320 North American suppliers by 1994. In that year, more than 80 per cent of its parts were purchased locally.[109]

Start of car manufacturing in the US

In January 1980, Honda announced its plan to manufacture cars in the US, with the construction of the necessary facilities starting in December 1980. The prime focus of this new operation was still to build high-quality products. In order to achieve this objective, Honda sent about 300 experts and veteran associates from its Sayama plant in Japan to the US. Additionally, many experienced workers involved in motorcycle production at HAM were transferred to the new HAM auto plant. HAM's first Accord rolled off the production line on 1 November 1982, with the promised high level of quality.[110]

Since then, HAM has become Honda's largest manufacturing plant, producing cars not only for the US, but also for Japan and other countries. In 2012, Honda employed more than 13,500 Ohioans and purchased more than US $16 billion in parts and materials from 600 suppliers in North America.

Following the 2008 financial crisis, favourable exchange rates and lower labour costs signalled a revival of the American automotive sector in 2012. In that same year, Honda announced intentions to invest US $218 million into expansion of two Ohio-based plants.[111]

Honda's legacy

Honda's successful entry into the United States was largely credited to the company's strategic and managerial expertise. Calling it the 'Honda Effect',[112] Richard Pascale noted that it was management's flexibility in reacting strategically to new challenges that allowed the company to be successful in a new market.[113] Because of this "strategic accommodation",[114] and "adaptive persistence",[115] Honda currently operates in Africa, Australia, China, Europe, the Middle East and South America.[116]

Today, Honda continues to establish itself in unfamiliar industries and markets. In 2012, Honda took further steps towards achieving Soichiro Honda's "long-standing dreams to advance human mobility".[117] In 2012 and following 26 years of aviation research, Honda reached the final stages of Federal Aviation Administration (FAA) certification for its HondaJet fleet in 2012. Honda Aircraft Co. CEO Michimasa Fujino expressed confidence the company would gain over a quarter of the market for small business jets thanks to logistics and technological efficiencies in manufacturing mass-market vehicles.[118] Dubbed the 'Civic of the skies,' HondaJet applies just-in-time inventory principles to manufacture 80 jets per year,[119] a figure almost double the industry average. Fujino attributes this edge to the company's manufacturing expertise: "We're doing with HondaJet what the Civic did to American cars from the 1960s. Our competitors are still producing with technology from the 1990s."[120]

Whether the 'innovative spirit'[121] Honda has applied to entering numerous international markets will also be successful in the aircraft industry is uncertain; Honda's aircraft manu-facturing plans were announced in the aftermath of a difficult 2011.[122] After reporting a 7 per cent drop in sales in 2011, and receiving uncharacteristically lukewarm reviews of the newest Civic model,[123] there was some speculation as to whether Honda was losing focus on its manufacturing edge and key product – the Civic. One industry analyst commented that, "Honda management has lost its way somewhat . . . Over the past decade, they've lost track of what the fundamental basis of their business is, and what appeal they hold on the market."[124]

QUESTIONS

1. What was Honda's distinct resource base, including elements of its administrative heritage, that provided internationally transferable FSAs?
2. Which value-added activities in which foreign location(s) permitted Honda to exploit and augment to the fullest its distinct resource base?
3. What were the expected costs and difficulties Honda faced when transferring this distinct resource base?
4. What specific resource recombination (associated with each alternative foreign entry and operating mode) was required so as to make the proposed international value-added activities successful?
5. Did Honda have the required resource recombination capability in-house?
6. What were the costs and benefits of using complementary resources of external actors to fill resource gaps?
7. What were the main bounded rationality and bounded reliability problems Honda faced when extending the geographic scope of the firm's activities, given the changed boundaries of the firm, the changed linkages with outside stakeholders and the changes in its internal functioning?

Case 1.2 Four Seasons' 'answers' to the seven basic questions in international strategy formation[125]

CASE

Four Seasons Hotels and Resorts, a Toronto (Canada)-based company founded in 1960, currently operates 86 properties in 35 countries. It is a leading player in the luxury hotel business worldwide, with several of its hotels routinely earning almost all major hotel quality recognition awards. In 2011, 45 Four Seasons hotels were among the 'Top 500 Hotels' according to *Travel + Leisure*, one of the most influential travel and lifestyle publications in the world. In 2012, 21 Four Seasons hotels won the AAA Five Diamond Award for hotels and restaurants, North America's symbol of excellence in the hospitality industry. Four Seasons has also been named one of *Fortune* magazine's top employers every year since the award's inception.

A detailed understanding of the routines required to satisfy sophisticated and demanding hotel guests drives this hotel chain's success. This knowledge took a long time to develop. The relevant routines also appeared deployable in the chain's international expansion, but some adaptation to local circumstances proved necessary.

Developing the four pillars – the foundation of Four Seasons' success

Isadore Sharp, founder of the Four Seasons hotel chain, started his career by joining his father's construction business in 1952 when he graduated with an architecture degree from Ryerson

Polytechnical Institute in Toronto. In the mid 1950s, when he built a motel for a friend in Toronto, Sharp felt it might be worthwhile to focus on the lodging business. However, the type of accommodation he envisaged was not a traditional motel, but rather a combination of the informality of a motel with the convenience of a conventional, downtown hotel. In 1961, Sharp opened the first Four Seasons in Toronto.

Exceptional luxury hotels as the first pillar

Sharp continued to build hotels during the 1960s, but the basis of the hotel chain's present philosophy surfaced only in the early 1970s. The Four Seasons London was opened in 1970. To compete against the old-fashioned grand hotels in London, Sharp established his London hotel as a luxury hotel of 230 rooms with then-modern amenities such as air conditioning. At the same time, the London hotel kept the essence of the combination of a motel and a downtown hotel: "luxury without formality, service without a class attitude".[126] The instant success of the Four Seasons London, together with difficulties in maintaining good service at the 1,600-room hotel in Toronto opened after the London hotel, resulted in Sharp's decision to develop and operate only midsized hotels of exceptional quality. It was then, in 1972, that the Four Seasons established an early version of its first pillar: "to specialize in small- to medium-sized hotels of exceptional quality, and to be the best wherever we are located".[127]

Uncompromising service as the second pillar

With the first pillar in place as the basic formula, Four Seasons slowly expanded in Canada. During this expansion, Four Seasons continued to refine its understanding of exceptional quality, with a focus on great service. Four Seasons was the first hotel chain in North America to provide 24-hour room service, hair dryers, overnight laundry and bathrobes. As the leader in innovative service, Four Seasons continued to upgrade the content of what was commonly understood in the industry as the 'five-star' hotel standard.

In 1976, Four Seasons formally decided to differentiate itself from its competitors on the basis of its great service, with uncompromising service becoming the second pillar of its success.

By 1978, Four Seasons had expanded to every major Canadian city large enough for a five-star hotel, and it faced a choice: enter the US market, or expand to secondary Canadian cities. Four Seasons chose to enter the US market, continuing to specialize in great service. In fact, it redefined luxury as great service, thereby explicitly linking its first two pillars. At that time, giant hotel chains dominated the US market, with luxury viewed mainly as an issue of architecture and decoration. Four Seasons clearly had to offer something more to defeat these competitors. Four Seasons surveyed its customers – most of whom were business executives – and discovered that they particularly valued time and productivity. Four Seasons therefore introduced new services to help their customers use their time as effectively as possible. For example, room service breakfast was redesigned from a simple leisurely activity to an instrument that helped customers save time and prepare for a busy workday.

Four Seasons also continued to redefine the concept of luxury in its operations. For example, it found that business travellers were interested in leisure and wellness services, such as workout options. In 1986, Four Seasons introduced a full-service spa at the Four Seasons Resort and Club Dallas. This type of service has now become a component of the luxury experience at every Four Seasons hotel.

Intuitive and caring culture as the third pillar

With many new employees joining Four Seasons during its expansion in the 1970s, control emerged as a major internal problem for the chain to maintain its positioning as a set of exceptional luxury hotels with uncompromising service. Four Seasons established detailed service standards as a part of its solution. In addition, Sharp decided to make the chain's implicit operating philosophy explicit. Its 'golden rule' became: "to treat others as we would wish to be treated".[128]

In contrast to other firms that had adopted similar credos, Four Seasons made great efforts to enforce the corporate culture down to the front-line employees. These efforts included a strong focus on hiring the right employees, establishing clear career paths within the firm, encouraging self-discipline and setting performance standards. For example, in terms of hiring process, Four Seasons hired employees for attitude rather than experience or appearance, with each applicant interviewed four or five times within a very strict hiring process. Sharp believed that it would be easier to teach the chain's philosophy to an employee with the right attitude than to change an employee with an ingrained but wrong attitude. When Four Seasons invested in Maui, Hawaii, the large number of hotels in that location made it hard to find capable employees. Four Seasons carefully screened workers from the sugarcane and pineapple fields, hired those workers with positive attitudes, and trained them extensively. Within a year, Four Seasons Maui became the number one hotel on the island.

Specializing in hotel management as the fourth pillar

In the 1980s, when demand for luxury hotels soared in North America, Sharp agreed to build Four Seasons hotels in over a dozen cities. However, the recession in the early 1990s greatly affected real estate and luxury hotels. In 1993, plummeting stock prices and big losses at Four Seasons drove Sharp to conclude that Four Seasons was good at running hotels, but not at building and owning them. Since then, Sharp gradually sold the ownership of almost all the Four Seasons hotels and refocused on hotel management only. By 2005, Four Seasons owned only two hotels: the Pierre in New York and the Four Seasons in Vancouver.

Building upon the four pillars in international expansion

By the early 1990s, Four Seasons had around 20 Four Seasons hotels in major North American cities and popular resort areas large enough to support five star hotels, and it again faced a choice: expand internationally, or expand to somewhat smaller North American cities. Four Seasons chose to expand internationally, for three main reasons. First, the smaller North American cities had fewer high-paying guests, and therefore fewer potential customers for luxury hotels. Second, if Four Seasons opened lower-priced hotels in North American cities, that could threaten its image as both a luxury hotel chain and a provider of outstanding hotel service. Finally, attractive markets for luxury hotels were still available in many foreign city centres in Europe, Asia and the Middle East. Such attractive markets resulted either from a rapidly rising demand for luxury hotels or from a lack of luxury hotels comparable to Four Seasons hotels.

However, overseas expansion also had its own problems. In order to provide a consistent, great service experience in its overseas hotels, Four Seasons needed to not only replicate the four pillars, but also adapt to the local environment. Four Seasons' experience in Paris demonstrated the difficulty of striking this balance between replicating a successful formula and adapting the formula to a foreign market.

The F. S. George V was one of the top six luxury and historic hotels in Paris, the other five being the Bristol, Crillon, Meurice, Plaza Athenee and Ritz. Although the reputation of the George V was falling in the 1980s and 1990s, it was located in one of the most fashionable districts in Paris, close to the Champs Élysées. Moreover, obtaining the necessary permits to build a new hotel was very hard in Paris, so the George V gave Four Seasons an easy way to enter the Paris market.

In November 1997, Four Seasons signed a management agreement with HRH Prince Al Waleed Bin Talal Bin Abdulaziz al Saud, who had bought the hotel in December 1996. With the fourth pillar in place (hotel management), Four Seasons had to look for ways to replicate the other three pillars while adapting to the French market.

A medium-sized Four Seasons luxury hotel with a French flavour

The George V was already a luxury hotel, with standard rooms priced between US $400 and US $700. However, to be a luxury Four Seasons hotel, both the physical appearance and service quality had to be raised to Four Seasons' standards. At the same time, the façade had to be retained, as it was a landmark building designed in the 1920s.

Four Seasons had to conduct a two-year physical renovation. The façade was kept, with the art deco windows, wood panelling and seventeenth-century Flemish tapestries restored. The interior part was redesigned by the French designer Pierre Rochon, who married up-to-date technology with the hotel's French heritage. Four Seasons reduced the number of rooms and suites from 300 to 245, in order to enlarge rooms.

At the same time, Four Seasons also had to upgrade some of the more tangible amenities to meet the French standards of luxury hotels. For example, French guests would expect a luxury hotel to have a world-class restaurant with floral arrangements, while Four Seasons restaurants were normally understated, providing excellent food, but in most cases not of Michelin Star quality. To meet the French standard, Four Seasons recruited Chef Philippe Legendre from Taillevent, a world-class Parisian restaurant.

Replicating Four Seasons' service at the George V

Transferring both its consistent high-quality service and its corporate culture were the major challenges in overseas expansion at Four Seasons. Four Seasons took several steps to facilitate the international replication of its service and culture.

First, Four Seasons clearly defined 7 international service culture standards and 270 international core operating standards. The seven service culture standards included greeting guests (SMILE), making eye contact (EYE), using guests' names (RECOGNITION), speaking in a natural and courteous manner (VOICE), being informed of the hotel and its product (INFORMED), appearing clean and well-fitted (CLEAN) and showing appropriate care for guests at any time (EVERYONE).

The operating standards included work rules and exceptions. For example: phone calls will be answered before the fourth ring; no guest will wait longer than 60 seconds at the reception desk or the cashier desk. There were 800 rules until 1998, but some rules proved to be overly complex or unnecessary in some overseas markets. Four Seasons therefore allowed exceptions to the standards. For example, Four Seasons normally requires waiters and waitresses to leave the coffee pot on the table for guests, so that they can refill their cups themselves, but this approach was viewed as poor service in France. Therefore, this rule was cancelled in France.

Second, Four Seasons enforced its strict hiring policies in France for new recruiting, while retaining a large number of the George V's former employees. According to French regulations, Four Seasons had to keep all former employees of the George V unless they wanted to leave. When the Four Seasons George V reopened, many of the best employees had already found jobs elsewhere, and at least 40 of the 300 former employees who did come back did not pass the Four Seasons' hiring process. For the 400 jobs not filled by former employees, Four Seasons screened more than 10,000 applicants to find employees with the right attitude. The critical mass of the new employees who met the Four Seasons' standards overcame the 'rotten apple'[129] of the inferior employees that Four Seasons was forced to keep.

Finally, Four Seasons chose Didier Le Calvez, the former general manager of the Pierre in New York, to be general manager. He knew the Four Seasons culture well and, because of his French origin, also knew how to deal with French uniqueness. Moreover, Four Seasons sent a 35-person task force to Paris to help Le Calvez to establish norms, as Four Seasons did for every new hotel. The task force consisted of experienced Four Seasons staff/managers trained to identify and mitigate specific problems.

The Four Seasons Hotel George V Paris successfully opened on 18 December 1999, with all rooms occupied. It has continued to do very well. It appeared on Condé Nast Traveler's 2012 Gold List for exceptional service, and was named the best hotel in France in 2011 by the same publication. Also in 2011, it received a 'Palace'[130] title from French tourism authorities – the equivalent of a five-star hotel rating and one of only nine hotels to receive the distinction. Le Calvez was named World's Best Hotel Manager in 2006 by the Hospitality Awards. In addition, one of the dining venues, Le Cinq, has earned two Michelin stars. Within the hospitality industry, these are all major, widely acknowledged signs of success.

Despite Le Calvez leaving Four Seasons in 2007, the staff at the George V Paris continued to receive recognition for excellence in service. In 2011, Céline Bodo of the George V Paris, was named France's receptionist of the year; an indication of the successful integration of Four Seasons' high-quality service values. In the same year, the George V was also recognized for bartending and sommelier services.

The eighth pillar

Following the global financial crisis in 2008, many luxury brands such as Tiffany & Co began offering more affordable product lines in response to increasingly cost conscious consumers. Despite the luxury class hotel sector experiencing a 21.8 per cent drop in revenue per available room between 2008 and 2009, Four Seasons did not opt to launch a low-cost line of hotels. Susan Helstab, Executive Vice President of Marketing at Four Seasons commented that the "growing accessibility of luxury brands means that wealthy buyers are now looking even harder for one-of-a-kind purchases".[131] Citing digital media as a means of providing personalization to their core consumer group, Helstab also noted that "luxury brands that do not commit to a holistic digital media strategy will not survive; it is no longer a nice-to-have but an essential pillar of branding".[132]

Four Seasons devoted fifty per cent of the marketing budget to digital media platforms in 2011, with an emphasis on developing a family travel blog and a social media presence. Online sales rose by 10 per cent from 2010 to 2011, with online bookings accounting for 12 per cent of revenue. In 2012, Four Seasons redesigned its official international website and published the *Luxury Trend Report*, an overview of the luxury goods industry.[133]

QUESTIONS

1. What was Four Seasons' distinct resource base, including elements of its administrative heritage, that provided internationally transferrable FSAs?
2. Which value-added activities in which foreign location(s) permitted Four Seasons to exploit and augment its distinct resource base to the fullest?
3. What were the expected costs and difficulties Four Seasons faced when transferring this distinct resource base?
4. What specific resource recombination (associated with each alternative foreign entry and operating mode) was required so as to make the proposed international value-added activities successful?
5. Did Four Seasons have the required resource recombination capability in-house?
6. What were the costs and benefits of using complementary resources of external actors to fill resource gaps?
7. What were the main bounded rationality and bounded reliability problems Four Seasons faced when extending the geographic scope of the firm's activities, given the changed boundaries of the firm, the changed linkages with outside stakeholders and the changes in its internal functioning?

Notes

1. Stephen Hymer wrote about the additional costs of doing business abroad in his doctoral dissertation, *The International Operations of National Firms: A Study of Direct Foreign Investment* (Cambridge, Mass.: MIT Press, 1976). This concept has since received considerable attention by international business scholars, see the outstanding synthesis by Lorraine Eden and Stewart R. Miller, 'Distance matters: liability of foreignness, institutional distance and ownership strategy', in M. A. Hitt and J. L. C. Cheng (eds.), *The Evolving Theory of the Multinational Firm: Advances in International Management* (Amsterdam: Elsevier, 2004), Volume 16. Obviously, MNEs can reduce the liability of foreignness by forging alliances, such as joint ventures, with local partners in host countries.

2. I view this observation of international FSA transfer, leading to economies of scope if the FSAs are transferred as intermediate goods, as the fundamental insight of modern international business theory.

3. An enormous literature exists on international entry mode choice, including the classic work of Peter J. Buckley and Mark Casson, *The Future of the Multinational Enterprise* (London: Macmillan, 1976); John Dunning, *International Production and the Multinational Enterprise* (London: Allen and Unwin, 1981); Jean-François Hennart, *A Theory of Multinational Enterprise* (Ann Arbor: University of Michigan Press, 1982); Alan M. Rugman, *Inside the Multinationals: The Economics of Internal Markets* (New York: Columbia University Press, 1981). Each of these five authors has continued to develop an impressive oeuvre on entry mode choice and international business strategy after the publication of the above studies. Academic outlets such as the *Academy of Management Journal*, the *Journal of International Business Studies, Management International Review* and the *Strategic Management Journal* have published numerous articles on entry mode choice challenges.

4. Chris Bartlett and Sumantra Ghoshal, in their book *Managing Across Borders: The Transnational Solution* (Boston: Harvard Business School Press, 1989), made a distinction among three rather than four archetypes, probably for convenience of presentation and to keep their framework easily understood. They did recognize the international exporter (which they called the global firm), the international projector (which they called the international firm), the multi-centred MNE (which they called the multinational firm). Unfortunately, they did not include the international coordinator in their framework, though many vertically integrated MNEs, especially in the resource-based sectors, conform exactly to that archetype. In addition, their terminology is confusing because the terms 'global', 'international' and 'multinational' had often been used, before the publication of their book, by multiple other authors, but with very different meanings. In addition, the prescriptive model they propose, the so-called 'transnational solution', adds further to the confusion, because the term 'transnational' corporation is a generic term, used by the United Nations Centre on Transnational Corporations (UNCTC, set up in 1974 and presently an arm of the United Nations Conference on Trade and Development – UNCTAD) to describe all firms with operations outside their home country and engaging in FDI.

5. See, for example, Marc Levinson, *The Box: How the Shipping Container Made the World Smaller and the World Economy Bigger* (Princeton: Princeton University Press, 2006).

6. NEC, company information.

7. *Ibid.*

8. David Germain, 'Harry Potter Box Office Record: $168.6 Million Opening Weekend, "Harry Potter and the Deathly Hallows Part 2" beats Batman "The Dark Knight"', *Huffington Post* (17 July 2011).

9. Mira Wilkins and Frank Ernest Hill, *American Business Abroad: Ford on Six Continents* (Detroit: Wayne State University Press, 1964), 18.

10. *Ibid.*, 50.

11. *Ibid.*, 100.

12. Geoffrey A. Fowler and Merissa Marr, 'Disney's China Play; Its New Hong Kong Park Is a Big Cultural Experiment; Will "Main Street" Translate?' *Wall Street Journal* (16 June 2005), B.1.

13. *Ibid.*, B.1.

14. *Ibid.*, B.1.

15. Paul Wiseman, 'Miscues mar opening of Hong Kong Disney', *USA Today online* (10 November, 2005).

16. Keith Bradsher, 'A trial run finds Hong Kong Disneyland much too popular for its modest size', *New York Times (Late Edition (East Coast))* (8 September 2005), C.1; Keith Bradsher, 'At Hong Kong Disneyland, the Year of the Dog starts with a growl', *New York Times (Late Edition (East Coast))* (4 February 2006), A.5; Henry Fountain, 'The ultimate body language: how you line up for Mickey', *New York Times (Late Edition (East Coast))* (18 September 2005), 4.4; Justine Lau, 'HK Disneyland gives Mickey Mouse lessons', *Financial Times* (London First Edition) (4 September 2006), 27.

17. BP company information, 2006.

18. Logitech company information, 2011.

19. Logitech company information, 2006.

20. Frederik Philips, *45 Years with Philips* (Poole, Dorset: Blandford Press, 1978), 187.

21. *Ibid.*, 187.

22. Lafarge company information, 2005.

23. *Ibid.*

24. *Ibid.*

25. *Ibid.*

26. Mira Wilkins and H. G. Schröter, *The Free-standing Company in the World Economy, 1830–1996* (Oxford: Oxford University Press, 1998). During the nineteenth century, free-standing companies represented a sizeable proportion of European firms. Thousands of British firms, and hundreds from the Netherlands and other European countries, were set up to operate directly abroad. They were predominantly in the natural resource and service industries. Typically, their head office was very small, with a board of directors, a corporate secretary, and little else. The directors were given the mandate by the shareholders to select managers to head overseas investments and to monitor overseas operations. Basically, they were "the men who stand to be shot at in the event anything goes wrong" (E. T. Powell, *The Mechanism of the City* (1910), pp. 144–5, cited in Mira Wilkins, 'The free-standing company, 1870–1914: an important type of British foreign direct investment', *The Economic History Review* 41 (1988), 264). Harrisons & Crosfield (H&C) was a typical freestanding company. Established in 1844 in Liverpool, H&C bought tea in China and India and sold it in Britain. H&C quickly expanded by opening branches in both tea-producing and tea-consuming countries, including respectively Sri Lanka and Malaya, and the United States, Canada and Australia. Moreover, H&C diversified into the plantation business. In 1903, H&C invested in its first rubber plantation in British Malaya. Later investments in Malaya, Java and the Dutch East Indies made it one of the largest plantation

companies in Southeast Asia. The overseas branches of H&C, as agents for shipping and insurance, managed business on the spot and collected and transmitted information back to the London head office. The London head office was responsible for recruiting expatriates as well as providing plantation management services. For further reading on free-standing companies, see Mira Wilkins, 'The free-standing company, 1870–1914: an important type of British foreign direct investment', *The Economic History Review* 41 (1988), 259–82; M. Wilkins and H. G. Schröter, *The Free-standing Company in the World Economy, 1830–1996* (Oxford: Oxford University Press, 1998); Geoffrey Jones, *Multinationals and Global Capitalism: From the Nineteenth to the Twenty First Century* (New York: Oxford University Press, 2005); G. Jones and J. Wale, 'Diversification strategies of British trading companies: Harrisons & Crosfield, c. 1900–c. 1980', *Business History* 41 (1999), 69–101.

27. See, for example, Alvaro Cuervo-Cazurra and Mehmet Genc, 'Transforming disadvantages into advantages: Developing-country MNEs in the least developed countries', *Journal of International Business Studies* 39 (2008), 957–979; Mauro Guillen and Esteban Garcia-Canal, 'The American model of the multinational firm and the "new" multinationals from emerging economies', *Academy of Management Perspectives* 23 (2009), 23–35; Ravi Ramamurti, 'What have we learned about EMNEs?', in Ravi Ramamurti and Jintendra Singh (eds.), *Emerging Multinationals from Emerging Markets* (Cambridge: Cambridge University Press, 2009).

28. I expanded on this point in the context of increased regionalization, whereby institutional arrangements such as the EU and NAFTA have allowed firms to increase the geographic deployment potential of their location-bound FSAs. However, outside their home region, most large MNEs do appear to suffer from a rapid decay of the transferability, deployment and exploitation of their FSAs, as reflected in their modest sales volumes, relative to total sales, in host regions; see Alan M. Rugman and Alain Verbeke, 'Regional and global strategies of multinational enterprises', *Journal of International Business Studies* 35 (2004), 3–18.

29. 'Japanese consumer goods: should we kow-tow to Kao?', *The Economist* 338 (1996), 60–1; Kao, company information.

30. Kao, company information, 2011.

31. 'A tale of tellers in distant places', *The Economist* 316 (1990), 77.

32. *Ibid.*, 78.

33. Quentin Hardy, 'Banking: Citicorp seeks niche among rich in Japan', *Wall Street Journal (Eastern Edition).* (1 November 1993), B1.

34. William V. Rapp, 'International retail banking: The Citibank Group', *Center on Japanese Economy and Business Working Paper Series*, Columbia University (2000).

35. Citibank Japan company information, 2012.

36. Eric Tegler, 'Designs a Europe', *Business Life* (October 2002), 37–40.

37. Yao-Su Hu, 'The international transferability of the firm's advantages', *California Management Review* 37 (1995), 73–88.

38. Yumiko Ono, 'U.S. superstores find Japanese are a hard sell', *The Wall Street Journal (Eastern Edition)* (14 February 2000), B.1.

39. Office Depot, company information, 2011.

40. Most international business opportunities and challenges for MNEs are thus positioned in a context situated between true globalization, which would allow the unfettered exploitation across borders of internationally transferable FSAs, and extreme localization, whereby only location-bound FSAs without international deployment potential would be relevant. This phenomenon can be called 'semi-globalization'; see Alan M. Rugman and

Alain Verbeke, 'Extending the theory of the multinational enterprise: Internalization and strategic management perspectives', *Journal of International Business Studies* 34 (2003), 125–37.

41. Pete Engardio and Peter Burrows, 'Acer: a global powerhouse', *Business Week* (1996), 95.

42. Martyn Williams, 'Acer to privatize Latin America PC Unit', *Computerworld* (13 January 2000).

43. Location advantages, and the differences in such advantages among nations, remain the foundation of modern international economics, with MNEs mostly treated as a black box; see James R. Markusen, 'International Trade Theory and International Business', in Alan M. Rugman and Thomas L. Brewer (eds.), *The Oxford Handbook of International Business* (Oxford: Oxford University Press, 2001), 69–87.

44. TMX company information, 2012; Rio Tinto Alcan company information, 2012; Barrick Gold Corporation company information, 2012; Xstrata company information, 2012; Potash Corp company information, 2012; Adriana Brasileiro and Heloiza Canassa, 'Vale buys Control of Canadian Nickel Miner Inco (Update 4)', *Bloomberg* (24 October 2006).

45. Hans Decker, 'Master craftsman, no college required', *The Wall Street Journal (Eastern Edition)* (18 March 1991), A14.

46. Michael Berger, 'Japanese firms testing more high-tech gadgets', *The Ottawa Citizen* (8 May 1989), D.2.

47. Karl Lohmann, 'The scents of the cities', *The American City & Country* 114 (1999), 54.

48. E. S. Browning, 'At Guerlain, marketing makes scents – Paris perfumer's products no longer led by nose', *The Wall Street Journal (Eastern Edition)* (19 February 1991), B.7; Robert Graham, 'Town thrives most fragrantly: PERFUME by Robert Graham: despite competition from artificial fragrances, Grasse, with its remarkable ability to adapt, still has to be watched closely by other producers', *Financial Times* (21 October 1998), 3.

49. Dan Primack, 'Biotech hotbeds: where are they, and how do you get one?', *Venture Capital Journal* (1 October 2004), 1.

50. Jones Lang LaSalle, Life Sciences Cluster Report, 2011.

51. Pricewaterhouse Coopers/ MoneyTree Report, Biotechnology & Medical Devices and Equipment Industry Reports, 2010.

52. Dan Primack, 'Biotech hotbeds: where are they, and how do you get one?', *Venture Capital Journal* (1 October 2004), 1.

53. Vanessa Fuhrmans and Rachel Zimmerman, 'Leading the news: Novartis to move global lab to U.S. – Swiss drug maker follows other European companies shifting strategy abroad', *The Wall Street Journal* (7 May 2002), A.3.

54. *Ibid.*

55. *Ibid.*

56. Gary Sawchuk and Aaron Sydor, 'Mexico and Canada: changing specializations in trade with the United States', *North American Linkages: Opportunities and Challenges for Canada* (2003), 169.

57. The four motivations included here have been well documented in the international business literature: see John Dunning, *Multinational Enterprises and the Global Economy* (Reading, Mass.: Addison-Wesley, 1992).

58. 'ExxonMobil announces first production from Usan field offshore Nigeria', *ExxonMobil* (24 February 2012).

59. 'Rosneft and ExxonMobil announce progress in strategic cooperation agreement', *Rosneft* (16 April 2012).

60. Philip F. Zeidman, 'The biggest market in the world', *Franchising World* 26 (1994), 60.

61. Richard Martin, 'China's size, economic boom lure US chains despite uncertainties', *Nation's Restaurant News* 29 (1995), 50.
62. Zeidman, 'The biggest market', 60.
63. In principle, an MNE could restructure its existing network of affiliates and engage in rationalization investments without the prior occurrence of substantial environmental change, but in practice such environmental change is usually the key driver of restructuring.
64. J. M. O'Brien, 'Logitech grows up', *Marketing Computers* 15 (1995), 77–81; China Daily, 'Logitech expands mouse manufacturing facility', *China Daily* (2005).
65. 'Business: Growing pains; Carrefour, Tesco and Wal-Mart', *The Economist* 375 (16 April 2005), 60.
66. Miriam Jordan, 'For many generic antibiotics, the supply line starts in New Delhi – little-known Ranbaxy makes a splash in look-alike drugs, seeks its own breakthroughs', *The Wall Street Journal* (28 December 1999), B.1.
67. *Ibid.*
68. Asian Business Review, 'Jollibee: the company that beat McDonald's', *Asian Business Review* (September 1997), 26–8.
69. Gertrude Chavez, 'The buzz: Jollibee hungers to export Filipino tastes, dominate Asian fast-food', *Advertising Age International* (9 March 1998), 14.
70. Chavez, 'The buzz: Jollibee', 14.
71. Mary Lou Egan and Marc Bendick, Jr, 'Workforce diversity initiatives of U.S. multinational corporations in Europe', *Thunderbird International Business Review* 45 (2003), 716.
72. Egan and Bendick, 'Workforce diversity initiatives', 717.
73. Pete Engardio, Manjeet Kripalani and Alysha Webb, 'Smart globalization; being first and biggest in an emerging market isn't always the best way to conquer it. A better tactic: learn local cultures – and build a presence carefully', *Business Week* (27 August 2001), 132.
74. *Ibid.*
75. Allen J. Morrison and Kendall Roth, 'Developing global subsidiary mandates', *Business Quarterly* 57 (1993), 108.
76. *Ibid.*
77. Paul Ingrassia, 'Global reach: industry is shopping abroad for good ideas to apply to products – foreign research units use latest local technology; the case of Liquid Tide – on the fringes of the swamp', *Wall Street Journal* (29 April 1985), 1.
78. *Ibid.*
79. *Ibid.*
80. Julian Birkinshaw, 'Entrepreneurship in multinational corporations: the initiative process in foreign subsidiaries', unpublished PhD thesis, University of Western Ontario (1995).
81. Ingrassia, 'Shopping Abroad', *Wall Street Journal* (29 April 1985), 1.
82. Birkinshaw, 'Entrepreneurship in multinational corporations', 300.
83. *Ibid.*
84. Darren McDermott, 'Citibank uses Latin American lessons in Asia', *Wall Street Journal (Eastern Edition)* (29 December 1997), 1.
85. Oliver Gassmann and Maximillian von Zedtwitz, 'Trends and determinants of managing virtual R&D teams', *R&D Management* 33 (2003), 248.
86. Thomas W. Malnight, 'The transition from decentralized to network-based MNC structures: an evolutionary perspective', *Journal of International Business Studies* 27 (1996), 55.
87. Malnight, 'The transition to network-based MNC structures', 55.

88. Christopher A. Bartlett, Sumantra Ghoshal and Julian Birkinshaw, *Transnational Management: Text and Cases*, 4th edition (Boston: Irwin/McGraw Hill, 2004), 478.

89. *Ibid.*

90. Robin Yale Bergstrom, 'Global issues demand taking teams global', *Automotive Production* 108 (1996), 61.

91. Bergstrom, 'Taking teams global', 61.

92. Benjamin Gomes-Casseres, 'Joint ventures in the face of global competition', *Sloan Management Review* 30 (1989), 17–26.

93. ConocoPhillips company information, 2006.

94. 'EnCana partnership worth $15 billion', *Times Colonist* (6 October 2006), A.17; Ian Austen, 'Conoco and EnCana plan oil sands venture', *New York Times* (6 October 2006), C.10; Diana Lawrence, Sheila McNulty and James Politi, 'Energy groups to link in Canadian oil sands', *Financial Times* (6 October 2006), 30.

95. The bounded rationality concept was popularized by Herbert Simon, *Models of Bounded Rationality and Other Topics in Economics, Volume 2: Collected papers* (Cambridge, Mass.: MIT Press, 1982), and *Models of Bounded Rationality, Volume 3: Empirically Grounded Economic Reason* (Cambridge, Mass.: MIT Press, 1997). Alain Verbeke and Wenlong Yuan provide an extension of the bounded rationality concept, with an application to the MNE context, 'Subsidiary autonomous activities in multinational enterprises: a transaction cost perspective', *Management International Review*, S.I. 2 (2005), 31–52.

96. David Leonhardt, 'It was a hit in Buenos Aires – so why not Boise? U.S. companies are picking up winning product tips from consumers in faraway places', *Business Week* (7 September 1998), 56.

97. Shelly Branch, 'Dulce de Leche Takes a Spot in Vocabulary and Pantries of U.S.', *Wall Street Journal* (12 October 2001), B.8.

98. Leonhardt, 'Picking up winning product tips', 56.

99. Ginny Parker, 'Wal-Mart gets high-cost lesson on low-price strategy in Japan', *Wall Street Journal* (2 February 2005), 1.

100. IATA, 'Alliances', *IATA* (June 2010).

101. Alain Verbeke and Sarah Vanden Bussche, 'Regional and global strategies in the intercontinental passenger airline industry: The rise of alliance-specific advantages', *Internalization, International Diversification and the Multinational Enterprise: Essays in Honor of Alan M. Rugman* 11 (Amsterdam: Elsevier, 2005), 119–48.

102. Bartlett, Ghoshal and Birkinshaw, *Transnational Management*, 574.

103. Benjamin Gomes-Casseres, 'Competing in constellations: the case of Fuji Xerox', *Strategy and Business* (1997), 4–16.

104. See Oliver E. Williamson, *The Mechanisms of Governance* (Oxford: Oxford University Press, 1996).

105. Alain Verbeke and Nathan Greidanus, 'The end of the opportunism vs trust debate: Bounded reliability as a new envelope concept in research on MNE governance', *Journal of International Business Studies* 40 (2009), 1471–95.

106. Alain Verbeke and M. Zaman Forootan, 'How good are Multinationality-Performance (M-P) empirical studies?', *Global Strategy Journal* (2012) forthcoming.

107. Honda, company information, 2005.

108. *Ibid.*

109. Kevin R. Fitzgerald, 'For superb supplier development – Honda wins!', *Purchasing* 119 (1995), 32–9.

110. Honda, company information, 2005.

111. Boudette, N, 'New U.S. car plants signal renewal for manufacturing', *Wall Street Journal* (26 January 2012), B.3.
112. Robert Pascale, 'The Honda effect', *California Management Review*, 38(4) (1996), 80–91.
113. *Ibid.*
114. *Ibid.*
115. *Ibid.*
116. Honda, 'Timeline', *Honda Worldwide* (2012).
117. Michimasa Fujino, *HondaJet* (2012).
118. Chang-Ran Kim, 'Honda out to shake up market with 1st biz jet next year', *Reuters* (31 January 2012); Chester Dawson, 'Why Honda says it can fly (and GM won't)', *Wall Street Journal* (30 January 2012).
119. *Ibid.*
120. *Ibid.*
121. Michimasa Fujino, *HondaJet* (2012).
122. Chang-Ran Kim and Ben Klayman, 'Insight: After Civic bruising, Honda fights for its soul', *Reuters* (2012); John Reed, and Bernard Simon, 'Honda faces challenges in US market', *Financial Times* (6 January 2012), 14.
123. *Ibid.*
124. *Ibid.*
125. Elena Cherney, 'Four Seasons Hotels looks abroad for ambitious overseas expansion', *Wall Street Journal (Eastern edition)* New York, N.Y. (30 October 2000), A.22; Matthew Garrahan, 'A new spring for Four Seasons', *Financial Times* (26 November 2004), 12; R. Hallowell, D. Bowen and C. I. Knoop, 'Four Seasons goes to Paris', *Academy of Management Executive* 16 (2002), 7–24; Isadore Sharp, 'The unseen but decisive factor in entrepreneurial success', address to The Canadian Club of Toronto (25 May 2004); Isadore Sharp, 'Remarks at the 14th Annual Ivey Business Leaders Award Dinner' (21 September 2006); Joseph Weber and John Rossant, 'The whirlwind at the Four Seasons; luxury hotel chain founder Issy Sharp is on a global tear', *Business Week* (13 October 1997), 82.
126. *Ibid.*
127. *Ibid.*
128. *Ibid.*
129. Hallowell, Bowen and Knoop, 'Four Seasons goes to Paris', 15.
130. France Tourism Development Agency, 'Palaces in France – Hotel Four Seasons George V in Paris joins the select few', *Maison de la France*.
131. *Marketing Week*, 'Q&A', 34(12), 18–19.
132. *Ibid.*
133. Four Seasons, *Luxury Trend Report*.

2

The critical role of firm-specific advantages

Five learning objectives

1. To describe the four characteristics of core competencies, which are the higher-order firm-specific advantages (FSAs) of the firm.
2. To explain the importance of the corporation's 'strategic architecture' in the context of core competencies.
3. To develop an understanding of the influence of an industry's national environment on competitive positioning strategies and firm-level core competencies.
4. To identify the bounded rationality problems associated with an MNE expanding internationally and trying to transfer its FSAs across borders.
5. Based on the conceptual framework in Chapter 1, to analyse the managerial implications of an ill-conceived sole focus on core competences.

This chapter explores Prahalad and Hamel's idea that 'core competencies' constitute the most important source of an MNE's success. Core competencies are really any company's most important FSAs: its vital routines and recombination abilities. According to Prahalad and Hamel, the company's main strategy should be to build or acquire core competencies. This idea will be examined and then criticized using the framework presented in Chapter 1.

Significance

C. K. Prahalad and *Gary Hamel* have provided the clearest exposition of the importance of higher-order FSAs in their path-breaking *HBR* article 'The core competence of the corporation', published in 1990.[1]

Prahalad and Hamel suggest that senior managers need to rethink the very concept of the large, diversified firm seeking worldwide leadership. This type of firm is more than a group of independently managed strategic business units

(SBUs), or in the case of MNEs, more than a set of independent subsidiaries or subsidiary-groupings (e.g., in geographic or product divisions) in various countries. Senior managers should view their firm as a portfolio of 'core competencies', which are its higher-order FSAs, i.e., the firm's routines and recombination capabilities. These higher-order FSAs include the company's shared knowledge (organized into routines), its ability to integrate multiple technologies (reflecting the recombination of internal resources) and the routines/recombination abilities carried by key employees (the so-called competence carriers) that can be deployed across business units. In the authors' words: "In the long run, competitiveness derives from an ability to build, at lower cost and more speedily than competitors, the core competencies that spawn unanticipated products. The real sources of advantage are to be found in management's ability to consolidate corporate-wide technologies and production skills into competencies that empower individual businesses to adapt quickly to changing opportunities."[2] According to Prahalad and Hamel, core competencies are more important than stand-alone FSAs.

What do these core competencies do? They produce the physical, tangible things that the authors call 'core products'. Core products represent areas of technological leadership in the form of key **components** from which end products are developed and created (for example, highly reliable engines in automobiles, or sophisticated data drives and lasers in compact audio disc systems).

The third and final level in the hierarchy of sources of competitiveness (in addition to core competencies and core products) is the level of 'end products'. End products are finished goods. Core products are integrated into these finished goods, establishing a visible corporate brand presence with end users.

To summarize: according to Prahalad and Hamel, *core competencies*, meaning the firm's routines and recombination capabilities, produce components called *core products*, which are put together to create *end products*.

The authors cite several examples to illustrate core competencies. Honda, for example, has developed a core competence around designing and building a versatile core product: compact engines. Honda is good at "exploiting what it ha[s] learned from motorcycles – how to make high-revving, smooth-running, lightweight engines"[3] and then applying and extending these routines to make end products in a range of related businesses, including automobiles, lawn mowers and electric generators. Sony's core competence of recombination in electronics miniaturization has allowed it to anticipate and pioneer a wide range of new features (i.e., core products) in consumer electronics goods.

Identifying core competencies and differentiating them from other FSAs is an intricate process. Stand-alone FSAs such as technological know-how and strengths derived from vertical integration are not core competencies. In practice, core competencies in the form of routines and recombination capabilities involve collective learning, communicating, harmonizing multiple streams of technology, and organizing value-creation skills across departmental boundaries. Prahalad and Hamel outline three characteristics to help managers identify core competencies. A core competence should:

- be difficult for competitors to imitate in terms of achieving the required internal coordination and learning (which points to the distinctiveness of the firm's routines and recombination abilities);
- provide potential access to a wide variety of markets (which points to the capability's contribution towards combining or recombining resources for success in new environments, as discussed in Chapter 1); and
- make a significant contribution to the perceived customer benefits of the end product (which points to satisfying the needs of customers, a key stakeholder group).

To these three characteristics we should add a fourth, assumed implicitly in Prahalad and Hamel's analysis, and especially important for a large MNE: the loss of a core competence would have an important negative effect on the firm's present and future performance, in terms of value creation and satisfying stakeholder objectives. This last criterion is essential. If senior corporate-level managers do not apply this fourth criterion, then every SBU, every functional area in the firm – and every foreign affiliate – could claim it is the home of a number of core competencies. This would divert senior management's attention from the elements that are truly critical to the firm's performance, and might lead to ineffective resource allocation to support the exploitation, further development and deployment throughout the firm of alleged core competencies.

According to Prahalad and Hamel, the primary role of senior management should be to develop the 'strategic architecture' to guide the corporation in building and acquiring core competencies, either through internal resources or external acquisitions and alliances. The strategic architecture is a "road map of the future that identifies which core competencies to build and their constituent technologies".[4] Such a strategic architecture is necessary to overcome the challenge of decentralized units acting in their own self-interest, which is a critical intra-organizational bounded reliability problem. In the long term, a strategic architecture will also help foster company-wide innovation, competitiveness and success. In the international context, this vision of the ideal corporation obviously implies a rejection of the multi-centred approach to foreign operations, as well as a deep suspicion of firms that operate with powerful product and geographic divisions.

Prahalad and Hamel argue that the firm's resource allocation process and incentive systems should support the firm's strategic architecture. For example, corporate-level senior management should reallocate the individuals who carry core competencies, i.e., have deep knowledge of routines and can be instrumental to resource recombination across functional and business units so as to yield the highest return for the firm as a whole. Lower-level units such as divisions or subsidiaries should be made to justify the continued location of competency carriers in their operations in the same way that they need to justify new capital spending. In addition, the incentive system should be designed to reward divisional or subsidiary managers for acting in the interest of the firm rather than their own unit, thereby reducing bounded reliability problems. For example, unit managers should be rewarded for volunteering competence carriers – often their most valuable employees – to a central pool for reallocation.

Finally, the authors address the issue of acquiring FSAs through external strategic alliances rather than through internal, organic development. In this case, the firm intends to internalize the knowledge and skills of the alliance partner(s), thus furthering the creation of the company's own technological and process-related FSAs. However, the authors caution against two dangers. First, the company must have a clear understanding of the FSAs it is trying to build through the partnership, and those it is seeking to protect from being transferred to potential competitors. Second, outsourcing strategies for key components, as a shortcut to increased short-term profitability, may lead to the loss of FSAs. Outsourcing often means that no more FSA development occurs in the outsourced areas, thereby leading to the atrophy of knowledge and skills embodied in the firm's employees and, in a broader sense, the firm's routines and recombination capabilities in the outsourced areas.

Context and complementary perspectives

Prahalad and Hamel's work was published in 1990, a time when much attention was devoted to the unbridled success of Japanese companies (more than to the Japanese economy as a whole) with their strong focus on scale and scope economies in product development and marketing. Many Asian MNEs were on the rise, while those in North America and Europe seemed to be declining in terms of innovation and world market share in a variety of industries.

Consistent with this setting, many of the positive examples cited in their work are derived from the small sample of the most successful Japanese companies, such as NEC, Canon, Sony, Honda and Matsushita. These are contrasted with lower-achieving competitors from the US and Europe, such as GTE, Xerox, Chrysler and Philips. The authors focus almost exclusively on consumer manufacturing industries such as computers, photocopiers, automobiles and electronics (TVs, VCRs, etc.), where the redeployment potential of technology from one set of products to another plays a key role in long-term success and a global approach to product development and marketing, typical for **centralized exporters** and **international projectors**, is well suited.

William G. Egelhoff wrote a complementary article in *SMR*, where he contrasted the mainstream Japanese and US approaches to strategy.[5] Comparing eight American and eight Japanese semiconductor firms, Egelhoff observed that most of the American companies attached substantial importance to product differentiation and a high diversity of product-market niches, with a view to achieving short-term profitability from these niches. Short-term profitability considerations also led to the frequent repositioning of products, the rapid move to licensing of standardized products and the exit from niches with strong price competition. In contrast, the Japanese companies systematically focused on improving process technology for standard products as the key source of competitive advantage, and adopted a long-term perspective on the profitability potential of their business. By focusing on the core competence of process technology, the Japanese companies thereby achieved both low costs and high quality for their rather standardized products.

In addition, the Japanese companies moved from relying heavily on external sources of process technology to becoming largely self-sufficient in this area. This confirms Prahalad and Hamel's suggestion that Japanese companies view end products more as an outcome of underlying competencies, and therefore focus their efforts on the underlying competencies. These firms view the continuous repositioning of end products in narrow niches as devoid of much value. Egelhoff concluded that the Japanese firms are more skilled at strategy implementation than the American ones, and that their approach is particularly appropriate in the semiconductor industry, where competitive positioning strategies at the level of end products are easily imitable. In this industry, firms gain competitive advantage not by frequent, short-term repositioning in the markets for end products, but by a long-term focus on core competencies.

A similar situation can be observed in the automobile industry. In the 1970s and 1980s, the American firms still relied largely on economies of scale and changes in styling and marketing to compete, whereas the Japanese firms aimed for superior performance in terms of productivity, quality and production time by emphasizing manufacturing excellence. A survey conducted by the MIT International Motor Vehicle Programme in the late 1980s found that the time to manufacture a car at an average Japanese plant was 16.8 hours, much less than the 25.1 hours at an American plant or 36.2 hours at a European plant. The adoption of Japanese best practices by American firms in the past 20 years appears to have helped them little, as Japanese lead manufacturers have continued to improve their production routines. From 1997 to 2003, the combined market share of Detroit's Big Three in the US fell from 73 per cent to 60 per cent, whereas the share of Japanese auto makers rose by 17 per cent to 29 per cent. Richard E. Dauch, past Chairman of the National Association of Manufacturers in the US, commented: "if Detroit's Big Three [had not created] the innovative products that launched the craze of minivans, pickups and SUVs for the last 20 years, the job loss tallies could have surged even higher".[6] Here, the question arises whether Detroit's ability to manufacture minivans, pickups and SUVs is a competence that is difficult to imitate. Recent market share increases of Japanese automobile manufacturers in each of these end-product segments indicate that these firms' underlying routines can relatively easily be redeployed in these new segments. Therefore, by definition, Detroit's expertise in manufacturing these particular end products is not a core competency.

Egelhoff did acknowledge, however, that the US approach may be more appropriate in industries characterized by fundamental technological change and the related commercial breakthroughs and early profits. In such industries, it is not the fine-tuning of strategy implementation through a focus on process technology routine that counts, but rather the correct anticipation of the future dominant industry standard, as well as rapid profit building by attracting buyers to customized niches. Different industries require different FSA types.

One implication of Egelhoff's analysis is that an industry's national environment will largely determine the way firms compete in that industry. In the case of the semiconductor industry, the Japanese business and technological environments were conducive to a focus on core competencies as the appropriate route to compete. In contrast, the US environment, with its focus on end-product differentiation, rapid strategic repositioning and short-term profitability, was helpful to firms in many other economic sectors, such as the e-commerce industry. This issue will be discussed further when Chapter 3 examines the impact of location on FSAs.

In industries that change rapidly, core competencies can become core rigidities. In those cases, it is the flexibility and adaptation of strategy – so well mastered by American firms in knowledge-based and consumer goods industries – that counts, and to a lesser extent the Japanese ability to achieve superior implementation of predetermined and only incrementally adaptable routines.

Andrew Bartmess and *Keith Cerny* have provided a second perspective complementary to Prahalad and Hamel's.[7] Their *CMR* article explains in great detail the implications of a core-competencies approach when the MNE expands internationally. Many MNEs mistakenly think they can access location advantages of foreign nations by setting up specific functional activities such as manufacturing in those nations. These activities will then hopefully 'absorb' the coveted location advantages. For example, low wages and material costs, and the promise of lower overhead costs, often lead to a relocation of manufacturing activities from high-cost countries.

Here, MNEs transfer manufacturing FSAs from the home country, hoping to reduce overall costs. Unfortunately, according to the authors, this approach builds upon two wrong assumptions, reflecting the bounded rationality problem faced by senior MNE management in the home country. First, it assumes that manufacturing knowledge is a stand-alone FSA. Second, it assumes that this FSA can be effortlessly recombined with foreign location advantages. We shall address the second assumption in Chapter 4.

As regards the first assumption, Bartmess and Cerny argue that manufacturing knowledge – in fact, any type of knowledge embedded in a single functional area such as R&D or marketing – is not a core competence in and of itself. Core competencies involve the combination of stand-alone knowledge bundles found in different functions into routines, as well as the further recombination of existing resource bundles with new resources. Therefore, in order to be successful, the entire set of functional activities involved in a routine or recombination capability should be transferred abroad. The heart of the core competence may actually reside in the superior interfaces between functional activities, or even superior interfaces with outside stakeholders. For example, a recombination capability in continuous quality improvement may rely on supporting links between design and manufacturing, between design and demanding customers, between manufacturing and demanding customers and between production workers and managers. At a more general level, at the customer end of the value chain, in-depth customer knowledge flowing to customer-focused design teams may be critical to national responsiveness. At the back end of the value chain, the linkages between manufacturing and logistics may be critical, especially if the products manufactured in a host country are subsequently exported to other nations, including the home country.

Co-locating all activities and supporting linkages involved in a routine and especially a recombination capability, so as to satisfy communication and coordination requirements, may thus be critical to international success.

The attractiveness of foreign locations, whether for input markets (e.g., specialized labour or R&D knowledge), specific functional activities or the markets for end products, must take into account the complexities of successfully exploiting and further augmenting FSAs. Managers must assess for each FSA the criticality of co-locating specific activities, as well as all relevant inter-functional linkages and linkages with specific stakeholders.

Bartmess and Cerny give five criteria to assess the need for co-locating activities instrumental to further recombination. (To assess what constitutes a recombination capability, the four-fold test described in the earlier discussion of Prahalad and Hamel should be applied.) Assuming a given volume of information that must be exchanged between two distinct activities, these five criteria together determine the scope of the bounded rationality problem that must be solved:

1. **Complexity**: if the information that must be communicated between the activities has a higher complexity, this requires geographic proximity for communication to be effective and efficient. This usually also implies the use of several communication modes, including face-to-face communication.
2. **Required level of interaction**: here, a lower predictability of the information content (meaning higher uncertainty) and the need for two-way information

flows (meaning mutual adjustment) requires closer geographic proximity of activities.

3. **Similarity of background and expertise** of the individuals involved: less similarity makes it more difficult to communicate from a distance, in terms of understanding what information is most important, and its significance in terms of required managerial action.

4. **Requirement of a prior relationship**: some types of sensitive communication between related activities require a prior relationship among the communicating parties, which is a precondition for the parties having confidence in each other that the information provided will not be used against them (for example, in cases of communication about production problems, cost overruns and delays). In addition, prior relationships are also important when communicating with external stakeholders (e.g., major customers) who cannot be forced to communicate with employees inside the firm. The absence of a prior relationship suggests a need for closer geographic proximity.

5. **Concreteness of information**: concreteness does not simply refer to the tacitness of information in a technical sense, but also to the meaning of the information beyond its verbal content (emotions, feelings and cultural values may be embedded in the information transmitted). The less concrete the information, the greater the need for face-to-face communication, and thus geographic proximity.

Only after all the activities associated with a recombination capability have been assessed in terms of their co-location needs can decisions be made about foreign expansion in particular locations. As explained above, managers also need to decide whether the geographic proximity of specific external stakeholders (such as leading-edge buyers at the customer end, or R&D labs at the back end of the value chain) is critical to the success of an international expansion project, taking into account the contemplated scale of the international project (for example, a foreign manufacturing plant may be too small to sustain the required linkages with foreign R&D facilities).

Only if the above approach is followed can resource recombination across borders be successful: the MNE's higher-order FSAs are embedded in specific functions, inter-function linkages and linkages with external stakeholders. For effective and efficient resource recombination, all the economic activities that require geographic proximity must be co-located. Such co-location requirements, including the need to access specific external stakeholders in the host country, determine which locations make sense beyond their attractiveness at the macro-level. Importantly, these co-location requirements may also lead to a hierarchy of locations, with scale considerations dictating that some bundles of activities be co-located at the regional level, such as the EU or the South-East Asia level, rather than at the country level.

Applying the concepts developed in Chapter 1, we see that Prahalad and Hamel's notion of core competencies is largely equivalent to the higher-order FSA concept, with a strong focus on routines and recombination capabilities. Recombination capabilities are especially critical for Prahalad and Hamel, but, as they correctly point out, these can be difficult to define exactly or to deconstruct. These FSAs are also affected by the administrative infrastructure or heritage that has evolved over the life of the company. However, the key ingredients are similar to the ones described in Chapter 1: an *entrepreneurial attitude* of senior corporate-level managers and competence carriers, critical to identifying and pursuing new *market opportunities* and to uncovering *resources that are not yet fully utilized* and can be deployed in other markets, and an *organizational ability* to *meld extant and new resources* in novel ways.

In terms of the patterns of FSA development discussed in Chapter 1, the authors paradoxically focus largely on Pattern I (see Figure 1.7 in Chapter 1), with core competencies typically developed in the home country (guided by corporate-level senior management) and then diffused to the rest of the firm. Here, the firm has been very effective in recombination at home, across product lines and units, but there is little need for further recombination abroad. The authors assume that North American and European firms are less effective than Asian companies in implementing Pattern I. As the authors see it, internationally transferable FSAs are typically developed in the home country, but their exploitation is, unfortunately, usually bounded to one unit, rather than shared across the company. The authors advocate that North American and European firms shift their strategic focus to align with that of Japanese MNEs, but observe that North American and European firms are hampered by an administrative heritage of 'bounded innovation'. Bounded innovation means that innovation activities and resulting resource recombinations are guided by decentralized unit goals rather than corporate goals, and innovation outcomes remain within the unit, rather than being deployed throughout the firm. The authors also criticize the presence of imprisoned resources, whereby the different units fully control specific individuals and technologies underlying core competencies. The authors thereby point to extensive bounded rationality problems in Western firms, since corporate-level senior management lacks the insight to engage in corrective action.

To some extent, this corporate structure also produces a bounded reliability problem, because individual units have sufficient power to block the transfer of knowledge from other units inside the firm (this is an expression of the 'not invented here' syndrome: whatever innovation comes from outside the unit must be bad or irrelevant). In addition, SBUs often refuse to cooperate with other units on joint innovation, and jealously guard their own resources, including valuable employees, so as to preclude these resources from helping other units. In other words, the unit's commitment to the pursuit of corporate goals is diverted towards the pursuit of local goals. In the authors' view, the resource allocation process

MANAGEMENT
INSIGHTS

Figure 2.1
Non-location-bound
(or internationally
transferable) FSAs as
drivers of economies
of scope across
markets and
products

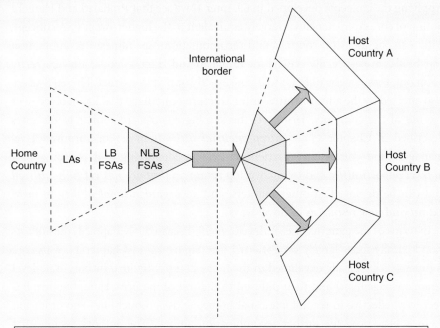

The shading of the NLB FSA area in the home country and the dotted outline of the rest of the home country triangle indicate the emphasis on NLB FSAs and the assumed irrelevance of home country LAs and LB FSAs in this model. The dotted middle section of the triangle in each host country reflects the lack of emphasis on the development of LB FSAs by host country operations. Extant NLB FSAs suffice to access and benefit from host country LAs.

should therefore not just limit itself to capital, but should also include the key, competence-carrying individuals. Corporate-level senior management should have the power to reallocate these individuals to serve corporate goals.

Figure 2.1 illustrates how Prahalad and Hamel's argument relates to the conceptual framework outlined in Chapter 1.

The triangle on the left of Figure 2.1 represents the domestic base of a firm that relies equally on all three forms of resources: a foundation of location advantages (LAs), from which location-bound FSAs and internationally transferable FSAs are built, but Prahalad and Hamel really emphasize the internationally transferable component. The authors also suggest that competitiveness in the global economy requires a focus on the higher-order FSAs. Specifically, firms need to expand continuously their resource base by developing new routines, permitting economies of scope across products and markets, and engaging in recombination. When expanding across markets, the relevant FSAs are internationally transferable. Prahalad and Hamel's view is reflected in the set of non-location-bound FSA triangles on the right-hand side, each representing how core competencies developed in the original home base are transferred to – and exploited in – a distinct host country market. The dotted lines in the rest of the figure highlight the fact that the authors do not address the need for the MNE to develop additional strengths to access the location advantages of home or host nations in the form of location-bound FSAs in these foreign markets.

On a critical note, the conceptual framework in Chapter 1 helps to identify five main weaknesses in Prahalad and Hamel's analysis.

First, they do not explicitly touch on the issue of location advantages (general or firm-specific) and geographic determinants of FSAs, nor do they consider the feasibility and cost in practice of transferring non-location-bound FSAs to other locations. They suggest that developing a firm's higher-order FSAs can be pro-actively planned and moulded by senior management through what they call a strategic architecture. However, their underlying assumption is that FSAs are non-location-bound and can be seamlessly transferred and exploited internation-ally, which is often not the case in practice.

Second, the authors overlook the importance of the geographical embedded-ness of competence carriers, i.e., the individuals and groups with a deep know-ledge of the company routines and the ability to drive resource recombination. Prahalad and Hamel go as far as to suggest that managers in decentralized units should be made to compete for the allocation of this talent carrying core com-petencies. This intra-firm competition should occur irrespective of where the competence carriers are located, similar to the way business units compete for capital resources in an annual budgeting process. In reality, however, individuals and even teams designated as competence carriers are embedded in specific locations, and their geographic reassignment may lead to the loss of this embedd-edness, causing the loss of the (often routinized) mutually enriching exchange of knowledge between the individual or team inside the firm and specific comple-mentary actors, both in the affiliate itself and in the local, external environment. Co-location matters! Losing this exchange of knowledge can lead to a loss of value for the firm as a whole. From an international perspective, the authors thus neglect the link between location advantages and the more intricate internal processes of FSA creation, developed as a result of the unique external environ-ment in which each business unit operates and its own internal functioning.

Third, the authors overlook the (sometimes critical) role of subsidiary-level capabilities for MNE competitiveness and the problems associated with trans-ferring these to other units in the MNE. Prahalad and Hamel suggest that decentralized units often develop unique competencies over time, which they should not be allowed to keep for themselves at the expense of value creation for the firm as a whole. The difficulties in the relationship between corporate-level senior management and decentralized unit management in general are similar to those prevailing in the relationship between the MNE's central headquarters and its foreign subsidiaries. Here, the concept of SBU or decentralized unit evolution over time mirrors that of developing autonomous subsidiary initiatives in host country subsidiaries. While Prahalad and Hamel mention the advantages of transferring one unit's competencies to other units, once again there is no discussion of the difficulties involved in this transfer.

Fourth, the authors overlook important bounded rationality and bounded reliability problems. In terms of hierarchical control within the corporation, Prahalad and Hamel implicitly suggest that strongly centralized decision making by corporate-level senior management is preferred over the decentralization of independent units. However, there are reasons why most large MNEs are organized into multiple divisions with relative autonomy and only limited, selective intervention from central headquarters. One important reason is that extensive intervention by central headquarters will face important bounded rationality and bounded reliability problems when trying to identify a set of competence carriers, assert control over these competence carriers and then reallocate them according to the perceived contribution they can make in each location.

The sheer volume of information used by a large MNE also produces bounded rationality and bounded reliability problems for Prahalad and Hamel's highly centralized MNE. While it is true that economies of scope can often be gained by interactions among decentralized units, it is also true that inter-unit communication, coordination and FSA-sharing must remain limited: companies are divided into divisions precisely as a governance mechanism to reduce bounded rationality and bounded reliability problems caused by information overload.

Fifth, the authors fail to make a distinction between the back end and customer end parts of the value chain. It makes sense to build upon core competencies at the back end of the value chain (i.e., all activities where no direct interface is required with customers, such as sourcing, the manufacturing of intermediate goods and logistics). At the back end, the MNE should attempt to streamline operations and to earn economies of scope by sharing knowledge across borders as much as possible, much in line with Prahalad and Hamel's recommendations. Here, overall efficiency considerations should in many cases trump individual subsidiary preferences. However, this does not hold for the customer end of the value chain, where a strong focus on national or regional responsiveness is often critical to exploit profitably core competencies. Here the firm has to make sure that its home-grown core competencies do not turn into core rigidities – i.e., barriers to necessary adaptation and profitable expansion in foreign markets.

Five management takeaways

1. Identify and nurture your company's core competencies, and differentiate their treatment from that given to less critical FSAs.
2. Develop a 'strategic architecture' to guide your company in building and acquiring core competencies.

3. Understand the economic potential and drawbacks of acquiring FSAs through external strategic alliances.
4. Do not overestimate the transferability of your FSAs across borders, and understand the costs of successful resource recombination.
5. Reflect on co-location requirements when expanding internationally and investing abroad.

Case 2.1 3M, the spirit of innovation

CASE

The US-based conglomerate 3M has been famous for decades for its culture of innovation. Its rule of allowing 15 per cent of its employees' working hours to be spent on their own projects has been widely cited as the symbol of tolerance for experimentation. However, there is more to the firm's core competences than this tolerance.

The development of the spirit of innovation

3M was incorporated in 1902, as Minnesota Mining and Manufacturing. In the late 1910s, when its annual sales exceeded US $1 million and it started to earn profits, President William McKnight decided the time had come to strengthen 3M's research function and its linkages with manufacturing and engineering activities. In 1921, Richard Carlton, a calculated risk-taker, was hired to lead 3M's research activities and to integrate research, manufacturing and engineering objectives. At the same time, Dick Drew, a rule-breaker, and Francis Okie, an inventor, joined the 3M lab staff. The shared characteristics of this trio shaped 3M's climate of innovation. This climate includes an 'electric atmosphere', the freedom to pursue any opportunity, the sharing of ideas, the presence of extensive mentoring and patience regarding investment returns. For example:

1. In addition to time (the 15 per cent rule), 3M also supplies money for independent research projects. In 1984, for example, 3M launched the Genesis Program to fund research projects unable to go through the regular funding channels. Genesis Grants could be worth up to US $100,000 and were often awarded to develop unconventional projects that would not otherwise receive funding in the outside world. Other grants were also introduced to spark innovation, such as Alpha Grants, the Technical Circle of Excellence and Innovation, the Carlton Society and the Engineering Achievement Award of Excellence.
2. Technology and ideas are shared through both informal channels, such as conversations in hallways, and formal channels, such as the 'R&D Workcentre' internal networking website and the so-called 'Tech Forum' (officially known as the Technical Information Exchange). The Tech Forum has specialty subgroups in each scientific discipline, so that engineers and chemists can share their expertise. By 2001, the Tech Forum had 9,500 members around

the world. 3M also facilitates informal and formal networking at the Tech Forum's annual symposium, where researchers can collaborate and share their work.

3. Mentors and sponsors help younger colleagues by listening to their ideas, giving them advice and assistance, and acting as their champions.

4. Patents give 3M the power and time to protect the growth potential of its business. For example, in the 1990s, 3M introduced the unique surface material called brightness enhancement film (BEF), which enhances the brightness of liquid crystal displays (LCDs). Its major customers were Japanese LCD manufacturers, which sold LCDs to computer manufacturers in both Japan and the US. However, 3M also provided BEF directly to several US computer manufacturers, for which it had US patents. By using these sales as leverage, 3M convinced two US computer manufacturers not to buy products which broke 3M's patents.

Together with the development of the spirit of innovation, William McKnight laid out the McKnight principle of management in 1948, which covers the essence of a corporate culture espousing initiatives: "As our business grows, it becomes increasingly necessary to delegate responsibility and to encourage men and women to exercise their initiative. This requires considerable tolerance. Those men and women, to whom we delegate authority and responsibility, if they are good people, are going to want to do their jobs in their own way."[8] This principle was critical not only to the spirit of innovation inside the firm, but would also guide the firm's international expansion in later years.

Diversification

While keeping the functions of engineering, research and development, finance, and human resources strongly centralized, 3M organized the rest of the company into many small divisions. When a division grew so big that it tended to overlook the development of new businesses, new businesses were removed from the division, which then had to look for new products to meet its growth objectives. For example, Magnetic Recording Materials was a spin-off from the Electrical Products Division, but it later grew to become a division and several new divisions later spun off from it. This was called the 'divide and grow' approach.

The direction of the growth was based on innovation. The company's philosophy was that "[I]nnovation tells us where to go; we don't tell innovation where to go".[9] Thus, the company followed the technology into new products and markets. "By the millennium, 3M had world-class expertise in about 30 technologies and excellent grounding in about 100 more."[10]

For example, its 'nonwovens' technology started with ribbon in the 1940s, but developed into such products as tape backings, low-density abrasives, medical products, and insulations and filters.

The fluorochemical technology also evolved a long way from its roots. In 1944, 3M acquired fluorochemical patents from a Penn State University professor, even though "no one knew how to use the compound".[11] After more than ten years of investment, 3M realized its first profits in fluorine research when it introduced Scotchgard fabric and upholstery protector to the textile industry in 1956.[12] By 2000, the Scotchgard line had grown to "100 commercially applied and six consumer applied protectors and cleaners".[13] Initially, 3M's Fluorel fluoroelastomers were used only in the automotive industry, to make "fuel line hoses, O-rings, oil seals for engines, engine valve seals, little rubber molded 'elbows' for crank case ventilation and other prosaic pieces and parts". By the late 1990s, the technology had evolved into a wide range of applications related to diverse products, including nonstick coatings on cookware.

This process of diversifying into numerous and varied applications was accompanied by the discipline of eliminating those businesses that could not sustain annual sales growth of 10 per cent and profit targets of 25 per cent. For these reasons, 3M sold its Duplicating Products business in 1988 and spun off its data storage and imaging systems businesses in 1995.

Internationalization and the global presence

The formative years

3M developed its international activities in stages, starting with exporting to foreign countries, establishing sales subsidiaries, setting up warehouses after learning about the local market, repackaging products shipped from the US, building plants and setting up R&D labs to provide technical support. As business abroad grew, a steady flow of new products from 3M's research labs created new export possibilities for foreign subsidiaries.

3M started to export sandpaper to Britain in the 1920s, but McKnight had to halt his attempts to set up a manufacturing plant in Britain because 3M's major rival in the US threatened to follow 3M there by also building its plant in Britain. McKnight believed that Britain's market could sustain only one American abrasives firm. After the US legal system began to allow US firms to cooperate in foreign trade, nine American firms, including 3M, founded the England-based Durex Corporation in 1929 to grow the abrasives business overseas. When Durex was dissolved in 1951, 3M inherited a group of top managers, three plants in England, France and Brazil, and an office in Germany.

3M expanded its international reach even further in the 1950s, benefiting from its mature research base in the US. The international division was an entrepreneurial venture, and country managers basically did whatever was necessary to help their businesses survive and grow. Maynard Patterson, vice president of the international division, adopted a hands-off approach to managing the foreign businesses. He delegated major decision-making power to country managers, and also built fences to prevent either well-meaning help or possible 'red tape' from headquarters. For example, when Patterson sent Em Monteiro to grow the business in Colombia, Patterson told him to "go start a company . . . and no one from St. Paul is going to visit you unless you ask for them. We'll stay out of your way and if someone sticks his nose in your business, you call me."[14] In this way, the early leaders of the international division built an environment for line managers in each country conducive to growth and adaptation to local customers.

By the end of the 1970s, sales from the international division accounted for around 42 per cent of 3M's total sales, with operations in 51 countries.

Capitalizing on the global network

In the late 1970s, both the 3M CEO and the head of the international division believed that the international division would grow more if it were integrated with US operations. Integration between the two progressed slowly, starting with some exchange of information, people and technical assistance. Although many employees did not initially see the benefit of such integration, the interactions gradually compelled both the US operations and the international division to identify the "advantages of worldwide cooperation in selling and distributing 3M products".[15]

In the 1980s, group executives in the US and country managers at the international division started to work together to develop worldwide strategic plans and to prioritize 3M's roughly 40,000 products. Moreover, 3M looked for ways to improve efficiency in its network. For example, until the mid 1970s, each European subsidiary still hired its own truck lines, without any communication among themselves. 3M finally established a distribution centre in Breda, the Netherlands, functioning as a hub to ship products to the 19 European subsidiaries.[16] In the early 1990s, 3M gradually switched from country-by-country management to a regional structure by creating the first European Business Centre (EBC) to manage 3M's chemical business in Europe in 1991, and several other EBCs a few years later.

In the late 1970s and early 1980s, overseas innovations started to become important. By the late 1970s, most foreign subsidiaries still copied existing products developed in the US, but some started to churn out innovations in marketing, operations and product adaptations. Some innovations had been applied by sister companies, even the US operations. To "encourage new products and new business initiatives born outside the United States",[17] 3M started its Pathfinder Program in 1978, and by 1983, US $153 million of new sales came out of the winning projects. Awards and grants initially designed for innovations at US operations were extended to international employees. For example, international researchers started to sit on 3M's Circle of Technical Excellence, and 3M Italy and 3M Canada became the first two international companies to receive Genesis grants to support their new product development. As a result of such encouragement, international operations generated important innovations. For instance, 3M Brazil developed a low-cost adhesive using local raw materials.

Overseas innovations also resulted from international cooperation among 3M's companies. For example, when a Canadian marketer had a new idea for cleaning ships underwater, a 3M lab in St Paul invited him to collaborate, and together they developed the Scotch-Brite marine cleaning disc.

By the 1980s, international labs at 3M employed around 1,200 technical professionals on product and process development. Some labs had developed technical expertise in specific areas. For example, 3M's German lab specialized in electrical innovation, the Belgian lab focused on specialty chemicals and the Italian lab studied recording materials. A global effort to improve automation in abrasive manufacturing included 3M Japan, Brazil, Colombia and several European subsidiaries. By the turn of the century, 4,300 scientists were located internationally, compared with 2,200 scientists in the US.

Troubled innovations

Starting in the early 1990s, 3M's innovations seemed to stagnate, as new products became incremental rather than revolutionary. Profits also started to fall, leading to a restructuring in 1995, the biggest one in 3M's history. Some people started to question 3M's success formula, attributing the stagnating innovation to redundancy in R&D. 3M had around 8,300 researchers scattered among central R&D, 11 centres for particular technology platforms, and labs attached to sectors, groups or businesses. Research money was allocated by management, fellow scientists and many other sources.[18]

In 2001, 3M brought in Jim McNerney, a GE executive and Harvard MBA alumnus to rejuvenate the company. First, McNerney asked researchers to talk more to people in marketing and manufacturing, and to use those conversations to guide their lab work from the very beginning. Naturally, some people worried that 3M might lose breakthrough innovations because of such micromanaging.[19] Second, McNerney got rid of the 30 per cent rule – the company's longstanding goal to produce 30 per cent of its revenues from products less than four years old. McNerney believed that this rule led to dubious innovations introduced by managers solely to meet the target. Third, he implemented the 3M-acceleration programme, to evaluate new products in the pipeline and invest more money in those with a high probability of success while dropping others at the very beginning. Fourth, McNerney implemented Six Sigma management standards that streamlined processes and minimized defects. However, the efficiency payoffs of Six Sigma also had the unintended effect of placing undue pressure on researchers to generate innovations at an unrealistic pace.[20] The former legacy at 3M, that small ideas could become great innovations, seemed to have been given up.[21] Ronald Baukol, executive vice president for international operations and a 33-year veteran, argued against McNerney that "the most important thing about 3M – the single most important thing – is you get to do things your own way", though many others agreed with McNerney, noting that money was not always directed towards the most promising research programmes.[22]

By 2005, only 21 per cent of revenue was being generated from products less than four years old.[23] In the same year, McNerney left to take the top position at Boeing Co., and George Buckley became the new CEO. Buckley, who had a PhD in electrical engineering, restored emphasis on the 3M laboratories and devoted more than US $1 billion to R&D in 2009. Buckley kept Six Sigma in 3M factories but removed it from the labs, and revenues from new products returned to 30 per cent by 2010.[24]

Buckley focused mostly on internal growth through product development, improving efficiency and expansion into emerging markets. He allocated US $2 billion to acquisitions in 2010, a sizeable increase from US $69 million the company spent on acquisitions in 2009.[25] During Buckley's tenure, 3M's revenue rose 40 per cent to US $29.6 billion between 2005 and 2011.[26] When Buckley announced his retirement in 2012, 3M's board of directors selected former COO Inge Thulin as his successor. Thulin's expertise in "orchestrating profitable growth in international markets" was considered a key factor in his appointment.[27]

Like Buckley, Thulin viewed diversity as a cornerstone of 3M's philosophy: "This is a company that is many, many small companies, and I think that is an advantage for us."[28] When asked if 3M should be in the business of producing arguably trivial items such as fishing gear, Thulin stated, "if we [3M] can make money on it, we should".

QUESTIONS

1. Identify 3M's core competencies, core products and end products. How are these three sources of competitive advantage linked with each other?
2. How does 3M mobilize resources at the SBU level?
3. How does 3M address the problem of bounded innovation?
4. What is the strategic architecture at 3M? How did top management build it?
5. How did 3M internationalize? How did it exploit its core competencies developed at home? How did 3M try to diffuse its core competencies to its overseas subsidiaries?
6. What did McNerney and Buckley implement to improve 3M's R&D activities? Do you agree with these approaches? Why or why not?
7. Can you provide an update on 3M's core competencies, using materials available on the Web?

Case 2.2 IKEA

The Swedish home products retailer IKEA Group (IKEA) has grown from a one-man mail order company, established in 1934, into an operation with 301 IKEA stores in 37 countries/territories and 131,000 employees by 2011.

The development of the IKEA formula

The 'IKEA formula', critical to its international success, has developed gradually over time. Its main focus is the delivery of low-cost products to customers: "[A] low price is the result of a methodical, systematic approach from initial idea through product development, supply, distribution and retail all the way to the customer's home".[29]

The importance of selling at a low price was ingrained in Ingvar Kamprad, the founder of IKEA, even before he established IKEA in 1934. He grew up on a farm in Sweden and, as a kid, purchased matches in bulk from Stockholm and rode his bicycle around, selling matches to his neighbours. His bulk purchasing helped him to sell at a very low price while still earning a profit. His small business grew to include Christmas tree decorations, fish and pencils.

In the early days of IKEA, the firm sold products as diverse as watches, jewellery and picture frames whenever it was possible to sell such products at a low price. While his business grew, Kamprad started to advertise via both local newspapers and mail-order catalogues. Only in 1947 did IKEA add furniture into its product line, and it quickly became IKEA's main set of end products. Local manufacturers near Ingvar Kamprad's home produced the furniture from trees in the nearby forests. This line of products continued to grow, and in 1951 Ingvar Kamprad decided to end all the other products and to focus solely on low-priced furniture. At that point, "the IKEA that we know today was born".[30]

Low-cost service and the showroom/warehouse idea

The focus on low-price furniture in the early 1950s caused customers to be concerned about the quality of IKEA products, as traditionally customers could not see the furniture before they placed an order. To solve this information asymmetry problem, IKEA opened a furniture showroom in Älmhult in 1953, so as to allow customers to compare IKEA products with those from its competitors.

The showroom idea became a key part of the IKEA concept and was applied systematically in IKEA's international expansion. In 1964, IKEA opened a 45,800 square metre store in an attractive circular building in Stockholm, so appealing that thousands of people lined up for its opening. The building had four floors, and customers could move easily from floor to floor. However, neither the storage capacity nor the number of employees was sufficient to provide proper service to customers. To fix this problem, IKEA opened its warehouse so that customers could help themselves to what they wanted to purchase. The circular store, open warehouse and self-service approach became important components of the IKEA concept.

Low-cost, in-house design

The intense competition within Sweden in the early 1950s led to another innovation at IKEA in 1955: it started to design its own furniture. Similar to the opening of its warehouse, in-house furniture design at IKEA was initiated as a response to a problem: in this case, furniture supplier boycotts instigated by IKEA's competitors. Contrary to the expectation of its competitors, IKEA did not run into supply problems; rather, in-house furniture design proved very successful.

Flat packaging

The design of 'flat packaging' started to emerge, triggered by an IKEA employee who, afraid of damaging a table during transportation, removed its legs to fit it into a car. This act unintentionally initiated IKEA's novel business approach whereby customers could easily transport the products in their own vehicles and assemble them later. The assemble-it-yourself furniture, together with the flat packages, reduced space requirements in logistics operations (trucks, warehouses, etc.), and also lowered costs. IKEA incorporated the requirement of easily transportable flat packaging first into the design of kitchen products in 1959, and later into a variety of other products for use throughout the home.

Low-cost supply

In the early 1950s and 1960s, a suppliers' boycott in Sweden forced IKEA to seek help from Polish manufacturers, who could sell it furniture at a lower cost than the Swedish suppliers. In that period, IKEA started to search for international low-cost suppliers to sustain its low-cost strategy.

By 2008, IKEA's network of international low-cost suppliers had grown to the point where it had 46 trading service offices in 54 countries that managed 1,300 suppliers. It sourced 18 per cent of its products and materials from China and 14 per cent from Poland.[31]

To reduce logistics costs even further, IKEA attempts to build new stores around its central warehouses. By concentrating several stores in the same area, IKEA has been able to reduce both marketing costs and logistics costs, though potential competition among stores nearby might adversely affect performance. For example, in the US, IKEA started with four stores in the Philadelphia/Washington DC/New Jersey area to facilitate shipping products from the central warehouse to these stores.

Low-cost materials and designs

IKEA systematically searches for new materials and new designs to "fit the IKEA concept of form, function and price".[32] For example, IKEA initially used wood for the so-called OGLA chair, but later switched to composite, and finally to hollow composite, to make the chair affordable to most people. In 2011, IKEA switched its wooden shipping pallets for single-use paper composite pallets. At that time, IKEA was ordering over 10 million shipping pallets a year for shipping merchandise to its retail stores. The change to lighter paper pallets reduced transport costs by 10 per cent, resulting in over 143 million euros in cost savings.[33]

Mobilizing staff's intuition and learning

IKEA has described itself "as a learning and problem-solving organization that trusts the intuition of its staff".[34] IKEA tries to achieve this through both maximum decentralization and extensive internal training.

Diversification

IKEA has continued to diversify in terms of both product variety and geographical expansion.

Designing for children

Besides serving the needs of the entire family, IKEA launched the Children's IKEA concept in 1997. To create child-friendly products, the company consulted with child psychologists who specialized in playing and kids. In this way, IKEA applied its design expertise to respond to children's needs. IKEA also added more play areas and special kids' meals in its stores.

Learning and adapting in the international markets

IKEA started to expand internationally in 1963, opening its first international store in Norway. In the 1960s and 1970s, it focused on the European market, entering Denmark in 1969, Switzerland in 1973, Germany in 1974, Austria in 1977 and the Netherlands in 1979. Outside of Europe, it opened stores only in Australia (1975) and Canada (1976).

In its European expansion, IKEA used the same products and the same operational formulas. As suggested by Anders Moberg, IKEA's president between 1986 and 1999: "(W)e don't spend much money or time on studies. We use our eyes and go out and look, and say it will probably do quite well here. Then we may adapt, but quite often we stick to our opinions."[35]

However, this lack of adaptation to local circumstances caused serious problems when IKEA entered into the US. IKEA opened its first American store in 1985, followed by six more stores in the next six years. Many products sold in these stores were manufactured in Sweden – following Swedish designs – and then exported to the US. Some of these products did not appeal to American customers. For example, many Americans use bedroom chests to store sweaters, but the IKEA chests were too shallow. Many Americans add substantial quantities of ice to their drinks; IKEA's glasses were too small to allow for this. Noticing the problems, IKEA redesigned a fifth of its products and introduced larger glasses and chests with deeper drawers.

Besides redesigning its products, IKEA also adapted its routines in the US. For example, by 1994 its American stores purchased 45 per cent of their furniture from local American manufacturers, thereby significantly reducing costs. IKEA also added cash registers to reduce waiting times, as Americans profoundly dislike waiting at a cash register. Between 1990 and 1994 IKEA's sales tripled, and in early 1993 it finally started to make a profit in the US.

However, even when adapting to the specificities of the American market, IKEA stuck with its low-price focus.

Crafting IKEA's future as of the early 1990s

In the early 1990s, IKEA faced two major challenges, partially as a result of its rapid expansion. First, its administrative costs increased. Second, it got harder to manage its international operations, especially in terms of fostering local learning and efficient problem solving. IKEA made three decisions. First, it gave more autonomy to the CEO of IKEA America. Second, it gave up on central, internal budgeting in 1992, as the internal planning system became too cumbersome. In later years, each region only had to meet a fixed ratio of costs to turnover. Third, IKEA introduced internal competition by giving its franchise rights to Inter IKEA Systems B.V., thereby separating the IKEA Group and Inter IKEA Systems B.V. From then on, Inter IKEA Systems B.V. became the owner of the IKEA trademark, and franchised its business to all IKEA stores in the world. The IKEA Group was still the largest franchisee, owning most of the IKEA stores: of the 301 IKEA stores around the world by 2011, the IKEA Group owned 267. This franchising approach produced internal competition, as the IKEA Group had to compete with the other IKEA franchisees.[36]

In the 1990s and the early twenty-first century, IKEA continued its expansion, forging into Hungary (1990), Poland (1990s), the Czech Republic (1991), the United Arab Emirates (1991), Spain (1996), China (1998), Russia (2000) and Portugal (2004). In 2011, IKEA announced its intention to enter Lithuania, Latvia and Belarus.[37] Furthermore, IKEA is expanding its product lines. It has added a new line of IKEA-branded kitchen appliances, such as refrigerators, dishwashers and microwave ovens;[38] it plans to add a line of private label grocery specialities (2006), such as smoked elk sausage.[39]

As it expands overseas, IKEA continues to adapt to local requirements while trying to retain its low-cost strategy. However, this objective has proven challenging for IKEA in a number of countries. For example, in Warsaw, Poland, IKEA discovered that a full replication of its success formula would make IKEA stores too costly for the Poles, so it decided to install fewer toilets and eliminate air conditioning, essentially making the new stores look like "what IKEA stores looked like 20 years ago". Even with these adaptations, IKEA in 1993 reached only upper-class Poles.[40]

Similarly, IKEA has revised its recipe in China. It provides more fee-based assembly services, as assemble-it-yourself is not popular in China and labour is inexpensive; IKEA stores are located near transportation lines rather than in the suburbs, since most customers do not have cars; the store layouts reflect those of average Chinese apartments, with more focus on the living room and the dining room, and less on the kitchen. As in Poland, however, IKEA is having difficulty trying to be a 'low-cost' provider in the Chinese market: In spite of its endeavours to cut costs through local purchasing, IKEA's prices as of 2004 were considered mid-range, rather than low.[41] Nonetheless, by 2012, IKEA had decided to accelerate further its expansion into China.

In 2012, IKEA opted to delay entry into India due to local sourcing regulations.[42] Foreign companies were required to obtain at least 30 per cent of their products from small to medium sized Indian companies – a regulation inconsistent with IKEA's global, low-cost sourcing strategy.[43] 'Big-box' stores such as IKEA are rare in India. The 'kirana', or small shops offer special services such as credit, delivery (even for small orders) and are geared towards supporting the purchasing behaviour of local consumers.[44]

QUESTIONS

1. What are the core competencies and end products of IKEA? How are they linked with each other?
2. How did IKEA diversify?
3. How did IKEA expand internationally? How has the firm maintained a focus on core competencies while simultaneously adapting to local needs in host countries?
4. Can you provide an update on IKEA's core competencies, using materials available on the Web?

Notes

1. C. K. Prahalad and G. Hamel, 'The core competence of the corporation', *Harvard Business Review* 68 (1990), 79–91.
2. *Ibid.*, 81.
3. *Ibid.*, 89.
4. *Ibid.*
5. William G. Egelhoff, 'Great strategy or great strategy implementation – Two ways of competing in global markets', *Sloan Management Review* 34 (1993), 37–50.
6. Richard E. Dauch, 'Detroit – in the cross hairs', *Executive Speeches* 19 (2004), 14.

7. Andrew Bartmess and Keith Cerny, 'Building competitive advantage through a global network of capabilities', *California Management Review* 35 (1993), 78–103.
8. 3M company information 2007.
9. 3M, 'A Century of Innovation'.
10. *Ibid.*
11. *Ibid.*
12. *Ibid.*, 55
13. *Ibid.*
14. *Ibid.*, 143–4.
15. *Ibid.*, 158.
16. Robert L. Rose, 'Success abroad: how 3M, by tiptoeing into foreign markets, became a big exporter', *Wall Street Journal* (29 March 1991), 1.
17. 3M, 'A Century of Innovation', 158.
18. Thomas A. Stewart, '3M fights back', *Fortune* 133 (5 February 1996), 94–9.
19. Michael Arndt and Diane Brady, '3M's rising star: Jim McNerney is racking up quite a record at 3M. Now, can he rev up its innovation machine?', *Business Week* (12 April 2004), 62.
20. Marc Gunther, Marilyn Adamo and Betsy Feldman, '3M's innovation revival', *Fortune* 162 (5) (27 September 2010), 73–6.
21. D. Gayatri and T. Phani Madhav, 'Innovating 3M's innovations', *ICFAI Business School Case Development Centre* (2004), Case No. 304–357–1.
22. Michael Arndt, '3M: A lab for growth? CEO Jim McNerney – the first outsider boss – is overhauling a company long known for innovation', *Business Week* (21 January 2002), 50.
23. Marc Gunther, Marilyn Adamo and Betsy Feldman, '3M's innovation revival', *Fortune* 162 (5) (27 September 2010), 73–6.
24. *Ibid.*
25. Bob Tita, '3M to ramp up growth', *Wall Street Journal. (Eastern edition)* (10 September 2010), pg. B.1.
26. Thomas Black, '3M's Thulin to keep Buckley focus on research, emerging markets', *Bloomberg* (8 February 2012).
27. *Ibid.*
28. James R. Hagerty, Joann S. Lublin, 'Corporate news: 3M taps 33-year veteran and operating chief as CEO', *Wall Street Journal. (Eastern edition)* (9 February 2012), pg. B.3
29. IKEA company information.
30. *Ibid.*
31. Peter Wilke, with André Sobzcak and Isabelle Schömann, 'Codes of conduct and international framework agreements: New forms of governance at company; IKEA: a case study' *European Foundation for the Improvement of Living and Working Conditions* (2008).
32. IKEA company information.
33. Ola Kinnander, 'IKEA's paper pallet challenges wood dominance', *Bloomberg* (3 November 2011).
34. The Economist, 'Furnishing the world', *The Economist* 333 (1994), 80.
35. *Ibid.*, 79
36. IKEA company information.
37. Milda Seputyte, 'Ikea plans to open first shop in Lithuania's capital in 2013', *Bloomberg* (14 December 2011); Nerijus Adomaitis, 'Icelandic investors to bring first IKEA to Baltics', *Reuters* (15 December 2011).

38. Debbie Howell, 'Latest IKEAs debut self-checkout, branded appliances', *DSN Retailing Today* 44 (2005), 2–3.

39. David Wellman, 'Ikea adds more stores, more food', *Retail Merchandiser* 45 (2005), 7.

40. Stephen D. Moore, 'Sweden's IKEA forges into Eastern Europe – Retailer tests new markets via "lab" in Warsaw', *Wall Street Journal (Eastern Edition)* (1993), A.9.

41. Paula M. Miller, 'IKEA with Chinese characteristics', *China Business Review* 31 (2004), 36–8.

42. James Lamont, 'Ikea shelves entry to India over rules on local sourcing', *Financial Times* (23 January 2012), 21.

43. *Ibid.*

44. James Lamont, 'Who is afraid of the big bad box store?', *Financial Times* (7 December 201), 16.

3

The nature of home country location advantages

Five learning objectives

1. To describe the relationship between a firm's strengths relative to international rivals and the competitiveness of its home country.
2. To explain 'Porter's diamond' and the interaction among the four diamond attributes.
3. To develop an understanding of the different international expansion trajectories of newly established firms.
4. To identify the role of 'diamond connectors' in the context of location advantages held by different countries.
5. To discuss the managerial relevance of a 'national diamond-based' analysis on the competitive advantage of nations.

This chapter explores Porter's idea that the most important aspect of international business strategy is four key home country location advantages, often simply referred to as 'Porter's diamond'. Porter's idea is that, ultimately, an MNE's long-term competitiveness results from vigorous domestic pressure in its home base, forcing it to innovate and improve productivity. This idea will be examined and then criticized using the framework presented in Chapter 1.

Significance

In the early 1990s, **Michael Porter's** now-classic *HBR* article, 'The competitive advantage of nations' (and the identically named book) created substantial debate on the sources of international competitiveness.[1]

Porter argues that any company's ability to compete in the international arena is based mainly on an interrelated set of location advantages in its home country. A high level of pressure in its home base pushes the firm to innovate and to upgrade systematically, resulting in FSA creation. These FSAs are then instrumental to expansion in foreign markets. According to Porter, "a nation's competitiveness depends on the capacity of its industry to innovate and upgrade. Companies gain advantage against the world's best competitors because of pressure and challenge. They benefit from having strong domestic rivals, aggressive home-based suppliers, and demanding local customers."[2]

According to Porter, FSAs are primarily developed not because firms have a strong, internal entrepreneurial drive, or because they can easily access external resources, but because they face external pressure. Companies should therefore not rely on 'natural' factor endowments such as an abundance of raw materials, low labour costs, a large domestic market or favourable exchange rates provided by their home base, nor on playing a national champion role in their protected home market. This type of thinking leads firms to rely on short-term advantages. Such advantages are short-lived because replication by rival firms is usually easy to achieve, simply by accessing these natural advantages (e.g., by acquiring the sources of coveted raw materials). Alternatively, in the case of sheltered markets, these advantages depend on precarious political circumstances and priorities of public policy makers, who are themselves faced with enormous bounded rationality problems – for example, when attempting to select national champions. Building mainly upon natural factor endowments or a protected market environment is usually detrimental to innovation and growth; the firm then has an incentive to become complacent and interested mainly in the status quo.

In contrast, long-term competitiveness results from innovation and firm-level productivity improvements. Here, it is the interplay among various home market attributes (especially those pressuring firms to innovate and improve productivity), which acts as the key location advantage for firms embedded in this home base, and is instrumental to long-term competitiveness. Porter visualized the four key sets of country attributes as the points of a 'diamond of national competitive advantage'. Note that 'Porter's diamond' therefore refers to the four-sided geometric figure representing one of the four suits in a deck of playing cards in addition to spades, hearts and clubs, rather than the very hard native crystalline carbon valued as a gem. Porter's diamond consists of:

1. Factor conditions: these include not only factors of production in the home base such as natural resources, but also, and more importantly, created factor conditions such as skilled labour, scientific knowledge and infrastructure. These are particularly valuable if they are specialized, meaning customized towards effective deployment in very specific economic activities and companies.
2. Demand conditions: here, the focus is not on domestic market size alone, but also on domestic buyer sophistication.
3. Related and supporting industries: high-quality, internationally competitive home-based suppliers as well as companies in related industries are critical to the firm's international competitiveness.

4. Firm strategy, industry structure and rivalry: a highly competitive, home-based industry with efficient macro-level governance and several domestic rivals may help the firms in that industry become internationally competitive.

According to Porter, it is the synergetic interactions among these four attributes, along with two external variables – government and 'chance' – that determine the competitiveness of specific industries in the international marketplace. 'Chance' includes stumbling upon a new commercial application for an existing resource, or being lucky in an innovation process and coincidentally creating a valuable new product technology or process knowledge. The interaction among the four diamond attributes causes an industry-wide recombination capability not attributable to the actions of the individual firms in that industry.

Here, *factor conditions* accessible by domestic firms need to be continuously upgraded through the development of skills and the creation of new knowledge, not simply inherited from the country's natural endowments. Porter makes the point that, even where a country's natural endowments are limited, disadvantages can be turned into advantages when they spur creativity and ingenuity to overcome deficiencies. For example, in the case of Japan, firms in several industries such as steel, shipbuilding and automobiles developed technological and design expertise to overcome a lack of natural resources, and the just-in-time production process was pioneered in response to a lack of affordable warehousing space.

The presence of sophisticated ***demand conditions*** at home also incites companies to be innovative. Companies must respond to new customer demands by pushing the envelope of existing technology and design features. As a result, they gain early insights into the future needs of customers across borders, and thereby build the potential to achieve first-mover advantages on a global scale.

Highly competitive firms in ***related and supporting industries*** at home, especially suppliers, are crucial to enhancing innovation through more efficient inputs, the ongoing exchange of ideas, timely feedback and short lines of communication between sequential and parallel activities in the vertical chain.

Lastly, vigorous ***domestic rivalry*** is instrumental to international competitiveness. Such rivalry forces companies to develop unique FSAs, beyond the generally available location advantages in their home base. Firms then become motivated to enter international markets as an outlet for exploiting these FSAs.

While each of the four attributes of the diamond model can have a stand-alone impact on the competitiveness of a specific industry, their joint impact is even more important. The four determinants operate as an interdependent system, with each element affecting and stimulating the other ones, often in a small geographic space where most firms in the industry are concentrated, thereby forming a cluster.

According to Porter, a home country diamond cannot be identified for a national or regional economy as a whole, across industries. The diamond of competitive advantage will be different for each specific industry considered. Porter is adamant that *industry-specific* pressures, associated with particular interactions among diamond determinants, lead to innovation and productivity improvements, and thereby to international competitiveness. An MNE's FSAs are thus strengthened, not simply through easy access to favourable generic location advantages in the firm's home base, but rather through absorbing or building upon the complementary resources arising out of its industry context. Such complementary resources are provided by sophisticated individuals (whether skilled workers or demanding customers), other firms and a variety of industry-specific institutions, ranging from accepted rules of competition to educational facilities training specialized workers.

Porter's findings resulted from a four-year study of over 100 industry groups in ten nations, including Denmark, Germany, Italy, Japan, Korea, Singapore, Sweden, Switzerland, the UK and the US. In each of the sample nations, industries were chosen based on their domestic importance and international competitive success as measured by substantial and sustained exports as well as outward FDI, arising from advantages created in the home country. Examples include automobiles and chemicals in Germany, semiconductors and electronics in Japan, banking and pharmaceuticals in Switzerland, footwear and textiles in Italy, aircraft and motion pictures in the US, TVs and VCRs in South Korea and healthcare in Denmark. We should note, however, that Porter developed his diamond concept prior to directing the empirical work. The empirical work was aimed mainly at validating the diamond framework, rather than augmenting it further or refining it in a substantive fashion.

Context and complementary perspectives

Porter worked on the diamond-based approach to international competitiveness throughout the late 1980s when many academics, managers and policy makers were reflecting on the sources of sustainable competitive advantage at the macro-level. How could a resource-poor nation like Japan achieve astounding competitive success while the mighty economic engine of the US sputtered? During this time, a fascination developed about Japanese business practices and the question was raised whether these practices were built upon a superior management system, a starting point similar to that adopted by Prahalad and Hamel in their work on core competencies, discussed in Chapter 2. Porter argued against this trend in thinking, stating that "no one managerial system is universally appropriate – notwithstanding the current fascination with Japanese management".[3]

Another important contextual element was the ongoing debate as to how the US should respond to the alleged threat of declining competitiveness. One option being considered at that time was increased protectionism through trade barriers in an attempt to shelter US companies in the domestic market and keep out foreign competition. In Porter's view, that was not the solution to the problem. According to Porter, sources of competitive advantage do not lie in conventional comparative advantage, nor in specific management styles or trade barriers, but rather are achieved through the promotion of domestic rivalry. Vigorous rivalry leads to long-term innovation and productivity improvements. Here, the home country diamond represents a fertile basis for FSA development, much of it of the recombination type, since individual firms systematically interact with other actors in this diamond, thereby absorbing and benefiting from complementary resources that strengthen their own FSAs.

Porter focuses primarily on the rise of industries at the national level, and less on firm-specific challenges. As a result, his work provides relatively little practical guidance to the managers or owners of newly established firms, in terms of what location advantages can – or should – mean to them. **Walter Kuemmerle** provided such a complementary perspective in an *SMR* piece on the entrepreneur's 'path to global expansion'.[4]

Kuemmerle analysed 27 cases of international expansion by newly established firms. In many cases, these new firms started as responses to local opportunities (mostly driven by domestic demand), and built upon local resources to achieve domestic success, much in line with Porter's thinking. However, somewhat in contrast to Porter's perspective, very early internationalization often occurred, with even the initial business models foreseeing access, either to foreign input markets for valuable resources, or to foreign output markets for delivery of end products (as frequently observed in newly established software companies, for example). This early internationalization usually entailed low-cost, low-risk experiments in neighbouring countries, whereby the firms' mix of internationally transferable knowledge and location-bound knowledge required only incremental change.[5]

Importantly, though, Kuemmerle also identified two patterns of more aggressive international expansion, beyond the simple incremental accessing of a neighbour's input or output markets. In a first set of cases, still consistent with Porter's perspective, save the early timing of internationalization, home country resources were used to exploit substantial cross-border opportunities in output markets. This works well if the internationally transferable FSAs embodied in the product offering can immediately be used to access and satisfy demand in foreign markets, without the requirement of investing in location-bound FSAs (such as distribution channels or high-cost retail outlets) in foreign markets.

In a second set of cases, newly established firms tapped into foreign input markets to find (usually stand-alone) resources such as (venture) capital, while maintaining their operations and sales primarily in the home country. Here, foreign resources were instrumental to accelerated domestic expansion (and subsequent international expansion), demonstrating that there may be more to competitive success than domestic diamond conditions, even at the early stages of firm growth.

However, Kuemmerle generally cautioned against both these patterns of aggressive international expansion (i.e., the ambitious search for foreign market opportunities or foreign resources at the early stages of a firm's development). Such expansion may reflect an overly optimistic view of the firm's internationally transferable FSAs, especially its recombination capabilities. It also underestimates the magnitude of linking investments needed to access foreign location advantages or complementary resources of foreign business partners (such as suppliers or providers of management skills). This is a typical bounded rationality problem, with managers incapable of understanding properly the international logistics problems associated with rapid international expansion. The effective coordination and control of multiple input and output markets is the key strength of the international coordinator, described in Chapter 1. However, the necessary recombination capabilities to coordinate and control activities in multiple input and output markets, as found in international coordinators, require extensive international experience. This experience can only be built up over time. Therefore, foreign input markets for resources and foreign output markets for end products need to be accessed and further developed in a selective and piecemeal fashion.

By recommending against aggressive international expansion for newly established companies, Kuemmerle generally accepts Porter's view that newly established companies will benefit from sustained exposure to vigorous domestic competition and should first focus on creating FSAs by attempting to become major players in the domestic market. However, Kuemmerle also finds, somewhat in contrast to Porter, that newly established companies can often successfully expand internationally, as long as they use a low-cost, low-risk, incremental approach in neighbouring countries.

David Teece provides a second complementary perspective to Porter's. Teece published an article in *CMR* focused on inward FDI in Silicon Valley, one of the world's best-known technological clusters.[6] The location advantages provided by the Silicon Valley cluster in the San Francisco Bay area will be discussed in more detail in the case study at the end of this chapter. Teece, however, focused primarily on the rationale for Japanese FDI in this cluster and its effects. His analysis suggests two things. First, Porter-type single diamond thinking breaks down when foreign investors can provide complementary resources not provided by the domestic diamond itself, but instrumental to domestic, firm-level sustainability and expansion (see also the critical analysis below). Second, foreign MNE activity through inward FDI can act as a bridge between the location advantages provided by two very different nations, in this case the US and Japan.

Japanese investors entering Silicon Valley through mergers, acquisitions, alliances and venture capital vehicles bring to local, high-technology firms a set of FSAs these firms cannot develop themselves by simply building upon the location advantages embedded in the US diamond. These FSAs, injected by Japanese companies into Silicon Valley, result themselves from the location advantages provided by the Japanese diamond: "patient capital, engineering talent, manufacturing excellence, and access to the Japanese market".[7] From a Porter-type perspective, some of these resources provided by Japanese companies could be interpreted as reflecting inadequacies of the US diamond. For example, a lack of patient capital means the US diamond fails to provide the proper capital market conditions conducive to success in long-gestation sub-sectors of biotechnology, computers and semiconductors. However, the real story is not one of failure. Japanese FDI in Silicon Valley leads to substantial benefits to the US firms and to the Japanese actors involved: "With technological competence and capabilities put centre stage, Japanese companies are free to focus on the long run, and to imagine constellations of future products deriving from technological capabilities."[8]

The Japanese companies benefit from these arrangements in many ways. Silicon Valley provides Japanese companies with unique access to US entrepreneurial capabilities, early-stage technology developments in innovation-driven sectors and a more general window on new trends in these sectors – location advantages sorely missing in Japan. In addition, conducting these types of entrepreneurial activities in Japan itself would be problematic. Managers who engage in initiatives characterized by substantial ignorance about future industry conditions would be ostracized, and the initiatives would probably fail. In contrast, experimenting in Silicon Valley is much more legitimate, and carries the promise of diffusion to Japan of any successful new technologies, and the further development thereof in Japan itself. Finally, Japanese companies can sometimes gain privileged access to US distribution channels and other stakeholders – location advantages embedded in the US diamond – through investing in these Silicon Valley ventures.

However, the effective melding of location advantages provided by the US and Japanese diamonds through Japanese FDI in Silicon Valley is not easy to achieve in practice. It requires long-term efforts to develop personal relationships between the Japanese and US actors with the intent to achieve international technology exchange and absorption. Importantly, it is not the higher cost of capital in the US that explains Japanese FDI, but rather differences in governance mechanisms: Japanese firms are much less interested in short-term profits, dividends and stock buybacks, and much more interested in long-term capability development. Here, the Japanese MNEs perform the role of diamond connectors: they act as a conduit for injecting Japanese-style governance mechanisms into Silicon Valley companies, while aiming for knowledge transfer to their Japanese operations.

Turning now to the framework developed in Chapter 1, it is clear that Porter holds a rather narrow view about how FSAs are created. According to Porter, the home country national diamond attributes determine a firm's innovation capabilities and related productivity improvements. Any company's FSAs thus systematically result from location advantages found in its home base. This home base is the location where the firm retains effective strategic, creative and technical control of its operations. This is usually the firm's original home country, unless it decides to move this home base to a more attractive foreign diamond for specific business units. Porter thereby makes a sharp distinction for each business unit between the home base, as the primary source of location advantages critical to innovation and productivity improvements, and other nations, which are selectively tapped into for certain diamond attributes but are primarily a channel for exploiting or incrementally extending FSAs developed at home. The MNE is thus either a **centralized exporter** or an **international projector**. Given his focus on a single home base per business unit, Porter implicitly rejects the relevance of a **multi-centred MNE** or an **international coordinator**.

Figure 3.1 shows Porter's interpretation of international business strategy in terms of the general framework outlined in Chapter 1. For Porter, location advantages in the home base are the key source of location-bound FSAs, including a company's stand-alone FSAs such as its technical knowledge, as well as its routines and recombination capabilities. The latter precisely derive from the interplay among the various diamond determinants in the home base.

In the case of a weak diamond, as shown at the top of Figure 3.1, the firm is unable to develop non-location-bound FSAs, and thereby unable to expand internationally. In contrast, at the bottom of Figure 3.1, the pressures arising from the strong home country diamond lead to innovation and productivity improvements, and ultimately to non-location-bound FSAs that can be exploited internationally, whether embodied in final products (exports), or transferred as an intermediate product and then exploited by host country subsidiaries. As regards the patterns of FSA development from this book's framework, Porter focuses mainly on Pattern II, in which location-bound FSAs are developed in the home base and then upgraded to become internationally transferable; see Figure 1.7 in Chapter 1.

An implicit normative message for managers is that they should cherish their domestic home base and reflect on what they can do themselves to improve diamond conditions in their industry beyond what would be immediately beneficial to their own firm.

Porter's analysis, while intuitively plausible, especially for technology-driven industries in large economies such as the US, unfortunately suffers from five main weaknesses.

First, Porter's perspective does not address fully the complexities of international management, especially for MNEs based in smaller countries with large

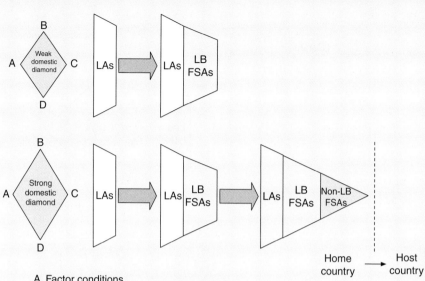

Figure 3.1
Domestic 'diamond'
determinants as
drivers of home-base
location advantages,
and subsequent FSAs

A. Factor conditions
B. Related and supporting industries
C. Demand conditions
D. Firm strategy, industry structure, and rivalry

Where the domestic diamond is strong (pictured here as a large diamond),
this model predicts the creation of NLB FSAs will be stimulated, while this
will not occur where the diamond is weak (pictured here as a small diamond).

neighbours, such as Canada, Belgium or New Zealand. In such cases, a 'single
diamond' approach fails to recognize the significant impacts on a country and its
firms exercised by the diamond attributes of one or several – often larger –
neighbouring countries or trading partners.

Take Canada as an example. The US economy is ten times larger than the
Canadian one. A single diamond approach would predict little good for
Canadian-based firms, having to compete with US-based ones; see Figure 3.2
(top part). However, firms in Canada benefit from unlimited market access and
national treatment in the US through NAFTA. For these reasons, Canadian firms
are often forced from their inception to work with – and react to – the various
national diamond determinants present in both Canada and the US, or they risk
missing out on key strategic signals and pressures in an increasingly integrated
regional market. Canadian companies often consider the US as a 'natural' component of their output market, and in many industries face largely the same
demand pressures and consumer sophistication as US firms. Since industries such
as the automotive sector are organized at the North American continental level,
sector-based rivalry in many cases is also almost identical, with the exception of
some protected sectors such as those related to maritime transport or Canadian
health care (and save the problem of the so-called fair trade laws, including
countervail and anti-dumping regulations, which can still be applied against the

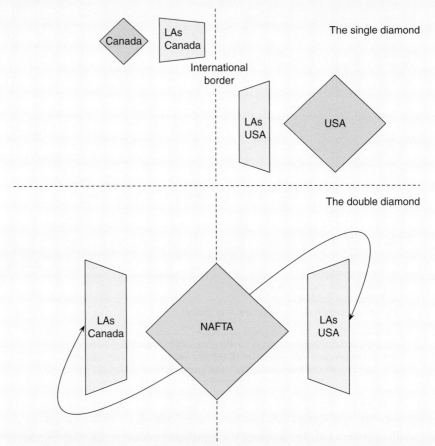

Figure 3.2
Porter's single
diamond model and
the double diamond
model

With the single diamond model, the home country LAs determine whatever FSAs a company may develop. With the double diamond model, firms also draw on LAs of other nations than the home country to strengthen their own FSAs. Trade and investment liberalization (as with NAFTA) institutionalizes this possibility of freely accessing and drawing upon the resources present in a host country diamond to strengthen FSAs. This is why the trapezoids representing Canadian and US location advantages are shown as being similar in size, though NAFTA obviously does not eliminate completely country borders.

other country's firms, as has occurred in the softwood lumber industry). Finally, Canadian firms have the same access as US firms to most production factors and inputs from related and supporting industries in the US. One could even argue that Canadian firms will not be hindered by any ineffective intra-US diamond interactions inherited from the past, but will selectively access US diamond determinants to satisfy present, urgent FSA development needs. In other words, they will take from the US diamond any elements not provided fully by their Canadian diamond; see Figure 3.2 (bottom part).

The same is also true for countries within the EU, where a firm's home base may not provide all of the necessary ingredients to develop the FSA bundles a company's top management wishes to control. The MNE must therefore remain attuned to conditions in the other, closely linked national markets. In this case, the close linkages among nations result from the single EU market, which is much more economically integrated than NAFTA.

These EU and NAFTA cases suggest a 'double diamond' (or 'multiple diamond') model, in which the attributes of two or more countries are critically important to the FSA development process. This contrasts sharply with Porter's view. Porter states that "relying on foreign activities that supplant domestic capabilities is always a second-best solution",[9] and "[u]ltimately, competitive advantage is created at home".[10]

The double diamond model has important managerial and policy implications. For example, in his 1990 book on the competitive advantage of nations, Porter describes in detail both the Singaporean and Korean diamonds.[11] His conclusions on the Korean diamond across industries are largely favourable, whereas he is less impressed by the Singaporean diamond. In reality, Singapore's GDP per capita has consistently been much higher than Korea's (it was approximately 50 per cent higher than Korea's in 2005). This implies that Singapore has a stronger economy than Korea. If we abandon Porter's model and apply double diamond thinking instead, we can see why Singapore has done better than Korea. Singapore's outward FDI has allowed it to access inputs (such as natural resources) from other countries. In addition, inward FDI by foreign MNEs (attracted by Singapore's attractive geographic location and its well-run institutions) has allowed Singapore's domestic economy to access foreign MNEs' knowledge bases.

Second, in line with the above point about the need for double diamond thinking, inward FDI as a force for upgrading a local economy, as described by Teece in his *CMR* piece, is not given the attention it deserves. Though Porter acknowledges that foreign-owned firms could in principle be part of a domestic cluster, at least if the domestic operation can function independently from the foreign parent, he focuses on home-grown firms, with domestic suppliers and buyers, using the home country diamond as a lever for subsequent international success. He thereby largely neglects the important issue of a country's location advantages being instrumental to inward FDI (rather than only outward FDI), and therefore to economic growth and prosperity. When adopting Porter's mindset, large-scale inward FDI in an industry is obviously not entirely healthy, as it can be interpreted as a failure to develop successful, home-grown firms in the same industry. That is, it results from a national diamond with intrinsic weaknesses.

However, developing advanced new knowledge within a robust national diamond does not necessarily create more wealth for a country's citizens than exploiting and further augmenting such knowledge through inward FDI. The latter case also adds value, benefiting workers and consumers in the host country as much as it may benefit the firm's shareholders in its home base. In addition, the knowledge complementarities and exchanges with other economic actors in a host country may be as intensive as in the home country, even if these complementarities and exchanges are likely to occur to a larger extent in downstream value chain activities. For example, if the US experiences substantial inward FDI in the automotive industry, this does not simply reflect the relative failure of domestic firms to remain competitive or hold on to their market share. It also signals that the US is perceived by foreign producers as an attractive location to engage in value creation. What counts is how consumers and other stakeholders, especially skilled workers, in the US benefit from this inward FDI. Foreign firms such as the Japanese automotive companies also benefit, because they gain proximity to large numbers of consumers, unchained from past loyalties, and willing to try new products and services. The consumers' willingness to explore new products may well be one of the United States' greatest location advantages across industries.

Third, Porter ignores the need for location-bound FSAs in host countries. Porter's model assumes that FSA development depends initially on domestic market factors, but can then be decoupled from the home location, when the FSAs are transferred for exploitation in host countries. This is in line with Ray Vernon's international product life cycle thinking.[12] As noted above, this approach is represented by Pattern II in Figure 1.7 in Chapter 1, whereby location-bound FSAs are created in the home base, and subsequently transformed into internationally transferable FSAs. This diffusion process can take the form of exports or transfers of intermediate outputs, such as technological knowledge or brand names, to subsidiaries. As outlined in Chapter 1, however, even strong FSAs from the host country may need to be complemented with location-bound FSAs in every country where the firm operates in order to achieve a balance between integration and local responsiveness. Porter neglects this necessary process of linking existing knowledge bundles with new knowledge in host countries and regions.

Fourth, Porter's framework is fundamentally tautological. Porter argues that selective factor disadvantages may actually drive domestic innovation and upgrading, as long as the disadvantages send signals to innovate to domestic companies (e.g., given a lack of natural resources at home, domestic firms may need to focus on developing brand-named products) and the other diamond determinants are strong. Unfortunately, this point fundamentally undermines the value added (and explanatory and predictive power) of the single diamond approach. It implies that, *ex post*, any domestic industry's international success in terms of exports or outward FDI can always be explained by Porter's diamond determinants. If one of the four diamond determinants shows an obvious weakness, this weakness can be simply reinterpreted as a driver for domestic firms to upgrade and to increase productivity. The diamond framework is thus fundamentally tautological, as there is no way to disprove it. *Ex post*, success follows from strong home country determinants, unless some of these determinants happen to be weak, in which case they are interpreted as selective factor disadvantages that have pushed domestic firms to overcome this weakness through innovation.[13]

Fifth, Porter places too much emphasis on **the country** as the appropriate geographic level of analysis. Consider a manager trying to operationalize Porter's diamond. It is actually feasible to operationalize the diamond, while overcoming the problems outlined above.[14] For each of the diamond determinants, managers should compile a list of all the parameters that can affect a firm's competitiveness (assuming that a diamond-driven analysis is conducted at the level of a firm, rather than an entire domestic industry). For example, within the determinant **factor conditions**, and the sub-factor **human resources**, a distinction could be made among scientists with R&D knowledge, skilled blue-collar workers, multilingual managers with advanced marketing, organizational and financial knowledge, etc. The question then arises as to the relevant geographic area where the firm can access each relevant type of personnel.

As noted above, Porter's work focuses primarily on the national level, and on the distinction between home country and host countries. The present book also makes a similar distinction, but without assuming that, in terms of access to location advantages, an MNE is constrained to whatever the home country diamond has to offer, with access to the strengths of host country diamonds largely off-limits. Porter's work simply misses one of the most basic points in international business: firms expand abroad only if they can establish a match between their FSAs and the location advantages of the host environments they penetrate, whether input markets or output markets. If international expansion involves more than the pure exploitation of extant FSAs, i.e., some form of resource recombination, the firm can actually improve on its existing strengths.

Conceptually, it is helpful to distinguish between the local level, the state/provincial level, the domestic national level, the regional level of one or more foreign nations (e.g., NAFTA or the EU), and the global level, as the relevant geographic spaces where parameters may be accessed by the MNE. Consider the case of a petrochemical firm located in Rotterdam, the Netherlands. Its highly skilled technical workers may be available largely as a result of educational facilities at the local and provincial levels. The relevant competitors producing similar chemicals may operate primarily out of Germany. The suppliers used by the MNE may be scattered around the European Union. Finally, demand for the products may be global, i.e., the firm's products can in principle be sold around the world.

Some of the above parameters, **at each geographic level**, can be interpreted as either a strength or a weakness, namely if the firm can directly influence the parameter (e.g., quality control systems adopted by suppliers). Similarly, other

Figure 3.3

A multilevel analysis
of the diamond
determinants

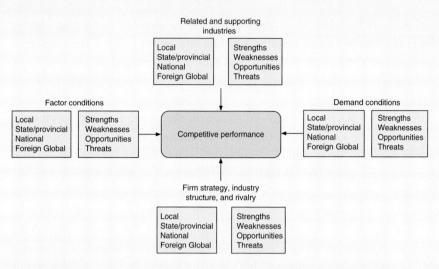

Figure 3.3
A multilevel analysis of the diamond determinants

parameters can be viewed as either an opportunity or a threat, to the extent that these parameters are largely exogenous to the firm (e.g., domestic taxation regimes or global energy prices). Figure 3.3 shows a stylized version of this approach, in which Porter's original diamond model has been transformed into a tool to classify in an intuitively appealing fashion a variety of environmental parameters that can affect a firm's international competitiveness. This classification can then be supplemented with an analysis of dynamics, i.e., the interactions among various critical parameters, leading to virtuous cycles of making the firm stronger or vicious cycles of downgrading.

Five management takeaways

1. Apply the 'diamond' framework to evaluate the sectorial strengths and weaknesses of your domestic industry.
2. Reflect on the relevance of national diamond characteristics to explain – at least partly – the short- and long-term competitiveness of your own firm.
3. Define industry-specific pressures that can strengthen your FSAs through absorbing – or building upon – the complementary resources present in your industry environment.
4. Analyse the economic potential of foreign diamonds, i.e., foreign input markets for providing resources to your firm, and foreign output markets for absorbing its end products.
5. Assess the suitability of the diamond framework for analysing your industry and adjust/add determinants and sub-factors according to your firm-specific needs.

Case 3.1 The rise, fall and resurgence of industrial hot spots: The experience of Silicon Valley and Boston's Route 128[15]

CASE

The success of high-technology industries in Silicon Valley and the Boston Route 128 region has attracted many followers, both domestically and internationally. In 1999, there were as many as 88 'Silicon Wannabes': one 'Silicorn Valley' (Fairfield, Iowa), one 'Silicon Sandbar' (Cape Cod, Massachusetts), ten 'Silicon Prairies' (e.g., Lincoln, Nebraska; Payne County, Oklahoma) and five 'Silicon Islands' (e.g., Long Island, New York).

Both Silicon Valley and Route 128 prospered after WW II and faced downturns in the early 1980s, though Silicon Valley regained its vitality in the early 1990s, with Route 128 resurging only in the late 1990s. Today, Silicon Valley remains an innovation hub, while Route 128 has succeeded in other industries. The similarities and differences between the two regions help to explain the functioning of industrial clusters, especially the roles played by venture capital, local universities, local culture, industry structure and technology.

Silicon Valley

Silicon Valley did not establish a name for itself in semiconductors or any other core technology until the mid 1950s, though lucrative military contracts during WW II and the Cold War, and the engineering expertise at Stanford University, helped establish the electronics industry in the region, with the formation of firms such as Hewlett-Packard (HP), Litton Industries and Varian.

The semiconductor industry in Silicon Valley started in 1955, with the founding of Shockley Transistors by William Shockley, co-inventor of the transistor at Bell Laboratories. In 1957, the eight scientists and engineers at Shockley Transistors resigned together and set up Fairchild Semiconductor. Fairchild led the transition from the transistor to the integrated circuit, which was widely adopted in the consumer electronics and computer industries in the 1960s.

The high profits in the transistor and integrated-circuit industries attracted not only firms from other industries, but also start-ups funded by early employees who had become very wealthy. For example, by 1986, at least 124 start-ups could be traced back to Fairchild, including Intel, National Semiconductor and Advanced Micro Devices. Moreover, the founders and key employees of Fairchild's spin-offs earned enormous capital gains, some of which were reinvested in new start-ups or venture capital funds. The availability of venture capital and the creation of successful new firms thus created a self-perpetuating process. By 1969, the San Francisco Bay Area had 150 active venture capitalists.

By the late 1970s, Silicon Valley had become synonymous with the semiconductor industry. However, in the mid 1980s, Silicon Valley's established chipmakers faced strong competition from Japanese firms, who literally took away the semiconductor market. Throughout the 1980s, the leading chipmakers continued to struggle to compete with Japanese firms. As a result, the Silicon Valley region lost 25,000 jobs.

However, by 1991, Silicon Valley regained its prosperity, with a new wave of successful semiconductor start-ups. During the 1980s, more than 85 new semiconductor firms were started in Silicon Valley.

By 1990, electronics products exported by Silicon Valley represented almost one third of the total US exports of electronics products.

Route 128

Close industry–government interactions heavily influenced the development of Route 128 through spin-offs from government-funded research at Harvard and the Massachusetts Institute of Technology (MIT) during WW II and the Cold War. In the 1950s and 1960s, about 156 firms spun off from MIT, including Digital Equipment Corporation (DEC) in 1957. Wang Laboratories spun off from Harvard's Computation Laboratories in 1951.

Many of these early firms became the source of later start-ups. For example, during the late 1960s and early 1970s, nearly 60 minicomputer producers were founded by engineers who used to work at DEC or other minicomputer producers. The expansion of the minicomputer industry attracted an infrastructure of support firms, including suppliers, software firms and consultants. By the late 1970s and early 1980s, Route 128 had become the centre of the minicomputer industry, representing 60 per cent of total US minicomputer production in 1982.

However, during the 1980s, the number of start-ups declined, as the customers of minicomputer companies shifted to workstations and personal computers. By 1998, Route 128 no longer had any large, dominant electronics firms.

Success factors

The two industrial hot spots shared many similarities, which distinguished them from other US regions.

Educational infrastructure

The two areas are both near excellent technical universities and business schools. Silicon Valley is near Stanford and the University of California, Berkeley. Route 128 is near Harvard University and MIT. These universities provided not only spin-off opportunities through their pioneering research, but also top scientists, engineers, technicians and managers. Between the end of WW II and the mid 1980s, four major MIT labs (the Electronic Systems Laboratory, Instrumentation Laboratory, Lincoln Laboratory and Research Laboratory for Electronics) and five academic engineering departments (Aeronautics and Astronautics, Chemical Engineering, Electrical Engineering, Materials Science and Mechanical Engineering) together produced a staggering 181 spin-offs.[16] In the late 1980s, MIT formalized the spin-off process via the MIT Technology Licensing Office, which had recorded more than 250 spin-offs by the end of 2003.[17] The Technology Licensing Office offers mentorship and patent assistance to entrepreneurs and inventors. In 2009, the Technology Licensing Office was issuing around "500 new invention disclosures" per year as a part of its mission "to benefit the public by moving results of MIT research into societal use via technology licensing".[18] The roughly 25,800 companies started by MIT alumni employed around 3.3 million people worldwide and generated US $2 trillion in yearly revenue in 2009.[19]

Venture capital

The two areas have easy access to large amounts of venture capital. For example, in 1981, Silicon Valley led all high-tech regions by receiving 32 per cent of the total venture capital in the US. Route 128 received 15 per cent. In 1985, Silicon Valley firms received US $800 million in venture capital, while Route 128 firms received US $300 million. The numbers just continued to grow, and between 1990 and 2000, the average annual amount of venture capital invested was US $1.767 billion for Silicon Valley, and US $493 million for Route 128.

The influence of the initial leading firm

Fairchild provided success stories, experienced engineers/managers and spinoffs, all of which spurred the development of the semiconductor industry in Silicon Valley. DEC and Wang Laboratories played similar roles for the microcomputer industry in the Route 128 area.

Government funding as the catalyst

The two areas received early and heavy support from US military and space programmes, which functioned as the catalyst for high-technology innovation. Between 1958 and 1974, the Pentagon spent US $1 billion on semiconductor research. Between 1990 and 2000, the average annual US federal government investment in R&D was US $883 million in Silicon Valley, and US $764 million in Route 128.

Explaining the difference

During the mid and late 1980s, both Silicon Valley and Route 128 were in crisis, although by the early 1990s, Silicon Valley rebounded while Route 128 failed to do so. The divergent perform-ance between the two regions has been attributed to their different internal functioning, including:

Corporate culture – conventional organization versus 'the HP way'

With an established industrial tradition and many experienced managers, firms on Route 128 were characterized by conventional, centralized hierarchical structures, with formal decision making and conservative work procedures. In most firms, including RCA, Honeywell and Raytheon, senior committee members retained the final authority on all major decisions. Such a structure facilitated vertical information flows, but largely neglected horizontal communication. Moreover, stability and company loyalty were highly valued, even more than experimentation and risk taking.

In contrast, firms in Silicon Valley were organized using a participative management style, professional autonomy and informality, known as 'the HP way'. In Silicon Valley, firms eliminated many traditional status symbols, such as reserved parking spaces and differentiated office furniture for top managers. Informal luncheons, intramural sports teams and hallway conversations reinforced the participatory culture.

Attitude towards entrepreneurs and risk

While both regions support entrepreneurship and innovation from outside sources, subtle cultural difference may have affected their respective development. Mark Zuckerberg, the founder of Facebook attempted to secure funding in the Boston area in 2004, and was rejected by various venture capitalists. Route 128's delay in embracing social media and networking was partly affected by the fact that investors in the area were generally older. In 2011, angel investors in Boston were on average 55 years old, while in California this average age was 32. Said one professor at MIT's Sloan School of Management: "It became a generational issue. ... To understand things like Facebook, you have to be 19 to 24 years old. If you're 56, you don't quite get it."[20]

Regional network – self-sufficient corporations versus relational networks

As far back as the early 1970s, Route 128 was dominated by a small number of self-sufficient and highly vertically integrated firms, such as DEC. Most of these producers designed their own computers, manufactured as many of their components and peripherals as possible, assembled their own computers and controlled all sales, after-sales service and marketing. Outsourcing was kept to a minimum, and the boundaries between firms were quite distinct. Moreover, the military contracts gained by Route 128 firms reinforced secrecy rather than open collaboration.

In contrast, Silicon Valley was not organized around a few dominant established firms. Rather, it was organized around its dense networks of social and professional relationships. These relationships strengthened repeated informal interactions. For example, after Wilf Corrigan resigned as Chairman of Fairchild Semiconductor in 1979, he started to contact his former customers and colleagues for their ideas regarding semi-customized integrated circuits. He met a former employee, Robert Walker, who had just completed some research on the custom chip business. Together, Corrigan and Walker established a new firm, LSI Logic Corporation, with venture capital financing. Later they hired a number of Walker's former colleagues at Fairchild to develop their business. LSI went public in 1985, assisted by technical consultants, local research firms and trade associations. This exemplifies how relational networks facilitated the diffusion and exchange of intangible technical knowledge.

Engineers in Silicon Valley were more committed to the concept of advancing technology than to the firm where they worked, and they therefore moved easily from one employer to another. California law did not support 'post-employment covenants not to compete', in contrast to Massachusetts law. Thus, inter-firm rivalry was not critical to individual scientists, engineers or managers, as today's competitor might become tomorrow's customer or colleague.

Dominant design – minicomputer versus semiconductor

Silicon Valley and Route 128 had a different 'dominant design', instrumental to each region's technological trajectory.[21] For Route 128, the minicomputer represented only one segment of the computer industry. Because a minicomputer is an assembled machine – an end product, to use Prahalad and Hamel's terminology – the minicomputer industry allowed companies to innovate new and better components, but otherwise provided few additional opportunities. In contrast, the semiconductor is a component, not an end product. As such, the semiconductor industry allowed Silicon Valley companies to innovate to create new applications in diverse areas such as consumer electronics, communications and programmable logic devices. Thus, the early entry into the two different industries determined, to a large extent, each region's technological pathway.

The question arises: with each region locked in on the path of a very specific technological trajectory, will that trajectory lead to future success or failure?

The current situation

Silicon Valley is thriving. Of the US $23.3 billion in total US venture capital investments in 2010, Silicon Valley firms received over US $9 billion.[22] Silicon Valley accounted for 39 per cent of US venture capital investments in 2010, a 5 per cent increase since 2003. In contrast, Route 128 only received about 3 per cent in 2010. In previous years, Route 128 would typically receive about an 11 per cent share in total US venture capital. In terms of individual firms, Silicon Valley start-ups raised almost triple in capital what equivalent Route 128 firms raised between 2006 and 2011.[23]

Silicon Valley is still one of the most attractive places in the world to run a business, though high housing prices have become a concern. Single-family home prices in Palo Alto rose 20 per cent in 2011 from 2010 to an average of US $1.63 million.[24]

Although Route 128's electronics business never regained its former glory, the region has successfully embarked on biotechnology as a new development path. In 2003, it ranked second after San Diego among all the biotech hotbeds in the US, according to a study by the Milkin Institute applying 44 different metrics.

The biotech industry along Route 128 has developed into a true regional network. Back in 1988, most local biotech firms were heavily dependent on formal collaboration with six public research organizations (MIT, Harvard, Tufts, Boston University, Massachusetts General Hospital and the New England Medical Center) and large pharmaceutical firms located elsewhere. At that stage, those local firms were largely isolated from each other. However, by 1998, local biotech firms had begun to work directly with one another, and public research organizations played a less dominant role in the local network.[25]

Foreign investment in Silicon Valley and Route 128

The reputations of Silicon Valley and Route 128 as advanced electronic technology clusters and proximity to major customers have attracted many foreign firms that have engaged in traditional foreign direct investment as well as indirect investment, e.g., through venture capital funds. In Silicon Valley, foreign direct investment transactions rose from 31 in 1976 to 244 in 1987, with a total of 1,343 transactions and a total value of US $30 billion.[26] In the Route 128 area, many high-technology firms invested without any government incentives. For example, in 1986, Toshiba opened a procurement office to buy electronic equipment in the Route 128 area.[27]

Although many foreign firms initially only located marketing and administrative operations in Silicon Valley and Route 128, an increasing number of foreign firms has opened technology and design centres. For example, some Japanese firms opened semiconductor design centres in Silicon Valley and Route 128 to work closely with their customers and to tailor their products to customers' needs.[28]

Some foreign firms have also invested in Silicon Valley and Route 128 to absorb and develop new knowledge. For example, Samsung built an R&D lab in Silicon Valley in 1983 to develop its own DRAM technology after it failed to license the technology from major American and Japanese chip manufacturers. Samsung hired over 300 experienced Korean engineers from companies such as Intel and IBM, and these engineers led the development of 256K DRAM, trained many Korean engineers and served as information posts to identify and acquire new technologies. Samsung also built a parallel unit in Korea to facilitate the transfer of technology from California to Korea. As a result, Samsung quickly improved its technological position.[29] Since then, Silicon Valley has continued to gain prominence as a research and development hub, especially within communications-technology research. For example, Huawei, a Chinese maker of communications equipment, set up an R&D office in Silicon Valley in 2011. That year, the firm employed about 430 engineers and technical employees, with the intent to increase staff by more than 120 in the following years.[30]

At the same time, telephone handset manufacturer Ericsson was also setting up shop in Silicon Valley. Rather than working from the firm's headquarters in Sweden, chief technology officer Håkan Eriksson (CTO) chose instead to base himself in Silicon Valley. In 2011, Ericsson had more than 1,200 employees working in R&D, with the intent to continue expanding. Eriksson noted that the location has proved advantageous for facilitating collaboration with other communications giants such as Apple and Google. "The epicenter for the handset industry has shifted from Finland to Silicon Valley," Mr. Eriksson said, "to be globally competitive, you really need to have a footprint here."[31]

Foreign firms have continued to invest in the two areas, but some noticeable differences exist. In 2003, the number of foreign firms in computer hardware in California almost doubled that of Massachusetts, suggesting that Route 128 has lost some of its lustre in this technology area. However, the percentage of foreign firms in Massachusetts in photonics and pharmaceuticals rose from 10 per cent and 11 per cent in 1997 to 16 per cent and 14–15 per cent in 2003 respectively, indicating that Massachusetts has developed new strengths.[32]

Replicating Silicon Valley and Route 128 elsewhere

Aspiring regions have tried to replicate the 'success formula' of Silicon Valley and Route 128, by developing key elements such as educational infrastructure and an environment conducive to venture capital investments. These regions (or more specifically publicly funded, regional development authorities) believe that the presence of universities will spark local start-ups and thus drive regional economic development.

However, it remains unclear whether intensifying industry–university relationships, similar to those in Silicon Valley and Route 128, is likely to create new clusters. Recent research[33] suggests that during the formative years of Silicon Valley Stanford University worked with both local start-ups and established firms, but Stanford's critical contribution was its linkages with established firms headquartered elsewhere. Further, Stanford did not proactively sponsor local start-ups in those formative years. Rather, the main driver of industry–university programmes was to bring money to the university from the deep pockets of business firms. Similar to Stanford University, neither MIT nor Harvard pursued an intended strategy to promote industry concentration or local growth on Route 128.[34]

In the case of Silicon Valley, Stanford established four major outreach programmes between 1945 and 1965, including the Stanford Research Institute (SRI), the Stanford Industrial Park, the Honors Cooperative Program and the Industry Affiliates Programs. Most participants in all four programmes were established firms. Take, for example, the Stanford Industrial Park – the Stanford programme with the greatest degree of local involvement. Of the 30 tenants in 1960, only 9 were local high-tech firms. Nine were branches of established firms (including GE), four were publishers and one was a book distributor, with the remainder including an architect, a bank, a mining company and a realtor. Moreover, the main purpose of building the park was to lease endowed land to bring revenue to the university, rather than to sponsor local start-ups.

Therefore, in the formative years of Silicon Valley, the main role of Stanford University was to connect with established firms located elsewhere, rather than to promote or incubate high-tech firms in the region. Other regions aiming to replicate Silicon Valley's 'success formula' should thus be very careful when attempting to copy what they think constitutes the heart of the clustering success. These regions should not assume that, e.g., industry–university cooperation is the key driver for successful industrial clustering.

QUESTIONS

1. Do Silicon Valley and Route 128 function as diamond-based clusters? Why or why not? What are their similarities and what are their differences?
2. What caused the development, decline and resurgence of the two regions? What is your understanding of the different explanations for the two regions?
3. How have Silicon Valley and Route 128 helped the establishment of start-ups?
4. Can the 'success formulas' provided by Silicon Valley and Route 128 be adopted as templates for other, would-be clusters?

CASE

Case 3.2 Shiseido: Becoming an insider in the perfume business in France[35]

Initially founded as a pharmacy in Japan in 1872, Shiseido expanded into the cosmetics business in 1897 by introducing a skin lotion. Shiseido then gradually expanded its product offerings in the makeup and skin care business. It also started to expand internationally, entering the Taiwan market in 1957. By the 1970s, Shiseido had established itself as the market leader in the makeup and skin care business in Japan.[36]

However, Shiseido was still weak in the fragrance business. At that time, Japan had a limited tradition of perfume use: the fragrance market in Japan accounted for only 1 per cent of the entire cosmetics market, much lower than the 30–40 per cent characteristic of most Western countries. Because of its limited tradition of perfume use, Japan lacked domestic fragrance experts and senior management with fragrance business experience.

Shiseido's small domestic fragrance market did not prepare it adequately to compete in the international market. In 1964, Shiseido launched the perfume Zen in the US. Driven primarily by the marketing concept of 'oriental mysteriousness with a subtle fragrance', Zen's US sales increased rapidly because of its novelty, but then quickly declined.

Because the fragrance market represented about 30–40 per cent of total cosmetics sales in Europe and America, Shiseido's lack of a significant position in the fragrance market also created barriers for the firm to secure strong distribution networks internationally. Thus, in spite of its limited domestic experience with fragrances, Shiseido felt it had to develop strengths in the fragrance business in order to become a truly world-class cosmetics company.

In the late 1970s and early 1980s, Shiseido decided to learn more about the international fragrance business. The lack of a favourable domestic environment in Japan pushed Shiseido to seek solutions in the very markets it wanted to penetrate.

France was identified as the ideal place to gain expertise, because it was the heart of the international fragrance industry. However, simply being in France did not ensure that the firm would automatically gain access to the local knowledge network. In fact, Shiseido had to spend a long time learning how to become an insider in this industry.

Shiseido's initial failures

Following expansion into Italy and Germany through 100 per cent subsidiaries, Shiseido chose a different strategy for its entrance into France.[37] In order to absorb French perfume development techniques, especially the subtle interactions between laboratory development and consumer tests, Shiseido established in 1980 a 50/50 joint venture with the French cosmetics company Pierre Fabre S. A. Faced with substantial market hostility in France at that time, Shiseido chose a joint venture as its entry mode in order to reduce risks, especially in terms of potential financial losses. At the same time, in order to collect information related to the fragrance industry, it also established the Shiseido Europe TechnoCentre as the 'eye' of its headquarters in France. Japanese expatriates were sent to the centre to collect vital local information and transmit it to headquarters.

Unfortunately, the Japanese expatriates did not have access to the social networks required to gain deep insights into the complex and tacit knowledge aspects of local perfume development and exploitation. Consequently, the information transferred back to Shiseido's headquarters tended to be superficial and did not truly help product development in Japan. Gradually, Shiseido realized that its strategies so far had not made it a player in France. Shiseido learned that, in order to learn the intricacies of perfume development, it would have to become an insider in the French fragrance industry.

Becoming an insider

To access the required tacit local knowledge, Shiseido decided to establish wholly owned operations in France to develop and sell perfumes, rather than simply collecting information there. This also involved, within the context of the firm's multi-brand strategy, a focus on acquisitions and the creation of new, non-Shiseido brands.[38]

Local operations (plants and salons)

In 1990, Shiseido established a 100 per cent subsidiary in Paris called BPI (Beauté Prestige International) to develop and sell fragrances in France. In 1992, Shiseido also set up a plant in Gien, a town south of Paris.

Shiseido also ran salons in France to learn how to provide beauty services. In 1986, Shiseido acquired two high-end French beauty salons, Carita and Alexandre Zouari. Carita and Alexandre Zouari were among the top five salons in Paris, the other ones being Alexandre Paris, Maurice Franc and Claude Maxim. In 1992, Shiseido opened a prestigious parlour called Les Salons du Palais Royal ('Les Salons') in Paris. These operations helped Shiseido understand the world of sophisticated French customers and the importance of local adaptation. At that stage, Shiseido's products were of high quality from a manufacturing perspective, but they lacked the cultural dimension of a fragrance as a story/concept, which was a crucial element driving French customers' tastes.

In 1992, BPI launched two perfumes branded after the names of their designers: Eau d'Issey and Jean Paul Gaultier. The former was designed by the famous Japanese fashion designer Issey Miyake and the latter by the well-known French fashion designer Jean Paul Gaultier. Both products were manufactured at the Gien plant and marketed to French customers.

Building local relationships

Shiseido used several techniques to build relationships with major stakeholders in France, including celebrities, journalists, bankers and local communities.

First, Shiseido invited leading celebrities in Parisian high society to its receptions held at 'Les Salons'. For example, the celebrations at the 1992 opening of 'Les Salons' lasted two days, with numerous parties, including a reception for journalists, a reception for VIPs and a reception for bankers. Such events at 'Les Salons' were not only covered by articles in newspapers and magazines, but also widely discussed in Parisian high society. The exposure in the media connected 'Les Salons' and Shiseido's brands with sophisticated customers and supported the firm's efforts to establish its brands as premium fragrances. More importantly, this exposure helped Shiseido build strong linkages with beauty and fashion journalists, local celebrities and bankers.

Second, Shiseido became actively involved in local communities, especially by sponsoring various cultural events in France. For example, Shiseido was active as a patron for the Festival International de Sully-sur-Loire, where Shiseido's Val de Loire factory was located. Such activities with local communities increased the connection between Shiseido and French consumers.

Local hiring

Rather than sending Japanese expatriates to direct its French operations, Shiseido hired local experts to manage several important positions throughout the value chain.

First, Shiseido hired a French creator, Serge Lutens, to craft Shiseido's overseas brand image. Before joining Shiseido in 1980, Lutens had worked for Christian Dior for 14 years. Serge Lutens contributed substantially to Shiseido's becoming an insider in France, by designing ads and posters that created a mysterious and artistic image for the firm. Even though his work was viewed as too indirect and artistic in Japan, he achieved his goal: his work became well accepted in Europe and America.

Second, a French CEO, Chantal Roos, headed BPI. Involved in launching the famous Opium perfume when she was marketing vice-president of Yves Saint Laurent, she was an expert in creative marketing and fragrances, and well known in the French fragrance industry. It was very rare for a Japanese company to hire a local person to head a strategically important subsidiary, but it was a wise move. Chantal Roos brought to the company a much-needed creative and artistic culture. She led Shiseido's credible entry into the French fragrance industry by leading the development of Eau d'Issey in 1992. Moreover, she insisted on creating a separate BPI division in each host country to distribute BPI's high-end fragrances.

Finally, Shiseido hired locally at its Gien plant. The plant, though managed by a Japanese president, had a French vice-president. In 1998, the plant employed only 6 Japanese expatriates out of 180 local full-time staff and 80 temporary workers. By 2005, Shiseido operated 12 organizations in France, with 12 Japanese nationals out of 1,300 employees. By 2010, France had become Shiseido's central operational platform for Europe and had more than 1,000 displays throughout the country. To celebrate 30 years of activity in France, Shiseido created a contemporary art installation at the Hôtel de l'Industrie in Paris. With over 1,400 employees throughout France, Shiseido's local hiring policy helped the firm truly to become an insider in the French market.[39]

Local success

Although the major objective of the French operations was to plug into the local fragrance knowledge, Shiseido did not assess its success simply based on the amount of knowledge transferred back to Japan.

Rather, success was assessed by the company's competitiveness in France itself. Perfumes such as Eau d'Issey and Jean Paul Gaultier were launched first in France and marketed first to French customers. These premium fragrances did very well there. For example, Jean Paul Gaultier Le Mâle produced by BPI became the leading brand among men's premium fragrances in France, with a market share of 4.8 per cent in that country in 2005. Among all fragrances in France, Jean Paul Gaultier Le Mâle was ranked tenth in 2005 with a market share of 1.2 per cent. This was good penetration, considering that the leading (down market) brand Yves Rocher had a market share of only 2.6 per cent in the same year.[40] In 2011, Jean Paul Gaultier Le Mâle received the Fragrance Hall of Fame award from The Fragrance Foundation, a highly regarded award within the industry. That same year, BPI's Eau d'Issey Pour Homme was nominated for the same award.[41] In 2012, Jean Paul Gaultier Le Mâle was the leading men's fragrance in the European Union based on sales and achieved high market shares in Australia and the United States.[42]

Similarly, the quality of the perfumes produced at the Gien plant was also evaluated against the French standard of perfume quality. In this context, Chantal Roos was very satisfied with the quality of Shiseido's products when benchmarked against high profile French rivals such as Christian Dior's Svelte.

Local decisions and autonomy

Shiseido granted substantial autonomy to BPI, because it realized that Japanese headquarters lacked sufficient understanding of the French artistic style in the fragrance industry. Therefore, product development, packaging and labelling of BPI products were all performed by BPI and the Gien plant's R&D division, without intervention from Shiseido.

The subsequent autonomy of the French branch of Shiseido led to a successful, but very 'locally rooted' perfume house.[43] From the outset, executives at Shiseido had consciously allowed their French operations to apply their expertise in the local environment freely. As a result, there were limited channels in place to facilitate cross-cultural knowledge sharing. Knowledge gained in France was not supposed to be readily adapted and applied to other markets, since formal channels had not been established. The integration of knowledge gained from the French market has remained a strategy issue at Shiseido.[44]

Subsequent developments

Brands such as Eau d'Issey and Jean Paul Gaultier have given Shiseido a solid position in Europe, and some of the knowledge learned by the expatriates has been transferred back to Japan for the development of future perfumes. However, in 2011, Spanish competitor Puig Group acquired 55 per cent of Jean Paul Gaultier. Puig will likely assume control over the production of Jean Paul Gaultier Le Mâle when BPI's licence expires in 2016.[45]

In 1997, Shiseido decided to spend US $30.5 million building a new plant at Ormes, France, to meet the expected rising demand in Europe for its fragrances and skin care products.

In 2004, Shiseido ranked 14th in the fragrance business with a market share of 1.8 per cent – still far behind L'Oréal Groupe, the market leader in fragrances with a market share of 8.9 per cent.[46]

In recent years, Shiseido has continued to increase its presence in the European market and has expanded its businesses with a wholly owned subsidiary in Switzerland and a joint venture in Greece in January 2010. Furthermore, in the months after, the brand Shiseido was launched in three Balkan Peninsula countries, namely Albania, Kosovo and Macedonia, via a distribution network and in Moldova, Armenia and Belarus via Shiseido Europe S. A. S. Shiseido also internationalized into countries outside of Europe and, in May 2010, it acquired 100 per cent of the shares of Shiseido Dah Chong Hong Cosmetics Ltd., its previously consolidated subsidiary in Hong Kong. In addition, the Japanese firm partnered with distributors in order to enter into emerging markets such as Mongolia, Georgia, South Africa, Columbia, Panama, Brazil, and Tunisia. In early 2012, Shiseido started operations through the joint venture company Shiseido Kozmetik Anonim Şirketi in Turkey and established a Shiseido representative office in India for market research.[47]

As of 2012, Shiseido's products were being sold in 88 countries.[48] In terms of Shiseido's continuing expansion, the company began selling its cosmetic products in Argentina from May 2012 and had ambitions to develop greater market presence in European, North American and Chinese markets.[49] Hisayuki Suekawa, Shiseido's President and CEO commented that Europe and North America had high potential for the company's luxury business, while China's rapid market growth was also a draw for the company. Moving forward, Suekawa hoped to strengthen Shiseido's position as a global brand beyond Japan; "In the past, we tended to be very Japan-centric . . . That was fine back then, but as we move forward we need to have a global standard that is common to all markets in which we operate."[50] In 2012, Japan still accounted for 55.7 per cent of Shiseido's sales.[51] Suekawa had intentions to decrease dependence on the Japanese market to 50 per cent by 2017.[52]

QUESTIONS

1. How did Shiseido finally become an insider in Paris? What factors had been instrumental to its initial failure?
2. What does Shiseido's experience imply for those companies not born in a cluster?
3. Which patterns of FSA development did you observe in the case?
4. Drawing on the discussion of Porter's single diamond framework versus the double diamond framework, what suggestions would you give Shiseido to help it to develop further its perfume business?

Notes

1. Michael E. Porter, *The Competitive Advantage of Nations* (New York: Free Press, Macmillan, 1990). Michael E. Porter, 'The competitive advantage of nations', *Harvard Business Review* 68 (1990), 73–93.
2. Porter, 'The competitive advantage of nations', 1990, 73.

3. *Ibid.*, 81.
4. Walter Kuemmerle, 'The entrepreneur's path to global expansion', *Sloan Management Review* 46 (2005), 42–9.
5. This is of course fully consistent with the research findings several decades ago from the Uppsala school; see Johansson and Vahlne (J. Johansson and J.E. Vahlne, 'The internationalization process of the firm: a model of knowledge development and increasing foreign market commitments', *Journal of International Business Studies* 8 (1977), 23–32), as well as extensive follow-up work during the past 30 years.
6. David J. Teece, 'Foreign investment in Silicon Valley', *California Management Review* 34 (1992), 88–106.
7. *Ibid.*, 100.
8. *Ibid.*
9. Porter, 'The competitive advantage of nations', 92.
10. *Ibid.*, 93.
11. Porter, *The Competitive Advantage of Nations.*
12. R. Vernon, 'International investment and international trade in the product life cycle', *Quarterly Journal of Economics* 80 (1966), 190–207.
13. Leonard Waverman, 'Critical analysis of Porter's framework on the competitive advantage of nations', in A. Rugman, J. Van Den Broeck and A. Verbeke (eds.), *Research in Global Strategic Management: Beyond the Diamond*, Vol. 5 (Greenwich: JAI Press, 1995), 67–95.
14. Alan M. Rugman and Alain Verbeke, *Analysis of Multinational Strategic Management* (Cheltenham: Edward Elgar, 2005), 206–22.
15. Anna Lee Saxenian, 'Regional networks and the resurgence of Silicon Valley', *California Management Review* 33 (1990), 89–112; Anna Lee Saxenian, 'Comment on Kenney and von Burg, "Technology, entrepreneurship and path dependence: Industrial clustering in Silicon Valley and Route 128"', *Industrial and Corporate Change* 8 (1999), 105–10; Anna Lee Saxenian, 'Lessons from Silicon Valley', *Technology Review* 97 (1994), 42–51; Dan Primack, 'Biotech hotbeds: where are they, and how do you get one?', *Venture Capital Journal* (2004), 1; Harald Bathelt, 'Regional competence and economic recovery: divergent growth paths in Boston's high technology economy', *Entrepreneurship & Regional Development* 13 (2001), 287–314; Hilary Stout, 'The new map of high tech: Sili-Come lately?', *Wall Street Journal (Eastern Edition)* (1999), B.1; Jim Kerstetter, 'Still the center of this world but Silicon Valley remains a ferociously expensive place to do business, and something's got to give', *Business Week* (2003), 76; Martin Kenney and Urs Von Burg, 'Technology, entrepreneurship and path dependence: Industrial clustering in Silicon Valley and Route 128', *Industrial and Corporate Change* 8 (1999), 67–103.
16. Edward B. Roberts, *Entrepreneurs in High Technology: Lessons from MIT and Beyond* (New York: Oxford University Press, 1991).
17. Scott Shane, *Academic Entrepreneurship: University Spinoffs and Wealth Creation* (Northampton, Massachusetts, USA; Cheltenham, UK: Edward Elgar, 2004).
18. Edward B. Roberts and Charles Eesley, 'Entrepreneurial impact: The role of MIT', *MIT Sloan School of Management* (2009), 56–8.
19. MIT Museum, 'Entrepreneurial MIT'. http://museum.mit.edu/150/80
20. Laura Keeley, 'Facebook "shock" has Boston firms searching for next Zuckerberg', *Bloomberg* (7 July 2011), www.bloomberg.com/news/2011–07–07/facebook-departure-prompts-boston-venture-capital-firms-to-return-to-city.html
21. Kenney and Von Burg, 'Technology, entrepreneurship and path dependence', 67–103.

22. Dan Levy, 'Home prices exploding in Silicon Valley amid more millionaires', *Bloomberg* (16 June 2011), http://www.bloomberg.com/news/2011–06–15/tech-ipos-boost-demand-for-silicon-valley-million-dollar-homes.html

23. Laura Keeley, 'Facebook "shock" has Boston firms searching for next Zuckerberg', *Bloomberg* (7 July 2011).

24. Dan Levy, 'Home prices exploding in Silicon Valley amid more millionaires', *Bloomberg* (16 June 2011), http://www.bloomberg.com/news/2011-06-15/tech-ipos-boost-demand-for-silicon-valley-million-dollar-homes.html

25. Jason Owen-Smith and Walter W. Powell, 'Knowledge networks as channels and conduits: the effects of spillovers in the Boston biotechnology community', *Organization Science* 15 (2004), 5–21.

26. Teece, 'Foreign investment in Silicon Valley', 90.

27. Barnaby J. Feder, 'Route 128: strength through diversity', *New York Times* (19 November 1986), http://query.nytimes.com/gst/fullpage.html?res=9A0DE4D81730F93AA25752C1A960948260&sec=technology&spon=&pagewanted=print, accessed on 10 October 2007.

28. R. Florida and M. Kenney, 'Silicon Valley and Route 128 won't save us', *California Management Review* 33 (1990), 68–88.

29. T. S. Frost, 'Imitation to innovation: the dynamics of Korea's technological learning', *Journal of International Business Studies* 28 (1997), 868–72.

30. Don Clark, 'Overseas tech firms ramp up hiring in Silicon Valley', *Wall Street Journal* (23 June 2011).

31. *Ibid.*

32. Michael Best, Albert Paquin and Hao Xie, 'Discovering regional competitive advantage: Massachusetts high tech' (2004), www.h-net.msu.edu/~;business/bhcweb/publications/BEHonline/2004/BestPaquinXie.pdf, accessed on 9 October 2007.

33. Stephen B. Adams, 'Stanford and Silicon Valley: lessons on becoming a high-tech region', *California Management Review* 48 (2005), 29–51.

34. Nancy S. Dorfman, 'Route 128: the development of a regional high technology economy', *Research Policy* 12 (1983), 299–316.

35. Kazuhiro Asakawa and Yves Doz, 'Shiseido France 1998', *INSEAD case 04/2002–4934* (2002); Yutaka Goto, 'How Shiseido succeeded in Europe: history and international strategy', *Japan Society Lecture* (12 January 2005); Yves Doz, Jose Santos and Peter Williamson, *From Global to Metanational: How Companies Win in the Knowledge Economy* (Boston, Massachusetts, USA: Harvard Business School Press, 2001), 65–7; Tara Rummell, 'What's new at Shiseido?', *Global Cosmetic Industry* 165 (1999), 20–3.

36. Shiseido company information, 2006.

37. Yutaka Goto, 'How Shiseido succeeded in Europe: history and international strategy', *Japan Society Lecture* (12 January 2005).

38. *Ibid.*

39. Invest in Francy Agency, 'Shiseido in France – celebrating 30 years of success', *The IFA Blog* (1 October 2010), http://blogs.afii.fr/en/2010/10/shiseido-in-france-celebrating-30-years-of-success, accessed on 15 April 2012.

40. Euromonitor International, 'The market for cosmetics and toiletries in France', August 2006.

41. 40th Anniversary FIFI Awards, 'Fragrance hall of fame – Men's', (2011) accessed on 15 April http://fifiawards.wordpress.com/finalists/fragrance-hall-of-fame/fragrance-hall-of-fame-mens/ accessed on 15 April 2012.

42. Wikipedia, 'Jean Paul Gaultier', Wikipedia (2012).

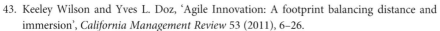

43. Keeley Wilson and Yves L. Doz, 'Agile Innovation: A footprint balancing distance and immersion', *California Management Review* 53 (2011), 6–26.
44. *Ibid.*
45. Vanessa Friedman, 'Spain's Puig Group succeeds by swimming against the stream', *Financial Times*, (6 June 2011), 6.
46. Euromonitor International, 'The market for cosmetics and toiletries in the world', August 2006.
47. Shiseido, 'Shiseido to exhibit corporate culture in Greece and Switzerland to mark the 140th anniversary of the company's founding', Shiseido (29 March 2012).
48. Shiseido, company information 2012.
49. Shiseido, 'Shiseido to commence sales of cosmetics products in the Argentine Republic', Shiseido (25 April 2012).
50. WWD, 'Shiseido's global growth blueprint', *Women's Wear Daily*, 202 (5 August 2011), 7–1.
51. Shiseido company information 2012.
52. *Ibid.*

4

The problem with host country location advantages

Five learning objectives

1. To describe the four main dimensions of 'distance' (cultural, administrative, geographic and economic) in the context of host country location advantages.
2. To link these various dimensions of 'distance' to bounded rationality problems faced by MNEs.
3. To develop an understanding of the alternative perspective of 'distance' as an opportunity, rather than a problem.
4. To highlight the importance of paying sufficient attention to the challenges posed by high-distance markets.
5. To identify the managerial implications of 'distance' on the international transferability of FSAs.

This chapter explores Ghemawat's idea that, even in the contemporary era of advanced communications technology and enormous international trade, senior managers still need to take into account 'distance' when assessing host country location advantages and making decisions about global expansion. As Ghemawat uses the term, the 'distance' between two countries includes differences in culture, societal institutions, physical location and economic status. According to Ghemawat, senior managers often overestimate the attractiveness of foreign markets because they fail to take into account the risks and costs associated with distance. Ghemawat concludes that higher inter-country distances correspond with lower inter-country trade levels, implying a lower probability of success. This idea will be examined and then criticized using the framework presented in Chapter 1.

Significance

In 2001, **Pankaj Ghemawat** wrote an insightful *HBR* article, 'Distance still matters: the hard reality of global expansion', demonstrating that distance still matters: "Technology may indeed be making the world a smaller place, but it is not eliminating the very real – and often very high – costs of distance."[1]

Ghemawat convincingly demonstrates that companies often overestimate the attractiveness of foreign markets, focusing solely on macro-level measures of market size and growth, while neglecting to address the risks and additional costs associated with entering a new market. These risks and additional costs arise from what he calls 'distance':

> Much has been made of the death of distance in recent years. It's been argued that information technologies and, in particular, global communications are shrinking the world, turning it into a small and relatively homogenous place. But when it comes to business, that's not only an incorrect assumption, it's a dangerous one. Distance still matters, and companies must explicitly and thoroughly account for it when they make decisions about global expansion. Traditional country portfolio analysis needs to be tempered by a clear-eyed evaluation of the many dimensions of distance and their probable impact on opportunities in foreign markets.[2]

Ghemawat's term 'distance' encompasses various components, which he organizes into four basic categories:

1. **Cultural distance**: this distance component results from differences in national cultural attributes such as language, religious beliefs, social norms and race.
2. **Administrative (or institutional) distance**: this distance component reflects differences in societal institutions. This distance can be low (or lowered) if two or more countries share a common history (including colonial relationships), have political ties, have engaged in efforts towards economic and monetary integration or preferential trading arrangements, and synchronize government policies.
3. **Geographic (or spatial) distance**: this distance component represents the physical distance between countries, taking into account the ease of transport between the countries. Having a common border or easy access via river and ocean waterways may keep this distance low. Differences in topography or climate may make this distance higher. Human intervention, such as the creation of efficient transportation and communication links, can reduce this distance.
4. **Economic distance**: this distance component represents differences in consumer wealth, income level and distribution, infrastructure characteristics, the cost and quality of natural, financial and human resources, and prevailing business practices.

Ghemawat's general conclusion is that higher distances correspond with lower inter-country trade levels, implying a lower probability of success.

Ghemawat describes in some detail these four dimensions of distance and outlines how they can affect different industries in different ways.[3]

While some aspects of **cultural distance** may be readily apparent, such as differing languages, Ghemawat suggests that other aspects may be more difficult to discover. He offers two examples of how prevailing attitudes in China create a high cultural distance for Western firms doing business there. The first is the failure of media mogul Rupert Murdoch's Star TV, which rebroadcast English language programming directly by satellite in an effort to overcome geographic distance constraints. Star TV underestimated the market's preference for locally produced, Chinese language content. The second is the tolerance for copyright infringements, which contrasts sharply with the protection of intellectual property rights in Europe and North America. The underlying causes for the prevailing Chinese attitude reside not only in the country's recent communist ideology in the second part of the twentieth century (the People's Republic of China was established in 1949), but also in deeply rooted social norms from "a precept of Confucius teaching that encourages replication of the results of past intellectual endeavours".[4] In general, 'soft' consumer goods such as food items, selected on the basis of personal tastes and cultural identity, are more sensitive to cultural distance than 'hard' items such as industrial machinery and bulk commodities.

Along with cultural distance, Ghemawat also argues that businesses often overlook **administrative (or institutional) distance**. He demonstrates that common historical and political ties significantly increase trade levels: "Colony-colonizer links between countries, for example, boost trade by 900% ... Preferential trading arrangements, common currency, and political union can also increase trade by more than 300% each."[5]

He points out that governments can be very effective at creating administrative distance. In order to protect domestic industries, host countries raise barriers through trade tariffs, quotas, restrictions on foreign-owned companies and preferential treatment of domestic firms. A firm's home country can create distance through unilateral measures, such as US policies prohibiting US-based firms from trading with Cuba, or from engaging in bribery anywhere in the world, irrespective of host country laws. Lastly, 'institutional infrastructure' characteristics such as corruption and systemic social upheaval have an important impact on administrative distance. According to Ghemawat, the firms most affected by administrative distance are large employers (including national champion companies), are vital to national security, produce essential goods and services, or exploit the country's key natural resources.

The third attribute, **geographic (or spatial) distance**, involves more than just physical proximity. Geographic distance also encompasses other aspects affecting the separation of countries in space (and therefore in time), including man-made elements such as transportation networks and communication infrastructure. Ghemawat argues that products with 'low value-to-weight' ratios (such as steel and cement) and highly perishable items incur the greatest cost increases as transportation distances increase.[6] Surprisingly, his research shows that trade in services and investment capital are also negatively correlated with greater geographic distance, largely because of diminished levels of information infrastructure.

The fourth and final dimension of distance, *economic distance*, relates to differences in wealth, income and standard of living between consumers in different countries. In his discussion of economic distance, he identifies two broad approaches to expanding abroad: replicating existing competitive advantages, building upon scale and scope economies and exploiting differences in input costs or prices between markets through 'economic arbitrage'.[7] If a firm focuses on scale or scope economies, typical for *centralized exporters* and *international projectors*, this strategy is likely to be more effective if the economic distance between home and host countries is small. Both scale and scope economies require standardization, meaning that there is no requirement to adapt to host country requirements. In contrast, if a firm focuses on economic arbitrage, typical for *international coordinators*, the firm embraces economic distance because it possesses FSAs that allow it to exploit and link the diverse location advantages of high distance countries. This is the strategy adopted by, for example, vertically integrated MNEs in resource industries.

Ghemawat's methodology is based on a thorough analysis of economic data concerning international trade. To reach the conclusion that increased distance generally corresponds with reduced inter-country trade, his research team "regressed trade between every possible pair of countries in the world in each of 70 industries on each dimension of distance".[8] To demonstrate how his distance framework can improve a firm's analysis of foreign market potential, Ghemawat provides a case study of US-based Tricon Restaurants International, the parent company of fast-food chains such as Pizza Hut, Taco Bell and KFC. (Tricon Restaurants changed its name to YUM! Brands, Inc. in 2002. YUM! Brands is headquartered in Louisville, Kentucky.) When the four dimensions of distance are factored in to complement traditional country portfolio analysis, a revised and more accurate picture of the opportunities and risks becomes clear. Countries with lower distance factors vis-à-vis the US, such as Mexico and Canada, become obvious top choices; countries that are seemingly attractive in terms of market size and growth, such as Japan and Germany, become less so when their higher levels of distance are taken into consideration. According to Ghemawat, "The results confirm the importance of distinguishing between the various components of distance in assessing foreign market opportunities."[9] Each distance component compounds the bounded rationality problem faced by the MNE's senior management: the problem of uncertainty increases, as does the problem of imperfect processing of information.

Context and complementary perspectives

Ghemawat's article demonstrates that the extent of globalization has been vastly exaggerated. The dot-com boom – i.e., the speculative stock market bubble built upon growth in the Internet sector between 1996 and 2001 – was supposed to signal the end of distance. The possibility of Web-based sales, instant communication within and between firms, and technology-supported, seamless, global supply chains was supposed to eliminate former barriers of time and space. A truly global marketplace would materialize thanks to information technology, with unlimited potential for firms to expand into foreign markets, develop centres of global excellence and experiment with cross-border structures of management and reporting. Ghemawat's article acts as a wake-up call, dismissing the belief that distance has finally been conquered. Cultural, administrative, geographic and economic differences between countries are here to stay, and will present continuing barriers to international business.

Till Vestring, Ted Rouse and *Uwe Reinert*, three partners with the consulting company Bain & Co., wrote a complementary perspective in *SMR*.[10] Their message is that MNEs intending to be cost leaders in their industry should establish portfolios of low-cost countries to which selected activities can be outsourced. They observed that many cost leaders in industries ranging from automotive and chemicals to consumer products and technology do not simply outsource to a few high-profile, low-cost destinations such as China and India, but attempt to reduce risk by including a broader set of countries in their offshoring strategy. Though the authors also caution against undisciplined fragmentation of offshoring activities, they focus on the benefits of accessing multiple, 'high-distance' input markets.

Note the contrast with Ghemawat: whereas Ghemawat focuses on the risk of penetrating too many high-distance output markets, Vestring, Rouse and Reinert focus on the risk of using too few high-distance input markets. For Ghemawat, distance is fundamentally a barrier; for Vestring, Rouse and Reinert, distance is fundamentally an opportunity.

Vestring, Rouse and Reinert argue that a large MNE would be insufficiently diversified if it outsourced all of its inputs to, for example, China. Whereas China's factory labour cost of US $1.36 per hour (2008) represents a global cost leadership position, China has more political uncertainty than several offshoring alternatives (such as a number of Eastern European nations) with higher labour costs. In addition, if transport costs and time-to-market are factored into the equation, and these cost components are more important than labour costs for particular products, many offshoring locations with substantially higher labour costs than China may become more attractive. Vestring, Rouse and Reinert conclude that large MNEs should create a portfolio of offshoring countries based upon the particular bundle of location advantages offered by each country, often a function of the specialized skills offered:

> The Boeing Co., for instance, has a centre that does design and technical work in Russia, a country with deep aerospace engineering skills. Procter & Gamble Co. has its taxes done in Costa Rica, which has a strong cadre of workers with accounting skills. General Electric Co. has built an R&D centre in India with more than 4,000 employees, many of whom are locals with doctorates.[11]

Vestring, Rouse and Reinert argue that large MNEs should develop a particular recombination capability: an FSA in offshoring. In practical terms, that means that strategic offshoring decisions are not left to individual business units, but are handled in a centralized fashion, so as to create cost advantages across business units by pooling resources, jointly developing new suppliers or expanding economies of scale in low-cost countries.[12]

However, in spite of advocating expansion into high-distance locations, the authors implicitly take on board Ghemawat's cautionary suggestions about the risks of distance. They argue that MNEs must be well informed on all relevant cost categories and other relevant country characteristics such as the availability of specialized skills, both now and in the future, before selecting particular offshoring locations. In addition, firms must make substantial investments in location-bound FSAs – including local logistics, engineering and manufacturing capabilities – before starting local production.

Bernd Schmitt and *Yigang Pan* provide a second complementary perspective to Ghemawat's analysis.[13] Their *CMR* article focuses on the cultural distance component, and provides guidance to Western MNEs selling branded consumer products (e.g., soft drinks, entertainment, consumer financial services, apparel and health care) when penetrating the high-distance Asian markets. They describe in detail the various dimensions of the cultural distance component relevant to managing the MNE's corporate and brand identities. Schmitt and Pan convincingly demonstrate that, in order to overcome the cultural distance, MNEs must invest substantial time and effort in developing a pan-Asian branding strategy. Their point is that various branding elements, conventionally considered to be internationally transferable by Western MNEs, must be carefully adapted and augmented by a location-bound component valid for the entire Asian market, as well as its individual countries and regions.

First, attention must be devoted to selecting the right corporate and product brand names. Most Asian countries use languages with (Chinese) characters that themselves are meaningful linguistic units, each composed of various strokes. Firms must therefore investigate whether the contemplated corporate and product brand names as a whole, the individual characters and even the strokes forming the characters are associated with positive connotations in all the relevant Asian submarkets. Corporate and brand names should also have desirable sound and tonal associations, and their written form should be attractive in all Asian submarkets. The reason is that sounds, tones and the visual representation of language characters also convey meaning, and typically carry desirable or undesirable associations.

Second, attention must be devoted to creating the right image. Here, the corporate image is often more important than the image created for an individual product. This contrasts with the US, where the corporate brand name may mean little to consumers in terms of the value they attribute to it, divorced from a particular product. Elements such as an upscale image, positive mystical connotations (e.g., respecting feng shui principles) and aesthetics perceived as valuable by Asian customers should be taken into account in the branding process. For example, with respect to aesthetics, Asian customers value symbols of natural objects such as mountains or rivers, as well as complex, decorative features.

Third, senior managers should note that Asian perceptions of 'quality' can be different from those in the West. Asian perceptions are affected by the 'collectivist' nature of Asian society[14] – meaning, *inter alia*, that specific reference groups may be critical in persuading customers to purchase a product, and that comparative advertising, including criticism of other firms, is considered inappropriate. Extensive community involvement and sponsorship are important to demonstrate the positive role the company intends to play in society. Attention to highly personalized service and consistent service rituals (with special attention to movement and gestures) are critical for service providers. The focus on highly personalized service is reflected in the branding of Asian airlines such as Singapore Airlines, where the attention is mainly on the quality of the airline personnel, rather than on flight schedules, number of destinations or mere pricing.

Schmitt and Pan's article could be viewed as somewhat pedantic, given their emphasis on several branding items that would undoubtedly be considered mere operational details by many senior managers in Western MNEs. Nevertheless, these details do reflect the complexity and pervasiveness of cultural distance, as well as the sophisticated recombination capability required to overcome such distance.

Schmitt and Pan's implicit message is that senior management must either pay sufficient attention to these shopping lists of distance components or else follow Ghemawat's prescription and avoid such high-distance markets altogether.

The most important connection between Ghemawat's work and the framework developed in Chapter 1 is the limits on the transferability, deployability and exploitation of FSAs across borders. Ghemawat cautions against the assumption that FSAs developed in the home country can be easily exploited in other markets regardless of distance. When firms try to transfer, deploy and exploit abroad their home-grown FSAs or create new FSAs and engage in resource recombination, they face additional barriers and complexities not faced by local competitors in the host country. While Ghemawat does not explicitly discuss the distinction between location-bound and internationally transferable FSAs, he emphasizes that the international exploitation potential of FSAs depends critically upon the type and level of distance among countries. Here, because of bounded rationality, managers often overestimate the international profit potential of their companies' FSAs, and underestimate the efforts required to create location-bound FSAs in high-distance host countries, as a precondition for accessing those countries' location advantages. Figure 4.1 and Figure 4.2 illustrate the point, highlighting the diminishing effectiveness of transferring, deploying and exploiting FSAs to foreign markets, and the increasing requirements for new FSAs, as the various distance components grow between the firm's domestic base and the host location considered.

Ghemawat's perspective initially appears similar to Pattern III of this book's framework (see Figure 4.3) insofar as allegedly internationally transferable FSAs developed in the home country are susceptible to difficulties when operating abroad because of the distance between the home and host country.

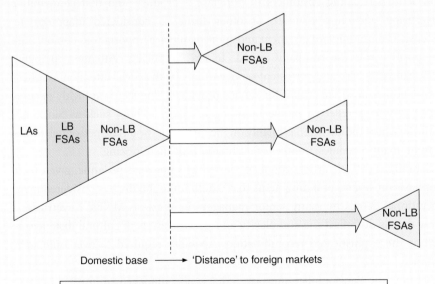

Figure 4.1
The MNE's diminishing stock of internationally transferable FSAs as a function of 'Distance'

Non-LB FSAs

LAs | LB FSAs | Non-LB FSAs

Non-LB FSAs

Non-LB FSAs

Non-LB FSAs

Domestic base ⟶ 'Distance' to foreign markets

Greater 'distance' leads to weaker transferability and exploitation potential of NLB FSAs, as indicated by the smaller NLB FSA triangles.

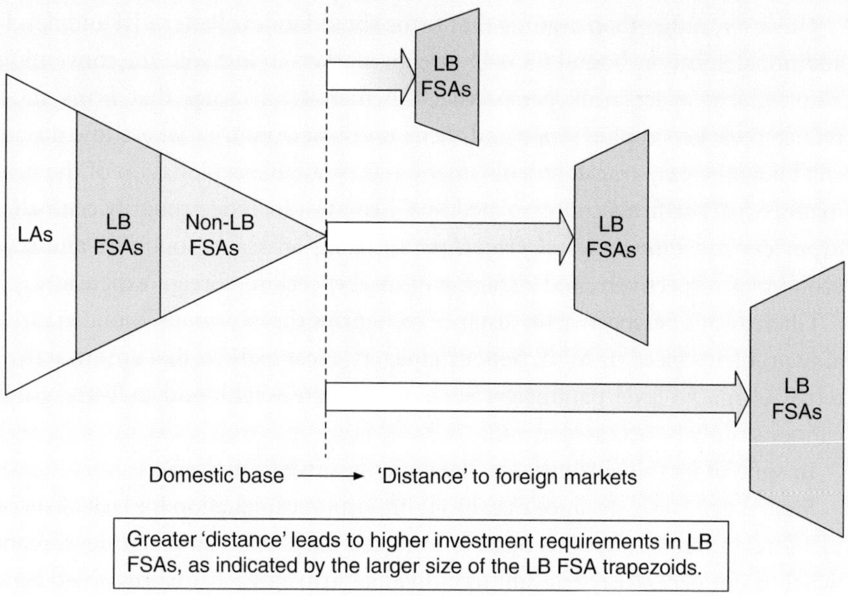

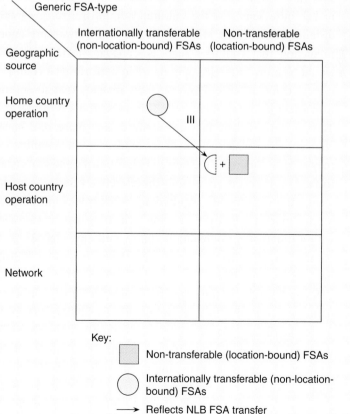

Figure 4.2
The need for LB FSAs as a function of 'Distance'

LB
FSAs

LAs

LB
FSAs

Non-LB
FSAs

LB
FSAs

LB
FSAs

LB
FSAs

Domestic base ⟶ 'Distance' to foreign markets

Greater 'distance' leads to higher investment requirements in LB FSAs, as indicated by the larger size of the LB FSA trapezoids.

Figure 4.3
Ghemawat's perspective of FSA development in MNEs

Generic FSA-type

Internationally transferable (non-location-bound) FSAs

Non-transferable (location-bound) FSAs

Geographic source

Home country operation

III

Host country operation

Network

Key:

Non-transferable (location-bound) FSAs

Internationally transferable (non-location-bound) FSAs

⟶ Reflects NLB FSA transfer

However, rather than arguing that firms should follow Pattern III and develop additional, location-bound FSAs in foreign markets in line with the conventional 'think global – act local' perspective, Ghemawat advocates that firms should reduce their geographic scope and focus on those countries where low distance will allow the easy transfer, deployment and profitable exploitation of the firm's main FSAs. The firms contemplated by Ghemawat include primarily **centralized exporters** and **international projectors**, focusing on scale economies and scope economies respectively, and engaging in market seeking foreign expansion.

Ghemawat's perspective on distance recognizes the enormous bounded rationality problems faced by MNE senior managers. Host markets that are attractive in terms of macro-level parameters such as absolute wealth and industry growth cannot simply be accessed at will.

In spite of its valuable insights, the paper has five limitations.

First, macro-level distance may be an important explanation for lack of success in a foreign market, but this observation itself only reflects a macro-level reality, which is not necessarily relevant to individual firms. In other words, the distance for a particular firm may be much less than the distance for the home country as a whole. Consider a US-based consumer goods company contemplating an expansion into Taiwan. A Ghemawat-type analysis would likely conclude that this makes little sense, as the cultural, administrative, geographic and economic distance components between the US and Taiwan are enormous. It is a safe prediction that countries such as Canada, Mexico and several EU countries would be more attractive options when performing a country portfolio analysis, corrected for distance. However, now imagine that several members of the US firm's senior management have Taiwanese roots. They were born and raised in Taiwan, earned their first university degree there, and have maintained close contacts with a wide social network in their mother country. In this case, the firm may already command the necessary location-bound FSAs (meaning here limited to Taiwan) to access successfully the attractive Taiwanese market. In more general terms, the investments required to develop location-bound FSAs to access a foreign market will be different for each company, because each will be equipped with a different recombination ability, and any analysis limited to macro-level parameters, whether or not corrected for macro-level distance components, neglects firm specificity.

Second, similar to the suggestion made by Vestring, Rouse and Reinert, companies can develop their recombination capabilities, improving their ability to overcome distance barriers. Simply abandoning the playing field and restricting the firm's geographic scope to low-distance locations is not the only appropriate strategy. For example, increasing the diversity in the senior management's (cultural) background lets the firm benefit from multiple cognitive bases. In addition, a higher functional diversity of senior management may allow a better estimation of the challenges likely to occur in each functional area when penetrating a host country. A larger senior management team, with some managers developing or sustaining expertise in specific geographic areas, may also be useful. In general, if a firm is on a trajectory of international expansion, it should build into its human resources base and key decision-making routines a deep knowledge of foreign markets, including cultural affinity and experience-based business knowledge. For firms that do this, some of the location-bound knowledge required to penetrate a new host market will already be available in-house. In this context, we should also mention that international experience in foreign markets, sometimes built over many decades, may eliminate the macro-level distance problem altogether if a newly entered country has a low overall distance vis-à-vis the firm's existing network of operations. Here, it is not necessarily the distance from the home country that counts, but rather the distance between the host country and the MNE's affiliate most closely resembling that host country.[15]

Third, the impact of macro-level distance may be very different in the different parts of the value chain: Ghemawat's conclusions are less persuasive at the upstream end than they are at the downstream end. Most MNEs indeed show a sales distribution oriented towards low-distance countries, e.g., Europe-based companies focusing on other European nations, Canadian companies focusing on the US and Japanese companies focusing on Asia. However, these same MNEs appear relatively unconstrained in the geographic location of upstream activities such as sourcing and sometimes even production.[16]

Consider, for example, the upstream and downstream activities of the US-based clothing company Levi Strauss. The North American region accounted for US $2.5 billion of Levi Strauss' US $4.4 billion in total sales in 2010,[17] showing a strong concentration of sales in the home region. However, by 2004, Levi Strauss had shut down all its manufacturing factories in North America and moved these comparatively high-cost, upstream activities to Asia and Latin America.[18] In this example, high distance does not appear to hinder relocating all upstream activities. In recent years, many MNEs have relocated entire upstream activity bundles, as described extensively in the popular business press.

What is the reason for this asymmetry between upstream and downstream activities? In the case of market seeking FDI (see Chapter 1), the MNE commits resources and creates location-bound FSAs to link its existing FSAs with location advantages, in this case the presence of a large market, in the high-distance host country. Unfortunately, the resource commitments made to attract potential foreign customers are completely one-sided, coming only from the MNE. Thus, effective resource recombination is difficult. This contrasts with, e.g., strategic resource seeking FDI, in which the MNE also engages in location-specific linking investments in the high-distance host country. In this case, however, the resource commitments are made to acquire knowledge or reputational resources and are made by all the relevant parties: foreign suppliers, workers and acquired companies themselves engage in reciprocal commitments to make these investments worthwhile. With this input from host country actors, resource recombination is much easier. This analysis suggests that resource recombination is generally harder for downstream activities than for upstream ones. Ghemawat's analysis may thus be particularly appropriate for **centralized exporters** and **international projectors**, focused on expansion in foreign output markets, but less so for **international coordinators**, attempting to access and coordinate multiple input and intermediate output markets.

Fourth, Ghemawat assumes that FSAs are developed in the home country and subsequently exploited in other markets. He does not address the role of host countries, including high-distance ones, in fostering FSA development. Ghemawat's conclusions are useful for companies looking to transfer and exploit their bundles of internationally transferable FSAs in foreign markets, and facing restricted access to the location advantages of high-distance host countries. However, they are less useful for companies seeking to enter foreign markets to cultivate new FSAs within the host location environment. For example, in the case of strategic resource seeking investment, a high-distance location, though creating high costs for the firm, may also be instrumental to learning opportunities unavailable in low-distance locations. (This is ultimately the strategy adopted by the **international coordinator** archetype discussed in Chapter 1. The **international coordinator** combines the location advantages provided by a variety of locations, including high-distance ones, and ultimately benefits from recombining these geographically dispersed resources.)

Unfortunately, Ghemawat's model relies heavily on macro-level trade statistics, which show only that – **lumping together all motivations for investing abroad** – higher distance attributes correlate with lower inter-country trade levels, and therefore seem to imply a lower probability of success. However, this approach overlooks the differences among foreign entry motivations. The managerial prescription of reduced geographic scope at the firm level is not valid for all foreign entry motivations: the required resource recombinations may be easier to achieve with some entry motivations than with others.

Fifth, Ghemawat's model does not address how cooperative entry modes, such as strategic alliances and joint ventures with host country firms, can affect, and perhaps soften, the impact of high distance. Very often, such arrangements are set up precisely to overcome the various macro-level distance components when the MNE does not have the resource recombination capability to address the distance challenge on its own. Here, the partner firm's complementary resources may reduce distance. Micro-level distance may remain, however, especially cultural differences with host country partners, and this raises the question whether the reduction in macro-level distance achieved is sufficient to overcome the micro-level distance associated with a cooperative entry mode. Do cooperative entry modes alleviate or compound the challenges posed by high distance? Ghemawat's model assumes that companies enter foreign markets on their own, primarily to exploit FSAs developed in the home market. The model does not address how cooperative entry modes can facilitate foreign entry.

Five management takeaways

1. Pay attention to the four key dimensions of 'distance' when evaluating the attractiveness of foreign markets.
2. Analyse your company's position in the realm of cost leadership and thereby your potential (or need) to develop an FSA in offshoring.
3. Consider the right corporate and product brand names, the right image and the creation of the right perception of quality when launching branded consumer goods in high-distance markets.
4. Reflect on the transferability, deployability and profitable exploitation of your FSAs across borders, as well as on the need to create new FSAs, and on the possibilities of resource recombination. Do not overestimate the profit potential abroad of FSAs that worked well at home.
5. Before making a final decision about entry in potential host markets, do assess several firm- and host country-specific characteristics, which amount to 'distance': evaluate whether strong but hypothetical profit potential in foreign markets can actually be achieved in practice, given the presence of distance.

Case 4.1 Coping with the four dimensions of distance in the international expansion of Starbucks[19]

CASE

US-based Starbucks, established in 1971, is the largest coffee house company in the world. When it decided to leave its North American base, it opened its first overseas locations in Japan and Singapore in 1996, and it quickly expanded throughout Asia, Europe and Latin America. By early 2003, Starbucks had 1,532 coffee houses outside the US and Canada – 23 per cent of its 6,526 stores worldwide. However, these international stores accounted for less than 10 per cent of its total revenue. Returns on its overseas investments varied from country to country, but by 2003, it had not yet earned a net profit on its international investments as a whole. Nonetheless, Starbucks continued to expand into international markets despite slower profit growth and lower profit margins in these markets. In 2008, the global recession forced the company to refocus its strategy. Starbucks had expanded into too many low-profitability locations and this led Howard Schultz to resume his position as CEO, after spending eight years as chairman.[20] Starbucks re-evaluated locations in terms of growth potential and closed 800 stores in the US, and 61 out of 84 locations in Australia.[21] Most of these store locations had been open for less than two years and were established to drive incremental revenue rather than market share growth.[22] In 2012, Starbucks is continuing to focus on innovation and branding to expand internationally into Africa, the Middle East and its new market in India. These emerging markets are attractive to Starbucks as they have a growing middle class with greater disposable income to spend on high-quality beverages. Starbucks is using its past experiences in the US to guide its expansion in these foreign markets. The company will be extremely disciplined in selecting locations by using statistics and models to identify and quantify business opportunities.[23] Most importantly, it will strive to create the expected Starbucks experience while remaining locally relevant to the markets it operates in.[24]

Cultural distance

The most important feature of cultural distance for Starbucks is the consumers' relative preference for coffee vis-à-vis other drinks. Japanese and Chinese consumers are so used to drinking tea that it was not easy to cultivate a preference for coffee; most Latin American countries do not have an established mass consumer coffee market either.

Even in countries with a deeply engrained coffee drinking culture, local tastes are sometimes very different from what Starbucks offers. For example, Starbucks coffee appears to be more bitter than the classic Italian espresso and milder than the usual Austrian brew.

Yet, another cultural barrier is that the Starbucks brand has been associated with globalization and the export of American culture. For some Austrians, Starbucks coffee damages European values more than Coca-Cola. Even harder to overcome has been the perception in France of a linkage between Starbucks and American cultural imperialism.

Europe's café traditions are entrenched and subtly different from those in North America. For example, in many Italian cafés, customers can purchase light lunches, cigarettes and pastries, as well as coffee. In Austria, people meet in coffee shops, smoke and drink there, and read free newspapers. These traditions contrast with Starbucks' 'take-to-go' approach and its non-smoking policy.

Administrative (or institutional) distance

Administrative distance in some host countries has also hurt Starbucks' operations. For example, Starbucks registered its trademark in Russia in 1997, but did not immediately open any cafés there. In 2002, a filing was made by Sergei Zuykov to annul the trademark because it had not been used for the registered purpose, and he registered the name on behalf of a Moscow company. In 2005, Starbucks finally won its case as Russia aimed to join the World Trade Organization and inevitably enforced stronger intellectual property laws.[25] However, as a result of the long legal battle, Starbucks suffered delays entering into Russia, one of the fastest growing retail markets in Europe.

Similarly, in Shanghai, China, Shanghai Xingbake registered its name as the standard Chinese translation for Starbucks in 1999, and also used the green-and-white Starbucks logo; in Qingdao, China, another coffee shop used the same Chinese name. Starbucks had to file a lawsuit, which it finally won against Shanghai Xingbake in early 2006.

Geographic distance

Geographic distance has affected Starbucks' international expansion path. Starbucks opened Canadian stores as early as 1987, operating them essentially as domestic stores. In its Latin American expansion, Starbucks launched its first stores in Mexico, the Latin American country closest to the US, both geographically and culturally.

Geographic distance has also affected the choice of cities within host countries. In developing countries, major cities usually have better information infrastructure, thus facilitating information flows between overseas cafés and corporate management, and reducing bounded rationality.

Economic distance

To expand, Starbucks required a consumer base with a certain level of wealth. In many developing countries, Starbucks encounters problems because it is comparatively expensive. In Shanghai in 2001, for example, an espresso drink at Starbucks sold for CAN $4.90, nearly double the price of an entire meal combo at McDonald's.

Moreover, economic differences affect Starbucks' operational costs. For example, real estate costs in some host countries are far higher than those in the US.

How Starbucks reduced distance from foreign markets

Starbucks has used various tactics to reduce its distance from foreign markets. To reduce cultural distance, Starbucks has conducted extensive research in each country, using focus groups and quantitative analysis, to evaluate local cultural sensitivities and preferences. To reduce its cultural distance vis-à-vis Japan and China, for example, Starbucks decided to market its chic western image, rather than its coffee. In Europe, especially in those markets with a long coffee tradition such as the Scandinavian countries, France, and Austria, Starbucks has behaved very deferentially and diplomatically, stressing its respect for local cafés. To reduce the appearance of cultural imperialism, Starbucks has expanded into Europe in a low-key, humble and subdued way.

To reduce economic distance, Starbucks has expanded primarily into developed countries. In developing countries, it has focused on major cities first (e.g., Beijing, Shanghai, Mexico City, Lima, Santiago) and only later expanded into smaller cities when confident that the smaller cities had consumers with the necessary disposable income.

To reduce criticism in the area of corporate social responsibility, Starbucks has established a policy of paying premium prices for coffee beans from local farmers in Mexico and Peru who use environmentally friendly techniques.

To reduce its own overall 'foreignness', Starbucks has sometimes partnered with local businesses.

Starbucks' patience and tactics appear to have paid off. CEO Howard Schultz noted in 2004 that the firm's international operations had finally started to show a profit.

Starbucks and Italy

Starbucks has never entered Italy despite this country being an important source of inspiration for the firm's functioning. Howard Schultz envisioned evolving Starbucks coffee rosters into coffee shops after experiencing the Italian coffee culture in the 1980s. However, Italian customers have very different expectations as to what a 'coffee experience' should be, as compared to what is offered at Starbucks locations. Many variables, including the beans used, the size of the drink, the nature of the cups, and the speed of the service make the Italian market a challenge for Starbucks to enter. Criticism from local consumers is also a concern as many Italians consider Starbucks to be a symbol of American imperialism.[26] Finally, the highly saturated coffee market in Italy makes this location unattractive from an expected profitability perspective. For these reasons, Starbucks has shied away from Italy with Howard Schultz claiming "we haven't looked at it as seriously as we had other markets, but at some point we will go".[27] However, the deep rooted traditions of the Italian coffee culture are slowly changing with competitors successfully offering coffee experiences that are similar to Starbucks'. Younger Italian consumers are looking for coffee shops that offer more than just a good cup of coffee; they want a casual atmosphere where long breaks can be taken. Despite this changing market place, the company has not taken concrete steps to enter into Italy.

Starbucks moving forward

In 2008, Starbucks' sales began to decrease in several key North American and international markets as consumers' income levels had been affected by the recession. Howard Schultz resumed his role as CEO to refocus the company's strategy and brand, which he felt had become 'commoditized' by the rapid expansion.[28] As a result, underperforming stores were closed and a greater focus was placed on customer experience and innovation. In the years following, Starbucks successfully introduced VIA, an instant coffee product, and released Starbucks K-Cups to provide clients with alternatives to their coffee experience. K-Cups provide Starbucks' consumers with the opportunity to brew their very own cup of Starbucks coffee at home using the Keurig single brew system. The company also removed 'Starbucks Coffee' from its logo to better position itself for moving into new product lines and international markets.

By January 2012, Starbucks was operating over 17,000 stores in 55 different countries.[29] Starbuck's international operations have continued to expand despite providing lower profit margins than its North American operations.[30]

The company announced in January 2012 a joint venture with Tata Global Beverages to enter the Indian market. The initial plans are to establish coffee houses in 50 locations in major cities to capitalize on a newly booming coffee culture within the traditionally tea-dominated country.[31] Partnering with Tata, a company with a strong tea heritage and presence in India, will help to bridge the cultural gap. India provides a unique challenge for Starbucks because of the changes the company will need to make to its products to adapt to local tastes. For example, when

McDonald's entered India the company was forced to remove all items that contained beef products to cater to the local religion (Hinduism). Starbucks' Indian operations will also source 100 per cent of their coffee and food products from India, a first for any of its international operations.[32] Indian regulations stipulate that any foreign entity can own a maximum 51 per cent stake in an Indian venture and must source at least 30 per cent of its inputs from local suppliers.[33] Starbucks' joint venture with Tata Global will source coffee entirely from the latter firm's subsidiary Tata Coffee Ltd in Bangalore. Starbucks hopes that support from local suppliers will help build a positive image for the company inside India.

Both in countries with a coffee drinking heritage (such as Austria), and in countries without such a strong heritage (such as Japan and China), Starbucks appears to have become successful.

QUESTIONS

1. What are the four dimensions of 'distance' in Starbucks' international expansion?
2. How did Starbucks reduce the 'distance' vis-à-vis host countries?
3. Looking only at the four dimensions of distance, should Starbucks invest in Japan or China? If yes, give the reasons why; if no, why not?
4. If you had been in charge of the international expansion of Starbucks, what would you have changed (e.g., the pace, the choice of host countries)?
5. Ghemawat left company-specific questions unanswered, but see if you can answer this one: in the case of Starbucks, what are the interactions between company-specific features and the four dimensions of distance?
6. Can you provide an update on Starbucks' international expansion, using materials available on the Web?

Case 4.2 Wal-Mart's retreat from Germany: How distance made the replication of a domestically successful model impossible[34]

CASE

US-based Wal-Mart, the world's largest retail firm, announced in 2006 that it would sell its 85 stores in Germany to its German rival Metro, after nine years of struggle there. Why did Wal-Mart's successful US retail model fail in Germany? What lessons can Wal-Mart gain from its experience in Germany to help it succeed in other international markets?

The history of Wal-Mart

Sam Walton opened the first Wal-Mart Discount City in Arkansas, USA, in 1962. By 2012, Wal-Mart had nearly 8,970 stores and wholesale clubs across 27 countries. In 2011, its global revenue rose to more than US $419 billion, with nearly US $15.4 billion in net income.[35] The key to its success is the Wal-Mart culture, particularly its 'every day low price' (EDLP) philosophy and its so-called 'exceptional service'. EDLP is based on efficient distribution systems, very innovative technology, low prices negotiated with suppliers and efficient processes with suppliers. The so-called 'exceptional service' includes smiling at customers, assisting them and exceeding their expectations.

Wal-Mart started its international expansion in 1991 when it opened a Sam's Club near Mexico City. Since then, Wal-Mart has expanded rapidly into countries such as Argentina, the UK, China, Brazil, Canada and Germany by transferring its domestic retailing model and corporate culture to each country while trying to adapt to local conditions.

Wal-Mart entered Germany by taking over 21 Wertkauf stores in 1997 and 74 Interspar hypermarkets in 1998. However, unique features of the German market meant that Wal-Mart could not just replicate its US model.

Unique characteristics of the German market for US retailers

The German retail market is characterized by fierce competition, strict regulations and a distinctive union and co-determination system. Specifically for Wal-Mart Germany, the locations of its warehouses and the distance between the headquarters of the two former chains brought additional problems.

Fierce competition based on price

In the early 1990s, German retailers competed fiercely with each other by focusing on low prices. The hard discounters, who offered around 600 to 700 products with a large share of store brands, sold products at very low prices with ultra-thin margins. On average, retailers' profits varied between only 0.5 per cent and 0.8 per cent of sales.

Parsimonious consumers

As a result of this price-based competition, German consumers became used to shopping based strictly on price. For example, they might go to one store to buy soap and then to another one to buy better-priced laundry detergent.

Although Germany is a highly developed country with affluent consumers, many Germans have shifted a large share of their expenditures to non-retail products such as housing and travel. That desired spending pattern gives them another reason to try to spend as little as possible on products typically found in retail stores, such as packaged household products. German consumers have become very parsimonious.

Regulations

Three major regulations affecting the German retail market are German zoning laws, German laws regarding store hours, and German fair trading and antitrust laws.

First, German zoning laws required retail facilities larger than 1,200 square metres (12,903 square feet) to be located only in zoned areas where their likely impact on the surrounding facilities and population has been assessed as minimal. Because of these regulations, opening a new hyper-market in Germany could take five years or more. Wal-Mart used precisely this kind of very large store: the average size of a traditional Wal-Mart supercentre in the US was 187,000 square feet.[36]

Second, the German government limited store hours to a maximum of 80 hours per week. Stores had to be closed on Sundays and holidays, and after 4 pm on Saturdays.

Third, Germany's fair trading and antitrust laws prohibited retailers from selling products below cost on a permanent basis.

Unionization and the co-determination system

The high prevalence of worker unionization and the co-determination system in Germany were also new for Wal-Mart. 'Co-determination' means that companies and unions are closely connected, and employees participate in corporate decision making that might affect working conditions.

Geographic locations of warehouses and headquarters

The geographic locations of warehouses and headquarters also affected Wal-Mart. Wal-Mart relied on only two warehouses, located in the western part of Germany, nearly 500 kilometres away from its stores in the eastern and southern parts of the country. Furthermore, the physical distance between the headquarters of the two former companies forced Wal-Mart to consolidate and shut down one of the former headquarters, leading some infuriated execu-tives to quit.

Wal-Mart's difficulties in the German market

The unique characteristics of the German market hindered the replication of the successful Wal-Mart model. To make things worse, Wal-Mart was not sufficiently prepared to cope with all the liabilities of foreignness it faced in Germany. Beth Keck, an international spokeswoman for Wal-Mart, commented shortly after Wal-Mart's retreat from Germany: "Germany was a good example of that naiveté ... We literally bought the two chains and said, 'Hey, we are in Germany, isn't this great?' "[37] Germany's uniqueness affected key parts of Wal-Mart's successful business model, including EDLP and the so-called exceptional service approach.

The impact of Germany's uniqueness on EDLP

Because Wal-Mart had to source locally or regionally for some of its product offering, the small size of Wal-Mart Germany and its inability to expand rapidly made it impossible to reduce costs so as to provide everyday low prices. In addition, Wal-Mart Germany's loss-leader strategy (a pricing strategy in which one item is sold below cost in order to stimulate other, profitable sales) was judged illegal, making it very difficult to create an EDLP image.

Many products had to be purchased from local or regional producers. For example, food like bratwurst and beer was primarily local, and many European brands in the non-food area, such as Fischer bicycles and Vernel fabric softener, were very different from what Wal-Mart sold in the US.

Wal-Mart did not command as much market power in Germany as in the US, although it benefited from scale economies and low-cost production economies for some products such as toys and clothing imported from countries like China and India. In 2003, Wal-Mart had only 92 stores in Germany, much less than the German discounter Aldi, which operated 3800 stores. Even though the average Wal-Mart store was ten times larger than the equivalent Aldi store, Wal-Mart had less market power.

The small size of its German operations prevented Wal-Mart from exercising power over suppliers when purchasing German or other European products. For example, when Wal-Mart Germany asked its suppliers to switch to a new supply system and to supply directly to its centralized warehouse, a number of suppliers did not comply with the request.

In its effort to expand and gain purchasing power, Wal-Mart was hampered by German zoning laws. Because the planned stores were so large, the zoning laws required that the stores' impact be assessed. In 2000, Wal-Mart Germany announced the construction of another 50 stores within the next three years, but by August 2003, it had opened only four new stores. Unable to expand rapidly, the relatively small size of its German operations affected the firm's purchasing power, negatively influenced its operating costs and ultimately diminished its ability to keep prices low for consumers.

Furthermore, Wal-Mart was not allowed to replicate the loss-leader strategy that had been so successful in the US. Wal-Mart Germany tried to sell milk, butter and similar products as loss-leaders by pricing them below cost to lure shoppers, but in September 2000, the German Cartel Office judged such activities illegal, and Wal-Mart was forced to raise its prices.

The impact of Germany's uniqueness on service

Wal-Mart Germany was not only unable to supply truly low-cost products – it was also unable to provide customer service perceived as particularly good. A survey in 2002–2003 conducted by Gerhard and Hahn in Würzburg, Germany, reported that only 8.7 per cent of customers viewed Wal-Mart staff as friendly and helpful.[38] The reason was simply that several of Wal-Mart's basic operating principles were only partially compatible with German stakeholder expectations.

First, Wal-Mart required sales clerks to smile at customers when they came within ten feet (the so-called 'ten foot rule'). However, the smile was interpreted as flirting by some male shoppers, and some shoppers even complained about being harassed. This practice was therefore terminated.

Second, Wal-Mart offered services such as grocery bagging. However, German consumers had been used to self-service bagging for decades, and they therefore assumed, at least initially, that they had to pay for any staff assistance. Indeed, as an important side effect, the additional personnel for such services did increase the labour costs at Wal-Mart Germany. In addition, many German customers did not like strangers handling their groceries.

Third, as noted above, the two retailers bought by Wal-Mart had headquarters in different cities, with Wertkauf's headquarters in Karlsruhe and Interspar's headquarters in Wuppertal. Wal-Mart therefore decided to consolidate the headquarters' activities in Wuppertal. In the US, this consolidation would have been routine, as 'being transferred' is a common employment practice in the US, and moving is part of the US culture. However, moving to another city was too big a step for some German executives, leading many talented managers to resign. The exodus of these executives made it even more difficult to learn the nuances of the German marketplace.

Finally, to make things worse, Wal-Mart had four local CEOs in the first four years of being active in Germany. The first two – one from the US and the other from the UK – lacked adequate knowledge about the German market. The second CEO even tried to run Wal-Mart Germany from his office in England. This turnover in leadership slowed the possible adaptation of Wal-Mart's prevailing service routines to German market conditions.

Lessons learned

Wal-Mart appears to have learned from its mistakes in the German market and is using this experience as a guide for future growth. In 2006, Mike Duke, Head of International Operations and current CEO, realized an overhaul of Wal-Mart's international strategy was needed to avoid the mistakes made in both Germany and South Korea.

Wal-Mart implemented a new system to evaluate international locations with a stronger focus on government restrictions, management requirements, cultural differences, and the specificities of the competitive landscape. The company also shifted its focus to put greater emphasis on the transition and integration stages of the acquisition process after new locations are selected.[39]

The German experience highlighted areas of concern in management functioning and the need to make some decisions locally. For example, product buyers in Walmart's German operations were actually Americans who may not have fully understood the needs of German consumers.[40] Wal-Mart now leaves more of its buying functions and management decisions to local personnel. Greater autonomy for local management and more rigid financial goals have also improved Wal-Mart's international operations.[41] When the company bought the British chain ASDA in 1999, local managers were given substantial autonomy to run the business, allowing it to remain essentially a British operation. Successful executives were moved around and senior executives were brought in from outside to add constructive perspectives.

Wal-Mart now focuses on locations with a greater opportunity for growth.[42] The German market was already saturated with discount retailers, leaving little room for growth and hindering expectations to gain immediate scale for EDLP. Wal-Mart has since pursued new opportunities in India, Central and South America where the market is less developed and provides an attractive competitive landscape.

In 2009, Wal-Mart entered into the lucrative Indian market by partnering with Bharti Enterprises to establish its wholesale presence as BestPrice Modern Wholesale. Government regulations restricted Wal-Mart's ownership of this joint venture to 51 per cent. Learning from its mistakes in Germany, Wal-Mart has paid greater attention to local preferences by filling 90 per cent of shelf space with products that the Indian population knows and loves.[43] The company has also invested for years building relationships with suppliers and farmers to ensure that the quality and quantity of demand can be met. Responding to industry challenges in supply chain management, whereby wasted fresh produce amounts to 35 per cent, Wal-Mart has established the rule that fresh fruits and vegetables must be sourced from distribution centres within 200 kilometres of wholesale locations.[44] Reinforcing Wal-Mart's stance on adapting to local markets, Raj Jain, President of Wal-Mart India stated "India is not a homogenous market, so ours is not a cookie-cutter approach from the U.S."[45]

It appears that Wal-Mart is successfully moving forward and using its failure in Germany as a positive learning experience.

QUESTIONS

1. What are some of Wal-Mart's FSAs? To what extent are these FSAs location-bound or internationally transferable?
2. What distance components (relative to the US) do American retailers face in Germany? Give examples. How did these distance components affect the exploitation of Wal-Mart's FSAs transferred to Germany?
3. Did Wal-Mart overestimate the transferability of its FSAs?
4. Can you provide an update on Wal-Mart's international expansion, using materials available on the Web?

Notes

1. Pankaj Ghemawat, 'Distance still matters: the hard reality of global expansion', *Harvard Business Review* 79 (2001), 147.
2. *Ibid.*, 138.
3. *Ibid.*, 142.
4. *Ibid.*
5. *Ibid.*
6. *Ibid.*, 145.
7. *Ibid.*, 147.
8. *Ibid.*, 142.
9. *Ibid.*
10. Till Vestring, Ted Rouse and Uwe Reinert, 'Hedge your offshoring bets', *MIT Sloan Management Review* 46 (Spring 2005), 27–9.
11. *Ibid.*, 29.
12. *Ibid.*
13. Bernd H. Schmitt and Yigang Pan, 'Managing corporate and brand identities in the Asia-Pacific region', *California Management Review* 36 (Summer 1994), 32–48.
14. For an insightful discussion of the differences among national cultures, and their implications for international business, see Bradley L. Kirkman, Kevin B. Lowe and Cristina B. Gibson, 'A quarter century of *Culture's Consequences*: a review of empirical research

incorporating Hofstede's cultural values framework', *Journal of International Business Studies* 37 (2006), 285–320.

15. This also implies that international experience may be largely useless if, for example, the institutional distance between the host country and the MNE's affiliates is particularly large. A similar conclusion was proposed by Verbeke and Yuan (Alain Verbeke and Wenlong Yuan, 'Subsidiary autonomous activities in multinational enterprises: a trans-action cost perspective', *Management International Review* 45 (2005), 31–52) when assessing the economic potential of autonomous subsidiary initiatives in large MNEs.

16. Alan Rugman and Alain Verbeke, 'A perspective on regional and global strategies of multinational enterprises', *Journal of International Business Studies* 35 (2004), 3–18; Alan Rugman and Alain Verbeke, *Analysis of Multinational Strategic Management: The Selected Papers of Alan M. Rugman and Alain Verbeke* (Cheltenham, UK, and Brookfield, US: Edward Elgar, 2005); Alan Rugman and Alain Verbeke, 'Regional multinationals: the new research agenda', in Peter Buckley (ed.), *What is International Business?* (New York: Palgrave Macmillan, 2005), 110–32.

17. Levi Strauss company information, 2010.

18. Alan Rugman, Alain Verbeke and Wenlong Yuan, 'Re-conceptualizing the classification of subsidiary roles in multinational enterprises', *mimeo* 2005.

19. John Authers and Mark Mulligan, 'Coffee culture comes to the coffee-growers', *Financial Times* (2003), 14; Ariane Bernard, 'New American beachhead in France: Starbucks', *New York Times* (2004), A.5; Paul Betts and John Thornhill, 'Starbucks steams into Italy', *Financial Times* (2000), 17; Keith Bradsher, 'Starbucks aims to alter China's taste in caffeine', *New York Times* (2005), C.3; John Murray Brown and Jenny Wiggins, 'Coffee empire expands reach by pressing its luck in Ireland', *Financial Times* (2005), 27; Mure Dickie, 'Starbucks wins key Chinese lawsuit over brand', *Financial Times* (2006), 24; Steven Erlanger, 'An American coffeehouse (or 4) in Vienna', *New York Times* (2002), A.1; Stanley Holmes, Irene M. Kunii, Jack Ewing and Kerry Capell, 'For Starbucks, there is no place like home: its overseas expansion is running into trouble', *Business Week* (2003), 48; Andrew Kramer, 'He doesn't make coffee, but he controls 'Starbucks' in Russia', *New York Times* (2005), C.1; Glen McGregor, 'Starbucks empire finds it a hard grind in China', *Times – Colonist* (2001), C.7; Mark Pendergrast, 'Career journal – manager's journal: Starbucks goes to Europe … with humility and respect', *Wall Street Journal (Eastern Edition)* (9 April 2002), B.16; New York Times, 'Starbucks in European venture deal', *New York Times* (2000), C.28; New York Times, 'Starbucks sees overseas profit', *New York Times* (23 May 2003), C.9; Andrew Yeh, 'Starbucks aims for new tier in China CAFES', *Financial Times* (2006), 17.

20. Howard Schultz, 'Health growth', *Leadership Excellence* (May 2011), 6.

21. Susan Berfield, 'Starbucks: Howard Schultz vs. Howard Schultz', *Bloomberg Businessweek Online* (2 July 2008).

22. Howard Schultz, 'Health growth', *Leadership Excellence* (May 2011), 6.

23. Allen Webb, 'Starbucks' quest for healthy growth: An interview with Howard Schultz', *McKinsey Quarterly* (March 2011).

24. *Ibid.*

25. Andrew Kramer, 'After a long dispute, a Russian Starbucks', *New York Times* (7 September 2007).

26. Adrian Michaels, 'Starbucks bows to Italy's baristi', *Financial Times* (27 December 2007), 9.

27. Stephan Faris, 'Grounds zero: a Starbucks-free Italy', *Bloomberg Businessweek* (9 February 2012).

28. Maureen Morrison, '2011 marketer A-List: Starbucks', *Advertising Age* (7 November 2011), 30.

29. Starbucks Corporation, Annual report 2010–2011 (2011).

30. *Ibid.*

31. Geetanjali Shukla and K. R. Balasubramanyam, 'All perked up: The entry of Starbucks will probably segment the Indian market, but existing cafe chains are unlikely to cede any ground', *Business Today* (4 March 2012).

32. Starbucks Corporation, 'The coffee we serve will be completely sourced locally', *Mint* (31 January 2012).

33. Sapna Agarwal, 'Starbucks will enter India in joint venture with Tata', *Bloomberg* (31 January 2012).

34. Ulrike Gerhard and Barbara Hahn, 'Wal-Mart and Aldi: two retail giants in Germany', *GeoJournal* 62 (2005), 15–26; Andreas Knorr and Andreas Arndt, 'Why did Wal-Mart fail in Germany (so far)?' *mimeo* (2003); Kate Norton, 'Wal-Mart's German retreat', *Business Week Online* (28 July 2006); Gerrit Wiesmann, 'Why Wal-Mart decided to pack its bags in Germany', *Financial Times* (2006), 21; Mark Landler, 'Wal-Mart to abandon Germany', *New York Times* (29 July 2006), C.1; Mark Landler and Michael Barbaro, 'No, not always', *New York Times* (2 August 2006), C.1; Ann Zimmerman and Emily Nelson, 'With profits elusive, Wal-Mart to exit Germany; local hard discounters undercut retailer's prices; 'basket-splitting' problems', *Wall Street Journal* (29 July 2006), A.1; Wendy Zellner, Katharine A. Schmidt, Moon Ihlwan and Heidi Dawley, 'How well does Wal-Mart travel? After early missteps, the retailing giant may finally be getting the hang of selling overseas', *Business Week* (3 September 2001), 82; The Economist, 'Business: Heading for the exit; retailing', *The Economist* 380 (5 Aug 2006), 54.

35. Wal-Mart, 'About Us' (2012).

36. *Ibid.*

37. Landler and Barbaro, 'No, not always', C.1.

38. Gerhard and Hahn, 'Wal-Mart and Aldi', 15–26.

39. Mike Troy, 'Wal-Mart bids auf wiedersehen, ends nine-year grind in Germany', *Retailing Today* (7 August 2006), 45–14.

40. Mark Choueke, 'Leader: Marketing at heart of all retail success', *Marketing Week* (11 June 2009), 3.

41. Matthew Boyle, 'Wal-Mart's painful lessons', *Business Week (Online)* (13 October 2009).

42. Mike Troy, 'Wal-Mart bids auf wiedersehen, ends nine-year grind in Germany', *Retailing Today* (7 August 2006), 45–14.

43. Emily Wax, 'India's first Wal-Mart draws excitement, not protest', *The Washington Post* (13 July 2009).

44. Vikas Bajaj, 'In India, Wal-Mart goes to the farm', *The New York Times* (12 April 2010), B1.

45. Nandini Lakshaman, 'Why Wal-Mart's first India store isn't a Wal-Mart', *Time* (15 May 2009).

5

Combining firm-specific advantages and location advantages in a multinational network

Five learning objectives

1. To describe the challenges associated with centralizing strategic decision making and control in MNEs, and to highlight the possible ineffectiveness thereof.
2. To develop a framework for classifying MNE subsidiaries as a function of the location advantages they can access and the unique bundles of FSAs they command inside the firm, but with due consideration to the value chain activities involved.
3. To foster reflection on the 'procedural justice' concept and to highlight the impact thereof on decision making and organizational effectiveness.
4. To outline the strengths and weaknesses of prevailing, Japanese MNE subsidiary management.
5. To highlight the managerial implications of assigning differentiated roles to MNE subsidiaries.

This chapter explores Bartlett and Ghoshal's idea that large MNEs are making a mistake when they adopt the two simplifying strategies of homogenization (treating all their subsidiaries the same) and centralization (making all their strategic decisions at central headquarters). According to Bartlett and Ghoshal, this is poor strategy: by selectively decentralizing elements of strategic decision making and control, these companies could instead optimize the deployment and exploitation of their present FSAs and support the development of new FSAs in their multinational subsidiary network. Bartlett and Ghoshal offer a model that helps senior corporate managers differentiate among their subsidiaries and decide which subsidiaries should do more than merely implement centrally determined strategy. These ideas will be examined and then criticized using the framework presented in Chapter 1.

Significance

In 1986, *Chris Bartlett* and *Sumantra Ghoshal* wrote an important article in *HBR* on how MNEs should manage their subsidiary network.[1] The substance of this paper was included three years later in their now classic book on the so-called 'transnational solution'.[2] The paper discussed here is actually the most important part of the book, as it contains a practical tool for senior managers to allocate specific roles to subsidiaries.

The authors suggest that many MNEs mistakenly view host country subsidiaries simply as recipients and distributors of company knowledge and products. These MNEs do not recognize their subsidiaries' potential to develop unique strengths in their own right and to augment further the MNE's existing FSA bundles. For these centralized MNEs, strategic decision making and control reside solely in the home country corporate headquarters, which can become isolated and oblivious to changing conditions in key international markets. This can lead to enormous bounded rationality and bounded reliability challenges (the latter in the sense of senior managers not making sufficient efforts to increase the subsidiaries' potential value). Bartlett and Ghoshal argue that by selectively decentralizing elements of strategic decision making and control, companies can optimize the deployment and exploitation of their present FSAs and support the development of new FSAs in their multinational subsidiary network.

In their study of 21 MNEs based in the US, Europe and Japan, Bartlett and Ghoshal found that senior management frequently adopted two simplifying strategies. The first strategy is what the authors call the 'United Nations model' of multinational management. MNEs adopting this approach treat each subsidiary in a similar manner in terms of the roles and responsibilities these units will have, and the coordination and control systems they will be subjected to, regardless of these subsidiaries' specialized resources or the strategic importance of the host market in which they are located. Usually this homogenized approach involves either complete subsidiary independence (as found in *multi-centred MNEs*) or complete dependence (as found in *centralized exporters* or *international projectors*). For *centralized exporters* and *international projectors*, this simplifying strategy is often adopted to offset the increasing complexity of managing large-scale international operations, even though "[as] a company reaches for the benefits of global integration . . . there is little need for uniformity and symmetry among units".[3]

The second assumption is what the authors term the 'headquarters hierarchy syndrome'. Here, senior management views the organization as consisting of two distinct levels – one dominant and one subordinate. The dominant central corporate headquarters control key decision-making processes and overall company resources in order to implement a consistent global strategy. In contrast, all the national subsidiaries are subordinate and merely "act as implementers and adapters of the global strategy in their localities".[4]

These two simplifying strategies – homogenization and centralization – cause tensions between headquarters and subsidiaries, as corporate headquarters attempt to maintain control of the subsidiary network, while entrepreneurial subsidiary managers fight for more independence and freedom of action in their local markets.

Bartlett and Ghoshal conclude that these two simplifying strategies have other dysfunctional effects on the MNE as well. As a result of the first strategy, important markets and subsidiaries are treated in the same way as unimportant ones, and therefore the opportunities they provide are not optimally exploited. As a result of the second strategy, subsidiaries with a distinct, specialized resource base are unable to escape from an implementer role and unleash their entrepreneurial abilities. In other words, Bartlett and Ghoshal acknowledge that the corporate headquarters of a large MNE face serious bounded rationality problems, but they argue that responding to these problems by adopting these two simplifying strategies will trigger bounded reliability challenges (as senior managers in central headquarters do not make sufficient efforts to maximize the potential value of each subsidiary, and senior managers in the subsidiaries attempt to deviate from their prescribed role).

In response to the above problems, the authors observe, a number of MNEs have moved towards "an organizational model of differentiated rather than homogenous subsidiary roles and of dispersed rather than concentrated responsibilities".[5] The authors offer two examples – one negative and the other positive – to illustrate the point. The first is the case of the UK-based firm EMI and its development of the CAT scanner. Although this technology revolutionized the medical industry, earned a Nobel Prize (awarded to the EMI scientist Godfrey Hounsfield) and established EMI as the market leader in this business, the company was not able to sustain its position over time and eventually was forced to sell the business. According to Bartlett and Ghoshal, the core problem resided in an ineffective and overly centralized organizational structure and related decision-making processes. Senior management in the UK headquarters maintained centralized control, and their strategy was overly focused on domestic market needs, at the expense of key foreign markets such as the US. For example, the firm filled all backlogged orders worldwide in the order they had been received, rather than giving priority to key customers or markets (e.g., important US customers). Corporate headquarters also refused to allow subsidiaries to engage in local sourcing to alleviate bottlenecks in production, and focused product-development efforts on British demands for improved image resolution rather than US demands for lower times per scan. As a result of these decisions, EMI was unresponsive to changing needs outside its home market, was unaware of emerging competitive threats in the US and left its national managers without the resources to address growing competitive threats.

The second example is Procter & Gamble's (P&G) innovative approach to creating 'Eurobrand' teams. Earlier efforts to launch a Europe-wide campaign controlled by regional headquarters in Brussels had failed. The failure was caused by neglecting the specialized resources – especially local market knowledge – held by the subsidiaries, and by demotivating local managers. For its new effort, P&G instead identified the most successful national subsidiary for each product and put that subsidiary's managers in charge of the pan-European team for that product. The goal was to move beyond P&G's traditional multi-centred approach – whereby countries operated independently of one another – in order to capitalize on greater scale efficiencies and effectiveness in promotional campaigns and product development. By delegating responsibility and authority for specific products at the pan-European level to specific lead countries, the head office created a new system of interdependence and reciprocal cooperation among the network of national subsidiaries. As a result, P&G "captured the knowledge, the expertise, and most important, the commitment of managers closest to the market".[6] The key point of this example is that P&G rejected both a global and a local/national approach to strategy. A global approach dictated out of the US would have been unworkable, given the bounded rationality constraints facing senior management at corporate headquarters. This bounded rationality challenge resulted from the substantial cultural, economic, institutional and spatial distance separating the US and Europe, whereby inappropriate, centrally made decisions would also have been a source of new bounded reliability challenges, with sub-sidiaries opposing centralized decision making. At the same time, a local/national approach to strategy would have prevented the firm from earning scale and scope economies at the regional level. In this case, the potential to earn scope economies – benefits from sharing the knowledge base of successful lead subsidiaries – was critical. Senior managers of lead subsidiaries at the regional level faced far fewer bounded rationality challenges when setting strategy for their region, and their proximity to national subsidiary managers also reduced bounded reliability.

Bartlett and Ghoshal offer a simple normative model to help senior management assign differentiated subsidiary roles. First, senior corporate management should assess each market according to its strategic importance (e.g., its market size, demand sophistication or technological innovation). Next, senior corporate management should rate each subsidiary's resource base in terms of sales and marketing achievements, production capabilities, research and development, or any other strength contributing to competitiveness. The result is a simple sub-sidiary classification system (see Figure 5.1), which distinguishes among four subsidiary types.

1. **Black Hole:** this is a rather weak unit in terms of specialized resources, but it is located in a strategically important market. The MNE can use this unit to maintain a presence in a key market in order to keep abreast of new

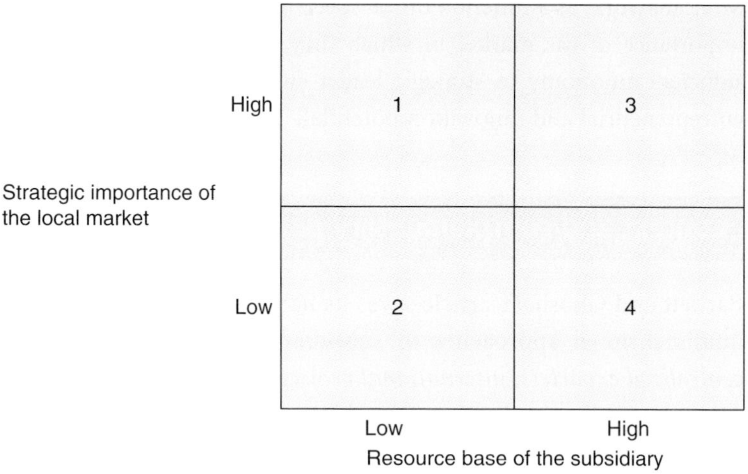

Figure 5.1
A classification of
subsidiary roles
in the MNE

innovations or strategic moves by competitors, despite a lack of specialized resources or even profitability in the local subsidiary unit itself. The black hole status does reflect, however, an undesirable competitive position in a key market. In the longer run, MNEs may want to commit more resources to such markets in order to build up their subsidiary, or they may want to engage in acquisitions or strategic alliances in order to access complementary resources and improve market success.

2. **Implementer:** this is a subsidiary with weaker (or absent) specialized resources, and located in a market of lesser importance with respect to the MNE's long-term survival, profitability and growth. The authors suggest that most MNE subsidiaries are in this category. Implementers are often key to a firm's overall success, however, because they may generate a steady stream of cash flow, and may help build competitive advantage by contributing to company-wide scale and scope economies.

3. **Strategic leader:** this is a highly competent local subsidiary in a strategically important market. The role of this type of business unit is to assist corporate headquarters in identifying industry trends and developing new FSAs in response to emerging opportunities and threats.

4. **Contributor:** this is again a highly competent national subsidiary, but one located in a less important market. This subsidiary type has typically developed new FSAs, often as the result of an entrepreneurial host country management team. Its subsidiary-specific, specialized resource base might then benefit other units in the firm if corporate headquarters understands its potential economic value to the entire MNE.

Keeping these four subsidiary categories in mind, senior management at corporate headquarters must provide a clear sense of overall strategic direction, and allocate appropriate roles and responsibilities to the different subsidiaries in the

MNE network, as a function of the specialized resources they command and the importance of the market in which they are located. This includes providing sufficient autonomy to strategic leader subsidiaries in order to stimulate their entrepreneurial and innovation potential.

Context and complementary perspectives

Bartlett and Ghoshal's article saves its harshest criticism for the homogenized, unidimensional approaches to subsidiary management commonly used by *centralized exporters, international projectors* and to some extent *multi-centred MNEs* expanding in the post-World War II period up to the mid 1980s. While the Iron Curtain was still in place across Eastern Europe and communist countries such as China remained essentially closed to foreign MNEs, many firms continued to grow their international operations. Their expansion into foreign markets typically followed the blueprints and conventional 'cookie cutter' patterns of FSA development and exploitation that had been set by the founders of the firm or its senior management in the early stages of its international growth.

A first complementary perspective to Bartlett and Ghoshal was provided by *W. Chan Kim* and *Renée Mauborgne*, two INSEAD-based scholars. Their important article on making global strategies work, published in *SMR*, is only one of several influential articles these authors have published on the topic of due process in MNEs.[7] 'Due process' here refers to the way strategic decisions are made, irrespective of their outcome. Kim and Mauborgne start from an observation similar to Bartlett and Ghoshal's: senior managers at MNE corporate headquarters, faced with the need to make difficult, company-wide strategic management decisions, including resource allocation decisions, often centralize the decision-making process, presenting subsidiary managers with a demotivating fait accompli. This strategy is especially problematic if the host country unit has grown very large relative to the home country operations and has accumulated substantial specialized resources. Destroying the entrepreneurial spirit and motivation in such subsidiaries is especially detrimental to the firm if those units are supposed to contribute to knowledge transfers and inter-subsidiary learning inside the MNE network. In such cases, the bounded reliability problem faced by senior managers at corporate headquarters becomes worse because they cannot take for granted anymore the commitment of subsidiary managers to pursue company goals, nor these subsidiary managers' willingness to implement company strategy wholeheartedly. Consistent with the above observation of subsidiary network growth, Kim and Mauborgne also noticed a more limited ability of corporate headquarters to evaluate appropriately each unit, to exert hierarchical power and to establish a common corporate culture.

Problems of bounded rationality and bounded reliability arise, requiring new managerial and organizational solutions.

However, rather than focusing on treating subsidiaries differently as a function of their specialized resources and the strategic importance of their location, as advocated by Bartlett and Ghoshal, Kim and Mauborgne propose a different solution. They note that subsidiary managers attach substantial importance to due process and will usually accept an allocation of MNE resources that does not benefit their unit if they believe that due process was observed in making that strategic decision.

Due process (also called 'procedural justice') implies that decision making respects five simple principles.

1. Corporate headquarters' familiarity with the local situation at the subsidiary level: this implies that senior managers at corporate headquarters understand – or at least appear to understand – all the implications of specific decisions for the subsidiaries affected.
2. Effective two-way communication between corporate headquarters and subsidiaries: in particular, the bottom-up part of this two-way communication signals that senior managers at corporate headquarters take subsidiary managers' views seriously and are willing to engage in a dialogue with these subsidiary managers.
3. Consistency in decision making across subsidiaries: consistency – in the sense of adopting clear and transparent criteria and routines to make decisions across the entire subsidiary network – prevents perceptions of politicized decision making and favouritism advantaging one subsidiary over another.
4. Possibility for subsidiary managers to challenge the dominant perspective at corporate headquarters: this signals to subsidiary managers that senior management at corporate headquarters – even if confident in its perspective – is nonetheless willing to hear its assumptions and conclusions challenged by individuals in the trenches, knowledgeable about the local situation in host countries.
5. A transparent explanation of final decisions made by corporate headquarters: here, senior management at corporate headquarters makes a serious effort to explain in depth the rationale for the decisions made, thereby pre-empting any second-guessing or rumours on the substantive reasoning behind these decisions.

Kim and Mauborgne explain why adhering to the above principles of due process is so important. First, following due process can reduce *bounded rationality* problems in the MNE. For example, by actively seeking input from host countries (through an investment of time and resources), senior management at corporate headquarters can make fundamentally better-informed decisions. Good relations with subsidiary management will also create new (informal) channels to access critical, bottom-up information from foreign units in the future.

Furthermore, following due process can also reduce *bounded reliability* problems in the MNE:

> ... those managers who believed that due process was exercised in their firms' global strategy-making process were the same executives who trusted their head offices significantly, who were highly committed to their organizations, who felt a sense of comradeship or unity with the corporate centre, and who were motivated to execute not only the letter but also the spirit of the decisions.[8]

These subsidiary managers behave this way because they feel that they have been treated with fairness and respect. Furthermore, by receiving full disclosure of the reasons for specific decisions affecting subsidiaries, these subsidiary managers become better informed on the views of corporate headquarters, and are more likely to align their own decisions with corporate headquarters' views.

Kim and Mauborgne tested their ideas on a sample of 119 subsidiary top managers in 19 MNEs. Their main conclusion: procedural justice has a tangible positive impact on reducing bounded reliability. Reducing bounded rationality (better information obtained and processed by senior managers at headquarters, and better information disseminated more effectively to subsidiary managers) was undoubtedly instrumental to reducing bounded reliability. As procedural justice increases, the 'losers' in the corporate resource allocation process (i.e., those subsidiaries that do not receive the resources they request) refrain from dysfunctional behaviour. Increased procedural justice, Kim and Mauborgne found, reduces the negative impact of unfavourable resource allocation decisions on (1) commitment, (2) trust and (3) subsidiary managers' willingness to execute centrally made decisions (whether such execution was compulsory or voluntary). This beneficial effect of procedural justice on bounded reliability was systematically larger for disfavoured subsidiaries than for subsidiaries that had experienced favourable resource allocation decisions, except for the voluntary execution parameter (see Figure 5.2). (With a higher level of procedural justice, it does not matter whether subsidiaries are winners or losers: in both cases, managers will try to go beyond the call of duty to implement voluntary strategic decisions.)

Anant Neghandi, Golpira Eshghi and ***Edith Yuen*** also wrote an article that complements Bartlett and Ghoshal's study. This complementary perspective, on the strengths and weaknesses of Japanese MNE subsidiary management, was published in *CMR* in 1985, thus actually predating Bartlett and Ghoshal's article.[9]

Neghandi and his colleagues note the widely recognized Japanese MNE superiority in engineering and production management in many industries, as well as these firms' ability to develop excellent relationships with host country governments. The authors point out, however, that Japanese MNEs nonetheless have highly problematic subsidiary management practices. Many admirers of the

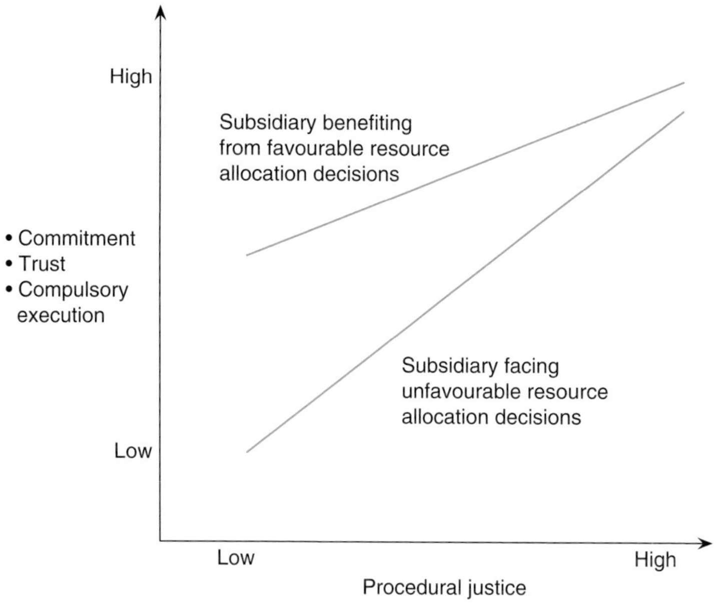

Figure 5.2
The impact of procedural justice

Japanese management system trumpet the benefits of approaches such as seniority-based human resources management, lifetime employment and consensus-based decision making. However, this does not imply that their MNE subsidiary management is particularly effective. Neghandi and his colleagues identify five main problems found in many Japanese MNEs:

1. Japanese MNEs adopt a centralized, autocratic approach vis-à-vis their foreign subsidiaries, without much evidence of a consensus-based management style. In many cases, foreign subsidiaries are simply informed after the fact about important decisions made by senior management at corporate headquarters.
2. Japanese MNEs have relatively little confidence in the ability of non-Japanese managers in host countries.
3. Relationships of trust established between corporate headquarters and foreign subsidiaries are usually confined to a few key managers in these subsidiaries.
4. Japanese staffing policies are often ethnocentric. Compared with their Japanese counterparts, non-Japanese managers frequently face unofficial ceilings on promotion, as well as different career paths, job security, training options and fringe benefits.
5. Japanese MNEs, though particularly sensitive to host government regulation and the rule of law in general, try to avoid unions and frequently discriminate against women and minorities.

The main conclusion of the analysis is that strong FSAs in technology, production and government relations do not imply a strong FSA in managing a foreign subsidiary network. In fact, tendencies towards homogenization and centralization prevent many Japanese MNEs from developing strategic leader subsidiaries, especially in the realm of upstream activities such as R&D.

Admittedly, Japanese subsidiary network management has become substantially less ethnocentric in the decades since the publication of the paper by Neghandi and his colleagues, largely as the result of more attention devoted to developing location-bound FSAs in host countries. However, decision making on critical strategic issues, especially at the upstream end of the value chain, has often remained centralized in Japan, with little room for bottom-up initiatives from foreign subsidiaries.

In their *HBR* article, Bartlett and Ghoshal caution against homogenization and centralization and provide a model that helps senior corporate managers differentiate among their subsidiaries. The authors thereby provide a useful perspective on FSA development, particularly by noting the dispersed nature of FSA development and the roles of both host country location advantages and specialized subsidiary resources in this process (see Figure 5.3). In Figure 5.3, the size of each subsidiary's base of location advantages, location-bound FSAs and internationally transferable FSAs is different, which determines the subsidiary's type in the typology. Bartlett and Ghoshal suggest that firms need to move beyond the conventional **centralized exporter**, **international projector** and **multi-centred MNE** models (interestingly, they neglect the very existence of the **international coordinator** model). With the first two approaches, internationally transferable FSAs are developed in the home country and subsequently diffused to foreign markets, either embodied in exported goods (**centralized exporters**) or as intermediate goods, typically technological and marketing know-how (**international projectors**). This reflects Pattern I in this book's framework, as shown in Figure 5.4. The authors also reject the pure **multi-centred MNE** approach, with its exclusive focus on Pattern IV – location-bound FSAs developed by individual foreign subsidiaries for their particular host country markets.

Instead, Bartlett and Ghoshal advocate a mix of FSA development processes, including Patterns I and IV, but with an additional focus on Pattern III, whereby internationally transferable FSAs are recombined with a location-bound component. Bartlett and Ghoshal also draw attention to a rather narrow version of Pattern VI, whereby some subsidiaries – especially strategic leader subsidiaries – are given a mandate to contribute to developing new, internationally transferable FSAs. This remains a narrow version of Pattern VI, however, because for Bartlett and Ghoshal even the strategic leader subsidiaries are not supposed to develop truly autonomous initiatives outside the realm of the MNE's 'dominant logic' (i.e., the prevailing mindset in the company

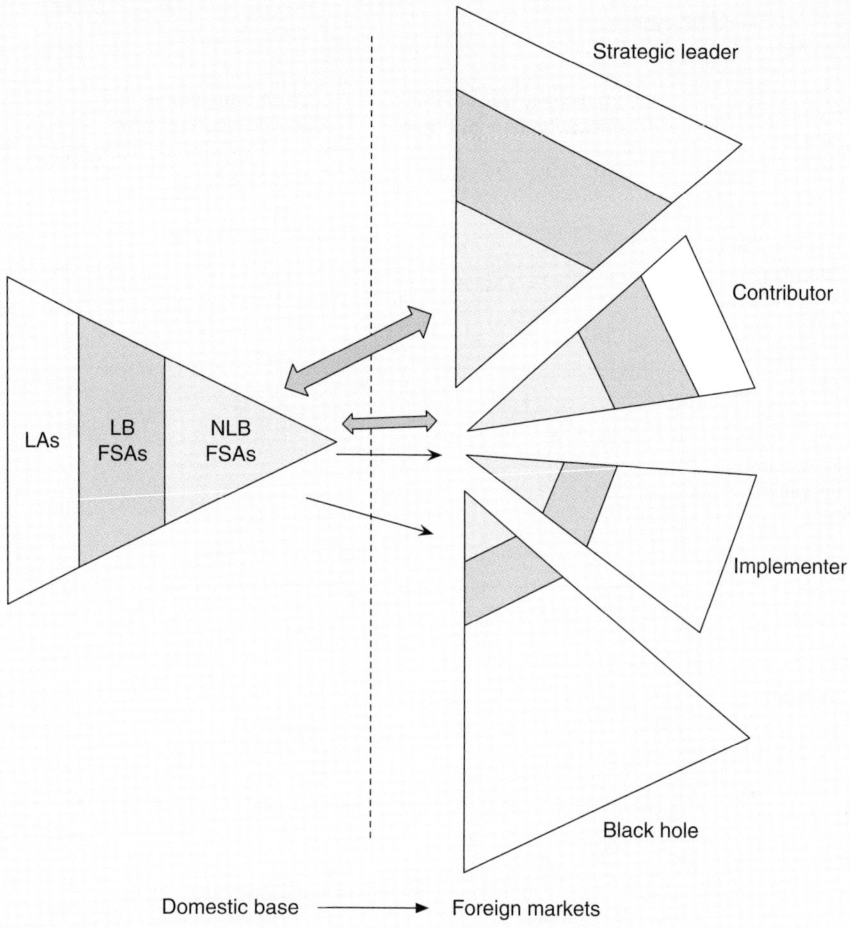

Figure 5.3
MNE resource
base – subsidiaries
as driving factor

Strategic leader

Contributor

LAs | LB FSAs | NLB FSAs

Implementer

Black hole

Domestic base ⟶ Foreign markets

Each type of subsidiary builds upon a different configuration and level of LAs, LB FSAs and NLB FSAs, as reflected by the different sizes of the segments in each triangle. The double-headed arrows reflect cases where the flow of NLB FSAs is two-way. Here, subsidiaries can play a key role in driving international FSA transfers (which could also occur between subsidiaries).

regarding the core businesses the firm should compete in and the required resource allocation processes to support those businesses). Resource recombination roles are still allocated by corporate headquarters and do not result from subsidiary initiatives.

In general, Bartlett and Ghoshal's work has four main limitations.[10]

First, senior managers at corporate headquarters need to recognize that good ideas can come from anywhere. In line with the observation above – that their version of Pattern VI is too narrow – Bartlett and Ghoshal assume that subsidiary roles and resources should be simply allocated to individual subsidiaries, as a function of the host market attractiveness/importance and the specialized

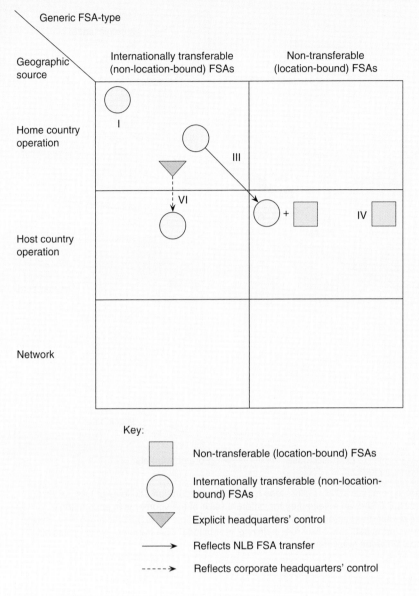

Figure 5.4
Bartlett and
Ghoshal's perspective
on FSA development
in MNEs

resources held by the subsidiary. In reality, however, valuable subsidiary initiatives often arise in spite of a particular, narrow charter given to a subsidiary. The key challenge for senior management at corporate headquarters is usually not to classify subsidiaries into four categories, but rather to craft a set of routines allowing valuable initiatives to arise from the bottom up and to provide support for such initiatives. Unfortunately, senior management at corporate headquarters faces substantial bounded rationality problems, in terms of its limited ability to assess appropriately new ideas and projects, especially if they come from the periphery, i.e., subsidiaries that have neither 'strategic leader' nor 'contributor' status. Thus, the problem is not simply to select those subsidiaries that should or should not contribute to FSA development. The challenge is to identify and then act on what constitutes potentially valuable knowledge, irrespective of its origin. Fortunately, several best practices have been identified to increase the likelihood that such subsidiary initiatives will contribute to FSA development.[11] These include the following mechanisms:

1. **Giving seed money to new initiatives**. Here, MNEs need to find a balance between focusing on short-term profitability expectations and allowing subsidiary managers the flexibility to pursue local new initiatives.

2. **Formally requesting proposals** (including proposals from the periphery) for projects that corporate headquarters wants to see implemented. Here, subsidiaries compete for funding through a process similar to the selection of arm's length, outside service providers.

3. **Using subsidiaries as incubators**. Here, subsidiaries are allowed to develop new products or services outside of the direct observation and control by corporate headquarters or by the senior management of core businesses. The lack of visibility keeps new initiatives safe from the so-called 'corporate immune system' (the set of forces that come into play inside the firm when new initiatives are perceived as threatening the company's prevailing dominant logic). The corporate immune system is valuable because senior management in a diversified firm can effectively manage only a limited number of distinct businesses at any given time. However, the corporate immune system can also destroy potentially valuable future businesses if the businesses are not protected from it in their early stages of development.

4. **Creating internal subsidiary networks** as the organizational centrepiece of the MNE's recombination capabilities. MNEs continually need to build formal and informal networks across foreign units. These networks are crucial for cross-pollinating ideas and providing a wider scope of connections from which innovators at the periphery can draw support. Such networking can be stimulated through multiple short-term overseas assignments and the use of idea brokers. Idea brokers are individuals who link innovators with the people who allocate resources (in this context, 'resources' include everything that is required to implement a subsidiary initiative – typically, financial or organizational support).

Second, Bartlett and Ghoshal's simple divisions into 'low' and 'high' are insufficiently fine-grained. They correctly recognize that the appropriate subsidiary role depends on both the strategic importance of the local market and the subsidiary competencies, but they fail to take that realization far enough. These variables should be measured as matters of degree, not just placed into the categories 'low' or 'high'. For example, if the local market has *extremely* high labour costs and taxes (suggesting very low strategic importance on the input side), then even if the subsidiary's competencies are high, senior management must ask whether the subsidiary's competencies are high *enough* to justify a role of 'contributor' (versus being closed down, moved, integrated or sold).

Third, another limitation of the Bartlett and Ghoshal typology is that it mixes the importance of host country environments as input markets versus output markets; this crucial difference often leads to very different resource recombination challenges.[12] It is no coincidence that the examples provided in the *HBR* article (EMI and Procter & Gamble) address primarily the output market. Little attention is devoted to the input market – for example, the local environment for specialized labour or R&D knowledge. When an MNE specifically wants to access foreign input markets, the subsidiary must play a different role: it contributes resources and capabilities at the upstream end (e.g., labour, technology, sourcing). When assessing a subsidiary's role, it is thus important to investigate the strategic importance of the local environment at both the input market and final products market side, as well as the subsidiary's capabilities at the upstream and downstream ends, with actual manufacturing activities potentially linked to either end. The strategic motivation/purpose of any FDI decision that leads to the creation or expansion of a subsidiary usually focuses on either the input or the output market in any given country, and either the upstream or downstream FSAs of the subsidiary. Senior managers need to recognize that many subsidiary roles will be defined primarily by the host country's input market rather than its output market, and by upstream FSAs rather than downstream ones. The Bartlett and Ghoshal model, shown in Figure 5.1, must thus be unbundled, as shown in Figure 5.5. Note that this creates a separate, previously overlooked Figure 5.5A, which will now be discussed quadrant by quadrant.

Figure 5.5
Unbundling
subsidiary roles in
Bartlett and Ghoshal
(1986)

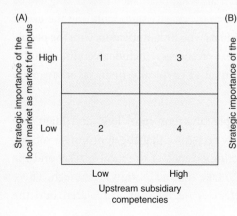

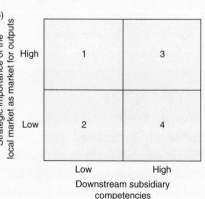

Quadrant 1 of Figure 5.5A contains subsidiaries with weak back-end competencies in a strategically important input market. Examples include subsidiaries unable to benefit fully from low-cost services in Eastern Europe or China because of poor relational networks, as well as subsidiaries that cannot acquire important technological expertise in key triad markets such as the US. One example is the European semiconductor manufacturer SGS-Thomson (which changed its name to STMicroelectronics in 1998) when it opened its Shenzhen factory, its first one in China, in 1996.[13] The lower salaries at this plant compared to the salaries received by the workers when they were trained in Malaysia led to a strike, which embarrassed the local government. To settle the strike, the plant eventually had to agree to house and feed its 600 workers, as well as raise its salaries. Expecting to benefit from lower wages, SGS-Thomson instead found that "the unit cost for chips out of the Shenzhen plant was about 10% higher than the cost at its Malaysian counterpart"[14] even though the costs arguably should have been much less (in nearby Guangdong province, costs were 40 per cent less than in Malaysia).[15] This is an example of a firm-level failure to benefit from a generally available input side location advantage (low wages) in a host country (China) due to a poor upstream recombination competence (poor management of local relational networks).

A subsidiary will also be in quadrant 1 of Figure 5.5A if weak upstream competencies preclude it from acquiring valuable knowledge in strategically important locations. For example, in the 1980s, the Swiss pharmaceutical giant Roche had poor success in biotech in the US, even though it operated biotech labs in New Jersey.[16] Thus, Roche's US operations in the 1980s were located in quadrant 1 of Figure 5.5A, characterized by weak upstream capabilities in the biotech industry's lead country.[17] (Incidentally, Roche's weak position in biotech in the US led it to purchase, in 1990, a major share in Genentech, the leading US biotech firm. Roche decided that, given its relative upstream weakness, acquiring US biotech firms was "the cheapest way . . . to catch up".[18])

Quadrant 2 of Figure 5.5A describes subsidiaries operating in input markets viewed as relatively unimportant to MNE competitiveness, and where the subsidiaries' upstream competencies are too weak to compensate for such deficiencies. One example is UK-based HSBC Banking Group's logistics, technology support and data centres in Great Britain. Despite Great Britain's strategic importance as an output market, it is strategically unimportant as an input market in these areas. When HSBC transferred these functions to India and mainland China, it reduced its overall service costs and improved the competitiveness of these back-end activities.

Quadrant 3 is the most desirable quadrant in Figure 5.5A. This position is achieved by finding input markets that contribute substantially to competitive advantage and then establishing (or acquiring) subsidiaries with strong upstream

FSAs there. Many manufacturing subsidiaries in low-cost countries such as China and India are located in this quadrant, but this quadrant also includes R&D centres in the most highly developed input markets, such as Silicon Valley for technological knowledge. For instance, as noted earlier, Logitech – the world's largest mouse manufacturer – closed its factories in Ireland and the US, consolidating manufacturing facilities in its Suzhou plant in China in 1994.[19] This showed both the confidence of the firm in the competencies of the Suzhou plant and the strategic importance of China as an input market. In recent years, products from this plant contributed to half of its global sales, and Logitech planned to expand its manufacturing base in China by launching a new factory in 2005.[20]

In contrast, many MNE activities in North America are located in quadrant 4 of Figure 5.5A: the input market does not contribute to MNE competitiveness, but the local upstream subsidiary compensates for this deficiency through highly efficient sourcing and manufacturing. This quadrant contains, for example, the major Japanese automakers' North American subsidiaries. Although North America does not complement these firms' FSAs with location advantages at the input side, the subsidiaries have still been able to stay competitive through the (partial) transfer to the US of the Japanese keiretsu-style management and modular production methods, as well as the use of transplanted Japanese suppliers.[21]

This last example also illustrates the importance of analysing subsidiary roles using both Figure 5.5A and Figure 5.5B. The Japanese subsidiaries in the US span both Figure 5.5A and Figure 5.5B, in terms of value activities performed, but on the input side – Figure 5.5A – they are largely 'contributors' (quadrant 4) rather than 'strategic leaders' (quadrant 3). They benefit from the transfer of upstream competencies developed in Japan, and may further develop those, but they operate in an environment with the relative location disadvantage of sourcing in the US rather than Japan. However, on the output side – Figure 5.5B – they are strategic leaders (quadrant 3). It is critically important to produce and market automobiles in the huge US market, and to be an insider there, because outsiders face the danger of rising trade protectionism. Thus, in this case a strategically unimportant input market is combined with a strategically important output market, and the subsidiary has both strong upstream and downstream FSAs. The point is that subsidiaries must be evaluated using both Figure 5.5A and Figure 5.5B. If a subsidiary's input and output side cannot be completely separated – as they cannot in the case of sourcing, building and selling automobiles in the US – then managers should take into account the results of both evaluations when assigning a role to that subsidiary.

Fourth, Bartlett and Ghoshal do not address fully the issue of subsidiary role dynamics. In reality, the situation is much more complicated than central headquarters simply deciding which role to assign which subsidiary. Subsidiaries often compete among themselves for roles, and central headquarters can also choose to restructure or reorganize, perhaps eliminating a subsidiary completely.

To illustrate some complexities of subsidiary role dynamics, let us examine the consequences of regional integration, one of the key drivers of external change throughout the triad markets of Europe, North America and Asia. Two variables stand out in determining the impact of regional integration on subsidiary role dynamics: the **extent of regional unification** of national environments as a market for inputs/outputs, and the **commodification of upstream/ downstream subsidiary competencies** in terms of resource recombination. The first variable refers to the overlap among the markets served by national subsidiaries. The second variable reflects the extent to which subsidiaries have similar strengths. High levels of regional market unification and competence commodification – see Figure 5.6 – both increase the internal competition among subsidiaries and provoke parent-driven rationalization programmes.

Let us look at a concrete example. In order to serve foreign markets, **international projectors** have historically engaged in market seeking FDI in each individual host country so as to overcome tariffs, with each national subsidiary typically designed as a replica of the parent firm. As a result, subsidiaries in different countries tended to have similar internal resources. However, once regional integration occurs, the subsidiaries find themselves in either quadrant 1 or quadrant 3 of Figure 5.6, depending on whether the subsidiaries have different strengths (i.e., depending on whether commodification is low or high). In either case, the dispersion of similar resources across different countries in the same region becomes unnecessary, and reduces the potential to earn scale economies. Typically, central headquarters then implements a rationalization programme, closing some subsidiaries and giving others extended charters, based on their respective strengths.

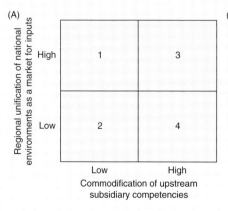

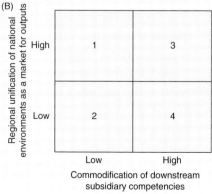

Figure 5.6

The impact of regional integration on subsidiary dynamics

As discussed earlier, it is important to decouple Bartlett and Ghoshal's framework into upstream and downstream competencies. For example, sales of branded consumer goods usually require proximity to the customer, because there are almost invariably differences among nations' consumers. In this industry, therefore, even if regional unification is high on the input side, it is likely to be low on the output side. The MNE that recognizes this difference between its input and output markets is unlikely to rationalize its operations.

In any case, a regionally unified market resulting from regional integration becomes a new geographic level relevant to multinational strategic management, in addition to the global and national levels.

As a final note, the essence of the Bartlett and Ghoshal's message remains pertinent. They state: "an international company enjoys a big advantage over a national one: it is exposed to a wider and more diverse range of environmental stimuli" in terms of customer preferences, competitive behaviours, government demands and sources of technological innovation and learning.[22] Their view contrasts sharply with Ghemawat's in Chapter 4. Ghemawat cautioned against rapid international diversification, since MNEs with a broad geographic scope face various distance barriers as compared to domestic firms and MNEs with a more narrow geographic scope. Ghemawat emphasized that the MNE's strengths in recombination should not be overestimated. Bartlett and Ghoshal, however, contend that an MNE can improve its FSA bundles by tapping into – and leveraging – the competencies found in its subsidiary network. In other words, an international presence and international experience through foreign subsidiaries may strengthen the MNE's recombination capability, if MNE senior management makes proper use of its internal network.

Five management takeaways

1. Assess the current organizational structure and decision-making processes in your firm and reflect on the different roles performed by your subsidiaries.
2. Classify your portfolio of subsidiaries as a function of the strategic importance of each market where they operate and the resource base they command.
3. Respect the five components of due process in each corporate head office decision that will affect subsidiaries.
4. Review the main problems faced by many Japanese MNEs and learn from their mistakes.
5. Analyse best practices (inside your firm and in industry) for FSA development in subsidiaries and reflect on the key drivers of subsidiary roles and dynamics.

Case 5.1 Organizational transformation at Nestlé[23]

Swiss-based Nestlé S. A., the world's largest food manufacturing company, employs around 281,000 people and has factories or operations in practically every country in the world.[24] However, Nestlé does not focus simply on building and exploiting global brands. As noted by former CEO Peter Brabeck-Letmathe, "There is a trade-off between efficiency and effectiveness in global brands . . . Operational efficiency comes from our strategic umbrella brands. But we believe there is no such thing as a global consumer, especially in a sector as psychologically and culturally loaded as food."[25] Although Nestlé does not believe in homogeneous consumer preferences, it has started to integrate its businesses at the regional level and even the global level – it has become much more than a holder of a portfolio of national units.

The inherited unique features at Nestlé

During his tenure as CEO from 1997 to 2008, Peter Brabeck-Letmathe as well as his predecessor Helmut Maucher, identified two unique features at Nestlé that should not change: first, the commitment to decentralization to cater to local tastes, and second, the minor role of information technology in everyday operations, relative to the importance of its employees, brands and products. At that time, Nestlé operated more like a holding company, with country-by-country responsibility for many functions.

Such an organization certainly helped Nestlé on the marketing side. Local managers could change the product taste, formulation and packaging according to local preferences. For example, Nescafé, Nestlé's instant coffee brand, had 200 different variants: in Russia, Nescafé was very thick, strong and sweet, totally different from the bitter flavour in Western Europe. In Britain, Kit Kat consisted of chocolate and wafers, but in Japan, Kit Kat had a lemon cheesecake flavour.[26]

However, such a decentralized organization leads to efficiency losses. Until the mid 1990s, 42 Nestlé factories located in the US still purchased their raw materials separately. As a result, a single supplier charged different Nestlé factories more than 20 different prices for vanilla. Moreover, the downplaying of information communication technology (ICT) aggravated the inefficiencies. For example, even though senior managers at Nestlé USA knew about the existence of different prices for vanilla, they had difficulty finding out which factories were over-charged, as each factory used a different purchasing code for vanilla.

Consolidating the business

As Nestlé expanded, competitive environments forced it to become more efficient. In spite of its status as the largest food manufacturing company in the world, its profit margins were lower than those of its main competitors, such as Unilever, Heinz and Danone. Starting in the late 1990s, Nestlé embarked upon a fundamental transformation of its business organization.

It shifted away from its longstanding geographic/functional focus to incorporate some product-oriented organization. The geographic focus still dominates, however.

A decentralized front end (markets and businesses)

Nestlé currently operates its downstream activities with three geographic zones and eight strategic business units (SBUs). Zone organizations refer to the major regions – Zone Europe, Zone Americas and Zone Asia, Oceania and Africa, with zone executive officers responsible for market/region business targets. The eight SBUs (Beverages; Milk products, nutrition and ice cream; Prepared dishes and cooking aids; Chocolate, confectionery and biscuits; PetCare; Pharmaceutical products; Water; and Nestle nutrition)[27] develop business strategies for selected market clusters, accelerate innovation and renewal, and introduce 'brand boards' to develop strategic brands.

To achieve focus in its branding, Nestlé operates with six umbrella brands: Nestlé, Purina pet foods, Maggi, Nescafé, Nestea and Buitoni. However, strong local brands are still kept, such as the Rossiya confectionery range in Russia and the Rolo brand in the UK. Moreover, the regional market head is responsible for the SBUs, and the country market head is responsible for the market/country performance. The country market head also functions as a business portfolio strategist in a given market. In this way, the former decentralized structure is still kept alive for many downstream activities.

In some countries, including many African countries, Nestlé still remains completely decentralized, with powerful country managers responsible for the operations in their host countries, as local features remain particularly idiosyncratic there.

A regionally or globally run backline (factories and shared services)

To be cost-efficient, Nestlé has streamlined its upstream/back office activities by integrating the management of its factories into regional and even global management units. For example, in four and a half years between the end of 1998 and mid 2003, Zone Europe closed or sold 68 factories, reducing the number of factories in Europe from 179 to 140 even after acquiring 29 factories during the period. The reduction in number of plants reflects the rationalization efforts at the back end of the value chain, in order to gain scale economies and better international coordination. Similarly, in New Zealand, Australia and the Pacific Islands, Nestlé integrated the functions of accounting, administration, sales and payroll.

Moreover, Regionally Shared Service Centres have also been established, to provide back-office functions for each region. For example, in the Americas Zone, Nestlé Business Services provides the purchasing, HR/payroll, retail sales execution, disbursement, general accounting, operations accounting, ICT maintenance, transportation, tax and legal services for all the operating companies in the region.

Finally, the three geographic units have started to implement regional ICT systems and common standards. For example, the three geographic units had been using different inventory, accounting and planning software; in 2001, Nestlé introduced a single company-wide resource planning system called 'GLOBE' (Global Business Excellence), in order to standardize company-wide ICT systems and to leverage scale economies in its back-end activities.

Results of the GLOBE project

The initiation of the GLOBE project in 2001 reflected a strong movement by Nestlé to improve on its apparent inefficiencies in operational and financial practices. Implementing a company wide SAP system required tremendous efforts, and though senior management initially faced resistance from employees, the system promised significant benefits.

By 2010, the GLOBE project had been implemented in over 90 countries, providing Nestlé with global 'data standards', a common IT platform, and improved operations.[28] Implementing data standards allowed Nestlé to consolidate data from all of its subsidiaries across each geographic region and to transfer information readily between counterparts in transactions. Strategic decisions could be made faster and with greater confidence as information could be gathered in minutes instead of days. The common IT platform allowed Nestlé to reduce the volume of data used by 65 per cent from 2006 to 2010.[29] In addition, Nestlé was able to leverage better its scale by consolidating purchases with suppliers across its multiple product lines, saving billions of dollars in the process[30].

Ultimately, the GLOBE project has helped Nestlé to identify areas within its value chain where inefficiencies were present. This organizational re-engineering at Nestlé has allowed the firm to become better positioned for future acquisitions, as part of its international expansion strategy.[31]

Grouping markets into clusters

Inside each SBU, Nestlé groups its markets into clusters, not by region but by other similarities, such as consumer preferences or the stage of market development. For example, in its coffee business, Nestlé has defined two clusters, according to consumers' coffee drinking habits. The first cluster, where soluble coffee is the norm, includes the UK, Japan and Australia; the second cluster consists of the USA, Germany, France and Spain, which are only emerging markets for soluble coffee. In those markets, roast and ground coffee are dominant. Similarly, Nestlé groups its confectionery markets into four different clusters based on consumers' eating habits.

Managers within the same cluster can develop strategies together, share best practices and innovations, and achieve synergies in manufacturing and some marketing services. Managers also transfer knowledge across clusters, although that is less common.

Moving away from the independent subsidiary model

Nestlé is transferring knowledge more between subsidiaries. For example, Nestlé Purina PetCare was the market leader in the US in 2004, with a 31 per cent market share of total pet food sales. However, in Europe, Nestlé Purina PetCare had only 24.5 per cent in 2004, well behind the 40.1 per cent market share of Mars, the market leader. To catch up, managers started to apply in Europe several concepts that had worked in the US, such as the 'small serving' concept. In the mid 1990s, US consumers still bought primarily multi-serve cans for their pets. In recent years, however, small serving cans (e.g., cans containing only a single serving) gradually became more popular. Accordingly, Nestlé Purina PetCare North America developed a very profitable small serving can called Fancy Feast. Nestlé Purina PetCare then introduced small serving cans in Europe, which helped it to narrow its market share gap with Mars.

In Europe, managerial attention in the past had usually not focused on the entire region, but unfortunately on only some of the national markets, thereby missing significant business opportunities. For example, the efforts of European PetCare focused on France and the UK, the top two markets in Europe, but not Germany, the number three European market. In Germany, Nestlé PetCare employed a specialist strategy by focusing on premium, high-end products. As explained by John Harris, the head of European PetCare, "We as a company have never been strong in Germany, we've never focused a lot of resources in Germany and it's not in our strategic plan to become a dominant player in Germany. In Germany we want to be a player but we are not willing to invest what is required to be the number one player."[32]

In 2004 and 2005, CEO Peter Brabeck-Letmathe stressed the need for substantial changes in organizational functioning at Nestlé, including a stronger business focus by delegating profit responsibilities to business executive managers or divisional managers and establishing regionally/globally shared services (see Figure 5.7 for the organizational structure in 2012).[33]

'Nestlé on the Move'

In 2002, after Nestlé started consolidating its decentralized management processes, it found that its organizational functioning included numerous dysfunctional incentives and systems. It placed value on seniority rather than skill; created loyalty to direct managers rather than to the organization; and fostered internal competition rather than value creation.[34]

Figure 5.7
Organizational structure at Nestlé in 2012

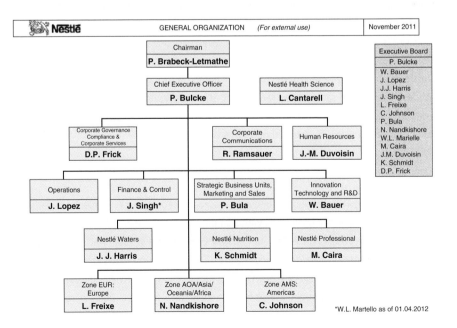

Nestlé realized that if it wanted to properly execute its long-term strategy it would need to change its modus operandi. Over a period of several years, a change process called 'Nestlé on the Move', shifted the company from a hierarchical structure to a network structure consisting of network 'hubs' (see Figure 5.8).[35] This horizontal approach allowed the company to become more flexible by making departments more autonomous when trying to meet business targets. Hierarchical levels within factories, for example, were decreased from an average of five to seven levels to just three or four.[36] The decrease in vertical levels reduced the probability of promotion; however Nestlé decided to place greater emphasis on moving employees across different regions and functions.

Nestlé's strategic direction also evolved to focus more on becoming a leader in nutrition, health and wellness. In 2007, the company announced that the role of CEO and Chairman would be separated. Previously held by Peter Brabeck-Letmathe, Paul Bulcke accepted the role of CEO, while Brabeck-Letmathe continued his role as Chairman. Paul Bulcke had achieved great success as head of Zone Americas and his younger age provided reassurance that Nestlé would be forward looking, building upon his strategic leadership.[37]

Moving forward

Nestlé's renewed control over its multinational network has led to significant benefits. However; Nestlé continues to struggle in terms of net income margins, despite having significantly higher gross income margins than those of its main competitor, namely Kraft. Nestlé still allows its international operations to command substantial decentralized power, in order to exploit optimally location advantages in host environments. In the future, Bulcke hopes that Nestlé can continue to look beyond national boundaries to best capitalize on its global presence.[38]

QUESTIONS:

1. What was Nestlé's initial organizational approach as an MNE (centralized exporter, international projector, international coordinator or multi-centred MNE)?
2. Has Nestlé transformed itself towards a less homogeneous, more multi-dimensional model? Can you identify certain Nestlé subsidiaries with specific roles – e.g., strategic leaders or contributors?
3. Has Nestlé been able to transfer knowledge from 'strategic leader' sub-sidiaries to other types of subsidiaries? Please identify an example in the case.
4. What is different between the subsidiary network discussed in this case and the model in the paper by Bartlett and Ghoshal?
5. Can you provide an update on Nestlé's international organizational approach, using materials available on the Web?

CASE

Case 5.2 Organizational transformation at the Tata Group[39]

The Tata Group is an Indian multinational corporation with headquarters in Mumbai, India, and counts 425,000+ employees.[40] In 2012, it was India's largest conglomerate with a share of 7.7 per cent of the total market capitalization of the Bombay Stock Exchange (BSE) and an operational presence in more than 85 countries.[41] In 2011, the total revenue of the entire group was US $83.3 billion, 58 per cent of which were generated abroad.

The Tata Group got its name from the firm's founder, Jamsedji Tata (1839–1904), who established the conglomerate in 1868. Since 1991, Ratan Naval (N.) Tata has acted as the Chairman of the Tata Group and has led the company in its fifth generation of family stewardship. At the end of 2012, Cirus Mistry took over the reins from Ratan N. Tata. In that year, the Tata Group consisted of 114 companies.[42] The high degree of diversification and internationalization as well as the complex ownership structure create a particular organizational setting, with each product unit commanding unique know-how and management skills.

The history of the Tata Group

In 1902, 44 years after the Tata Group's foundation, the firm acquired the Indian Hotels Company and built India's first luxury hotel, the Taj Mahal Palace & Tower. After the death of founder Jamsedji Tata, his son Dorab Tata became the chairman of the Tata Group and further promoted the group's diversification. Under his management, the group continued to expand its business and entered into a variety of sectors, including steel (1907), electricity (1910), education (1911), consumer goods (1917), and aviation (1932).[43] In 1907, the group opened its first international representative office in London, UK.

From 1932 to 1938, the only non-Tata chairman in the firm's history, Nowroji Saklatwala, directed the Tata Group. However, only after the appointment of Jehangir Ratanji Dadabhoy (J. R. D.) Tata in 1938, the group resumed its diversification strategy and expanded further in industries such as chemicals (1939), technology (1945), cosmetics (1952), marketing, engineering, and manufacturing (1954), tea (1962), and software services (1968). By increasing its scope of business activities, the Tata Group gained worldwide recognition and established its first representative office for North America and Latin America in New York, United States in 1945. In the same year, Tata Engineering and Locomotive Company (in 2003 renamed Tata Motors) was established to manufacture engineering and locomotive products. Later, in 1954, it further expanded to produce commercial vehicles. In 1968, based on internal needs the Tata Group set up Tata Consulting Services, India's first IT services company, which began to engage in external business in the 1970s. Under J. R. D. Tata's leadership, the Tata Group grew from only 13 companies in 1938 to 300 in 1991. Most of the subsidiaries and associated companies were managed independently and expanded into a variety of markets. The unstructured strategic development of Tata's affiliates created an overlap in businesses.

After J. R. D. Tata's resignation in 1991, the new chairman of the Tata Group, his nephew Ratan N. Tata, conducted an in-depth portfolio analysis of all the Tata businesses in order to increase the group's competitiveness and to streamline the businesses. In the ensuing restructuring process, Ratan N. Tata segmented the portfolio of businesses into seven industries, namely materials, engineering, energy, consumer goods, chemicals, services and information technology (IT) & communication.

Under Ratan N. Tata's leadership, the conglomerate accelerated its local and international expansion. For many years, the Tata Group's international activities focused on exports and the firm's international expansion was limited mainly to organic growth.[44] However, over time, the various industry groups broadened their operating platforms and began to source, produce and sell abroad. In recent years, the Tata Group has revisited further this approach by acquiring a substantial number of well-known companies outside of India. In line with this new internationalization approach, Tata purchased the British brand Tetley Tea in 2000. Today, this wholly owned subsidiary of Tata Global Beverages is the world's second largest manufacturer and distributor of tea after Unilever. In 2001, the group created the insurance company Tata-AIG, a partnership between the Tata Group and the American International Group (AIG). Three years later, Tata Motors acquired the Daewoo Commercial Vehicle Company, South Korea's second largest truck producer.[45] In 2007, Tata Steel expanded its production capacity and merged with the Anglo-Dutch steel manufacturer Corus Group, Europe's second largest steelmaker. The deal was the largest corporate acquisition by an Indian company ever.[46] In 2008, Ford and the Tata Motors agreed on the takeover of the two British car manufacturers Jaguar and Land Rover. In the same year, Tata Motors unveiled the Tata Nano, supposedly the world's cheapest car, which went on sale in 2009. Other major companies belonging to the Tata Group are Tata Steel, Tata Technologies, Tata Chemicals, Tata Power, Tata Communications and Tata Teleservices. The 31 publicly listed companies of the Tata Group have a combined market capitalization of about US $79.4 billion (as on June 21, 2012).[47]

Managing the business

Based on the historical background of the Tata Group, each operating company is responsible for its own international strategy forming "an integral part of its overall strategy, depending on the nature of the industry, opportunities available and competitive dynamics of the global stage".[48] The hierarchical functioning of companies within the Tata Group is driven by the ownership structure: "public philanthropic trusts endowed by the members of the Tata family" control the Tata Group.[49] These trusts hold 66 per cent of the equity capital of Tata Sons, "the holding company and promoter for the Group companies".[50] The two largest trusts are the Sir Dorabji Tata Trust and the Sir Ratan Tata Trust, which were both established from the estates of the founder of Tata Group.

In 1945, Tata Sons established Tata Industries serving as a managing entity for companies governed by Tata Sons. However, upon removing the management activities from Tata Industries, Tata Sons decided to make Tata Industries responsible for the group's expansion into emerging and high-tech businesses in the 1980s. Over time, the Tata Industries unit has become an independent entity with its own board of directors and is, next to Tata Sons, the second key holding company of the Tata Group. Today, Tata Industries consists of two operating units: Tata Strategic Management Group offers consulting services to Tata as well as non-Tata companies, while Tata Interactive Systems provides e-learning solutions for project management, design, etc. The main activities of Tata Industries have continued to focus on market expansion into novel technologies and on opportunities for new business ventures. Further, Tata Industries invests in Tata's operating affiliates to enhance growth and it secures control throughout the Tata Group by keeping at least a minority stake in a wide range of Tata companies.

The holding company Tata Sons also consists of two units, namely Tata Quality Management Services and Tata Financial Services. Both units give assistance to Tata companies in order to achieve business excellence and secure financial planning, respectively. Given that each company is managed as a stand-alone entity, Tata Group created the Group Corporate Center as Tata's main decision-making body. It reviews the growth of individual firms, and assesses possible further market entries and product diversification. Under Chairman Ratan N. Tata, this body has also provided guidance in terms of financial, legal, human resources and other operational policies, and it analyses the portfolio of the Tata Group across industries.

The rapid expansion under J. R. D. Tata was associated with a lack of corporate identity. In order to gain more control over its many affiliates and an improved ability to influence their operations, Chairman Ratan N. Tata increased Tata Sons' equity stake in all Tata companies from small minority stakes to a minimum of 26 per cent, thereby allowing (a) Tata Sons to exercise a veto right against potential takeovers and (b) the Group Corporate Center to oversee actively all business operations.[51] In the past, affiliates had automatic permission to use the Tata brand without compensating the group. However, Tata Sons owns the name 'Tata' as well as the Tata trademarks, and therefore has the right to authorize their use by Tata companies for their products and services. In the 1990s, Ratan N. Tata changed Tata's brand management so that all operating companies that make use of the Tata brand and trademarks have to pay a licensing fee.[52]

Figure 5.8 illustrates the holding structure of the Tata Group. The grey shaded region represents the Tata Group. All companies belonging to the Tata Group are under management of the Group Corporate Center and are supported by the holding companies Tata Sons and Tata Industries. The philanthropic trusts own 66 per cent of equity of Tata Sons, which in turn, jointly with Tata Industries, is a major shareholder in all Tata companies: e.g., Tata Sons has around 74 per cent in shares of Tata Consultancy Services[53]; Tata Sons and Tata Industries hold around 26 per cent and 3 per cent respectively of Tata Motors' equity[54] and Tata Sons owns around 29 per cent of Tata Steel's stocks.[55]

Tata Consultancy Services

As one example of a unit that has been characterized by rapid international expansion, Tata Consultancy Services (TCS) was established in 1968 as the result of internal demand for information related systems. In contrast to most other operating companies of the Tata

Group, TCS is a relatively young company in a fast-moving industry that rapidly expanded internationally and did not only rely on the domestic and export markets.

It was really twenty senior managers from various Tata companies who combined their forces to provide consulting services to Tata's businesses. Based on the increasing complexity of requests, TCS quickly expanded its consultancy business into information systems development (e.g., automation of the payroll and financial systems at Tata companies) and data services (e.g., data processing). Until 1990s, TCS had only limited competition in India, since its only rival, namely IBM, decided to exit the Indian market due to the 1977 regulations limiting foreign investors to a minority stake in Indian firms.

As the result of an agreement to become the exclusive marketing agent in India for Burroughs, a former leading US business equipment manufacturer that later merged with Sperry and resulted in Unisys, TCS would enter the US market in 1974 by exporting software services to the Detroit Police. In 1978, TCS refused an offer from Burroughs jointly to manufacture computers through a joint venture arrangement in India. Instead, TCS decided to focus on its own competences. Former Chief Executive Officer and later Vice Chairman of TCS, Mr. Subramaniam Ramadorai, explained: "When we gave up Burroughs, the pressure was on to build the business. Our strength was our line-of-business experience, our ability to learn quickly, and our confidence."[56]

As a result, in 1979, TCS' management established its first international representative office in New York, United States. From then on, TCS would not only build up its position in the US market, but, as its IT projects were related to a variety of new technologies, TCS would also gain access to the latest know-how across a variety of industries and rapidly enrich its employees' skills. After finishing a client's project, consultants were sent to India to share the acquired knowledge of new technologies with their colleagues and teach them. TCS called this process 'bootstrapping'.

With the introduction of software migration combining "an existing application that had 90 per cent of the functionality that the enterprise needed, and add[ing] the other 10 per cent after migration", TCS created a new, cost-efficient and less risky solution approach for US and European enterprises that had to upgrade their computer systems and transfer existing software from old to new servers.[57] After the first international migration project at a US bank consortium, TCS would further expand its international business, and its migration services quickly turned into a major source of TCS' international revenue.

In the late 1980s, the demand for domestic and international assignments began to change. While Indian companies asked for the automation of operations, software development and packaged application services, international clients demanded implementation of systems embodying the latest technologies and providing them a strategy edge. Despite the more promising outlook for revenues from abroad, TCS continued its activities on the domestic market. This strategy proved to be effective as local operations would regularly develop software packages that could then later be applied in international projects (e.g., the communications software 'C-Dot' was first introduced in the Indian market, but later used in communication projects abroad).

Driven by its domestic and especially its international successes, TCS aimed to strengthen its global footprint. With the Global Network Delivery Model allowing TCS "to seamlessly and uniformly deliver services to global customers from multiple global locations in India, China, Europe, North America and Latin America", TCS was able to establish global service standards.[58] In 2002, TCS established a global delivery centre in Uruguay, which became "one of the largest outsourcing operations in Latin America".[59] This centre has a leading role in TCS' operations in Latin America and interacts with global delivery centres in Argentina, Brazil, Chile, Columbia, Ecuador and Peru. TCS' investment decision to enter Uruguay resulted from generous government intervention: the TCS' affiliate was established in a new upscale technology park in a free trade zone, allowing operations at reasonable costs. Further, Uruguay offered strong government support in favour of the IT industry, a stable political and economic environment and highly skilled graduates.[60] Together with the TCS IT centres in Columbia and Argentina, Uruguay formed a cluster streamlining "internal processes, resulting in a synergy among the three companies that led to more efficient services of better quality".[61] Today, TCS operates three Uruguayan facilities specializing in business process outsourcing, IT project implementation and advanced IT services and offering its assistance to clients in the Americas and beyond. The implementation of the global network delivery model has created a competitive advantage. TCS is now able to send consultants to different parts of the world and can guarantee a structured business approach that is controlled by the head office and implemented in a disciplined fashion.

The above modus operandi, however, has created organizational challenges, as employees are constantly working on projects with changing geographic scopes: an average of 45 per cent of TCS' revenues is generated from projects conducted at client locations, 51 per cent is created at delivery centres in India (though much of this for foreign clients), and 4 per cent comes from global delivery centres.[62]

After 30 years of domestic and international organic growth, TCS made its first strategic purchase in 2001 when acquiring CMC (Computer Maintenance Corporation), an IT services, consulting and software provider, from New Delhi, India. In 2004, TCS bought three further Indian IT companies, namely Airline Financial Support Services India, Aviation Software Development Consultancy India, and Phoenix Global Solutions. In 2005, TCS completed its first international takeover with Sydney-based Financial Network Services. Thanks to this buyout, TCS gained knowledge about IT solutions and services at international financial institutions, secured access to a valuable global customer base and strengthened its position in the profitable banking, financial services and insurance sector.

In the same year, TCS and Pearl, a UK insurance company, agreed to a 'structured deal' that created a new subsidiary with TCS as the majority stakeholder. A further expansion in the financial services industry was the acquisition of Comicrom in late 2005. The Chile-based business process outsourcing company was focused on the banking and telecommunication sector, but was not capable of providing one-stop-shopping IT solutions. Here, combining resources from TCS' global delivery centers in Latin America and Comicrom created a powerful platform to serve this market.

In 2006, TCS absorbed Tata Infotech, a second IT company of the Tata Group, in order to create synergies and opportunities for cross-selling. Tata Infotech was specialized in the telecommunications and defence sectors and complemented TCS' capabilities in these areas. Still another acquisition was completed in 2008 when TCS acquired Citigroup's India-based Citigroup Global

Services, a business processing outsourcing company. Chief operating officer and executive director Natarajan Chandrasekaran outlined the synergies as follows: "This acquisition gives us the ability to offer an end-to-end, domain-led third-party solution for business operations to our large financial services clients. We will also work to create platforms for the future and integrate our strong domain expertise in operations along with our suite of products for the financial services sector."[63]

As of March 31, 2012, TCS controlled a total of 183 offices in 43 countries and 117 delivery centres in 21 countries.[64] In the financial year 2011–12, TCS derived 91 per cent of its US $10.17 billion in revenues from abroad, mainly from the Americas and Europe with 56 per cent and 25 per cent respectively.[65] With a headcount of 238,000+ employees, the company is organized in a way to combine technical (project-related) and location-specific expertise. *First* are the geographic units: (1) North America, UK and Europe, (2) Latin America, and (3) India, Asia-Pacific, Middle East and Africa. *Second* are the industry service units, specialized in: (1) banking and financial services, (2) insurance and healthcare, (3) telecom, media and hi-tech, (4) life sciences, energy, resources & utilities and manufacturing, (5) retail & consumer packaged goods and travel & hospitality. *Third* are the service units providing IT know-how about infrastructure services, enterprise solutions, assurance services, business process outsourcing etc. *Fourth* is the unit covering the corporate functions, namely marketing, R&D, finance, human resources, etc. Through this structure, chief financial officer and executive director of Tata Consultancy Services, Seturaman Mahalingam, aims to combine a global, industry-related approach to business and rely on a local network of highly skilled people: "Our business philosophy is based on our desire to make our customers feel that they are being serviced by a local organization."[66]

Corporate social responsibility at the Tata Group

As early as in 1912, the Tata Group integrated CSR in its working environment and implemented an eight-hour workday for employees, possibly being the first company worldwide to do so. In addition, in 1917, the Indian firm started to provide medical services and promoted, along with some other leading pioneers, the introduction of further social advantages for its employees such as pension funds, maternity aids and profit-sharing programmes.

Tata Sons receives around 66 per cent of Tata Group's profits. As an additional financial aid, the trusts receive 4 per cent of the operating income of each company belonging to the Tata Group and every generation of the Tata family passes a huge share of its inheritance on to the trusts. In addition to its function as a holding company, the main objective of Tata Sons is to improve social well being. This philanthropic approach helps to support a vast array of projects, to fund new initiatives and to finance charities in the areas of quality research, education and culture. Some of the organizations that have been established include the Tata Institute of Social Sciences offering undergraduate and postgraduate programmes in social work (e.g., rural development, health administration), the Tata Memorial Hospital specializing in cancer treatments and research, and the National Centre for the Performing Arts focusing on the performing and allied arts (e.g., it is the home of the Symphony Orchestra of India).

In addition to Tata's commitment to local philanthropy, the conglomerate is also actively engaged in international CSR initiatives. In 2010, Chairman Ratan N. Tata decided to donate US

$50 million to the Harvard Business School (HBS), the largest international donation in the school's history.[67] This gift is supposed to fund a new academic and residential building, the Tata Hall, for the executive education programs on campus in Boston, United States. Previously (in 1975), Ratan N. Tata attended one of the HBS advanced leadership programs and in 1995, he was honoured with the HBS's highest distinction, the Alumni Achievement Award.[68]

A more dramatic event led to the Tata Swach project, meaning 'clean' in Hindi. After the 2004 tsunami in the Indian Ocean, thousands of people lost their homes and did not have access to clean drinking water. Three Tata companies, namely Tata Consultancy Services, Titan Industries and Tata Chemicals joined forces and developed a compact, nanotechnology water purification device for use at home. With a capacity of 3 to 4 litres per hour, this water purifier enables families to filter their own drinking water as it removes "the minutest visible impurities in water".[69] The filters purify around 3,000 litres and hence last about one year for a family of five people. The device costs around US $21 and is therefore an affordable solution for families with no access to clean drinking water in their environment. A major plus of the Tata Swach is the fact that it does not rely on the use of electricity. Thanks to the product, Tata has helped to decrease the risk of infection of cholera, diarrhoea and other diseases. Mr Ashvini Hiran, Chief Operating Officer Consumer Products Business of Tata Chemicals, explained the driving forces behind this project: "Safe drinking water is a basic human right and Tata Swach combines technology, performance, design and convenience to serve this basic human right of millions of consumers. The company has made affordability an important part of its innovation efforts."[70] At present, the water purifier belongs to the product portfolio of Tata Chemicals. After focusing solely on the Indian market for a long time, Tata Chemicals studied the African continent for international sales of the Tata Swach. Additional enquiries from South America, China, South East Asia, etc. poured in and further stimulated Tata Chemicals' international activities. As Mr Sabaleel Nandy, head of the water purifier business at Tata Chemicals, explained: "International expansion needs to be carefully thought through. We will have to evolve an international model. We need to ramp up production considerably or set up a factory abroad."[71]

In addition, Tata Chemicals focuses on the business of LIFE – Living, Industrial and Farm Essentials. By covering niche markets and strongly investing in R&D capabilities, Tata Chemicals is attempting to strengthen its market position and to advance its knowledge in the emerging fields of nanotechnology and biotechnology.[72] Through a joint venture with Temasek Life Sciences Laboratory from Singapore, Tata Chemicals is trying to develop a special type of seedlings to produce bio fuel in India and at a later stage in other parts of the world.

Overall, most Tata companies invest heavily in R&D in local and international subsidiaries, as well as in strategic partnerships and joint ventures and promote sustainable solutions in a wide range of industries. A further example is the UK division of Tata Steel Research, Development and Technology that is involved in electrical steel making. Although modern electric arc furnaces at Tata Steel make use of recycled steel scrap, steel manufacturing has negative environmental effects to consider (e.g., from the use of cooling water, electricity generation, air released from production processes etc.). Therefore, the main focus of the research projects in Tata Steel's UK subsidiary in Port Talbot, is to design a more sustainable approach to steel making and to reduce related environmental harms.

False belief?

When studying Tata Group's CSR engagement, the image projected towards the outside world is that of one of the most visionary emerging multinational enterprises in the world. Tata companies pride themselves on avoiding 'dubious' businesses and of relying on honest deals. As Chairman Ratan N. Tatan explained: "You really have to take a view that you are above what, in the Indian context, is considered normal. If I had to pay a bribe to enter a particular business, I just wouldn't be able to live with myself. Today, the greatest strength we have is that we are known to be people who don't play dirty and rationalize our ethical lapses."[73]

However, Tata's history does include a number of less inspiring episodes. In the 1860s, Tata Group founder Jamsedji Tata established a private trading firm. He and his brother were opium traffickers and exchanged opium for tea, silks and pearls from China. The profits generated by Jamsedji Tata's family from the opium trade built the major share of the seed capital with which the Tata Group built several cotton mills in the province of Bengal, a leading producer of opium.

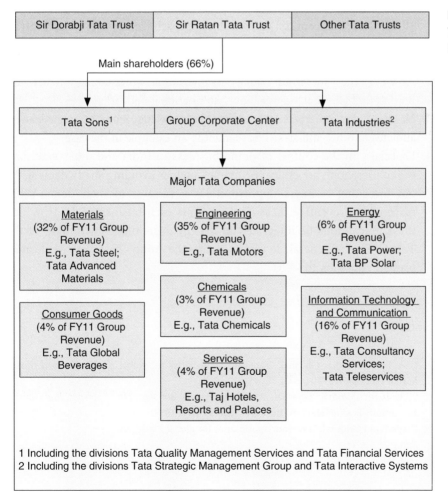

Figure 5.8
The Tata Group holding structure

With the launch of the Empress Mills in Nagpur, the Tatas began to prosper and as a result the Tata business empire could flourish.[74] This may appear somewhat at odds with founder Jamsedji Tata stating: "We do not claim to be more unselfish, more generous or more philanthropic than other people. But we think we started on sound and straightforward business principles, considering the interests of the shareholders our own, and the health and welfare of the employees, the sure foundation of our success."[75]

Despite the fact that opium trade was legal at that time in history, it somewhat contradicts the core values of the Tata Group, being integrity, understanding, excellence, unity and responsibility. After some negative publicity about the personal use of company funds among senior managers in the 1990s, Ratan N. Tata promoted the implementation of a written Code of Conduct. Today, this document comprises 25 clauses and "serves as the ethical road map for Tata employees and companies".[76]

QUESTIONS

1. What was the Tata Group's initial organizational approach at the beginning of the nineteenth century and did this approach change over time (centralized exporter, international projector, international coordinator or multi-centred MNE)? Please justify your answer.

2. How does the Tata Group manage its internal network, taking into account Bartlett and Ghoshal's views about multinational networks?

3. Has the Tata Group been able to transfer knowledge from "strategic leader" affiliates to other affiliates? Please identify an example in the case.

4. Especially in the context of doing business in India and other emerging economies, applying ethical principles such as avoiding shady deals without foregoing business opportunities, is easier said than done. What reasonable preventive measures can limit such business risk? How can these precautions be integrated in the organizational functioning of the Tata Group? In general, do you think that the group's past plays a role in its present approach to CSR?

Notes

1. C. A. Bartlett and S. Ghoshal, 'Tap your subsidiaries for global reach', *Harvard Business Review* 64 (1986), 87–94.
2. C. A. Bartlett and S. Ghoshal, *Managing Across Borders: The Transnational Solution*, 1st edition (Boston: Harvard Business School Press, 1989).
3. Bartlett and Ghoshal, 'Tap your subsidiaries for global reach', 88.
4. *Ibid.*
5. *Ibid*, 90.
6. *Ibid*, 89.

7. W. Chan Kim and Renée A. Mauborgne, 'Procedural justice, strategic decision making, and the knowledge economy', *Strategic Management Journal* 19 (1998), 323–38; W. Chan Kim and Renée A. Mauborgne, 'Implementing global strategies: the role of procedural justice', *Strategic Management Journal* 12 (1991), 125–43; W. Chan Kim and Renée A. Mauborgne, 'Effectively conceiving and executing multinationals' world wide strategies', *Journal of International Business Studies* (1993), 419–48; W. Chan Kim and Renée A. Mauborgne, 'Procedural justice, attitudes, and subsidiary top management compliance with multinational's corporate strategic decisions', *Academy of Management Journal* 36 (1993), 502–26; W. Chan Kim and Renée A. Mauborgne, 'Making global strategies work', *MIT Sloan Management Review* 34 (1993), 11–27; W. Chan Kim and Renée A. Mauborgne, 'A procedural justice model of strategic decision making: strategy content implications in the multinational', *Organization Science* 6 (1995), 44–61.
8. Kim and Mauborgne, 'Making global strategies work', 14.
9. Anant R. Neghandi, Golpira S. Eshghi and Edith C. Yuen, 'The management practices of Japanese subsidiaries overseas', *California Management Review* 27 (1985), 93–105.
10. Alan Rugman, Alain Verbeke and Wenlong Yuan, 'Re-conceptualizing the classification of subsidiary roles in multinational enterprises', *mimeo* (2006).
11. Julian Birkinshaw and Neil Hood, 'Unleash innovation in foreign subsidiaries', *Harvard Business Review* 79 (2001), 131–7.
12. A more extensive analysis can be found in Rugman, Verbeke and Yuan, 'Re-conceptualizing the classification of subsidiary roles'.
13. 'Chinese torture', *The Economist* 347 (1998), 59–61.
14. *Ibid*, 60.
15. *Ibid*, 61.
16. David J. Teece, 'Foreign investment and technological development in Silicon Valley', *California Management Review* 34 (1992), 91.
17. Christian Zeller, 'North Atlantic innovative relations of Swiss pharmaceuticals and the proximities with regional biotech arenas', *European Geography* 80 (2004), 83–111.
18. Teece, 'Foreign investment in Silicon Valley', 94.
19. J. M. O'Brien, 'Logitech grows up', *Marketing Computers* 15 (1995), 77–81.
20. 'Logitech expands mouse manufacturing facility', *China Daily* (2005).
21. Alan Rugman and Simon Collinson, 'The regional nature of the world's automotive sector', *European Management Journal* 22 (2004), 471–82.
22. Bartlett and Ghoshal, 'Tap your subsidiaries for global reach', 94.
23. Information from Nestlé company information and Carol Matlack, 'Nestlé is starting to slim down at last but can the world's No. 1 food colossus fatten up its profits as it slashes costs?', *Business Week* (2003), 56.
24. CNN, 'Global 500', (2011).
25. Alex Benady and Haig Simonian, 'Nestlé's new flavour of strategy: global selling: the world's largest food company has put marketing at the heart of its plans for future growth, says Alex Benady', *Financial Times* (2005), 13.
26. 'Daring, defying, to grow – Nestlé', *The Economist* 372 (2004), 64.
27. 'Very strong performance in 2006 first half – double-digit growth of sales, EBIT and net profit', *Nestlé press release*, www.nestle.com/Media_Center/Press_Releases/All+Press+Releases/2006 HallfYearResults. htm (23 August 2006).
28. '2010 Half year results roadshow transcript', *Nestlé press release*. www.nestle.com/Common/NestleDocuments/Documents/Library/Presentations/Sales_and_Results/2010_HYResults_Roadshow_Transcript.pdf (11 August 2010).

29. Deborah Ball, 'After buying binge, Nestlé goes on a diet; departing CEO slashes slow sellers, brands; "no" to low-carb Rolo', *Wall Street Journal* (23 July 2007). A.1.

30. Rudy Puryear, Bhanu Singh and Stephen Phillips, 'How to be everywhere at once', *Supply Chain Management Review* (1 May 2007). 11.

31. Deborah Ball, 'After buying binge, Nestlé goes on a diet; departing CEO slashes slow sellers, brands; "no" to low-carb Rolo', *Wall Street Journal* (23 July 2007). A.1.

32. Nestlé company information, 2006.

33. Peter Brabeck, 'Business focus and the organization', *Nestlé Investor Seminar*, www.ir.nestle.com/NR/rdonlyres/264B68C6-072A-46BE-9E60-69E22C82E0F1/0/PBL_presentation. pdf (15–16 June 2004).

34. Robert Hooijberg, 'Breaking out of the pyramid', *IMD International* (June 2007).

35. *Ibid.*

36. Robert Hooijberg, James G. Hunt, John Antonakis, Kimbery B. Boal, Nancy Lane Elsevier, 'Nestlé on the move', *Perspectives for Managers* 156 (April 2008).

37. 'Nestlé Board designated Paul Bulcke as future CEO', *Nestlé press release.* www.nestle.com/Media/PressReleases/Pages/AllPressRelease.aspx?PageId=171&PageName=AllArchivedPressReleases.aspx (20 September 2007).

38. Peter Grumbel/Vevey, 'Nestlé's quick', *Time Magazine* (14 November 2007).

39. This case was co-authored by Ms Jenny Hillemann and Professor Alain Verbeke.

40. Tata Group company information, 2012.

41. *Ibid.*

42. *Ibid.*

43. Tata Group, Company brochure 2012 (March 2012).

44. Tarun Khanna, Krishna G. Palepu and Richard J. Bullock, 'House of Tata: Acquiring a global footprint', *Harvard Business School* (2009), Case: 9–708–446.

45. Sanjay Singh, Meera Harish and Kulwant Singh, 'Tata Motors' integration of Daewoo Commercial Vehicle Company', Richard Ivey School of Business (4 December 2008)

46. Tata Group, Company brochure 2012 (March 2012).

47. Tata Group company information, 2012.

48. *Ibid.*

49. Tata Group, Company brochure 2012 (March 2012).

50. Wee Beng Geok and Ivy Buche, 'Tata Consultancy Services: A systems approach to human resource development', Nanyang Business School (30 March 2012)

51. Tarun Khanna, Krishna G. Palepu and Richard J. Bullock, 'House of Tata: Acquiring a global footprint'.

52. *Ibid.*

53. Tata Consultancy Services, Annual report FY 2011–2012, 2012.

54. Tata Motors, Annual report FY 2010–2011, 2011.

55. Tata Steel, Annual report FY 2010–2011, 2011.

56. Gary C. Mekikian and John D. Roberts, 'Tata Consultancy Services: Globalization of IT Services', *Stanford Graduate School of Business* (2009), Case: IB-79.

57. *Ibid.*

58. *Ibid.*

59. Pankay Ghemawat and Steven Altman, 'Tata Consultancy Services: Selling certainty', *Harvard Business Review* 2011, Case: PG0–004.

60. Tata Consultancy Services company information, 2012.

61. *Ibid.*

62. Tata Consultancy Services, Annual report FY 2011–2012, 2012.

63. Tata Consultancy Services company information 2008.
64. Tata Consultancy Services, Annual report FY 2011–2012, 2012.
65. *Ibid.*
66. Gary C. Mekikian and John D. Roberts, 'Tata Consultancy Services: Globalization of IT services'.
67. Harvard Business School, Harvard Business School receives $50 million gift from the Tata Trusts and Companies (14 October 2010).
68. *Ibid.*
69. Tata Swach company information, 2012.
70. Tata Group company information, 2012.
71. Tata Group company information, 2011.
72. Tata Swach company information, 2012.
73. Rohit Deshpande, 'Tata Consultancy Services', Harvard Business School (3 November 2009).
74. Mary L. Kienholz, *Opium Traders and their worlds – Volume Two* (2008), iUniverse, Bloomington, Indiana.
75. Tata Group company information, 2008.
76. Tata Group company information, 2012.

PART II

FUNCTIONAL
ISSUES

6

International innovation

Five learning objectives

1. To explain the reasons for the trend towards R&D decentralization and to describe the difference between 'home-base-exploiting' and 'home-base-augmenting' innovation sites inside the MNE.
2. To highlight the key stages in the development of foreign R&D units.
3. To explain the role of subsidiary initiatives in the innovation sphere and the functioning of the 'corporate immune system', geared towards destroying such initiatives.
4. To foster understanding on how to access another firm's knowledge base so as to create new upstream FSAs.
5. To examine the potential conflicts between host country research sites and the corporate office.

This chapter examines Kuemmerle's idea that many MNEs, particularly international projectors, are wisely decentralizing their R&D by building worldwide networks of R&D labs. He examines R&D labs in host countries, dividing them into two types: (1) home-base-exploiting sites, which primarily receive information from the central lab in the home country and adapt products to local demand, and (2) home-base-augmenting sites, which primarily access local knowledge and send information back to the central lab. Kuemmerle gives practical advice about how those two different roles imply different needs and requirements, including different location and management requirements. Kuemmerle strongly recommends that both types of labs should interact regularly with the firm's other R&D units. These ideas will be examined and then criticized using the framework presented in Chapter 1.

Significance

In his *HBR* article 'Building effective R&D capabilities abroad' **Walter Kuemmerle** shows that many MNEs are changing their strategic approach to R&D. In particular, **international projectors** are decentralizing their R&D: instead of keeping all their R&D activities in their home country, they are building international networks in which foreign R&D laboratories fulfil specific roles within the firm.[1]

There are two main reasons for this trend. First, many MNEs feel they need to be present in various knowledge and innovation clusters scattered around the world. Often, a host country presence is essential in order to monitor and absorb new developments – typically, complementary resources from foreign input providers such as competitors, host country universities and scientific communities. Second, given the commercial requirement of moving quickly from innovation to market, MNEs must integrate their R&D facilities more closely with host country manufacturing operations, so as to support complex production tasks. This often involves complementing existing, internationally transferable FSAs in the upstream, technological knowledge sphere with a set of location-bound FSAs in host countries.

Kuemmerle studied 32 MNEs in the pharmaceutical (13) and electronics (19) industries – two manufacturing sectors with substantial product innovation and a high technological R&D intensity. The MNEs' home countries/regions were the US (10), Japan (12) and Europe (10). The location of these firms' R&D labs initially reflected a triad-based, home region approach, with most of the fundamental innovation activity conducted in the home country. Kuemmerle analysed the development trajectories of these companies' international R&D networks, eventually involving 238 labs with nearly two-thirds (156) located in host countries.[2]

Kuemmerle observed the internationalization of the R&D function over time. Building upon the 'home base' concept developed by Michael Porter,[3] discussed in Chapter 3 of this book, Kuemmerle identified two distinct types of host country R&D facilities based on their primary strategic role inside the MNE: home-base-exploiting sites and home-base-augmenting sites.

Home-base-exploiting sites "support manufacturing facilities in foreign countries or . . . adapt standard products to the demand there". "[I]nformation flows *to* the foreign laboratory *from* the central lab at home".[4] In contrast, home-base-augmenting sites act as the firm's eyes and ears in host countries, and access knowledge from rivals and research institutions there. With these labs, information generally flows "*from* the foreign laboratory *to* the central lab at home".[5]

Building upon the above, Kuemmerle outlined three key stages in the development of foreign R&D units: first, selecting the decision makers; second, the set of decisions and actions that strengthen the facility's initial capabilities; and third, the decisions and actions designed to maximize the lab's contributions to the MNE's overall corporate strategic goals.

First, the MNE selects the decision makers. Most MNEs set up a technology steering committee, usually consisting of five to eight members, with extensive technical and organizational expertise, and representing a broad variety of educational backgrounds. The technology steering committee typically reports directly to the CEO. This approach reduces the bounded rationality problems faced by the MNE, by reducing the uncertainty involved in assessing alternative, high-distance locations.

Second, when trying to strengthen the lab's initial capabilities, senior management should bear in mind that home-base-exploiting and home-base-augmenting lab types have different needs and require different skills. **Home-base-exploiting labs** should be located close to key markets and the MNE's own foreign manufacturing units so that the firm's technological innovations can be rapidly adapted to host country requirements if needed, and absorbed by host country manufacturing operations. This is an example of how adapting to key markets sometimes requires building new, location-bound FSAs in host countries (in this case, produced by the home-base-exploiting lab) to link the MNE's internationally transferable FSAs more effectively with the location advantages of the host country's output markets. The initial leadership of such labs should be placed in the hands of "highly regarded managers from within the company – managers who are intimately familiar with the company's culture and systems ... to forge close ties between the new lab's engineers and the foreign community's manufacturing and marketing facilities".[6] One of the key bounded rationality problems facing the MNE is to reduce the 'distance' (see Chapter 4) between home country R&D operations and host country manufacturing operations, and a home-base-exploiting R&D operation – particularly if led by managers selected from within the company – will reduce this distance.

In contrast, **home-base-augmenting labs** should be located in critical knowledge clusters relevant to the MNE's businesses, where they will be well positioned to tap into new sources of innovations. The initial senior managers selected to guide this type of lab through the capability-strengthening stage "should be prominent local scientists ... to nurture ties between the new site and the local scientific community".[7] Here, the MNE's main problem is that it cannot access knowledge resources available in foreign locations without becoming an insider there.

Third, to maximize the lab's contributions to the MNE's strategic goals, each lab, especially the home-base-exploiting ones, should interact regularly with the other R&D units, as well as with the firm's manufacturing and marketing operations. The home-base-augmenting labs should, in addition, remain focused on strengthening their insider status in their host country scientific communities.

As regards the internal knowledge sharing required from all labs so as to maximize their impact on the firm as a whole, senior managers must ensure, in this third stage, that contributions complement the MNE's existing FSA base, including applications relevant to manufacturing operations. This goal cannot be achieved if the labs work as islands, isolated from the rest of the company. For effective knowledge recombination to occur, each lab must become integrated as quickly and seamlessly as possible with the other parts of the MNE. This entails substantial interaction, both with home country R&D managers in the central lab(s) and directly with other units in the company research network. In this context, Kuemmerle offers the following description of the ideal profile of R&D unit leaders, who will be instrumental to the necessary knowledge recombination:

> The best candidates for both home-base-augmenting and home-base-exploiting sites share four qualities: they are at once respected scientists or engineers and skilled managers; they are able to integrate the new site into the company's existing R&D network; they have a comprehensive understanding of technology trends; and they are able to overcome formal barriers when they seek access to new ideas in local universities and scientific communities.[8]

In short, senior R&D lab managers must be able to marshal the resources necessary for the lab to be successful in meeting its objectives, including new FSA development. The managers do this by connecting the lab with other resources inside the firm and, especially in the case of home-base-augmenting labs, effectively tapping the external environment in host markets for new knowledge.

Throughout his article, Kuemmerle describes real-world examples to illustrate his insights. In the case of US-based document services company Xerox, senior management decided to establish a home-base-augmenting site in continental Europe as it believed that the unique opportunities for new research and knowledge extraction in that area warranted a second lab to complement an existing one in the United Kingdom. Given the lab's proposed knowledge-augmenting role, the company decided to locate the lab in Grenoble, France, viewed as an established centre of scientific excellence. Xerox hired a renowned French scientist to head up the unit and integrate it within the local scientific community. This manager was instrumental in recombining the firm's existing FSAs with complementary resources in the French environment. Xerox also had new staff visit other company R&D centres in order to expedite the lab's integration into the firm's internal R&D network. This facilitated the transfer of non-location-bound FSAs across borders.

In another example, the US-based pharmaceutical firm Eli Lilly set out to increase sales in Asia by more effectively exploiting its research capabilities and adapting its portfolio of pharmaceutical products to meet needs in that region. The company decided to open a home-base-exploiting lab in the region and selected Kobe, Japan, for its proximity to existing MNE operations, as well as key markets in Japan and southeast Asia. To integrate the new lab as quickly as possible with the rest of the company, a senior research manager with extensive knowledge of both production and marketing activities was selected to lead the new unit. In addition, the firm implemented a staff transfer programme in which veteran R&D scientists were assigned to the new location, and new staff visited other labs to enhance the exchange of information. This approach to transferring the MNE's non-location-bound FSAs from the home base using a location-bound FSA was successful as the lab quickly passed through the capability-strengthening stage and began effectively commercializing R&D capabilities for the Asian market in a relatively short time period.

As a third example, Japan-based electronics giant Matsushita has set up an effective, international R&D knowledge network consisting of both home-base-exploiting and home-base-augmenting labs. Units can communicate directly with each other, formally and informally, rather than using a central R&D office as an intermediary. This process of direct communication increases the level of knowledge transfer and resource recombination within the company. Furthermore, R&D managers meet on a regular basis to discuss their current scope of technological capabilities and also participate in planning sessions with manufacturing and marketing managers to develop a more accurate sense of the types of R&D innovations that could be valuable in the future. Here, the focus is on the international transfer of non-location-bound FSAs in multiple directions.

These three examples illustrate Kuemmerle's view that MNEs are increasingly adopting an interlinked network of host country facilities to improve their R&D efforts, rather than relying on a centralized approach with all core R&D performed in the firm's home market. In addition, the labs can play different roles, depending on whether their primary purpose is to exploit knowledge or augment knowledge.

Context and complementary perspectives

When Kuemmerle published 'Building effective R&D capabilities abroad' in 1997, the previous decade had witnessed a proliferation of innovations in communications technology that changed how R&D could be performed. The emergence of the Internet and the adoption of email, wireless communications, electronic data transmission protocols and robust database management systems all significantly affected the R&D process, allowing researchers to communicate remotely and near-seamlessly across borders in new ways that removed previously existing barriers.[9] As a result, companies no longer had to rely on physical proximity within a centralized location in order to obtain the efficient communication necessary for effective R&D.

However, at the same time that advances in communications technology made physical proximity less important, new knowledge clusters sprung up around the world, and physical proximity to these clusters remained as important as ever (see Chapter 1). The benefits of spatial clustering in cases of abundant localized markets for specialized resources (e.g., specialized labour, local government support), as well as localized knowledge spillovers, caused MNEs to place knowledge-generating activities inside these foreign clusters in order to access these resources.

This combination of international transferability of FSAs and international accessibility of some resources with the need to have value-added operations physically embedded in specific locations to reap the full benefits of clusters is the 'sticky places in slippery space' paradox.[10] This phenomenon can also be interpreted as an expression of the double diamond model described in Chapter 3: site location matters, but the location advantages of several countries/regions may need to be combined to gain competitive advantage on an international scale. This points to the key strengths of the **international coordinator** archetype: coordination skills allowing the continuous recombination of internationally dispersed resources.

Overall, this change in thinking on how R&D should be approached mirrored a change in international business strategy in general, in particular the evolution of conventional **international projectors**. These MNEs realized that their value-generating activities, including R&D, should include tapping into host country input markets as new suppliers of valuable resources. They also understood the need for more adaptation in order to meet host market demand requirements.

Julian Birkinshaw and **Nick Fry** provide a first piece complementing Kuemmerle's analysis.[11] Their 1998 *SMR* article on subsidiary initiatives in MNEs focuses primarily on the drivers of new development activities in large, established MNEs, and it addresses one of the critical limitations in Kuemmerle's study, namely that Kuemmerle overlooks subsidiary role dynamics. The reality of international innovation, especially in large MNEs with large portfolios of foreign subsidiaries, is that corporate headquarters in the home country does not simply choose locations and assign roles to foreign sites in terms of R&D charters. In many cases, entrepreneurial managers in MNEs assume extended roles inconsistent with their unit's formal charter (which might specify whether the unit is to be home-base-augmenting, or merely home-base-exploiting).

Entrepreneurial subsidiary managers, especially in a well-established foreign affiliate, will often pursue a subsidiary initiative, defined as: "the proactive and deliberate pursuit of a new business opportunity by a subsidiary company, undertaken with a view to expand the subsidiary's scope of responsibility, in a manner consistent with the MNCs strategic goals".[12]

Birkinshaw and Fry make a key distinction between 'internal' and 'external' subsidiary initiatives. In the context of R&D, **internal** subsidiary initiatives reflect attempts by subsidiary managers to become the chosen location for new corporate R&D investments. Here, it is not simply the corporate steering committee that selects an 'optimal' location. Rather, subsidiary managers attempt to influence this decision through a process of internal competition. Subsidiary managers use their wide-ranging arsenal of formal and informal linkages with headquarters, including personal contacts, to sell their unit as the best place for the firm to invest. Subsidiary managers may thereby reduce significantly the bounded rationality problems faced by senior management in the home country, as those senior managers will be thoroughly updated about the foreign units' innovation potential and broader capabilities.

In contrast, *external* subsidiary initiatives result from foreign subsidiary managers identifying an opportunity in their business environment. Often, this results from interactions with customers, suppliers or competitors. To the extent that subsidiaries benefit from high autonomy, some slack resources and discretion in resource allocation, they may fund pilot projects themselves, sheltered from corporate headquarters. After some initial positive results have been achieved – for example in the form of customer buy-in or a successful technical prototype – they may go to corporate headquarters with a strong case for funding and for formal acknowledgement of the de facto upgrading of their original corporate charter.

Both internal and external initiatives reflect attempts to earn home-base-augmenting innovation charters. Such attempts will likely become even more important in the future given the rise of internal benchmarking in many MNEs, whereby corporate headquarters allocates resources based on the subsidiary initiatives' potential to contribute to internal network optimization or to external market expansion. Chapter 5 discussed several best practices that corporate headquarters can use to increase the likelihood that subsidiary initiatives fulfil their potential (giving seed money, formally requesting proposals, etc.).

The corporate immune system is a key problem facing entrepreneurial subsidiary managers interested in pursuing novel resource recombinations. This resistance to subsidiary initiatives is largely due to bounded rationality problems facing senior managers at corporate headquarters. Here, the lack of proper understanding of subsidiary initiatives by headquarters leads to false attributions of empire building or opportunistic sub-goal pursuit by subsidiaries. In addition, individuals at corporate headquarters and other MNE units may actually engage in opportunistic behaviour themselves: because every subsidiary initiative ultimately reflects a reallocation of resources away from present priorities, perverse incentives may exist, even for senior managers, to kill valuable initiatives.[13] The corporate immune system, designed to protect merely the MNE's dominant logic (so as to avoid, e.g., excessive diversification), becomes instead an instrument of powerful stakeholders inside the firm, who do not want to see their existing charter and responsibilities challenged by foreign subsidiaries, especially if those subsidiaries are located in peripheral countries and lack an established reputation for work similar to the new initiative. In such cases, the major bounded reliability problem inside the MNE is not subsidiary empire building whereby subsidiary managers pursue their own goals at the expense of overall MNE goals. Rather, the major bounded reliability problem is that individuals and groups outside of the subsidiary and driven by their own interests falsely portray the initiative as detrimental to overall MNE goals. The great challenge for the MNE is then to create an environment empowering subsidiaries to go forward with innovative and valuable initiatives while maintaining an appropriate level of initiative scrutiny to economize on bounded reliability problems, including empire-building attempts by subsidiaries and more benevolent forms of "scarcity of effort to make good on open-ended promises".[14]

Andrew Inkpen provides a second complementary perspective to Kuemmerle's analysis. Inkpen's important *CMR* piece on alliances demonstrates that a firm does not always need to set up its own labs in order to acquire knowledge; it can access another firm's innovation if it can persuade that other firm to form an alliance.[15] Inkpen studies how the largest US-based car manufacturer, General Motors (GM), learned about the Toyota Production System (TPS), especially its 'lean manufacturing' principles, through the NUMMI (New United Motor Manufacturing, Inc.) alliance. NUMMI, established in 1984, operated a car manufacturing plant in Fremont, California. It was a joint venture between GM and the world's third largest automobile manufacturer, Japan-based Toyota. However, after having produced nearly 8 million cars and trucks together, the partnership was terminated and the production plant closed in 2010, a decision which should be understood in the context of GM's bankruptcy in 2009 and subsequent restructuring.

In this particular case, the MNE being studied (GM) wanted to innovate and learn about Japanese production methods, but it did not set up a home-base-augmenting or exploiting R&D site in Japan, a country with expertise in automotive innovation and enjoying the world's highest manufacturing productivity. Rather, a host country firm at the forefront of such innovation and with enviable productivity levels (Toyota) invested in the MNE's home base and, through a joint venture, gave GM access to the desired knowledge.

Inkpen convincingly demonstrates that GM needed to overcome two main bounded rationality challenges to tap effectively into the TPS knowledge base. First, GM needed to understand the routines that drove the TPS system. These routines had a large tacit component that could not readily be codified into easily imitable best practices, e.g., in the form of a manual or blueprints to guide managerial action. Only after several years of learning and the establishment of a large-scale learning system did GM fully understand the TPS routines. Second, the TPS routines needed to be recombined with the extant GM car manufacturing knowledge, which led to substantial resistance and other adoption problems inside GM's operations.

The first problem above – difficulty in understanding the TPS routines – resulted from causal ambiguity (namely, a failure to understand the linkages between specific actions and outcomes/performance).

The second problem – difficulty in recombining the TPS routines with existing knowledge within GM – resulted from GM's lack of absorptive capacity and a 'not invented here' mentality. The former problem reflected the absence of an effective learning system within GM, which is really a bounded rationality problem.

The latter problem was the lack of motivation at the level of domestic operations to assimilate the TPS knowledge, which is more of a bounded reliability problem.

GM personnel generally underestimated what there was to learn, as indicated by the following quote from a GM manager:

> We [managers in GM] started with denial that there was anything to learn. Then we said Toyota is different, so it won't work at GM. Eventually we realized there was something to learn. The leaders initially said: 'implement lean manufacturing', but they did not understand it . . . We went to Japan and saw kanban and andon, but people did not understand why they work. We did not understand that the TPS is an integrated approach and not just a random collection of ideas . . . We implemented parts of the system but did not understand that it was the system that made the difference . . . We did not understand that the culture and behaviour had to change before the techniques would have an impact.[16]

Fixing this situation was a priority for Jack Smith, who became GM's CEO in 1992. Jack Smith had led the original NUMMI negotiations for GM and understood well the economic potential of transferring TPS principles to GM plants.

Inkpen describes in detail the learning system adopted by GM, especially after 1992, to understand effectively the TPS routines in their full complexity and to provide the basis for subsequent knowledge recombination. This learning system included: study teams at NUMMI focused on learning a specific task and paying attention to implementation and follow-up issues; various types of experiential learning at NUMMI itself; the documentation (codification) of TPS knowledge; and the careful preparation for re-entry into GM operations of so-called 'advisors' (a small cadre of individuals assigned to learn directly from NUMMI).

To further improve the absorptive capacity of its operations and the motivation of its employees to assimilate TPS knowledge, GM organized extensive tours of the NUMMI plant for its employees, set up formal training programmes, and promoted 'NUMMI alumni' to senior positions at GM. These steps were reinforced by the (informal) social network interactions among former NUMMI advisors and other individuals who had been exposed to NUMMI and were convinced of its merits.

Eventually, the TPS lean manufacturing principles were effectively recombined with dominant GM routines to produce GM's Global Manufacturing System (GMS). GMS aims to establish a common manufacturing system in all GM plants, and is largely inspired by TPS principles such as teamwork, continuous improvement, built-in quality and short lead times.

The NUMMI example suggests that innovation from abroad can sometimes be adopted at home, and may lead to new upstream FSAs in the technological knowledge area. However, even at home, tacit knowledge from abroad, in the form of sophisticated manufacturing routines, may be difficult to access, absorb and utilize effectively. This example shows that substantial problems can arise when managers at corporate headquarters underestimate the challenges and costs of transferring and absorbing new knowledge internationally.

Kuemmerle's work usefully describes the changes characterizing two of the key parameters set out in the conceptual framework in Chapter 1, namely location advantages and internationally transferable FSAs. The old model, according to Kuemmerle, is that of the *international projector*, with unidirectional flows of knowledge from the home country to host countries, building upon the location advantages of the home country. In Kuemmerle's new model, the old approach is complemented by knowledge transfer the other way: home-base-augmenting sites in the host countries also create internationally transferable FSAs, building upon the (input side) location advantages of their host countries. As Kuemmerle puts it, "[C]ompanies must establish a presence at an increasing number of locations to access new knowledge and to absorb new research results from foreign universities and competitors into their own organization".[17] The underlying assumption is that some knowledge bundles are embedded in specific locations and can only be accessed through being physically present in these locations. However, when such knowledge is combined with the MNE's extant resources, firm-level learning and new FSA development may occur, with these new FSAs being fully transferable to a central lab in the home country or to other affiliates.

Even Kuemmerle's home-base-exploiting sites are more than just recipients of parent company knowledge. These sites act as the vehicle through which companies transfer FSAs to foreign markets, but they must develop new (location-bound) FSAs in order to adapt the firm's goods and services to host country customers. Here, it is important to differentiate between stand-alone technical knowledge, which may be easy to transfer between R&D centres, and the related routines and recombination capabilities developed by the various centres, which may be more difficult to diffuse. Figure 6.1 displays the old and new approaches to R&D operations in MNEs.

The traditional approach of R&D activities centralized in the home base reflects Pattern I in this book's capability development model, whereby internationally transferable FSAs are developed in the home country and subsequently diffused internationally with the purpose of straightforward exploitation by subsidiaries in host markets.

The two types of labs Kuemmerle identifies reflect the growing trend towards additional, distinct patterns of FSA development. Home-base-augmenting research centres reflect Pattern VI in this book's framework (see Figure 6.2). Here, internationally transferable FSAs in the form of upstream, technological knowledge are generated by R&D operations in host countries but are closely linked to – and guided by – corporate headquarters. Close communication between the parent and subsidiary organization (or lab) is maintained – in fact, this communication is identified by Kuemmerle as a crucial component to ensuring that the lab is meaningfully integrated into the company's network. In contrast, home-base-exploiting R&D sites are more representative of Pattern III, whereby internationally transferable FSAs are developed in the home base but their diffusion to host country

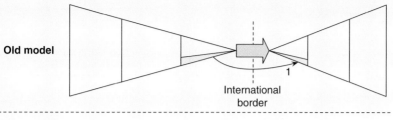

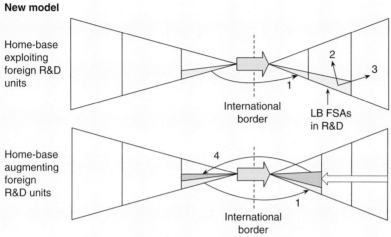

Figure 6.1
Home-base-
exploiting and
augmenting foreign
R&D units

Old model

International
border

New model

Home-base
exploiting
foreign R&D
units

International
border

LB FSAs
in R&D

Home-base
augmenting
foreign
R&D units

International
border

1. NLB FSAs related to R&D, transferred from home to host countries.
2. Internal links between host country R&D and local manufacturing.
3. External links between host country R&D and local output market.
4. Reverse transfer of new, NLB FSAs related to R&D, from host country
   operation to home.

subsidiaries is accompanied by regional modifications or enhancements in response to local market needs. Finally, Kuemmerle stresses the importance of the various host labs working directly together to create new FSAs without channelling through the home office: "Reducing the instances in which the central lab must act as mediator means that existing knowledge travels more quickly through the company and new ideas percolate more easily."[18] This scenario reflects Pattern VIII and Pattern IX, whereby internationally transferable FSAs are jointly created by a network of MNE affiliates, and then exploited internationally, either with or without the addition of location-bound FSAs for specific countries or markets.

Kuemmerle's analysis has two main limitations. First, he does not thoroughly examine the critical issue of ongoing tension between host country labs and central headquarters in terms of setting the research agenda.[19] Should the research agenda include only projects induced by corporate headquarters and consistent with the MNE's dominant logic, or should it include external initiatives driven by opportunities identified in host country subsidiaries, and to what extent? Who gets to set the research agenda? This tension mirrors the more general tensions between subsidiary managers and central headquarters across value chain activities, as

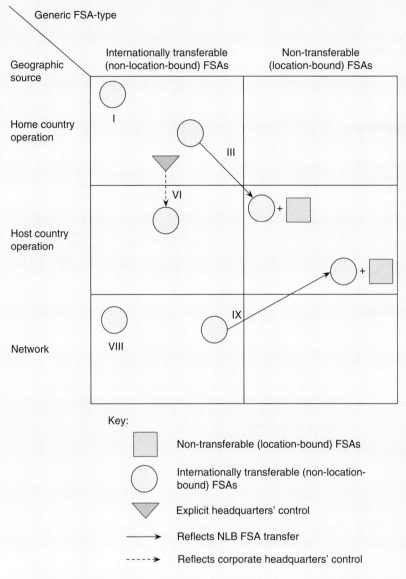

Figure 6.2
Patterns of FSA
development
in home-base-
exploiting and
augmenting research
centres in MNEs

described by Birkinshaw and Fry.[20] As noted above, senior managers in the central lab must determine whether subsidiary R&D initiatives are compatible with overall corporate strategy. Here, bounded rationality constraints facing these managers may lead to false attributions of severe bounded reliability problems to foreign labs, and thus a dysfunctional application of the corporate immune system. In fact, such dysfunctionality limits the MNE's recombination capabilities.

As a second limitation, Kuemmerle fails to discuss the role of joint ventures and strategic alliances in reshaping how MNEs conduct R&D internationally. As shown by Inkpen, such cooperative arrangements are contributing to changes in how MNEs engage in R&D and organize their international research network.

Indeed, what the MNE lacks, when attempting to become an insider in foreign knowledge clusters through a home-base-augmenting R&D lab, is often access to a social network. The MNE may be unable to access autonomously and utilize effectively this host country location advantage through market-based supplier contracts or acquisitions. This is especially troublesome when the MNE needs long-term, multilateral linkages (rather than static, bilateral linkages) with members of host country clusters in order to create reputational FSAs. In these cases, the MNE cannot just purchase resources or acquire activities from specific actors in order to reap the expected benefits of clustering. The R&D subsidiaries of US MNEs in Japan have often encountered this problem.[21] Primarily because of their inability to hire and retain top scientists, these subsidiaries have often been locked out of Japanese clusters. The US MNEs' inability was itself the result of insufficient understanding of the complex linkages prevailing in Japan among institutions such as universities and firms that hire scientific personnel. For example, professors from lead universities in Japan systematically 'allocated' graduates to a small set of leading domestic companies. In its most extreme form, a professor would send one letter of reference for a Master's student to a single firm, and this firm would then hire the graduate based upon the one recommendation it received. Foreign firms hoping to tap into this pool of young scientists had to emulate the human resources management practices of the large domestic companies, including long-term employment commitments, large R&D expenditures and well-funded labs, and the building of networking relationships with leading universities.

Another reason not to simply acquire R&D labs is that acquisition sometimes eliminates the opportunity for learning by destroying the complementary cognitive specialization and idiosyncratic resource bundles of the firms acquired. This happens if the MNE attaches too much importance to institutionalizing its own routines at the expense of using its recombination capabilities. In this context, a poor reputation for making good on promises, such as respecting acquired firms' knowledge bundles, may also negatively affect the MNE's ability to become an insider in host country clusters.

Five management takeaways

1. Analyse your firm's portfolio of international R&D facilities, and categorize these according to their home-base-exploiting versus home-base-augmenting status.
2. Assess whether your knowledge-generating activities are located in the best possible knowledge clusters with optimal access to specialized resources.
3. When exploring the drivers of innovation inside your firm, examine the potential contribution of subsidiary initiatives.

4. Reflect on the potential to partner in alliances, so as to absorb new knowledge in your industry.

5. Align your R&D initiatives in host country labs with the firm's overall corporate goals and consider alternative avenues for acquiring new knowledge (e.g., strategic alliances, acquisitions, etc.).

CASE

Case 6.1 Globalizing corporate R&D at Siemens[22]

Founded in Berlin in 1847, Siemens has grown from a small telegraph workshop to one of the largest electrical engineering and electronics companies in the world. Focusing on the businesses of Automation and Control, Power, Transportation, Medical, Information and Communications, and Lighting, Siemens has 360,000 employees in over 190 countries. In fiscal year 2011, Siemens had sales of more than EUR 74 billion with a net income of more than EUR 7 billion.

Research and development has always been important at Siemens. Innovation is one of the five core targets at Siemens, the other ones being taking responsibility, a focus on customers, a focus on people and a focus on value. As Siemens puts it on its website, "Innovation is our lifeblood, around the globe and around the clock." In 2011, 27,800 individuals were employed in R&D. In the 2011 fiscal year, Siemens spent EUR 3.93 billion on R&D, accounting for 5.3 per cent of its sales. In a ranking by business consultants Booz Allen Hamilton of the 1,000 companies around the world with the highest levels of R&D expenditures in 2011, Siemens ranked as number twenty.

Siemens has been decentralizing its R&D activities since the 1980s. Siemens increasingly performs research activities abroad: R&D is now being conducted in 30 countries. Of the 27,800 employees engaged in R&D, less than half (42.5 per cent) are employed in Germany. Other major R&D locations include the US, China, Austria, India, Slovakia, Switzerland and the UK.

The role and scope of Corporate Technology

Despite having only 6,400 employees worldwide, Corporate Technology (CT) still performs a leading role within Siemens' R&D operations. Its international network focuses on core technologies and international patent management, strategically important to Siemens. In Germany, CT's activities are mainly concentrated in Munich, Erlangen and Berlin. Internationally, CT's R&D units are located in Berkeley, California (US), Princeton, New Jersey (US), Vienna (Austria), Beijing and Shanghai (China), Singapore, Bangalore (India), Moscow and St Petersburg (Russia) and Tokyo (Japan).

The R&D units in China and Singapore were only established recently. For example, CT Beijing opened in 2006 and CT Singapore opened in 2008. Most of these units are relatively small. The total staff in Beijing, Shanghai, Singapore and Tokyo added together is just over 200.

Siemens corporate research

Employing 430 staff, Siemens Corporate Research (SCR) in Princeton, New Jersey, was Corporate Technology's first research institute outside Europe. It started in 1977 as a small development facility in New Jersey to support its US manufacturing operations. In the early 1980s, however, Siemens decided to invest heavily in SCR to solidify further Siemens' leading technology position. SCR is now a leader in the fields of information technology and software, computer graphics and imaging, and multimedia technology within Siemens.

Global technology fields

Within Siemens CT operations, the company has implemented the Global Technology Fields (GTF), to develop CT capabilities that stretch beyond divisional boundaries. Teams consist of highly specialized employees from across the world who possess strengths in specific research areas. An aspect of GTF includes 'lighthouse projects' whereby Siemens creates a team to focus on specific challenges entailing both new foreseeable demand and alternative resources. Examples of projects taking place in 2012 include energy storage and smart grids.[23] Lighthouse projects provide a good indication of where Siemens R&D is heading, as these areas are selected as beacons for the long-term focus of the company.

GTFs provide the opportunity for knowledge development and transfer within this diversified company. This programme creates a unique bond for employees as R&D responsibility is placed on the organization as a whole, rather than on specific divisions with traditional location advantages.

Building the R&D unit in India[24]

In October 2004, Corporate Technology opened a research laboratory (CT India) in Bangalore, placing it under the organizational umbrella of Siemens Information Systems Ltd (SISL).

For this new R&D unit in India, the objective was "to establish a leading industrial research center, which will attract the best talent, promote cooperation with universities and research facilities, and allow Siemens to tap into India's strengths, particularly with regard to information technology".[25]

Siemens chose Electronics City, one of the major industrial parks in Bangalore, as the site for the R&D unit. Bangalore is India's fourth largest market and 'India's Silicon Valley', hosting a large number of information technology companies. Electronics City is a location of choice for both major multinational companies such as 3M and Hewlett Packard, and major local Indian giants such as Infosys and Wipro.

In April 2004, 43-year-old Mukul Saxena was given the mandate to establish this new research centre. An engineer and manager, he first worked for General Electric's (GE) global research and development team in the US before returning to India in 1997 to work for an automotive supplier for four years. In 2000, he rejoined GE to lead a 140-member research team with members in both Bangalore and Niskayuna, New York, and was made a member of the Board of Directors of GE Medical Systems, India.

By 2005, Saxena had been able to attract a young research team of 39 members for the new Siemens research centre. Saxena's top priority was to work closely with SISL to apply its technology quickly to end products.[26] Close coordination with SISL would also help fulfil his ultimate goal of "doing research in India for the Indian market and successfully implement[ing] cost-effective solutions there". Saxena asked, "What's driving the local market? And how can we adapt solutions that cost $1,000 in the US to the Indian market, where they shouldn't cost more than $100?"[27]

At the same time, CT India was also working closely with Siemens researchers located elsewhere. Romain Moreau-Gobard, a French scientist who had worked at SCR in Princeton for four years, was the liaison with SCR. In addition, CT India also worked closely with other Siemens R&D units around the world. For example, a team headed by Rita Chattopadhyay worked closely with SCR and with Siemens researchers in Karlsruhe, Germany, on embedded software for security cameras and optimized solutions for camera systems in traffic monitoring.

The slogan of CT India for 2006 was 'Made for India – in India'. Looking into the future, Saxena expected that CT India would become more embedded as an insider in the Indian market and better integrated into Siemens' existing innovation network.

Siemens' Corporate Technology will continue to internationalize its R&D activities. According to Professor Claus Weyrich, a member of the Managing Board of Siemens AG and the head of Siemens Corporate Technology, "we also need to be represented in regions characterized by fast growing markets and dynamic innovation processes. Besides, Siemens needs more than 10,000 highly qualified young people a year. We therefore need to develop networks with foreign universities. Finally, it's a matter of corporate citizenship."[28]

Siemens moving forward

In 2008, Siemens continued its R&D expansion by opening a CT lab in Singapore. Singapore's unique conditions in terms of lack of fresh water for human consumption created an attractive area for Siemens to open up a research lab.[29] The company's research focuses on finding efficient techniques to desalinate water and remove organic material. The lack of local water resources has created positive pressure to find innovative solutions to meet the needs of Singaporeans. As R&D efforts begin to concentrate more on the demands of developing markets, research located in South East Asia is gaining in importance.[30] Siemens has also been tweaking its products with the goal to simplify them, and to decrease their prices in emerging markets. However, Siemens Chief Financial Officer, Joe Kaeser, has acknowledged that the R&D labs in Germany are still "a vital part of Siemens strategy".[31]

In 2012, Siemens remains dedicated to improving its R&D outputs and is currently developing over a thousand new partnerships a year, involving *inter alia* numerous universities from around the globe.[32] Universities are often selected based on their location advantages in terms of linkages with the local industry. By partnering with universities that have connections to local industry, Siemens can gain a better understanding of trends prevalent in the local market. Universities benefit through receiving funding and opportunities to study current industry issues.[33]

Siemens uses as incubators those universities that develop innovative technology and market this to the local industry[34]. The University of California, Berkeley and Shanghai have been designated as 'Technology-to-Business (TTB)' centres for Siemens. Research labs are operating in close proximity to these university campuses. Both TTB centres are located in areas where intensive innovation is prevalent within the businesses competing there. The University of

California, Berkeley is located in San Francisco where a thriving venture capital market exists that focuses mainly on technological developments. TTB Shanghai is a valuable location for Siemens as it provides access to the large Chinese market. The research lab aims to provide cost-effective solutions that can compete with technologies currently being used in China.

QUESTIONS

1. Can you categorize SCR and CT India as either home-base-exploiting sites or home-base-augmenting sites? Why? Did Saxena's priorities support your categorization?
2. Does Saxena meet the ideal profile of an R&D unit leader as described by Kuemmerle?
3. What is the rationale for the choices of the location and the leader at CT India?
4. Can you provide an update on the internationalization of Siemens Corporate Technology's R&D, using materials available on the Web?

Case 6.2 Sony: Managing the international R&D network

Sony Corporation (Sony), the Japan-based consumer electronics and entertainment group, has become synonymous with breakthrough technology products, including the Walkman, Trinitron TV, Compact Disc Player and PlayStation video consoles. Over the course of more than half a century, Sony has developed into a world-class brand representing high quality and advanced technology in consumer electronics. However, during the past ten years, and with the exception of the PlayStation (PS2 and PS3) consoles, Sony has been more of a laggard in consumer electronics innovation, for example in the fields of LCD technology and MP3 players. It has not been able to keep up in the marketplace with Sharp in LCD technology, or with Apple in MP3 players, or with Nokia in mobile phones, though it has remained successful in areas such as digital cameras and gaming consoles.[35]

Why was Sony unable to keep pace with changes in the consumer electronics industry? How does Sony manage its research and development?

Sony's history of technologically innovative products

During World War II, Masaru Ibuka, an electronics engineer, met Akio Morita, a physicist, and they became close friends. In 1946, together with Ibuka's father-in-law, Tamon Maeda, they established Tokyo Tsushin Kogyo (Totsuko), or the 'Tokyo Telecommunications Research Institute', with around 20 employees. The company conveyed its focus on developing technologically innovative products in its founding prospectus: "We shall be as selective as possible in our products and will welcome technological challenges. We shall focus on technologically sophisticated products that are highly useful in society, regardless of the quantity involved. Moreover, we shall not establish any clear demarcation between electronics and mechanics, but shall create our own unique products uniting the two fields, demonstrating a determination unmatched by other companies. We intend to keep our business operations small, go forward in technology, and grow in areas where large enterprises cannot enter because of their size."[36]

The company soon introduced Japan's first magnetic tape recorder in 1950 and Japan's first transistor radio in 1955. The company was renamed Sony in 1958. Guided by the philosophy set out in its initial prospectus, Sony invested heavily in R&D. For many years, Sony invested 6–10 per cent of its sales into R&D.

In the next three decades, Sony continued to launch innovative new products in the global market, such as the personal headphone stereo Walkman in 1979, the world's first compact disc (CD) player and a single-unit broadcast-use camera in 1982, the single-unit video camera in 1985, the HD Trinitron television in 1990, the 'Kirara Basso' series with Super Trinitron picture tube in 1991 and the PlayStation in 1994. Such innovations established Sony as the innovator in the consumer electronics industry.

Going international

Sony started to internationalize its activities as early as the 1950s, but in an incremental and cautious way. Morita explained the rationale for this strategy: "you must first learn about the market, learn how to sell to it, and build up your corporate confidence before you commit yourself. And when you have confidence, you should commit yourself wholeheartedly."[37]

Following this strategy, Sony started by exporting products through foreign agencies or its own sales offices when entering foreign markets. It set up manufacturing plants close to markets only when sales took off, and ultimately also internationalized its R&D activities. For example, Sony established Sony Corporation of America (SONAM) in 1960 to oversee Sony's marketing activities in the US, but only started to build its first US plant in San Diego in 1971, beginning with a simple assembly operation, with all components shipped from Japan. In Europe, Sony set up Sony Overseas, S. A. (SOSA), in Zug, Switzerland, in 1961, and a sales subsidiary in London in 1968. Only in 1974 did Sony establish it first European manufacturing facility, in Wales.

Again moving incrementally, Sony then established overseas technology centres (R&D centres) once the overseas sales and manufacturing subsidiaries were successful. Until the early 1980s, these centres were set up either by Japanese business divisions/labs, or by foreign subsidiaries without the direct involvement of corporate headquarters, as Sony believed that foreign subsidiaries should ultimately conduct their own manufacturing, marketing, service, financing and R&D activities. Sony established its first overseas R&D centre in San Jose, California, in 1977, and the second in Basingstoke, UK, in 1978. The main reason Sony's foreign subsidiaries established R&D activities was to solve problems faced by local sales and manufacturing activities, especially requirements to modify products for local markets and to provide technological support to overseas plants. For example, in the area of broadcast and industrial applications, Sony established Sony Broadcast

Ltd (SBC) in the UK in 1978, which initially focused on sales and service. SBC gradually expanded from sales and service to design and development serving local needs. Later, SBC and development teams in the US together developed broadcast-use video equipment.[38]

At that stage, top managers at the overseas labs had substantial autonomy. Even though the overseas labs were initially established with the support of Japanese business divisions/labs, the latter did not exercise stringent control over the overseas subsidiaries. As a result, top managers at the overseas labs could decide for themselves what R&D projects to pursue.[39]

During the 1980s and the early 1990s, Sony gradually internationalized its R&D activities. By the early 1990s, Sony operated around 20 overseas R&D centres, including 11 major labs. In 1996, these overseas labs employed approximately 500 workers. This represented only a small fraction of Sony's total R&D, whereas overseas production accounted for 30 per cent of Sony's total production and foreign sales represented 70 per cent of Sony's sales.

The majority of Sony's R&D takes place in Japan as the development process requires extensive coordination and communication among all parties involved. For example, when Sony developed the Viao 505 laptop in the late 1990s it required tremendous efforts from the R&D centre in Japan with little effort needed from foreign centres. These foreign centres were mainly required to aid in the process of adapting the product to local markets, and this usually involved translation of labels and product information. For Sony, the development process of the Viao 505 required all R&D activities to be located within a narrow geographic area. Face-to-face meetings between concept designers occurred daily to ensure effective communication and continuous evaluation. Once the product was in the stage of component development, designers and engineers were also required to meet face-to-face when developing the product. In addition, suppliers were selected that were located within a short train ride to the Sony technical centre to ensure a strong, ongoing relationship. It was also common for the Sony team to travel to supplier locations to ensure quality of inputs. Finally, monthly meetings took place among members of groups responsible for design, materials, product quality, applied technology, software application, and production. For the above reasons, Sony required its R&D activities to occur in a centralized location in Japan. Similar to Sony's approach, many firms, R&D activities and innovation development are concentrated in clusters, since tacit knowledge is difficult to transfer overseas.[40]

Sony's global R&D labs were developed to provide more sensitivity vis-à-vis end markets; however, the majority of Sony's R&D capabilities will remain in Japan.[41]

Managing R&D units

In 1989, at the opening ceremony of the Advanced Video Technology Center in San Jose (US), Morita stated: "We believe it is necessary to develop products locally in order to meet the needs and requirements of the local market. Also, if we could transfer local specialties such as digital technologies from the United Kingdom, or graphics and special effects technologies from the United States to other regions, we would realize a global synergy in R&D."[42]

In the late 1980s and early 1990s, two important elements affected the further internationalization of Sony's R&D. First, Sony felt the need to tap into the advanced knowledge embedded in various foreign locations. For example, the computer and telecommunications industries in the

US and a few other locations were much more advanced than in Japan. As Sony had expanded from its traditional audio-video niches into telecommunications, it needed to establish R&D bases in advanced technology locations so as to access the relevant knowledge. Second, Sony felt it had to increase internal coordination among R&D labs, to improve efficiency and to create synergies.[43]

In the early 1990s, Sony introduced a regional management system to improve the internal coordination of its worldwide R&D activities. In 1994, it designated the research laboratories in San Jose, California, as the US Chief Technology Office and allocated the role of European head office to its Stuttgart Technology Centre. The Chief Technology Officer (CTO) at the Japanese headquarters became responsible for worldwide R&D strategy, with CTOs in the US and Europe responsible for regional R&D strategy and coordinating R&D activities in their region. Moreover, Sony organized R&D coordination meetings twice a year for the three CTOs to discuss internal collaboration and resource allocation.

However, autonomy at overseas labs remained highly valued under the regional management system. To a large extent, overseas labs retained the power to plan and execute their own projects.

Sony's standards[44]

Prior to Japan signing the Technical Barriers to Trade (TBT) Agreement in 1995, Sony's products were developed to raise the level of standards and become a benchmark for others to follow. Most Japanese companies followed the 'de facto standardization' approach where firms with large market shares created products that consumers accepted as standards. As early on as 1993, Sony saw the importance of international standards also known as '*de jure*', and made a strong commitment to follow and establish such standards in Japan, North America and Europe. Japan's signing of the TBT Agreement and the World Trade Organization's enforcement of trade standards required individual country's standards to conform to the international standards.[45] This development was positive for Sony as the company's global R&D strategy had already committed to meeting and exceeding international standards. Sony's initiatives have created products instrumental to developing new international standards, unlike competitors who develop products to meet these standards. Setsuo Harada, head of Standards and Partnership Department, states that "In the future, international standardization will be an essential part of our efforts to gain widespread acceptance of our technologies and create a more convenient world for consumers."[46]

Sony's recent decline

Since the mid 1990s, Sony has shown signs of reduced competitiveness, exemplified by a drop in net income. A corporate restructuring in 1996 did not remediate this situation, nor did subsequent restructuring attempts in 1999, 2001 and 2009. Sony, the former technological forerunner, has become a laggard in many key product categories. Even its successful PlayStation gaming console has faced challenges with the release of the PS3 in 2007.[47] Due to the high investment costs required to develop the PS3, it took over four years for Sony to turn a profit on its gaming console. Sony has struggled to stay competitive as it relies on brand prestige to justify its higher prices in an industry that is evolving towards a dominant focus on cost competitiveness.

Not only has Sony faced challenges internally, but external events have also tested the firm. The 2008 recession hit Sony hard with the company posting a net operating loss of US $2.92 billion, its first full year operating loss in fourteen years. This forced Sony to restructure again and to cut costs by US $3.2 billion in 2009. Operational efficiency became the key focus of Sony as it closed plants in developed markets, cut suppliers, and implemented bids for supplier contracts.[48] Contracts were awarded for the best offers that suppliers put forth to gain the right to sell their products to Sony. This provided Sony with more competitive prices from their suppliers. In 2008, the Japanese yen also appreciated strongly against the US dollar putting a further strain on the export-reliant Japanese company. Over 70 per cent of Sony products are sold outside of Japan making foreign exchange risk management critically important.[49] Mr Chubachi, Sony's President, stated that each time the Japanese currency's appreciates with one yen against the US dollar, Sony would incur a loss of US $58.5 million.[50] Subsequently, in 2011, a devastating Tsunami hit Japan halting operations and causing plant closures and disruptions in supply change management.

The Sony brand appears to be losing its allure. Ichiro Morimune, marketing manager in the Tokyo region for Yamada Denki, a leading discount retailer, commented, "The strong Sony fans are declining. There are very few people who ask for Sony."[51]

Two major problems in the R&D sphere may have contributed to Sony's relative downfall. First, Sony has been dominated by a silo structure, with little coordination among divisional managers. There has been insufficient coordination of resource allocation in R&D for improving existing products. Different divisions and product groups under the decentralized structure have been allowed to pursue independent agendas, resulting in waste and duplicated effort. Second, irrespective of problems of duplication and insufficient coordination, Sony's R&D efforts have simply been less effective than those of rivals, pointing to major problems in the realm of strategic guidance and incentives: "Employees are paid more than peers at Matsushita but deliver less bang for their buck, as does the group's R&D budget."[52]

Sony's current strategy

The competitive environment is changing for the electronics industry and joint ventures are becoming a more common and important resource for fostering innovation.[53] Sony has started to form strategic alliances to increase its technological strengths. For example, Sony, IBM and Toshiba have joined forces to develop Cell, a semiconductor described as a supercomputer-on-a-chip. To compete with companies in Korea and Taiwan, Sony has teamed up with Toshiba and Hitachi by integrating R&D capabilities to develop small LCD screens.

Moreover, Sony has tried to restructure its R&D operations to create a sense of urgency and to shy away from complacency. In 2005, Sony formulated 'Project Nippon' to reduce management layers, improve coordination of R&D and refocus R&D on growth areas. Sony is attempting to create "an over-arching structure for research and development and software spending for all products, rather than the old piecemeal system".[54]

Improving operational efficiency will be extremely important for Sony in the coming years as the company tries to turn its profitability trend around. However; Sony is faced with a difficult trade-off between decreasing costs and increasing R&D spending to drive innovation. Due to the impact of the recession, the company has decreased its R&D expenditures from 2007 to 2011 but remains dedicated to fostering innovation. The company is increasingly focusing, both internally and externally, on 'open innovation'.[55] In 2012, Sony has invested R&D resources to improve the environmental performance of its products as part of its greater focus on corporate social responsibility. In addition, Sony is increasing its R&D spending in the healthcare sector to develop further the use of audiovisuals and magnetic technology.[56]

Sony has also begun to outsource specific parts of its value chain in order to decrease its costs. Sony has had difficulties turning a profit on its TV production, with losses for four straight years since 2008.[57] Sony has attempted to decrease costs by closing factories in Spain, Slovakia and Mexico, and has looked to outsource production. In December 2011, Sony dropped out of its joint venture with Samsung to develop liquid crystal display (LCD) screens and may move to cheaper suppliers in Taiwan. A movement towards outsourcing has led to varying opinions on where Sony is headed. Some believe that Sony will focus more on designing rather than manufacturing to compete with companies such as Apple.[58] However, others believe Sony will continue to focus on manufacturing high-end TVs but will outsource production of small and medium sized TVs.[59]

In April 2012, Kazuo Hirai replaced Howard Stringer as Sony's CEO. In the months preceding his new role, Mr Hirai alluded to shifting the strategic focus for Sony to put more emphasis on digital content and networks. Ultimately, Hirai hopes to "bring everything under the Sony Entertainment Network umbrella" and to integrate all of Sony's devices, users, and data.[60]

QUESTIONS

1. How did Sony internationalize its R&D activities? What were the initial motivations for Sony to establish technology centres abroad? How would Kuemmerle categorize the R&D centres at Sony?
2. How have the motivations for internationalizing R&D changed over time?
3. Why did Sony feel the need to internationalize its R&D activities in the late 1980s and early 1990s?
4. How did Sony manage its overseas R&D activities? How did the managerial approach evolve over time?
5. What have been the problems with Sony's way of managing R&D activities?
6. Besides in-house restructuring to strengthen its technological capabilities, what did Sony do to rejuvenate its businesses?
7. Can you provide an update on the internationalization of Sony's R&D activities, using materials available on the Web?

Notes

1. Walter Kuemmerle, 'Building effective R&D capabilities abroad', *Harvard Business Review* 75 (1997), 61–70.
2. *Ibid.*, 62, 70.

3. Michael E. Porter, 'The competitive advantage of nations', *Harvard Business Review* 68 (1990), 73–93.
4. Kuemmerle, 'Building effective R&D capabilities abroad', 62.
5. *Ibid.* Kuemmerle's sample had a slightly higher proportion of home-base-exploiting sites, representing 55 per cent of the labs studied compared with 45 per cent of home-base-augmenting labs.
6. *Ibid.*, 64.
7. *Ibid.*
8. *Ibid.*, 65.
9. The single most significant moment in modern communications history may well have been 6 August 1991, when CERN, the European Laboratory for Particle Physics located in Switzerland, placed online the first website, thereby publicizing the new World Wide Web. Two years before that date, Tim Berners-Lee, a CERN Fellow, had started developing the Hypertext Markup Language (HTML) and the Hypertext Transfer Protocol (HTTP), as well as the first Web pages.
10. Alan Rugman and Alain Verbeke, 'Location, competitiveness, and the multinational enterprise', *The Oxford Handbook of International Business* (2001), 150–77.
11. J. Birkinshaw and N. Fry, 'Subsidiary initiatives to develop new markets', *Sloan Management Review* 39 (1998), 51–62.
12. *Ibid.*, 52.
13. Alain Verbeke and Wenlong Yuan, 'Subsidiary autonomous activities in multinational enterprises: a transaction cost perspective', *Management International Review* 45 (2005), 31–52.
14. For a conceptual analysis, see Alan Rugman and Alain Verbeke, 'Extending the theory of the multinational enterprise: internalization and strategic management perspectives', *Journal of International Business Studies* 34 (2003), 125–37.
15. Andrew Inkpen, 'Learning through alliances', *California Management Review* 47 (2005), 114–36.
16. *Ibid.*, 120–1. Kanban is the instrument through which the just-in-time approach is implemented in manufacturing. It means that a signal from the demand side triggers action, i.e., a set of production activities. Andon is a system that signals problems in the production process requiring attention and support.
17. Kuemmerle, 'Building effective R&D capabilities abroad', 61.
18. *Ibid.*, 69.
19. *Ibid.*, 68.
20. Birkinshaw and Fry, 'Subsidiary initiatives', 51–62.
21. D. E. Westney, 'Cross-Pacific internationalization of R&D by U.S. and Japanese firms', *R&D Management* 23 (1993), 171–81.
22. Siemens company information, 10 March 2012.
23. Siemens, 'Global research at Siemens', (2011), 4.
24. Siemens company information, www.siemens.com/index.jsp?sdc_p=t15ls5o1372623i1372572cd1187 (5 January 2007).
25. Siemens company information, http://w4.siemens.de/ct/en/technologies/fue/index.html (5 January 2007).
26. Siemens company information, www.siemens.com/index.jsp?sdc_p=t15ls5o1372623i1372572cd1187 (5 January 2007).
27. *Ibid.*
28. Siemens company information, www.siemens.com/index.jsp?sdc_p=t15ls5o1320009i1319932cd 1187140fmu20n1319932pFEz3&sdc_sid=26004352353& (5 January 2007).

29. Siemens, 'Global research at Siemens', (2011), 32.
30. Daniel Schafer, 'Development tooled to fit the demands of emerging markets', *Financial Times* (17 March 2011).
31. *Ibid.*
32. Siemens, 'Worldwide cooperation with leading research institutions', (2012).
33. Siemens, 'Global research at Siemens', (2011), 34.
34. *Ibid.*
35. Daren Fonda, 'How Sony got game?' *Time* 168 (27 November 2006), 54; Michiyo Nakamoto, 'Sony looks to touch customers' hearts: the company is struggling to dispel concerns that it has lost touch with both its buyers and investors', *Financial Times* (30 June 2003), 26.
36. Sony company information, www.sony.net/SonyInfo/CorporateInfo/History/prospectus.html (26 September 2007).
37. Arun Khan and A. V. Vedpuriswar, 'Sony Corporation in 2004', *ICFAI Business School Case Development Centre* (2005), Case number 3050154, 6.
38. Sony company information, www.sony.net/Fun/SH/1-16/h1.html (27 October 2007).
39. Sadanori Arimura, 'How Matsushita Electric and Sony manage global R&D', *Research-Technology Management* 42 (1999), 41–51.
40. Yasuyuki Motoyama, 'Innovation and location: A case study of Sony's Vaio laptop', *The Industrial Geographer* 8 (2011) 1–25.
41. Sony Corporation, 'Chapter 19: Globalization of R&D Operations' (2012).
42. Sony company information, www.sony.net/Fun/SH/1-29/h3.html (27 October 2007).
43. *Ibid.*
44. Sony Corporation, 'Special interview Setsu Harada', www.sony.net/SonyInfo/technology/interview/sp01.html
45. *Ibid.*
46. *Ibid.*
47. Daisuke Wakabayashi and Juro Osawa, 'Sony PlayStation to mind budget', *Wall Street Journal (Eastern Edition)* (31 May 2011) , B.4.
48. Robin Harding and Robin Kwong, 'Sony to sell TV plant in Mexico', *Financial Times* (2 September 2009), 16.
49. Daisuke Wakabayashi, 'Sony's dollar-yen exposure now 'virtually zero', *Wall Street Journal (Online)* (3 March 2011).
50. 'Sony to cut costs in effort to mitigate yen's strength', *Financial Times* (4 April 2008), 15.
51. Michiyo Nakamoto, 'Screen test: Stringer's strategy will signal to what extent Sony can stay in the game', *Financial Times* (21 September 2005), 17.
52. 'Stringer's along THE', *Financial Times* (21 September 2005), 16.
53. Nicole Swengley, 'The shape of sounds to come', *Financial Times* (3 April 2010), 9.
54. Tim Burt and Joshua Chaffin, 'The streamliner in charge of "Project Nippon" ', *Financial Times* (22 June 2005), 11.
55. Sony Corporation, 'Sony Group corporate strategy update FY2008-FY2010', *Business Wire* (26 June 2008).
56. Nihon Keizai Shimbun, 'Interview: Sony aims for better use of R&D prowess', *Nikkei Weekly (*9 January 2012).
57. 'Sony sells its half stake in TV joint venture with Samsung', *The Guardian* (26 December 2011).
58. Kenji Hall, 'Can outsourcing save Sony?', *BusinessWeek* (30 January 2009).
59. 'Sony sells its half stake in TV joint venture with Samsung', *The Guardian* (26 December 2011).
60. Bryan Gruley and Cliff Edwards, 'What is Sony now?', *Bloomberg BusinessWeek* (17 November 2011).

7

International sourcing and production

Five learning objectives

1. To describe the changes in the international business environment leading to new roles assigned to international factories.
2. To explain the two key parameters underlying the roles of foreign manufacturing plants and to highlight the six generic factory roles.
3. To explain the contribution of tools such as flexible manufacturing systems, just-in-time and total quality management when making locating decisions for establishing production plants.
4. To develop an understanding of the difficulties associated with transferring manufacturing knowledge in high-technology firms.
5. To identify the limitations of a strategy aimed at upgrading foreign manufacturing plants.

This chapter examines Kasra Ferdows' idea that senior MNE managers should try to upgrade their host country factories to give them the ability to develop FSAs. For Ferdows, a factory's ability to develop FSAs is at least as important as low costs. In general, he argues, this will require that senior managers invest in each factory for the long term, and not move production based on changes in exchange rates, costs or government incentives. These ideas will be examined and then criticized using the framework presented in Chapter 1.

Significance

In an *HBR* piece entitled 'Making the most of foreign factories', **Kasra Ferdows** provides a detailed argument in support of the market seeking and strategic resource seeking arguments for FDI in the context of international manufacturing.[1]

Chapter 5 has already described how MNEs can tap their foreign subsidiaries as sources of competitive advantage, selectively giving certain subsidiaries increased control and decision-making power. Chapter 6 then extended this analysis, with a focus on foreign R&D centres. These centres can develop new knowledge that exploits or even augments the knowledge developed in the home country. This chapter will extend this analysis further, looking at how MNEs can tap their foreign factories.

Ferdows bases his research on a wide variety of sources, including his own consulting work with a dozen large manufacturing MNEs, a four-year study conducted with ten large MNEs (Apple, Digital Equipment, Electrolux, Ford, HP, Hydro Aluminum, IBM, Olivetti, Philips and Sony), industry surveys of companies (pharmaceuticals, food processing and paper machinery) and the Global Manufacturing Futures Surveys project, studying the practices of nearly 600 manufacturers operating in the triad regions of North America, Europe and Japan.

Ferdows attempts to answer one key question: "How can a factory located outside of a company's home country be used as a competitive weapon not only in the market that it directly serves but also in every market served by the company?"[2] The answer depends largely on the mindset of home country senior managers: what do they think is the proper role of foreign factories? Senior managers who view their factories merely as sources of efficient, low-cost production typically don't allocate their factories many resources, and these managers get only what they expect: efficient, low-cost production. In contrast, senior managers with higher performance expectations from their foreign factories require innovation and customer service as well: these managers "generally expect their foreign factories to be highly productive and innovative, to achieve low costs, and to provide exemplary service to customers throughout the world".[3] These managers allocate their factories more resources and get more in return.

In his study, Ferdows observes that the most successful manufacturing MNEs view their foreign factories as sources of FSAs beyond the ability to save costs as with conventional offshoring plants. Ferdows therefore concludes that, beyond the traditional motives such as "tariff and trade concessions, cheap labour, capital subsidies, and reduced logistics costs", MNEs should leverage their foreign factories "to get closer to . . . customers and suppliers, to attract skilled and talented employees, and to create centres of expertise for the entire company".[4]

Ferdows describes three changes in the international business environment driving the assignment of these new foreign factory roles. First, international trade tariffs declined substantially in the second half of the twentieth century, reducing the need to establish foreign plants merely to overcome trade barriers. Second, modern manufacturing is increasingly technologically sophisticated (meaning capital-intensive) and has complex supply-chain requirements. As a result, MNEs seldom select manufacturing locations based simply on the lowest possible

wages. Rather, the emphasis is on the overall productivity level, which is determined by several factors, including the available levels of infrastructure, technology, worker education and skills. Third, the time frame available to move from
development to actual manufacturing and marketing has become shorter. As a
result, MNEs increasingly co-locate development and manufacturing activities in
highly specialized plants, which then receive broad geographic mandates within
their areas of expertise.

These changes are consistent with the argument developed in Chapter 6,
that the successful penetration of foreign markets requires more than merely
transferring non-location-bound knowledge from the home country to the host
country. MNEs are increasingly attempting to augment conventional, host country production with at least some local R&D activities, rather than centralizing
such activities in the home country and then deploying this non-location-bound
knowledge to host countries as the basis of foreign manufacturing. A subsidiary
located in a specialized foreign knowledge cluster, as described in Chapter 3, must
become the company specialist for those knowledge areas in which the cluster has
core strengths. In other words, the subsidiary must develop, in its own right,
internationally transferable FSAs, building upon the location advantages of the
host country cluster.

The article distinguishes among six possible roles for foreign manufacturing
facilities, based upon two parameters. First, the strategic purpose of the plant,
which is intimately related to the host country location advantages the MNE
wants to access (e.g., proximity to market, access to low-cost production and
access to knowledge and skills). Second, the level of distinct FSAs held by the
plant (weak or strong). Here, the level of distinct FSAs refers to the additional
strengths added by the plant itself, augmenting the FSAs transferred from the
home country. Note also that this includes the plant's higher-order FSAs, such
as the ability to generate new knowledge and new FSAs. As regards purpose,
it was noted in Chapter 5 that a distinction should be made between the
subsidiary's role in accessing host country input markets (e.g., for skilled
labour) versus output markets (i.e., for selling the company's products).
Ferdows makes a similar distinction in the context of manufacturing activities.
His 'proximity to market' purpose reflects the importance of output markets for
selling the MNE's products (output market seeking investments). His second
purpose, 'access to low-cost production', reflects the factory's need to access
input markets. Finally, his third purpose, 'access to knowledge and skills',
is often closely tied to both input and output markets. By definition, it encompasses some need to tap into input markets, especially for sophisticated
production factors, but in many cases the ultimate goal is to serve (output)
markets with innovative products.

The two parameters above allow Ferdows to distinguish among six specific
factory roles (see Figure 7.1):

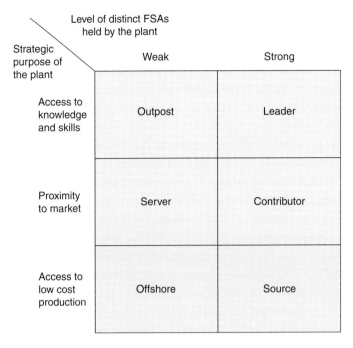

1. **Offshore factory:** this factory's primary purpose is simply to access low-cost production factors as an implementer on the input side. The plant's manufacturing output, typically predetermined by senior management in the home country, is then exported. This factory type typically does not develop new FSAs and receives minimum autonomy.

2. **Server factory:** this factory's primary purpose is to manufacture goods and to supply a predefined, proximate national or regional output market. Market imperfections such as trade barriers, logistics costs and foreign exchange exposure usually explain the establishment of such factories in specific host countries. A server factory may engage in some FSA development, but it ultimately has a narrow charter with relatively little autonomy or specialized capabilities.

3. **Outpost factory:** similar to the 'black hole' type subsidiaries discussed in Chapter 5, the primary purpose of this factory is to gather valuable information from advanced host country clusters, mainly on the input side. On the actual manufacturing side, this role is usually combined with that of an offshore (input market driven) or server (output market driven) factory.

4. **Source factory:** this factory's primary purpose is to gain access to low-cost production factors on the input side, similar to an offshore factory. However, it also receives resources to engage in resource recombination and to develop FSAs that will turn it into a 'best practice' plant in the MNE's network for the assigned product range. It therefore has more autonomy in terms of logistics, product customization, redesign, etc. The MNE sets up source factories in locations with good infrastructure and a skilled workforce. This type of

factory may be a strategic leader on the input side of the value chain, but nonetheless has a narrow charter.

5. **Contributor factory:** this factory type is oriented primarily towards the host country or host region output market, similar to a server factory, but it commands stronger capabilities than a server factory. More at the upstream end of the value chain, it is responsible for resource recombination in the form of process improvements, new product development, customizations, etc.

6. **Lead factory:** this factory type is the most important one in terms of resource recombination and new FSA development. It accesses valuable inputs from the local cluster where it is embedded and plays a key role in localized manufacturing innovation. It is also closely connected with both the key players on the input side (such as research labs) and the end users on the output side.

Overall, says Ferdows, the MNE should aim to upgrade its offshore, server and outpost factories so that they gain the ability to develop FSAs as source, contributor and lead factories. However, this upgrading process requires a high level of commitment, as it "entails a substantial investment of time and resources, as well as changes in a factory's culture and management style".[5]

Upgrading, according to Ferdows, involves substantial resource recombination spread over three stages: enhancing internal performance (e.g., through employee training and education, self-managed teams and adopting just-in-time manufacturing (JIT)), accessing and developing external resources (e.g., strengthening the plant's supplier network and improving the logistics integration with distributors) and developing new knowledge that can benefit the overall MNE network. As the MNE guides its foreign factories towards taking on upgraded, FSA-developing roles, it tends to place greater emphasis on intangible internal strengths and location advantages rather than tangible ones such as lower costs, taxes or the benefit of avoiding trade barriers. Intangible strengths include the factories' recombination capabilities, especially their capacity to absorb host country knowledge, to learn from customers, suppliers and rivals, and to attract new talent. The end result of the upgrading process is a 'robust network'[6] of factories with FSA-developing roles, able to adapt swiftly to changes in the marketplace. According to Ferdows, such a network is conducive to stability and security of internal MNE functioning over the long term, even if many plants are located in so-called 'high-cost' locations. This 'robust network' view of the MNE is in sharp contrast with the popular view that many MNEs should operate a so-called 'footloose' set of plants. Footloose operations imply low exit barriers, as well as the capability to relocate manufacturing operations and redeploy resources across geographic space rapidly in response to changing cost conditions.

According to Ferdows, MNE strategic manufacturing planning should focus on specializing foreign factories, with each plant taking on a leadership role in a specific area, and avoiding the duplication of R&D efforts: "The solution lies in specialization. Whenever feasible, a foreign factory's ultimate mission should include developing a world-class specialty."[7]

A number of examples illustrate this point. In the late 1970s, the US-based technology company NCR (set up in 1884 as the National Cash Register Company, acquired by AT&T in 1991 and re-established as a separate company in 1996) had closed down five factories in the area of Dundee, Scotland, and had one remaining, a server factory that was fighting for its survival. Building upon a structural change inside NCR that included a new focus on business units, the subsidiary management decided to refocus this factory, specializing in automated teller machines (ATMs) for the banking industry. The upgrading efforts included improving performance and speeding up product development cycle times. "By 1990, Dundee had become NCR's lead plant for ATMs, with primary responsibility for developing and manufacturing the products that the billion-dollar business needed."[8]

During the same period, Sony built a new plant in Wales (UK), initially intended as a server factory to overcome European trade barriers against outsiders. Over 15 years, however, the factory pioneered new quality control processes, both internally and with local suppliers, and eventually took on responsibility for R&D to customize television product designs for the European market. "Since 1988, the plant has designed and developed most of the products it has produced . . . It continues to be a strong and valuable contributor plant in Sony's global network."[9]

In closing, Ferdows cautions managers about four common obstacles that may prevent the upgrading of foreign factories: fear of relying on foreign operations for critical skills, treating overseas factories like cash cows and neglecting long-term investment, creating instability by shifting production in reaction to fluctuating exchange rates and costs, and the enticement of government relocation incentives to move factories to new locations that possess minimal potential for upgrading.

Context and complementary perspectives

Ferdows' article appeared in the same 1997 edition of the *HBR* as Kuemmerle's 'Building effective R&D capabilities abroad', discussed in Chapter 6. At that point in time, as noted above, it had become necessary for many firms to improve linkages between host country manufacturing and actual knowledge development activities, so as to command the required location-bound FSAs to function effectively in host country environments. In addition, senior MNE managers perceived the need to gain access to geographically dispersed innovation clusters as the basis for new resource recombinations, culminating in new, internationally transferable FSAs. For these two reasons, many MNEs created R&D labs in host countries, often in conjunction with host country factories.

The potential of host country subsidiaries as a source of both location-bound and internationally transferable knowledge provided the impetus for companies to review their international operations. Freer trade in the form of lower tariffs and non-tariff barriers alike resulting from institutions and agreements such as GATT, NAFTA and the EU had dramatically changed the landscape of international business. Companies were no longer forced to establish factories in local areas simply to overcome unnatural market imperfections imposed by governments. At the same time, fiscal instability, dramatic devaluations of currencies and political uncertainty in developing countries in Latin America, Asia and Eastern Europe created new bounded rationality problems for MNEs trying to reconfigure their dispersed subsidiary networks. The latter part of the 1990s also saw a halt in the seemingly endless boom of several Far East economies, as Japan and the developing Asian Tigers became mired in a prolonged recession. Senior MNE managers were thus forced to rethink the bigger picture when planning the location of their factory networks to achieve optimal efficiency and effectiveness. As Ferdows suggests, companies were beginning to realize that across-the-board relocation of activities to low-wage, off-shore production areas was not necessarily the panacea to achieve higher overall productivity, lower manufacturing costs and better access to customers.

A first complementary perspective is provided by practitioners (senior consultants) **Alan MacCormack**, **Lawrence Newman** and **Donald Rosenfield** in an *SMR* piece entitled 'The new dynamics of global manufacturing site location'.[10] The authors argue, much in line with Ferdows' analysis, that senior MNE managers in capital-intensive, mature industries should not neglect qualitative parameters when locating manufacturing plants. Senior managers, facing severe bounded rationality constraints, tend to favour easily quantifiable variables such as factor cost advantages, thereby neglecting what may be much more important in the longer run: the knowledge and skills held by the local workforce. It is this workforce's quality that ultimately determines the effectiveness of MNE subsidiaries in implementing skill-based process technologies.

The authors identify a trend towards regionalization, with many firms attempting to seek a manufacturing presence in each of the triad regions of North America, Europe and Asia to mitigate a variety of political risks (such as non-tariff barriers) and economic risks (such as foreign currency exposure) typically associated with the strategy of **international projectors**. The question then arises where to locate manufacturing plants in host regions. The authors observe a critical manufacturing trend.

The emergence of manufacturing technologies and methodologies such as flexible manufacturing systems, just-in-time manufacturing, and total quality management have reduced scale, increased the importance of worker education and skill, and placed demands on local infrastructure.[11]

Flexible manufacturing systems (FMS) are an efficient response to the reduction of product life cycles and the need to adapt products to satisfy idiosyncratic customer needs. An FMS "integrates computer-controlled tools and material handling systems with a centralized monitoring and scheduling function".[12] JIT allows an immediate response to specific customer demands and largely eliminates the need to hold inventories. Finally, total quality management (TQM) focuses on continuous improvement, whereby "heavy emphasis is placed on understanding and incorporating customer requirements into daily job routines at every level".[13]

The important point in the international context is that FMS, JIT and TQM all place significant demands on the host country workforce, which is viewed as an important location advantage, supposed to implement and perhaps improve these systems. For example, in MNEs that use these systems, engineers typically "outnumber production workers three to one".[14] In this context, the authors suggest the following human resources requirements be imposed on potential site locations:

> All employees must be highly flexible and multiskilled. For FMS, an ability to understand complex machinery and computers is essential. Successful JIT manufacturing requires that employees perform preventive maintenance, repairs, and complex planning activities. TQM . . . improvement tools make extensive use of mathematics and statistics. Softer skills such as team dynamics and proactive problem-solving techniques are also important.[15]

If these high-quality requirements are imposed on the workforce, then manufacturing plants will benefit from being located in places with sophisticated labour markets, an extensive educational infrastructure, and substantial experience with advanced manufacturing, including experience embedded in component suppliers, logistics services providers, etc. A critical point here is that an excellent site location must provide resources that can be combined with the MNE's extant set of FSAs. These resources can usually only be found in high-cost locations, which will thus still be attractive in the future. In turn, the MNE's recombination capabilities are crucial to access, exploit and augment such advanced human resources available in the highly developed sites selected for manufacturing operations.

Craig Galbraith provides a second complementary perspective with his *CMR* piece on the transfer of core manufacturing technologies in high technology firms.[16] He observes many firms locked into a situation of 'profitless prosperity', whereby continuous investment in innovation – combined with fierce international competition and short product cycles – brings little if any financial rewards. One way to escape from this situation, according to Galbraith, is to move towards a system of flexible, smaller manufacturing plants that can easily adapt to changes on both the demand and supply sides. For example, in terms of supply conditions, smaller plants can be set up to take advantage of lower input costs for simple value chain activities (e.g., final stages of assembly and testing) or to be closer to places of technology creation. As regards demand, a decentralized manufacturing network facilitates region-specific production (e.g., geared specifically towards the EU countries) and also allows the MNE to easily expand, contract or refocus plants in response to changes in demand.

In the context of this chapter's discussion of factories' ability to generate transferable FSAs, the question then arises: can manufacturing technologies be easily transferred, deployed and exploited across factories in a firm's network? Galbraith found, after investigating a sample of 32 manufacturing technology transfers (both domestic and international), that these transfers were accompanied by substantial resource costs as well as productivity and know-how losses. Resource costs include both pre-transfer planning and engineering costs, as well as post-transfer management and control costs. The productivity and know-how losses reflect the need for a start-up phase at the plant receiving the manufacturing knowledge, during which experiential knowledge from the source facility must be relearned at the recipient plant. There is a trade-off between the two above cost categories: higher resource costs (better planning and execution) should in principle reduce the productivity and know-how losses.

Even though Galbraith did not consider explicitly the complex issue of knowledge recombination, he observed that both stand-alone and routine-type manufacturing knowledge faced substantial transfer difficulties. Even though the transfers were all intra-firm and limited to proven technologies, initial productivity losses averaged 34 per cent, with some recipient facilities never achieving pre-transfer productivity levels, and most taking several months to attain the levels prevailing at the donor facility. Galbraith observed an important bounded rationality problem: more pre-transfer training did not reduce productivity losses. The two main reasons for the disappointing effects of training were: (1) the training team often lacked operational responsibility and operational ('on the floor') experience; and (2) insufficient attention was paid to production support activities such as ordering and inventory control procedures, and redefinition of personnel requirements and job responsibilities. Galbraith also observed a bounded reliability problem: in several technology relocation cases, donor facility personnel refused to provide long-term support to the recipient facility. Such lack of cooperation, obviously increasing productivity losses, occurred when manufacturing relocation was viewed as unfairly removing commercially viable production from the donor facility.

Ferdows' *HBR* piece focuses on the key issues of location advantages, the transferability of home country FSAs and the creation of FSAs in host country factories. The key assumption is that factories located in various host markets offer new bases from which to acquire and develop FSAs:

MANAGEMENT INSIGHTS

> Why spread these specialized units around the globe? Why not keep them in one location or close to one another? Why not keep them in the home country? Because a company would miss opportunities to collect and digest the expertise that other regions have to offer.[17]

As we have done with previous authors in previous chapters, we can classify Ferdows' recommendations as advice for senior managers to follow certain patterns of FSA development over others. His recommendation to upgrade off-shore, server and outpost facilities – established to access and exploit respectively low-cost production factors, proximity to markets and available skills and know-ledge – ultimately reflects a shift from the top part of Figure 7.2 (FSAs developed at home), towards its middle part (FSAs developed in a host country) and bottom part (FSAs developed by the internal network).

Overall, the FSAs held by the weaker foreign factories (i.e., offshore, server and outpost plants) are primarily the non-location-bound FSAs transferred from the

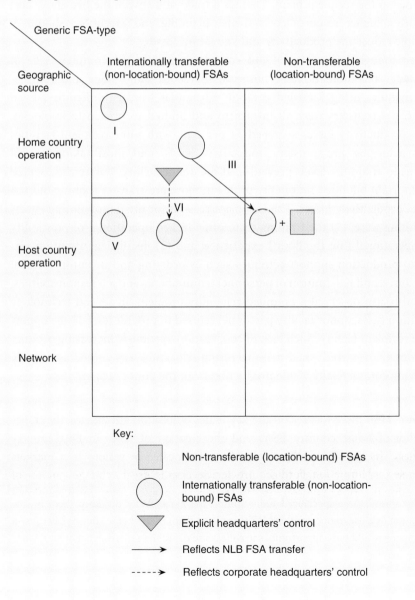

Figure 7.2
Ferdows' analysis
of FSA development
in MNEs

Generic FSA-type

Geographic source

Internationally transferable (non-location-bound) FSAs

Non-transferable (location-bound) FSAs

Home country operation

I

III

Host country operation

V

VI

Network

Key:

☐ Non-transferable (location-bound) FSAs

◯ Internationally transferable (non-location-bound) FSAs

▽ Explicit headquarters' control

⟶ Reflects NLB FSA transfer

----➤ Reflects corporate headquarters' control

home country, with little if any distinct knowledge added. This is consistent with Pattern I in this book's conceptual framework, the behaviour of the ***international projector***.

In contrast, the upgraded plants (i.e., source, contributor and lead factories) reflect other patterns in this book's framework. Contributor factories, which customize products to suit the host market, fit Pattern III: internationally transferable FSAs developed in the home country and diffused to host country plants are accompanied by regional modifications or enhancements in response to local market needs.

Finally, consider source and lead factories, both of which exploit valuable (input side) production factors present in host countries (with lead plants having a broader mandate). These types of host country factories are supposed to develop into centres of excellence with world-class competencies in specific product areas. These factories follow Patterns V and VI, whereby non-location-bound FSAs are generated through operations in host countries, either autonomously (Pattern V) or under close direction and guidance of head office (Pattern VI).

Ferdows' analysis has three main limitations. First, Ferdows ultimately believes that senior managers should try to upgrade ***all*** their factories. This homogenizing strategy flies in the face of what was suggested in Chapter 5 on giving subsidiaries different roles. Ferdows most definitely does not view the MNE as a portfolio of operations, with some of these acting as 'implementers' indefinitely. Even though he is correct that an internal MNE network of plants is a dynamic system, and that plants' roles can change, it would be somewhat naïve to assume, especially for large manufacturing firms, that all plants should be candidates for upgrading in the sense of becoming specialized centres of excellence with a distinct knowledge base inside the MNE. Here, the economies of scale and scope resulting from an approach with little plant upgrading obviously need to be weighed against the benefits of allowing plants to become increasingly embedded in host locations and to deviate substantially from adopting and applying the MNE's key routines. This trade-off must be assessed for each plant in the MNE network, and there is no guarantee that every single plant should be upgraded. In fact, most large MNEs operate with a number of 'strategic leader' plants (using the terminology from Chapter 5), positioned on the upper part of Figure 7.1, but usually also have many 'implementer' plants, consistent with the various roles described by Ferdows on the lower part of Figure 7.1.

The key differences among the six plant types identified by Ferdows are visualized in Figure 7.3.

As a second limitation, Ferdows' article does not discuss the changing nature of production in terms of outsourcing and the increased use of long-term, relational contracting with external suppliers. Especially within the sampled industries of technology-based companies, many of the market leaders such as Nortel, Lucent and Cisco have long pursued an outsourcing strategy. For these companies, manufacturing generally occurs in host country, emerging economies (see also

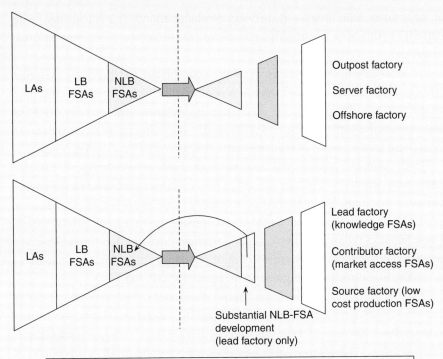

Figure 7.3
Key differences among the six plant types

Outpost factory

Server factory

Offshore factory

Lead factory
(knowledge FSAs)

Contributor factory
(market access FSAs)

Source factory (low
cost production FSAs)

Substantial NLB-FSA
development
(lead factory only)

The bottom, host country triangle has a larger middle area than the top one, because of greater LB-FSA development in these types of factories. The thin, curved arrow out of the bottom host country triangle, pointing to the left, means the NLB-FSAs developed in the host country can be transferred back to the home country or to other affiliates in the MNE network.

Chapter 14) by dedicated contract manufacturers or original equipment manufacturers (OEMs) such as Flextronics, Solectron and Sanmina-SCI, in exchange for long-term, exclusive contracts to manufacture products designed by the MNE. These large MNEs focus instead on the control of R&D on the upstream side and investments in branding on the downstream side.

A significant driver of outsourcing is the use of information communications technology (ICT) to monitor and coordinate with outside suppliers. Here, the MNE can easily and inexpensively identify poor quality, cost inefficiencies, delays in the logistics chain, etc. The result is increasingly blurred organizational boundaries between in-house product development and manufacturing and similar activities performed by manufacturing partners. This new division of labour may give the MNE full access to attractive production factors, including knowledge and skills in host environments, without the need to upgrade its own manufacturing facilities. The possibility of long-run, relational contracting adds a new trade-off to be considered when reflecting upon the upgrading of factories abroad: a 'robust network' may include 'robust' relationships with external contracting parties, rather than solely a set of upgraded factories.

The third limitation of Ferdows' analysis is that he underestimates the value of having low-cost, highly efficient factories in host countries, especially emerging markets that simply adopt and exploit both stand-alone technological knowledge from the parent as well as its key routines. On the one hand, this allows MNEs to improve their margins in their home country and other highly developed economies – markets where large and powerful distributors may try to squeeze the manufacturers' prices, and there may be strong competition and low growth rates. On the other hand, low-cost, highly efficient production may in some cases be the most practical tool to penetrate emerging, host countries – markets characterized by lower income levels and local low-cost manufacturers with lesser quality products.

Five management takeaways

1. View each of your foreign manufacturing plants as performing primarily one of six generic roles in your firm's portfolio of affiliates.
2. Consider the potential of 'upgrading' the existing, market seeking and resource seeking roles of individual foreign factories.
3. Re-evaluate your portfolio of international operations by recognizing changes in initial drivers for expansion and assess whether and how this portfolio could be improved further.
4. Assist source, contributor and lead factories to exploit their knowledge and to transform themselves into centres of excellence.
5. Take into account the quality of human resources when contemplating low-cost locations, and realize that successfully exploiting advanced production techniques requires access to a pool of sophisticated human resources.

Case 7.1 Defining the roles of manufacturing plants at Flextronics

CASE

As an electronics manufacturing services (EMS) company, Singapore's Flextronics International (managed from its headquarters in San Jose, California) may be an unfamiliar name to many, but it produces and delivers printers for Hewlett-Packard, cell phones for Sony Ericsson and Motorola, Xboxes for Microsoft and routers for Nortel, just to name a few of its customers. Its net sales in the fiscal year 2011 reached US $28.7 billion, with 29 per cent from the Americas, 19 per cent from Europe and 52 per cent from Asia. Its manufacturing facilities are dispersed over 30 countries in Asia, Europe and the Americas.[18]

Originally founded by Joe McKenzie and his wife in California in 1969, Flextronics initially soldered components into printed circuit boards (PCBs) for electronics firms (commonly referred to as original equipment manufacturers) in Silicon Valley. In 1980, the McKenzies sold Flextronics to a group of private investors, who expanded the firm's business from a mere 'stuffer' to a contract manufacturer. When Flextronics was just a 'stuffer', OEM customers shipped PCBs and components to Flextronics, which soldered components into the PCBs and then shipped the finished PCBs back to the OEM customers for further assembly. In contrast, when Flextronics became a contract manufacturer, OEM customers provided only the PCB design, and Flextronics took on the responsibility of purchasing the components and manufacturing the board.

In the 1980s, Flextronics expanded internationally. Setting up a facility in Singapore in 1981, it became one of the first American manufacturers to move offshore. By 1989, Flextronics' sales had reached US $202 million, with several operations in Asia and the US. However, the Silicon Valley downturn in the early 1990s seriously reduced the demand for Flextronics' services. A complex buyout privatized the firm in 1990, and the new owners moved the formal home base to Singapore and shut down US operations. Flextronics went public again in 1994.

Acquiring a global presence

Michael Marks became Flextronics' Chairman in 1993 and its CEO in 1994. He decided to rebuild the international presence of Flextronics through an aggressive strategy. Flextronics acquired manufacturing assets from OEMs and then used these assets to provide electronics manufacturing services, often to the very same OEMs. For example, Flextronics acquired manufacturing assets in Canada, Brazil, Malaysia and Mexico from Xerox, and then used these assets to manufacture copiers for Xerox. Flextronics moved aggressively, acquiring 53 operations between 1993 and 2001. Major acquisitions included the printed circuit board assemblies (PCBA) business from the Astron Group Ltd in Hong Kong in 1996, the assembly for industrial automation from ABB in 1999 and the systems assembly for GSM cell phones from Bosch Telecom in Denmark in 2000.[19]

Until the mid 1990s, Flextronics simply classified its manufacturing plants according to the complexity of PCB assembly and the technologies involved. In 1996, Flextronics manufactured complex PCBA by using the traditional pin-through-hole (PTH) technology, the more advanced surface mount technology (SMT) and the emerging multi-chip module (MCM) interconnect technologies. It had ten manufacturing facilities in 1996: one in Singapore, one in Malaysia, two in China, one in Hong Kong, four in the US and one in Wales. The plant in Singapore, for example, provided services with a "complex, high value-added PCB assembly using primarily SMT technology"; the Wales plant provided services with "medium complexity PCB assembly using both SMT and PTH technology"; and one US plant provided "advanced packaging and MCM design and fabrication".[20]

The large number of acquisitions led to a global network of manufacturing plants. In 1999, Flextronics started to report its facilities using a classification that included industrial parks, regional manufacturing facilities, product introduction centres and manufacturing and technology centres. After 2002, Flextronics changed its reporting, classifying its facilities into three types: industrial parks, regional manufacturing facilities and product introduction centres.

Industrial parks are located in low-cost areas close to major electronics markets. With facilities ranging between 270,000 square feet and more than 1.9 million square feet, these industrial parks contain both Flextronics' manufacturing and distribution operations and a number of its major suppliers, thereby reducing transportation costs and turnaround times in the manufacturing process. These parks were designed for fully integrated, large-volume manufacturing. In 2012, Flextronics had nine industrial parks located on three continents, with one in Poland, two in Hungary, two in Mexico, one in Brazil, one in India and two in China.

Regional manufacturing facilities engage in medium- and high-volume manufacturing in locations close to strategic markets.

Product introduction centres provide low-volume manufacturing services and a broad range of engineering services.

Finally, a fourth category, regional manufacturing and technology centres, are a combination of regional manufacturing facilities and product introduction centres. Regional manufacturing and technology centres were set up to launch new products, transform new products to mass production, and conduct medium- and high-volume manufacturing. Such regional centres include product introduction centres with advanced technological competencies, see below.

Industrial parks in focus

Industrial parks have been a major driver for the fast growth at Flextronics; former CEO Marks has even commented that "the future is big locations like these".[21] Since 2001, Flextronics has started to consolidate more of its production into its industrial parks. Already one year later, 30 per cent of Flextronics' business was performed through the parks.[22] Flextronics' approach has been to purchase extra land adjacent to its manufacturing facilities and then to attract suppliers and distributors to set up facilities in the park, where the supply of water, electricity and other services is readily available. Flextronics sometimes even takes responsibility for government relations, or puts up buildings and leases them to suppliers. Such services are especially crucial to its suppliers, many of whom are small American firms lacking Flextronics' recombination abilities.

While some industrial parks face internal competition, others do not. For example, the Chennai industrial park in India was built to be Flextronics' only industrial park for India. It serves the Indian market exclusively, though it could become part of Flextronics' global supply network in the future.[23] In contrast, other parks have already experienced internal competition. The Guadalajara industrial park in Mexico and the Hungarian industrial parks mainly targeted the North American market and European market respectively, due to their proximity to these markets. However, some of the jobs done at the Mexican and Hungarian parks were moved to the Doumen industrial park in China.

The Doumen industrial park has quickly moved from making simple mobile phone chargers, to advanced miniature printed boards, to Microsoft's sophisticated Xbox. Tony Capretta, Flextronics' resident general manager, acknowledged the technical capability and experience of the plant's workforce: "We can do anything here that we make anywhere else . . . The learning curve is a fast ramp."[24] The Doumen industrial park enjoys the proximity of a dense local supplier network, as almost all materials Flextronics needs are available from thousands of suppliers within a two-hour drive of the park. In contrast, many materials and components needed by the Guadalajara industrial park in Mexico and the Hungarian industrial parks have to be sourced from the Far East. Therefore, lower labour cost at the Doumen industrial park, strong local suppliers and rising technological capabilities have made the Doumen industrial park very competitive within Flextronics.

However, not all production is being moved to China. In a later comment on the disruption of its supply chain (including maritime shipping) in China caused by the SARS virus, former CEO Marks said, "Some companies are moving stuff to China that really doesn't belong there. It makes sense to make cell phones in China because they are inexpensive to air-freight. But personal computers don't travel well. If you start to air-freight PCs because of a supply disruption, your cost-savings disappear instantly."[25] In the case of Xbox game consoles, Flextronics initially centralized production for the European market in Hungary and production for the US market in Mexico, but one year later it shifted all production to China. However, after the shutdown of the Xbox production line in Hungary, Flextronics ramped up other production lines at its Hungarian industrial parks, hiring personnel to make other products such as TVs for France's Schneider Electric.[26]

Restructuring the global network of plants

The many acquisitions resulted in a wide variety of plants spread around the globe. With a booming EMS business in the 1990s, such a huge, internationally dispersed network met demand very well. However, since 2001, the slow growth of the US economy and the duplication of manufacturing have triggered restructuring efforts.

In 2001, Flextronics decided to consolidate its production by closing (or exiting from) some duplicate plants and concentrating similar activities into fewer locations. In mid 2001, Flextronics decided to lay off 11,168 employees.[27] At the same time, it shut down around 20 per cent of its factory space.[28] For example, it shut down its manufacturing plants in Singapore and changed the Singapore operation into a competency centre in design.[29]

However, this restructuring did not mean simply moving all manufacturing to low-cost countries. CEO Marks commented that "it's a great simplification – and a lot of people fall into this trap – to say that all manufacturing is going to get done in Mexico, Hungary, and China. Consumer products will be made there. But the infrastructure products – technically complex value-added products – are easy to manufacture in developed countries. That's why we also have big operations in the US, Germany, France, and Sweden, where you have high capabilities in engineering. The OEMs like us to be everywhere."[30]

As noted by Marks, Flextronics still operates plants in some high-cost locations, either to stay close to key customers or to gain advanced technological capabilities. For example, though shutting down 26 of its 40 regional plants in electronics enclosures, Flextronics still kept 14 regional plants to be close to customers and to offer specific value-added activities, focusing on new product introduction and design.[31]

Gaining technological competencies was the other reason to stay in some high-cost locations. This is reflected in Flextronics' revised acquisition strategy, whereby acquisition activities have focused primarily on companies that have the recombination capabilities to offer technological solutions customized to customer needs. One example of this new strategy is the acquisition of US-based Instrumentation Engineering, Inc. (IE, based in Oakland, New Jersey) in 2001, a systems test equipment developer and manufacturer. IE had experience in designing and building custom test systems for optical and wireless network equipment, which would enhance Flextronics' capacity and capabilities in the functional test market. IE's president has taken on a global role within Flextronics' test operations worldwide.[32]

After the recession in 2008, Flextronics took on another round of restructuring to cope with the impact of lower demand faced by its customers. This time, the restructuring focused on cost cutting and improving operational efficiencies. Flextronics aimed to save around US $230–260 million by shifting operations to more efficiently run locations and laying-off some of its workforce.[33] The company also consolidated its suppliers to leverage its economies of scale and develop more strategic relationships. Flextronics now makes 90 per cent of its purchases with just 10 per cent of its suppliers.[34]

Flextronics in Asia

Asia continues to be a stronghold for Flextronics' operations with an estimated 60 per cent of production being performed there.[35] Production locations can be found throughout China, India, Japan, Malaysia, Singapore and Taiwan. Each location has developed specific strengths derived from the environment it operates in. For example, in Singapore, where the country is known for its advances in healthcare, Flextronics has established a medical manufacturing facility to help benefit the firm from innovative medical technologies. In China, the future largest auto market in the world, Flextronics operates a product design centre to assist automotive clients with product development.

China in particular remains an important market for Flextronics with an estimated 600,000 employees across 17 locations.[36] Given the scale of Flextronics operations in this country, it was important for the company to develop specific skills in order to succeed in various Chinese markets. Target markets in China often consist of smaller, locally based customers, as opposed to the large multinational corporations that make up the majority of customers in western markets. To meet the needs of these smaller customers, Flextronics has developed the 'Flextronics Supplier Portal', which allows customers to effectively track supplies to better meet end user needs. Furthermore, Flextronics has also developed human resource practices aimed at retaining local workers in an industry that typically experiences high turnover after the Chinese New Year. By responding to local pressures in China, Flextronics may have been able to develop successful practices that can be transferred across Asia.

Moving forward, Flextronics aims to continue its successful growth in Asia; however, it also wants to focus on diversifying globally.[37]

In 2012, Flextronics still operated regional manufacturing and technology centres in Austria, Brazil, China, Denmark, Germany, Hungary, India, Indonesia, Ireland, Israel, Italy, Japan, Malaysia, Mexico, Norway, Poland, Romania, Singapore, Slovakia, Sweden, Ukraine and the US. These centres were distributed across both high-cost and low-cost manufacturing locations in Europe, the Americas and Asia. Roughly 74 per cent of production in 2011 was completed in low-cost manufacturing locations to provide customers with competitive prices.[38]

Flextronics "has one of the world's most comprehensive geographic footprints, service offerings, and sets of capabilities",[39] which has allowed it to play a valuable role in its customers' success. This role has continually allowed the company to garner industry awards and recognition, including the Emulex supplier of the year award, the Cisco Smart award for operational excellence and the prestigious Business Superbrands Award in 2011.

QUESTIONS

1. How did Flextronics classify its plants before the mid 1990s? What was the drawback of such a classification?
2. Define the strategic roles of the following plants mentioned in the case: the Chennai industrial park in India, the Guadalajara industrial park in Mexico, the Doumen industrial park in China, regional manufacturing and technology centres, and the plants acquired from IE.
3. Why does Flextronics still have manufacturing activities in some high-cost regions?
4. What changes happened at the Singapore operations? What changes happened at the Doumen industrial park in China? What was expected for the Chennai industrial park in India?
5. Can you provide an update on the strategic role of Flextronics' plants, using materials available on the Web?

Case 7.2 Internationalizing production at BMW: An unfortunate experience in the UK

Known throughout the world for quality and style, BMW as a manufacturer of luxury automobiles, motorcycles and engines, has built a strong reputation and brand image. For decades, the BMW trademark has been synonymous with quality German manufacturing and with attention to detail that caters to the refined consumer with a passion for driving.

Currently, the BMW group consists of three brands: BMW, MINI and Rolls-Royce Motorcars. All three brands are associated with quality, luxury and a design focused on the driver's experience. With 24 manufacturing facilities in 13 countries and operations headquartered out of Munich, Germany, BMW reaches customers in over 150 countries worldwide.[40] The automotive firm has a solid grip on the global premium automotive market, one that it is not willing to relinquish without a fight.

It may therefore be surprising for those familiar with BMW's quality and luxury status to hear that the firm may have been partially responsible for the demise of UK-based MG Rover in 2005. BMW owned the iconic British automotive group with a noble history including the MG series, the Land Rover and the MINI from 1994 to 2000. BMW's efforts to integrate the Rover Group in the BMW group were not successful and BMW ultimately decided to sell the underperforming Rover Group in 2000. Only the MINI brand remains with BMW today.[41]

A brief history of BMW[42]

BMW's roots can be traced to aeronautical design and manufacturing. Bayerische Flugzeugwerke (BFW) was founded in 1916, and was combined with the Bayerische Motoren Werke (BMW) GmbH, created in 1917 from the restructuring of the military aircraft engine manufacturer Rapp-Motorenwerke. This combination would eventually become BMW AG, which was established in 1918. BMW AG was created as a stock corporation, and one third of the 12 million Reichsmark share capital was held by Camillo Castiglioni, an Italian-Austrian financier, with the reputation of being the richest person in Central Europe at the time of World War I.

The impact of World War I and World War II

With the end of World War I came a ban on aircraft engine manufacturing; in the 1920s BMW experienced a shift in focus to producing rail vehicle brakes and engines, and in 1922 relocated to the BFW factory in Munich. The 1930s–40s and World War II witnessed a surge in demand for aircraft engines, resulting in a flurry of activities for BMW, the dispersion of the aircraft engine manufacturing and the automotive production to smaller companies, the acquisition of a number of new plants, and the takeover of Brandenburgische Motorenwerke GmbH and its aircraft engine facilities.

Air raids in the 1940s caused damage to BMW's main Munich plant, and the US government seized control and dismantled most of the company's assets. In exchange for providing repairs to American military vehicles, BMW was allowed to resume manufacturing of spare parts, equipment, and, most importantly, motorcycles. By 1948, the company was back on its feet and began production of its first post-war motorcycles. By 1950, nearly one fifth of this motorcycle production was being exported outside of Germany.

BMW's perseverance pays off

BMW's new foothold in the automotive and motorcycle industries remained tenuous throughout the 1950s, and by the end of the decade Daimler-Benz made an offer to take over the company. This offer was declined largely due to shareholder Herbert Quandt's faith in the company; he increased his equity holdings in the firm and took control with some governmental financial aid. The Quandt family has retained the controlling majority of the BMW Group.[43]

During the 1960s, global demand soared for BMW automobiles and motorcycles. In order to relieve some pressure on the firm's overwhelmed plants, motorcycle production was moved to the old aircraft engine facility in Berlin-Spandau in 1969 and the Munich facility expanded production of automobiles. The 1970s were a period of major change, including the arrival of

Chairman Eberhard von Kuenheim, who led the company out of Europe and into global waters. He remained at BMW's helm until 1993, when he became Chairman of the Supervisory Board. Subsidiary BMW Kredit GmbH was established in 1971 to provide financing for the company and BMW dealers, as well as financing and leasing for customers.

The mid-to-late 1970s marked an important evolution in BMW's company structure: responsibility for sales was shifted to subsidiaries being established across the world. BMW was making the transition from being a German exporter to developing foreign subsidiaries. The year 1979 was a landmark year for BMW: in a joint venture with Steyr-Daimler-Puch AG, an engine plant was established in Steyr, Upper Austria, where just three years later the first diesel engine was developed. In the 1980s, massive new plants were added to BMW's production facilities in Germany, and a 'think tank' was established for new concept development and design innovation. By that time BMW had earned global recognition for its groundbreaking engine development and quality automobiles; a few concept vehicles had even gone into small-scale production with some success.

Maintaining a foothold in the global marketplace

Building upon its successes of the 1980s, BMW began to make massive strides to establish itself as a dominant player in the global luxury automotive market throughout the 1990s. Innovation and design became key strengths for the company, as illustrated by the establishment of BMW's Research and Innovation Centre in Munich in 1990. In 1992, BMW launched its US operations with a manufacturing facility in South Carolina; this plant serves as the sole production facility for the Z3 roadster and the X5 SUV.

While BMW was experiencing dramatic success and had developed powerful brand equity, it was still struggling in some markets, particularly in the UK. It was becoming increasingly apparent to then Chairman, Bernd Pischetsrieder, that BMW's small size and specialized product offering would not be enough to remain a global player in the automobile market which was becoming flooded with mass-produced models of increasing quality and decreasing prices.[44] Pischetsrieder recognized that BMW needed to appeal to new markets, including the UK market. The solution to this problem came in an unusual form: in what was hailed at the time as a brilliant strategic move, BMW purchased an 80 per cent controlling interest in Rover Group from British Aerospace for GBP 800 million, or approximately US $1.2 billion, in 1994.[45] BMW hoped to gain new strengths in mass production through the purchase of Rover, thereby realizing manufacturing economies of scale, additional branding power coming from the Rover brand name, and design and production capabilities specific to small-sized automobiles produced at a reasonable cost. BMW also stood to gain significant location advantages through the acquisition, primarily those of lower labour and manufacturing costs in the UK as compared to Germany. This acquisition would double BMW's production scale from 440,000 units to more than 800,000 automobiles per year,[46] which would represent a major step towards solving BMW's perceived size problem. According to one observer, this purchase "turned Europe's Big Six auto makers into the Big Seven and laid to rest the fear previously voiced by company chief Bernd Pischetsrieder that 'in 10 years' time, BMW might be too small to compete in the world auto industry.'"[47]

The Rover Group

The pre-BMW years

The Rover Group was an amalgamation of UK automobile companies with a noble and iconic heritage such as Austin, Rover and Triumph, most of which were founded in the late 1800s and early 1900s. Throughout the 1950s, 60s and 70s, most of the original UK auto manufacturers consolidated into one group, the British Motor Corporation (later the British Leyland Motor Corporation – BLMC), in order to compete with the increasingly dominating American multinational automobile companies such as Ford.[48]

The integration of these consolidated companies was not successful, and by 1975, the BLMC was nationalized and received GBP 2 billion in government financial aid. Even this large amount of resources was insufficient to rescue the failing company, and in 1979, Honda took a 20 per cent stake in Rover in exchange for the right to produce a Honda model rebranded as the Triumph Acclaim and services for the production of some Honda automobiles at Rover facilities. Throughout the 1980s, British Leyland was renamed as Austin Rover, and a number of auto models were developed in collaboration with Honda.[49] British Aerospace purchased the remaining 80 per cent stake in Austin Rover in 1988, and remained in control until it decided to sell the company in 1994. Rover doggedly attempted to convince Honda to increase its 20 per cent holding and take over the company, but Honda refused and BMW successfully purchased the remaining 80 per cent stake.[50,51]

BMW's acquisition of Rover

During its years of ownership of Rover, BMW invested heavily in development, hoping to revive flagging sales and capitalize on the Rover brands' iconic status as well as the firm's portfolio of small, front-wheel drive cars (an area of the market BMW had not been able to penetrate). The purchase positioned BMW as the world's largest specialty auto manufacturer and allotted the group previously unattainable economies of scale. Following the acquisition, in May 1994, BMW's shares rose in value from DM 740 to DM 927, an indication of investors' early support of the investment decision.[52] BMW hoped to drive down its high costs of production by offshoring some of its manufacturing to the newly acquired facilities in the UK.

In the first few years following the acquisition, both Rover and BMW experienced some success. Rover experienced increases in both domestic and export sales in 1996 and 1997, and heavy investments were made in research and development for new product offerings.[53,54] In 1997 and 1998, BMW's share price continued to rise dramatically, despite the drain of massive financial investments into Rover's development[55]. Even with increased sales, Rover continued to make financial losses throughout this period.

The end of Rover

In spite of all the 'positivity' and efforts to turn around the British manufacturer, the Rover Group continued to lose money, and by 2000, BMW had to rid itself of the lagging company. There is little consensus amongst industry analysts as to what exactly happened.

The beginning of the end

Despite the positive reception by the public of a new model launched under the Rover brand (the '75') in 1998, BMW chief Pischetsrieder publicly indicated frustration with Rover's continued financial losses and overall sluggish performance.[56] This marked the beginning of the end, as this announcement spawned a flurry of media reports that Rover was in trouble. That year, the reason for Rover's continued decline offered to the public by BMW and Rover spokespeople was the decreasing value of the British pound (i.e., an unfavourable exchange rate). However, this explanation has been explicitly rejected by a number of industry experts, who ranked Rover as the poorest performer in the European automotive industry based on both productivity and quality levels.[57,58]

The end – BMW's move to part ways with Rover

By 2000, a deeply embarrassed BMW cut its losses and divvied up and sold the Rover Group, retaining only the MINI brand. Land Rover was separated and sold to Ford for GBP 185 million, while the remaining group was renamed MG Rover and sold to the Phoenix Group for the rather shocking nominal sum of GBP 10.[59] Despite Phoenix's promises to turn a profit within two years, MG Rover continued to spiral into debt, haemorrhaging money throughout the next five years. In April 2005, the company was dissolved, leaving thousands of workers jobless.[60] This spectacular failure leads to a particular question: did BMW help contribute to Rover's decline, or did it do all it could to save the ailing company in an effort to diversify the geographic scope of its manufacturing base?

BMW's participation in Rover's destruction

BMW's management suffered from information problems in its decision making prior to the acquisition of Rover. Even BMW management admitted, following the failure of the Rover acquisition, that more information should have been gathered and a closer examination of the actual advantages to be gained should have been undertaken. Had such scrutiny taken place, it is unlikely that BMW would have gone through with the purchase in the first place.[61] It appears that the German firm overestimated Rover's brand equity, its production capabilities and the possibility to gain scale economies and manufacturing synergies with the remainder of the company.

Rover was suffering from productivity and quality issues problems prior to BMW's takeover in 1994, and it would appear that one major source of the group's failure to turn things around was

BMW's over-estimation of its own capabilities to revitalize/reengineer Rover, both financially and managerially.[62,63]

Production decisions

A key factor cited as a potential source of BMW's problems with Rover, was BMW's choices in the production sphere during its years of control. While the new model '75' was launched with some degree of success, BMW failed to develop other products to serve the demands of the very market segment it was targeting. In fact, the planned replacement for Rover's midrange platform was never actually launched, partially due to BMW's untimely dissolution of the company. By the time BMW sold Rover, it was left with an inadequate product portfolio that failed to meet the demands of growing market segments.[64]

Managerial deficiencies

After acquiring Rover, BMW initially gave the incumbent management a great deal of autonomy to continue production operations in the UK in a 'business as usual' fashion. BMW's attempt to avoid 'stepping on Rover's toes' resulted in a disastrous blindness to many of the troubles faced by Rover. For example, it has been heralded as a foolish neglect by BMW not to exploit the US' frenzied appetite for premium SUVs via the Land Rover brand, and an even greater mistake may have been to let the Land Rover unit go to Ford following the dissolution of the Rover Group; this failure was due in large part to slow strategic issue recognition and slow strategic response on the part of BMW management. By the time, BMW realized the problem and tried to regain control of the Rover operations, it was too late.[65]

From the perspective of Rover management, everything seemed to be going well at first but when BMW suddenly tried to impose its own administrative systems and was sending senior management from Germany to the UK to alter manufacturing operations, tensions began to run high. By 1996, Rover's CEO Towers had resigned, and BMW appointed a new CEO from the company's German board.[66] An article criticizing BMW for failing to come to terms with its small size and specialty orientation states:

> On a deeper level, a key factor in Rover's demise was that BMW believed – either through arrogance or naïveté – that it could turn Rover into a British version of itself. What the executives in Munich didn't realize was that the Rover brand had suffered too many quality problems over time, and consumers weren't going to come back – not even for a BMW-vetted product.[67]

It seems that one of BMW's largest failures during its time with Rover was its inability to achieve successful resource recombination in the host country. BMW's main problem in this case was not an inability to transfer its existing strengths from Germany to the UK, nor an inability to create knowledge through its newly acquired subsidiary, but rather an inability to integrate Rover-based knowledge with its existing knowledge base. Whether it was because BMW leadership lacked the skills necessary to perform this essential integration or whether it simply did not see the need,

BMW did not recombine its existing strengths with the potential new advantages brought by Rover. It would appear that the entire acquisition process was driven by top line concerns, i.e., the perceived need to increase scale, and by the rather naïve view that adding UK manufacturing plants to the BMW network of factories would somehow make for a more healthy and diversified production base. According to Grogaard, Verbeke and Zargarzadeh, such "lack of creative resource recombination as a precondition for market success reflects the absence of effective entrepreneurial action".[68]

QUESTIONS

1. What are some of BMW's FSAs? Was BMW able to diffuse these FSAs to Rover?
2. Did the acquisition of Rover provide substantial location-bound and non-location-bound FSAs to the BMW group?
3. Using Ferdows' framework, define the strategic role of the intended versus realized BMW-Rover manufacturing activities in UK.
4. Did BMW invest sufficiently in resource recombination after the Rover acquisition?
5. Can you provide an update on the strategic role of the various BMW manufacturing plants spread around the world, using materials available on the Web?

Notes

1. K. Ferdows, 'Making the most of foreign factories', *Harvard Business Review* 75 (1997), 73–88.
2. *Ibid.*
3. *Ibid.*
4. *Ibid.*, 73.
5. *Ibid.*, 86.
6. *Ibid.*
7. *Ibid.*, 87.
8. *Ibid.*, 83.
9. *Ibid.*, 84.
10. Alan David MacCormack, Lawrence James Newman and Donald B. Rosenfield, 'The new dynamics of global manufacturing site location', *Sloan Management Review* 35 (1994), 69–80.
11. *Ibid.*, 72.
12. *Ibid.*
13. *Ibid.*
14. *Ibid.*, 73.

15. *Ibid.*
16. Craig S. Galbraith, 'Transferring core manufacturing technologies in high-technology firms', *California Management Review* 32 (1990), 56–70.
17. Ferdows, 'Making the most of foreign factories', 76.
18. Flextronics company information, 2012.
19. Flextronics, Annual report (1996–2006).
20. Flextronics, Annual report (1996), 9.
21. Kerry A. Dolan, 'The detour economy', *Forbes* 169 (2002), 52.
22. *Ibid.*
23. Vankatesha Babu and Rahul Sachitanand, 'Heralding a hardware boom', *Business Today* (6 November 2005), 98.
24. Peter Wonacott, 'Talent Pool – China's secret weapon: smart, cheap labor for high-tech goods – beyond toys and garments, country raises the bar again in manufacturing – view from Mr. Li's balcony', *Wall Street Journal* (14 March 2002), A.1.
25. 'Weathering the tech storm: How Michael Marks boosted efficiency at contract manufacturer Flextronics', *Business Week* (5 May 2003), 24B.
26. Geri Smith, 'Wasting away despite SARS, Mexico is still losing export ground to China', *Business Week* (2 June 2003), 42.
27. Flextronics, 3rd Quarter Report (2001).
28. Dolan, 'The detour economy', 52.
29. Claire Serant, 'Singapore no longer an EMS magnet – Mainstay Flextronics latest to look for lower cost destination', *EBN* (2001), 3.
30. Gene Bylinsky, 'Heroes of U.S. manufacturing', *Fortune* 141 (20 March 2000), 192A.
31. Claire Serant, 'Flextronics consolidates EMS empire', *EBN* (2001), 1.
32. John Shedd, 'Flextronics to acquire Telcom, expands business unit', *Circuits Assembly* 12 (2001), 16.
33. 'Flextronics announces restructuring plans', Flextronics press release. http://news.flextronics.com/phoenix.zhtml?c=235792&p=irol-newsArticle&ID=1469515&highlight= (10 March 2009).
34. James Carbone, 'Flextronics focuses more spend with fewer suppliers', *Purchasing* (17 December 2009), 30.
35. 'The Flextronics effect', *Supply Chain Asia Magazine* (19 March 2012).
36. *Ibid.*
37. *Ibid.*
38. Flextronics, Annual report (2011), 10.
39. Flextronics, Annual report (2011), 2.
40. The BMW Group company information 2009.
41. M. Holweg and N. Oliver, 'Who killed MG Rover?', Centre for Competitiveness and Innovation, Cambridge: University of Cambridge (2005).
42. The BMW Group company information, 2005.
43. The BMW Group company information, 2008.
44. B. Gould, 'The BMW acquisition of Rover', *The Antidote* 3 (2) (1998), 37–38.
45. P. Bingham, 'BMW buys Rover', *Motor Trend* 46 (5) (1994), 18.
46. *Ibid.*
47. *Ibid.*
48. M. Holweg and N. Oliver, 'Who killed MG Rover?', Centre for Competitiveness and Innovation, Cambridge: University of Cambridge (2005).
49. *Ibid.*

50. *Ibid.*

51. P. Bingham, 'BMW buys Rover', *Motor Trend*, 46 (5) (1994), 18.

52. B. Gould, 'The BMW acquisition of Rover', *The Antidote* 3 (2) (1998), 37–8.

53. *Ibid.*

54. M. Holweg and N. Oliver, 'Who killed MG Rover?', Centre for Competitiveness and Innovation. Cambridge: University of Cambridge (2005).

55. B. Gould, 'The BMW acquisition of Rover', *The Antidote* 3 (2) (1998), 37–8.

56. M. Holweg and N. Oliver, 'Who killed MG Rover?', Centre for Competitiveness and Innovation, Cambridge: University of Cambridge (2005).

57. G. Robinson, 'The great Rover disaster', *New Statesman* (27 March 2000) 13–14.

58. M. Holweg and N. Oliver, 'Who killed MG Rover?', Centre for Competitiveness and Innovation, Cambridge: University of Cambridge (2005).

59. *Ibid.*

60. *Ibid.*

61. S. Zesiger, 'Why is BMW driving itself crazy?', *Fortune Magazine* (26 June 2000).

62. M. Holweg and N. Oliver, 'Who killed MG Rover?', Centre for Competitiveness and Innovation. Cambridge: University of Cambridge (2005).

63. G. Robinson, 'The great Rover disaster', *New Statesman* (27 March 2000), 13–14.

64. M. Holweg and N. Oliver, 'Who killed MG Rover?', Centre for Competitiveness and Innovation, Cambridge: University of Cambridge (2005).

65. S. Zesiger, 'Why is BMW driving itself crazy?', *Fortune Magazine* (26 June 2000).

66. P. Crush, 'When HARRY met BMW', *Human Resources* (November 2010), 41–2.

67. S. Zesiger, 'Why is BMW driving itself crazy?', *Fortune Magazine* (26 June 2000).

68. B. Grogaard, A. Verbeke and M. A. Zargarzadeh, 'Entrepreneurial deficits in the global firm', in A. Verbeke, A. Tavares-Lehmann and R. Van Tulder (eds.), *Entrepreneurship in the Global Firm* (Emerald, 2011), 117–37.

8

International finance

Five learning objectives

1. To define economic exposure and its strategic significance for the MNE.
2. To describe the various approaches to manage and minimize economic exposure.
3. To explain the short- and long-term effects of a global cash management system.
4. To justify why MNEs try to overcome market imperfections by using financial management tools.
5. To explain the linkages between the MNE's administrative heritage and its organization of the risk exposure management function.

This chapter examines Lessard and Lightstone's recommendations for how MNEs should deal with economic exposure. Economic exposure (also known as operating exposure) is the impact (i.e., the effect on the net present value of the MNE's future income streams) of changes in real exchange rates relative to the MNE's competitors. To minimize this impact, Lessard and Lightstone recommend that senior managers strive to (1) have a flexible sourcing structure (i.e., be able to shift production from one country to another quickly and efficiently), and (2) attain the capability to engage in exchange rate pass through (i.e., the capability to raise prices in response to exchange rate fluctuations without losing sales volume). To obtain this second capability, senior managers should try to obtain a market leadership position with highly differentiated products. According to Lessard and Lightstone, senior managers at MNEs should take economic exposure into account when determining their international business strategy (e.g., the likelihood of negative currency fluctuation should be taken into account when assessing location advantages). Lessard and Lightstone also present other specific strategies that senior managers at MNEs can use to minimize their economic exposure. These ideas will be examined and then criticized using the framework presented in Chapter 1.

Significance

D. R. Lessard and **J. B. Lightstone's** classic *HBR* article on the risk created by volatile exchange rates adds useful aspects of international finance to the discussion of MNE strategies.[1] Though this article is more than twenty years old, its substance remains important for multinational strategic management today. In essence, the authors observe that fluctuations in foreign exchange rates create the risk of net present value reduction of the firm's future income streams. This potential value reduction is called economic exposure. It is different from the more conventional transaction exposure (reflecting the risk of financial losses resulting from outstanding but unfulfilled contractual commitments, such as sales contracts in a foreign currency to be fulfilled at a later date; here, the relevant income streams are known, and can often be secured fully in the home country currency through simple hedging instruments) and translation exposure (reflecting the risk of losses resulting from the translation of accounting statements expressed in foreign currencies into the home country currency at consolidation date).

In strategy terms, economic exposure refers to the possible negative effects of largely unexpected changes in exchange rates on a firm's competitiveness relative to rivals. A firm's economic exposure is affected by the geographic configuration of its input and output markets: "The measurement of [economic] exposure requires an understanding of the structure of the markets in which the company and its competitors obtain labor and materials and sell their products and also of the degree of their flexibility to change markets, product mix, sourcing, and technology."[2]

Here, the issue is not simply to understand how fluctuating foreign exchange rates directly affect a company's income stream through immediate price changes, but rather to gain insights into the longer-term relative impacts of these fluctuations on the income streams of the various firms competing in an industry. If two firms have the same structure in terms of sourcing production inputs from a foreign country and command a similar position in the market in terms of market share, product differentiation, flexibility to shift production, etc., then any changes in the corresponding exchange rates will impact both firms equally and advantage neither firm relative to the other. If, however, one of these firms or a third competitor sources its inputs from a different country, or is very differently positioned in terms of market share, product differentiation, flexibility to shift production, etc., then fluctuating exchange rates will affect the firms differently. Here, the firm with the strongest market position, most differentiated products and the greatest flexibility to shift production will incur the lowest negative impact on the net present value of its future income stream. It is important to note that even purely domestic firms without foreign operations or production imports can incur economic exposure if their market rivals include MNEs whose competitive position is positively affected by exchange rates for internationally sourced inputs.

When assessing economic exposure it is important to distinguish between 'real' versus 'nominal' exchange rates. Nominal rates refer to the direct exchange ratio between currencies – e.g., how many euros or Yen one US dollar will buy – while real exchange rates refer to "changes in the nominal exchange rate minus the difference in inflation rates" between two countries. So, for example, a nominal rate change of 4 per cent with an inflation difference of 3 per cent implies a 1 per cent change in the real exchange rate. Here, the country faced with the higher inflation should experience an equivalent drop in the value of its currency, mirroring the fact that a unit of this currency can now only purchase a lower volume of goods and services.[3]

The distinction between changes in nominal and real exchange rates is important, as it is changes in real exchange rates that affect the level of economic exposure for firms. If, in the very long run, purchasing power parity holds, then (starting from an equilibrium situation) differences in inflation rates and resulting price levels between countries should be precisely offset by corresponding changes in their nominal exchange rates. In that case, changes in real exchange rates would be negligible or close to zero. However, casual empiricism teaches that differences do persist in the medium term (sometimes spanning several years), and it is these real exchange rate fluctuations that create economic exposure risk for companies: "In the short run of six months to several years, however, exchange rates are volatile and greatly influence the competitiveness of companies selling to the same market but getting materials and labor from different countries."[4]

For example, a US manufacturer of durable consumer goods that sources, sells and finances its operations entirely domestically would not be considered exposed to contractual foreign exchange risk in the form of transaction exposure, nor to translation exposure. However, if its main competitors in the market are Japanese, centralized exporters sourcing from Asia, the company is actually exposed to economic risk through the US dollar to yen exchange rate. While the Japanese firms price and sell their products in US dollars, their underlying competitiveness may be largely dependent on yen-based costs. As a result, if the US dollar depreciates against the yen in real terms, then the US manufacturer will enjoy an improved competitive position vis-à-vis its Japanese competitors. But if the dollar's real exchange rate increases, the company's position will be weakened through higher relative costs, and its economic exposure will become visible in the form of a negative impact on its income streams.

Only in cases (again starting from an equilibrium situation) whereby the nominal exchange rate changes between the dollar and yen correspond exactly with differences in inflation rates between the US and Japan, is purchasing power parity maintained. In this (unlikely) scenario, the companies do not experience any change in their competitive positions due to exchange rate changes, since the real exchange rate does not change and no negative impact on the income stream occurs during that period.

The authors observe, *inter alia*, that economic exposure depends not only on decision making inside the individual firm, but also on choices made by rivals in terms of the geographic configuration of their investments and their sourcing policies. As noted above, a substantial economic exposure may thus result entirely from the international sourcing patterns and foreign production operations of rivals, irrespective of whether the particular firm in question itself engages in any international sourcing and/or has foreign production operations.

In terms of this book's framework, three elements are important. First, economic exposure should be viewed as a parameter that adds uncertainty to the value of a firm's location advantages. It implies that even unfettered, privileged access to location advantages in a desirable geographic area may not lead to long-run competitive advantage if the economic value attributed to these location advantages depends on the evolution of macro-level parameters such as currency exchange rates. Second, the economic exposure concept also implies that the location advantages benefiting an MNE should be considered, not solely in a positive sense, and on a country-by-country basis, but also as a portfolio of potential risks for future cash flows. Third, MNEs can choose to develop specific FSAs allowing risk mitigation in the foreign currency area by 'immunizing' their products to economic exposure, thereby allowing full 'exchange rate pass through' (see below).

Companies occupying a market leadership position with highly differentiated products will generally be best positioned to engage in exchange rate pass through, meaning that they can adjust their pricing if necessary to offset any increased costs arising from economic exposure without incurring a loss in sales volume. For such firms, economic exposure is minimal. In the case of an MNE with a geographically dispersed subsidiary network, each subsidiary may face a unique level of economic exposure depending on the industry and geographic market in which it operates, its sourcing policies and the market power it commands.

Figure 8.1, inspired by the Lessard and Lightstone paper, describes the situation faced by each MNE unit in terms of two parameters.

First, there is each unit's capability relative to rivals to adjust its sourcing structure, and thus its cost position, to a potential new exchange rate reality. This is weak or strong exposure absorption capability on the input market side, measured on the vertical axis. It is important to realize that the value of the unit's exposure absorption capability needs to be assessed relative to competitors: even if the unit's sourcing structure is relatively inflexible, its absorption capability would still be 'strong' if its rivals are faced with the same situation of having to import materials from the same input markets, characterized by real exchange rate increases.

Second, there is each unit's capability to 'pass through' changes in real exchange rates: is the subsidiary in a position to pass any price changes on to its customers,

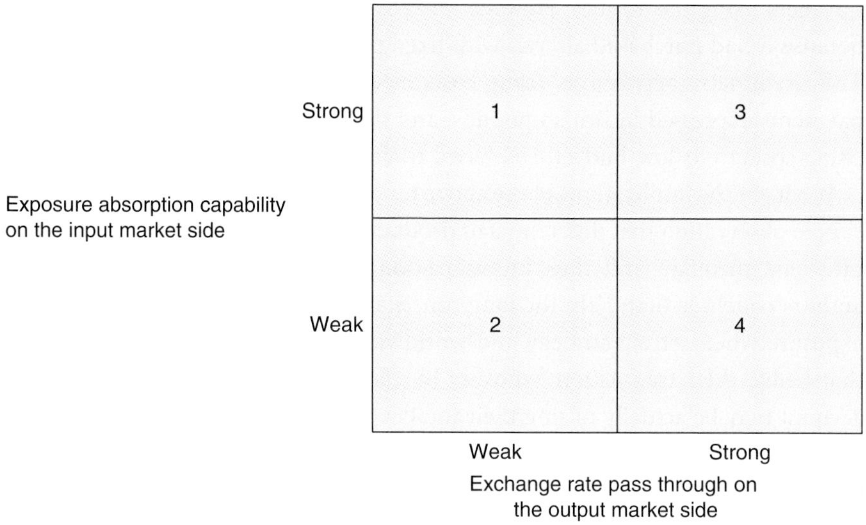

Figure 8.1
A classification of
operating exposure at
the subsidiary level

without a loss of volume and thus income? This is weak or strong exchange rate pass-through capability on the output market side, measured on the horizontal axis.

Quadrant 3 describes the most desirable situation, where economic exposure effects are absent. The MNE unit is able to make the necessary adjustments on the input market side relative to rivals to reduce the effect of real exchange rate changes. At the same time, its market position is sufficiently strong that any cost increases can be translated into price increases for customers without a loss of business.

Quadrant 2 is clearly the least favourable (1 and 4 being intermediate cases), since the MNE unit lacks any exposure reduction capability in its supply chain. MNEs in this quadrant typically sell commodity-type products, the sales of which can be greatly affected by even a small price increase (i.e., there is high price elasticity of demand). This is typical for subsidiaries that import products from the parent company home base (e.g., in retail), and that lack a strong market position in the host country (e.g., are faced with other, larger providers of similar product). If the home country real exchange rate increases and the subsidiary is fully dependent on supplies from the home country, whereas rivals in the host country source domestically, then economic exposure may substantially affect the subsidiary's profitability and growth, since any price increase imposed on customers will lead to a substantial drop in sales volume. Hence, the subsidiary will need to engage in a difficult trade-off between reduced profitability and lower sales.

The authors provide the example of Laker Airways, a UK-based airline that was instrumental in creating a commodity-type market for air travel in the early 1980s. Because it targeted primarily UK-based customers, its income was primarily in UK currency, i.e., in British pounds. When the real exchange rate of the pound decreased vis-à-vis the US dollar, Laker Airways' income, expressed in British pounds, did not increase substantially (given the relative lack of US-based travellers using the airline). However, its costs expressed in British pounds did, because it had purchased aircraft with fixed payments to be made in US dollars. This asymmetry between its rising costs in US dollars, leading to much higher payments expressed in British pounds, and the impossibility of passing on these rising costs to its low-budget, UK-based travellers, led to the firm's bankruptcy.

What are the implications of the above for MNE strategy, apart from the rather simple observation that differentiated products are more likely to allow exchange rate pass through, and thus immunization against economic exposure? The authors conclude that: "[i]n the long run, managers should consider [economic] exposure when setting strategy and worldwide product planning".[5] Companies that hedge their transaction exposure but fail to take economic exposure into account may be actually raising their total exposure.[6]

From their research, they suggest that companies typically manage economic exposure through one of three approaches, which tend to be more strategic in nature than the more administratively oriented, currency hedging instruments available for managing contractual exposure.

In the first approach, each business unit is assessed individually, and each unit therefore configures its own operations in such a way as to reduce its specific economic exposure. This strategy entails a trade-off between increased production costs and lowered risks (e.g., a higher number of operating plants can be established in various countries or regions at the expense of gaining economies of scale).

The second approach reflects a company-wide perspective, whereby a portfolio of businesses and operational structures is selected with offsetting exposures, which balance each other (similar to investment management principles under-lying the creation of diversified mutual funds). The result of such diversification is a lower total rate of exposure across the company, even though individual units may continue to have higher levels of risk on their own.

The third and final approach incorporates flexibility in operational planning. Here, the company exploits fluctuating exchange rates by switching production between factories. Here again, a trade-off is necessary between the increased costs of carrying excess capacity (so as to allow production transfers) on the one hand, and reduced economic exposure risks on the other.

As a final note, the authors suggest that managers who cannot set company policy on economic exposure should not be held responsible for the economic exposure effects of volatile exchange rates. When assessing the performance of these managers, senior management should reduce their own bounded rationality problem by adjusting either performance indicators or goal-based expectations to eliminate the economic-exposure effects on performance of fluctuations in real exchange rates. The authors note, however, that these types of administrative adjustments will be insufficient, and that real bounded rationality reduction will require substantial investment in communication:

Highly reliable models and hence correct performance or budget adjustments will probably be impossible. This uncertainty underscores the need for open and continuing communication between top executives and operating managers to improve understanding of these exposures and also to anticipate responses to possible exchange rate scenarios.[7]

Context and complementary perspectives

Lessard and Lightstone's article was written in 1986, more than twenty-five years ago. At that time, floating exchange rates were becoming more volatile than they had been in previous decades when many currencies in developing countries were pegged to benchmarks such as the US dollar. There was currency instability in Latin America and Asia, and several countries – including Mexico, Argentina and Thailand – experienced acute financial crises and sudden devaluations of their currencies.

The demise of the Soviet empire in the early 1990s also brought new volatility to the currencies of Eastern Europe and Central Asia, which had previously been pegged to the Russian rouble under a centrally planned communist system. Lessard and Lightstone also observed that countries were increasingly following divergent monetary policies in managing their own domestic economies. One significant exception to this trend emerged in the decade following the publication of their article, when several member states of the European Union decided to link their currencies and national monetary policies more closely together through the European Monetary Union and the introduction of the Euro, though this currency itself has been under fire as of 2011, thereby increasing volatility of European financial markets.

The authors also noted the move away from American hegemony, and the rise of triad power: "The United States no longer has a 70% or 80% world market share in key industries but shares markets more equally with Europe and Japan."[8] This statement is still valid today. In the present, triad-based regional system with large MNEs from Asia, Europe and North America competing internationally in the same industries, fluctuations in the currencies of both traditional powerhouse economies and newly emerging low-cost production regions continue to impact the operating profits and exposure risks of MNEs around the globe.

A first complementary perspective on this issue of international financial management is provided by the *SMR* piece 'The evolution of a global cash management system', co-authored by **Christopher Holland**, **Geoff Lockett**, **Jean-Michel Richard** and **Ian Blackman**.[9]

In this article, the authors describe how US-based electronics and telecommunications giant Motorola's cash management system evolved from an internal cost-reduction tool into a strategic, supply chain management instrument. Motorola started with an internal 'currency netting' system under central control by the company's treasury department in 1976. Internal currency netting means that each subsidiary's outstanding accounts receivable and payable to other subsidiaries are aggregated periodically by a netting centre (in Motorola's case weekly). The netting centre receives all the information on outstanding foreign currency obligations, computes the net amount receivable or payable by each affiliate, and then informs each affiliate about the net, single payment it will have to make to – or will receive from – the centre in its own, domestic currency. In the early 1990s, the yearly savings in bank charges and foreign exchange costs were calculated to be in the order of US $6.5 million (largely due to the enormous US $3 billion reduction in foreign exchange transactions handled by banks), excluding administrative costs saved through this streamlined internal accounting, and not taking into account the value of the newly created organizational FSA, in the form of a routine fostering information transparency and accountability among affiliates.

In 1980, Motorola moved to extend its system by including its suppliers, i.e., by engaging in external netting:

> After netting incoming payments with outgoing payments and combining common currencies, an approximate foreign exchange position is reached in which surplus currencies are sold and deficit currencies are bought ... Two first-tier banks and one from a pool of other banks are asked to quote for the foreign exchange dealings.[10]

Again, the immediate effect was cost savings, but the more long-term effect was improved coordination with suppliers, especially after 1992, when its suppliers were given additional services, such as electronic money transfer and value date notification. The improved efficiency and accuracy in supplier payments allowed more focus on discussing strategic, production-related issues with suppliers rather than on redressing payment errors or related problems, as had been the case before. The creation of this new FSA for Motorola was strongly aided by its partner for this project, Citibank. Citibank's interests were aligned with Motorola's, since enhanced payment services would create an FSA in its own right for Citibank.

For the banking sector in general, as the supplier of foreign currency exchange services, this meant a step towards recognizing the needs for 'just-in-time money', and therefore an adaptation of their internal management systems to the requirements of large, internationally diversified MNEs. This reduced the MNEs' bounded reliability problems, as the banks worked harder to provide favourable exchange rates and to make payments promptly.

When implementing its currency netting initiatives, Motorola's affiliate managers faced bounded rationality problems caused by imperfect understanding of the benefits. Resistance to the cash netting initiative led to a one-year delay and disappeared only after extensive internal information diffusion on the expected benefits of the practice.

Apart from a bounded rationality problem, caused by imperfect information, implementation may also have been hindered by an issue related to bounded reliability. A netting system has the potential to improve significantly the transparency of cash flows, and to expose inefficiencies in internal administrative systems. Therefore, resistance to introducing such a system can be expected as it exposes subunits' unreliability in terms of payments, and constrains their ability to blame exogenous factors.

Importantly, in this case the cash-netting approach was perceived as much more beneficial in Europe than in the US home base. Recall that this was in the pre-European Monetary Union era: international, foreign currency transfers and exchanges within Europe were expensive. Here, it is useful to note that a treasury management centre was set up in London because of its location advantages as the world's premier financial centre for foreign exchange services, and because of Motorola's extensive production operations in Europe. This suggests a mix of company-wide and regional considerations in treasury management activities, as found in many of today's large MNEs.

The point is that MNEs can develop FSAs in functional areas such as international financial management, and these FSAs can have important implications for MNE strategy beyond the functional area itself. In the case of Motorola, the new FSA improved coordination with suppliers, eventually leading to more high-level strategic collaboration with those suppliers.

A second complementary perspective was provided by **Alan Rugman** in an insightful, but totally neglected, 1980 *CMR* piece on international financial management.[11] This article is the oldest one discussed in the book, but its insights remain particularly relevant for today's MNE senior managers.

According to Rugman, MNEs come into existence when their FSAs can be exploited only through foreign direct investment rather than through licensing agreements (as a result of imperfections in intermediate product markets) or through exports (in case of government-imposed trade barriers). He describes the MNE as a governance mechanism allowing international diversification, and with that the promise of more stable sales and returns over time. He then reinterprets various MNE financial management instruments, such as transfer pricing, as efficient responses to imperfections in external markets. Here, he distinguishes between natural market imperfections, such as the 'public goods' nature of valuable knowledge, which may invalidate the option of foreign market penetration through licensing, and government-imposed market imperfections, such as an ineffective property-rights regime to protect technological knowledge, tax rate differentials among countries, etc. Internal MNE markets can overcome such imperfections, since senior managers set the transfer prices themselves, in the best interest of the firm as a whole, through administrative fiat. The internal MNE market also lets all domestic and foreign investment projects be evaluated using a single cost of capital, and this internal market, run by a centralized financial management function, acts as a 'proxy' for an external, internationally integrated capital market.

Importantly, Rugman argues against the suggestions of some finance scholars that economic exposure should drive strategic decisions such as plant location. For Rugman, financial transactions should not dominate 'real-world' transactions: "The exposure of MNEs to foreign exchange risk is not a problem in itself ... Instead, the MNE should determine its long-run profit maximization strategy by producing and selling in optimal locations. Its economic decisions should include exchange risk as only one element in the location decision."[12]

Lessard and Lightstone's analysis should be considered not simply as the study of one specific, functional area in international business. Rather, it sheds additional light on the nature of location advantages: any configuration of location advantages, whether in input or output markets, carries risks, in this case the risk of unexpected exchange rate fluctuations affecting future cash flows. In response, MNEs should aim to develop, as an FSA, a central routine that integrates economic-exposure information into the capital budgeting evaluation of large investment projects. This is especially relevant in the context of large-scale foreign expansion. The development of this type of FSA reflects Pattern I in this book's framework (see Figure 8.2). However, especially for large subsidiaries, it may be useful to combine this internationally transferable knowledge with local capabilities in the particular affiliates, following Pattern III. Obviously, especially in the absence of a central economic-exposure policy, one would also expect Pattern IV to occur, whereby individual affiliates learn how to protect themselves against the hazards of economic exposure.

This last pattern allows us to identify a first limitation of Lessard and Lightstone's story line, namely the suggestion that operations managers not responsible for setting economic-exposure policy should not be held accountable for performance differentials resulting from such exposure. The problem is that many large MNE subsidiaries, operating without strict firm-wide economic-exposure policies or guidelines, have substantial autonomy in their supply chain management processes and targeting of markets – actions that create economic exposure. Chapters 5, 6 and 7 addressed precisely this issue of strategic leader-type subsidiaries benefiting from substantial autonomy and in some cases developing their own knowledge bases. Why should the managers of such subsidiaries be exempted from the risks resulting from economic exposure? How is this different from any other type of external risk facing the entrepreneurial MNE subsidiary, such as unexpected new restrictions on business imposed by government agencies, or technological changes making existing product lines obsolete? The reality is that subsidiary managers who can influence the supply chain management of their own operations, as well as the geographic markets where they will operate, should be held responsible for the economic exposure they have created. The key managerial challenge is not to exempt individuals who have

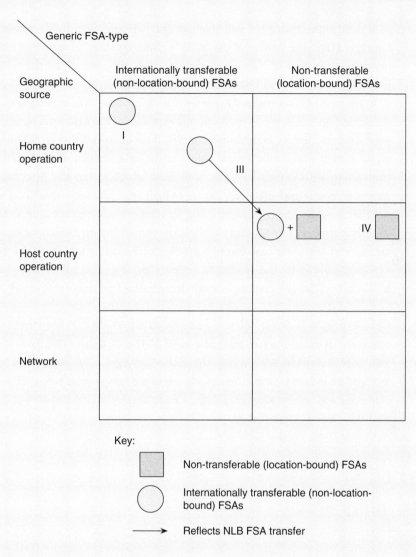

Figure 8.2
Patterns of FSA
development
from managing
operating
exposure in MNEs

somehow been forced to accept the economic-exposure policies of the MNE corporate headquarters from being accountable for the consequences thereof. On the contrary, the much more common challenge, arising in the absence of a strictly imposed firm-level economic-exposure policy, is to make subsidiary managers responsible for the economic exposure they create themselves through their own decision making at the affiliate level. This averts a bounded reliability problem whereby these subsidiary managers could argue that poor results are the outcome of unfortunate external circumstances.

A second limitation of Lessard and Lightstones' *HBR* piece, much in line with Rugman's comments in his *CMR* article above on the linkages between strategy and the finance function, is that the way to address economic exposure – and how to link it with strategy – will depend critically on the MNE's administrative heritage. Here, the nature of the MNE's FSAs, its internal organization and its historical trajectory of location decisions will largely determine the content and process of international financial management decisions.

In the case of a ***centralized exporter*** (e.g., a Japanese firm exporting to the US), shown in Figure 8.3, the main economic exposure at the firm level results from all production occurring in the home country. Two questions then arise. First: on the input market side, is the firm's supply chain, often managed primarily through contracting with external parties, sufficiently flexible that the firm can change suppliers rapidly and effectively in case of high economic exposure? This is usually not the case if the main part of the cost structure is incurred at home, in the home country currency. Second, and usually more important: on the output market side, are the exchange rate pass-through problems (caused by a high price elasticity of demand) sufficiently threatening to support moving production into a particular host country, thereby creating a more decentralized production system?

Case example American film producers suffered in 1999 and 2000 when the Euro plunged against the US dollar. The Euro slumped from US $1.17 on 1 January 1999 to US $1.07 in mid 1999, and then to US $0.89 in mid 2000. This was bad for American film producers, as Europe was an important market for them. They usually pre-sell the foreign rights before a film goes into production, and presales to major continental European distributors often account for nearly a third of the movie's total revenues.

Figure 8.3
Centralized exporter:
Operating exposure
from changes in the
real exchange rate
between the
currencies of
countries A and B

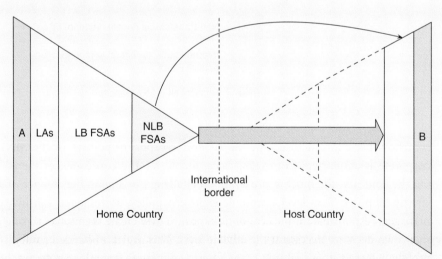

The thin, curved arrow out of the home country triangle, pointing to the host country's LAs, means that the firm's NLB FSAs allow for a strong exchange rate pass-through capability in the output market: unfavourable changes in exchange rates, leading to price increases in the host country's currency, are simply passed on to host country customers without loss in exported sales volume. The areas A and B reflect macro-level location characteristics affecting the real exchange rate between the currencies of countries A and B.

The international movie business is almost exclusively priced in US dollars. The rise in the value of the dollar made American movies too expensive for European distributors. As a result, American producers found it hard to pre-sell the foreign rights.

In response, both American producers and European distributors tried to look for ways to deal with exchange rate fluctuations. European distributors sought creative financing, such as stretching out payments or setting a floor price with additional payments for future currency appreciation; American producers talked about lowering prices or switching to contracts in euros for their foreign rights.[13] ∎

In the case of a ***multi-centred MNE***, shown in Figure 8.4, the economic exposure challenge is really the opposite of the one characterizing the ***centralized exporter***: here, the firm's overall economic exposure results from the individual exposures of all the foreign affiliates. In a conventional firm of this type, there is no powerful, centralized treasury function because all host country subsidiaries have substantial autonomy. Here, economic-exposure challenges will usually be addressed at the subsidiary level, and solutions are more likely to involve changing international suppliers on the input market side rather than making changes on the output market side. A change in this decentralized approach is likely to occur only as one ingredient of a much larger move towards more balance between the centre and the subsidiaries. Here, location-bound FSAs become increasingly complemented by an infusion of non-location-bound capabilities where useful; a centralized exposure management tool may be part of such a move.

Case example As discussed in Chapter 1, Lafarge is a typical multi-centred MNE. One of the world's largest manufacturers of building materials, Lafarge manages exposure using both its central treasury department and its subsidiaries. Due to the local nature of its business, in most cases operating costs and revenues are in the same currency. When purchase and sale transactions are performed in currencies other than this prevailing functional currency (usually the domestic currency) at the subsidiary level, the subsidiary managers themselves address the economic exposure. Lafarge also expects each subsidiary to borrow and invest excess cash in its functional currency. At the same time, the corporate treasury department attempts to reduce the overall exposure by netting purchases and sales in each currency on a global basis when possible.[14] ∎

The growth of ***international projectors*** (shown in Figure 8.5) can produce substantial new economic-exposure problems. This occurs when new subsidiaries replicate not only home country production patterns, but also home country supply chain strategies (with contracts in foreign currencies from the perspective of the host country subsidiary). This may create economic-exposure challenges if the subsidiaries' exchange rate pass-through capabilities are much weaker than those in the home country, especially if the subsidiaries' market position is much weaker than in the home country. The upshot is that it may be much easier to

Figure 8.4
Multi-centred MNE:
Overall exposure
from the individual
exposures of all
foreign affiliates

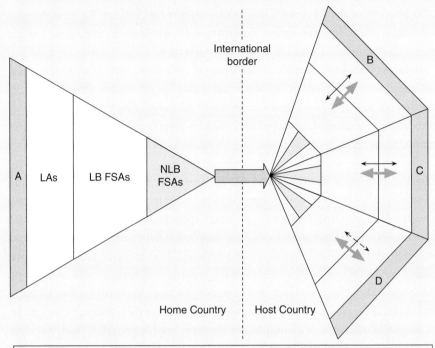

Figure 8.4
Multi-centred MNE:
Overall exposure
from the individual
exposures of all
foreign affiliates

Each subsidiary commands its own exchange rate pass-through capability (weak or strong) when serving its host country market, as shown by the three thin, double-headed arrows. The dotted arrow for country D suggests a weak exchange rate pass-through capability in that country. A and B, A and C and A and D reflect macro-level location characteristics affecting the real exchange rates between the currencies of countries A and B, A and C, and A and D, respectively.

introduce a centralized economic-exposure management system in these companies than in ***multi-centred MNEs***.

Case example Before 1994, Goodyear mostly imported supplies for its Mexican plant and then sold the plant's output to local Mexican customers. However, in December 1994, the crash of the peso dramatically decreased the domestic demand for Goodyear tyres by more than 20 per cent, or 3,500 units a day. Goodyear managers had only two options: to downsize or to look for new export markets. The headquarters and the Mexican subsidiary managers worked together to export the Mexican production, mostly to the US but also to Europe and South America.[15] ∎

Finally, for ***international coordinators***, shown in Figure 8.6, managing economic exposure is usually completely integrated into their overall strategy. This MNE type's main strength is precisely the coordination of internationally dispersed operations, with substantial product and knowledge flows that may be traded internally and externally in a variety of currencies and may be exposed to a broad spectrum of external risks. In the case of commodities, as in many resource-based industries, the main protection against economic exposure is to add value

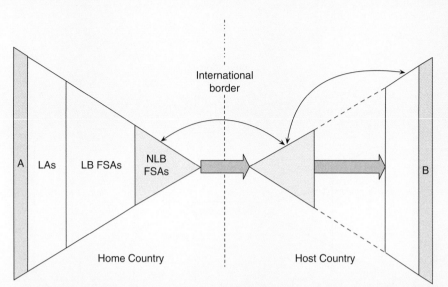

Figure 8.5
International
projector:
Centralized
exposure
management

The firm operates a centralized exposure management system, meant to reduce overall operating exposure risks faced by the firm, but the unique currency exposure position of each subsidiary co-determines the functioning of this central system (shown by the thin, curved double-headed arrow connecting home and host country). The exchange rate pass-through capability of each subsidiary depends on the specific inputs it is mandated to access in the host country and/or on the specific outputs it must sell in the host country (shown by the second double-headed arrow). A and B reflect macro-level location characteristics affecting the real exchange rate between the currencies of countries A and B.

that makes the products more differentiated (a common strategy in the petro-chemical and chemical industries), so as to improve the firm's exchange rate pass-through capabilities. Of course, if no such value is added and the products remain commodities (in the extreme case with a single, world market price), then there is no issue of exposure pass-through capability. The firm has to accept the world price, and its only defence against economic exposure (assuming its cost structure is not incurred in the same currency as the world price) is the use of financial instruments such as currency swap agreements.

Case example Statoil, a Norwegian company and one of the largest oil firms in the world, does business in all the vertical industries associated with petroleum and petrochemical products, such as exploration, production, processing, transport, sales and trading of crude oil, natural gas and refined products.

Statoil's petroleum and petroleum products are priced on world markets primarily in US dollars. However, costs and cash disbursements are to a large extent denominated in Norwegian kroner. Thus, fluctuations in exchange rates could have significant effects on the operating results of Statoil. To manage its exchange risk, Statoil utilizes different types of foreign exchange contracts such as hedges, forward foreign exchange contracts and non-functional currency

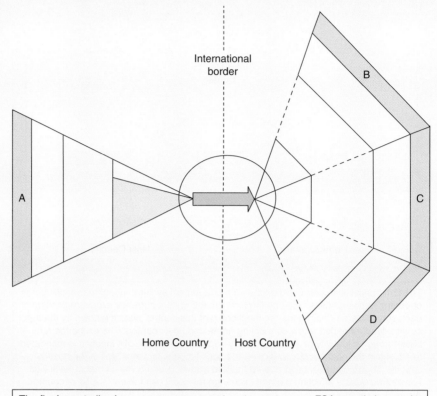

Figure 8.6
International coordinator: Network optimization

International border

Home Country | Host Country

The firm's centralized exposure management system acts as an FSA to optimize results for the network as a whole (shown by the circle). Impacts of this central system on individual subsidiaries are considered secondary. A, B, C and D reflect macro-level characteristics affecting real exchange rates, and can influence the complex network linkages that exist among subsidiaries in countries A,B, C and D.

swaps. At the same time, Statoil also enters into commodity-based derivative contracts (e.g., futures, over-the-counter forward contracts, market swaps).[16] ∎

A third limitation is that Lessard and Lightstone detail the benefits of a flexible sourcing structure without also addressing its costs. They are correct that a flexible sourcing structure (the capability to quickly shift production from one country to another) yields a strong exposure-absorption capability on the input market side, with all the benefits they discuss.

However, exposure-absorption capability is not the only legitimate goal of international business strategy. As we saw in Chapter 7, Ferdows would strenuously object to Lessard and Lightstone's view, pointing out that at least some factories should be considered long-term investments. A factory that is no longer the low-cost producer due to exchange-rate fluctuations can still make contributions in other ways. For example, it can be the company specialist in a knowledge area, develop best practices in a product area, innovate or develop new FSAs.

Realizing these benefits typically requires long-term commitment. Thus, there is a trade-off between the benefits of a flexible sourcing structure and the benefits of long-term commitment. This trade-off must be assessed for each plant in the MNE network.

Five management takeaways

1. Analyse how your company can reduce its economic exposure and achieve the lowest possible negative impact on the net present value of its future income stream.
2. Assess your operating exposure at the level of each subsidiary with regard to the possibility of making adjustments at the input as well as the output market side.
3. Consider the implementation of a global cash management system or, if already existing, its possible extension and its implications for your corporate strategy.
4. Discuss the degree of responsibility for economic exposure to be held at the subsidiary level and define clear guidelines on what the head office versus the subsidiaries are responsible for.
5. Examine the relationship between your corporate strategy and international financial management tools.

Case 8.1 Avon: Dancing with volatile exchange rates[17]

CASE

Famous for selling cosmetics door-to-door through 'Avon ladies' sales representatives, Avon is the world's largest direct seller of beauty products, with more than US $11 billion in annual revenues from over 100 domestic and foreign markets.[18]

Avon was founded as the California Perfume Company by David McConnell in 1886 and named Avon in 1939. In 1914, it opened its first international office in Montreal, Canada. By 1986, more than a third of its US $3 billion sales came from abroad.[19] By the end of 2011, the foreign share of its total consolidated revenue from outside North America had risen to 81 per cent.[20]

Extensive cross-border activities expose Avon to all kinds of effects brought about by volatile exchange rates. For example, in the mid 1980s, the dollar reached a peak in 1985. As the dollar rose to its 1985 peak, converting foreign earnings from weakening currencies into dollars reduced Avon's profits. However, as the dollar fell between 1985 and 1987, conversion from strengthening currencies increased the profits from foreign markets. During the Asian crisis of 1997–8 and the Latin American currency crisis in the 1990s, sharp devaluations of currencies, such as the baht (Thailand), the peso (Mexico) and the real (Brazil), also hit Avon.

Such volatile exchange rates forced Avon to introduce effective tools to reduce the risk of losses resulting from changes in exchange rates. However, with Avon's key markets being located outside of the United States, the firm will continue to face challenges when attempting to mitigate foreign exchange risk.

Sources of operating exposure

The market position of Avon vis-à-vis its competitors, including the geographic sourcing of its inputs, the geographic dispersion of its outputs and its comparative flexibility at switching locations, largely determines the firm's operating exposure.

Because of its market position, Avon has sometimes outperformed the competition during currency crises. For example, during the Mexican peso crisis in 1994, when the peso was devalued, Avon's main competitors in Mexico faced much more expensive imports when expressed in pesos, leading their prices to almost double. Unlike its main rivals, however, Avon relied mainly on domestic producers in Mexico for its supplies. As a result, Avon was able to raise its prices higher than required by inflation rates, but still lower than its competitors.

Managing exposure

Besides using financial options to reduce its transaction exposure risk, Avon has configured its international business activities to reduce the potentially negative effects of volatile exchange rates. More importantly, Avon's senior financial managers communicate extensively with operating managers and help them to understand the possible impacts of operating exposure.

Financial options

When the dollar declined against the yen in late 1987, John E. Donaldson Jr, then Avon's treasurer, reduced the transaction risk of losses by using various tools, including purchasing forward contracts from foreign exchange brokers, buying options contracts from brokers and applying stop-loss orders.

To effectively manage the financial risk arising from its international business activities, Avon now utilizes a combination of tools such as forward contracts, swaps and options. These financial instruments help to reduce Avon's "exposure to fluctuations in cash flows associated with changes in interest rates and foreign exchange rates".[21]

Although Avon has successfully managed its foreign exchange exposure in the past, the firm has faced many challenges in recent years. In particular, Avon's operations in Latin America underperformed as compared to expected sales projections, despite being a key market for the company. The situation was exacerbated when Venezuela devalued its currency after a prolonged period of high inflation, which negatively affected Avon's net profits in 2010 and 2011. This impact is expected to continue into the foreseeable future.[22]

In 2011, the bulk of the company's foreign exchange exposure was to "the Argentine peso, Brazilian real, British pound, Canadian dollar, Chinese renminbi, Colombian peso, the Euro, Mexican peso, Philippine peso, Polish zloty, Russian ruble, Turkish lira, Ukrainian hryvnia and the Venezuelan Bolivar".[23]

Configuring manufacturing activities

Prior to 2007, most of Avon's cosmetics were manufactured within the country where they are sold. When viable, Avon would try to source materials from local suppliers, but the company has recently moved to take more advantage of economies of scale. The company's strategy is to move towards a 'globally coordinated' approach to sourcing, rather than one that is locally oriented.[24] This Strategic Sourcing Initiative (SSI) was implemented in 2007 and had provided a cumulated value of US $300 million by 2010. This initiative allowed Avon to decrease the costs of materials and to select suppliers with complementary capabilities. The SSI and price increases on selected products helped to mitigate the foreign exchange effects faced by Avon in 2010.[25]

Avon has also shifted production in response to fluctuating exchange rates. For example, during the Asian crisis, Avon replaced its European lace supplier (with the lace being used to make bras) with a Thai company, so as to reduce the negative impact of having to pay for inputs in a strong European currency.

Continuing communication between finance officers and operating managers

In 1997, Avon treasurer Dennis Ling was in daily contact with Jose Ferreira Jr., head of the Asia-Pacific region for Avon. Together, the two chose financial options and other reconfiguring activities to manage potential risks. Such communication with finance specialists helped operating managers to understand the threats and opportunities brought by currency volatility.

Transferring knowledge to manage exposure

In countries throughout Latin America, such as Brazil, Venezuela, Mexico and Argentina, senior managers have developed specific knowledge to cope with economic crisis, political crisis and hyperinflation. Avon has used this knowledge to develop a set of responses to deal with volatility. Further, Avon can also move these experienced managers to help Avon managers in other countries in crisis. For example, when Russia experienced a currency crisis in 1998, Avon called in Miguel Salbitano and Richard Foggio to give a hand. The former was the head of the Central America region, and the latter spent eight years in Latin America. Similarly, a team of Latin American executives was brought to visit Avon's Asian units country by country to help them out in 1997 during the Asian crisis.

Future outlook

With the impact of the 2008 recession still felt across the globe, Avon has had a difficult time trying to turn around its operating performance since 2009.[26] Avon's strong presence in emerging markets continues to be a key driver in its success, which opens the company up to significant operating exposure.[27] Avon must continue to manage its foreign exchange risks to ensure these markets continue to contribute to their growth.

Avon has faced an uphill battle since 2008 with allegations coming forth regarding participation in bribery in China. Numerous executives were fired and an investigation by the Securities and Exchange Commission was imposed for many of Avon's international operations, costing the firm millions of dollars. In 2012, Avon's debt rating has also been downgraded from a triple-B-plus to a triple-B by Standard and Poor's. Weak operating results and bribery allegations have negatively affected the firm.[28]

In December 2011, the company announced that its current CEO, Andrea Jung, would be stepping down to take on the sole position of executive chairman. This move created significant debate amongst employees, ex-employees and the public. Past CEOs made public statements disagreeing with Mrs Jung staying on as executive chairman as they felt a new direction needed to be taken.[29] Former executives indicated whom they felt should have been appointed, signalling to the public that dissatisfaction had existed with the internal functioning of the firm.[30] After a five-month search, Avon announced that Sherilyn S. McCoy, a former executive of Johnson & Johnson, would replace Andrea Jung as CEO, effective 23 April 2012.[31]

On 2 April 2012 Avon was presented a buyout offer from Coty Inc., a 'global beauty company' for US $10 billion.[32] The offer was priced at a 20 per cent premium from the closing price on March 30th. However, Avon rejected the offer stating that the company was undervalued. Avon hopes the appointment of a new CEO will help to revive and realign the struggling firm.[33]

QUESTIONS

1. How do volatile exchange rates affect Avon's operations? What are the major risks and benefits?
2. Explain Avon's position in Mexico as described in the case. Please explain the effects of both Mexican inflation and the peso devaluation on Avon Mexico and its competitors, who rely on imports to service the Mexican market. (Note: to answer this question, you have to know the inflation rates in both Mexico and the US, and the exchange rate between the peso and the dollar.)
3. Please apply your understanding of location-bound FSAs and non-location-bound FSAs to describe the Avon case.
4. Can you provide an update on Avon's management of its operating exposure, using materials available on the Web?

Case 8.2 Porsche: Fighting with currency swinging[34]

CASE

Porsche's concern about operating exposure arising from changes in the exchange rate of the dollar can be traced back to heavy financial losses incurred in 1992–3. In one year, Porsche's global sales dropped by 38 per cent to 14,000 units; in the US, its largest market, Porsche sold less than 4,000 units. The large losses were attributed not only to the global recession in the early 1990s, but also to the weak US dollar.

Founded in 1931 by Ferdinand Porsche, Porsche is a legendary German manufacturer of luxury sports cars. In 1972, Ferry Porsche and Louise Piëch, the two children of Ferdinand Porsche, changed the firm's legal form from a limited partnership to a private limited company (German AG). An executive board and a supervisory board were set up, with executives from outside the Porsche family on the former and members mainly from the Porsche family on the latter.

The Porsche family members didn't get along very well with their appointed chief executives in the 1980s. The feuding between the family and the executives ended only in the early 1990s when financial losses hit the company. In 1993, the family brought in Wendelin Wiedeking to head the company. Wiedeking largely remade the company by improving its efficiency and launching new products. However, the financial losses, partly resulting from exposure to the dollar, are a lingering and lasting memory, and Porsche has been watching its foreign exchange exposure very carefully since that time, implementing various exposure management strategies.[35]

Porsche's sourcing structure

Porsche manufactures cars in only two countries: Germany and Finland. Manufacturing in Finland occurs under a licensing agreement with Finland's Valmet Automotive Inc. With plants in only two countries – both Euro-denominated – Porsche does not have much room to adjust its cost structure when the euro fluctuates vis-à-vis other currencies, as most of its costs are incurred in euros. However, Porsche owners and senior managers believe that the brand name stands for 'Made in Germany', and reflects core capabilities in engineering and manufacturing. The firm has no plan to build production plants beyond its current European facilities.

Porsche's rivals, by contrast, have attempted to engage in 'natural' hedging (i.e., having revenues in the same currency as expenses). For example: since 1995, the major Japanese automakers have vastly increased their overseas production. In 2005, Japanese automakers produced for the first time more vehicles abroad than at home, with 10.93 million vehicles made at their overseas factories and 10.89 million vehicles produced in Japan. Moreover, production by these Japanese companies had become very dispersed across major regions, with "4.08 million vehicles made in the United States, 3.96 million in Asia, 1.55 million in Europe, 645,000 in Latin America, 226,000 in Africa, 135,000 in

Australia and 10,500 in the Middle East".[36] Like the Japanese automakers, Ford and GM have also expanded their overseas production into Asia and Latin America.

Even when compared only with other European automakers, Porsche still faces a higher operating exposure. BMW opened its first plant in South Carolina in the US in 1994, and has plans to double its US-based capacity. Mercedes plans to expand its Alabama manufacturing facility. Volkswagen, though having closed its US plant in 1988, believes that it will be able to hedge its US dollar exposure through its operating base in Brazil.

Most importantly, when compared with other European automakers, Porsche has the largest discrepancy between the location of production and the location of markets. In 2011, sales in the United States accounted for 25 per cent of Porsche's total car sales, with no cars produced in this region.[37] In contrast, in 2011, the US market accounted for 18 per cent of BMW's car sales and 19 per cent of its production[38]; and 18 per cent of Mercedes' car sales and 12 per cent of its production[39].

Besides factory location, sourcing strategy is another way to naturally hedge against operating exposure. For example, BMW has not only set up plants in the US, but has also used it as a base for procuring parts and materials for its German-made vehicles. Although these parts and materials incur transportation costs, they have still been cheaper than equivalent domestic purchases in Germany or in other European countries, taking into account the exchange rate and lower production costs. By incurring costs in North America, BMW has created 'natural' hedges against operating exposure, though "BMW says that its decisions on where it locates production are driven by market needs, not currency considerations."[40]

In short, Porsche's rivals are better positioned on the input market side to handle unexpected exchange-rate fluctuations.

Porsche's exchange rate pass-through capability

Porsche's ability to pass through to US consumers at least part of the cost of exchange-rate fluctuation varies according to the product type. Porsche's portfolio includes three vehicle platforms: the 911 series, the Boxster and the Cayenne.

The 911 series is a premier luxury sports car. To some extent it is the only player in its own market segment. Although its sales have gone up and down, demand has been largely price inelastic, as the series has commanded high prices from the outset, and demand has depended mainly upon the potential buyers' disposable income. In the US, Porsche could probably increase prices of the 911 series to a certain extent, in the context of exchange rate pass through, without experiencing a decrease in sales volume.

The Boxster roadster was introduced in 1996 to compete in the lower price end of the sports car market. It is priced substantially lower than the 911 series. However, this market segment is also very price sensitive and competitive, with several alternatives such as the BMW Z3 and Z4. Therefore, any increase in the Boxster's price resulting from exchange rate pass through would probably hurt its sales.

The Cayenne is an off-road sports utility vehicle (SUV) priced at the top end of this market segment. Although the Cayenne has been a huge success, especially in the SUV-crazed American market, Porsche quickly introduced a lower-priced version as it was afraid that the high-end market segment was not a growth market. The Cayenne has since become Porsche's most successful model, with sales of 59,873 units in 2011.[41]

In a 2011 Automotive Performance, Execution and Layout (APEAL) study, Porsche's 911 and Cayenne models were identified as the best cars in their segments.[42] The APEAL study surveys 73,000 new vehicle buyers annually, and aggregates data across categories such as design, handling and comfort.[43] The popular success of these models allows for some pricing flexibility.

Overall, Porsche's portfolio allows some exchange rate pass through. However, if the Euro appreciated strongly against the US dollar, Porsche would not be able to pass on to North American customers the full price change required without a significant reduction in sales. If Porsche wanted to avoid a significant reduction in sales, it would have to reduce its profit margins on sales in the US.

Porsche's exposure management strategy

Instead of natural hedges, Porsche uses other strategies to manage its exposure. The first major strategy at Porsche is to compete not on price but on quality. Unlike its rivals, Porsche does not offer price rebates or discounts.[44]

The second major strategy is an aggressive 'put options' hedging strategy, introduced in 2001, when the Euro bottomed out against the US dollar. With around 40 per cent of total sales in North America, Porsche feared the potential damage of a strengthening Euro in the medium term. To minimize this potential damage, Porsche purchased a set of put options, which allowed Porsche to exchange at will its US dollars from sales in the US into euros, at pre-specified exchange rates. This hedging has been so aggressive that the firm's 2011 and 2012 sales have been hedged for 100 per cent. Porsche is typically able to cover every current and upcoming year at 100 per cent. Unfortunately, this medium-term strategy has required Porsche to forecast sales and future exposures, and it has also become very costly due to the option premiums associated with such a large options portfolio. Porsche has had to estimate sales into 2016 to hedge against the US dollar.

Porsche continues to mitigate its foreign exchange exposure by means of hedging against ten different currencies. Residual risk is mitigated through forwards, simple options and more complicated structured products. The company even experimented with options on top of options on top of options to give 'flexibility'. Goldman Sachs has estimated that Porsche currency hedging techniques manage to generate roughly €250 million a year.[45]

However, Porsche's hedging strategy has been criticized for being a 'second-best solution'. As noted by Citigroup Smith Barney, "Porsche has the heaviest US exposure (and this is increasing), yet it has the lowest level of natural hedging in the sector."[46]

Foreign exchange exposure in China is also increasing as Porsche aims to expand its market share in China. During the past few years, the Chinese automotive market has experienced substantial growth and is now the largest market in the world. The demand for premium cars is also rising with expected growth in 2012 reaching 15–20 per cent.[47] For Porsche, the Chinese market is now its second largest behind the United States. The company is responding with plans to expand from 41 dealerships in 2011, to 60 by the end of 2012.[48] Porsche is continuing to pay close attention to the fluctuations of the Chinese currency to hedge against the foreign currency exposure.

Former CEO Wiedeking was confident about Porsche's future profitability: "In the long term, we will have to live with an adverse dollar. There is no way out. We have to have a strategic answer for currency fluctuations . . . Our currency hedging strategy had one single purpose: we buy time to prepare ourselves for the situation when the currencies run against us."[49] Porsche has started to engage in a cost-cutting programme. Industry analysts view such an approach as feasible if Porsche can reduce its cost by 2–3 per cent on the input side.[50]

Structural changes in Porsche

At the annual general meeting in 2007, Porsche, legally operating as Porsche AG, established Porsche Automobil Holding SE (Porsche SE), to be the umbrella holding company for Porsche. Shareholders voted in favour of establishing the holding company to manage Porsche's equity investment and to legally register as a 'Societas Europaea', a term that refers to a European Public Limited Liability Company. Porsche SE would own Porsche Zwischenholding GmbH, a holding company that in turn has a 100 per cent stake in Porsche AG, its automotive manufacturing arm (see Figure 8.7)

Volkswagen takeover

Porsche's and Volkswagen's joint history dates back to the 1930s, when Ferdinand Porsche designed the Volkswagen Beetle. He later established his own company, namely Porsche, but the ties between the two companies continue to exist today. Executives overlap between Porsche and Volkswagen as Martin Winterkorn is the CEO of both Volkswagen and Porsche SE. In addition, Ferdinand Piëch, the grandson of Ferdinand Porsche, is the chairman of the supervisory board of the Volkswagen Group. Throughout the years, the two companies have often worked together to integrate their operations by sharing factories and even car parts. Porsche's best-selling Cayenne model shares platform components with the VW Touareg and the Audi Q7.[51]

Figure 8.7
The current Porsche holding structure

Holding Structure

¹ voting rights

It came as no surprise to the public when in the mid 2000s Porsche started to increase its ownership in Volkswagen.

In October 2008, Porsche SE shocked the markets by revealing it had control over 74 per cent of the shares in Volkswagen. The move had signified that Porsche was in the process of attempting a takeover of a company fourteen times its size.[52] The announcement drastically drove up the share price of Volkswagen, so much so that at one point it was the most valuable company in the world. Conversely, some hedge funds lost an estimated US $10–40 billion and many speculated that the company had participated in market manipulation.[53] Porsche reaffirmed that its move towards acquiring Volkswagen was purely strategic, rather than motivated by financial gains.

In 2009, Porsche and Volkswagen agreed to merge and in December of that year Porsche sold 49.9 per cent of Porsche Zwischenholding GmbH, the holding company for its automotive operations, to Volkswagen.[54] An agreement for a complete merger was in place until the end of 2011. However, collecting debt amounting to EUR 10 billion made it difficult for Porsche to gain the support of lenders during the financial crisis.[55] Additionally, pending lawsuits against Porsche SE eventually made it too arduous to value the company, and the merger agreement was aborted. Porsche stated that "preparations for the merger were terminated, because in the merger negotiations the companies could not agree on the exchange ratio".[56] Both companies are still willing to continue a collaborate relationship as a stepping stone towards an 'integrated automotive group'.[57] Moreover, Volkswagen does hold the opportunity to exercise options to buy the remaining stake of Porsche Zwischenholding GmbH between November 2012 and January 2015.[58] If Volkswagen does decide to purchase the remaining stake, the automotive operations of Porsche will be integrated into Volkswagen's.

Volkswagen's foreign currency exposure

Volkswagen, like Porsche, manages its foreign currency exposure utilizing derivatives such as forwards, options and swaps. However, a major difference lies in Volkswagen's reliance on developing a natural hedge with 54 international production sites across Africa, Asia, Europe, North America and South America.[59] Within each location, Volkswagen has been able to adjust its production levels to accommodate fluctuations with currency exchange. The firm has also established larger operations in areas where currency can have a significant impact on its operations. For example, the United States is a substantial market for Volkswagen, so to further reduce currency exposure, the company has established local production facilities and procurement relationships. Given the flexibility of its international production, roughly 50 per cent of Volkswagen's foreign currency exposure is mitigated through its natural hedging strategy.[60]

If Volkswagen were to purchase the remaining stake in Porsche's automobile operations, it could affect Porsche's currency hedging strategy. The brand that signifies 'made in Germany' could be fully integrated into Volkswagen's international production operations. It is unknown how much more and exactly how the two companies will integrate their operations. However,

Volkswagen estimates that the move could create savings of around EUR 700 million.[61] Volkswagen's ultimate goal is to integrate Porsche's manufacturing and R&D capabilities into its own.

QUESTIONS

1. How would you position Porsche's US operations in Figure 8.1? What is the exposure-absorption capability on the input market side? What are the exchange pass-through capabilities on the output side?
2. Compared with other European automakers, what is the magnitude of Porsche's exposure in the US? Why?
3. What is the current exposure management strategy at Porsche?
4. Porsche has relied on currency hedging to protect itself. Can Porsche continue to do so in the long run? What would be your strategic answer for currency fluctuations for Porsche in the future?
5. What did BMW do to manage its exposure in the US? Can Porsche follow BMW's approach?
6. Could a strengthened relationship between Porsche and Volkswagen affect Porsche's economic exposure and/or its exposure reduction strategies?

Notes

1. D. R. Lessard and J. B. Lightstone, 'Volatile exchange rates can put operations at risk', *Harvard Business Review* 64 (1986), 107–14.
2. *Ibid.*, 111.
3. *Ibid.*, 108.
4. *Ibid.*, 107.
5. *Ibid.*
6. *Ibid.*, 108.
7. *Ibid.*, 114.
8. *Ibid.*, 107.
9. Christopher Holland, Geoff Lockett, Jean-Michel Richard and Ian Blackman, 'The evolution of a global cash management system', *Sloan Management Review* 36 (1994), 37–47.
10. *Ibid.*, 40.
11. Alan M. Rugman, 'Internalization theory and corporate international finance', *California Management Review* 13 (1980), 73–9.
12. *Ibid.*, 78.
13. Charles Goldsmith, 'Moguls rewrite script at Cannes as euro tanks', *Wall Street Journal (Eastern Edition)* (19 May 2000), B.1.
14. Lafarge, 20-F Report (26 March 2004).
15. Michael H. Moffett, Arthur I. Stonehill and David K. Eiteman, *Fundamentals of Multinational Finance* (Boston, Mass.: Pearson Education), 244.
16. Statoil, Annual report (2005).

17. Fred R. Bleakley, 'How U.S. firm copes with Asia crisis – Avon moves to protect against volatile currencies', *Wall Street Journal* (26 December 1997), 1; Thomas C. Hayes, 'Puzzling out foreign profits', *New York Times* (12 September 1987), D.1; David Whitford, 'A currency drowns – can you stay afloat?' *Fortune* 139 (1999), 229–35.
18. Avon, company information, 2012.
19. Avon, company information, 2006.
20. Avon, Annual report (2011), 29.
21. Avon, Annual report (2011), 42.
22. Avon, Annual report (2010) 10.
23. Avon, Annual report (2010).
24. Avon, Annual report (2010), 6.
25. Avon, Annual report (2010), 28.
26. 'S&P cuts Avon Products Inc' *Thomson Reuters* (16 March 2012).
27. M. Gottfried, 'Avon needs more than lipstick', *Barron's* (19 December 2011).
28. Emily Glazer, Gina Chon and Anupreeta Das, 'Scarred Avon is takeover target', *Wall Street Journal (Online)* (3 April, 2012).
29. Joann S. Lublin and Emily Glazer, 'Corporate news: Avon ex-CEOs push alumnus for post', *Wall Street Journal (Eastern Edition)* (30 March 2012), B.4.
30. *Ibid.*
31. Jenna Goudreau, 'Avon names Sherilyn McCoy as new CEO', *Forbes* (9 April 2012).
32. Coty Inc., 'About Coty', (2012).
33. Phil Wahba, 'Wanted: one makeover; Avon ladies looking for a new look amid executive changes, bribery probes', *National Post* (19 March 2012), FP.5.
34. Michael H. Moffet and Barbara S. Petitt, 'Porsche exposed', *Thunderbird Case A06–04–0004* (2004), 1–13; 'Grappling with the strong euro', *The Economist* 367 (7 June 2003), 65; David Woodruff, 'Porsche is back – and then some', *Business Week* (15 September 1997), 56; Martin Fackler, 'Japan makes more cars elsewhere', *New York Times (Late Edition (East Coast))* (1 August 2006), C.1; Porsche company information (2007); Guido Reinking, 'Porsche will cut costs to cover hedging expiry', *Financial Times* (20 October 2004), 26.
35. Woodruff, 'Porsche is back', 56.
36. Fackler, 'Japan makes more cars elsewhere', C.1.
37. Porsche SE, Annual report (2011), 50–1.
38. BMW, Annual report (2011), 24–8.
39. Mercedes Benz Cars, Annual report (2011), 130.
40. The Economist, 'Grappling with the strong euro', 65.
41. Martha Lagace, 'Porsche's risky roll on an SUV', *Harvard Business School* (5 September 2006); Porsche SE, Annual report (2011).
42. Porsche SE, Annual report (2011).
43. *Ibid.*
44. Porsche, Annual report (2006).
45. *Ibid.*
46. Citigroup Smith Barney, Porsche (24 September 2003), 5, cited in Moffet and Petitt, 'Porsche exposed', 5.
47. 'Porsche plans to accelerate China dealership openings this year', *Bloomberg* (22 April 2012).
48. *Ibid.*
49. Reinking, 'Porsche will cut costs', 26.
50. *Ibid.*

51. Porsche SE, Annual report (2011).
52. Emily Hughes, 'Fast bucks: how Porsche made billions', *BBC* (22 January 2009).
53. *Ibid.*
54. Christoph Rauwald, 'Volkswagen calls off Porsche merger', *Wall Street Journal* (12 January 2012).
55. Tony Czuczka, 'Volkswagen clears tax hurdle on Porsche integration WiWo says', *Bloomberg* (9 June 2012).
56. Porsche, Annual report (2011), 12.
57. Porsche, Annual report (2011), 41.
58. Andreas Cremer and Karin Matussek, 'Porsche plunges after VW merger fails over pending lawsuits', *Bloomberg Businessweek* (9 September 2011).
59. Porsche, Annual report (2011), 75.
60. Uta Harnischfeger, 'VW increases its hedging', *Financial Times* (10 September 2003), 29.
61. Chad Thomas, 'Volkswagen aims to combine with Porsche as soon as economically "sensible"', *Bloomberg* (22 January 2012).

9

International marketing

Five learning objectives

1. To define the term global standardization and to understand the intellectual arguments in favour of global standardization.
2. To describe the revenue-enhancing and cost-reducing effects of using the Internet in international operations.
3. To explain the new types of intermediaries and to highlight the limitations and restrictions of the Internet and online sales.
4. To examine the potential and the constraints of global account management.
5. To identify the managerial challenges associated with simplistic views on the globalization of markets.

This chapter examines Levitt's idea that MNEs should not worry very much about customizing to cultural preferences. According to Levitt, technology has largely homogenized consumer preferences – most consumers simply want quality, reliability and low price. Therefore, MNEs should focus on offering such products and services. MNEs should standardize their products and services worldwide in order to achieve economies of scale, and should implement global strategies across all markets. These ideas will be examined and then criticized using the framework presented in Chapter 1.

Significance

"The world's needs and desires have been irrevocably homogenized. This makes the multinational corporation obsolete and the global corporation absolute."[1] This statement sums up ***Theodore Levitt's*** bold assertions in his well-written, landmark *HBR* article, 'The globalization of markets'.[2]

In terms of this book's framework, Levitt sees the ***multi-centred MNE*** being gradually replaced by ***centralized exporters*** and ***international projectors***. He argues that advances in technology, communications and travel have revolution-ized commerce and trade in all parts of the globe, basically conferring additional value to non-location-bound FSAs, and strengthening the MNE's ability to deploy and exploit such non-location-bound FSAs, irrespective of cultural, economic, institutional or spatial distance.

Customers throughout the world are thirsty for new products that can now be made available universally. While MNEs have traditionally customized their products to cater to perceived cultural differences across countries and regions, these preferences are converging as technology brings the world closer together into one global market. According to Levitt, the majority of the world's consumers want the same thing: high-quality, reliable products at low prices. They are often willing to accept globally standardized products without expensive customization or modifications for cultural preferences if the three above attributes of quality, reliability and low price are present. Companies that grasp this new 'global' reality, and that can inject these attributes into simplified products coming out of scale-efficient manufacturing processes, will win the competitive battles against those rivals that continue to pursue a polycentric approach of customizing products for different markets, thereby incurring higher costs simply to cater to what are in Levitt's view superficial local preferences.

Levitt's argument in favour of global standardization rests on two foundations. The first is that cultures and national societal tastes are not fixed, but subject to continuous change, with technology guiding such change towards homogeniza-tion. According to Levitt: "technology drives consumers relentlessly towards the same common goals – alleviation of life's burdens and the expansion of discre-tionary time and spending power".[3] The force of technology and the allure of modern goods create converging global preferences, and overpower traditional differences rooted in national cultures and historic customs. As a result, cultural preferences follow one of two paths: they eventually lose relevance to economic decision making, or they diffuse to other groups and become the substance of global trends. This is true not only for commodities and high-tech products, but also for 'high touch' goods and services, which are gaining popularity with large consumer groups. ('High touch' refers to items where personal interactions among individuals remain critical, either at the moment of purchase or later, during consumption/usage.) Levitt offers examples such as the worldwide diffu-sion and gain in popularity of certain ethnic foods (pizza, pita bread, Chinese food), music (jazz, country and western) and product brands (Coke and Pepsi soft drinks, McDonald's fast food, Sony TVs, Levi jeans).

Levitt's second point builds on the first. Converging tastes now allow com-panies to offer globally standardized products, harnessing economies of scale to deliver high-quality, dependable goods at low cost. According to Levitt, high quality and low cost are not mutually exclusive objectives: they represent com-plementary goals achievable through innovation and efficiency. The key is standardized products that allow for economies of scale in production, as well as in downstream activities such as distribution and marketing and in management activities in general. Scale efficiencies translate into lower prices, which are a powerful draw for consumers everywhere. Levitt gives the example of Japanese firms who, despite commanding limited domestic resources, suffering from a high cultural distance vis-à-vis Europe and North America, and lacking traditional marketing departments or market research, have nevertheless 'cracked the code of Western markets', meaning they have found a way to cater to the above-mentioned demand for high-quality, reliable, aggressively priced goods, and have beaten rivals on their own, home region turf.

No matter how small or niched a product area may be, there are always equivalent segments in other markets worldwide that allow for a global approach satisfying the above three criteria (quality, reliability and low price). As a result, neither MNEs nor local firms can continue to rely on their domestic markets as safe havens from global competition.

As an example, Levitt discusses the European strategy of US-based Hoover, a manufacturer of vacuum and laundry machines. The company conducted research on national markets in Europe and identified a number of differences in consumer preferences among countries. Accommodating these preferences through product customizations resulted in shorter production runs and higher costs than if one standardized machine had been produced for the whole region. In contrast, Italian competitors offered lower-cost machines with far fewer of the allegedly preferred features, yet still managed to gain market share, even in high-end markets such as Germany. Levitt concludes that "Two things clearly influenced customers to buy: low price regardless of feature preferences and heavy promotion regardless of price."[4] To Levitt, this example demonstrates that companies need to avoid conforming in a slavish fashion to the different cultural preferences expressed by consumers in various markets.

In fairness to Levitt, he does not in fact "advocate the systematic disregard of local or national differences".[5] Nor does he propose that customization based upon fundamental differences such as language or regulatory systems be ignored. Some customization may thus still be required, if all efforts to achieve acceptance of standardized products and to change local preferences have been exhausted.

Finally, despite his uncompromising assertions regarding the need for a global approach to strategy, Levitt concedes that administrative heritage and corporate culture play a large role in determining the success or failure of a firm's managerial efforts: "There is no one reliably right answer – no one formula . . . What works well for one company or one place may fail for another in precisely the same place, depending on the capabilities, histories, reputations, resources, and even the cultures of both."[6] This warning acts as a reminder that even when adopting a global approach to marketing, it is effective organization and implementation – i.e., the MNE's routines and recombination capabilities – that count.

Context and complementary perspectives

'The globalization of markets' was published in 1983, when computers were in their infancy and cell phones had not yet taken the world by storm. Trade barriers between most countries were still significant, reinforcing national borders and hindering the development of a truly global marketplace. As discussed in earlier chapters, exchange rate volatility and environmental uncertainty were increasing. One could interpret such environmental conditions as conducive to an increased focus on national responsiveness through developing location-bound FSAs. Yet, Japanese firms had proved successful in pioneering a 'global' approach in a variety of industries, including steel, automobiles and home electronics. Here, export-based strategies (using standardized goods) and international-projector-type strategies appeared to be sure-fire recipes for rapid international expansion.

Levitt, not surprisingly, draws heavily on such Japanese examples, but also outlines successful 'imitators' from all over the world, including even the US and Western Europe. From his perspective, these successes substantiate his theory that "If a company forces costs and prices down and pushes quality and reliability up – while maintaining reasonable concern for suitability – customers will prefer its world-standardized products."[7]

Given the above, a first complementary perspective is provided by **John Quelch** and **Lisa Klein** in an early (1996) *SMR* article on the potential offered by the Internet to change the face of international marketing.[8] The authors suggest that the Internet can have both revenue-enhancing and cost-reducing effects in international operations. On the revenue-enhancing side, however, they focus neither on Levitt-type scale economies, nor on conventional scope economies associated with internationalization, but on network effects, including network externalities. A key network effect benefiting a rapidly internationalizing MNE is that services with a broad geographic scope often become more valuable to the MNE's customers precisely because of these services' international availability and accessibility (e.g., with banking, insurance, air travel and courier services). In other words, the number and distribution of existing customers affects the value that the service has to the next customer. In addition, every new international customer leads to a network externality: this customer further contributes to the overall quality and value of the MNE's service offering. Here, new customers may contribute to removing glitches in an international delivery system or to increasing frequency of services as in the airline and shipping industries, or to increasing network coverage as in the mobile telecommunications industry, thereby leading to improved service levels benefiting all other customers.

For example, in the computer industry, US-based Sun Microsystems benefits from network effects. As Quelch and Klein note, "Sun Microsystems provides global product support, software updates, and hardware service to its worldwide network of internal and external hardware users and software developers."[9] The availability of both these stand-alone technical capabilities and service-oriented routines that can be accessed by Sun Microsystems' customers around the world is particularly valuable to business customers with widely dispersed operations. MNEs that use Sun's information and communication technology services run more efficiently because those services are standardized across borders and can benefit all of the MNE's affiliates.

Similarly, the courier company Federal Express' global tracking service – allowing customers to track their packages and assess delivery times instantaneously at any time of day – is another example of a valuable routine brought about by the Internet and made more valuable because of its international coverage. In this context, the authors also note the cost-reducing effects of this tracking service, as a formerly labour-intensive, heterogeneous service provided by only moderately reliable employees has been largely replaced by a standardized, automated tracking system.

Consistent with Levitt, Quelch and Klein predict that companies that offer standardized (i.e., not culturally customized) products using the Internet will have certain advantages, with the result that customers worldwide will both demand and receive more standardized products. First of all, the Internet provides better access to international customers. In addition, the Internet allows immediate, worldwide information diffusion about new product offerings, and sometimes also immediate access to these offerings by host country consumers around the globe. Especially for fashion-type goods, supply can thus cater to a global audience. This immediate linkage between supply and geographically dispersed markets may be especially important for smaller firms, who may be 'born global', not in the sense of achieving a truly balanced distribution of sales around the world, but in terms of customers from around the world having access in principle to the firm's product offering from day one.

Quelch and Klein also predict that the Internet will reduce prices, because it lets customers rapidly compare prices electronically, resulting in smaller price differentials across geographic markets (at least in the absence of regulatory barriers, such as international trade restrictions).

In terms of this book's framework, the Internet should be viewed as a tool to reduce bounded rationality problems faced by the MNE and its potential customers in host countries. More specifically, the MNE may need to invest less in developing location-bound FSAs in host countries, since the Internet provides an inexpensive communication tool for many interactions with potential customers, especially in terms of informing and persuading these customers to purchase the MNE's products. In this context, the authors advocate the use of single, centrally managed websites for each brand name used by the MNE, as well as the provision of standardized service bundles so as to avoid confusion in the minds of customers as to what service level can be expected in a specific geographic sphere, except where the creation of location-bound FSAs and the tailoring of the product offering to customers in host countries remains critical (e.g., in the automobile industry, some brands have a very different market image and reputation from country to country).

The authors also predict the growth of new types of intermediaries acting as international projectors. For example, one type of intermediary will need to provide the necessary, standardized logistics services to support Internet-based sales of physical products (e.g., international courier companies). Another type of intermediary will reduce the information overload facing Internet users (e.g., firms that collect, assess, synthesize and present information on product offerings, and the quality thereof, from various alternative suppliers).

In contrast with Levitt's analysis, Quelch and Klein exhibit a keen understanding of the limits of standardization brought about by the Internet. One major cost is the risk that brand names will become increasingly vulnerable to even isolated instances of problems with quality, price and availability. Worldwide dissemination of information about such problems may lead to a worldwide decline in sales. Therefore, a worldwide approach to crisis management and maintaining reputational resources is required.

Government imposed restrictions may limit international, Internet-based sales, and an MNE providing worldwide coverage through the Internet must have: "(1) twenty-four hour order taking and customer service response capability, (2) regulatory and customs-handling expertise to ship internationally, and (3) in-depth understanding of foreign marketing environments to assess the relative advantages of its own products and services".[10] In this context, senior managers should not make the mistake of assuming away cultural distance between home and host country environments. The absence of direct, personal contact with customers may lead managers to assume (wrongly) that foreign customers are very much like home country customers, and this may result in under-investment in location-bound FSAs in host countries.

Here, the authors note the special difficulty of after-sales service provision, in cases where this service can only be provided locally, building upon a physical infrastructure and with localized human resources, rather than electronically.

Finally, the authors identify a potential, internal challenge inside the MNE: Internet-based sales through specialized, central websites should not be at the expense of more conventional, foreign affiliates' sales: to recognize the affiliates' contributions, clear rules should be established regarding how to credit Internet-based sales.

David Arnold, Julian Birkinshaw and **Omar Toulan** provide a second complementary perspective to Levitt's on the globalization of markets. Their *CMR* article discusses the potential and the limits of global account management.[11]

Global account management can be defined as dedicating specialized resources, typically involving non-location-bound routines, to serve internationally operating customers in an integrated fashion. This implies a move towards standardized supply contracts with these customers, as well as a consistent international platform of predetermined service content and processes. In many cases, this may mean host country subsidiaries lose their ability to alter the marketing mix when serving local operations of international customers with global account status (much in line with Levitt's approach discussed above). Host country subsidiaries must be willing to give up this control: "Global account relationships cannot work unless both partners are committed to global marketing … [I]t is important that there is a compelling demand for a consistent global platform for the agreement."[12]

On the positive side, global account management, with its focus on standardization, can be interpreted as a logical reaction to the internationalization of large customers eager to gain a tighter grip on their supply chain. From the supplier's perspective, this practice is also in line with the strategy of crafting a stronger customer orientation across borders.

However, Arnold *et al.*, building upon research conducted with 16 large companies, conclude that there are two main pitfalls to effective implementation of global account management. First, if the customer/potential global account is more internationally coordinated than the supplier, then the main effect of global account management may be price squeezes, with little benefit accruing to the supplier except perhaps more certainty about future sales volumes. In this case, the customer has more knowledge than the supplier about pricing in the various international markets. The customer will automatically demand that the lowest price be applied across the board, and may ask for additional volume discounts. The authors observed several instances of this unfortunate outcome for the supplier.

Only if the supplier engages in international coordination to the same level, can this type of bounded rationality problem (i.e., the supplier incorrectly predicting the customer's response to a global account management value proposition) be avoided. If the supplier engages sufficiently in international coordination, then price reduction requests by the global account customer can be appropriately anticipated and resisted. Here, the focus of negotiations on the substance of the global account agreement can be redirected from mere cost considerations to strategic issues such as additional value-added services that could be provided by the supplier, including a more streamlined and transparent supply chain, customized services and help in new product development. This strategic approach to global account management usually only makes sense if the vendor is one of the customer's main suppliers for a specific product range, and the customer is a 'lead user' of the vendor's products.

Second, important internal problems of bounded rationality and reliability occur if the supplier pays insufficient attention to implementation details. Global accounts should be assigned to experienced executives with a long-term vision, rather than to mere salespeople interested in maximizing short-term sales irrespective of profit margins and without an interest in building lasting relationships with the customer.

It is equally critical to recognize that the supplier's local marketing and sales organizations in host countries will often remain active in fulfilling specific contracts with local affiliates of the global account (e.g., distribution and after-sales servicing). In fact, when serving a global account in a specific host country, it may be impossible to separate precisely the value added by the supplier's global account management team from the value added by the local marketing and sales organizations. This is a typical intra-organizational bounded rationality problem that may cause, as a dysfunctional outcome, more bounded reliability challenges at the local level. If local marketing teams feel that the global account management team is just taking business away from them, they may experience severe alienation and may not commit themselves to the accounts. To counter such bounded reliability problems, senior MNE management must communicate clearly to their local marketing organizations what role the global account managers will play, including their interaction routines with the local marketing and sales organizations. Senior MNE management must also provide adequate administrative support at corporate headquarters for their global account managers, who are often physically located close to their assigned customer's international headquarters, in the customer's home country. Finally, senior MNE management must spend sufficient time and energy to enlist the commitment from local marketing and sales organizations in host countries to the principles of global account management, especially through adopting the common best (though expensive) practice of allocating sales commissions to both global account management teams and local marketing and sales organizations (formalized incentive splitting).

MANAGEMENT INSIGHTS

Levitt's work advertised the 'global' approach to international business strategy for MNEs, with centralized exporting and international projection taking on a worldwide scale. This approach builds upon a key assumption regarding MNE FSAs: the key FSAs of relevance are non-location-bound ones, predominantly developed in the firm's home market. Figure 9.1 illustrates the concept as it relates to this book's framework. Recall that in earlier figures the three elements on the left-hand side of the figure represent the conventional triad of location advantages, location-bound FSAs and non-location-bound FSAs. Figure 9.1 shows Levitt's perspective: non-location-bound FSAs (the dark, shaded region), embodied in globally standardized products, largely if not exclusively determine the MNE's competitiveness. This is very similar to the Prahalad and Hamel model on the core competence of the corporation discussed in Chapter 2. The difference between the two approaches is that Levitt focuses on high-quality, low-cost, reliable products, whereas Prahalad and Hamel emphasize the knowledge bundles underlying these products.

According to Levitt, successful global companies "sell in all national markets the same kind of products sold at home or in their largest export market".[13] This perspective mirrors Pattern I from this book's framework, whereby internationally transferable FSAs are developed in the home country and subsequently diffused to national subsidiaries for exploitation in foreign host markets (as with *international projectors)* or embodied in final products exported to the rest of the world (as with *centralized exporters*) (see Figure 9.2). Levitt explicitly contrasts this with the polycentric approach represented by Pattern IV, the pattern most representative of the *multi-centred MNE*. Levitt views this last pattern of international expansion, whereby location-bound FSAs are developed to cater systematically to host country preferences, as a relic of the past.

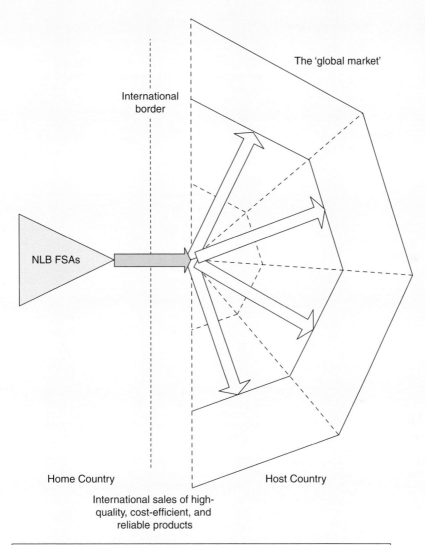

Figure 9.1
Product standardization as the driver of global competitiveness

The 'global market'

International border

NLB FSAs

Home Country

International sales of high-quality, cost-efficient, and reliable products

Host Country

Absence of LA and LB FSA segments of the home country triangle, reflects the model's exclusive emphasis on NLB FSAs as drivers of MNE competitiveness. The similar sizes of the host country triangles and their weak separation, using only dotted lines, reflect the model's emphasis on treating all host countries in a similar fashion using standardized products to serve the 'global market'.

These characteristics of Levitt's model allow us to identify its five main limitations. First, Levitt pays relatively little attention to the role of either home country location advantages or host country location advantages in the development of new FSAs. However, as we have explored extensively in earlier chapters, the MNE's presence in particular locations often plays a key role in the company's FSA development processes, and its resulting international competitiveness.

Second, Levitt argues that firms should implement a global strategy across all markets rather than respond excessively to distinct customer preferences in host

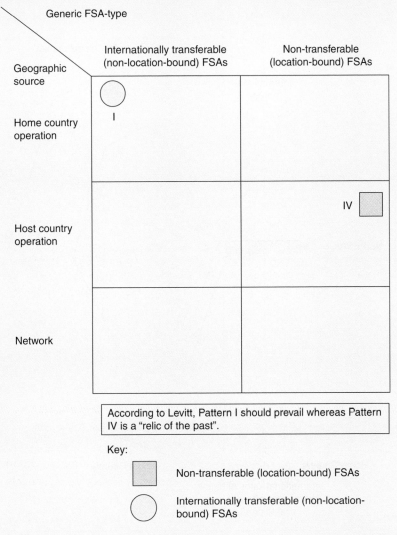

Figure 9.2
Levitt's perspective of
FSA development in
MNEs

Generic FSA-type

Geographic source	Internationally transferable (non-location-bound) FSAs	Non-transferable (location-bound) FSAs
Home country operation	I	
Host country operation		IV
Network		

According to Levitt, Pattern I should prevail whereas Pattern IV is a "relic of the past".

Key:

■ Non-transferable (location-bound) FSAs

○ Internationally transferable (non-location-bound) FSAs

countries. Even though he does not completely dismiss customization, he views it as a sign of weakness that increases costs, rather than as a strength. However, companies that go too far in implementing a top-down standardized decision-making process risk overlooking both the unique location advantages of various host markets by curtailing subsidiary initiatives, and the need for new location-bound FSAs as a precondition for value creation in those host markets. It is of course a question of balance between standardization and customization, as Levitt recognizes, but his suggestion that existing customer preferences in host markets can often be altered to conform to standardized products perhaps oversimplifies the time and effort required to achieve such a change.

Third, and related to the two previous points, when adopting Levitt's mindset, a serious bounded rationality problem may be created: senior managers may well become overoptimistic about the international transferability, deployment and exploitation potential of their FSA bundles. These bundles may actually contain unnoticed location-bound components, and thus may have a much more limited international deployability and exploitation potential than anticipated.

Fourth, Levitt's perspective on the substance of scale economies appears relatively simplistic. In most industries, there is a minimum efficient size of production, but this minimum efficient size may represent only a small fraction of the world market for a product. In other words, the minimum efficient size and the lowest marginal cost per unit may often be achieved in a single, large economy such as the US, or in an economic region such as the EU or the NAFTA zone. In these cases, increasing the scale by 'going global' will not decrease the marginal cost per unit. There may also be vastly differing scale economies in the different value chain activities, with upstream activities typically providing the greatest potential for scale economies. Finally, scale can evolve from being the expression of a key FSA to a potential liability or core rigidity, especially in industries where a very high capacity utilization is required to make profits. Here, customizing the MNE's product offering across geographic markets can stabilize sales volumes and profitability.

Fifth, Levitt identifies and contrasts only two types of corporations: 'multinational' ones, engaged in excessive national responsiveness, and global ones, striving to maximize scale economies. However, in reality there are many shades of grey, in the sense of more complex strategies available to MNEs, such as international strategies focused more on scope economies (through international knowledge transfers) than scale economies, and strategies building upon the exploitation of national differences, as found in ***international coordinators***.

In this context, it is important to mention that Levitt's suggestion of technology forcing convergence and global commonality is only partly correct: in many sectors, technology has enabled the customization of services and products, through computer-aided design and computer-aided manufacturing (CAD/CAM) and sophisticated logistics, and has reduced the importance of conventional scale economies. Levitt, however, dismisses the benefits of such customization, arguing that the large-scale production of standardized goods is systematically cheaper than smaller-scale production runs. Here, he neglects the fact that in many industries, customization – building upon tools such as CAD/CAM – is actually demanded and highly valued by customers.

Five management takeaways

1. Study your firm's product portfolio and assess its potential for global standardization.
2. Examine the potential of the Internet to increase your revenues and to reduce your costs in international markets.

3. Carefully monitor your Internet activities in order to avoid any infringement of the law and subsequent loss of reputation, and make sure online sales do not cannibalize foreign affiliate sales.
4. Determine the potential and limitations of global account management in your firm.
5. Reflect on your own industry and firm-level context (e.g., administrative heritage, internationalization strategy) to determine the limits of product standardization as the preferred vehicle for international expansion.

CASE

Case 9.1 International marketing at beer brewer Anheuser Busch – InBev[14]

Anheuser Busch (AB) – InBev is the largest beer brewing company and was formed in 2008, when InBev acquired St. Louis-based Anheuser-Busch to become one "of the world's top five consumer products companies".[15] Belgium-based InBev, at that point in time, the world's number one brewer, was itself formed in 2004 through a complex merger arrangement between Interbrew of Belgium and Companhia de Bebidas das Américas (AmBev) of Brazil.

Interbrew (we will use 'Interbrew' to refer to the period before the AmBev acquisition, 'InBev' to refer to activities prior to the Anheuser-Busch acquisition, and 'AB InBev' to refer to events thereafter) traces its origins to a brewery called Den Horen, established in 1366 in Leuven, Belgium. In 1717, the brewery changed its name to Artois when it was acquired by Sebastien Artois, its master brewer. In 1987, Brasseries Artois, then the second largest brewer in Belgium, and Brasseries Piedboeuf, then the largest brewer in Belgium, merged to create Interbrew. In 1988, Interbrew was the 17th largest brewer in the world.[16]

Before the 1987 merger, both Brasseries Artois and Brasseries Piedboeuf had expanded through acquisitions. Brasseries Artois acquired the Leffe brand in 1952, the Dommelsch Brewery in the Netherlands in 1968 and the Brasseries Motte Cordonier in France in 1970. Similarly, Brasseries Piedboeuf purchased the Lamot brewery in Belgium in 1984.

Interbrew continued with this acquisition strategy. It acquired Belgian brewers Hoegaarden in 1989 and Belle-Vue in 1990. In the early 1990s, Interbrew expanded extremely rapidly, pursuing more than 30 acquisitions and strategic joint ventures throughout the world. Examples of such acquisitions included Labatt in Canada in 1995, SUN Interbrew in Russia and Ukraine in 1996, Oriental Breweries in South Korea in 1999, and Diebels and Beck & Co. in Germany in 2001. More recent acquisitions included the Malaysian Lion Group in China and the Apatin Brewery in Serbia.

Interbrew's traditional brand strategy: Local branding

As a way of managing its large number of acquired firms, Interbrew traditionally left most decisions to local managers, and it even intentionally prohibited the usage of 'Belgium' in its ads. Its slogan was 'the world's local brewer'.

Traditionally, Interbrew applied a geographic structure with major decision-making power decentralized to local managers. Following the acquisition of Labatt in 1995, Interbrew managed the group through two geographic zones: the Americas and Europe/Asia/Africa. Although it shifted to an integrated structure in 1999, in less than a year it switched back to a geographic structure with five regions reporting directly to the CEO. Interbrew allocated major decision-making responsibilities in each country to the individual country teams. Such a decentralized approach was viewed as crucial to Interbrew's strategy.

Interbrew's corporate strategy in the 1990s was to develop a complete portfolio in both mature markets and growth markets through acquiring and developing existing local brands. In both markets, whenever possible, Interbrew focused on acquiring established, high-quality local brands, such as Labatt Blue in Canada. In some cases, Interbrew acquired local brands, upgraded their product quality and developed them into strong local brands, such as Borsodi So in Hungary and Ozujsko in Croatia. Essentially, the international expansion was "brand, rather than brewery, driven".[17]

In addition, Interbrew identified certain local brands with regional potential and developed them across a group of markets. For example, Hoegaarden and Leffe became leading brands in France and the Netherlands.

Interbrew adds global brands

In 1998, the executive management committee decided to change strategy and add some global brands to its portfolio, for three reasons.

First, consumer demand was expected to converge on a global basis. There was growing demand for premium beers from the rising number of affluent consumers worldwide, as well as increasing demand for low-priced beers from the rising number of poorer consumers. In contrast, the market for mainstream (i.e., expensive and local) beers was expected to shrink gradually. Although the market for global brands was still small, this market was expected to grow in the next few decades.

Second, the beer business was becoming more international, and the international media had made it more viable to build global brands than in the past. For example, Heineken, Budweiser and Corona had become global brands. Interbrew believed that a global strategy would add synergies through global advertising and marketing, thereby improving operating efficiency.

Third, it was thought that a global brand would raise the company's profile, which in turn would boost the company's stock performance. As a downside of its strategy of being 'the world's local brewer', Interbrew's profile was so low internationally that "some beer analysts nicknamed the company 'Interwho'?"[18] This low profile was thought to damage Interbrew's stock performance, with Interbrew's stock trading 10 per cent below that of rival Heineken.

Thus, reducing its sole emphasis on local strategy and developing some global brands seemed to be the solution to fix the firm's problems on the stock market and to anticipate expected market changes. An Interbrew annual report explained the new core strategy well:

Beer is a business of local brands, so brewers need to be big in local brands, culturally adept at being local. That is the basis of our strategy. Yet if all we had was strong local platforms, it would be good – but not great. And if all we had was globally famous names, it would be pleasing – but not good enough. With no local platforms, an international brand has to pay its own infrastructure costs. The picture brightens considerably if you have strong local brands with critical scale, which covers overhead costs, then add premium brands on top. This is the more profitable way – the local platform plus the premium portfolio. In other words, the Interbrew model.[19]

In 1998, the executive management committee chose Stella Artois as Interbrew's global flagship brand.

Launching Stella Artois as the global flagship brand

Tracing its origins back to 1366, Stella Artois was launched as a Christmas beer in 1920 in its home market of Belgium. In the 1970s it became a strong market leader in Belgium. By the 1990s, though, Stella Artois was considered somewhat old-fashioned within Belgium, and it experienced declining domestic sales. However, Stella achieved great success in two international markets, namely the UK and France. Performance in the UK was particularly strong, and by 1998 Stella occupied 7.6 per cent of the lager market share. In 1998, the UK market accounted for 49 per cent of Stella's total brand volume, France 18 per cent and Belgium 13 per cent. Besides these three markets, Stella was also sold in Italy, Sweden, Australia, Croatia, Hungary and Romania through licensing agreements, joint ventures and Interbrew subsidiaries.

The initial stage

In September 1998, Interbrew started to apply a centralized Stella brand management approach, which quickly faced implementation barriers.

Interbrew had operated on a regional basis, and country management teams had become used to making most decisions by themselves. Not all country management teams were convinced it was a good idea to adopt a global approach, especially in those countries where they had already established an image for Stella Artois. For example, in the UK market, Interbrew's licensee Whitbread did not want to change its successful 'reassuringly expensive' advertising slogan. In Belgium, Interbrew's local advertising programme had carefully positioned Stella Artois as a mainstream lager, rather than a premium lager, as designed by the centralized Stella brand management team.

Moreover, even for those countries most likely to adopt the global approach for Stella Artois, Interbrew still needed time to improve the coordination system between the centralized management team and country management teams.

For the above reasons, Interbrew included only the less established markets in its initial global campaign. The campaign intended to position Stella Artois as a sophisticated, contemporary European lager with an important brewing heritage. The global advertising framework included a television concept and a series of print and outdoor executions that had been researched to be effective across borders. In 1999, with both local and corporate funding, the advertising campaign was rolled out in 15 markets, including the US, Canada, Italy, France and Croatia.

In 1999, Stella grew strongly. For example, sales rose by 14 per cent in Croatia, 37 per cent in Hungary and 88 per cent in Romania.[20]

Switch to a new branding plan

Despite making good progress, establishing Stella Artois as a global brand experienced a major challenge in early 2000. Rolling out the brand at the global level required a huge amount of funding – in the US market, Interbrew's corporate marketing department allocated several million dollars to Labatt USA for launching Stella Artois within the single year 1999. Further market development in the next few years would require additional funding, thereby leading to substantial financial pressures. At the same time, the benefits of a global brand did not appear to materialize in the short run, at least not consistently in every market.

Thus, in 2000, Interbrew revised its initial approach to global branding, deciding to be more selective when identifying its global target market for Stella Artois. Interbrew established four strategic filters. *First*, any potential market targeted had to be a large and/or growing market with a current or potential premier lager segment no less than 5 per cent of the total market.

Second, Interbrew's resources and commitment had to be sufficient to make Stella one of the top three brands in the local market, and achieve attractive margins after an initial period of around three years.

Third, a committed local partner had to be available both to provide high-quality distribution and to invest in the brand.

Fourth, the success in the chosen markets had to have potential spillover effects benefiting the firm in other national or regional markets.

These market selection criteria shifted what was included in the 'global' markets for Stella Artois from national markets to around 20 international cities, such as London, New York, Hong Kong, Moscow and Los Angeles. These major cities had a concentration of affluent consumers, potentially allowing Interbrew to benefit from scale and scope economies in sales and marketing.

The new city-by-city global branding plan required a new management approach. Interbrew established a corporate marketing group, comprised of the brand management team, a customer service group, regional sales managers, a cruise business management group and a Belgian beer café manager. These group members worked together to identify top cities, develop brand positioning for local execution, design marketing programmes and allocate resources. Because the corporate marketing group was responsible for both the development of core marketing programmes and local support, Interbrew brought all crucial resources under the global brand development director to ensure an integrated effort. Still, the central marketing group had to rely on the commitment of local managers. This was relatively easy to achieve in the case of wholly owned subsidiaries, but not so for licensees and joint ventures.

The new global plan also incorporated the launch of Stella in other countries. In the late 1990s, Stella had already been successfully introduced in various central European urban centres, such as Budapest and Sofia, with a large presence of the targeted group of consumers of premium beer. In these cities, Interbrew strictly controlled the choice of distribution channels and promotion programmes, choosing only a few high-end bars in order to build up Stella's premium image. Further, Interbrew opened Belgian Beer Cafés in these markets to showcase how to serve Stella Artois, e.g., to serve Stella at 38 degrees Fahrenheit in branded glasses and shaving off foam with a spoon. The Beer Cafés greatly helped Stella Artois build up a reputation as a premium beer. In addition, the stature of Stella Artois in the UK and its marketing programmes there also helped, as the image in the UK was very similar to the global positioning of Stella intended by the corporate marketing team.

The new global plan copied this strategy in other markets. For example, in New York, Interbrew chose around 20 of the most exclusive bars, including Madonna's favourites, Chez Esaada and Markt. Stella was priced at about US $100/keg, much higher than Heineken's US $85/keg, and the media campaign included only prestigious outdoor advertising (e.g., a Times Square poster) and high-end celebrity events. In Chicago, Interbrew opened 'beer academies' to showcase Stella etiquette.

These marketing efforts seemed to work very well around the world. Although Stella Artois cost only US $1.10 a pint in Belgium in 2002 and was sold in plastic cups, it successfully established its image as a modern, sophisticated lager, selling for as much as US $8 a glass in Manhattan. Interestingly, Belgians were surprised by Stella's international image. One Belgian, a 62-year-old Mr De Boek, commented in 2002, "In Belgium, Stella is a beer fit for old peasants . . . Americans must be insane."[21]

Anheuser-Busch

The history of Anheuser-Busch dates back to 1852 when German immigrant Eberhard Anheuser invested in a local brewery in St. Louis, Missouri. By 1957, it had become the leading brewery in the United States and has continued to hold that position in 2012. The success of the company created an attractive target for InBev, which was looking to expand its global position. An acquisition would create the world's largest brewing company and provide InBev with access to Anheuser-Busch's established markets. The takeover process resulted in a long battle between the two firms. When InBev's initial offer was rejected, InBev moved to take over the board. The acquisition was finally completed on November 1, 2008 with Anheuser-Busch becoming a wholly owned subsidiary.

Selling the American dream

Budweiser, the 'American style lager', was introduced to America in 1876 by Adolphus Busch. Brewed in St. Louis, Missouri and known for its 'American' lager characteristics of being a light and thin brew, Budweiser gradually became the best selling beer in America. However, its popularity in its home market eventually started to fade, with volume sales decreasing from

1988 on. This trend can be attributed to Americans' increasing demand for lower caloric alcoholic beverages and the rising popularity of micro brews.[22]

Thus in 2010, AB InBev responded by launching a new campaign to push Budweiser into international markets. In the past, Budweiser had encountered difficulties in European markets as American beer had a reputation for being 'watery'.[23] However, this quality was appealing to other international markets such as Asia and South America. AB InBev adopted a strategy for marketing Budweiser internationally that was similar to Interbrew's promotion of Stella Artois as a premium beer. Capitalizing on its American roots, AB InBev promoted Budweiser as the 'American dream in a bottle' to appeal to international consumers.[24] The global 'Grab Some Buds' campaign used optimism to create a sense of promise even if it was just a great night out with friends. The success of this campaign in foreign markets was astounding giving rise to double-digit growth in sales volume in 2010 and 2011.[25] The campaign managed to be relatively cohesive across international borders with only minor changes required to address cultural preferences. For instance, in Canada, the slogan was reworked as "Why Not Grab Some Buds" in response to research indicating that Canadians were less comfortable with being instructed to drink.[26]

Budweiser continues to grow in foreign markets; AB InBev recently launched Budweiser in Russia (2010) and Brazil (2011). In Brazil, AB InBev is attempting to respond to the demand for premium beer, since it already controls 70 per cent of the market for lower priced brews. Chris Burggraeve, Chief Marketing Officer, foresees that Brazilians will take a liking to the American lager, stating "We're bringing abroad to them. They're hungry for the world."[27]

Global marketing with social media

Social media have become a useful tool for managing brand health. The creation of an interactive medium for AB InBev to communicate with consumers has had a significant impact on how the company markets to global consumers. Approximately one fifth of AB InBev's marketing budget is dedicated to the use of social media to build its brand. However, Chris Burggraeve firmly states that AB InBev does not have a "social media strategy".[28] It prefers to use a "connection strategy", which focuses on connecting with consumers in the most "efficient, effective and relevant" manner.[29]

In fact, AB InBev hopes to use social media to create a social environment that inspires consumers to move away from online interaction and return to more personal, face-to-face social settings. This aim is revealed in Mr Burggraeve's rhetorical questions, "Isn't beer, in today's speak, the best and most 'real' social network ever?"[30] Its pursuit can be seen in AB InBev's sponsorship of live events such as the 2006 FIFA World Cup and the Beijing Olympics, with these sponsorships serving as a positive way to promote shared experiences. This philosophy is facilitated by the company's Facebook platforms, which promote cultural events and encourage followers to share locations of social events.[31]

AB InBev way of marketing

The effectiveness of InBev's present global marketing strategy requires a cohesive integration of three pillars: brand portfolio management, consumer connection and consistent innovation.[32]

Any marketing concept must pass through these three pillars, which encompass 23 different modules to create effective marketing. Mr Burggraeve sums up the AB InBev Way of Marketing as 'art, science, and discipline' to deliver successful brand health.[33]

To manage its portfolio of international brands, AB InBev applies a strategy known as 'Freedom in a Framework'. This strategy stipulates that, for a given brand, the positioning, the campaign and the look and feel of the product are controlled, with some flexibility being allowed between countries.[34] For 'local jewel' brands the framework is less stringent and local marketing executives have substantial control over how the brand is marketed.

Regardless of the brand level, AB InBev is committed to marketing that exemplifies a 'fans first approach'.[35] This approach ensures that marketing investment connects first with those consumers who are loyal to their brews. CEO Carlos Brito describes this approach as "helping [AB InBev] to stay relevant to beer lovers around the world and sustainably grow [its] business".[36]

AB InBev has largely adopted Interbrew's branding strategy, offering more than 200 regional and local brands. By 2012, AB InBev had developed three global brands: Stella Artois, Beck's and Budweiser. The firm aims to have its global, regional and local brands "work cohesively together to optimize relevance for different consumers".[37] In 2012, AB InBev employed around 116,000 people in 23 countries across the Americas, Europe and Asia Pacific, with a worldwide market share of close to 18.8 per cent.[38] AB InBev aims to become "The Best Beer Company in a Better World".[39]

QUESTIONS

1. How did Interbrew view consumers' demands across different markets? What changes occurred to Interbrew's perspective? What would be Levitt's perspective?

2. Did Interbrew offer high-quality, cost-efficient, globally standardized Stella Artois in a global market?

3. What were the differences in Stella Artois' positioning in Belgium, the UK and the US?

4. To what extent did the firm's administrative heritage affect the global launch of Stella Artois?

5. What was the source of Interbrew's knowledge for the 'global marketing' of Stella Artois? What would Levitt's model suggest?

6. What happened with the firm's international branding strategy after AB Inbev was formed?

7. Can you provide an update on AB InBev's branding strategy, using materials available on the Web?

Case 9.2 A rising star from China: Haier Group[40]

After almost going bankrupt in 1984, the Qingdao General Refrigerator Factory from Qingdao (China) was restructured. Presently known as the Haier Group (in the following: Haier), it has become one of the leading consumer electronics and home appliances manufacturers in the world. In 2011, Haier's sales[41] reached almost US $23.8 billion a year-on-year increase of more than 11 per cent.[42] A share of 27 per cent of revenues came from washing machines, 7 per cent from water heaters and 66 per cent from integrated channel services. The latter comprise the product distribution and logistics services business of the Haier Group and account for the sales of the "non-Haier" brands. However, the products sold through Haier's integrated channel services include mainly refrigerators, air conditioners, televisions and computers of the group itself.[43] Since 2009, Haier has been consistently ranked as the world's largest major appliance brand, with a global retail volume share of 7.8 per cent.[44]

Success stories such as Haier's are not an exception anymore, yet Haier can be seen as an exemplary MNE from an emerging economy that worked its way up to become a renowned global brand in over 100 countries.[45] Thanks to the high skill level of its management, its focus on knowledge generation, and well-thought-out strategy execution, Haier's local and international expansion turned out to be more than satisfying. However, in its early internationalization stage, Haier had to face many challenges, related mainly to the company's poor reputation and low quality standards. Some drastic changes were necessary to improve Haier's market positioning and save it from bankruptcy.

The early years: Improving product quality and reputation

In 1984, then-35-year-old Zhang Ruimin, deputy manager of a home appliance company in Qingdao, China, was appointed director of Qingdao General Refrigerator Factory. At that time, the firm was deeply in debt and suffered from decreasing demand; employees were notably demotivated. Zhang identified a need to introduce far-reaching measures in order to manage a successful turnaround.

While investigating a client's complaint about the poor quality of a refrigerator purchased from the firm, Zhang discovered that 76 out of 400 refrigerators in stock were of inferior quality, reflecting a failure rate of close to 20 per cent. Zhang asked for all defective models to be lined up and ordered his staff to destroy these. This incident represents the turning point in the firm's history and marked the beginning of the company that is known today under the brand name Haier.

Under Zhang's management, employees began to understand the importance of product quality and reliability, and Haier established a successful brand strategy. With the goal of providing high-quality products and services, Zhang established his "always cautious, always meticulous"[46] philosophy of achievement that shaped Haier's corporate culture, and is largely responsible for Haier's reputation for innovation as well as for the enthusiasm of its 70,000+ employees.[47]

Diversification through joint ventures and M&A

One of Zhang's strategies was to learn from best business practices in developed countries such as the United States, Germany and Japan. Following this strategy, Zhang revolutionized his company: He tied salary to performance, sent technical personnel abroad for advanced training, and developed a worldwide supply chain system. Zhang was aware of the fact that Haier could best improve its image by partnering with a foreign company. Therefore, in 1985, he entered into a joint venture with the German firm Liebherr, a leading home appliance manufacturer.[48] During this partnership, the Chinese manufacturer benefited from access to Liebherr's refrigerator technology, improved product quality and built up its reputation. Moreover, several years later, the firm was renamed after the second part of the Chinese translation of its partner Liebherr to receive its current name, Haier.

The first signs of the joint venture's success became apparent as early as 1988, when Haier gained a dominant position in the Chinese refrigerator market.[49] In the same year, the firm completed its first acquisition and integrated a small electroplating firm, the Qingdao Electroplating Company, from Qingdao, China, later transforming the newly acquired division into a microwave producer.[50]

Over time Zhang's drive continuously to improve products and services did not fade ... Haier took an impressive step forward when it achieved internationally recognized accreditations such as the Underwriters Laboratories Inc. certification from an American independent product safety certification organization, the Technischer Überwachungsverein accreditation from the German technical inspection association, and the qualification of the International Organization for Standardization, a non-governmental organization with headquarters in Switzerland. These certifications marked Haier as an accredited supplier for the international markets.[51]

However, in the 1990s, Zhang realized that quality alone was insufficient to achieve sustained corporate growth. He decided to spread Haier's corporate risk by diversifying into various new product lines. Therefore, in 1991, Haier merged with the Qingdao Freezer Factory and the Qingdao Air Conditioner Factory, two financially challenged companies from Qingdao, China, that flourished with rising sales shortly after Zhang's restructuring was completed.[52] Considering high growth forecasts for the acquired businesses, Zhang made a decision to expand production facilities by buying land for a new industrial park, which would house corporate headquarters and 66 subsidiaries. In order to finance this large-scale project, Zhang listed Haier on the Shanghai Stock Exchange in 1993. The IPO became a big success, raising sufficient capital to establish Haier Industrial Park in Qingdao, China, two years later.[53]

In the same year as going public, Haier started cooperating with the Japanese firm Mitsubishi in order to gain more expertise in air conditioners.[54] Haier also partnered with the Italian firm Merloni Elettrodomestici, at that time the third largest home appliance producer in Europe.

Together, the partners built a washing machine production plant for the Chinese market in Qingdao, China. This joint venture enabled Haier not only to acquire valuable technology necessary to produce washing machines, but also to implement its diversification plans. It consequently paved the way for Haier's subsequent acquisition of the Red Star Electric Appliance Company in 1995, which was turned around "from money-losing to profit-generating" within three months.[55]

Thanks to the acquisitions of the Huangshan Electronics Group and the Yellow Mountain Television Company in 1997, Haier expanded into the television business.[56] Haier's diversification strategy led to a total of 18 Chinese enterprises in a range of industries being acquired. By the end of the century, Haier's offerings included traditional home appliances (e.g., washing machines, electric irons, microwaves) as well as the latest consumer electronics goods (e.g., mobile phones, televisions, computers).[57]

Internationalization

Following the success of Haier's diversification strategy and continuously increasing exports, Zhang started to implement his plans for more sophisticated international expansion. While earlier-stage exports relied mainly on licensing agreements (e.g., with Liebherr in Germany) and sales alliances (e.g., with Welbit Appliances in the United States), Zhang aimed to increase Haier's independence and degree of internationalization with the help of a multichannel strategy. "To achieve its balanced country portfolio", Haier defined three stages:[58]

- Stage one: 'Seeding' – a sales-volume-based approach that emphasizes reputation building and foreign distribution through local sales agents;
- Stage two: 'Rooting' – key aspects are rising market share and creating wholly owned production subsidiaries abroad;
- Stage three: 'Harvesting' – represents the implementation of subsidiary-based local sales and location of R&D capabilities abroad.[59]

In guiding the international expansion of Haier, Zhang followed his credo: "difficult things first, easier steps later"[60]. He initially intended to enter markets in developed countries first, and to expand into developing countries afterwards. However, this strategic approach, that aimed to gain strong managerial, technological and reputational competences in developed economies and to apply these newly acquired competencies subsequently in emerging countries, was not strictly followed.[61] After Haier's initial market entry in the United States, the firm established itself in emerging countries as 'Haier ASEAN' (abbreviation for the Association of Southeast Asian Nations). Haier followed its initial exports to Indonesia in early 1992 with opening its first foreign production site there four years later. In 1997, Haier furthered its expansion into emerging economies by establishing subsidiaries in the Philippines and Malaysia.

During the same year, Haier approached foreign distributors at the World Household Appliances Expo in Cologne, Germany, with the intention to take a share of the world market in home appliances. In contrast to its internationalization strategy in the Americas, Haier had to hire external sales agents to import its refrigerators from China and to sell these in the European market, mainly in Germany, the Netherlands and Italy.

Having gained self-confidence as well as reputational and financial strength, Haier re-focused on the US market a few years later. Based on Haier's previous sales alliance with Welbit and the US market's complexity, Zhang opted for a cautious market expansion strategy. Instead of offering Haier's full product range, Zhang targeted two niche categories, namely small-sized compact refrigerators and electric wine coolers. Zhang believed that those markets were underdeveloped and therefore remained below the US-based producers' radar, yet offered a lot of growth potential. Zhang's assessment proved to be right: Haier developed into a renowned brand in these previously ignored product niches. Along with this success, Zhang considered a stronger, long-term oriented commitment in the US by diversifying Haier's product offerings and establishing a local production. Expansion into the market for full-size refrigerators placed Haier in direct competition with the big four American appliances brands: GE, Whirlpool, Frigidaire and Maytag. In 2000, with the help of its former local distributor, Haier established its first wholly owned production subsidiary in Camden, United States.[62]

Within a 12-month time frame, Haier demonstrated its ambitious growth strategy by building three industrial parks: Haier Qingdao Economic and Technological Development Zone (QETDZ) Industrial Park in Qingdao, China, for export-oriented production; Haier Information Park in Qingdao, China, for the expansion into information technology; and Haier American Industrial Park for local production and research and development (R&D) in Camden, United States. It also built a university, namely Haier University in Qingdao, China.[63] By the end of 2000, Haier had grown tremendously and controlled six production plants overseas.[64] By 2001, Haier's contribution to the US economy was recognized by the naming of a street located near the Haier American Industrial Park as "Haier Road".[65] Haier was the only Chinese company to receive this honour in the United States, which was particularly important for the company's reputation in its home country, where these types of favours are considered an important sign of respect and deference.

In Europe, Haier tried yet another approach. Having relied solely on local sales agents in the past, Haier founded a European trading company that would receive the exclusive distribution of Haier products in seventeen European countries.[66] In 2001, Haier's first transnational merger with an Italian refrigerator company, owned by Meneghetti, took place. As part of Haier's localization strategy, this deal contributed substantially to its ambitious goal of conquering the European market of refrigerators and freezers.

In the same year, Haier established further production sites in Pakistan and Bangladesh.[67] Moreover, Haier established a joint venture in Nigeria, Africa, centralizing the entire production of home appliances for the African continent.[68] Furthermore, in 2001, Haier partnered with OBI, the German market leader in the Do-It-Yourself sector that is called after the phonetic spelling of the French pronunciation for hobby.[69] Their joint venture, China Homeworld Company Limited, focused on the retail business of construction and home furnishing materials and generated synergies for both partners.[70] On the one hand, OBI predicted potential for its own Chinese retail stores through the access to Haier's local distribution and logistics networks in China. On the other hand, Haier would benefit from extended domestic and overseas market access through OBI's sales channels. In addition, OBI's stores in China started to offer Haier's home appliances and electronics.[71]

One year later, in 2002, the firm expanded to Jordan and reinforced its strong market position in the Middle East. In the same year, Haier built trading subsidiaries for air conditioners in Italy and Spain, and in the UK one year later.[72] Following the Nigerian joint venture, Haier opened its second joint African production plant in Tunis, Tunisia, in 2002.[73]

Japan and the entire Asian region were also of great importance to Haier. To strengthen its position in the Asian markets, Haier formed a partnership with Sanyo, a leading Japanese electronics company. The objective of this cooperation was "to exchange market resources with higher efficiency and thus create a larger market".[74]

By the end of 2002, Haier had grown into an international company that managed thirteen production plants abroad, generating sales of US $1 billion. Haier's year-on-year revenues growth was 37 per cent in 2002.[75]

In 2003, Haier leveraged its joint venture with OBI in China to enter the German home appliance market by establishing a brand alliance with its German partner. In 2004, Haier's Pakistani subsidiary achieved the ISO9001 accreditation as the first of Haier's overseas production facilities and the first foreign home appliance manufacturing facility in Pakistan. In the same year, Haier's Jordan Industrial Park started operations and expanded its capacity with a second production facility in 2006. This was a large project, representing an annual production capacity of 150,000 air conditioners, 250,000 refrigerators, 300,000 washing machines and 450,000 televisions.[76]

During the following years, Haier continuously increased its product offerings worldwide, established more and more foreign sales and trading offices, and negotiated with potential joint venture partners, especially in Eastern Europe.[77]

The Cuban government started cooperating with Haier in 2006 following Cuba's 'Energy Revolution' programme.[78] In return for the approved market entry, Haier announced a donation of energy-efficient street lamps to Cuba, creating a win-win situation for both parties.[79] After four years of successful cooperation, Haier and Japanese Sanyo deepened their commitment by forming a joint venture in Osaka, Japan. One year later, in 2007, Haier entered into strategic cooperation with Intel, a leading American semiconductor chip producer, and Cisco, a worldwide leader in networking equipment. In the same year, Haier established its first India-based production plant in Pune, India, by acquiring the appliances production of the company Anchor Daewoo, a joint venture between Anchor Electricals, a subsidiary of the Japanese Panasonic Corporation, and Daewoo Electronics from South Korea.[80] With this acquisition, Haier took the next step in implementing its localization strategy. The acquisition allowed Haier to circumvent import tariffs, and to achieve reduced delivery times, and better customer service.[81]

Haier had already achieved top sales volumes in the global refrigerator market. The collaboration with numerous partners and various acquisitions only strengthened Haier's position on the world market. In 2008, Haier became the world's largest refrigerator manufacturer in terms of sales, surpassing its US rival Whirlpool.[82]

In the beginning of 2009, Haier and the Venezuelan government signed a cooperative agreement on household appliances. Plans were made to establish a local production site in partnership with a publicly owned consortium from Venezuela.[83] During that time, Zhang exchanged ideas for further strategic partnerships with Samsung and Dell, however, no agreement was reached on any bilateral cooperation. In 2009, in an attempt to strengthen its position in the New Zealand market, Haier acquired a 20 per cent stake in Fisher & Paykel, New Zealand's largest domestic home appliances producer. As a high-end white goods brand, Fisher & Paykel offered a great opportunity for Haier, which was previously under-represented in this upscale segment due primarily to fierce competition, especially from Germany. With the mutual trade agreement, Haier became the exclusive distributor of Fisher & Paykel products in China, whereas Fisher & Paykel took responsibility for Haier's products in the Australian and New Zealand markets.[84] In early 2010, Haier agreed to a strategic alliance with Hewlett-Packard (HP), a leading multinational information technology company. The goal of the agreement was to enhance both companies' competitive position. Haier's distribution network offered HP broad access to China's rural areas.[85] In 2011, Haier and Panasonic initiated a takeover of Sanyo's refrigerator and washing machine unit in Japan and South-East Asia. This acquisition, to be consumed in 2012, will increase Haier's access to the highly competitive market of white goods and give the firm inroads into the challenging Japanese market where domestic brands are typically favoured over foreign ones.[86]

Zhang has turned Haier into one of the most successful EMNEs that has produced over 100 million refrigerators worldwide and "achieved world-class production and marketing scale among the global refrigerator enterprises".[87] To keep up with the speed of international innovation, Haier developed an international R&D network consisting of six research centres in Qingdao and Beijing, China; Seoul, South Korea; Tokyo, Japan; Milan, Italy; and Los Angeles, United States, as well as eight global design centres in Seoul, South Korea; Osaka, Japan; Los Angeles and Camden, United States; Copenhagen, Denmark; Amsterdam, the Netherlands; Munich, Germany; and Milan, Italy.[88]

Product portfolio and market share

Once a modest refrigerator producer, Haier is presently playing an important role in various types of home appliances. In the course of Haier's early diversification strategy in the 1990s, numerous acquisitions and joint ventures worldwide helped it establish a strong product portfolio that is presently divided into five main categories. The *first* group targets the white goods, covering refrigerators, air conditioners, washing machines, water heaters and electric kitchen appliances.[89] *Second*, the Haier Digital and Personal Product Group covers home appliances, computers and mobile phones for entertainment, "interconnection and interaction".[90] The *third* segment focuses on integrated kitchens, with the full spectrum of Haier's home electric appliances. Haier was the first local company in China to offer to consumers "integrated kitchen cabinets and home appliances, (with the) one stop service satisfaction".[91] Haier Real Estate is the *fourth* industry group. As a wholly owned subsidiary of Haier, it manages property development projects and thus benefits from the significant economic potential of China's real estate market.[92] The *fifth* group, Home Appliances, includes more than 200 products in 14 categories (e.g., rice cookers, microwave ovens, induction cookers, etc.) in the high-end home appliances sector.[93]

Haier's position as the world's leading major appliances brand was largely enabled by the company's relentless expansion and commitment to innovation, but is particularly owed to the success of four major product categories. By 2011, Haier had become the world's number one manufacturer of refrigerators, freezers, home laundry appliances and electrical wine coolers.[94]

Haier's strategy

Today, Haier's journey to the top league of international home appliances producers represents a great Chinese success story, and an inspiring example for MNEs from emerging countries worldwide. After several near escapes from insolvency, the formerly small Chinese refrigerator manufacturer was revitalized and established as a world brand. Haier's extraordinary transformation, however, was not magical, but was based on hard work, endurance and insight on industry functioning. Haier's development path can be subdivided into four major phases.

First, in the immediate period after Zhang's appointment as a director, Haier's reputation suffered due to past quality problems. As his first order of business, Zhang aimed to improve the quality of Haier's refrigerators and implemented a 'brand building strategy' (1984–1991). In partnership with foreign companies, Haier built up advanced technological knowledge and updated its production equipment. In addition, Zhang created a strong focus on quality and implemented Total Quality Management (TQM), a proven method borrowed from quality-driven Japanese manufacturers. From then on, Zhang asked all employees to participate in continuously improving Haier's products and processes.

Second, with the new strict quality standards, Haier achieved huge success on the Chinese refrigerator market in the late 1980s and embarked on a diversification path. In the beginning of the 1990s, Haier started to expand into related businesses by acquiring and integrating numerous (and often struggling) local enterprises (1991–1998). While competitors tried to gain market share through price wars, Haier stuck to its principle of superior quality, which eventually allowed the company to achieve competitive advantage. Moreover, Zhang established Haier's own management control system ("OEC") that aimed to "accomplish what's planned each day; evaluate and improve what's accomplished each day".[95] According to "Haier's definition, 'O' stands for 'Overall', 'E' stands for 'Everyone', 'Everything' and 'Every Day', and 'C' stands for 'Control' and 'Clear'."[96] This managerial approach focuses on "overall control of everything that every employee does every day" and suggests that all employees finish their daily assignments with an increase of one per cent in volume of work each day.[97]

Third, Haier's diversification phase was followed by internationalization (1998–2005). By introducing a "Three-in-One" strategy, namely the co-location of design, production and marketing, Zhang was able to achieve customization of products to fit local needs. Haier's international expansion succeeded and this improved its market position vis-à-vis foreign rivals.[98]

Until today, Haier has followed the 'Three-in-One' principle. However, some managerial adjustments were needed in order to implement successfully Zhang's 'global brand strategy': to keep up with the speed of globalization, Haier decided to consolidate its resources in R&D, production and sales on a global scale.

Fourth, in 2010, Haier announced its strategic transformation from a production-focused company to a service-focused one, with an emphasis on meeting customer needs in a tailored, customized fashion.[99] Driven by complex customer demand and a fierce competitive environment, Haier became one of the most innovative home appliances companies worldwide. Its achievements in innovation were recognized with the Industrie Forum Communication Design Award in 2011.[100] Haier's strategic plan for the next five years includes the goal of remaining the number one home appliances brand in the world, and to be among the top five international electronics brands.

Zhang Ruimin

Zhang Ruimin is one of the most respected and powerful executives in Asia. Zhang's role in turning little-known Haier into an award-winning, innovative corporation prompted widespread analysis of his managerial practices. Zhang managed to build a successful corporate culture, which he infused with his personal values of modesty, search for knowledge and a firm commitment to quality. Following best global practices and focusing on continuous product innovation, Zhang updated Haier's business model and integrated the concept of zero inventory, thus achieving "a subversion of traditional management".[101] In the later step of Haier's internationalization, Zhang pushed Haier's independent operational entities to produce following "individual-goal combinations".[102] Like the OEC-approach, this management tool focuses on the individual employee. The individual-goal combination defines each employee as "an independent and innovative strategic business unit with the collective goal of achieving primacy in the marketplace".[103] By assigning more responsibility to employees, they get involved in setting business objectives, manage business resources and create shared value for the company and clients likewise.[104]

Even after Haier became a successful global brand, Zhang never lost sight of the company's Chinese roots. Respect for Chinese culture and politics remains an integral part of Haier's corporate values. In return, the Chinese government honoured Zhang's achievements by appointing him to the alternate committee for the 16th and 17th Central Committees of the Communist Party of China.[105]

QUESTIONS

1. What are Haier's FSAs? How did Haier exploit these in its international expansion?
2. Which specific resource recombinations have helped Haier to achieve international success?
3. Which market entry strategy did Haier choose for its various international markets?
4. Most manufacturing companies move to China to gain advantage of cheap labour. However, Haier – a Chinese company – opened production plants around the world. Why?
5. Based on Haier's case, please discuss differences (if any) between developed economy MNEs and emerging economy MNEs. Can you name specific examples from the case?
6. Haier's CEO, Zhang Ruimin has been the key decision maker in the company for almost 30 years. What has been his unique contribution to the firm's success? Do you think he could have achieved the same level of success in an MNE from a developed country? Please explain.
7. Can developed country MNEs learn from Haier's worldwide success? Are there any best practices that developed country MNEs could 'copy' from Haier?

Notes

1. T. Levitt, 'The globalization of markets', *Harvard Business Review* 61 (1983), 93.
2. *Ibid.*, 92–102.
3. *Ibid.*, 99.
4. *Ibid.*, 98.
5. *Ibid.*, 97.
6. *Ibid.*, 100.
7. *Ibid.*, 94.
8. J. A. Quelch and L. R. Klein, 'The Internet and international marketing', *Sloan Management Review* 37 (1996), 60–75.
9. *Ibid.*, 64.
10. *Ibid.*, 69–70.
11. D. Arnold, J. Birkinshaw and O. Toulan, 'Can selling be globalized? The pitfalls of global account management', *California Management Review* 44 (2001), 8–20.
12. *Ibid.*, 16.
13. Levitt, 'The globalization of markets', 94.
14. Paul Beamish and Anthony Goerzen, 'The global branding of Stella Artois', *Ivey Case 9B00A019* (2000); Dan Bilefsky, 'How Belgium's "peasant" beer became "premium" in U.S. – Stella Artois's shrewd marketing in hip New York bars boosts draw; a

"reassuringly expensive" brew', *Wall Street Journal (Eastern Edition)* (12 April 2002), A.13.

15. 'InBev completes acquisition of Anheuser-Busch', AB InBev press release. www.ab-inbev.com/press_releases/20081118_1_e.pdf. (18 November 2008)

16. Bob Hagerty, 'Recognition for Belgium beer is sought – Artois Piedboeuf aims to be among top 10 world brewers', *Wall Street Journal (Eastern Edition)* (8 January 1990), 5.

17. Interbrew, Annual report (1999), 24.

18. Bilefsky, 'Stella Artois's shrewd marketing', A.13.

19. Interbrew, Annual report (2000), 12.

20. Interbrew, Annual report (1999).

21. Bilefsky, 'Stella Artois's shrewd marketing', A.13.

22. Simon Zekaria, 'Anheuser-Busch upbeat as profit jumps', *Wall Street Journal (Online)* (8 March 2012).

23. Carter Dougherty, 'How well will Budweiser Travel', *The New York Times* (27 June 2008).

24. Mike Esterl, 'Sudsy American dream sells abroad', *The Wall Street Journal* (9 March 2012). B1.

25. *Ibid.*

26. *Ibid.*

27. Clementine Fletcher, 'Rihanna to help sell Budweiser to Brazil as AB InBev aims for margin boost', *Bloomberg* (21 September 2011).

28. Ken Beaulieu, 'AB InBev CMO on marketing globally', *Marketing Daily* (2 March 2012).

29. *Ibid.*

30. *Ibid.*

31. Michael Barnett, 'Profile: AB InBev CMO Chris Burggraeve', *Marketing Week* (28 March 2012).

32. Chris Burggraeve, 'St. Louis Investor Conference – World Class FMCG: Marketing @ Ab InBev' *AB InBev* (2 June, 2010)

33. Chris Burggraeve, 'St. Louis Investor Conference – World Class FMCG: Marketing @ Ab InBev' *AB InBev* (2 June, 2010)

34. Ken Beaulieu, 'AB InBev CMO on marketing globally', *Marketing Daily* (2 March 2012).

35. 'World's largest brewer is a fan of real-life social networks', *Marketing Week* 14 (March 2012).

36. *Ibid.*

37. InBev company information, inbev.com, accessed on 5 March 2007.

38. Joel Baughman, Srinivas Chundi, Mikhail Kholyavko, Chintan Patel and Chris Vadner, 'Battle for world beer dominance: SABMiller enters Brazil', *Forbes India* (30 September 2011).

39. AB InBev, 'About out new identity', 2012.

40. This case was co-authored by Ms Jenny Hillemann and Professor Alain Verbeke.

41. Haier company information, 2012. Any indicated turnover in this case study reflects the turnover of the Haier Electronics Group, a subsidiary of Haier Group. The Haier Electronics Group is listed on the Hong Kong Stock Exchange. The turnover of the Haier Electronics Group is published on the company's official homepage.

42. Haier company information, 2012. Exchange rate as of March 15, 2012 (1RMB = 0.157908USD).

43. Haier company information, 2010.

44. Haier company information, 2012.

45. Haier company information, 2010.

46. 'Zhang Ruimin', *China View* (2003).
47. Haier company information, 2012.
48. Jeannie Jinsheng Yi and Shawn Xian Ye, *The Haier Way* (Dumony, New Jersey: Homa and Sekey Books, 2003), 32.
49. Haier company information, 2012.
50. Yi and Ye, *The Haier Way*, 64.
51. Haier company information, 2012.
52. Yi and Ye, *The Haier Way*, 32, 64.
53. Haier company information, 2012.
54. Ling Liu, *China's Industrial Policies and the Global Business Revolution* (Abingdon, UK: Routledge, 2005), 93.
55. Yi and Ye, *The Haier Way*, 63.
56. Yi and Ye, *The Haier Way*, 73.
57. Haier company information, 2012.
58. Sandra Bell, *International Brand Management of Chinese Companies* (Heidelberg, Germany: Physica Verlag, 2008), 162.
59. Bell, *International Brand Management of Chinese Companies*, 162.
60. Yi and Ye, *The Haier Way*, 90.
61. *Ibid.*, 188; Ling, *China's Industrial Policies and the Global Business Revolution*, 98.
62. 'Haier Group Corporation', *Funding Universe*.
63. Haier company information, 2012.
64. *Ibid.*
65. *Ibid.*
66. Yi and Ye, *The Haier Way*, 199.
67. Haier company information, 2012.
68. *Ibid.*
69. OBI company information, 2012.
70. Bell, *International Brand Management of Chinese Companies*, 165.
71. Shaohui Chen and Marie Wilson, 'OBI China: Going, going, gone', *CEIBS* (2006).
72. Bell, *International Brand Management of Chinese Companies*, 165.
73. Haier company information, 2012.
74. *Ibid.*
75. *Ibid.*
76. *Ibid.*
77. Bell, *International Brand Management of Chinese Companies*, 165.
78. Prensa Latina, 'China manufacturer Haier sells 300,000 refrigerators to Cuba', *Havana Journal* (16 March 2006).
79. Haier company information, 2012.
80. 'Hayer buys Anchor Daewoo's appliance biz', *The Economic Times* (10 August 2007).
81. Haier company information, 2012.
82. 'Haier tops Whirlpool in global refrigerator sales', *Alibaba* (20 January 2009).
83. 'Venezuela, China's Haier signs business deals', *Agence France-Presse* (14 May 2010).
84. 'Buying into Fisher & Paykel, Haier overseas expansion still relentless', *China Stakes* (31 May 2009).
85. Haier company information, 2012.
86. Reiji Murai, 'Haier to buy Panasonic's Sanyo white goods unit', *Reuters* (28 July 2011).
87. Haier company information, 2012.
88. *Ibid.*

89. *Ibid.*
90. *Ibid.*
91. *Ibid.*
92. *Ibid.*
93. *Ibid.*
94. *Ibid.*
95. *Ibid.*
96. Yi and Ye, *The Haier Way*, 40.
97. *Ibid.*
98. Haier company information, 2012.
99. *Ibid.*
100. Haier company information, 2011.
101. Haier company information, 2012.
102. *Ibid.*
103. Wenxian Zhang and Ilan Alon, *A Guide to the Top 100 Companies in China* (Singapore: World Scientific Publishing, 2001), 159.
104. Laurie Young, *The Marketer's Handbook: Reassessing Marketing Techniques for Modern Business* (Sussex, UK: John Wiley & Sons, 2011).
105. Haier company information, 2012.

10

Managing managers in the multinational enterprise

Five learning objectives

1. To identify best practices in managing expatriates and to outline the roles of these managers in FSA development and transfer processes.
2. To examine the main pitfalls when managing expatriates.
3. To explain how the purpose and usage of expatriates largely depends on the MNE's administrative heritage.
4. To describe how to craft effective organizational change in the MNE through following a rigorous eight-step process.
5. To show how successful MNEs can improve their organization-wide capacity to integrate interdependent international operations through 'managing managers'.

This chapter focuses on expatriate managers and examines Black and Gregersen's idea that, when it comes to successfully managing expatriate managers, there are three best practices: "[Successful companies] focus on creating knowledge and developing global leadership skills; they make sure that candidates have cross-cultural skills to match their technical abilities; and they prepare people to make the transition back to their home offices". In theory, expatriation is supposed to, *inter alia*, produce managers who have an in-depth knowledge of the MNE, understand the pressures leading to benevolent preference reversal in subsidiaries and can integrate geographically dispersed operations. These ideas will be examined and then criticized using the framework presented in Chapter 1.

Significance

MNEs must develop managers with a broad mental map covering the entirety of the MNE's geographically dispersed operations. This is critical to the MNE's long-term profitability and growth, especially in an era when foreign markets are becoming increasingly important contributors to innovation and cost reduction at the upstream end of the value chain, and to overall sales performance at the downstream end. In fact, managers commanding deep knowledge of internal MNE functioning – including the challenges of simultaneously addressing legitimate business objectives/interests at multiple geographic levels within the firm – represent the MNE's key resource to facilitate international expansion and to coordinate geographically dispersed, established operations. Such managers are best positioned to (a) engage in the international transfer of non-location-bound FSAs from the home nation; (b) identify the need for new FSA development in host countries and facilitate such development; and (c) meld both location-bound and non-location-bound FSAs. These managers are especially valuable when transferring the MNE's routines across borders if those routines include a substantial tacit component. Often, these managers are also the physical carriers of the MNE's recombination capabilities.

Expatriation is the most direct and rigorous way to give managers this in-depth knowledge of the MNE's internal network, as well as the abilities to transfer routines abroad and be a catalyst for recombining resources.

Furthermore, expatriate experience gives managers valuable experiential knowledge of the pressures for good faith local prioritization and other types of benevolent preference reversal in affiliates. Consequently, managers with extensive expatriate experience are often the best equipped to reduce bounded rationality problems in headquarters–subsidiary relations, and to anticipate bounded reliability problems arising in host country affiliates.

Unfortunately, while many MNEs incur high costs from sending managers abroad as expatriates, few reap the expected returns because of poor expatriate management practices. These are the main findings presented by **J. S. Black** and **H. B. Gregersen** in their compelling *HBR* article on the management of expatriates.[1]

The authors studied the expatriate management practices of nearly 750 US, European and Japanese firms over a decade. Their data gathering included feedback from the expatriates themselves and from the executives who sent them overseas. The research covered a range of subject areas, with a focus on selection and training, perceived value of the assignment, post-assignment return and integration back into the organization.

Overall, the authors consider their findings 'alarming'. They note that nearly 80 per cent of all mid- to large-sized MNEs send managers abroad, at a significant cost to the company. With full packages costing two to three times the average equivalent position at home, expatriation is "probably the single largest expenditure most companies make on any one individual except for the CEO".[2]

What is the return on such investments? Black and Gregersen's research shows that 10–20 per cent of US expatriates actually came back home early because of dissatisfaction or disillusionment with their new position and difficulties adjusting to a new foreign culture. The performance during the assignment of more than 30 per cent of those who stayed did not meet senior management expectations. Of those who completed their assignment, 25 per cent ended up leaving the company within a year of their return – double the average turnover rate in the companies studied.

Often, returning expatriates did not find suitable jobs awaiting them after repatriation. More than 30 per cent were still in temporary positions three months after returning home. Of those who came back to a permanent position, over 75 per cent experienced their position at home as a step down, often associated with substantially less independence than they had become accustomed to during their assignment abroad.

Finally, over 60 per cent of recent expatriates felt that there was little or no opportunity to leverage and productively apply the knowledge gained from their foreign experience once they were back in the home office.

Black and Gregersen attribute these unfavourable outcomes to four common problems in how firms manage their expatriates. First, senior managers in the home country often underestimate the impact of cultural distance on organizational functioning and, as a result, do not invest sufficiently in programmes to select and train properly potential candidates. Second, responsibility for expatriates is often assigned to human resources managers, very few of whom (only 11 per cent according to the authors' research) have any international experience themselves. Most human resources managers thus have little insight into the problems faced by expatriates and the ways to remedy them. Third, senior management in many MNEs view expatriates as being well paid and well looked after, and therefore as having little to complain about. Fourth, in many MNEs, a common misconception persists that expatriates do not need help readjusting after having returned home, despite the fact that changes will likely have occurred during their absence (e.g., company reorganization, appointment of new staff and decision makers, shifts in office politics and corporate culture, and changes to the expatriates' own family and personal life).

Black and Gregersen did identify a few firms with superior expatriate management practices, in terms of job satisfaction, performance and retention. This group includes MNEs of various sizes, in a variety of industries, but all tend to adopt three best practices in managing expatriates:

> Companies that manage their expats successfully follow the three practices that make the assignments work from beginning to end. They focus on creating knowledge and developing global leadership skills; they make sure that candidates have cross-cultural skills to match their technical abilities; and they prepare people to make the transition back to their home offices.[3]

A key component of the first best practice (creating knowledge and developing global leadership skills) is that both senior management in the expatriate's home country and the individual sent abroad share a clear understanding of the expatriation's purpose and related expectations. What types of knowledge should be acquired or disseminated by the expatriate and what areas of leadership skills should be honed? Black and Gregersen note that careful planning on these issues yields far more long-term benefits to both the company and the employees than expatriate assignments geared simply towards filling an immediate staffing shortage or business need abroad, rewarding successful staff or shipping unwanted employees to peripheral host country affiliates.

The authors identify Nokia as a best practice example. At Nokia, the Finnish telecommunications MNE with an internationally decentralized R&D function, creating knowledge (meaning recombining resources) instrumental to new product development is made an explicit objective of expatriate R&D assignments. This helps explain Nokia's success in bringing innovative ideas to market.

The second best practice involves selecting appropriate candidates whose "technical skills are matched or exceeded by their cross-cultural abilities".[4] Cross-cultural abilities are often overlooked, as companies tend to send people who are "capable but culturally illiterate".[5] In other words, effective resource recombination requires a mix of technical and social skills.

The third best practice involves devoting substantial attention to reintegrating expatriates into their home country after their assignment. Here, successful MNEs "end expatriate assignments with a deliberate repatriation process".[6] Such a process allows effective absorption of the former expatriate into the home country's professional and personal environment.

The authors suggest it is the simultaneous adoption of all three practices above that leads to successful expatriate management; adopting only one or two of these practices does not suffice to achieve successful assignments.

Honda of America Manufacturing is cited as "perhaps one of the best examples of a company that implements all three practices".[7] Its expatriation approach systematically includes clearly stated expatriate assignment objectives, personal strengths/weaknesses surveys completed by the individuals selected for expatriate assignments, a repatriation job-matching programme triggered six months before the end of the assignment, and a debriefing interview after the expatriate's return to capture what can be learned from the expatriate's experience. Honda's approach has resulted in consistently successful assignments that meet or surpass objectives and expectations, with a turnover rate of less than 5 per cent.

In addition to outlining the appropriate way to manage expatriate employees, Black and Gregersen also discuss the required personal characteristics for employees to be high-potential expatriate prospects. Successful companies look for five characteristics: a drive to communicate, broad-based sociability, cultural flexibility, a cosmopolitan orientation and a collaborative negotiation style.[8]

Through describing a few real-world examples, the article outlines three different successful approaches MNEs can use to select the most suitable candidates for expatriation. First, the authors give the example of a large, privately held chemicals company that utilizes an informal but efficient selection process. Here, a senior executive personally observes the actions, reactions and instincts of employees in various cultural settings, especially when they accompany the executive on international business trips. The information resulting from such direct observation is then used to determine whether a particular employee has the potential to become an expatriate.

Second, at the other end of the formality spectrum, LG Group, a large South Korean conglomerate (set up in 1947 as Lucky Goldstar) employs a much more formal approach. The firm uses an extensive survey early in the employee's career to assess individual preparedness for expatriate assignments. It then organizes discussions between potential candidates and senior managers to identify how personalized development and training plans might contribute further to honing the individual's strengths and shoring up weaknesses. This long-term approach to developing individuals ready for expatriation is costly and time intensive, but has led to a 97 per cent success rate in overseas assignments.

Third, Colgate-Palmolive, a US-based company established in 1928 as the result of a merger between Colgate and Palmolive-Peet, looks for prior international experience in new hires, thereby leveraging the investments and training in international management provided by previous employers. Colgate-Palmolive then sends prospects for expatriation on shorter-term, foreign training assignments (6 to 18 months). These training assignments are devoid of the costly perks and compensation packages normally provided to expatriates. Only after completion of such assignments are prospects given longer-term expatriate positions.

Black and Gregersen suggest that any MNE's expatriate selection process entails a trade-off between accuracy and cost. Here, a thorough assessment process in the form of carefully crafted routines – like those used by LG Group and Colgate-Palmolive – is costly upfront but also very accurate in terms of selecting the right individuals for expatriation. This approach reduces the risk of subsequent costs resulting from failed expatriate assignments. In the end, "the key to success is having a systematic way of assessing the cross-cultural aptitudes of people you may want to send abroad".[9]

Context and complementary perspectives

Published in 1999, Black and Gregersen's *HBR* piece predates the 11 September 2001 terrorist attack on the World Trade Center twin towers in New York. Thus, the article did not address the stress associated with the perceived and actual security risks of travelling and living abroad for expatriates, especially employees from US and UK-based firms in Muslim regions of the world (and more generally in many developing countries). This event has increased further the importance of properly selecting, training and managing expatriates along the lines suggested by Black and Gregersen. Many MNEs have indeed responded to heightened security concerns by improving their candidate selection processes and training programmes.

Other insights in Black and Gregersen's article are not necessarily new, but rather serve as a reminder of the importance of considering cultural distance challenges inherent in international business (discussed in detail in the classic works of researchers such as Geert Hofstede, dating back to 1984).[10]

C. K. Prahalad and *Yves Doz* provide a first complementary perspective on the management of managers in MNEs with a set of two related pieces published in *SMR*, where they propose a new approach to strategic control in MNEs (i.e., who actually determines the MNE's expansion and restructuring path). Their articles do not focus on human resources management in the narrow sense, but rather on the creation of an appropriate 'organizational context'. In cases where senior management lacks what the authors call 'conventional substantive control', the authors recommend that senior management instead implement change by gradually and collaboratively changing the organizational context.

'Organizational context', discussed in detail below, refers to "a blending of organizational structure, information systems, measurement and reward systems, and career planning and a fostering of common organizational culture".[11]

By contrast, conventional substantive control typically uses centralized financial resource allocation, and is often associated with unidirectional knowledge flows from the home country to foreign affiliates.[12] Furthermore, conventional substantive control is usually immediate rather than gradual, and hierarchical rather than collaborative.

One way that corporate senior management might lack conventional substantive control is if foreign subsidiaries have become too powerful. Prahalad and Doz describe the interesting paradox whereby higher effectiveness in home country FSA transfers to foreign affiliates, especially as regards technology and management capabilities, simultaneously makes foreign affiliates less dependent on the home country and corporate headquarters. This holds true especially if these affiliates grow in size and relative importance of their sales and assets vis-à-vis the rest of the company thanks to the initial FSA transfers. In fact, Prahalad and Doz describe the possibility of an unintended transformation over time from an *international projector* into a *multi-centred MNE*.

Other ways that corporate senior management might lack conventional substantive control include situations of high bounded reliability among subsidiaries, mistrust of corporate headquarters and warring factions with different strategic visions.

In these cases, what should senior management do when change is required? For example, suppose that increased international competition and an industry-wide focus on cost cutting impose rationalization of the internal MNE network.

To continue to be profitable, the company needs to rationalize product lines at the level of an entire region (e.g., the European Union) by closing down product lines, reallocating product lines among affiliates and bringing cost levels in line with those of other MNEs. Yet, corporate headquarters is unable to impose such rationalization, because they lack conventional substantive control over key resources. In such cases, a 'control gap' exists, which Prahalad and Doz suggest can be closed through creating an adequate organizational context. This can be achieved, they argue, only by following a particular sequence of steps.

Before discussing these steps, it is necessary to first explain how complex organizations such as MNEs can be described in terms of four orientations. Successful change requires changing all four orientations.

First, the **cognitive orientation** is the perception by managers of what constitutes the relevant business environment and the main competitive forces in this environment. Managers in different functional areas or operating at different hierarchical levels may not share the same perception of these parameters. Importantly, substantial differences may exist between senior management in the home country and managers in foreign affiliates on the substance of present and future environmental changes, and on the appropriate way for the MNE to respond to such changes.

Any successful change process in the MNE network needs to focus first on creating a shared cognitive orientation between senior management at corporate headquarters and subsidiary management.

Second, the **strategic orientation** is the managers' interpretation of the changes occurring in the relevant external environment – specifically, in terms of recognizing the business threats that need to be answered in a particular way and the business opportunities that can be exploited.

Here, successful change processes require senior management at corporate headquarters and subsidiary management to find common ground. A precondition for achieving a common strategic orientation is the prior development of a shared cognitive orientation, and both are required for major change.

Third, the **administrative orientation** refers primarily to the information management system within the MNE, particularly the management of accounting data and personnel performance-related data.

A proposed change such as closing down specific product lines and expanding other ones may require, for empirical support, a new administrative orientation in the form of detailed data on performance differentials. In turn, agreeing on the correctness and significance of specific analytical tools (such as internal accounting measures) and the resulting, actual performance data will contribute to commonality in strategic orientation. Thus, a new administrative orientation can bring about a new strategic orientation.

Fourth, the **power orientation** refers to who in the firm has the power to do what.

To effect change, it is not enough to simply have **_unanimous adoption of new cognitive, strategic and administrative orientations_** (as discussed above). The senior manager(s) responsible for – and capable of – reallocating resources (financial, human, etc.) must ultimately change the power orientation in the MNE. This means changing who gets to decide what. In the cases Prahalad and Doz examined, this typically involves taking away decision-making power from subsidiaries in cases where they have benefited from extreme decentralization.

Prahalad and Doz studied actual change processes in several large firms where corporate headquarters lacked formal resource allocation power. In each case, these MNEs were suddenly faced with the need to rationalize specific businesses, driven by competitive pressures such as the penetration by other MNEs of their subsidiaries' markets. Prahalad and Doz found that each successful change process focused on altering the organizational context and, ultimately, the four orientations discussed above.

Each successful change process included the same sequence of eight steps in the same order. First, each process started with the appointment of a new key executive, formally assigned the task of effecting change. The substantive purpose of the change process, from the perspective of the newly appointed key executive, typically included increased inter-subsidiary coordination, accompanied by substantial rationalization in manufacturing to reduce costs and gain scale economies.

Second, though external pressures in the form of increased competition typically legitimized the executive's appointment and role as change agent, this executive spent considerable time trying to alter the cognitive orientations of subsidiary managers. Here, the executive typically employed relatively 'soft' conflict resolution mechanisms, such as coordination committees and task forces involving senior subsidiary managers to achieve the required changes in cognitive orientation and to plant the first seeds in the subsidiary managers' minds for a subsequent shift in strategic orientation.

Third, after the second stage, and precisely thanks to that stage, the executive explicitly stated the consequences of new environmental threats for firm strategy. For example, an increase of low-cost foreign exports by Asian firms to Europe might imply that the highly autonomous subsidiaries in Europe of an American manufacturer must now engage in pan-European consolidation of manufacturing, i.e., must concentrate product lines in specific countries so as to serve the entire European market with scale-efficient production. In other words, the executive laid out the new strategic orientation.

Fourth, when supported by adequate data-management tools, generating credible comparative cost and performance data, it became possible to have a productive dialogue on specific changes in responsibilities held – and activities performed – by the different affiliates, thereby legitimizing minor reallocations of authority. Here, it was critical that the data systems provided sufficient accuracy and allowed appropriate differentiation among product lines and businesses, not all of which required the same level of inter-subsidiary coordination or rationalization. Often, new data-management tools had to be introduced (i.e., a new administrative orientation adopted) and applied selectively – namely, applied to those product lines and businesses in need of international rationalization, but not to the lines and businesses where a multi-centred approach was still appropriate. The resulting data on costs and productivity also had to be so clear and credible as to leave no room for alternative judgements on their implications for organizational restructuring (e.g., in the case of product interdependencies and related inaccurate cost allocations).

Fifth, on the basis of the above cognitive, strategic and administrative shifts, multiple minor reallocations of authority (i.e., changes in the firm's power orientation) became possible, often directly benefiting the affected subsidiaries, such as centralized export coordination or international knowledge transfer coordination.

Sixth, the cumulative effect of the multiple reallocations of authority established the key executive as a powerful actor in the change process.

Seventh, building upon the new position of power, the key executive was then able to engage in more drastic changes that typically included changes in the status and career paths of specific managers, new approaches to incentive systems, etc., thereby altering more fundamentally the MNE's power orientation.

Eighth, the key executive systematically supported and validated the newly created cognitive, strategic and power orientations using finely tuned data-management tools, including performance measurement systems, resource allocation procedures and budgeting procedures (i.e., using the new administrative orientation).

The above led Prahalad and Doz to conclude that "[w]hat can be accomplished organizationally sets limits on what is feasible as a strategy".[13] If an organization's control mechanisms are dysfunctional, then attempting to exert 'brute force' conventional substantive control over subsidiary managers using immediate, hierarchical decision making will be unsuccessful. Instead, senior managers should use a gradual, sophisticated, eight-step approach that takes into account the organizational context and the firm's cognitive, strategic, administrative and power orientations.

A second complementary perspective was written by **Christopher Bartlett** and **Sumantra Ghoshal** and published in *CMR*.[14] In this piece, the authors describe how large MNEs attempt to shed some of the dysfunctional characteristics imposed by their administrative heritage as a **centralized exporter** (or, to some extent, as an **international projector**, if the firm has marketing and sales operations abroad) or a **multi-centred MNE**, when those characteristics cease to be effective in a changed external environment. MNEs that move away from these pure archetypes require managers who can integrate geographically dispersed operations and can manage interdependent (rather than hierarchical or independent) operations in several countries. Bartlett and Ghoshal discuss how to give managers these necessary organizational capabilities.

For example, the authors describe how the Japanese electronics firm Matsushita, which traditionally exhibited the characteristics of a **centralized exporter**, has attempted to reduce the dominance of unidirectional knowledge and decision-making flows (from Japan to all other countries) so as to become more responsive to foreign markets. This did not occur through sweeping changes in structure, but rather through a number of subtle adjustments to the organizational context. Here, Matsushita's use of expatriates who can benefit from extensive personal networks in Japan, and sometimes maintain a cross-appointment with Matsushita in the home country, allows continuous interaction between home country and host country decision makers. The expatriates become a cornerstone of the firm's information and communication system. They are also critical to the creation of a common organizational culture, and may be instrumental to shared cognitive, strategic and administrative orientations across borders.

Importantly, the use of expatriates with strong links to Japanese operations occurs at multiple levels (including both senior management and more junior-level managers). Besides developing a cadre of managers with strong international organizational skills, the use of expatriation allows the subsidiary voice to be heard throughout the manufacturing side in the home country – even, for example, in the realm of detailed product specifications for the host country market. It also allows appropriate adaptation of product designs in the home country, so as to guarantee subsequent success in the host market.

This international coordination affecting the manufacturing side is comple-mented by coordination mechanisms influencing the most downstream activities. For example, through internal trade shows, managers representing Matsushita's sales companies from around the world are able to "pick and choose among proposed models, order specific modifications for their local markets, or simply refuse to take products they feel are unsuitable".[15]

Furthermore, in both home country and international operations, Matsushita attaches substantial importance to personnel transfers across functions, thereby ensuring that foreign marketing organizations have a sufficient number of man-agers with deep product expertise.

For Matsushita, these three mechanisms (infusion of subsidiary input into home country manufacturing, infusion of subsidiary input in marketing and cross-functional personnel transfers) all facilitate the successful transfer and exploitation abroad of non-location-bound FSAs present in the home country, and embodied in the products shipped to the sales organizations across the world. In addition, these mechanisms allow the bundle of non-location-bound FSAs to be augmented with a location-bound component to adapt the product specifications and product mix to host country requirements. This (Pattern III, see Figure 1.7) is ultimately one of the most common forms of recombination found in international business strategy.

The Dutch electronics firm Philips started from a very different position than Matsushita's (with the latter moving towards more flexibility and giving host country managers more input and decision-making power). Philips convention-ally operated as a ***multi-centred MNE*** with largely autonomous subsidiaries (see Chapter 1), but has in the past decades attempted to increase coordination within its affiliate network.

The key tool adopted by Philips to achieve such coordination in this multi-centred organization has been the use of expatriates. Expatriates at Philips are not individuals simply completing one or a few foreign assignments. Rather, they are managers following a long-term career trajectory abroad and sharing strong social linkages with a network of fellow expatriates, somewhat similar to what is expected in many countries' diplomatic services. Given that they are the carriers of Philip's corporate culture across borders and rarely suffer from bounded reliability problems, they can credibly and effectively advocate for national sub-sidiary interests when they think central corporate strategy is wrong.

Because central headquarters takes the expatriates' opinions very seriously, this in turn attracts complementary resources in host countries in the form of com-petent local managers, as these individuals know the subsidiary is viewed as much more than an appendix to the company, merely executing central directives. These competent local managers, combined with the expatriates themselves, make a highly skilled management team.

The effectiveness of local management is strengthened further by explicitly seeking synergies among the technical, marketing and finance functions in each subsidiary, e.g., by the formal use of 'three-headed' management at the level of products, product groups and within the subsidiary management committee.[16]

In these and other examples provided by Bartlett and Ghoshal, they dem-onstrate the importance of legitimizing different perspectives in the MNE, and the simultaneous fostering and melding of non-location-bound and location-bound knowledge. In implementation terms, there are costs of moving away from being a 'pure' ***centralized exporter*** or ***multi-centred MNE***. In both cases, the MNE explicitly fosters interdependencies among operations in several countries, thereby requiring extensive use of decision-making instruments such as coordination committees and conflict resolution forums with real influence to align goals and actions of the corporate headquarters and the various subsidiaries.

Effective integration of geographically dispersed operations in large MNEs, irrespective of their original administrative heritage, requires the development of new organizational capabilities carried by each firm's cadre of managers with international experience and an international mindset. Building this capability requires the extensive use of expatriation, international assignments and inter-national team formation. Here, host country operations are infused with know-ledge from central headquarters and their employees learn to appreciate the company's culture, while the MNE's corporate headquarters and home nation operations are made more sensitive to the needs of the international affiliates.

The most relevant element in Black and Gregersen's *HBR* article, in terms of this book's framework, is that using expatriate managers is a key channel through which MNEs – especially **international projectors**, **multi-centred MNEs** and **international coordinators** – can diffuse their FSAs from the home country to host country affiliates and among internationally operating affiliates in general. Of course, in each of the MNE archetypes, the purpose and scope of expatriates is different (see Figure 10.1, Figure 10.2 and Figure 10.3).

With **international projectors**, the purpose of expatriates is to transfer knowledge, especially technical knowledge and routines, from the home country to host country affiliates. With **multi-centred MNEs**, expatriates constitute part of the minimal glue to hold the internal MNE network together through fostering the sharing of core values and acting as trusted communication channels between corporate headquarters and the foreign affiliates. In the case of **international coordinators**, expatriates are the most important: they are instrumental to creating effective international value chains, linking economic activities across borders. They thereby constitute an integral part of the MNE's recombination capability. Black and Gregersen described the source of this capability as the MNE's "focus on knowledge creation and global leadership development",[17] the first of their three recipes for successful expatriate management. Here the emphasis is clearly on new FSA development and the use of the expatriates themselves as key resources to meld internationally transferable FSAs with location-bound FSAs

Figure 10.1
International projector: Expatriates as knowledge carriers

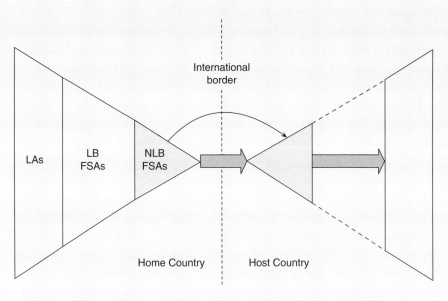

The thin, curved arrow represents the role of expatriates in facilitating the transfer of home country NLB FSAs to the host country.

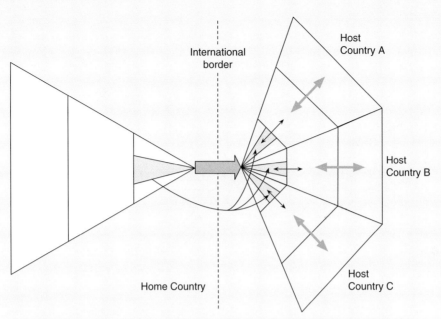

Figure 10.2
Multi-centred
MNEs: Expatriates
as carriers of core
values and trusted
communication
channels

The thin, curved arrow represents the role of expatriates in facilitating the transfer of home country routines to the host country. The thin, double-headed arrows represent the dual role of expatriates sent to host countries A, B and C: they both foster the sharing of core values and knowledge from the home country and act as trusted communication channels between corporate headquarters and the foreign affiliates.

in host locations. Expatriate managers thus (a) facilitate the process of transferring existing FSA bundles across borders; (b) improve the exploitation potential of such FSAs in host country environments by augmenting them with locally developed FSAs; and (c) engage in the appropriate melding of internationally transferable FSAs and location-bound FSAs into effective value-added activities and products.

In addition to these roles of transferring and implementing FSAs, high-quality, experienced expatriates constitute a non-location-bound FSA in their own right. They can be deployed anywhere in the network to – as discussed above – transfer and implement other FSAs, foster the sharing of core company values, help communication between subsidiaries and central headquarters, facilitate the management of the MNE's internal network and integrate geographically dispersed operations.

It is important to note that the FSA diffusion processes facilitated by expatriates are multidirectional. Expatriates not only facilitate the process of disseminating FSAs from the home office (or other high-competence units) to host country subsidiaries, but they also acquire new knowledge and international experience abroad that can be redeployed to other units inside the MNE. This latter process is largely an emerging phenomenon, which cannot be exactly predefined in the form

Figure 10.3
International coordinator: Expatriates as key resources to link internationally transferable FSAs and location advantages of host nations

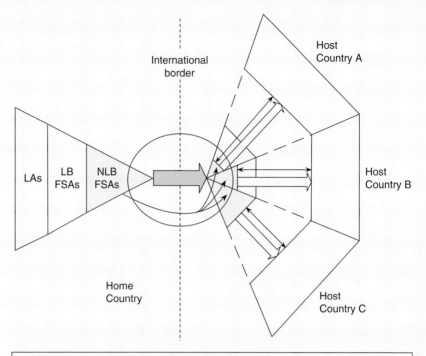

The thin, curved arrow out of the home country represents the roles of expatriates in facilitating the transfer of specific bundles of home country NLB FSAs to each host country. The double-headed arrows represent the expatriates' role in facilitating the alignment between the firm's NLB FSAs and the LAs sought in each host country. The circle represents the expatriates in countries A, B and C being connected to create effective international value chains.

of detailed expatriation objectives, but is largely crafted through many interactions with other employees in a variety of affiliates.

This leads to the first of the three major limitations of Black and Gregersen's piece. As noted by Bartlett and Ghoshal in their analysis of the Dutch MNE Philips, expatriation can be a permanent way of life for managers, analogous to the diplomatic service in government, whereby a career trajectory is essentially a series of foreign assignments. In Black and Gregersen's article, expatriation ends with reintegration of the expatriate back into the home country, but this neglects the point that extended (if not permanent) expatriation is critical in creating executives with a widely dispersed informal social network, very high cross-cultural skills and a profound understanding of the multiple perspectives in the MNE's geographically dispersed operations.

The second limitation is related to Black and Gregersen's observation that the process of knowledge creation and dissemination by expatriates may not always proceed as smoothly as planned. Black and Gregersen observed that a substantial number of expatriates either return home early or perceive only limited opportunities to leverage their overseas knowledge when returning to their home country environment. However, in addition to the reasons presented by the authors, this lacklustre record of expatriation may be indicative of the inherent friction in home country–host country relationships. Established foreign affiliates may be reluctant to accept guidance from the head office through expatriate managers, especially when procedural justice is perceived to be lacking (see Chapter 5). Senior subsidiary managers may also be unwilling to share freely with the rest of the company, via expatriates, the specialized knowledge and processes developed by the subsidiary if they do not expect a fair return for such diffusion or at least proper recognition of their contributions. Similarly, attitudes and prejudices within the home office may limit the flow of information back to the top after an expatriate returns home. In each of these cases, the end result is missed opportunities in terms of new FSA diffusion and exploitation across the MNE's internal network. Here, the prior creation of a receptive organizational context may contribute to the success of subsequent expatriate management.

As a third limitation, Black and Gregersen do not discuss 'external' expatriation. In addition to expatriate assignments internal to the organization, joint ventures and strategic alliances give rise to another form of expatriate placement, as managers are seconded abroad to partner firms or international joint venture projects. In such cases, the best practices outlined by Black and Gregersen are likely to remain valid, but the requirement to outline clear objectives for knowledge creating may need to be augmented so as to prevent the unintended leakage of FSAs to partner firms, who may be competitors in particular market or industry areas (see also Chapter 12).

Five management takeaways

1. Reflect carefully on the common problems of expatriate management faced by every MNE.
2. Learn about best practices to manage expatriates, including experiences from competitors.
3. Given your firm's administrative heritage, explore the various possible purposes and forms of expatriation (e.g., 'external' expatriation, overseas knowledge transfers, extended/permanent expatriation).
4. Focus strategic change processes on fine-tuning the MNE's organizational context, and follow a sequence of eight implementation steps that have proven successful in many firms.
5. Train your managers to integrate successfully the activities of interdependent but geographically dispersed international operations.

CASE

Case 10.1 Managing expatriates at LVMH

Think for a moment about the brand names of high-end fashion and leather goods – names such as Louis Vuitton, Donna Karan, Fendi, Loewe, Céline, Marc Jacobs, Berluti, Rossimoda and StefanoBi; alcoholic beverage brand names such as Moët et Chandon, Hennessy and Dom Perignon; perfume brand names such as Christian Dior, Guerlain, Givenchy and Kenzo; and watch brand names such as TAG Heuer, Zenith and OMAS. The world's largest luxury goods group, France-based Moët Hennessy Louis Vuitton (LVMH), controls all of these brand names.

LVMH was created in 1987 as the result of a merger between Moët Hennessy and Louis Vuitton. As of 2011, the company was a highly internationalized conglomerate with annual revenue of 23.7 billion euros and an international retail network of more than 3,040 stores. Geographically, 12 per cent of its revenues came from France, 21 per cent from the rest of Europe, 22 per cent from the US, 8 per cent from Japan, 27 per cent from the rest of Asia and 10 per cent from other markets,[18] making it one of the world's few truly global companies in terms of geographic sales dispersion.

With a presence in 62 countries and 79 per cent of its 97,500 worldwide employees based outside of its French home base, LVMH has had to carefully design its international human resources management. A crucial component of international human resources management at LVMH is the management of international assignments, with expatriates occupying key strategic positions. Such assignments are often a stepping towards even more important jobs in the future.

In 2001, LVMH had 260 expatriates, and the number of expatriates is rising. In 2011, one fifth of all transfers within the LVMH group were to a different country. Additionally, 1500 executives were transferred to various brands across the LVMH portfolio.[19] What is the current approach to expatriate management at LVMH? How can LVMH improve further its expatriate management approach to facilitate its international expansion?

History and organizational structure

The 1987 merger that created LVMH combined companies from two different industries. On the one hand, Louis Vuitton founded his 'House of Louis Vuitton' Company in Paris in 1854, specializing in creating extraordinary quality bags. The Louis Vuitton Company had a tradition of using multiple marketing instruments, with campaigns that included the use of famous photo models and actresses, print ads in magazines and billboards in cities. Interestingly, counterfeit Louis Vuitton products have something of a cult-like following among (often middle-class) consumers. In 2004, counterfeit Louis Vuitton products made up 18 per cent of counterfeit accessories seized in the EU.[20] The company is best known for its fashion and leather goods.

Hennessy, on the other hand, was started as a liquor trading business by Irishman Richard Hennessy in Cognac, France, in 1765. The successive generations of Hennessy continued to expand the business into brandy production and established the firm as the leading manufacturer of cognac. In 1971, Hennessy merged with Moët et Chandon, a leading cham-pagne producer.

After the 1987 merger, LVMH expanded rapidly through both organic growth and acquis-itions. For example, LVMH acquired Kenzo in 1993, the jeweller Fred and the perfume manu-facturer Guerlain in 1994, Céline in 1996, and the world's number one distributor of luxury products, Duty Free Shoppers, in 1997. The expansion resulted in the world's largest luxury goods company with more than 60 major brands.

To manage this diversity of brands, LVMH emphasizes the importance of decentralization in its organizational structure. As stated on its website: "The Group's organizational structure is decentralized, which fosters efficiency, productivity, and creativity."[21] LVMH is organized into five business groups and around 50 companies. The business groups are: wines and spirits, fashion and leather goods, perfumes and cosmetics, watches and jewellery, and selective retailing. Each business group includes a collection of brands. The 50 companies represent the substantive foundation of LVMH, and manage around 450 subsidiaries around the world. With major responsibilities delegated to these companies and their subsidiaries, senior management expects entrepreneurial initiatives from managers at both the company and subsidiary levels.

Organizing human resources management[22]

Human resources managers at LVMH operate at four levels: corporate, regional, business group and company. Corporate human resources managers mainly provide adaptable guidelines and procedures to be adopted by the business groups and companies. These guidelines are not strict rules, and business groups and companies normally have substantial flexibility to introduce the routines they see fit. At the regional level, regional human resources managers provide the guidelines for each region. The five regions at LVMH are France, Europe, the Americas, Pacific Asia and Japan, with France and Japan (though only single countries) regarded as important zones because of their market size for the company. Employees are hired directly by either companies or subsidiaries.

From the time of its creation in 1987, LVMH realized that it needed a pool of managers with international skills and working knowledge of international markets. However, too many of its managers were not even fluent in English, and even less competent in terms of being multilingual or having an affinity with multicultural issues.

To develop a pool of competent managers with international skills, senior management decided to rely primarily on what they called 'international mobility' rather than formal training. 'International mobility' refers to the systematic expatriation and repatriation of individuals on a limited time basis. The International Transfer Department formalized an 'international transfer policy' charter in 2000, delineating all company routines to be followed in the context of the firm's international mobility practice.

LVMH decided, however, that the implementation of these procedures had to be accom-panied with sufficient flexibility to address the particular concerns of each expatriate. LVMH felt that flexibility was particularly important because its international assignments often involved senior managers.

Reasons to send people overseas

Each year, the brands under LVMH participate in developing the firm's strategy and outline the impact it will have on the upcoming year.[23] Human capital requirements are evaluated and development plans for internal employees are created to ensure that the requirements will be met. These development plans consist of internal mobility and training programmes to further advance employee growth. An annual evaluation for each brand was implemented in 2006 to help develop a more cohesive outlook for the company as a whole in the upcoming year.

Moreover, at monthly meetings each business group's human resources director and the companies' human resources directors within the business group identify the group's need for expatriates throughout the world. The main reasons for sending people overseas at LVMH include the control of foreign subsidiaries and the development of expatriate managers' skills. Most expatriates are responsible for operating a smaller subsidiary, infusing corporate culture in that foreign subsidiary and training local nationals. A need for talent in a host country may also drive expatriation. For example, it is sometimes very hard to find talented fashion designers in host environments and LVMH has had to expatriate some of these designers.

Most LVMH expatriates remain in the assigned host country for three years on average, with only a few of them staying longer, as LVMH does not want to disconnect expatriates from their home bases. Moreover, locating expatriates permanently in a host country is not cost effective for LVMH.

Whom to send abroad

As noted above, one major reason for expatriation at LVMH is to develop expatriate managers' skills. Many expatriates are viewed as high potentials (HPs), likely to climb up the corporate ladder. LVMH has created two classes of high potentials, called 'HP1' and 'HP2'. HP1 includes those elite individuals who may have the ability to move up to a top management position such as that of subsidiary/regional president or member of a board committee; HP2 comprises individuals likely to advance one or two steps above where they are now. LVMH also identifies individuals classified as 'Ready to Move', meaning that senior management views them as candidates for a new assignment within a year (not necessarily abroad).

The Organizational and Management Review (OMR) at LVMH reviews the main human resources management objectives annually, and establishes the HP and 'Ready to Move' lists. Individuals on these lists receive development opportunities, including international assignments for career development. The OMR also reviews and evaluates the current performance of individuals included on the HP and 'Ready to Move' lists of the previous years.

While very few employees at LVMH turn down an international assignment, senior management take into account the willingness of employees to take on an international assignment. If senior management foresees reluctance or potential problems, it does not normally offer an international assignment to the employee.

LVMH has found over the years that some nationalities are more willing to take on international assignments. French, British, Italian and Spanish employees are typically keener to participate in internal mobility placements across borders.[24] Integration amongst European countries is often more common given the closer administrative and cultural distances.

Preparing for expatriation

The preparation of LVMH's expatriates for international assignments is largely limited to language courses, taken either before the expatriate leaves for a new position or immediately after starting the new job. LVMH also funds preparatory field trips before expatriates take on a new job. In some cases, subsidiaries provide some help, but expatriates cannot expect too much support, given the small number of human resources management staff at the subsidiaries. A few companies provide intercultural training after expatriates take on a position, simply because of their past experience with expatriates or because of the uniqueness of the host country. To put it simply, expatriates at LVMH are largely expected to learn by themselves.

LVMH provides this limited training for four reasons. First, all candidates for international assignments already have acquired some international experience, either through earlier professional assignments or their studies abroad. In other words, they are considered to be ready based on such prior experiences. Second, international vacancies must usually be filled quickly, thereby leaving little time for LVMH to train expatriates. Third, LVMH does not expect expatriates to demonstrate stellar performance immediately in the host country to which they are assigned. On the contrary, senior management feel that expatriates should be given sufficient time to adjust on their own. Fourth, expatriates at LVMH are usually assigned to cosmopolitan locations, such as Hong Kong, Tokyo, New York or Paris, where adjustment costs are assumed to be rather low.

On occasion, though, LVMH's senior management provides more training for its expatriates and their families, so as to accelerate the adjustment process in the host country. Furthermore, although LVMH generally provides only limited support for intercultural training, it offers substantial logistical support when it comes to new accommodation searches, administrative procedures, finding experienced furniture movers, etc.

Repatriation

LVMH does not intend to create permanent expatriates. To prevent expatriates from losing contact with their home country, LVMH normally limits international assignments to three years. Usually, at least six months to one year before expatriates return home, the repatriation process kicks in to prepare expatriates' positions to be taken up after their return, and to address compensation and career progression. In some cases, expatriates may be transferred to a third country after several years of an international assignment.

Compensation

LVMH's senior management applies the 'balance sheet' approach as the main guideline to set compensation packages for expatriates, but compensation packages vary among business groups.

According to the balance sheet approach, expatriates should neither gain nor lose as a result of international assignments. When using this approach to calculate the expatriate's salary in the host country, LVMH starts with the expatriates' gross salary in the home country and then converts this gross salary into the host country currency, after which LVMH deducts home country taxes and pension contributions to obtain the net salary. LVMH then adds or deducts a cost of living allowance and family allowance differentials. Finally, LVMH adds taxes and social contributions in the host country to arrive at the expatriate's salary in the host country.

A disadvantage of this balance sheet approach is that it fails to address salary differences among countries. For example, wages in France for senior managerial positions are systematically lower than in the US. Thus, French expatriates sent to the US would actually receive a low and uncompetitive salary compared to their US peers. While this may be fair in one sense, it nonetheless often leads to employee dissatisfaction. To minimize this problem, LVMH now adopts a hybrid approach by incorporating the host market employment compensation situation in its assessments.

Compared with other major MNEs, LVMH does not offer a competitive compensation package, especially regarding housing allowances, though it provides some benefits such as temporary housing and paid education for the expatriate's children. The appeal of expatriation at LVMH is thus the fact that it is instrumental to career development and an increased salary at the time of a future promotion, rather than an advantageous compensation during the actual expatriation.

Employee development beyond international mobility

Beyond opportunities for employees to participate in international mobility placements, LVMH is dedicated to developing a more diverse and multicultural workforce.[25] With LVMH's global consumer reach, having diverse employees is a valuable resource in understanding the needs of consumers. LVMH has increased its focus on gender equality, youth development, and staff development to become a "true learning organization".[26] In 2011, LVMH continued to send HR personnel to attend the annual International Human Resource Convention in Paris. This event focuses on challenges and understandings in the global community of human resource management. LVMH has also strived to improve the number of women in management positions, since over two thirds of its employees are women. In 2011, roughly half of all managers were women, however there was only one woman on the executive committee. LVMH is also developing its team by aligning with universities in France to unveil potential future talent. Scholarships and opportunities for students to work across the globe within LVMH are made available to further develop multiculturalism. Other continual staff development programmes include international forums, training sessions and the creation of the 'LVMH Experience'.[27] The 'LVMH Experience' involves collaboration between managers and creative leaders to foster multicultural integration throughout the LVMH group.

Future challenges

LVMH now faces new challenges, especially given its dual focus on strengthening further its leading position in the luxury goods industry and on developing new markets such as Asia.[28] In the early 1990s, LVMH expanded to China and South Korea; a decade later, it entered India. Many of the Asian economies have been predicted to continue to grow at the rate of 7–8 per cent in GDP every year.[29]

A key challenge for LVMH is to use its international mobility policy to support its international expansion. Such an international mobility policy should also fit with its administrative heritage. At the same time, LVMH should also keep pace with changes in the 'market' for expatriation. For example, currently most senior expatriates are male with a non-working spouse, but more and more women have been appointed to high positions, and dual careers have become more common. Therefore, LVMH now has to cope with spousal hiring and other spousal issues. On a separate note, the number of expatriates at LVMH is currently rising; LVMH is trying to determine what is the 'right size' of the pool of expatriates.

QUESTIONS

1. What is the administrative heritage of LVMH? How does the practice of international assignments reflect this heritage? What roles do expatriates play in LVMH's organization?
2. Does LVMH pay much attention to cross-cultural differences in its international assignments? What should it do to better prepare its expatriates for adjustment in the host country they are sent to?
3. Does LVMH send expatriates abroad for the right reasons?
4. How can LVMH further improve its international assignments strategy?
5. Can you provide an update on LVMH's international assignments strategy, using materials available on the Web?

Notes

1. J. S. Black and H. B. Gregersen, 'The right way to manage expats', *Harvard Business Review* 77 (1999), 52–63.
2. *Ibid.*, 53.
3. *Ibid.*, 61.
4. *Ibid.*, 53.
5. *Ibid.*, 58.
6. *Ibid.*, 54.
7. *Ibid.*, 62.
8. *Ibid.*, 58.
9. *Ibid.*, 60.
10. Geert Hofstede is Professor Emeritus of Organizational Anthropology and International Management at the University of Maastricht in the Netherlands. His comprehensive and influential study (e.g., G. H. Hofstede, *Culture's Consequences: International Differences in Work-related Values* (Sage Publications, 1984); G. H. Hofstede, *Culture's Consequences:*

Comparing Values, Behaviors, Institutions, and Organizations Across Nations (Sage Publications, 2001)) identified five independent dimensions of national culture differences. Hofstede's work has had far greater impact on later cultural studies than other frameworks. For example, Google Scholar indicated that Hofstede's 1984 book has been cited 4334 times (accessed on 26 March 2007). At the same time, Hofstede's work has been criticized for being overly simplistic for having only five dimensions, ignoring intra-country cultural differences, etc. For a recent review of Hofstede's work and related empirical research, see Bradley L. Kirkman, Kevin B. Lowe and Cristina B. Gibson, 'A quarter century of Culture's Consequences: a review of empirical research incorporating Hofstede's cultural values framework', *Journal of International Business Studies* 37 (2006), 285–320.

Hofstede analysed a large data base of employee values scores collected by IBM between 1967 and 1973, covering more than 70 countries. He first used only the 40 largest countries, and then later extended the work to 74 countries through replications and extensions of the IBM study on different international populations.

Hofstede developed a model that identifies five primary dimensions to differentiate cultures: Power Distance – PDI, Individualism – IDV, Masculinity – MAS, Uncertainty Avoidance – UAI and Long-Term Orientation – LTO. PDI refers to the extent of equality/inequality between people in a country; IDV indicates to what extent individuals are integrated into groups; MAS focuses on the distribution of roles between the genders; UAI reflects the tolerance for uncertainty and ambiguity within a society; and LTO shows the degree to which the society values long-term, forward thinking.

Hofstede's cultural values between countries have led to research on cultural distance and its impact on organizational outcomes. For example, as the cultural distance between countries increased, the tendency to choose a joint venture over an acquisition increased (B. Kogut and H. Singh, 'The effect of national culture on the choice of entry mode', *Journal of International Business Studies* 19 (1988), 411–32); as cultural distance increased, the amount of US FDI decreased (e.g., J. Li and S. Guisinger, 'The globalization of service multinationals in the "triad" regions: Japan, Western Europe and North America', *Journal of International Business Studies* 23 (1992), 675–96).

11. Prahalad and Doz, 'An approach to strategic control in MNCs', 5.
12. Y. Doz and C. K. Prahalad, 'Headquarters influence and strategic control in MNCs', *Sloan Management Review* 23 (1981), 15–29; C. K. Prahalad and Y. Doz, 'An approach to strategic control in MNCs', *Sloan Management Review* 22 (1981), 5–13.
13. Doz and Prahalad, 'Headquarters influence and strategic control in MNCs', 28.
14. Christopher A. Bartlett and Sumantra Ghoshal, 'Organizing for worldwide effectiveness: the transnational solution', *California Management Review* 31 (1988), 54–74.
15. *Ibid.*, 59.
16. *Ibid.*, 63.
17. Black and Gregersen, 'The right way to manage expats', 54.
18. LVMH, Annual report 2011 (2012), 7.
19. LVMH, Annual report 2011 (2012), 24.
20. Angus McCrone, 'Special report: trying to stub out the fakes, counterfeiters sell £10bn worth of fakes – from cigarettes to scent – every year', *The Sunday Times* (11 June 2006), http://business.timesonline.co.uk/tol/business/law/corporate/article673534.ece.
21. LVMH, www.lvmh.com, accessed on 21 March 2007.
22. Jean-Luc Cerdin, 'LVMH career development through international mobility', *Groupe ESSEC* (2003), Reference no. 403–050–1.
23. LVMH, Annual report 2011 (2012), 04/24.

24. Anonymous, 'Why France's LVMH sets common HR rules', *Business Europe* 33, 43 (8 November 1993). 7.

25. Paola Vee, 'LVMH: Total luxury stars- part 2', *Les Cahiers* (01 August 2011).

26. *Ibid.*

27. LVMH, Annual report 2011 (2012), 05/24

28. Ben McLannahan, 'The luxury goods industry lost its lustre after 9/11. Now it's posting near-record profits. What happened?', *CFO* (November 2005), www.cfoeurope.com/displayStory.cfm/5107936.

29. Yigang Pan, 'LVMH Moët Hennessy Louis Vuitton: Expanding brand dominance in Asia', *Asia Case Research Center* (2005), Reference no. 505–079–1.

PART III

DYNAMICS OF GLOBAL STRATEGY

11

Entry mode dynamics 1: Foreign distributors

Five learning objectives

1. To explain the reasons why MNEs establish long-term relationships with local distributors, even when they also command a wholly owned distribution network.
2. To foster an understanding of the role foreign distributors can play in the FSA development process.
3. To provide concrete guidelines to MNEs on how to manage local distributors in host countries.
4. To describe the challenges facing large MNEs in dealing with mega-distributors such as Wal-Mart and the benefits of direct sales.
5. To define the 'bullwhip effect' and to illustrate how manufacturing companies should manage uncertainty on the input and output sides of the supply chain.

This chapter examines Arnold's idea that, when selling in foreign markets, MNEs should maintain relationships with local distributors over the long term even after establishing their own local network to handle major clients. In theory, local distributors provide insight into the local market, knowledge of local regulations and business practices, existing major customers at low cost, and the ability to hire appropriate staff and develop relationships with potential new customers. Selecting and managing distributors is difficult, though, and Arnold provides a list of seven best practices. These ideas will be examined and then criticized using the framework presented in Chapter 1.

Significance

In an important *HBR* article, **David Arnold** studied the role of external actors, specifically foreign distributors, in international strategy.[1] Arnold focused on the evolving role of local distributors when MNEs first establish themselves in new markets and then try to grow in these markets. He observes that many MNEs initially establish relationships with local distributors in order to reduce costs and minimize risks. In other words, the local distributor's complementary capabilities (e.g., knowledge of local regulations and business practices, ability to hire appropriate staff and relationships with potential customers) substitute for developing new, location-bound FSAs required to access the host country market, in cases where market success is highly uncertain. Unfortunately, however, after enjoying some early market penetration, sales often flatten and may even start declining. Typically, the MNE then responds by calling into question the effectiveness of the local partner and its ability to make good on performance commitments and expectations. The MNE's reflex may even be to take control of local operations by buying out the distributor or by reacquiring the distribution rights in order to build a self-owned, dedicated distribution network. The resulting transition period is often difficult, disruptive and costly – problems that could be avoided, according to Arnold, through better strategic planning of distributor selection and governance of the relationships with local distributors.

Arnold's research included a two-year field study of the international distribution strategies of eight MNEs active in the consumer, industrial and service sectors as they entered nearly 250 new host country markets. Arnold observed, perhaps surprisingly, that MNEs often select new countries for market seeking purposes in a largely unplanned or reactive way. This approach typically begins with a positive response to unsolicited proposals from local distributors, advertising the location advantages of the host country in which they operate and their own capabilities to help the MNE serve that market.

The MNE then aligns itself with an independent local distributor in order to minimize up-front risk and to tap existing knowledge about the local market and potential major customers at low cost. Here, the distributor is supposed to add complementary capabilities to the MNE's internationally transferable FSAs, which are embodied in the products it wishes to export.

Typically, the MNE invests very little in marketing and business development, as it assumes that the local distributor will take care of these areas critical to foreign market penetration. But in doing so, "companies cede control of strategic marketing decisions to the local partners, much more control than they would cede in home markets".[2] Arnold calls this minimal, low-risk, low-investment strategy the 'beachhead strategy'. The MNE's attitude is to wait and see what can be achieved with such minimal commitment.

Behind this hands-off 'beachhead' approach may be the MNE's longer-term intent to eventually take direct control of local operations and to integrate these into the MNE's existing international network after some initial market penetration has been achieved. Arnold notes that "for many multinationals, it's a foregone conclusion that local distributors have merely been vehicles for market entry, temporary partners incapable of sustaining growth in the long term".[3] Observing this past behaviour by MNEs, many local distributors conclude, quite reasonably, that the relationship will only be temporary. In such cases, the local partners may be unwilling to make the significant investments in strategic marketing and business development that are necessary to grow the business over the longer term. Thus, a vicious cycle of increasing bounded reliability challenges is set in motion: the distributor's expectation of MNE unreliability (to provide adequate long-term support) in turn creates distributor unreliability (to invest for the growth of the business).

If sales growth falters, once the initial 'low-hanging fruit' (selling the MNE's core products to the distributor's existing customer base) has been captured, each side may embark on a path of blaming the other for the disappointing results. Typically, the MNE laments that the local distributor "didn't know how to grow the market … didn't invest in business growth … [and] just wasn't ambitious enough",[4] whereas the local partner counters that the MNE did not provide enough support to match its overly high expectations.

In reality, both parties may share responsibility for the relative failure of the distribution agreement. Arnold's research shows that "the same themes repeatedly emerge: neither party – the multinational nor the distributor – invests sufficiently in strategic marketing or in aggressive business development".[5]

However, according to Arnold, senior MNE managers usually deserve the main burden of responsibility, as they should realize that: "distributors are implementers of marketing strategy, rather than marketing departments in the country-market".[6] Arnold's point is that MNEs often relegate too much of their strategic marketing planning activities and the control thereof to local distributors when first entering new markets without providing proper direction and resources. In addition, the local market's life cycle stage typically changes after entry, but the MNE often fails to adjust its market strategy or market commitments to reflect the evolution from early penetration to rapid growth. Instead, the MNE sticks with its initial market-entry strategy (i.e., the beachhead strategy) for too long.

What is the solution to these common problems between MNEs and their international distributors, especially in developing countries? According to Arnold, "The key to solving the problems of international distribution in developing countries is to recognize that the phases are predictable and that multinationals can plan for them from the start in a way that is less disruptive and costly than the doomed beachhead strategy."[7]

Interestingly, Arnold finds that companies usually have success when they evolve from a beachhead strategy to a mix of direct distribution by the MNE itself and long-term relationships with local distributors. This mixed strategy often lets the MNE retain control of distribution where feasible, while relying on the complementary capabilities of distributors where necessary:

> It seems probable that some national distributors will become part of a mixed distribution system, in which the multinational corporation will manage major customers

directly, while other, independent, distributors will focus on discrete segments of national markets or smaller accounts . . . independent local distributors often provide the best means of serving local small and medium accounts.[8]

In other words, MNEs are advised to maintain relationships with independent local partners for distribution activities over the long term even after establishing their own local network to handle major clients. The key for the MNE is to find the correct balance between three competing objectives: strategic control over important customers, benefits from the local partner's market knowledge and market access, and risk reduction when faced with high demand uncertainty in the new market.

Arnold's research also contains recommendations for local distributors who want to continue to work with the MNE as it gains market share. Arnold's research shows that, in the cases where distributors successfully maintained their relationship with an MNE over the longer term, these local partners shared a number of characteristics: they did not distribute competing product lines from rivals, they shared market information with the MNE, they initiated new projects and they collaborated with other distributors in adjacent markets. They also invested in areas such as training, ICT and promotion to grow the business.[9]

The article concludes by offering a list of seven guidelines for MNEs when dealing with local distributors. These guidelines should help MNEs avoid the commonly observed pattern of local market underperformance as a result of underinvestment and over-reliance on distributors, followed by an over-correction in the form of complete internalization of all distribution activities:

1. Proactively select locations and only then suitable distributors. The MNE should identify for itself the countries it wants to enter, in relation to its strategic objectives (and the related country-level location advantages), and then suitable partners in those countries, rather than expanding internationally to particular locations in response to unsolicited proposals from local distributors (e.g., in the context of trade fairs). The best partners are not necessarily the largest distributors, as the latter may already have contracts with (competing) MNEs for similar product lines, and may thus have an interest in dividing the existing local market among MNE rivals, rather than rapidly building the market for one firm.

2. Focus on distributors' market development capabilities. It is critical to find the best 'company fit' in terms of strategy, culture, willingness to invest and to train staff, etc., rather than merely a 'market fit' with those distributors already serving key target customers with related products.

3. Manage distributors as long-term partners. This approach, which may include incentives related to actual sales performance, will make distributors willing to invest more in strategic marketing and long-term development. Using distributors for short-term market penetration purposes only, and making this clear through distribution rights buy-back clauses in the contract, takes away the

incentive for distributor investment in market development and may even increase bounded reliability problems. For example, if the buy-back price depends on sales volumes, irrespective of profit margins achieved, the distributor may attempt to position the MNE's product as a commodity, rather than extract the highest possible price from customers. The distributor may thereby harm the product's future positioning in the local market.

4. Provide resources (managerial, financial and knowledge-based) to support distributors for market development purposes. Arnold's research indicates that MNEs rarely withdraw fully from a new export market. Committing more resources earlier may therefore foster better relationships with local partners as well as higher performance. The resources provided may include skilled support staff, minority equity participations (e.g., to co-fund investments) and knowledge sharing (e.g., to augment simple equipment selling with related service provision to customers).

5. Do not delegate marketing strategy to distributors. While distributors should be able to adapt the MNE's strategy to the needs of local markets, it is up to the MNE to provide clear leadership in terms of the choice of products to be marketed, the positioning of these products and the size and use of marketing budgets.

6. Secure shared access to the distributors' critical market and financial intelligence. In many cases, local distribution partners may be the only economic actors holding such valuable information in the host country, and their willingness to share this information signals their commitment to becoming a solid, long-term partner. At the same time, the distributors reduce the MNE's bounded rationality problems by improving its limited understanding of the idiosyncrasies of the local market.

7. Link national distributors with each other, especially at the regional level (spanning several countries). Such linkages, in the form of regional headquarters to coordinate distribution efforts, or autonomous distributor councils, may lead to the diffusion of best practices inside the distributors' network, and act as an internal monitoring mechanism, stimulating more consistent strategy implementation throughout the region.

Context and complementary perspectives

Arnold's work can be interpreted as a complement to Bartlett and Ghoshal's perspective, discussed in Chapter 5, which addressed the MNE's need to tap its foreign subsidiaries as new sources of competitive advantage. It is also consistent with Kuemmerle's view on innovation, discussed in Chapter 6, that foreign R&D centres are key to acquiring new sources of advanced knowledge, and Ferdows' assessment, discussed in Chapter 7, that successful manufacturers should develop their foreign factories into sources of new FSAs.

Whereas Bartlett and Ghoshal's, Kuemmerle's and Ferdows' views are applicable in principle to all MNE types, but especially to the **international projector**, Arnold's article is especially relevant to the **centralized exporter**. For the latter MNE category, neither simple market contracts with foreign distributors nor the full internalization of international distribution operations may be the optimal way to bring exported products to the overseas customer. In cases where the key to success in a host market is continued, long-term access to the (not generally available) market knowledge and management expertise of local partners to reach customers, strategic partnerships with distributors may be the optimal entry mode.

Arnold's 'seven rules of international distribution' are in line with a key theme in international business thinking throughout the past 20 years, namely that companies may benefit from strengthening their international linkages with external parties that command complementary FSAs, rather than trying to develop such FSAs within the company, especially if such FSAs would take a long time to develop internally and cannot be simply purchased in the host country market.

Andrew R. Thomas and *Timothy J. Wilkinson* provide a first complementary perspective on international distribution, suggesting that MNEs may also face a critical distribution challenge at home, with implications for international strategy.[10] Their *SMR* piece argues that many US manufacturing MNEs, especially those active in consumer goods industries, have made an important strategic mistake in managing their domestic distribution system, and should try to avoid a similar mistake abroad. They observe that, since the early 1970s, many large manufacturing firms have focused on their so-called 'core competencies' and have adopted total quality control systems in production, thereby largely neglecting the distribution and sales side of their business. The dual outcome has been increased efficiency in production, where allegedly (according to business gurus and consultants) the firm's core competencies are located, and outsourcing of distribution, often to non-dedicated distributors.

Unfortunately, a problem may then arise when these non-dedicated, downstream partners include mega-distributors such as Wal-Mart and The Home Depot – partners that represent a substantial portion of the firm's total sales volume. For many US manufacturers this has meant the evolution from "having a global network of loyal and faithful dealers and strong brand loyalty to becoming the manufacturer of a commodity that could be purchased at an ever-growing number of outlets for a lower price".[11] Importantly, the market power of the mega-distributors has led to continuous downward pressures on prices, and therefore to almost forced offshoring of production to low-cost locations such as China. Unfortunately, according to the authors, such offshoring mainly serves the profit margins of the mega-distributors, not the manufacturers, as any cost reductions on the input side yield only further price squeezes at the output side.

The authors urge manufacturers to regain control over domestic distribution and to engage in direct marketing, citing US-based computer manufacturer Dell

Inc. as one example of a company that successfully controls its own distribution, bypassing conventional distribution channels and selling directly to consumers. In the international context, manufacturers should avoid their past domestic mistakes: "In high-growth emerging markets around the world, manufacturers still possess the ability to directly influence what happens to their products once they enter the distribution chain."[12]

This view is consistent with Arnold's recommendation to keep control of the strategic marketing aspects of foreign distribution, and not give foreign distributors free rein to grow market share using any means they wish. In fact, if large manufacturers had applied Arnold's prescription of not relegating strategic marketing to distributors in the domestic context, they might have been able to avoid the tyranny of mega-distributors. Note, however, an important difference: where Arnold emphasizes the advantages of using distributors if managed properly, Thomas and Wilkinson emphasize the disadvantages of using distributors and the benefits of direct sales.

Thomas and Wilkinson's point is that long-term relationships with distributors can lead to an almost irreversible and undesirable lock-in for the manufacturer, when these distributors transform the product's positioning into that of a commodity and purchase a large part of the manufacturer's entire output.

Hau L. Lee provides a second complementary perspective in an insightful *CMR* paper on how manufacturing companies should manage uncertainty on both the input market and output market sides of the supply chain.[13]

Obviously, demand and supply side uncertainties are detrimental to the firm's ability to serve customers effectively and efficiently. For example, even if demand were predictable, the **bullwhip effect**, meaning "the amplification of order variability as one goes upstream along a supply chain",[14] could occur if there is poor planning or execution by the foreign distributor. Only if sufficient information on demand is shared – and replenishment/distribution planning and execution aligned – with the MNE's supply chain management, can this effect be avoided, and distributor-driven demand uncertainty removed.

Lee notes that another way to manage demand uncertainty is to adopt a postponement strategy, whereby some production activities are performed at the end of the production process, thereby maximizing this process' flexibility. In this way, customization of end products is done as late as possible, in line with changing customer demand. For example, Benetton, the Italian clothing retailer, delays dying its sweaters with particular colours until very late in the production process. In the international business sphere, the optimal location for postponed activities such as final assembly, testing and packaging is often a distribution centre close to the final customer, e.g., European Distribution Centres (EDCs) in the European Union.

On the supply side, the MNE must also attempt to eliminate unnecessary uncertainty. Here, risk hedging is critical, e.g., by setting up inventory pools at the regional level, close to the customer, to mitigate supply interruptions and to stabilize order fulfilment.

Lee's main point is that much of the uncertainty on the input and output market sides can be reduced or avoided by effective supply chain management. Here, vertical integration need not substitute for strategic partnerships with a variety of actors on the input market side (suppliers) or output market side (distributors). However, the management of such uncertainties requires substantial efforts in information sharing, joint coordination and planning with suppliers and distributors. Here, the MNE can develop a new, non-location-bound FSA in the form of an 'agile supply chain', common among **international coordinators**. For example, Cisco Systems, a US-based supplier of networking equipment and network management for the Internet, created an 'e-Hub' that uses 'intelligent planning software' allowing "the identification of potential supply and demand problems early, with proper warning given to the appropriate parties and resolution actions taken promptly via the Internet".[15]

Even though the argument in Lee's paper addresses only specific types of uncertainty, Lee's recommendations and his conceptual analysis have broad applicability to all manufacturing firms. His recommendations are particularly relevant in the context of MNE supply chain challenges when penetrating foreign markets, because such penetration has enormous uncertainty surrounding both demand and the optimal supply chain to link sourcing, production and distribution.

In the case of penetrating foreign markets, demand uncertainty on the output market side is not primarily the consequence of innovative product characteristics (in contrast to Lee's paper). Rather, demand uncertainty results from the MNE's limited capability to understand beforehand what set of new location-bound FSAs in the distribution sphere will need to be developed to penetrate the new market, as a complement to its internationally transferable FSA bundle, embodied in its exported products.

Supply uncertainty on the input market side, in the context of MNE management, is not primarily the consequence of a lack of maturity and stability of the supply chain in a technological sense (as it is in Lee's paper). Rather, uncertainty in the supply chain, starting on the input market side, results from bounded rationality challenges faced by senior MNE managers in their quest to optimize logistics when a new country needs to be linked to the existing supply chain.

Whereas Arnold's *HBR* piece addressed the broad, strategic challenges in MNE–distributor relationships, Lee's *CMR* piece usefully proposes adopting an agile supply chain in cases of high demand and supply uncertainties. With an agile supply chain, the MNE, its suppliers and distributors can all benefit from concerted action to reduce such uncertainties. Furthermore, Lee agrees with Arnold that vertical integration (i.e., ownership of the entire supply chain) is not necessary to manage uncertainty – with effective information sharing, joint coordination and planning, the MNE can effectively manage uncertainty together with (external) suppliers and distributors.

One of Arnold's main points in his *HBR* piece on foreign distribution is that, when penetrating a host country, MNEs should develop location-bound FSAs. Arnold's research essentially reveals that in the early stages of an MNE's entrance into a new market, FSA development is usually neither the main focus of the MNE's strategy, nor of its local distribution partner. Rather, the MNE's primary goal is typically to reap the benefits of its bundle of existing, internationally transferable FSAs, embodied in its exported products, while minimizing costs and investment risks associated with foreign market penetration. This is made possible by using the existing, location-bound FSAs of distributors that allow easier market access.

As Arnold points out, however, MNEs thereby often cede strategic decision-making control to the local partner, assuming that this partner will handle critical areas of marketing and business development. The local distributor, however, often remains focused on short-term sales growth, knowing that this is the MNE's primary interest. The local distributor assumes (often correctly) that little MNE support or long-term commitment will be forthcoming to improve the outcome of the distribution arrangement, and that great market success might actually lead to MNE attempts to internalize the distribution activity, especially in cases whereby both parties would need to invest heavily in proprietary knowledge (e.g., brand name development) to sustain and further strengthen such success. The development of new FSAs suffers because of this lack of credible, mutual commitments.

By contrast, in the few examples Arnold provides of successful, long-term distribution partnerships and in his recommendations for properly building such partnerships, both sides place greater importance on new FSA development, even in the short run, especially in terms of effectively linking the MNE's and the distributor's knowledge base. Distributors who have managed to remain successful over the long run have contributed to MNE competitiveness by sharing market intelligence and helping to build new FSAs, e.g., by initiating new projects and working collaboratively with other distributors in neighbouring markets. Such distributor commitments have been associated with similar commitments from the MNE, in terms of managerial, financial and knowledge-based resources to develop the market.

Such credible, mutual commitments only make sense, according to Arnold, if there is an overall 'company fit' between the MNE and its local distributor. That is, they must be willing and able to work together as partners in building new FSAs, rather than focusing solely on the immediate 'market fit' when linking the MNE's products (and thus the MNE's underlying, internationally transferable FSAs) with the distributor's existing customer base (and thus its location-bound FSAs, providing local market access). The linking of internationally transferable FSAs held by the MNE and location-bound FSAs held by the distributor should thus not be assessed merely in static terms, at the time of the agreement. Rather, such linkages must be crafted over time, and initial similarities between the MNE and the distributor (e.g., in terms of corporate culture, incentive systems or supply chain routines) can greatly facilitate this crafting process.

This idea of distributors – actors external to the MNE – contributing to the generation of FSAs provides an interesting extension of this book's framework for analysing patterns of FSA development. In earlier chapters, we assessed whether FSA development took place through the parent organization in the home country or through subsidiaries in host markets. Arnold's article adds another level to the analysis by assessing whether, and to what extent, FSA development in foreign host markets should take place internally, through wholly owned subsidiaries, or externally, through partnerships with local distributors.

Arnold's prescription for the long term is to adopt a mix of the two governance mechanisms: establishing subsidiaries to control the company's international marketing strategy, especially in the context of serving key global customers, while also retaining external distributors as partners to service optimally smaller, local customers. The normative conclusion is thus clearly to establish long-term strategic alliances with external partners, in this case local distributors, to benefit from their FSAs – a concept covered in greater depth in Chapter 12.

Following Arnold's advice – adopting a mix of 'internal' and 'external' distribution operations – would allow an MNE to pursue a mix of strategies of FSA development, which can be analysed using our framework of FSA development patterns. According to Arnold, the subsidiary should play to its strengths (i.e., transferable FSAs) and adhere to a more standardized approach focusing on large international accounts. By contrast, the local distribution partner should play to its strengths (i.e., location-bound FSAs) and should be nationally responsive in providing service coverage that is unique and adapted to each host market. These strategies correspond to Pattern I and Pattern IV of our framework, respectively (see Figure 11.1).

Pattern I builds upon standard, internationally transferable FSAs in the realm of distribution that the MNE can deploy in its foreign subsidiaries around the world to manage large global clients (this is really the equivalent of global account management, discussed in Chapter 9). In contrast, Pattern IV here involves external distributors, who are supposed to provide unique, location-bound FSAs to satisfy the requirements of smaller, local customers, but with their exploitation potential largely confined to the specific host country market.

Arnold's fifth guideline for MNEs, that they should maintain control over strategic decision making, is a warning against domination of international distribution by Pattern IV, with independent local distributors afforded such a high level of autonomy and control that each country operates independently of the others, with market success determined by each national distributor's FSAs. This outcome would reduce the MNE's potential to reap economies of scope by sharing valuable knowledge across borders.

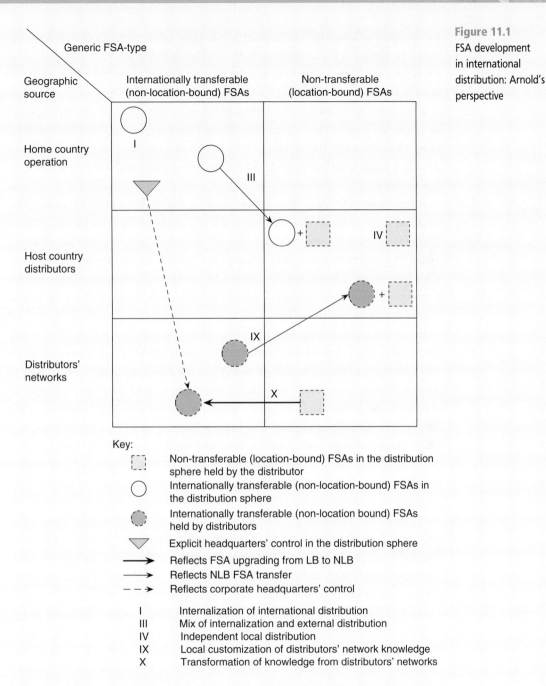

If the MNE relies solely on independent, foreign distributors – and if strategic control exerted by central headquarters remains weak – FSA development is unlikely to occur through Pattern V or Pattern VIII, even in the longer run, since the independent distributors will have little incentive to act as entrepreneurs and to generate new FSAs either autonomously (Pattern V) or collectively (Pattern VIII), to be shared subsequently with other MNE distribution partners or MNE subsidiaries. In this case, the independent distributors will not generate and share such FSAs because they know they will receive no benefit from successes achieved outside of their local markets.

If the MNE subsidiary cooperates with the local distributor, FSA development in the broad sense may end up resembling Pattern III, with the MNE introducing internationally transferable FSAs to the market and the local distributor adding unique location-bound FSAs to optimize sales and distribution within the country.

Arnold's seventh guideline, recommending the crafting of linkages between national distributors at the regional level, is a pitch for Pattern IX and Pattern X. Here, subsidiaries and local distributors work together as a network to create new FSA bundles that can then be customized with location-bound additions for each host market, in the case of Pattern IX, or transformed into internationally transferable FSAs and exploited internationally under the guidance of central headquarters, as in Pattern X.

In spite of its useful managerial prescriptions, Arnold's work has two major limitations. First, Arnold mistakenly recommends internalizing some customers and outsourcing others based primarily on the customer's size. According to Arnold, larger (and thus presumably more important) customers should be served by the MNE itself. In reality, however, parameters other than size may be more strategically important. The key question is whether a customer requires extensive interaction and customization, and expects continuous product adaptation. These customers should be dealt with internally, because such attention requires substantial resources, and because continuous product adaptation will probably be easier and more efficient if carried out directly by the MNE subsidiary rather than the distributor. (The subsidiary will have a closer and more direct relationship to the production facilities than the distributor will.) On the other hand, if a customer just purchases large quantities without any need for customization or continuous technical improvements, the use of an external distributor with strong location-bound FSAs may be the optimal solution.

Figure 11.2 incorporates this modification of Arnold's work. The figure shows two parameters critical to deciding the optimal governance of international distribution.

The vertical axis measures the final customer's needs for technical customization/adaptation of the product offering (low or high). Note that the word 'technical' is used here to indicate that these customer requirements are intrinsically unrelated to the customer's location. In other words, the MNE's success in meeting technical customer requirements depends upon its proprietary technical capabilities, which are in principle non-location-bound. In contrast, the horizontal axis measures the level of customer requirements that are location-determined

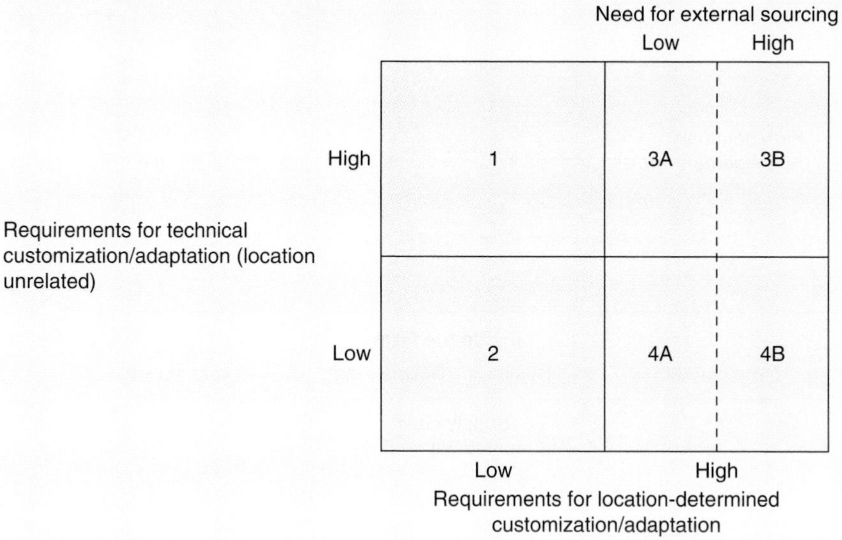

Figure 11.2
Optimal governance of international distribution

(low or high), e.g., so as to meet prevailing health and safety standards considered normal in the host country. A high level of location-determined customer requirements on the right-hand side of Figure 11.2 implies that the necessary customization/adaptation cannot be performed simply by recombining and deploying internationally transferable knowledge, but necessitates deep knowledge of the local situation. The right-hand side of the horizontal axis is further subdivided into two segments, which address the need for external sourcing to develop the required location-bound knowledge (versus the ability to develop it internally). The latter need is again expressed as being low or high.[16]

In cell 2 of Figure 11.2, exports can occur without major governance complications, perhaps using simple market contracts with distributors if these can operate with low costs, since the customer imposes no requirements to alter the product offering. In cell 1, substantial technical customization/adaptation to customer requirements is necessary, thus providing an incentive for the internalization of distribution to facilitate smooth adaptation. In cells 3A and 4A, there is an additional need to satisfy location-determined customization/adaptation, and this need can be met internally by the MNE, i.e., by developing new, location-bound FSAs inside the company. Note that in cell 3A, the MNE has exceptional recombination capabilities: it can develop further and recombine both technical knowledge (internationally transferable) and location-bound knowledge. Finally, in cells 3B and 4B, only external parties can satisfy the need for location-determined customization/adaptation. Cell 3B represents perhaps the most intriguing case: here, the MNE can customize/adapt its product offering to purely technical customer requirements, but it must also meet location-determined requirements for customization/adaptation which cannot be met internally.

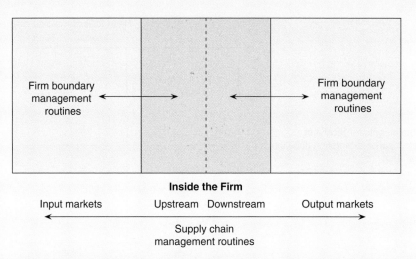

Figure 11.3
An integrative
approach to
coordinate various
components of the
supply chain

This is likely to lead to complex distribution arrangements, perhaps in the form of equity joint ventures, since both the MNE and its distributor need to engage in customization/adaptation processes to satisfy customer requirements.

Second, Arnold's sole focus on distribution leads to a relative neglect of the remainder of the supply chain, especially the input market side and the need for an integrative approach to the various supply chain components. Figure 11.3 displays such an integrative approach: here, the value chain consists of three main components – the left-hand side describes the input market, whereby external actors provide at least some inputs to the MNE. The middle section describes the upstream and downstream activities performed by the MNE itself. Finally, the right-hand side describes the output market, where distributors may play a key role, as discussed above.

For reasons of simplicity, Figure 11.3 does not show explicitly the dispersed geography that may characterize this supply chain. However, dispersed geography imposes additional needs for combination capabilities to coordinate the various components of the supply chain.

To increase efficiency, the MNE will typically try to adopt similar routines on the input market and output market sides. For example, if JIT systems are adopted on the input market side, a similar system will probably be used on the output market side. If production coordination occurs to a large extent through the use of sophisticated ICT systems, then sophisticated ICT will probably be used at the boundaries with suppliers and distributors. The point is simply that understanding a relationship with a foreign distributor, in terms of why and how it was set up, and how it should be managed in the future, may require an understanding of the MNE's entire supply chain setup, rather than simply an understanding of the distributor and the MNE's distribution needs. Figure 11.4 illustrates the case of routine-type FSAs (which may span the entire supply chain) being transferred to

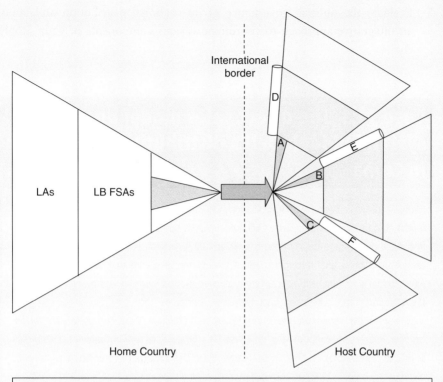

Figure 11.4
Managing foreign
distribution

International
border

D

A

E

B

LAs   LB FSAs

C

F

Home Country   Host Country

The NLB FSAs in the realm of distribution transferred to foreign operations in different
host countries are indicated by A, B and C. The complementary resources provided by
distributors in each of these host countries to meet local requirements, are indicated by
D, E and F.

host countries, where these are then augmented with complementary resources of
distributors.

Five management takeaways

1. Review your international distribution strategy and portfolio of relationships
   with local distributors.
2. Follow the seven guidelines for MNEs when using local distributors in
   international expansion.
3. Consider the disadvantages of using distributors and the benefits of direct
   sales.
4. Assess in a comparative fashion the uncertainty in your input and output
   markets in your supply chain.

5. Evaluate the optimal governance of international distribution and apply an integrative approach to coordinate various components of your supply chain.

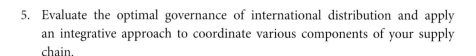

CASE

Case 11.1 The direct sales model or a 'dual system' model: Dell's distribution strategy in China

Many people have been very skeptical about Dell's ability to replicate its famous direct sales model abroad. According to Dell's CEO, when the US-based computer hardware company first expanded internationally (into the UK in 1987), "of the twenty-two journalists who came to our press announcement, about twenty-one predicted that we would fail. The direct model is an American concept, they claimed; nobody will buy computers direct from the manufacturer . . . It's a bad idea, they said. Go home."[17]

Similar doubts were expressed when Dell entered China. In China, Dell gradually evolved from an indirect sales model to a 'dual system' model (i.e., a system that uses both direct sales and distributors). At first, in the early 1990s, Dell exported PCs to China using only distributors. Then, in 1998, Dell set up a manufacturing base in Xiamen, China, and applied a dual system model. In August 2004, Dell pulled out of the low-end PC market in China, thereby reducing the weight of distributors in its dual system model.

In the US, Dell has evolved in the opposite direction, from a direct sales model to a dual system model: Dell USA started to sell PCs at Wal-Mart in 2007.

What future changes should we expect for Dell China?

The direct sales model

A college dropout after his freshman year, Michael Dell capitalized on the opportunity of selling PCs directly to consumers when he noticed a number of anomalies in the computer business. For the components of an IBM PC, manufacturers would pay around US $700; for the assembled PC, retailers would pay US $2,000; and customers would then pay US $3,000 without receiving much technical support. This was the traditional channel model followed by the biggest players in the industry such as IBM and Apple: manufacturers built computers, distributed them to dealers, and dealers sold them to businesses and individual consumers.

Michael Dell thought that end users paid too much. He thought that he could make the process of buying a PC easier and better. In 1983, when Michael was only a freshman, he bought PCs at retail stores, upgraded them by purchasing components, and sold upgraded PCs to people he knew. For him, this was a good opportunity: he could bypass much of the retailer's markup and pass savings on to end users. In 1984, Michael Dell created Dell Computer Corporation, the first computer manufacturer to sell PCs directly to end users. By the end of 1986, Dell's annual sales had reached US $60 million.

Much of the success was attributed to the direct sales model. Dell redesigned and integrated its supply chain: it received orders from end users first, then ordered components from its suppliers, assembled PCs and finally shipped PCs directly from Dell's factories to end users. Compared with the traditional supply chain in the computer industry, the direct model had two major advantages. First, the closeness to end users helped Dell better understand users' needs, forecast demand more accurately and build long-term relationships with end users. Second, the elimination of distributors helped Dell reduce not only its selling cost, but also its inventory through both accurate forecasting and integration with components suppliers.

The direct sales model seemed to meet two trends in the 1980s very well. First, corporate customers and individuals were becoming very sophisticated and experienced technology users. They often knew exactly what they wanted and did not need intense personal selling. Second, mass customization was also becoming viable as components became standard modules.[18]

In 1990, Dell experimented with selling computers through retail stores like CompUSA, Best Buy and Sam's, but pulled out of the retail distribution channel in mid 1994. Dell made a core decision to stick to the direct sales model: 'never sell indirect' finally became one of the three golden Dell rules, the other two being 'disdain inventory' and 'always listen to the customer'.[19]

International expansion and exporting to China: pre-1998

Although Dell always stressed the direct sales model as a 'golden' Dell rule, the company applied this golden rule selectively in its international expansion, assessing each host country individually. Dell's decision as to which model to adopt depended on characteristics along the country's whole value chain. First, to what extent would end users accept direct sales, especially given Dell's reputation in the host country? If end users had neither heard of nor seen Dell computers, it would be difficult to convince customers to buy via telephone. Second, to what extent would Dell be able to recruit a skilled sales force for direct sales? Third, were capable suppliers and carriers available to meet just-in-time management? Fourth, was the market size large enough?

International forays began in June 1987 when Dell started its business in the UK. In spite of wide scepticism, Dell's business in the UK was profitable from the very beginning.[20] In the next four years, Dell established subsidiaries in 14 countries. In 1995, Dell established the Asia Pacific Customer Center in Penang, Malaysia, which functioned as the hub for sales and marketing in Australia, China, Hong Kong, India, Indonesia, Korea, Malaysia, New Zealand, the Philippines, Singapore, Taiwan and Thailand.

Dell's history in China can be traced back to 1993, when Dell chose Star Advertising Corporation as its sole agent in mainland China and set up a network of four resellers.[21] The cooperation lasted less than a year. In 1995, however, Dell re-entered mainland China. From this time until late 1998, Dell imported PCs from other countries and then sold Dell PCs through its distributors. The distribution system included four first-tier distributors located in metropolitan areas including Beijing, Shanghai, Guangzhou and Xi'an, as well as second- and third-tier resellers. Dell's representative office in China decided on the sales plan, designed promotion strategies such as sales rebates and coordinated the relationships among the distributors.

However, Dell's performance was not very good. By 1996, Dell sold only 20,000 PCs in China, giving it only a 1 per cent market share and putting it in tenth place among PC vendors.[22] These unimpressive results were largely due to the country's relatively small market size and the lack of effort from both Dell and its distributors. Dell was waiting for the right time to apply its direct sales model, with no intention of keeping a long-term relationship with the distributors. At the same time, these distributors did not want to invest much in developing the market, anticipating that Dell would soon switch to its famous direct model.

Replicating the direct model in China: 1998–2004

Phil Kelly, President of Dell Asia Pacific, had been pushing Dell headquarters to build a manufacturing base in China and to sell directly. Finally, the tremendous growth of the Chinese PC market convinced the headquarters. In 1998, Dell set up a China Customer Centre (CCC) in Xiamen to manufacture and sell PCs, as well as to provide service and technical support.

Characteristics of the mainland China PC market

The PC market in China grew significantly during the mid and late 1990s: sales rose from RMB 7.6 billion in 1990 to RMB 66.2 billion in 1996.[23] In 1998, China became the fifth largest PC market in the world, behind only the US, Japan, Germany and Britain. According to the prediction of the Market Information Centre (MIC) in June 1998, the PC market of mainland China would continue to grow and was very likely to become the third largest PC market in the world by 2000.

The Chinese market was distinctive in two important ways.[24] First, retail buyers accounted for only about 10 per cent of total sales, and a PC would cost nearly two years of an average person's savings. Thus, buying a PC was something very big for average Chinese families, and the whole family would want to go to a store, touch the machine and test it. Therefore, Dell targeted the corporate market, including MNEs and government institutions. The information officers in these organizations were usually technologically savvy, and they already knew what they needed. Seeing and touching the machine was not necessary. Moreover, these firms did not need much service either.

Second, credit cards in China were issued primarily to corporate bodies and people of high social status. Most Chinese people were not used to credit card sales.

Replicating the direct sales model with minor adaptations

Dell was confident that its direct sales model would work well in China if it focused on the corporate segment.

Dell thus divided its customers into three groups: relationship companies (companies with more than 3,000 employees), mid-sized companies (companies with 500–3,000 employees) and small-sized companies and family customers (companies with less than 500 employees and individual customers). The first two segments were the major targets.

After selecting its target markets in China, Dell modified its direct sales model in two ways to meet China's distinctive characteristics. First, to contact corporate customers in China, Dell relied more on door-to-door sales and telephone sales rather than Internet sales. Normally, a sales team was comprised of an external salesperson and an internal one, with the former responsible for developing and retaining big accounts and the latter answering customers' inquiries and handling purchase orders. On average, the salespeople made three to four calls a day and spent one third of the day visiting customers.

Second, Dell recognized that most Chinese people were not used to credit card sales, so it did not insist on pre-payment through the Internet. Instead, Dell signed agreements with several banks to facilitate payments; Dell's delivery men could also collect cash or transfer money through wireless debit card machines carried by them.

Dell worked hard to reduce its costs in China, as a door-to-door sales channel was very costly, given salespeople's salaries and commissions "commensurate with those paid in Hong Kong and the US".[25] Dell tried to improve efficiency across the whole value chain. For example, in 1999, the time from order to delivery in China was about the same as the 9-day period in the US. In addition, Dell tried to draw on local talent. Although Dell brought in some Dell employees from Southeast Asia, the company soon hired local talent for most positions, even for many managerial ones.

Dell's direct sales efforts resulted in a much improved market penetration.[26] By 1999, Dell was ranked seventh among the top PC manufacturers in China, with a market share of 2.3 per cent. By 2004, Dell became the top company in sales of servers and commercial computers.

The dual system model: 1998–2004

While replicating its direct sales model in China, Dell continued to sell PCs and provide technical support through a network of authorized distributors, creating the first 'dual system' business model for Dell anywhere in the world. Dell named these authorized distributors 'system integrators'. They received orders from their customers and then ordered PCs from Dell.

These system integrators played an important role. When retail buyers in the form of small-sized businesses and family customers lacked technological knowledge and wanted advice, Dell could not meet their needs, but system integrators could. Moreover, the sales volume through system integrators was too large for Dell to simply dismiss. In 2001, Foo Piau Phang, President of Dell's operations in China, announced that around 75 per cent of Dell's sales in China came from direct sales,[27] although some insiders said that the percentage of direct sales was only around 60 per cent.[28]

However, Dell was never completely happy with the system integrators. Obviously, they partially competed with Dell's direct Internet and telephone sales. When system integrators bundled orders from retail buyers, the resulting large orders would win the system integrator better per-unit prices than what retail buyers would pay through Internet purchasing. For example, some notebooks from system integrators could be RMB 1000–2000 cheaper than the listed price on Dell's website.[29] As a result, the system integrators took some sales volume away from the direct channel.

Dell was willing to put up with this, though, because the system integrators helped Dell to maintain and expand its market. What Dell did not tolerate, however, was when system integrators placed large orders with Dell (thereby earning prices below retail) and then sold the PCs to resellers/agents rather than end users. Dell tried to stop these unofficial agents. In 2003, the collision between Dell and these unofficial agents led to a widely reported lawsuit.[30] Shanghai Zhiqi Corp. ordered 53 PCs from Dell and prepaid for these at the price of RMB 5,699, but after one week Dell China contacted Shanghai Zhiqi and cancelled the order, arguing that Dell had offered an inaccurate price and needed to triple the price. According to Dell's spokesman, Dell suspected that Shanghai Zhiqi was selling these PCs not to end users but to smaller distributors. The lawsuit ended with a private settlement between the two parties.

Despite such occasional problems between Dell and its distributors, the dual system worked very well when the retail buyer segment was negligible in the mainland Chinese PC market. Between 2000 and 2002, Dell was delighted to see its market share in the retail market rise from 0.2 per cent to 4.7 per cent, most of which came from system integrators (because Dell itself focused on large and mid-sized companies).

However, the lawsuit case in 2003 signalled to Dell that its dual system model, with the main focus on direct sales, did not fit the market conditions very well anymore. Given the rapid market growth in China, the good reputation of the Dell brand and the impossibility of exercising proper control over independent distributors, the likelihood of opportunistic behaviour by some of these partners was considerable.

Faced with the growth of the retail market: after 2004

The mainland Chinese PC market continued to grow in the new millennium, but most of the growth has come from the retail market. The growth rate of PC demand in urban centres such as Beijing and Shanghai fell to an annual rate of 2–3 per cent in 2004, while the growth rate in mid-sized cities and small towns soared to around 40 per cent. Compared with retail buyers in big cities, end users in rural areas had less savings to spend, knew less about computers, preferred to receive advice from retailers before they made the important decision to buy a computer, and required convenient technical service after bringing the PC back home.[31] Commentators noted that businesses were also requiring these services that Dell did not traditionally supply: "demand is emerging elsewhere – in hundreds of smaller cities . . . where even some business customers want to see products before they buy".[32]

In China, Dell's performance started to fall after 2004. From being second in 2003, it fell to fourth in 2004 with a market share of 7.2 per cent, even though PC shipments rose by 29 per cent. In 2006, Dell still lagged behind three local vendors: Lenovo, Founder and Tongfang. Lenovo, the market leader, had a market share of 25.1 per cent with around 4,800 retail outlets in China. In addition,

Acer was catching up in China, totally relying on distributors and outsourcing all production to factories in China.[33] Compared with these rivals, Dell was still doing very well in the corporate segment, but was falling further and further behind in the retail segment.

In 2003, Dell rejected a plan from its executives in China to sell computers online, but then accepted the plan one year later when statistics showed that more than 90 million people in the coastal cities in China had access to the Internet, either at home or work.[34] At the same time, Dell exited the low-end PC market, because that market required distributors with physical access to local consumers. In 2005 and 2006, the presidents of Dell China and Dell Asia-Pacific, together with four top executives in Asia, left Dell to join Lenovo. A major reason for the exodus was that Chinese executives wanted to focus much more on distributors and resellers, while Dell headquarters disagreed.

In China, Dell has started to focus on low-end consumers again by designing a new computer in 2007, priced at US $335 to meet the needs of novice users in this emerging market.[35] However, the lingering problem for the firm is that, according to one consultant, " 'Dell needs to establish more of a presence on the street' either through kiosks or retailers."[36]

Dell's retail move

In 2006 and 2007, Dell lost its position as the largest PC maker in the world to Hewlett-Packard.[37] Additionally, Dell lost its top ranking for highest notebook and LCD shipments to Acer and Samsung respectively. Its reputation was also jeopardized with recalls of over four million laptops and allegations of fraud in financial reporting. Michael Dell, who had resigned as CEO in 2004, resumed this role in 2007 to help turn around the struggling company. In an email sent to Dell's worldwide staff in April 2007, Michael Dell indicated that Dell would pursue new models of manufacturing and distributing computers. "The Direct Model has been a revolution, but is not a religion . . . We will continue to improve our business model, and go beyond it, to give our customers what they need."[38] Dell's restructuring plan was to centre around the consumer.[39]

The year 2007 was a time of change for Dell as the company stepped away from its core strategy of direct 'modeling' and moved towards the more traditional retail approach. Dell recognized that its built-to-order strategy had been key to its success in the past, but acknowledged the fact that the PC industry was changing and that Dell would need to change with it.[40] PCs were now being used as more of a 'hub for multimedia', creating a greater need for consumers to physically evaluate a product before making a purchase.[41] In addition, the growing demand for PCs in emerging markets shifted attention to these new consumers. With its experience in China, Dell recognized that consumers in emerging markets did not benefit from the direct model as much as they did in developed markets. Although the direct model was still expected to be the primary method for selling in mature markets, the need to open up other distribution channels in emerging markets was evident.[42]

Dell initiated a change to its model in the US in June 2007. Moving away from its traditional reliance on the direct sales model, it started selling computers through Wal-Mart.[43] Internationally, Dell opened retail locations in Russia and Hungary and partnered with retail chains in various countries including the UK, Japan, and China. By 2008, Dell products were located in roughly 10,000 retail locations. This was still significantly lower than Hewlett-Packard, whose products were found in over 110,000 locations.[44]

Rethinking retail in China

Effectively capturing the market in China required Dell to compete in a similar retail fashion to its main competitors Lenovo and Hewlett-Packard. Selecting the right retailer was imperative for Dell as it wanted to pursue a selective strategy. Michael Dell stated "[Dell didn't] want to just show up everywhere".[45] In 2007, Dell partnered with Gome, the largest electronics retailer to provide the face-to-face contact that the Chinese consumers' desired. Gome is found extensively throughout China, with over 1,000 stores in 168 cities.[46] Inventory in each store varies depending on the location, with some retail locations requiring no inventory.

The move to partner with a large retailer like Gome has been met with some criticism from industry executives as the majority of electronics is bought from small retailers located in IT malls. With close to 100 retailers, consumers are able to get access to numerous products at one location. It is estimated that around 80 per cent of all PC purchases are made in these IT malls, however Dell's Consumer VP Michael Tatelmen foresees a consolidation in the industry.[47]

To establish more commercial clients, Dell has developed its service capabilities to compete better with rivals in the market. Hardware has become a struggling sector in terms of its capacity to make profits, so services such as storage and cloud computing have taken on a stronger focus. In 2009, Dell acquired Perot Systems, an IT service provider, for US $3.9 billion to further develop its service competencies.[48] Steve Felice, President and Chief Commercial Officer, describes Dell's service and customer focus as a "[return] to a value-products oriented company. At the same time, [Dell is] transforming into a solutions company."[49]

In 2010, Dell started to see its efforts pay off with record growth in China that has been unmatched by any other country. In the first quarter, Dell experienced 81 per cent growth over the previous year's results.[50] An increase in Dell's commercial clients in 2011 can be attributed to turmoil at Hewlett-Packard after that company announced its intention to sell off its PC segment, causing customers to switch to more stable competitors even though Hewlett-Packard inevitably cancelled the initiative months later.

To continue its growth, Dell is now putting efforts into capturing the rural market in China. Although this segment has generally not been seen as containing many PC consumers, the vast number of potential customers is attracting attention from many PC manufacturers. Accessing this segment requires Dell to display its technology and educate villagers on the benefits of using a Dell PC. By tapping into new customer segments, increasing service capabilities and improving distribution tactics, Dell hopes to cling to its position as the second largest PC manufacturer in China.[51]

QUESTIONS

1. What are Dell's FSAs? What are the macro-level requirements for the direct sales model to be successful? What are the major advantages of the direct model, compared with the traditional channel strategy in the computer business?
2. How did Dell treat its distributors in China during its re-entry into China in 1995? Was there a vicious cycle of bounded reliability involved? Who should be blamed for Dell's initial failure?
3. According to Arnold's seven guidelines, discussed in Chapter 11, what mistakes did Dell make?
4. Given Dell's FSAs and China's location advantages in the late 1990s, why was the direct model successful? What has changed since?
5. With the changing market situations after 2004, what new location-bound FSAs should Dell develop to cater to retail buyers in China? Or, alternatively, what complementary capabilities should Dell expect from its distributors?
6. Did demand and supply uncertainties affect Dell's channel strategies in China? How?
7. Arnold recommends simultaneously internalizing some distribution activities and outsourcing other activities to external distributors. This is the 'dual system' model already followed by Dell in China. Please use Figure 11.2 to analyse possible channel strategies Dell could use in the future.
8. Can you provide an update on Dell's distribution strategy in China, using materials available on the Web?

Notes

1. D. Arnold, 'Seven rules of international distribution', *Harvard Business Review* 78 (2000), 131–7.
2. *Ibid.*, 132.
3. *Ibid.*
4. *Ibid.*, 133.
5. *Ibid.*
6. *Ibid.*, 137.
7. *Ibid.*, 134.
8. *Ibid.*, 133.
9. *Ibid.*
10. Andrew R. Thomas and Timothy J. Wilkinson, 'The outsourcing compulsion', *MIT Sloan Management Review* 48 (2006), 10–14.
11. *Ibid.*, 12.
12. *Ibid.*, 14.

13. Hau L. Lee, 'Aligning supply chain strategies with product uncertainties', *California Management Review* 44 (2002), 105–19.

14. *Ibid.*, 108.

15. *Ibid.*, 118.

16. Here, we assume for simplicity that the required location-bound knowledge can actually be sourced externally – albeit not through simple market contracts. Such possibility of external sourcing is not always present, however, especially not in emerging economies. We also assume that knowledge acquisition does not entail the acquisition of a host country firm. This assumption is reasonable because MNEs often are not interested in absorbing another company because it would lead to the internalization of – and perhaps subsequent need to dispose of – unwanted assets, the need to create a more uniform corporate culture after the acquisition, etc.

17. Michael Dell and Catherine Fredman, *Direct from Dell* (New York: HarperCollins, 1999), 28.

18. Anil K. Gupta and Vijay Govindarajan, *Global Strategy and Organization* (New York: John Wiley & Sons, 2004), 155.

19. Dell and Fredman, *Direct from Dell*, 43.

20. *Ibid.*, 28.

21. 'Business briefs', *Wall Street Journal* (7 October 1993), B.4.

22. Wayne Arnold, 'Dell feels the heat in computer dispute with Chinese buyer', *Wall Street Journal (Eastern Edition)* (18 April 1997), B.16.B.

23. B. Buchel and S. Raub, 'Legend Group and the Chinese Computer Industry', *Asian Case Research Journal* 3 (May 1999), 51.

24. Neel Chowdhury, 'Dell cracks China', *Fortune* 139 (21 June 1999), 120–4.

25. *Ibid.*

26. *Ibid.*

27. Mingshun Li, 'What is hidden under the direct model', *21 Century Economic Report* (5 June 2003).

28. 'Misery of Dell – the story from an insider', *IT Times Week* (23 March 2004).

29. Li, 'Hidden under the direct model'.

30. *Ibid.*

31. Mure Dickie and Scott Morrison, 'In China the agent enters the equation', *Financial Times* (26 August 2005), 13.

32. Louise Lee, Peter Burrows and Bruce Einhorn, 'Dell may have to reboot in China', *Business Week* (7 November 2005), 46.

33. Bruce Einhorn and Olga Kharif, 'A racer called Acer', *Business Week* (29 January 2007), 48.

34. Evan Ramstad and Gary McWilliams, 'Computer savvy: for Dell, success in China tells tale of maturing market', *Wall Street Journal (Eastern Edition)* (5 July 2005), A.1.

35. Gordon Fairclough and Jane Spencer, 'Dell's PC for China marks developing-market rush', *Wall Street Journal (Eastern Edition)* (22 March 2007), B.3.

36. Lee, Burrows and Einhorn, 'Dell reboot in China', 46.

37. Michael Kanellos, 'Global PC shipments grow, but revenue remains flat', *CNET News.com* (17 January 2007), accessed 12 June 2007.

38. Christopher Lawton, 'Dell could go beyond its direct-sales model in bid to bolster growth', *Wall Street Journal (Eastern Edition)* (28 April 2007), A.6.

39. Cliff Edwards, 'Dell's extreme makeover', *BusinessWeek* (15 October 2009).

40. William Hoffman, 'Redirecting Dell', *Traffic World* (21 April 2008).

41. Kevin Allison and Robin Kwong, 'China chapter of Dell's retail adventure opens NEWS ANALYSIS Computer maker's latest move is part of the overhaul of its longheld direct sales model', *Financial Times* (25 September 2007), 26.
42. William Hoffman, 'Redirecting Dell', *Traffic World* (21 April 2008).
43. Kevin Allison and Chris Nuttall, 'Dell to sell its computers at Wal-Mart', *Financial Times* (25 May 2007), 24.
44. Christopher Lawton, 'Dell treads carefully into selling PCs in stores', *Wall Street Journal Eastern Edition* (3 January 2008), B.1.
45. *Ibid.*
46. Mark McSherry, 'Dell to sell computers through China's Gome', *Wall Street Journal* (23 September 2007).
47. Bruce Einhorn, 'Dell goes retail in China with Gome', *BusinessWeek* (24 September 2007)
48. 'Dell to acquire Perot Systems for $3.9 billion, creating comprehensive, customer-focused IT-solutions company', Dell Inc. press release. http://content.dell.com/us/en/corp/d/secure/2009-09-21-Perot-Systems (21 September 2009).
49. Gaurav Raghuvanshi, 'Dell Counts on Local Leaders', *Wall Street Journal (Online)* (4 April 2012).
50. Loretta Chao, 'Dell intends to extend services unit in China', *Wall Street Journal Eastern Edition* (25 March, 2010), B.8.
51. Gaurav Raghuvanshi, 'Dell Counts on Local Leaders', *Wall Street Journal (Online)* (4 April 2012).

12

Entry mode dynamics 2: Strategic alliance partners

Five learning objectives

1. To describe the meaning of 'strategic alliances' and their main benefits.
2. To explain the concept of 'dependency spiral' and the ways to avoid it when outsourcing.
3. To develop an understanding of the risks of dependence, exploitation and abuse in strategic alliances.
4. To support a reflection on the meaning of the 'learning race' and 'learning asymmetry' concepts in the alliance context.
5. To illustrate how MNEs select wholly owned affiliates versus alliances in the emerging economy context.

This chapter examines Hamel *et al.*'s idea that, when pursuing strategic alliances with partners who are also rivals, firms should try to learn as much as possible from their partners while giving away as few of their FSAs as possible. In theory, strategic alliances have three main benefits: they allow firms to share risks and costs (particularly R&D costs), they allow firms to benefit from their partner's complementary resources, and they allow the quicker development of capabilities to deliver products and services valued by the output market. Hamel *et al.* provide other advice on carrying out strategic alliances, including the advice to keep developing FSAs independently and to avoid a vicious cycle of dependency on the partner. These ideas will be examined and then criticized using the framework presented in Chapter 1.

Significance

In 1989, **Gary Hamel**, **Yves Doz** and **C. K. Prahalad** wrote an influential *HBR* article on the dynamics of international strategic alliances.[1] They focused on the phenomenon whereby large MNEs form strategic alliances with equally large foreign firms that are also rivals in the international marketplace.

Such 'competitive collaboration' occurs because MNEs find it increasingly difficult to bear alone the enormous R&D costs – and singlehandedly gain easy access to the scarce resources required – to launch new products. These problems are amplified in the context of the compressed time frames necessary to stay ahead of rivals. Hamel *et al.* attempt to explain why some MNEs benefit greatly from these partnerships, in terms of new FSA development, while others do not.

Hamel *et al.*'s methodology involved a five-year study of fifteen international strategic alliances at various levels within the organizations involved, covering industries such as automotive manufacturing, semiconductors, computers and electronics. The sampling reflected a triad-based approach with a mix of cross-region alliances including: seven US–Japanese cases, four US–European ones, two European–Japanese ones and two intra-European ones. Wherever possible, both partners in the alliance were carefully investigated to uncover the role of strategic alliances in corporate strategy and competitive positioning, as well as the factors affecting the company either gaining or losing relative advantage by collaborating with a rival.

The benchmark adopted for evaluating alliance success was not how long the alliance lasted, which the authors claim is a commonly used, but misguided, performance parameter. Rather, they focused on the change in each partner's competitive strength: "We focused on how companies use competitive collaboration to enhance their internal skills and technologies while they guard against transferring competitive advantages to ambitious partners."[2] The authors focused on how to win the so-called 'learning race' – i.e., how to learn more from your partner than your partner learns from you.

The authors identified four key principles that successful companies adhere to when forming strategic alliances:

1. Collaboration is competition in a different form . . .
2. Harmony is not the most important measure of success . . .
3. Cooperation has limits. Companies must defend against competitive compromise . . .
4. Learning from partners is paramount . . .[3]

Their study revealed that, overall, Japanese MNEs – and Asian firms more generally – benefited the most from their strategic alliances with MNEs from other areas of the world. Hamel *et al.* provided four reasons why Asian MNEs tended to win the learning race. First, Asian firms tended to be intrinsically more receptive and more willing to put effort into learning from their alliance partners. This aspect is rooted in cultural and historical differences; the authors suggest that "Western companies won't realize the full benefits of competitive collaboration until they overcome an arrogance born of decades of leadership."[4]

Second, the Asian MNEs viewed alliances as an opportunity to develop new FSAs, and not primarily as a convenient tool to reduce investment costs and risks, (usually) on the upstream, technology development and manufacturing side, in contrast to several Western firms.

Third, Asian MNEs usually defined clear learning objectives regarding what they wanted to achieve from a partnership, and focused their efforts on acquiring new knowledge and observing their partners' practices in order to support such learning.

Fourth, the Asian MNEs' contribution to alliances often involved complex, tacit process knowledge that is not easily imitated or transferable, whereas the Western partners' contribution often involved easily transferable, codified product and marketing knowledge.

While some companies gain competitive strength from alliances, others fall behind as their FSAs are transferred to – and absorbed by – the alliance partner. For example, the authors noted that Western companies in particular often fall behind when they form alliances with Asian MNEs that are largely outsourcing arrangements, whereby manufacturing and technology development become the responsibility of the Asian partners, who essentially act as original equipment manufacturers (OEMs). This can cause a dangerous ratchet effect, since out-sourcing to an OEM leads to lower investments in R&D (and in product and process design) by the Western firm until eventually not only manufacturing but all the upstream, FSA-developing activities have been transferred to the Asian partner. The risk is that the Asian partner firm can then enter markets on its own and compete outside the realm of the alliance agreement because of what it has learned inside the alliance.

The authors also observed that companies positioned as 'troubled laggards' often pair up with 'surging latecomers' to the market.[5] The lagging companies are trying to find a quick fix for their own deficiencies, especially in terms of their inadequate innovation capabilities (e.g., their lack of 'manufacturing excellence' routines, such as appropriate total quality control systems), whereas the new-comers are seeking to fill specific capability gaps, often in the realm of stand-alone knowledge (e.g., product or market knowledge) that can more easily be absorbed. With this starting position, the weaker firms (in practice, usually the 'troubled laggards') may become trapped in a 'dependency spiral'. Here, their attention may shift from continuously reassessing the merits of the alliance vis-à-vis strategic alternatives (such as a wholly owned subsidiary or market-based contracting), towards trying to keep the present partner satisfied with the relationship, which may become increasingly critical to the survival of the dependent company.

When outsourcing, senior MNE managers should respect four principles in order to avoid a vicious cycle of increasing dependency on a partner, and to maintain a focus on developing the FSAs required for competing in the inter-national marketplace. First, outsourcing to provide a competitive product cannot replace the need to build FSAs over the long term. Second, senior managers should consider the negative consequences of outsourcing in terms of capability losses, and not just the short-run beneficial cost effects of de-internalizing key value-creating activities. Third, senior managers should be aware of the cumulative effects that individual outsourcing decisions can have, in terms of creating a vicious cycle of deepening dependence on outside actors. Fourth, if FSAs do dissipate towards a partner in an outsourcing relationship, they must be rejuvenated and strengthened as quickly as possible.[6] Hamel *et al.* note that, while ending up with a winner and a loser in an alliance is a common scenario, it is nonetheless possible for both MNEs to benefit from working together. The key condition here is each MNE's willingness and ability to learn from its partner, so as to allow new capability development, while avoiding excessive transfer and diffusion of its own proprietary knowledge. Moreover, the new knowledge obtained from the external partners must be effectively disseminated internally: "Knowledge acquired from a competitor-partner is only valuable after it is diffused through the organization."[7]

In order for both MNEs to benefit from the alliance, each must share some but not all of its knowledge and skills. Each partner must acquire new knowledge and skills and foster new FSAs without transferring its proprietary strengths:

> The challenge is to share enough skills to create advantage vis-à-vis companies outside the alliance while preventing a wholesale transfer of core skills to the partner. This is a very thin line to walk. Companies must carefully select what skills and technologies they pass to their partners. They must develop safeguards against unintended, informal transfers of information. The goal is to limit the transparency of their operations.[8]

The nature of the FSAs contributed by an MNE to an international alliance affects how easily these FSAs will diffuse to a partner. One important variable here is called 'mobility'. Mobility refers to the ease of moving the complete physical instructions of how to duplicate an FSA. For example, if FSAs in the realm of technical knowledge can be represented in their entirety in easily understandable technical drawings and manuals, these FSAs are highly mobile. The more mobile the FSA, the more easily it may diffuse. A second relevant variable is called 'embeddedness'. An FSA is embedded if it cannot easily be shared through communication with actors outside the firm, without problems of interpretation or absorption across cultures. For example, stand-alone knowledge is usually less embedded than integrated skills or processes. The more embedded the FSA, the less easily it may diffuse.

Hamel *et al.* advise companies to take steps to limit the easy replicability and unintended diffusion of FSAs to their alliance partners. Such steps might include limiting the formal scope of the alliance to a well-defined learning area. They might also include carefully considering where the alliance should be physically located, with a preference for a location away from the MNE headquarters, so as to avoid providing the alliance partner with a window on all the MNE's key FSAs (e.g., critical technologies), even those unrelated to the alliance's scope of activity.

Still another step may entail establishing incremental, performance-related checkpoints, whereby specific knowledge bundles valuable to alliance functioning are shared only within the alliance context, and only when the alliance has achieved some preset performance benchmarks.

A last step consists of empowering company 'gatekeepers' to control and moderate informal information transfers at lower operational levels to the partner. Here, easy access to key people and facilities must be prohibited, employee discipline and loyalty must be stimulated and cultural differences that affect information flows must be carefully assessed. For example, as regards the last point on cultural differences, Western engineers often like to share information on their technical achievements, driven by their enthusiasm and professional pride. Their Japanese counterparts, on the other hand, are generally more likely to keep their company's proprietary knowledge confidential.

Context and complementary perspectives

Hamel *et al.* published their *HBR* article in 1989, one year before Prahalad and Hamel's classic *HBR* piece 'The core competence of the corporation', which we discussed in Chapter 2. The context for these two articles is similar in terms of the level of attention devoted in the academic literature at that time to the competitive strengths of Japanese (and more generally Asian) manufacturers, relative to US and European MNEs. As in the other *HBR* article, many of the examples cited in the article on strategic alliances were drawn from manufacturing industries such as automobiles, semiconductors, computers and electronics, where strong international competition prevails, and where the potential of reaping cost efficiencies through incremental innovation, as well as scale and scope economies, is compelling. In these industries, however, it is difficult to access the required volume and span of the diverse resources needed to achieve such benefits. Therefore, risk mitigation is critical. Here, strategic alliances may provide a way rapidly and efficiently to access the required resources, as compared to the other governance alternatives available to MNEs, such as internal development of the relevant FSAs or purchase of the required knowledge through market-based contracts.

During the twenty-five years since this article was written, the trend towards collaborative partnerships among large, international firms vis-à-vis other governance alternatives has persisted, motivated by the same three factors identified by Hamel *et al.* First, alliances allow partners to share high R&D costs and the risks thereof. Second, alliances allow each partner to benefit from complementarities in scarce talent and related capabilities brought to the table by the other partner. Third, with shortened time frames to bring new products to the market, alliances may also reduce the risk of being too late to develop the capabilities to deliver products and services valued by the output market.

At the same time, concerns about unintended knowledge dissipation as a result of alliances have become even more severe over the past twenty-five years, given the proliferation of Internet and cellular communication technologies, which make information easier to transport and disseminate (i.e., more mobile).

Erin Anderson and **Sandy Jap** provide a first complementary perspective to Hamel *et al.*'s piece on strategic alliances. Anderson and Jap's *SMR* article addresses the so-called 'dark side' of alliances: dependence, exploitation and abuse.[9]

Recall that Hamel *et al.*'s *HBR* piece explicitly noted that a superficially harmonious relationship may not be a good indicator for alliance success, as surface harmony may hide deep dysfunction such as one partner becoming overly dependent on the other, or dissipating too much proprietary knowledge to its alliance partner.

Anderson and Jap take this perspective a step further. On the basis of a number of large-scale research studies, they argue that the best relationships on the surface – i.e., the most stable and long-lasting ones, with excellent personal ties among alliance partner managers – are often the *most* vulnerable to problems of bounded reliability. If one partner engages in continuous, strong alliance-specific investments, whereas the other does not, then the incentive for the latter partner to start abusing the relationship grows stronger. This observation is similar to the one made in Chapter 11, which discussed the problem of manufacturers becoming too dependent upon mega-distributors. In that case, once the dependency relationship is established, mega-distributors increasingly squeeze the manufacturer to reduce prices, even when the manufacturer cannot realistically make the necessary productivity improvements. Anderson and Jap's perspective provides a useful antidote to the somewhat naïve view, often promulgated in business schools, that longer-term relationships usually lead to trust and therefore better alliance performance through improved knowledge transfer and joint FSA development processes. The reality may be quite the opposite: high levels of trust make a relationship more vulnerable to bounded reliability, whether in the form of benevolent preference reversal or opportunism, unless safeguards are introduced to prevent it.

Anderson and Jap advocate the use of six types of safeguards to avoid the dark side of close relationships from creeping into alliance functioning:[10]

1. Regular re-evaluation of the alliance relationship. One particularly effective way to re-evaluate the relationship is to bring in new evaluators. The rotation of employees and managers, similar to the rotation observed in many countries' diplomatic services, may contribute greatly to avoiding – and mitigating the effects of – bounded reliability problems. This is because bounded reliability can be a problem not only on the partner's side (e.g., the partner purposely overbilling for contributions to the alliance), but also inside the firm itself (e.g., a manager misguidedly trusting the partner's cost estimates for contributions

to the alliance based on a harmonious relationship with an associate in the partner firm).

2. Continued focus on profitability rather than volume. Especially in supply chain relationships, senior managers often attach great importance to the absolute and relative size of their relationship with particular suppliers and distributors. However, relationship size can be a poor indicator of the relationship's contribution to profitability, especially when it is abused by the partner (for example, when the promise of loyalty by a customer or distributor is accompanied by unreasonable demands for volume discounts, thereby negatively affecting the firm's profitability).

3. Continued attention to alternatives ('back-ups'). By focusing on realistic alternatives (and even moderately investing in such alternatives), which can be tapped into if the relationship sours, managers can avoid becoming too dependent on one specific alliance partner, thereby reducing the possibility of sustained abuse by that partner. This is a form of risk minimization, equivalent to assessing the possible loss that could occur in case the alliance fails to perform, and then making sure such potential losses are minimized by ensuring access to non-alliance alternatives.

4. Swapping hostages. This means that both partners should invest resources that cannot easily be redeployed outside of the alliance without significant loss of value. Irreversible, alliance-specific investments create an incentive for each partner to make the alliance a success. However, such investments must be made by both partners. If only one partner provides a 'hostage', and the other does not, then the failure of the alliance would have less serious economic consequences for the latter partner. This gives the latter partner undue leverage, which can cause bounded reliability problems. In the ideal case, the hostage provided by each firm constitutes a credible safeguard for the other.

5. Setting and reassessing common goals. Strategic alliances typically face substantial uncertainty about the future, sometimes more so than when a firm expands alone, because the value of the resources contributed by the partner is difficult to estimate in advance. This value will depend to a large extent on the firm's evolving ability to recombine the partner's resources with those already present in the firm itself. Setting clear goals and re-evaluating these goals based on actual alliance performance is critical, especially after the dust has settled over the initial unrealistic expectations regarding the economic potential of resource recombination within the scope of the alliance.

6. Avoiding vicious cycles of suspicion and the resulting buildup of bounded reliability. If one firm in the alliance suspects that its partner will not make good on its promises and systematically interprets its partner's moves as attempts to abuse the partnership, or as signs that the partner is no longer committed to the alliance, this may lead to the alliance's breakdown. A breakdown is especially likely if such suspicion leads to signals that the alliance is not functioning

properly and if the partner reacts negatively to such signals (e.g., new company policies to withhold technical information from the alliance upsets the alliance partner, who then retaliates by introducing a similar policy). Transparency of all available information (especially in the realm of cost accounting) and open communication, together with the first five guidelines above, are critical to avoiding such vicious cycles of suspicion.

Although Anderson and Jap do not focus specifically on international alliances, their study of the dark side of alliances is particularly useful in the international context, especially in the context of expansion to high-distance countries (e.g., alliances among North American and Asian MNEs), for three reasons. First, the goals of the alliance partners, and the time frame adopted by managers from high-distance countries, are likely to differ more than in the case of a single-country partnership, because of greater cultural, economic, institutional and spatial differences than would be found within a single nation. Hence, extra attention must be devoted to joint goal setting and the regular reassessment thereof, so as to bridge the additional bounded rationality problems (especially information processing issues). Second, higher distance is likely to be a driver of suspicion, especially when alliance performance problems occur that are (erroneously) attributed to the alliance partner's different country culture (as in "firms from country X cannot be trusted to respect intellectual property rights"). Third, higher distance between partners may also have important effects in the realm of resource combination. The impact of various distance components may be underestimated when transferring and melding FSAs from different companies, especially when a large tacit component is involved, as well as routines that are affected by cultural, institutional and economic norms prevailing in the different countries. When the alliance is between high-distance countries, the firms need to make special efforts to recognize such potential problems beforehand, and to continuously monitor these areas so as to identify any problems early.

Prashant Kale and ***Jaideep Anand*** provide a second complementary perspective to the Hamel *et al.* piece. Building upon Hamel *et al.*'s insights, Kale and Anand describe in their *CMR* article the problems associated with establishing alliances, typically in the form of joint ventures set up for market-seeking purposes in emerging economies such as India.[11]

Kale and Anand observe that such joint ventures are often set up when they are the foreign MNE's only penetration option, given a restrictive regulatory regime preventing wholly owned operations. Deploying and exploiting the MNE's FSAs then requires the use of a local partner, whose main substantive contribution may result from FSAs in government relations (especially if the local venture partner is state-owned) and from other location-bound FSAs allowing national responsiveness (e.g., reputational resources). If the MNE is trying to learn from a local partner without giving away too many of its own FSAs, building upon the advice of Hamel *et al.*, which kind of partner should the MNE select? Kale and Anand suggest that, in the short term, the MNE can learn more from a privately owned local partner than from a state-owned partner, because with a state-owned partner, the MNE's learning efforts will be diverted by its overriding need to maintain a harmonious relationship simply to secure continued access to the local market. Because of its government connections, a state-owned partner will typically have more leverage in this area than a privately owned partner. In the long term, however, this state-owned partner may still be the better option, because an ambitious, privately owned partner may face stronger incentives to enter into a competitive learning race with the MNE, and to try to absorb the MNE's proprietary knowledge in order to upgrade its own FSA bundles. Senior managers must thus balance these short- and long-term concerns when choosing alliance partners.

In 1991, when the rigid regulatory system restricting FDI in India was liberalized, Kale and Anand observed five important changes in a majority of the joint ventures, based on their study of 69 cases in India, in a variety of manufacturing industries, including chemicals, pharmaceuticals, engineering, information technology and consumer goods:[12] stronger MNE involvement in strategy setting, an increased MNE equity stake (which had previously been restricted), greater MNE control over joint venture operations, an increase in MNE board representation and the replacement of the local CEO by an expatriate.

Importantly, with ongoing liberalization, the incentive to form alliances with a local Indian partner in many cases disappeared, except in special cases of strong resource complementarity. In those cases where there remained an incentive to form an alliance, Kale and Anand found that the MNEs usually appeared much better equipped to win the 'learning race' against the local partner. The reasons for this better learning performance included three key elements: first, a systematically stronger MNE intent to learn from the partner; second, the better preparedness of the MNE to identify valuable learning opportunities on the basis of prior experiences with local partners elsewhere; and third, the existence of learning routines underlying the MNE's learning capability. Such routines included, *inter alia*: (1) explicitly assigning specific individuals or units to manage the learning function within the alliance, e.g., through formal working teams with the partner firm's managers and employees; (2) rotating managers and employees between the MNE and the joint venture, so as to facilitate knowledge flows into the MNE network; and (3) fostering systematic interactions between alliance personnel and personnel in the MNE parent and other MNE affiliates to diffuse knowledge gained in the joint venture.

Kale and Anand make the important observation that this learning asymmetry between the MNE and its local partner creates an inherent instability in the joint venture. Once the MNE learns what it needs to learn, this often eliminates the very resource complementarity that may have existed at the outset. Thus, there will be a growing incentive to transform the joint venture into a wholly owned subsidiary, especially for MNEs that operate as *international projectors* or *international coordinators*. Such firms may want to improve operational efficiency by changing the role of their affiliates and rationalizing international operations. Such changes may be more difficult to achieve when a joint venture partner is involved, namely when reassigning roles leads to perceived losses of activity bundles previously performed by the joint venture. There may also be discrepancies in the alliance partners' interests, e.g., when the MNE engages in transfer pricing to maximize overall profitability, or when it attempts to transfer internal best practices across borders.

The instability of the joint venture may thus lead to its termination, possibly through the forced exit of the local partner. This dynamic – and the MNE's strong bargaining position – is the opposite of the one observed in the conventional international business literature, whereby the MNE faces the problem of 'obsolescing bargaining', meaning a rapid decline of its bargaining power once it has engaged in irreversible investments (in this case, investments that are location-specific and cannot be redeployed elsewhere without a large loss in value). This has been typical in the past for MNE investments in resource-based industries (e.g., mining and petroleum), whereby governments of developing countries (rather than local companies themselves) often reneged on agreements concluded with the MNE once the latter had engaged in large, irreversible investments. However, in many contemporary cases, much of the MNE's value added may reside in internationally transferable, intangible FSAs, which can easily be redeployed across borders without loss of productive value.

MANAGEMENT INSIGHTS

The Hamel *et al. HBR* article focuses on the process by which firms align themselves with their competitors to develop jointly new FSAs, but with each firm driven by the ulterior motive to appropriate for itself the largest possible part of the benefits arising from the alliance. In this process, each partner attempts to absorb as much knowledge as possible from the other, while protecting against the diffusion of its own FSAs. As the authors point out, an MNE's strategic goal in entering an alliance must always stay focused on new FSA creation – by definition, strengths specific to the firm itself – while guarding against FSA dissipation benefiting the partner. It is a challenge to stay focused on such long-term goals, as many senior managers have an incentive to pursue short-run cost reductions through the alliance, e.g., through outsourcing activities, even if those activities have FSAs embedded in them.

Importantly, the authors observe that some FSAs by their nature are more readily transferable to alliance partners than other ones, depending upon how easily they can be transported, interpreted and absorbed across cultures. Different FSAs have different levels of mobility and embeddedness. In the examples provided, complex skills and processes such as Japanese systems of manufacturing tend to be much more embedded, and thus more difficult to absorb, than the discrete, stand-alone FSAs held by Western MNEs.

This analysis is displayed visually in Figure 12.1.

At the top (Figure 12.1A), we see two MNEs, one on each side of the conventional border line. The actual alliance is shown simply as a set of FSA bundles around the border line, because the essence of the alliance's dynamic functioning lies in the knowledge transfer processes among the MNEs involved and the alliance they have set up, irrespective of which specific international market(s) is to be served with the knowledge involved. The top firm in Figure 12.1A is the typical Asian company in Hamel *et al.*'s analysis. It is supposed to contribute routines, such as knowledge about total quality control processes, to the alliance. The bottom firm is the typical Western firm, providing stand-alone technical knowledge to the alliance. The alliance, located between the top and bottom MNEs, benefits from the knowledge provided by each partner (see the arrows in bold), and engages in recombination. Within the alliance, recombination occurs among the various types of knowledge involved, possibly taking into account location advantages of the geographic area where the alliance is physically placed. However, the bold arrow pointing up to the Asian MNE suggests

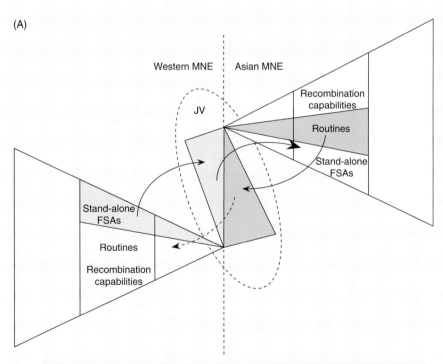

(A)

Figure 12.1
Dissipation of FSA
bundles to alliance
partners

The two thin, curved arrows pointing to the quadrilateral representing the joint venture, indicate that the Western MNE contributes stand-alone FSAs and the Asian MNE contributes routines to the JV. The thick arrow pointing right and the dotted arrow pointing left indicate that more of the JV's contribution to knowledge can be captured by the Asian MNE as compared to the Western one.

Figure 12.1 (B)
(cont.)

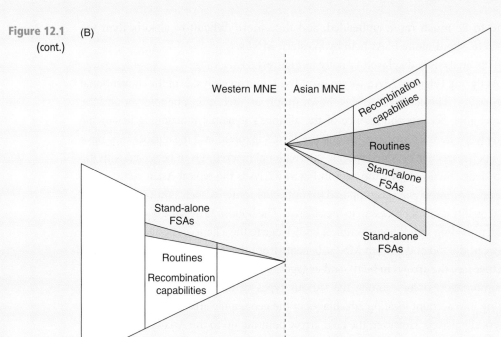

The LB and NLB FSAs of the Asian MNE have grown due to the absorption of its partner's stand-alone FSAs, while the Western MNE's stand-alone FSAs have shrunk in relative terms due to the dissipation of its knowledge base to the Asian MNE.

substantial knowledge transfer from the alliance to that company, whereas the narrower dotted line pointing downwards to the Western MNE suggests only limited knowledge transfer to that company. Once the Asian firm has absorbed all the knowledge it needs from the Western one, we can see the new situation visualized in Figure 12.1B. The Asian firm can exit from the alliance, possibly leading to the alliance's closure, having achieved its learning goals, as shown at the top of Figure 12.1B, with a vastly increased amount of location-bound and non-location-bound knowledge. In contrast, the Western firm at the bottom is now left with fewer FSA bundles, because the alliance distracted it from pursuing independent FSA development, and because part of its relevant knowledge base is now in the hands of its previous partner, a major international rival.

Given the two different kinds of FSAs contributed, should the Western MNE have rejected such an alliance in the first place? This question is difficult to answer. On the one hand, the Western firm clearly came out second-best relative to the Asian firm. On the other hand, it nonetheless was able to access the Asian firm's complementary resources for the duration of the alliance. If it had been possible to replicate easily the Asian firm's complementary resources inside the Western

MNE or to acquire them in the external market through simple contracting, there would have been no need for the MNE to engage in the international alliance. International alliances are formed when an MNE is unable to replicate the same or equivalent FSAs as those provided by a foreign alliance partner within an acceptable time frame or cost structure. Therefore, given these benefits, the alliance may have been good for the Western firm in an absolute sense as measured by profits, revenues, etc., compared to what would have happened if the alliance had not been formed. That is the appropriate standard. The answer as to whether the alliance was a good idea will depend on the specific case.

Once firms have decided to cooperate, they can choose among a range of different strategic alliance types, and the possibility of a merger or acquisition, as discussed in Chapter 13. Alliances will be preferred over mergers and acquisitions (M&As) when two conditions are satisfied. First, each firm needs only a subset of the resources/FSAs held by the partner. Second, it is difficult to dispose of the prospective partner's unuseable resources because those resources are firm-specific. Thus, the advantage of strategic alliances is to have access to precisely those resources/FSAs bundles that are really needed. In addition, strategic alliances may be preferred if the synergistic potential of the human and organizational resources is likely to be eliminated or diminished under the new identity in the case of a complete merger or takeover. Of course, greenfield investments and M&As may be legally prohibited in the first place, as a result of anti-trust policy, restrictions on foreign ownership, etc. In such cases, firms form alliances as a second-best solution.

Kale and Anand's *CMR* story line on alliances in emerging economies describes a conceptually similar challenge for the MNE. If the MNE faces a competence gap when operating internationally, and is unsuccessful in linking its FSAs with location advantages in host countries, the question arises whether this problem can be solved through cooperating with local firms that do have the resources required to establish such a link. Here, cooperation is a valid strategy, especially for customer-end activities, if the required resources cannot be acquired in the market and replicated within an acceptable time frame and cost structure. More specifically, strategic alliances can lead to rapid local embeddedness and access to social network ties in ways that are not possible by acting alone.

Alliances can help link the MNE's FSAs with location advantages abroad or other coveted resources in two ways (see Figure 12.2 and Figure 12.3). First, the alliance can facilitate access to the **location-bound FSAs** of the local partner, similar to Kale and Anand's story line described above, as shown in Figure 12.2. Cooperation lets the MNE avoid high-cost location-specific adaptation investments. Second, the alliance facilitates the combination of the MNE's non-location-bound resources and existing FSAs with the equivalent resources of the partner (who may be another MNE) to create new **non-location-bound FSAs**, for example in the realm of

Figures 12.2
Alliance in emerging
economies

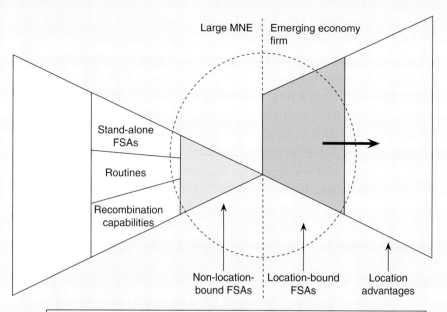

In a typical alliance in an emerging economy, represented here by a dotted circle, the foreign MNE transfers NLB FSAs to the alliance, whereas a local partner in the host country contributes LB FSAs. Together these FSA bundles deployed through the alliance allow accessing and benefiting from the coveted LAs in the host country, as indicated by the bold arrow.

Figure 12.3 (A)
Alliance in emerging
economies

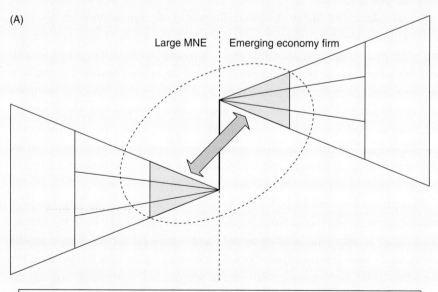

Both the foreign MNE and the emerging economy MNE contribute NLB FSAs to the alliance in the emerging economy (represented by the dotted circle) as equal partners.

Figure 12.3
(cont.)

(B)

Large MNE | Emerging economy firm

The outcome of this emerging economy alliance is that both the foreign MNE and the emerging economy MNE have been able to strengthen their NLB FSA base by learning from their partner through the alliance activity. This learning has two parts: first, the absorption of the existing knowledge of the partner (ordinarily shaded extension of each triangle); second, new knowledge creation arising from the alliance activity (light-green-coloured extension of each triangle).

technological innovation, as shown in Figure 12.3A. To the extent that strategic alliances reduce the needed resource commitments from a single MNE, they enable the MNE to obtain broader geographic coverage with the same resources.

The benefits of cooperative agreements must always be weighed against the two significant costs. First, the MNE's FSAs could be appropriated by the alliance partner, which means that the MNE must introduce sufficient safeguards against such dissipation, as explained in this chapter by Hamel *et al.*

Second, an alliance may reduce coherence within the MNE, if the MNE becomes biased towards maintaining its initial arrangements with the alliance partner at the expense of long-term profit or cost considerations. Fortunately, steps can be taken to ensure that profit goals are not subordinated to other considerations, and that strategic alliances are not maintained without effective monitoring of their value added, as explained in this chapter by Anderson and Jap.

The partners' objectives have important implications for the alliance's stability. If each partner simply aims to extract resources from the other partner, alliances result in a learning race, as described above. The partner who first acquires the desired resources may dissolve the alliance even if the other partner has not completed its learning. If, however, the main purpose of the alliance is to create value by combining the resources of both firms, the resulting synergies can take the form of new FSAs that can be exploited globally but are not necessarily amenable to being captured fully by individual alliance members (e.g., if the FSAs require the sustained infusion of resources from each partner).

This analysis suggests that we introduce the concept of alliance-specific advantages (ASAs), which cannot be classified using the old distinction between endogenous FSAs (originating inside the firm) and exogenous location advantages (originating outside the firm). ASAs have international exploitation potential, but are embedded in alliances and cannot be simply transferred to the individual partner firms.

ASAs are thus somewhat similar to subsidiary-specific advantages (SSAs), which are advantages that have international exploitation potential, but are embedded in subsidiaries and cannot be simply transferred to the rest of the MNE network. (As Bartlett and Ghoshal noted in Chapter 5, if a particular subsidiary has this kind of special expertise, it is sometimes wisest to let that subsidiary expand beyond its initial, assigned market to exploit its advantages internationally.) In contrast to SSAs, conventional FSAs are either non-location-bound FSAs (easily transferable and deployable across borders in foreign affiliates, and providing benefits of global exploitation, typically through scope economies) or location-bound FSAs (difficult to transfer to other affiliates across geographic space, but providing benefits of national responsiveness).

Like SSAs, ASAs can be exploited globally, e.g., through world product mandates given to the alliance, but they cannot be simply diffused within the partner firms because of alliance-specific isolating mechanisms. Isolating mechanisms or mobility barriers exist, *inter alia*, because knowledge is tacit (difficult to codify), context-specific (each individual alliance partner's contribution may actually be locally embedded and these individual contributions may depend on the alliance's own technological and organizational trajectories), and dispersed across several individuals within the alliance (embedded in teams with members belonging to the different partner companies).

We now see that the concept of a 'transferable' advantage is more complicated than we thought. To this point, it has meant that the advantage can be transferred to another **economic actor** in another **location**. We now see that we must treat these two elements separately. While conventional transferable FSAs are transferable to other economic actors in other locations, ASAs and SSAs are transferable to other locations, but are not transferable to other economic actors.

ASAs enhance an alliance's stability. With an ASA, the advantage depends upon the synergies gained by combining, in an evolutionary process, the partners' resources. These advantages would be lost to the individual firms if they left the alliance or if the alliance were dissolved. As ASAs grow stronger, the partner companies have greater incentives to stay in the alliance.

Turning to our framework of FSA development patterns, alliance formation takes various forms, consistent with a number of patterns from our framework.

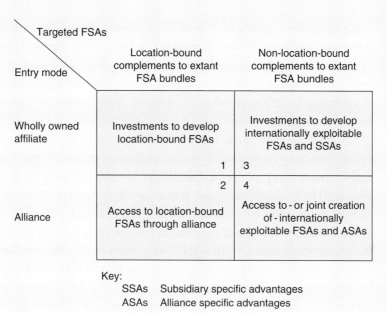

Figure 12.4
MNE foreign market penetration via wholly owned affiliates versus alliances

The difference between alliance formation as an entry mode to penetrate foreign markets and going in alone is shown in Figure 12.4.

Quadrants 2 and 4 are the quadrants relevant to alliance formation. Quadrant 2 reflects the main case described in Kale and Anand's *CMR* article, whereby an MNE partners with a local firm in an emerging economy, largely driven by government restrictions on entry-mode choice and other regulations of MNE activities. However, from a dynamic perspective, the MNE may soon learn all that is required to operate independently in the foreign market. Therefore, if FDI is liberalized, the MNE may shift its longer-run entry mode to quadrant 1, thus making the alliance only an intermediate market penetration option.

Quadrant 4 reflects the content of Hamel *et al.*'s *HBR* article, whereby two firms may engage in a learning race, with one of them coming out as the winner and having little incentive to continue with the alliance. However, if ASAs have been created, e.g., within multi-partner global airline alliances such as Oneworld and Star Alliance, partners in the alliance cannot simply exit from the alliance and take their learning with them, as several sources of competitive advantage are embedded in the alliance itself. For example, in the case of the global airline alliances, the MNEs involved share brand names, operational bases, computer reservation systems, and external relationships across markets. These ASAs resulting from the pooling and recombination of the FSAs of the individual companies simply cannot be replicated by individual companies that have left an alliance.

Hamel *et al.*'s prescription to learn more from your partner than your partner learns from you has three major limitations. First, senior managers who pay too much attention to that goal may overlook the important goal of creating ASAs. ASAs are simply not the sort of things that either partner can learn from the other.

Second, attempts to win such a learning race may cause dysfunctionalities: if each partner attempts to learn as much as possible through the alliance, while contributing as little as possible, the intent to limit knowledge sharing may itself be instrumental to a vicious cycle of ever-increasing bounded reliability problems.

For example, individuals and subunits may engage in resource commitments to the alliance and then be told by dedicated gatekeepers that they are out of line, and that what was promised to the alliance would jeopardize the firm's competitiveness. The problem for gatekeepers assigned to regulate knowledge flows is to identify the fine line between information that is critical to the alliance's success and information that is not required to achieve such success, but simply makes the partner/rival stronger. An aggressive gatekeeper may thereby hinder valuable recombination of resources coming from the two partners and thus reduce the learning capability of the alliance itself, ultimately reducing its value to both partners. Gatekeepers who limit knowledge transfer without knowing all the relevant information (e.g., facing bounded rationality problems caused by geographical distance from the alliance activity centre) may trigger a vicious cycle of suspicion, as described in Anderson and Jap's *SMR* article. This vicious cycle can then produce bounded reliability problems (including opportunistic behaviour), which would not otherwise have occurred.

A third and related limitation of Hamel *et al.*'s *HBR* article is that it insufficiently addresses the impact of culture on alliance dynamics. Their article observes, e.g., that Japanese firms often appear to be the winners in international alliances, at the expense of their Western partners. However, it is not entirely clear what role culture plays in this superior learning performance, nor how cultural differences leading to learning performance differentials should be addressed.

One simplistic interpretation could be that MNEs from some cultures are more inclined to engage in opportunistic behaviour than those of other cultures, thus implying that the latter should avoid engaging in alliance formation with the former, irrespective of the economic and technical complementarity of FSAs. A second, equally simplistic interpretation is that some cultures are simply not conducive to competent cooperative behaviour in business, and should for that reason try to abstain from alliance formation. A third, more sophisticated view of the impact of culture is that some countries may have developed, at the macro-level, a superior ability to successfully manage alliances, because of a variety of historical events, such as a multi-decade long tradition of absorbing and adopting foreign knowledge bundles (e.g., through licensing, as the Japanese did after World War II).

Finally, the question arises whether country-level culture is necessarily relevant to alliance success or failure, as compared to the corporate cultures of the respective firms engaged in alliance formation. Here, a corporate culture suggesting that alliance functioning is little more than a learning race and advocating the protection of proprietary knowledge against diffusion to alliance partners, especially those of a high-distance culture, may jeopardize alliance success. This is especially the case if the alliance is established in a context whereby opportunistic behaviour (cheating) by the partner is expected: culturally determined, false attributions of cheating may lead to genuine attempts to cheat, as the result of a vicious cycle of suspicion build-up.

Five management takeaways

1. Remember the four key principles of how to establish successful international partnerships and how to prevent excessive dependency on an alliance partner.
2. Limit the unintended diffusion of FSAs by assessing their 'mobility' and 'embeddedness'.
3. Examine whether sufficient safeguards have been established in your alliance agreements.
4. Evaluate your learning performance in alliances.
5. Consider the impact of your own strategic decisions on the quality of your relationship with your alliance partners.

Case 12.1 Danone's affair in China

CASE

From 2007 to 2009, Danone, the French multinational food company, was in a fierce battle with China-based Wahaha Group (the largest beverage producer in China) to win control of their joint ventures (JVs) in China. The fight is reported to have started in 2005 when Danone uncovered some unusual financial figures at the JVs, but this did not become known to the public until 2007, when Danone and Wahaha Group failed to resolve their disputes on the selling price of Wahaha-related non-joint ventures (non-JVs).

The quarrel between Danone and Wahaha Group escalated. It involved disputes on brands, as well as on perceived unequal commitments to the JVs. Lawsuits were launched, both in China and internationally. How did cooperation turn into a large-scale battle? How did the story unfold?

Danone and its international expansion

Originally named Boussois-Souchon-Neuvesel (BSN), Danone was founded in 1966 when two glass companies, the Souchon-Neuvesel glassworks and Glaces de Boussois, merged to compete in the expanding Common Market. The setback in the glass industry prompted BSN to switch its focus to its downstream business, namely the beverages industry. In 1969 and 1970, BSN acquired Evian, Kronenbourg and the European Breweries Company, becoming the leading manufacturer of beer, mineral waters and baby food in France in 1970. In 1973, BSN merged with Gervais DANONE, creating the largest French food group. In the mid and late 1970s, BSN Gervais DANONE gradually retreated from the lagging glass sector, focusing solely on food after the group divested Boussois in 1981.

After establishing its leadership position in France in the 1970s, BSN Gervais DANONE started to expand in the European market in the 1980s, through a series of acquisitions, joint ventures and partnerships, including the cross-shareholding arrangement with the Agnelli empire in Italy in 1987, the alliance with the Fossati family in Italy in 1989, the acquisition of Generale Biscuit in 1986 and the takeover of Nabisco's European subsidiaries in 1989. By 1989, Danone had become the third largest food group in Europe, behind only Nestlé and Unilever. It was very well established in southern Europe, England and Germany.

During its European expansion, especially in Italy and Spain, Danone used a low-cost, low-risk and relatively rapid market entry approach. Danone established relationships with powerful local businesses by acquiring minority shareholdings, thereby creating beachhead positions for its further expansion into the host country. For example, the alliance with the Agnelli family in Italy helped Danone to acquire Galbani (Italy's number one fresh cheese producer) and Agnesi (a pasta producer), and to start a cooperative relationship with Peroni (a brewer).

In the late 1980s and early 1990s, BSN Gervais DANONE expanded into formerly communist Eastern Europe. Initially, it exported goods from Western Europe, but it soon manufactured the same goods in these host countries by either cooperating with or taking control of local firms such as cookie producers Cokoladovny in the Czech Republic and Bolshevik in Russia.

To assess the international potential of its brands and the appropriate locations for its marketing expatriates, BSN Gervais DANONE set up a specialized export division in 1993. Its partnerships and buyouts helped it expand quickly in emerging markets such as Asia, Latin America and South Africa. In June 1994, it changed its name to Groupe DANONE. Since 1998 Danone has sped up its international expansion, with around 40 acquisitions in Central Europe, Asia, Africa, Latin America and the Middle East. Danone currently has four divisions: Fresh Dairy Products, Medical and Nutrition, Baby Nutrition and Waters. It employs 100,995 people in more than 120 countries and is the world leader in fresh dairy products and medical nutrition.[13]

Danone in China

Danone entered China in 1987 by founding Danone Yogurt Company in Canton. Not knowing much about the peculiarities of the Chinese market, Danone brought almost identical French products to the Chinese market, only to find out that just a few consumers had refrigerators to store fresh dairy products, Danone's products were too expensive for the average Chinese consumer and many Chinese consumers were lactose intolerant.

This initial setback with dairy products drove Danone to copy in China the alliance strategy used with great success to expand into Italy and Spain in the 1980s. Danone decided to capitalize successful local businesses rather than build its own businesses from scratch, resulting in a strong focus on joint ventures and acquisitions. Unlike most multinationals, Danone gave these acquired local businesses a great deal of autonomy. The joint ventures and acquired firms continued to sell their products under their own brands. Until late 2002, 80 per cent of Danone's sales in China were under local brands. Furthermore, Danone let the former executives run the businesses and didn't get involved much in daily operations. In fact, Danone functioned more like a capital investor, linking its joint ventures through capital investment rather than joint products.

This expansion strategy in China worked very well. In 2001, Danone had become one of the largest food concerns in China, with US $1.2 billion in sales, more than 50 plants and around 25,000 employees.[14] Accounting for 9 per cent of Danone's international sales in 2003, China became Danone's third largest market, tied with the US after France and Spain. More importantly, not only did sales grow strongly, but operating profit margins were also much higher than the global average of 12.2 per cent.[15]

Danone and Wahaha appeared to have a perfect marriage

The history of the Hangzhou Wahaha Group Co., Ltd can be traced back to the Hangzhou Shangcheng District School-Run Enterprise Sales Department, founded by Qinghou Zong in 1987. Its early success selling nutritional drinks to students won the favour of the Hangzhou city government, whose support paved the way for the firm to acquire the Hangzhou Canned Food Product Co. in 1991. The Hangzhou Wahaha Group Co. was established in 1991, with 'Wahaha' referring to the sound of a baby laughing. In 1994, the Wahaha Group acquired three other companies in the province of Sichuan.

In the mid 1990s, the Wahaha Group did very well in the Chinese market, with around 2,000 employees, RMB 1 billion in sales (around US $200 million), and RMB 200 million (around US $40 million) in profits. However, it was afraid that it would soon lose its competitiveness in an era when foreign multinationals were entering China, so it was eager to expand its scale and market share in China. Unfortunately, the Wahaha Group lacked the necessary financial capital to expand. Then Danone came into the picture through the introduction of the Hong Kong-based Peregrine Group.

Both Wahaha and Danone expected to gain something from the cooperation. Wahaha needed cash, and it also hoped to adopt new technology and managerial techniques from Danone. Meanwhile, joint ventures with a strong local firm in a fast-growing emerging market were a perfect opportunity for Danone, especially considering Danone's disastrous 1987 solo efforts in China. Moreover, Danone "lacked the management depth and size to grow quickly".[16]

The cooperation between Danone and Wahaha started in 1996. Danone and Peregrine Group set up a Singapore-based firm called Jinja. Jinja and the Wahaha Group then set up five JVs in 1996, with Wahaha controlling 49 per cent of the shares, Danone 41 per cent and Peregrine 10 per cent.[17] Jinja invested US $45 million in the JVs, while the Wahaha Group gave the JVs the assets from five of its subsidiaries. All three parties agreed to let the Wahaha Group take full control of the everyday operations of the JVs.

Even after Danone took the position of majority shareholder in 1998 (when Peregrine Group sold its shares in Jinja because of Peregrine's financial problems during the Asian crisis), Danone did not have a single executive in the joint ventures and Zong ran the joint ventures with a high degree of autonomy.

The cooperation appeared to work well. The new cash from Jinja enabled Wahaha to invest in both marketing and advanced production lines. In 2003, Wahaha had 15.6 per cent of China's total beverage production, and its income reached US $1.24 billion. Since 1997, Wahaha had been China's number one domestic, non-alcoholic beverage producer in both production volume and sales revenue. With annual sales of around US $1.35 billion, the JVs accounted for 75 per cent of Danone's sales in China and about 3 per cent of its total global sales.[18] By 2007, 39 JVs between the Wahaha Group and Danone had been established.

However, the JV agreements included several clauses that became the seeds of future disputes between Danone and Wahaha:

1. Only 5 out of 10 Wahaha subsidiaries became real JVs, with the other ones (non-integrated companies) still using Wahaha brands.
2. Wahaha agreed to transfer Wahaha brands to the JVs, but the modalities of the transfer were neither precise nor transparent.
3. Danone agreed to a vague non-compete clause with the joint ventures.

Things become ugly

The disputes between Danone and Wahaha became known to the public on 3 April 2007, when Zong told Chinese reporters that Danone wanted to take over the RMB 5.6 billion assets of the non-JVs for only RMB 4 billion. These non-JVs had been established by the Wahaha Group and had not been integrated into the JV system.

Other long-time conflicts between Wahaha and Danone were also exposed, dating back to the very beginning of the JVs. Zong further accused Danone of designing a trap in the original JV agreement to win control of both the Wahaha brands and the JVs. On 5 April, Emmanuel Faber, President of Danone Asia-Pacific, said that Danone strictly followed the agreements/contracts between Danone and Wahaha. He also urged Zong to continue with the negotiations related to transferring the non-JVs to Danone.

On 7 April, a JV sued the three of its directors appointed by Danone, arguing that these three directors also functioned as directors of the JV's rival companies in China.[19] On 11 April, the Chinese Ministry of Commerce asserted it would remain neutral and not get involved in the disputes, though Wahaha and Danone were later reported to have provided the Ministry with related materials to explain their stand in early July.

The negotiations on the use of Wahaha brands and the takeover conditions did not lead to a positive outcome. On 9 April, Zong stated that, if necessary, he was prepared to establish another brand to replace Wahaha brands. Danone hinted that it might pursue litigation. On 11 April,

Emmanuel Faber stated at a press conference that Danone had notified Zong that the JVs would sue the non-JVs for using Wahaha brand names within 30 days if Zong did not take measures against the illegal use of Wahaha brands by the non-JVs.

On 9 May, Danone filed an arbitration request at the arbitration institute of the Stockholm court of commerce. On 4 June, Danone filed a complaint in the Superior Court for the County of Los Angeles, USA, against two companies and two individuals (US citizens or US green card holders) related to the non-JVs, alleging that these non-JVs illegally used Wahaha brands and marketed products similar to those of the JVs. The two companies controlled some of the non-JVs; and the two individuals, reported later to be Zong's wife and Zong's daughter, were major shareholders of the two companies. On 7 June, Zong resigned from his position as Chairman of the Wahaha joint ventures, accusing Danone of hurting his family and hiring surveillance companies to trace him illegally. Zong remained Chairman of Wahaha Group, and Emmanuel Faber, previously Vice Chairman, became the interim Chairman of the Wahaha joint venture companies.

However, Emmanuel Faber found it hard to regain control of the JVs. First, the board meetings were wracked with divisions and disagreements. Second, Wahaha's employees and distributors showed strong support for Zong, even asking Emmanuel Faber to pull out of the JVs. Some distributors refused to sell Wahaha brand products anymore and, as a result, some factories in the JVs had to cut production. As the same time, the Wahaha Group started to sell its products under two new brands.

What happened: Wahaha's view

The Wahaha Group argued that it was the sole owner of Wahaha brands, that both the Wahaha Group and the JVs had equal rights to use Wahaha brands, that the non-JVs were established because Danone was not interested in the JVs' expansion in China and that Danone violated the JV agreement by investing in Wahaha's competitors in China.

Brands

The Wahaha Group filed two requests to transfer Wahaha brands to the JVs at the National Brand Bureau of China in April 1996 and September 1997, but the requests were rejected by the Bureau in order to prevent the loss of national brands. Knowing the difficulty of transferring the brands to the JVs, the Wahaha Group and Danone signed two contracts, a simplified version filed with the National Brand Bureau with the objective of bypassing administrative hurdles, and a complete version determining the rights of Danone and Wahaha. The simplified version did not limit the JVs' use of Wahaha brands, while the complete version allowed the JVs to legally use Wahaha brands only for a period of 50 years. Revisions of the complete version in 1999 and 2005 again specified that the Wahaha Group was the owner of Wahaha brands.

The Wahaha Group argued that the complete version of the contract should be invalidated because the period of 50 years for the JVs to use the Wahaha brand names did not respect the Chinese brand laws. Danone had not paid the Wahaha Group in the form of either brand transfer fees or brand usage fees. From the perspective of the Wahaha Group, therefore, both the JVs and the Wahaha Group had rights to use Wahaha brands.

On 8 July 2007, Zong admitted that the Wahaha Group and Danone had not been entirely forward with the National Brand Bureau by designing both a simplified contract and a complete contract.[20]

The lack of commitment from Danone

From Zong's perspective, the Wahaha Group had not received any technological or managerial expertise from Danone. Moreover, because of Danone's lack of understanding of the Chinese market at the early stage of the cooperation Danone had even created barriers when Wahaha tried to expand the JVs' business, such as when Wahaha tried to launch Feichang Kele (translated as 'Future Cola'), tried to expand their production of bottled water and tried to invest in the western regions of China. When such businesses succeeded and created much cash flow for the JVs, Danone started to let Zong and his team run the business in their own ways.

Interestingly, in late 2000, Danone took control of Robust Group, Wahaha's largest competitor in China. Afterwards, Danone showed little interest in Wahaha's request for further expansion. Considering that Danone had shares in several of Wahaha's major competitors, the Wahaha Group reasoned that it should not expect Danone to provide more resources for investment. This is why the Wahaha Group set up many of the non-JVs.

Non-JVs

Wahaha argued that some of the non-JVs were already in existence at the very beginning of the cooperation with Danone. When Zong realized that Danone was not interested in further investment in the JVs, Zong decided to expand the non-JVs on his own. Zong argued that Danone was fully aware of the non-JVs, as annual audited reports of the JVs reported the connections between the JVs and the non-JVs.

Wahaha felt that Danone suddenly wanted to purchase the non-JVs simply because they appeared to be very profitable.

What happened: Danone's view

Danone disagreed with the Wahaha Group's view on both the ownership of the Wahaha brands and the legal status of the non-JVs. Moreover, according to Danone there was no formal non-compete clause at all in the JV agreement that would prevent Danone from investing in any other company in China.

Brands

Danone emphasized the actual content of the agreements/contracts. According to Danone, the initial JV agreement, the brand transfer contract and the two brand usage contracts all confirmed that the Wahaha Group had transferred the usage rights of Wahaha brands to the JVs and that

Danone had paid usage fees to the Wahaha Group. Thus, the JVs were the sole owner of the Wahaha brands and the Wahaha Group did not have the rights to use Wahaha brands in another business context such as the non-JVs.

Danone suspected that the Wahaha Group had not filed any request to transfer Wahaha brands through the National Brand Bureau at all.[21] Moreover, as of 2001, the Wahaha Group had illegally permitted 87 companies to use Wahaha brands.[22] In 2005, Danone itself allowed 27 non-JVs to use Wahaha brands,[23] but Danone stressed that it did not know that these non-JVs would compete with the JVs.

Commitment from Danone

Danone rejected the Wahaha Group's allegation that Danone had not contributed to the JVs in the prior 11 years. Emmanuel Faber also explained that Danone chose not to increase its investments in the JVs simply because Danone had uncovered the existence of the non-JVs competing with the JVs.[24] Moreover, Danone did send marketing and R&D personnel to the JVs, but they were kicked out by Zong.[25]

Finally, Danone felt that the agreements/contracts with Wahaha Group did not contain clauses preventing Danone from investing in other companies in China, even if these companies competed directly with the Wahaha Group.

Non-JVs

Danone discovered the allegedly illegal, Wahaha-related non-JVs in 2005, when these companies expanded aggressively and manufactured a growing share of the JVs' products. Upon investigation, Danone discovered that Zong and his family members had started to operate these parallel companies around 2003.

It appeared that around 60 Wahaha-related non-JVs had illegally manufactured and sold products similar to those of the JVs through the JVs' distributors and suppliers. In 2006 and 2007, the business of the non-JVs expanded significantly. In late 2006, the Wahaha Group set up a separate sales/marketing company. Distributors were asked by the Wahaha Group to pay the sales/marketing company separately, though the non-JVs had until then used the JVs' sales channel and even received cash through JVs' banking accounts from the distributors. For Danone, the non-JVs had created a totally independent and complete business system and the JVs were in danger of losing a substantial portion of their business.[26]

This is why Danone negotiated with Zong to take control of the non-JVs in 2006. In late 2006, Zong actually agreed to sell a majority share in the non-JVs to Danone and to integrate the non-JVs into the JVs system, but he finally pulled out of the deal in 2007.[27]

What happened: Commentators' view

Most commentators in China agreed that the JVs were the owners, or at least the legal users, of the Wahaha brands, according to the agreements/contracts between Danone and the Wahaha

Group. The Wahaha-related non-JVs were therefore viewed to have used Wahaha brands illegally. However, the agreements/contracts did leave substantial room for alternative interpretations.

Some commentators suspected that Danone and the Wahaha Group actually conspired to transfer the state-owned Wahaha brands to the JVs, with the intent of facilitating the privatization of the Wahaha Group.[28]

Emmanuel Faber argued that Zong agreed in the JV agreement to include Wahaha brands in the JVs and that the brands would be a part of Zong's stake brought into the JVs.[29] Thus, it is not entirely clear whether the financial resources contributed by Danone were to be used as its investment in the JVs or as usage fees for Wahaha brands, or both.

Finally, Danone was widely accused of trying to secure a monopoly position in the Chinese market. In 2005, Danone had already invested in five of the top ten domestic beverage companies, gaining a controlling position in three of them. Danone, however, argued that its market share was less than 15 per cent, which was still below the 20 per cent threshold specified in Chinese monopoly laws, and that it still faced strong competitors such as Coca Cola and PepsiCo.[30]

By 11 July 2007, Danone and Wahaha Group had not reached any agreement on how to proceed further. In June 2007, Emmanuel Faber asserted that "at the end of the day, we want a fair share of the pie . . . we don't want to destroy the pie".[31] However, Danone was in a very difficult situation: it might win in court and remain the legal owner of the Wahaha brands, but then be unable to run the JVs by itself. Danone had never operated the JVs, did not have the management resources to control the JVs and did not have much experience in running successful businesses in China on its own. For example, Robust, Wahaha's former major competitor, reported a loss of RMB 157 million in 2005 and an expected loss of RMB 150 million in 2006 after Danone took over the operation from the entrepreneurs who started Robust.[32]

Danone acknowledged that it took a risk by letting Zong run the JVs, but it believed that JVs would make Danone move forward at a faster pace than its competitors. Laurent Sacchi, Danone's spokesman, said that "if we now have 30% of our sales in emerging markets and we built this in only ten years, it's thanks to this specific tactic . . . [W]e have problems with Wahaha. But we prefer to have problems with Wahaha now to not having had Wahaha at all for the last ten years."[33]

At the same time, the Wahaha Group had also benefited from the strategic alliance. It was also likely to be in a better position to do business in the post-litigation period than if no alliance had been struck with Danone. Both the JVs and non-JVs had been managed together in their daily operations. Marketing and sales had been controlled by the same management team. Even if Danone had won control of the JVs and the Wahaha brands, the Wahaha Group would have been able to move some of the key human resources to the non-JVs.[34]

How it unfolded . . .

In November 2007, the Hangzhou Arbitration Commission ruled that there was no legal requirement for the trademark of the Wahaha Group to be transferred to the joint ventures. Supporting the judgment, the Commission stated that there was a lapse in time for a justified case to be made against Wahaha. Controversy over the ruling quickly transpired as the local trademark office in Beijing supported Danone's stance by confirming that the 1996 trademark agreement had never been declined.[35] Danone quickly moved to appeal the decision and waited on other trials to present rulings. The appeal to the Hangzhou Intermediate People's Court in China failed and left Danone with little hope of success in Chinese courts.[36] Additional lawsuits were filed elsewhere in China, as well as in Los Angeles, The British Virgin Islands and Samoa against companies connected to Wahaha.[37] The lawsuits became extremely personal when Danone sued Mr Zong's family for aiding in transfers to the non-JV businesses. The company even went as far as assisting the US tax authorities when an investigation was underway for a property belonging to Mr Zong.[38] Danone did have some success with its international lawsuits, but it was evident that the situation in China was unlikely to turn for the better.[39]

The intensity of the legal battle between Danone and the Wahaha Group eventually reached beyond just the companies involved. With strong nationalistic ties between Danone and the French government, and between the Wahaha Group and Chinese authorities, political leaders from each country became interested in the outcome of this case. In late 2007 while visiting China, French President Nicolas Sarkozy pressed the issue over a dinner hosted by Chinese President Hu Jintao. Soon after, a joint statement was released by the two companies stating "Both parties agree to temporarily suspend all lawsuits and arbitrations, stop all aggressive and hostile statements, and create a friendly environment for peace talks."[40]

Negotiations continued into 2008 with the help of government mediators; however an agreement was never reached during the courtroom truce period, which ended on 10 April 2008.[41] Appeals and reviews continued throughout 2008 with Danone earning little support for its allegations. On 30 September 2009 the Stockholm Chamber of Commerce's Arbitration Institute ruled that the majority of claims against the Wahaha Group and Mr Zong be discarded. The only violation found was on the grounds that Mr Zong had broken compliance on confidentiality and non-competition agreements.[42]

After a tedious two-year dispute, Danone announced in October 2009 that it would sell its 51 per cent stake in the JVs. Danone received an estimated 300 million euros from the sale, despite the stake having a book value of 380 million euros.[43] This announcement marked the end of all legal allegations between the two parties.

Interestingly, in 2007 Danone had also been embroiled in a fight about brands in India with the Wadia Group, an Indian conglomerate. Danone and the Wadia Group have been equal partners in Associated Biscuits International Holding, which controls Britannia, India's largest biscuit maker and the owner of the Tiger brand. In 2004, Britannia found that Danone had registered the Tiger brand in around 70 countries and that Danone had been selling biscuits under the Tiger brand in other countries, such as Indonesia and Malaysia. Danone argued that it had disclosed to Britannia's board what it had done.

In a further sign of strained relations, the Wadia Group also claimed that the dairy business in which Danone invested in India would compete with Britannia, thereby violating the non-compete clauses in the joint venture agreement between Danone and Wadia.[44] Danone was reported to have agreed to return the Tiger brand to Britannia,[45] and exit Britannia, in order to obtain the freedom to invest in the dairy business in India.[46]

Ironically, it was Danone standing accused of violating intellectual property in India, whereas it was this same firm that accused Wahaha of violating its intellectual property rights in China. Moreover, Danone had argued that the Britannia board and management had full knowledge of the international registration of the Tiger brand, using the same argument as Wahaha arguing that Danone had been fully aware of the non-JVs. Danone eventually sold its 51 per cent stake in the joint venture with Wadia Group in April of 2009.[47]

National governments have played a role in Danone's international business strategy. PepsiCo was prevented from taking over Danone two years ago partly because the French government did not want foreigners to control Danone "as a matter of national security" consistent with the French yogurt policy.[48] Similarly, Danone has been unable to purchase the Wahaha brands, partly because the Wahaha brands are viewed as national brands in China.

QUESTIONS

1. What were the intentions of Wahaha Group and Danone when setting up joint ventures in China?
2. How did the relationship between Wahaha Group and Danone change during the 11 years of cooperation? How did the bargaining power of both parties change?
3. Did the long-term cooperation between both firms lead to more trust? Did you observe any problems of bounded reliability with the two firms' cooperation? Was there a vicious cycle of suspicion? Was there a vicious cycle of increasing dependency on a partner?
4. Was there a learning asymmetry in the joint ventures?
5. Has Danone been able to access the location-bound FSAs of the Wahaha Group? Should Danone have rejected the joint venture entry mode in the first place?
6. Can you provide an update on Danone's activities in China after the sale of its joint venture assets to the Wahaha Group, using materials available on the Web?

Notes

1. G. Hamel, Y. L. Doz and C. K. Prahalad, 'Collaborate with your competitors – and win', *Harvard Business Review* 67 (1989), 133–9.
2. *Ibid.*
3. *Ibid.*, 134.
4. *Ibid.*, 138.
5. *Ibid.*, 135.
6. *Ibid.*, 137.
7. *Ibid.*, 139.

8. *Ibid.*, 135–6.
9. Erin Anderson and Sandy D. Jap, 'The dark side of close relationships', *MIT Sloan Management Review* 46 (2005), 75–82.
10. *Ibid.*, 79–81.
11. Prashant Kale and Jaideep Anand, 'The decline of emerging economy joint ventures: the case of India', *California Management Review* 48 (2006), 62–76.
12. *Ibid.*, 66.
13. Danone company information, www.danone.com, accessed on 3 May 2012.
14. Leslie Chang and Peter Wonacott, 'Cracking China's market', *Wall Street Journal* (9 January 2003), B.1.
15. Leslie Chang, 'Danone's China sales and profit make the country a top market', *Wall Street Journal* (10 March 2004), B.4H.
16. James T. Areddy and Deborah Ball, 'Danone's China strategy is set back; dispute with venture partner highlights the risks of not going it alone', *Wall Street Journal* (15 June 2007), A.10.
17. However, Danone was the controlling shareholder of Jinja.
18. http://finance.sina.com.cn/chanjing/b/20070411/17433492856.shtml, accessed on 12 July 2007. However, a Chinese news agency reported that the JVs accounted for around 5 per cent of Danone's global operating profits in 2006, Xinhua, 9 May 2007, 'Danone starts legal procedures against Wahaha after talks break down', http://news.xinhuanet.com/english/2007-05/09/content_6077320.htm, accessed on 6 July 2007.
19. http://finance.sina.com.cn/chanjing/b/20070710/14573770710.shtml, accessed on 11 July 2007.
20. http://finance.sina.com.cn/g/20070708/23403764003.shtml, accessed on 12 July 2007.
21. http://finance.sina.com.cn/chanjing/b/20070621/01053709694.shtml, accessed on 12 July 2007.
22. http://finance.sina.com.cn/review/observe/20070612/04293681956.shtml, accessed on 12 July 2007.
23. http://finance.sina.com.cn/chanjing/b/20070617/09503698289.shtml, accessed on 12 July 2007.
24. http://finance.sina.com.cn/chanjing/b/20070411/17503492870.shtml, accessed on 12 July 2007.
25. http://finance.sina.com.cn/g/20070419/14203518054.shtml, accessed on 12 July 2007.
26. http://finance.sina.com.cn/review/observe/20070612/04293681956.shtml, accessed on 12 July 2007.
27. David Barboza and James Kanter, 'A Chinese company fights its French partner', New York Times (13 June 2007), C.8.
28. http://opinion.news.hexun.com/2168067.shtml, accessed on 12 July 2007.
29. http://finance.sina.com.cn/g/20070708/23403764003.shtml, accessed on 12 July 2007.
30. http://finance.sina.com.cn/g/20070419/14203518054.shtml, accessed on 12 July 2007.
31. Barboza and Kanter, 'A Chinese company fights its French partner', C.8.
32. http://finance.sina.com.cn/chanjing/b/20061230/07183210427.shtml, accessed on 12 July 2007.
33. Areddy and Ball, 'Danone's China strategy is set back', A.10.
34. http://finance.sina.com.cn/chanjing/b/20070615/03203693838.shtml, accessed on 12 July 2007.
35. Geoff Dyer, 'Danone blow in China brand dispute', *[Asia Edition]. Financial Times* (11 December 2007), 21.

36. Geoff Dyer, 'Danone offers truce in legal fight with Chinese partner Wahaha', *[Asia Edition] Financial Times* (17 December 2007), 17.

37. Michelle Ng, 'International Business: Danone's Wahaha appeal is dismissed', *Wall Street Journal (Eastern Edition)* (6 August 2008), B.2.

38. James T. Areddy, 'Partners fight over Wahaha in China, firm's founder, Danone appear headed for split', *Wall Street Journal (Eastern Edition)* (28 July 2008), B.1.

39. James T. Areddy, 'Danone loses dispute in trademark case', *Wall Street Journal (Eastern Edition)* (11 December 2007), B.5.

40. Mure Dickie, 'Danone and Wahaha agree legal ceasefire in attempt to end feud', *[Asia Edition]. Financial Times* (24 December 2007), 11.

41. J. Tao and E. Hillier, 'A tale of two companies', *The China Business Review* (May 2008), 35(3), 44–47.

42. Tom Mitchell & Geoff Dye, 'Danone learns perils of doing business in China', *Financial Times* (9 November 2009).

43. Scheherazade Daneshkhu, Sundeep Tucker and Patti Waldmeir, 'Danone ends Wahaha tie-up', *Financial Times* (1 October 2009), 17.

44. Jenny Wiggins, 'Danone faces India brand suite', *Financial Times* (13 April 2007), 27.

45. 'Danone to return Tiger brand to Britannia, investment dispute may go on – report', *AFX News Limited* (20 April 2007), www.abcmoney.co.uk/news/20200759780.htm, accessed on 12 July 2007.

46. 'Danone may exit Britannia Industries; to pursue dairy, beverage plans – report', *Thomson Financial* (21 June 2007), www.abcmoney.co.uk/news/21200791147.htm, accessed on 12 July 2007.

47. Jenny Wiggins, 'Danone and Wadia part ways' *Financial Times* (15 April 2009), 15.

48. 'Yoghurt turns sour Troubled Asian ventures. Will Wahaha have the last laugh?', *Financial Times* (14 April 2007), 8.

13

Entry mode dynamics 3: Mergers and acquisitions

Five learning objectives

1. To develop an understanding of international mergers and acquisitions (M&As) as instruments to create economic value for the firm.
2. To explain the challenge of 'management biases' when contemplating M&As, and the possibility of pursuing potentially superior alternatives that focus on developing and profitably exploiting FSAs.
3. To describe the challenges of effective governance in the post-acquisition process.
4. To support a reflection on the barriers to success and the common mistakes in M&A implementation processes.
5. To describe the process of integrating extant FSAs of the acquirer with the FSAs of the acquired company in international M&As.

This chapter examines Ghemawat and Ghadar's idea that global M&A transactions usually do not make economic sense. The authors note several management biases that lead to inefficient M&As, and they recommend several alternative strategies as superior to global M&As. These ideas will be examined and then criticized using the framework presented in Chapter 1.

Significance

Pankaj Ghemawat and **Fariborz Ghadar** wrote a classic *HBR* article in 2000, criticizing the observed trend towards international M&As, especially those among large MNEs from different regions of the world (the so-called 'global mega-mergers'). Such M&As typically aim to create a company with a much wider geographic reach than that commanded by each partner individually.[1]

Ghemawat and Ghadar ask whether such large-scale M&A transactions between MNEs, attempting to create firms with interregional or even worldwide market coverage, make economic sense. According to the authors, a general belief persists in many industries that increasing internationalization, in the sense of growing interdependence of markets in the world economy, will ultimately lead to industry consolidations whereby only a few large firms, commanding impressive scale economies, will survive. The obvious implication for senior managers is to get big in order to survive. This view is exemplified by the main strategy rule introduced at General Electric by former CEO Jack Welch. This rule, which still prevails in this highly diversified, US-based MNE, states that the firm should be active only in businesses where it can be the number one or two in the world in terms of size, and should divest businesses in which it cannot achieve that goal.

Ghemawat and Ghadar argue that this approach is inappropriate, since the underlying conceptual rationale for it is weak, and the predicted consolidation is, in many industries, simply not happening. Their empirical research reveals that several industries characterized by increasing internationalization have actually also witnessed *de*creasing levels of market share concentration over the past half-century. In light of this observation, they argue that MNEs should contemplate alternatives to strategies of increased geographic reach through large-scale, international M&As.

Their *HBR* article starts by briefly discussing some of the economic theories underlying the perceived link between internationalization and industry concentration. The conventional theory of comparative advantage argues that specific production activities will become concentrated in those countries that possess advantages relative to other countries. But, as the authors correctly point out, this theory "simply predicts the geographic concentration of production, not concentration of the number of companies in an industry".[2]

While the conventional theory of comparative advantage does not account for economies of scale, which is a key factor in the trend towards global consolidation, other mainstream economic models, such as the theory of monopolistic competition, do. However, application of the latter models usually does not lead to the conclusion that increased internationalization triggers extreme consolidation. The exception consists of some rare (mainly theoretical) cases of industries characterized by very large R&D expenditures, whereby a few firms are expected to win the learning race and drive out their less successful rivals (as occurred in the 1960s with US-based Kodak and Japan-based Fuji, who won the innovation race in colour photo technology).

Ghemawat and Ghadar's methodology involved examining data relating to the worldwide market share of companies in over 20 industries, going back more than 40 years to the 1950s. From this work, they computed a so-called 'modified Herfindahl index' for each industry, based on data from the ten largest companies in each industry (rather than including all the companies in each industry). A Herfindahl index is a measure of market share concentration. The index is smaller than – or equal to – the number 1.00. In this particular case, a modified

Herfindahl index was calculated for each industry, as the sum of the squares of the market share of the ten largest companies. A higher number reflects a higher degree of market share consolidation (the extreme case being the hypothetical scenario of one firm commanding 100 per cent market share, meaning the index would take the value 1.00), while a lower number implies a lower level of concentration. If there were only ten competitors, each with an identical market share, the index would be 0.1. If there were many more competitors, again with the largest firm(s) holding 10 per cent of the market, but the smallest of the ten firms included in the index commanding much less than 10 per cent market share, the index could be substantially lower than 0.1.

The article presents a sample of the results by industry. For example, calculations for oil production and refining show an increasing number of companies and decreasing market concentration since the 1950s, rather than a consolidation of companies into a few global energy giants, as is commonly perceived. The only exception to the trend is the observation, in the late 1990s, of a number of mega-M&As that created some of today's largest oil majors (e.g., BP Amoco, now BP, formed in 1998 by UK-based British Petroleum and US-based Amoco). The modified Herfindahl index calculated for the oil industry in 1997 stood below 0.05, implying the equivalent of more than twenty significant rivals in terms of market share. Such industry structure is far removed from a conventional monopoly or oligopoly with a small number of dominant firms.

Other natural resource industries such as zinc, bauxite, copper and aluminium also showed a similar increase in the number of international competitors and a decrease in market concentration over the same time period. The automobile industry displayed a trend similar to that of oil with decreasing market concentration for decades, with the exception of the years characterized by a few mega-M&A consolidations in the 1990s (e.g., the now defunct merger of Daimler-Benz of Germany with US-based Chrysler Corporation to form DaimlerChrysler in 1998).

Even in high-tech industries, the examples of computer hardware, software and telephony also suggest a decrease in the market share of the largest firms during the 1990s.

As an aside, the authors do concede that their concentration measure does not include other forms of inter-company concentration such as strategic alliances, but they argue, in line with the 'competitive collaboration' discussion in Chapter 12, that such partnerships often fail or otherwise dissolve over the long term, and are therefore not indicative of a sustained consolidation trend.

Of course, not all industries exhibit this decrease in concentration. In those industries, Ghemawat and Ghadar argue that even if some level of consolidation is observed, and this results mainly from M&As rather than from organic growth, there is not necessarily a sound economic rationale for it. Ultimately, the aim of consolidation must always be to create value. "To profit from dominating in a concentrating industry, a company needs to extract value by pushing certain economic levers – for example, reducing production costs, reducing risk, or increasing volume."[3]

Creating value through consolidation, however, is often harder to accomplish successfully than might be expected by senior managers contemplating an M&A. In fact, consolidation often **reduces** value because of the pre-integration (negotiation) challenges, purchase price premiums and post-integration barriers associated with M&As.

Having reached these anti-M&A conclusions, Ghemawat and Ghadar then attempt to discover why some industries have an ineffective and inefficient tendency to consolidate through international M&As:

Why are cross-border consolidations pursued even when they destroy economic value? It seems there is often a pathology involved. Management appears to suffer from one or more of several motivational and cognitive biases towards mega-mergers, which can lead to irrational decision making and large-scale destruction of value.[4]

The authors provide a list of six senior management biases, which can all be interpreted as reflections of bounded rationality and, in some cases, also bounded reliability:[5]

1. 'Top Line Obsession' This occurs when senior managers focus too much on growing revenues (the top line of an accounting statement) rather than profits (the bottom line of an accounting statement) because corporate goals for growth are formulated in terms of revenue, and performance incentives are tied to achieving such top line goals. The bounded reliability problem is that, given these ill-conceived incentives, managers neither pursue shareholder interests, nor the interests of consumers or workers, but solely their own interests.

2. 'Stock Price Exploitation' Senior managers are likely to engage in M&A activity if the firm has an overvalued stock price that makes it more affordable to engage in large M&A transactions, or if the managers are looking to maintain an elevated share price based on the promise of operational (cost-reducing) synergies, even if few of these synergies will actually materialize over time. To the extent that senior managers know that the promise of substantial synergies is unlikely to occur and provide false information to relevant stakeholders, there is again a problem of bounded reliability, in this case akin to opportunistic behaviour.

3. 'Grooved Thinking' Senior managers will often follow the traditional mindset within an industry even if it has become obsolete (e.g., the focus of conventional telecoms on maximizing the number of telephone lines under their control, even in the age of the new communication possibilities provided by the Internet).

4. 'Herd Behaviour' Senior managers tend to follow and imitate the actions of their main competitors, especially in oligopolistic industries (e.g., M&A activity in the European banking industry). Herd behaviour can also reduce managers' individual risk of underperforming rival firms. This is another example of bounded reliability, whereby senior managers engage primarily in self-serving behaviour.

5. 'Personal Commitments' Individual senior managers may hold fast to their own personal views in favour of M&As even in the face of evidence that M&As in their industry systematically lead to underperformance.

6. 'Trust in Interested Parties' Outside parties such as investment bankers and consultants can influence companies to engage in M&As, thereby furthering their own interests in earning commissions and fees. Here, the source of bounded reliability problems resides with the external parties to the transaction; these parties have an incentive to further their own interests, rather than act in the best interest of the firm that hired them.

As an alternative to pursuing international M&A deals, the authors offer a host of alternative strategies that senior managers can pursue. As a general point, they caution that companies must remain focused on developing and profitably exploiting FSAs, rather than on attaining a particular scale as measured by revenues:[6]

1. 'Pick Up the Scraps' Spin-offs and divestments that arise from the mega-M&As of other companies can offer profitable growth opportunities for the firms that refrained from engaging in large-scale M&As themselves, if the assets are complementary to the buyer.

2. 'Stay Home' Many companies have ample opportunity to improve their competitive position locally or in their home region, rather than pursuing large-scale, interregional M&As to expand their geographic reach.

3. 'Keep Your Eye on the Ball' Companies can improve their competitive position by remaining focused on developing and exploiting their key FSAs, while their competitors become consumed with pursuing M&A deals and struggle with post-M&A integration.

4. 'Make Friends' Strategic alliances offer an alternative expansion trajectory, often with less resistance internally and from external parties such as government regulators. See Chapter 12 for a discussion of the relative merits of alliances versus M&As.

5. 'Appeal to the Referee' Assuming a company cannot, or will not, pursue a mega-M&A itself, it may be able to slow those of its competitors by calling on regulators to review antitrust implications.

6. 'Stalk Your Target' In industries where first-mover advantages associated with international market expansion, especially outside the home region, are dubious, it may be best to wait and observe as others test the waters, rather than trying quickly to increase the MNE's geographic reach through M&As.

7. 'Sell Out' If consolidation is economically justified, it may prove more profitable to be the seller rather than the buyer, given purchase price premiums, integration difficulties, etc.

Context and complementary perspectives

The timing of Ghemawat and Ghadar's article is highly significant: it was published in 2000 at the height of the 'dot-com' boom. The implausible escalation of technology and Internet-related share prices through the latter part of the 1990s had temporarily turned some industries upside down, with new entrants commanding enormous market capitalization overnight. Many of these firms leveraged their overvalued stock to fuel buyout sprees of other companies in a frenzy of M&A activity that focused primarily on size and revenue growth rather than profitability. The authors' reference to America Online's huge acquisition of Time Warner helps recall the context of the era: "Some think AOL will eventually recover what it paid, but others believe this may be the deal that brings some rationality to the valuation of Internet stocks."[7] Although the dot-com bubble was indeed about to burst, the epic events in the e-business world had spillover effects in other industries, creating a desire to pursue similar blockbuster-type M&As in order to compete for the attention of investors' heightened expectations. In an environment where companies were pressured to produce double-digit yearly growth percentages, even in mature industries, many larger firms turned to mega-M&As, especially on an interregional scale, in order to meet otherwise unattainable targets.

By way of additional context, it should be noted that the large-scale interregional M&As of the 1990s were possible only because the previous two decades witnessed a trend towards freer trade and investment. These M&As would have been infeasible in an era of high, protectionist trade and investment barriers.

In an *SMR* article, **James K. Sebenius** provides a first complementary perspective to Ghemawat and Ghadar's article.[8] Rather than criticizing the rise of large-scale, interregional M&As, Sebenius focuses on the success story of the Italian copper producer Societa Metallurgica Italiana (SMI, operating under the name KME Group since 2006), which grew rapidly and profitably during the 1990s as a result of cross-border acquisitions throughout Europe (involving France, Spain and Germany), and was able to solve most of the pre- and post-acquisition problems observed by Ghemawat and Ghadar.

There were two reasons for SMI's sustained acquisition success. First, for every transaction contemplated, senior management was always "very clear about the industrial and strategic logic behind [the] proposed acquisition and the genuine value it will create".[9] SMI carefully scrutinized outstanding acquisition targets, and pursued only related rather than unrelated diversification, thus reducing bounded rationality problems. SMI also had the patience to wait on purchasing these targets until several of the target's relevant stakeholders were predisposed towards shedding assets.

Second, senior executives engaged in careful stakeholder management. They adopted this approach long before starting negotiations. In those early stages, they attempted to develop good personal relationships with relevant actors working for the acquisition target and tried to understand salient governance issues in the macro-level context and at the level of the target, e.g., governance rules that could block the acquisition. Astute stakeholder management was even more critical during and after the acquisition negotiations. A target was never defined simply as a set of complementary FSAs, with the potential of synergies and value creation, and therefore commanding a particular, appropriate price. A target was also, and foremost, a set of diverse stakeholder groups, covering an entire spectrum of attitudes towards being an acquisition target, from great enthusiasm to strong dismay. A key to success at SMI was its ability to craft acquisition transactions in such a way as to shift the negotiation focus from the economic valuation principles (i.e., the price of the targeted firm), from which SMI was unwilling to depart anyway, towards clauses allowing even the most critical stakeholder groups to see value in the acquisition for themselves. Such stakeholder-specific crafting of transaction clauses, representing attempts to develop a shared vision with each stakeholder group, sometimes included commitments towards senior staff, e.g., the promise of continued autonomy of the entity to be acquired, in the sense of respecting the value of its location-bound FSAs or involving it in new non-location-bound FSA creation, such as technology development. It sometimes involved commitments towards the selling firm's shareholders, e.g., by allowing the seller to remain a minority partner in the acquired entity and by involving the seller in setting pan-European strategy. In politically sensitive situations, as in the case of a French acquisition, the design of an industrial plan with specifics on the benefits of cross-border integration of fragmented, inefficient firms rather than the threat of plant closures, increased legitimacy vis-à-vis political stakeholders. Mostly, the crafting of a shared vision with the various stakeholder groups meant that agreement was reached about broad restructuring principles rather than detailed operational measures, with the latter being designed later, as part of the post-acquisition integration process.

As regards this post-acquisition process, effective governance meant on the one hand cross-border integration of operations through international product-type divisions with clear leadership, and on the other hand cross-border, horizontal coordination of functions such as ICT, finance and administration. This dual integration approach, with the most competent individuals in charge of divisions and intra-functional coordination across borders (including human resources from the acquired units) was superimposed on the conventional, national subsidiary structure kept for legal and tax reasons.

Andrew C. Inkpen*, *Anant K. Sundaram and ***Kristin Rockwood*** give a second complementary perspective in a *CMR* piece[10] addressing less successful cases than those discussed by Sebenius in his *SMR* article. Specifically, Inkpen *et al.* studied European acquisitions of technology-based firms in California. They observed, in the cases they studied, that usually the only winners of such transactions were the shareholders of the acquired entities, commanding stock price gains of more than 43 per cent (as compared to the stock price one month before the acquisition announcement), versus gains of only 14 per cent when the acquirer was a US firm.

In contrast, the European acquirer, typically a large MNE, usually ended up with negative value creation. Importantly, the staff and management of the acquired firm were often also negatively affected by the transaction (e.g., because the prevailing stock option packages for staff were cancelled).

Inkpen *et al.* described in some depth the various barriers that made these acquisitions so unsuccessful. These barriers were largely related to the difference between the general entrepreneurial culture, corporate governance practices and related routines prevailing in Silicon Valley versus those characteristic for the large European MNEs engaged in strategic resource seeking investments. For example, the European acquirers typically restricted the autonomy of the smaller firms they purchased and had little if any experience with stock option compensation packages for employees, thus alienating key personnel, often the carriers of the acquired firms' main FSAs (the so-called 'assets that walk out of the door every evening', with no guarantee that they will show up the next day), with ample opportunity to move to other companies in the same geographical area. One of the problems facing European MNEs was of course that allowing 'option package' type compensation in US-based, acquired operations could lead to demands elsewhere in the MNE network for the generalized introduction of such packages. This would disrupt prevailing compensation routines with proven, past effectiveness, as well as potentially drive up labour costs.

Given this overall difference in environmental and governance context, Inkpen *et al.* usefully discuss four ways that the European MNE displayed inappropriately slow integration and rigid decision making.

First, European MNEs typically adopted time-consuming consensus-building strategies before making a decision on changes to be effected in the acquired unit. This contrasted sharply with the rule of thumb adopted by some US firms to complete integration within 100 days (sometimes using formal integration teams). Senior management of European MNEs also made excessive use of so-called hard data (e.g., formal marketing plans instead of intuition about market opportunities) to guide decision making.

Second, the European MNEs involved typically neglected to convey quickly to the new staff a clear and credible picture of the future of the acquired entity, thus leading to high turnover rates. A much faster dissemination of a vision for the future would have been required to avoid such turnover, given the hot Silicon Valley labour market.

Third, the expatriates sent by the new European parent typically socialized only among themselves, rather than attempting to become insiders in Silicon Valley social networks, a key source of information about business and technology trends.

Fourth, immediately after acquisition, confusion often arose about who was actually at the helm of the acquired entity, and had responsibility for strategic decision making. Parent company managers typically just visited the acquired entity for short time periods without engaging in fundamental restructuring, another expression of slow post-acquisition integration.

Note that, in contrast to SMI's excellent job of managing all the stakeholders in the acquired company, these European MNEs did a poor job of managing one important stakeholder group: the employees of the acquired company.

Ghemawat and Ghadar's *HBR* piece focuses on the issue of whether firms actually improve their strategic position and truly acquire new FSAs through large-scale, international mega-mergers. The authors reject the widely held assumption that FSAs can be created solely through larger size and economies of scale, with a few MNEs eventually dominating all other firms in an industry. Ghemawat and Ghadar's research shows that many industries have actually experienced decreasing levels of concentration over recent decades, but this empirical result describing a historical trend obviously does not answer the question of when M&As are appropriate. What the article does describe very well is the challenges posed by bounded rationality (and bounded reliability) constraints – both at the individual manager's level and more generally, at the broader organizational level – that come into effect when considering mega-mergers.

As the authors correctly point out, firms must stay focused on developing and exploiting their FSAs, and not just on growing larger. On the one hand, it is true that FSA development can sometimes be strengthened through acquiring complementary capabilities of competitors. Complementary capabilities can, *inter alia*, broaden the scope of innovation, thereby minimizing the risk of falling behind competitors in terms of new FSA development. On the other hand, the melding of the FSAs of both companies may require hard work to make the new post-merger organization effective and efficient. Many earlier chapters in this book have made the point that senior MNE managers often overestimate the international transferability and profitable international deployment of the MNE's FSAs, even within the firm itself. In the present case of international mega-mergers, the key challenge is not really the large-scale transfer of FSAs across borders, but rather that FSAs of two MNEs must be combined and some key FSAs, such as overall routines, diffused throughout the merged entity. This challenge is shown in Figure 13.1.

Figures 13.1
M&A partners

(A)

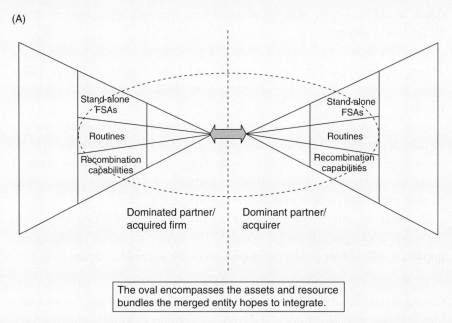

The oval encompasses the assets and resource bundles the merged entity hopes to integrate.

(B)

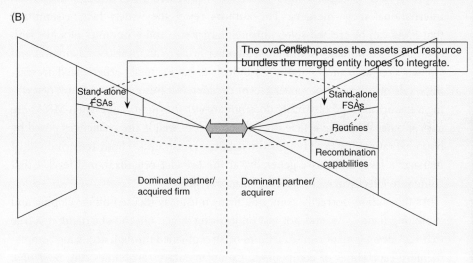

The oval encompasses the assets and resource bundles the merged entity hopes to integrate.

The dotted oval refers to the merger being completed, with the acquired entity retaining only a fraction of its initial resource base. The LB and NLB FSA segments of the acquired firm's triangle "shrink" due to conflicts when attempting to integrate this firm's routines and recombination FSAs into the merged entity's dominant routines and recombination FSAs, which are mostly inherited from the acquirer.

The top part, Figure 13.1A, shows the acquired and acquiring firms, respectively left and right of the country border, with their idiosyncratic structure of location advantages, location-bound FSAs and internationally transferable FSAs. When a merger or acquisition occurs, the FSA bundles are supposed to be melded, but this is difficult to achieve for two reasons. First, the FSA bundles found in each firm are often to some extent location-bound, grown out of location advantages and a unique company strategy building upon access to those location advantages. Severe post-M&A integration problems can therefore be expected when the distance between locations is large (as is usually the case with interregional as opposed to intra-regional M&As). Second, there can be problems even around completely transferable FSAs. Even though synergies may be created by combining resources held by each firm, it is particularly unlikely that all of the two firms' routines and recombination capabilities will be able to reinforce each other, or even to co-exist: there cannot be 'the two ways we do things in this firm'. Here, integrating an acquisition may be somewhat easier to achieve than integrating two entities in a merger, because specific resources and FSAs considered inconsistent with the acquirer's overall dominant logic can be legitimately shed, and the acquirer's own routines legitimately imposed on the acquired entity. Figure 13.1B shows the problem of integrating the non-location-bound routines and recombination capabilities; here, at least partial incompatibility can be expected.

It should also be noted that the integration of stand-alone FSAs is much easier to achieve in the case of related (rather than unrelated) diversification, because the carriers of these FSAs (ranging from groups of research scientists to marketing managers) will face much less difficulty creating shared cognitive and strategic orientations (see Chapter 10) and outlining a joint way forward.

On a somewhat more critical note, and moving back to Ghemawat and Ghadar's lucid *HBR* piece, three limitations of this work are worth noting.

First, in spite of the valid criticism voiced against 'global' M&As (in the sense of M&As with partners outside the home region), this type of expansion may actually be a realistic and worthwhile strategic option for large MNEs. Sometimes a global M&A is the right choice, picked for the right reasons. While Ghemawat and Ghadar are right that many senior MNE managers overestimate the potential for cost-cutting and synergies, and underestimate the integration difficulties, not all senior MNE managers are blinded by the thrill of the chase. Some correctly view an M&A as the best choice out of a number of imperfect, real-world alternatives (which may include other market entry mode choices, such as setting up wholly owned subsidiaries, licensing agreements and alliances).

This is especially true for MNEs that already command a dominant position in a highly competitive, slow growth industry in their home region, whereby any further attempts to grow with the present product lines may lead to price wars. The M&A transaction may then act as a trigger for implementing cost-cutting/synergy-seeking initiatives that might otherwise be foregone, given the preference for the status quo and the presence of vested interests typically found in any large organization.

There is an important general point here for senior managers to recognize: the benefits of a large-scale M&A do not derive solely from the FSA complementarity between the partners, though such complementarity constitutes an efficiency and effectiveness-related precondition for the M&A to occur in the first place. An additional key source of benefits is the legitimatization of deep, structural change throughout the entire MNE(s) involved. For example, an M&A may provide the only context within which shareholders and other stakeholders can be persuaded that the firm needs to contract.

Another important point to keep in mind is that it may be unfair to compare the stock market prices of the firms involved just before and after the M&A. The more important question is what would have occurred to the stock market prices (over both the short and long term) in the absence of an M&A. A small short-term dip is better than a large long-term decline.

Second, Ghemawat and Ghadar argue that the international consolidation of industry is often vastly exaggerated. However, if national markets are indeed increasingly interrelated, then data on low consolidation levels in industry may paradoxically provide a strong rationale for M&As. Through M&As it becomes possible for MNEs that previously dominated national and home region markets to continue being a major player in the industry. Intending to remain a major player in industry may be driven by efficiency and effectiveness considerations such as being able to have a voice in industry standard setting, preventing other MNEs from tying up suppliers and distribution channels, and broadening the scope of innovation to reduce the risk of falling behind in terms of new FSA creation. Note that these reasons are distinct from the more conventional scale economy rationale, in this case not in terms of single plant scale economies, but rather in terms of the new, larger firm's ability to spread R&D costs across larger production volumes.

Third, when a merger or acquisition is disappointing in terms of value creation, this does not imply that another entry mode would have been better. As Ghemawat and Ghadar note, a decision to engage in a large-scale, international M&A is often driven by information that underestimates the impact of distance. However, this is often a general bounded rationality problem that might have occurred irrespective of the entry mode chosen.

Some bounded rationality problems are common to every collaborative entry mode, like the correct identification and valuation of the partner's FSAs in the intangible asset sphere such as R&D resources, brand names and reputational resources, and in the organizational capability sphere (managerial strengths, employee loyalty, etc.). This difficulty is amplified by the fact that it is not the other firm's resources per se that should be assessed, but rather the value-creating potential of combining the two firms' complementary resources. On the other hand, as this book has noted, other bounded rationality problems await if the firm tries to enter a foreign market alone, particularly a high-distance market. Therefore, when an M&A is unsuccessful, senior management should sometimes be criticized for venturing outside of their home country or region at all, rather than for choosing an M&A per se.

Five management takeaways

1. Do not *over*estimate the potential for value creation and do not *under*estimate the potential for value destruction of international M&As.
2. Do not fall into the trap of typical senior management biases when deciding on possible M&A deals.
3. Trade-off the benefits and costs of international M&As vis-à-vis alternative uses of resources for expansion.
4. When assessing merger and take-over targets, always focus on the 'industrial logic' of the proposed M&A, and engage in comprehensive stakeholder management from the outset.
5. Try to understand how to benefit as much as possible from the complementary capabilities of acquired parties and focus on effective post-merger organization.

Case 13.1 CEMEX: Growing and growing stronger?[11]

CASE

Of all the countries and industries one could match, the combination of Mexico and cement does not necessarily sound like the ideal couple to produce an efficient organization, able to expand internationally, largely through effective acquisitions. Yet, CEMEX has done just that. It has grown from a local Mexican producer into one of the world's largest cement producers, in the same league as France's Lafarge and Switzerland's Holcim. During the 1990s, it reached a compounded annual growth rate of 26 per cent in operating cash flow, almost double the industry average.

Most of its international acquisitions have been successful, proving wrong the many commentators who doubted its ability to integrate the acquired firms. In April 2007, it acquired Rinker, the Australian building materials supplier with more than 80 per cent of its sales in the US, for a price of US $14.2 billion.[12] Was this perhaps one bridge too far?

How did CEMEX develop and exploit its FSAs? What drove CEMEX to the path of international acquisitions? And what was its formula for successful acquisitions?

The global cement industry

Historically, the cement industry has been highly fragmented and localized. The raw materials, such as limestone and clay, are inexpensive, heavy and abundant in many areas of the world. The major costs of production are energy, materials, labour costs and transportation. At first, high road transportation costs limited the service area to a distance of 300 km from any plant. However, waterborne transportation was very economical, particularly with specialized ships and new systems of loading and unloading. Therefore, by the mid 1950s, cement producers were able to serve more distant markets if waterborne transportation was available.

Cement demand is directly related to economic growth rates – more specifically, to construction investment. Since the early 1980s, the growth in world demand has been highest in developing countries in Asia and Latin America, but flat in Western Europe and North America. Major markets for cement in absolute terms include China, the US and Japan.

Since the early 1980s, the global cement industry has started to consolidate. From 1988 to 1997, the 13 major cement producers increased their aggregate share of world production capacity from 18 per cent to 30 per cent. In the past fifteen years, cross-border acquisitions reduced the six major international competitors to three: Lafarge, Holcim and CEMEX. Although the cement industry is still very fragmented with around 10,000 firms in the world, high capital investment to sustain competitiveness has made it increasingly difficult for smaller firms (which typically lack sufficient access to funding), and the industry is expected to become more concentrated as a result of international mergers/acquisitions.

Developing 'the CEMEX way'

CEMEX, headquartered in Monterrey, Mexico, was founded in 1906. In 1976, it started to trade on the Mexican Stock Exchange. It mainly expanded within Mexico by building and acquiring plants and, by the mid 1980s, CEMEX had become a major cement producer in Mexico with diverse businesses in mining, petrochemicals and tourism.

In 1985, Lorenzo Zambrano, an MBA from Stanford and the grandson of the founder, became CEMEX's CEO at the age of 41. He led the company to refocus on the cement business, and strengthened Cemex's position in Mexico by acquiring domestic competitors Cementos Anahuac in 1987 and Tolteca in 1989. As a result, CEMEX became the second largest local cement producer. More importantly, Zambrano was instrumental to the firm adopting two important principles: that cement can be branded, and that modern ICT can be incorporated into every aspect of the cement business.

As it expanded in Mexico, CEMEX developed a unique business model. Traditionally, cement had been a bulk product, sold to larger customers as a mere commodity without major service differences or price differentiation among producers. In contrast, CEMEX branded its cement and sold it in bags, to accommodate small and poor Mexican customers used to buying cheaper powdered cement in bags rather than pricier ready-mixed concrete. Thus, CEMEX differentiated itself from other producers in a fragmented market. Furthermore, CEMEX launched aggressive marketing campaigns to raise its profile in Mexico, via such tactics as sponsoring local football clubs. In addition, CEMEX convinced a large number of small local shops to join its franchise distribution network so that customers could easily buy a small bag of cement at a nearby store and carry it back home.

CEMEX also invested heavily in ICT systems, to improve the flow and the use of information. To improve its shipping efficiency, CEMEX adopted a satellite telecommunication system to coordinate its trucks in 1987. CEMEX also used computer systems to monitor each plant's performance and each store's sales.

CEMEX's success at home can largely be attributed to recognizing the unique market conditions in Mexico and developing a model to effectively meet the demands of its Mexican customers. CEMEX summarized its business model as 'the CEMEX way', meaning the "company wide effort to manage our global knowledge base efficiently, identify and disseminate best practices, standardize our business processes, implement key information and Internet based technologies, and foster innovation".[13] Generally speaking, the CEMEX model was quite centralized and efficient, with simplified and standard business processes. However, marketing was largely left to its affiliates in order to respond to local conditions quickly.

After the introduction of the 'CEMEX way' in 2000, the company saw improved results from its acquisitions in terms of cost savings and integration periods decreasing from 18 months to 4 months.[14]

Learning to acquire abroad

CEMEX started to feel the pressure of international competition in the mid and late 1980s, when the Mexican government began to liberalize the economy. Multinational cement producers began to penetrate the Mexican market. As Zambrano recalls, "We suddenly found ourselves competing with very large international companies at a time of consolidation in the global cement industry. There were few independent producers left. Either we became large and international, or we would end up being purchased by a bigger player."[15]

CEMEX chose to start its international expansion by exporting cement to the US, as the US market was adjacent, stable and highly fragmented. Moreover, CEMEX had shipping facilities on the Gulf of Mexico due to its earlier acquisitions of Anahuac and Tolteca. Unfortunately, the antidumping ruling imposed by the US government in 1990 as a result of the lobbying of a group of American cement producers hindered CEMEX's expansion in the US market.

CEMEX continued to look for international acquisition opportunities, switching its attention from geographically proximate markets to culturally proximate markets. In 1992, CEMEX acquired the two largest Spanish cement producers, Valenciana and LACSA. CEMEX chose Spain for four reasons. *First*, Spain was culturally proximate, with strong historical connections to Mexico. *Second*, Spain was less economically developed than other European countries and offered more opportunities for growth. *Third*, Spain's cement market was more similar to Mexico's than that of many other European countries. *Fourth*, as Spain had become an important market for major European companies, CEMEX could use Spain to 'counter' these companies' investments in Mexico, especially the heavy investment of the Swiss Holderbank (now Holcim) in Grupo Cementos Apasco, the number two cement producer in Mexico.

CEMEX faced a daunting task of integrating the two acquired companies. The market perception was that CEMEX not only overpaid for the two Spanish companies, but would also "suffer from indigestion".[16] CEMEX set up a post-acquisition integration team, consisting of

23 experienced functional managers. The team analysed managerial skills of local managers, information technology, business processes and the structure of functional areas in the acquired companies, and looked for ways to merge the CEMEX way with the current operations. During the 18-month integration process, Zambrano travelled to Spain every month to meet face-to-face with the team.

The team found that the two Spanish companies were very inefficient, especially in the areas of inventory management, energy consumption and plant automation. Moreover, the acquired companies did not use ICT effectively. For example, they still used paper to record orders and payment.

CEMEX engaged in a large-scale effort to bring the use of ICT up to CEMEX's standard. It brought in its ICT system to track everyday operational results. Moreover, CEMEX streamlined management, introduced more efficient fuel sources such as petrocoke and improved plant automation. By the end of the integration process, operation margins had risen from 7 per cent to 24 per cent.

The skyrocketing economic performance at the two acquired companies then gave CEMEX the confidence to integrate its own dispersed Mexican operations. In 1994, CEMEX consolidated its Mexican operations into one managerial unit by applying the integration processes developed during the Spanish acquisitions. As a result, CEMEX gained US $85 million in profits.

Systemizing the acquisition process

During the domestic and Spanish acquisitions, CEMEX gradually developed its own systematic acquisition processes, including a target selection process and a post-acquisition process.[17]

CEMEX is always alert to acquisition opportunities around the world, but it does not really target specific acquisitions in particular countries. As Hector Medina, executive vice-president of planning and finance, puts it: "when someone is ready to sell that's when we're ready to buy . . . So when we're offered an acquisition opportunity it can only be at the right price."[18] This is why CEMEX has not entered large growing markets such as India, as there have not been tempting opportunities so far in these countries.

Moreover, CEMEX carefully evaluates an acquisition/merger target when opportunities do present themselves. The target should meet three objectives. *First*, and most importantly, CEMEX should be able to integrate the target into its existing management structure and system of operations. Before any deal is closed, CEMEX's human resources division always collects all relevant information about the target and its products, and creates a booklet on key issues for due diligence. CEMEX also sends a team of experienced functional managers from the head office to the targeted company, and then the team interacts with managers of the targeted company to discuss CEMEX's post-acquisition approach. *Second*, the investment in an acquisition should not negatively affect CEMEX's financial performance benchmarks, and if it does, any negative impact on the capital structure and cost should be temporary. For example, the group level interest expense ratio should be maintained below 4.5 per cent, and the ratio of net debt to net earnings before interest, taxes, depreciation and amortization should be kept below 2.7. *Third*, acquisitions should be accretive, in the sense of increasing earnings per share, meaning, *inter alia*, that new purchases should not start until CEMEX has finished integrating current acquisitions and has started to pay off debt related to such acquisitions.

Once a target is selected, CEMEX addresses two key phases to aid in the acquisition process. After CEMEX's first acquisition in Spain, the company quickly realized that analysing the targets' IT infrastructure was the most pressing concern. CEO Mike Zambrano stated "information is your ally: you use it to detect problems more quickly and get better faster".[19] Integrating the acquired company's IT has become the first phase in CEMEX's acquisition process. The second phase involves analysing the acquired firm's business processes using ARIS (Architecture of Integrated Information Systems). ARIS was developed to set company-wide standards in processes for CEMEX's many departments. These standards are then compared with those of the acquisition to determine areas where the two firms face discrepancies. Based off of these results, CEMEX is able to determine the intensity of the post-acquisition process.

Finally, CEMEX has also formalized the post-acquisition/merger integration process. The post-acquisition/merger team, consisting of individuals known as 'CEMEX widows' because they are told not to take their families,[20] analyses the target firm, benchmarks the target against CEMEX's own operations and presents its findings, focusing on a list of improvements, to the firm's Executive Committee. If CEMEX uncovers unique and useful procedures adopted by the acquired companies, CEMEX attempts to take these and transfer them to other units within the company. After the acquisition, CEMEX sends operational teams to initiate changes in the acquired company, and to raise its performance to CEMEX's levels.

New areas of international expansion

In the past 20 years, CEMEX has continued to expand internationally through acquisitions. Geographically, it has moved from Latin-American-based emerging countries to other emerging countries, and finally to developed countries. Its long list of acquisitions includes Corporacion Venezolana de Cementos in Venezuela (1994), Cemento Bayano in Panama (1994–5), Cementos Nacionales in the Dominican Republic (1995), Cementos Diamante in Colombia (1996), Rizai Cement Company in the Philippines (1997), PT Semen Gresik in Indonesia (1998–9), Assiut in Egypt and Cemento del Pacifico in Costa Rica (1999). The company then acquired several firms in developed countries, including Southdown (US) in 2000, Pastorello (France) in 2001, Wangan (Japan) in 2001, RMC (UK multinational) in 2005 and Rinker (Australian multinational) in 2007. From 1980 to 2010, CEMEX spent an estimated US $29 billion on its acquisitions.[21] As of 2012, CEMEX had a highly diversified portfolio of markets stemming from its 20 acquisitions.

The acquisitions in developed country markets should be interpreted partly as a reaction to the critiques of some financial analysts and partly as the outcome of CEMEX's strategy to control its exposure to country-specific risk. As CEMEX operated almost entirely in emerging markets before 2000, some analysts considered CEMEX's portfolio too risky, given the possibility of political and social instability in those countries. CEMEX agreed, and it also wanted to reduce its reliance on any particular single country, especially after it weathered the tumultuous 1995 Mexican peso crisis.

CEMEX has also expanded its acquisitions along the value chain, to gain the benefits of vertical integration. In 2005, CEMEX acquired RMC, the troubled UK cement producer and the world's largest concrete producer, thereby positioning CEMEX as the third largest cement producer in the world. In this case, CEMEX expected to gain synergies by providing raw materials for RMC's ready-mix concrete. CEO Zambrano commented, "The whole point of buying RMC is to get vertical integration for CEMEX overall . . . not only in the US but everywhere – the UK, Germany, Croatia, everywhere."[22]

Although some analysts were sceptical about the likelihood of performance improvements at RMC, CEMEX achieved synergies of approximately US $360 million after only six months. CEMEX's ratio of net debt to net earnings before interest, taxes, depreciation and amortization also fell to 2.3, much lower than its threshold of 2.7.[23] During the process of integrating RMC, CEMEX sent around 400 people around the world to observe RMC operations.[24]

CEMEX had experienced great success with approximately 20 acquisitions since Zambrano became CEO. (The one significant 'failure' was CEMEX's withdrawal from Indonesia. However, in that case, CEMEX withdrew – selling its stakes in Semen Gresik in 2005 – simply because it was not able to gain majority control of the firm.) CEMEX gradually expanded its acquisition scope, both geographically and across the value chain, and acquired the Rinker Group in 2007.

CEMEX's struggle with the recession

The acquisition of the Rinker Group in 2007 drastically changed CEMEX's capital structure by tripling the amount of debt it held.[25] The Rinker Group was an Australian company that conducted the majority of its business in the United States. When CEMEX acquired the firm, it was aware of potential troubles in the American housing market. However, it did not foresee the substantial impact a collapse would have on the Rinker Group's operations. Zambrano commented "that every time we bought something, [the country where it was located] would go into recession. We called it the 'Cemex effect'".[26] This indeed often happened as CEMEX acquired firms that were actually choosing to be sold, not coincidentally at times when their home nation's economy was struggling. With earlier acquisitions, this had been only a minor issue for CEMEX, as it had typically been able to impose efficiencies and generate net benefits from its acquisitions within five years.[27] The expectation was no different when acquiring the Rinker Group and CEMEX continued to finance this acquisition as it had done before with other ones, using primarily short-term debt.

It did not take long before the American housing bubble burst and demand for new construction fell drastically. Not only was CEMEX's product demand affected, but the banks that held its loans were unwilling to renew these. By 2009, CEMEX was close to defaulting on US $21.7 billion of debt and was subsequently downgraded in terms of S&P's investment rating.[28] Negotiations with creditors resulted and a 'Financing Agreement' was reached outlining CEMEX's obligations for US $15 billion in refinancing. CEMEX eventually sold numerous assets in Australia,

Austria, The Canary Islands and Hungary to strengthen its balance sheet. The agreement capped spending on acquisitions at US $100 million annually and mandated that these be creditor approved.[29] These restrictions, along with the company's substantial debt, have left CEMEX with little room to continue its growth strategy since its last acquisition in 2007. This has raised some concerns for the company, as it is believed that the industry is approaching another consolidation period. In 2009, the number of acquisitions in the industry tripled as compared to the previous year.[30] Fernando Gonzalez, chief of planning and finance, warned that "The largest players might grow faster than what we can do in the next five years."[31]

Competitors have been shifting efforts towards the BRIC countries (Brazil, Russia, India and China) as demand for construction is expected to remain strong in these areas. Despite operating in 50 countries around the world, CEMEX has not yet entered Brazil or India and has only a limited presence in China and Russia. Its operations in China have only recently begun, mainly through strategic partnerships. By the end of 2011, CEMEX operated four concrete factories, namely in Tianjin and in Qingdao, and had been awarded a significant contract to supply cement for the construction of "one of the tallest buildings in Asia", namely a 117-storey building in Tianjin.[32] As regards Russia, CEMEX established a joint venture with a Russian construction group (TVA) in 2009, to form CEMEX Baltic Cement and started operating in that country. CEMEX has stated that it intends to move into Brazil and India, but the optimal entry opportunity has not been found.[33] Reports from 2010 suggested that CEMEX was evaluating Murli Industries, an Indian company, as a possible takeover target, but a formal proposal never transpired.[34] The question remains, in the post-Rinker Group acquisition era, whether CEMEX can and should revert to its previously successful acquisition strategy, when it patiently waited for the "right time to acquire the right target".[35]

QUESTIONS

1. What are the dynamics of industry concentration in the cement industry? Has internationalization led to higher concentration in the industry? Did the low consolidation level provide a rationale for international M&As?

2. What were the major objectives of CEMEX's international acquisitions? Did CEMEX show any of the six biases identified in Ghemawat and Ghadar's article? Did CEMEX pursue any of the alternative strategies proposed by Ghemawat and Ghadar?

3. What are CEMEX's key FSAs? Has it been able to diffuse these FSAs to all acquired entities?

4. How did CEMEX integrate the firms it acquired? Did CEMEX pay attention to the problems of distance during the integration process?

5. How did the acquisition of the Rinker Group ultimately affect CEMEX's international acquisition strategy? Please use materials available on the Web to update your response.

CASE

Case 13.2 Lenovo: A Chinese company grows an international brand[36]

In 1981, after nearly 100 years in business, IBM introduced the world to home computing through the launch of the IBM personal computer (PC). The relatively small machine offered home users the basics of personal computing, complete with two floppy disks, 16 kilobytes of memory (expandable to 256 kilobytes), an Intel processor chip, and a DOS operating system developed by a small, 36-person company called Microsoft.[37] This invention would launch a technological revolution and would help grow the company to the giant it is today, with nearly 400,000 employees worldwide.

Twenty-four years later, in December 2004, IBM shocked the industry by selling its US $1.75 billion pivotal PC business to Lenovo, a company partially owned by the Chinese state. IBM employees, competitors and management pundits were stunned. How could a relatively unknown company, operating only in China, come to swallow the PC business of "Big Blue"?[38] What did this mean for the PC industry?

Why would IBM want to exit the PC making business? In a word, margins. The PC industry is a low-margin, commodity-like industry. IBM realized it could increase its margins by selling the PC division and focusing on products with higher returns, such as servers and software, and technology services. Historically, IBM's PC division made little profit and in some years, lost money. IBM felt the division was negatively affecting the company's overall profitability. Over the next few years, IBM gradually sold its shares in Lenovo until its shares fell below the 5 per cent reporting requirement.

Lenovo, on the other hand, believed it knew the PC market well and was earning healthy returns in China. In an earlier attempt at an international venture, Lenovo failed to launch PCs in Spain, and thought the IBM purchase was an opportunity to introduce Lenovo to the world with the support of the trusted Big Blue brand. The deal instantly quadrupled Lenovo's revenues, and gave Lenovo access to an invaluable pool of highly skilled IBM researchers, product designers, sales professionals and support personnel.

Can Chinese brands sell internationally?

Building an international brand requires years of development and investment, and an understanding of global customers in their unique markets.[39] It takes time for a company to develop a reputation for quality and performance, and this is especially evident in technology industries. Some Asian companies, especially Korean (e.g., Samsung) and Japanese (e.g., Sony) ones, have built solid, thriving international brands. However, very few major brands have arisen from the emerging economic giants, China and India. When China and India liberalized their economies in the 1980s and 1990s, a widely shared fear in those countries was that foreign MNEs would enter local markets and destroy local, home-grown companies.[40] This did not happen. Instead, local companies have thrived and prospered, and have started acquiring the large MNEs that were originally thought to pose such a threat.

China's large market base provides companies with an opportunity to grow and build cash flow and experience before venturing overseas.[41] Increased foreign investments in local emerging markets have created a large base of prosperous citizens, with incomes to purchase both local and foreign products. This growing consumer mass has created a thriving base of small and medium sized businesses in emerging markets that are able to experiment, expand and build cash flow before venturing overseas.[42]

The first Chinese companies to take advantage of freer markets and more prosperous consumers tended to compete on price, taking advantage of lower labour costs and offering competitive products that were mass produced at discounted prices. Instead of producing innovative, new products, Chinese companies mass-produced inexpensive knock-offs for sale internationally. While this situation still exists today, over time companies have realized that in order to continue to grow, they could no longer rely on organic growth opportunities, but rather would have to look outside their own borders for acquisition targets.[43] The past few years have seen an increase in Chinese merger and acquisition activity. Recent prominent examples include Lenovo's acquisition of IBM's PC division and car manufacturer Geely's acquisition of Volvo. While low-cost manufacturing continues to play a prominent role, it is no longer the driving force behind Chinese economic growth. China has become a technological innovator, with heavy investments in research and development. However, according to the consulting company McKinsey, how Chinese firms innovate is different from the approach adopted by MNEs in developed economy markets.[44]

Gordon Orr and Erik Roth of McKinsey's Shanghai office find that Chinese companies are weaker in three main areas:[45]

1. They lack analytical tools for uncovering and understanding customer needs.
2. Their corporate cultures are risk-averse.
3. Corporate cultures tend to be authoritarian, with little of the internal collaboration that is necessary for the development of new ideas.

Chinese MNEs have attempted to remediate some of these problems, but often still lack a deep understanding of local foreign markets. However, Chinese companies excel at innovating through commercialization, which reflects a type of 'trial and error', and means they prefer to introduce products and see how these perform rather than doing extensive marketing research prior to market release.[46] Traditionally, most of the innovations developed in China have tended to stay there, and the 'trial and error' approach is then an 'analytically easy' way to try to expand abroad. In general, the "market is so large that domestic companies have little incentive to adapt successful products for sale abroad".[47] As China continues to grow and develop, it is reasonable to expect that this situation will not continue, and we will see an increasing number of Chinese companies targeting global acquisitions.

Lenovo: The making of China's first global brand

Liu Chuanzhi: Lenovo's Steve Jobs

Lenovo's founder, Liu Chuanzhi, is widely respected by Lenovo employees and Chinese citizens alike. Within Lenovo, he is referred to as "The Chairman", and throughout China he is revered as a pioneer of China's industrial and technological development.[48] Liu's road to success was not an easy one. In 1968, Liu graduated from military college and was sent to work for the Chinese government as a researcher for the Ministry of Defence.[49] Unfortunately, his tenure as researcher did not last long, as he was sent to work on a state-owned farm to be "re-educated" during the Cultural Revolution of Chairman Mao Zedong of the Communist Party of China.[50] The purpose of the Cultural Revolution was "to enforce socialism in the country by removing capitalist, traditional and cultural elements from Chinese society, and to impose Maoist orthodoxy within the Party".[51]

Liu's living conditions were dire, and he worried he would never be allowed to leave. He was fortunate that the Cultural Revolution ended two years later, and he was re-assigned to work at the Chinese Academy of Sciences in Beijing as a researcher. While he was lucky not to have been assigned to work in a factory, the job lacked fulfilment with no opportunities for movement or advancement.

With the death of Mao in the early 1980s, the new Chinese government began to introduce market reforms. The president of the Chinese Academy of Sciences was encouraged to visit the West and see if he could find ways to stimulate the economy. He chose to visit IBM, and brought back home his observations of how IBM commercialized its research and development initiatives. The Chinese government, intent on pushing forward reforms, invested RMB 200,000 (worth US $25,000 at the time) in seed funds for Liu's new technology venture with ten other engineers. This venture was called "The Chinese Academy of Sciences Computer Technology Research Institute New Technology Development Co"[52] and was based out of an old guard shack in Beijing. Fortunately, the company changed its name to Legend (Lianxiang), but unfortunately, none of the founding engineers had any experience running a business.

One of the most important technologies developed by the founders was a chip card that enabled Chinese characters to be accessible on foreign-made computers.[53] Legend formed a partnership with a US PC company called AST, and Legend distributed the computers to market. In short order, Legend became so well known in China that Liu decided to produce a "Legend-branded PC" in 1990.[54] Business took off.

In 1991, the Chinese government lowered import taxes on foreign goods. Suddenly, Legend's virtual monopoly evaporated, and a flood of competitors entered the market. Legend was in a loss position for the first time.

"The most dangerous thing is to be successful", said CFO Wong Wai Ming, "You then think every decision is the right one. That's why you have to review what you do."[55] Liu realized he had to make changes quickly. He promoted a young, 29-year-old sales superstar named Yang Yuanqing to reorganize and invigorate the company. Yang decided that Legend's next generation computer should have the fastest processor in the market, and in 1996 Legend was the first to introduce a Pentium-powered PC in China, at a lower price than that of competitive, slower PCs. Demand for the PCs exceeded expectations.

Legend made sure it was always one step ahead of the competition in China. When competitors introduced a comparable PC to the Pentium-powered Legend PC, Legend introduced an even faster one at a lower price. Legend strengthened its customer service and sales support, and became well known for its after sales service, which encouraged brand loyalty.[56] By 1997, Legend was the top-selling PC in China, a position it has never relinquished since.[57] But this wasn't enough for Liu, and in 2005 after changing Legend's name to Lenovo Group, Liu achieved his dream of running a global company. He acquired the PC business of giant multinational corporation IBM, in a deal that would stun IBM employees and competitors, and alarm the government of the United States of America.

The Asian tiger swallows a big blue giant

In 2004, IBM was the third largest PC vendor in the world, with a 5.2 per cent share of the market. Lenovo was the ninth largest, with 2 per cent of the market generated from sales in China (Figure 13.2).

Lenovo's sales in 2004 were approximately US $3.8 billion, whereas IBM's global PC sales were approximately US $10 billion.[58] The acquisition deal, worth US $1.75 billion, involved US $800 million in cash, US $450 million in securities and US $500 million in debt assumption.[59] Lenovo agreed to manufacture the PCs and was allowed to use the IBM brand for five years, namely the well-known and trusted Think Product Group. The Think products include the ThinkCentre PC and ThinkPad for commercial clients, and the IdeaCentre PC and IdeaPad for retail clients. IBM agreed to provide consumer financing, marketing and warranty, maintenance and sales support. The new Lenovo would have 10,000 former IBM employees and 9,200 Lenovo employees, with global headquarters in New York. Offices in Raleigh, North Carolina and Beijing were maintained.

The market was sceptical about the prospect that Lenovo, a low-end manufacturer with no international presence or experience, could be successful in a global market. How could two drastically different companies, from distinctly diverse cultures, merge with any degree of success?

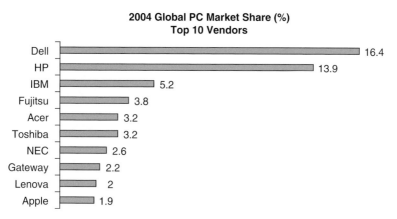

2004 Global PC Market Share (%)
Top 10 Vendors

Vendor	Share
Dell	16.4
HP	13.9
IBM	5.2
Fujitsu	3.8
Acer	3.2
Toshiba	3.2
NEC	2.6
Gateway	2.2
Lenova	2
Apple	1.9

Figure 13.2
The top 10 of the global PC market in 2004

Lenovo's customers were predominantly Chinese consumers (over 50 per cent), and IBM's customers were predominantly commercial entities (over 50 per cent). As Michael Dell, Chairman of Dell, stated, "We're not a big fan of the idea of taking companies and smashing them together. When was the last time you saw a successful acquisition or merger in the computer industry?"[60]

Lenovo definitely had a difficult road to travel. The road was ultimately steep, bumpy and with a few detours.

Lenovo's initial branding strategy: Preserve, educate, launch

Lenovo's first priority post-acquisition was to ensure that it preserved existing IBM and Lenovo customer bases. By allowing Lenovo to use the IBM brand for five years, IBM also had a vested interest in Lenovo's success. Not only did IBM own a significant number of shares in Lenovo, but there was an inherent risk in damage to IBM's own brand if the venture was unsuccessful. Aiming to achieve stability in the first year after the acquisition, Lenovo retained all employees of IBM's PC business despite their relatively high salary level compared to that prevailing at Lenovo. Lenovo's initial surveys of 4,000 global IBM customers found that customers would continue to purchase Lenovo computers if three key factors were maintained: "quality, innovation and service and support".[61] Based on the research results, Lenovo's branding strategy initially focused on a business as usual message, the "same people, same locations, same processes".[62] The IBM logo featured prominently in all advertisements and products. In this phase, Lenovo focused heavily on marketing to existing and potential large commercial clients and smaller business clients, given that this sector accounted for over 50 per cent of revenues.

In Lenovo's second phase of its branding strategy, the Lenovo brand was cautiously introduced to the market as the manufacturer of the Think and Idea groups by removing the IBM logo and replacing it with Lenovo's.[63] Advertisements emphasized the "Think" and "Idea" brands, and removed references to IBM. The intent was to assure clients that this is the product that they had come to know and trust, and "by the way, Lenovo is the company making this product".[64] Furthermore, the new company was restructured in order to reduce operational costs and improve Lenovo's efficiency in the supply chain. Lenovo laid off 1,000 and 1,400 US-based employees in two consecutive years (2006 and 2007), and 750 positions were relocated to emerging countries such as Brazil, China and India.[65]

In the third phase of Lenovo's post-acquisition process, the company focused on cultural integration. By forming an international leading team, offering global cross-training programmes and establishing a two-level research system that consists of central as well as business unit level research institutes, Lenovo enhanced the creation of competences and thus Lenovo's long-term success. In addition, the third phase involved the launch of the Lenovo master brand, particularly in consumer emerging markets, such as India and Russia. Lenovo's global tag line became, "Lenovo engineers exceptional PCs".[66] Lenovo wanted to highlight the importance innovation plays in the company, and believed using the word "engineer" would also appeal to its commercial client target market. The third branding phase involved an aggressive entry into the consumer segment in emerging markets. Lenovo believed it could leverage its successful Chinese strategy by adapting it to local emerging markets.

The first emerging market to be targeted was India. It was important for Lenovo to ensure its branding strategy did not emphasize low cost; otherwise, it risked losing the brand equity built with commercial clients. Lenovo understood that price is not the only driver for Indian customers; they are very brand-conscious. Lenovo's brand strategy in India utilized Bollywood stars, positioning Lenovo as a cool, young, trendy brand, while making sure that the messaging was not inappropriate for its commercial client base.[67] The strategy worked. Within 11 months, brand awareness soared from a nearly negligible base to approximately 70 per cent of consumers.[68]

Lenovo's strategy execution was a bit bumpy at times. In 2008, after disappointing international sales, Lenovo sold its mobile handset division to its parent, Legend Holdings, for US $100 million. Lenovo's CEO Bill Amelio was credited for successfully integrating Lenovo and IBM's operational and supply chain activities. However, the organization was still operating as two separate entities in terms of overall strategy development and execution, research and development, and marketing.[69] Analysts claimed Lenovo had focused too heavily on the commercial market and was too slow introducing popular consumer products, such as the netbooks (an inexpensive, smaller version of a laptop). As a result, Lenovo was hit hard during the financial crisis in 2008. Orders from commercial clients declined significantly during this time period, and Lenovo lost money and market share in its developed economy markets.[70]

In January 2009, Lenovo replaced CEO Bill Amelio and brought back its founding management team. The new team revisited its mobile strategy. PC competitors were beginning to offer mobile smart phones, and the industry expected demand for mobile computing devices to increase. Consequently, Lenovo bought back its handset unit from parent Legend Holdings for US $200 million, double the selling price from eighteen months earlier. Charles Guo from JP Morgan observed: "It makes you feel they are always a bit late. Also, the price tag is a bit high."[71]

With the founding management team back in place, Lenovo's global strategy underwent an aggressive transformation. In 2009, Lenovo launched a global line of Idea PC's targeting the consumer market. Lenovo calls this new strategy, 'Protect and Attack' and its new tag line is "Lenovo, for those who do[TM]".[72]

Lenovo's current strategy: Protect and attack

Protect the base

In Lenovo's developed economy markets, its strategy includes direct sales to commercial clients and global advertising in the consumer segment (e.g., sponsoring high-profile international sporting events). Lenovo also utilizes the Internet for advertising, since a majority of businesses and consumers are online. Developed economy markets represent 35.7 per cent of Lenovo's overall sales, over half of which are sales to commercial clients.

In China, which in 2012 accounted for approximately 46.4 per cent of Lenovo's overall revenues, Lenovo is focused on growing its share of the PC market, particularly in smaller cities and rural areas, and continuing to introduce new products, including mobile smart phones and tablets.[73] Lenovo is the number one selling smart phone in China, though it is largely unknown in developed economy markets. Lenovo's Chinese market base is critical, both for the country's contribution to Lenovo's revenues and as a test market for new products and services. Apple is Lenovo's most aggressive competitor in the mobile smart phone and tablet space in China.

Attack new markets

The 'Attack' component of Lenovo's strategy focuses on gaining market share in emerging markets, including Russia, Ukraine, India, ASEAN countries (Indonesia, Malaysia, Philippines, Singapore, Thailand, Vietnam, Laos, Cambodia, Brunei, Myanmar) and Latin America. Lenovo's sales have really taken off, with unit shipments increasing by at least 40 per cent in all markets, particularly in Russia and Ukraine (+141 per cent) and India (+64.9 per cent).[74] The emerging markets segment accounted for 17.9 per cent of Lenovo's overall revenues.[75] Local offices run marketing, sales and support initiatives, and though Lenovo has a common look and feel to its brand, country-specific advertising campaigns are strongly geared to local markets' preferences.

Acquisitions have played an important role in Lenovo's attack on the PC business in developed economy markets. Lenovo hopes it can make inroads into mobile computing with its ThinkPad and Idea tablets for commercial and consumer segments in developed economy markets. In 2012, it planned to release a new tablet that runs Windows 8 software.

Industry consolidation

Given the highly competitive nature of the PC industry and corresponding thin margins, industry consolidation is inevitable. In 2007, Acer acquired Gateway for US $710 million. In January 2011, Lenovo announced a joint venture with Japanese PC manufacturer NEC, whereby Lenovo would purchase 51 per cent of NEC for US $175 million.[76] The joint venture increased Lenovo's share of the Japanese market from 5 per cent to 25 per cent.[77] Lenovo also purchased Medion in Germany in 2011 for US $906 million.[78] Medion is a well-established consumer PC brand in Germany, and was a natural fit for Lenovo whose European customer base is primarily commercial. Lenovo's last two acquisitions reflect its desire to expand beyond commercial business and towards an increased consumer presence in developed economy markets.

Competitive landscape

Lenovo's 'Protect and Attack' global strategy appears to be paying off. In the fourth quarter of 2011, after years trailing in third or fourth place for total global PC market share, Lenovo overtook rival Dell for second place. The Top 5 PC manufacturers are displayed in Figure 13.3.

The market share graph presents an interesting illustration of the global PC market's top competitors. HP leads the pack with 16 per cent share. HP is a leading hardware (printers, PCs, servers, tablets, etc.) manufacturer, software developer and technology services consultant to both consumer and business clients. HP is the dominant player in developed economy markets such as the United States. Despite its market share dominance, HP has struggled to define its strategy in recent years, partially due to industry woes suffered during the financial crisis that began in 2008. In mid-2011, HP announced plans to spin off its PC business from the rest of the corporation,

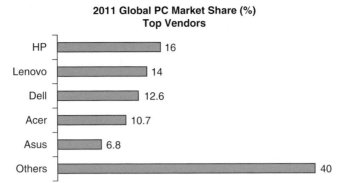

Figure 13.3

Top vendors in the global PC market in 2011

reminiscent of IBM's sale to Lenovo. No plans were announced for a sale, however, and the company stated that the split would allow focusing on "products that drive higher value solutions to enterprise, small and midsize business and public sector customers" while allowing the PC division to become more entrepreneurial and nimble.[79] The market reacted negatively to the news, and HP's stock lost more than 43 per cent of its value in less than a year.[80] HP subsequently dismissed its CEO, and new CEO Meg Whitman has reversed the spinoff decision, stating that it would be very difficult for a new PC company to develop such a strong brand, and recognizing the PC division's critical contribution to the corporation's overall technology strategy.[81]

Dell, Inc. is a large multinational computer technology company, with over 100,000 employees worldwide. The company, based in Texas, pioneered advancements in supply chain management and e-commerce PC sales. Consumers have since developed a keener interest in purchasing directly through retail outlets, which is hurting Dell's business model. Dell is one of the top three server manufacturers after IBM and HP, and has been investing in its data storage and technology services business. Dell has been criticized for relying too heavily on its low-margin PC business and being too slow to market with mobile computing devices such as its Streak tablet, which has not sold well.[82]

Acer is a large, multinational enterprise from Taiwan with over 8,000 employees, selling notebook and desktop PCs, servers, tablets, smart phones, LCD monitors and projectors.[83] While Lenovo has been focusing on business clients in developed economy markets, Acer's strategy is to target price-conscious PC consumers. Acer has done well with its netbook sales. A netbook is an inexpensive version of a laptop, and its initial popularity helped propel the company to many years of growth. However, Acer has struggled in the last year due to the financial crisis and consumer preference for tablets over netbooks, as well as inventory management issues. Acer has quickly moved to introduce ultra-thin notebooks and tablets to attempt to re-gain some of the business it has lost.[84]

Asus is a multinational computer company launched by four former employees from Acer, with a global workforce of 10,000 employees.[85] Asus sells PCs, servers, smart phones, tablets, and also specializes in manufacturing motherboards for its own computers and also for some of the firm's competitors. Asus has been praised for moving its innovations quickly to market, first with the Netbook, and then with tablets and ultra-thin notebooks.[86]

Apple Inc. is a multinational corporation with over 60,000 employees worldwide based in California that sells consumer electronics, computers and software. Apple is recognized as a leader in the mobile computing industry, and the iPad 2 has a commanding 55 per cent share of the tablet market.[87] Rivals running Google's Android mobile operating system and the upcoming Windows 8 touch screen software are expected to challenge Apple's higher-priced mobile phones and tablets in the future. As Lenovo's CEO Yang Yuanquing, stated, "Apple is very strong, but when IBM created the PC market there was just IBM, if you look at the PC industry now it is very diversified. I believe that will happen in tablets as well."[88]

What is the future for China's most successful international brand?

The IBM-Lenovo PC deal is one of China's most visible and successful forays into international brand extension. By all accounts, the acquisition was a success. Lenovo is the second largest PC vendor in the world, and is closing in on HP. Lenovo's return to its emerging markets roots has played a big role in Lenovo's current success, as do strategic acquisitions in Japan and Europe. Lenovo is well known for quality and customer service/support.

Lenovo's biggest test will be to determine whether it is able to penetrate the consumer base in developed economy markets such as North America and Europe. Competitors in developed economy markets have developed strong consumer brands, including HP, Dell, Apple, Acer, Asus and Toshiba. Can Lenovo build brand awareness and loyalty in these markets organically, or should it pursue acquisition targets?

Experts argue that PCs will continue to be the preferred product for meeting commercial and consumer computing needs for some time to come. Tablets and mobile smart phones are currently ancillary devices to a laptop or PC, but as Lenovo and competitors begin to develop fully functional, powerful hybrids that combine the functionality of both PCs and tablets, will these devices replace PCs?

QUESTIONS

1. What are Lenovo's FSAs? How have these evolved over time?
2. Was IBM's decision to sell its global PC business to Lenovo a good one?
3. Should Lenovo have focused on the commercial business in developed economy markets, or should it have targeted both commercial and consumer customers? Will it be able to gain lost ground organically in developed economy markets, or will it need to target another acquisition?
4. As Lenovo continues to build its global brand, what potential consumer perception barriers may Lenovo encounter as a brand from China?
5. What did Lenovo do well in terms of its global branding strategy? What could Lenovo have done better?
6. Is Lenovo's 'Protect and Attack' strategy positioning the firm properly for the future of the PC and mobile computing industry? What will this future look like, and what should Lenovo be doing now to prepare?

Notes

1. Pankaj Ghemawat and Fariborz Ghadar, 'The dubious logic of global megamergers', *Harvard Business Review* 78 (2000), 65–74.
2. *Ibid.*, 66.
3. *Ibid.*, 68.
4. *Ibid.*, 69.
5. *Ibid.*, 69–70.
6. *Ibid.*, 72.
7. *Ibid.*
8. James K. Sebenius, 'Case study: negotiating cross-border acquisitions', *Sloan Management Review* (Winter 1998), 27–41.
9. *Ibid.*, 40.
10. Andrew C. Inkpen, Anant K. Sundaram and Kristin Rockwood, 'Cross-border acquisitions of U.S. technology assets', *California Management Review* 42 (2000), 50–71.
11. 'Cemex 2005 Annual report' (2006), 1–2.
12. Adam Thomson, 'Shareholders accept Cemex bid for Rinker', *Financial Times* (9 June 2007), 9.
13. Lorenzo Zambrano, 'Remarks to the "CEMEX Americas" global analyst meeting', (Houston, Texas: 19 July 2001), 13.
14. Donald Marchand, 'Into the CEMEX Womb', *Go India* (December 2008), 56–9.
15. Leslie Crawford, 'Long reach opens new sources of finance: Leslie Crawford on how thinking big helped the group survive', *Financial Times* (7 November 1997), 16.
16. *Ibid.*
17. Steven Prokopy, 'A conversation with CEMEX's President of U.S. Operations Gilberto Perez', *Cement Americas* (1 July 2002), http://cementamericas.com/mag/cement_conversa tion_cemexs_president/, accessed on 29 July 2007.
18. 'Emerging titans: Mexico, India', *FDI Magazine* (2 December 2003), www.fdimagazine.com/news/fullstory.php/aid/185/Emerging_titansMexico,_India.html, accessed on July 29, 2007.
19. Donald Marchand, 'Into the CEMEX Womb', *Go India* (December 2008), 56–9.
20. 'Success at home has bred victory abroad', *Financial Times* (9 May 2007), 6.
21. Thomas Black, 'Cemex says debt terms create "nightmares" of missing cement acquisitions', *Bloomberg* (14 June 2010).
22. Sara Silver, 'Cemex waits to cement its gains', *Financial Times* (18 November 2004), 33.
23. Adam Thomson, 'Cemented: a reputation for efficiency', *Financial Times* (11 April 2007), 26.
24. Financial Times, 'Success at home has bred victory abroad', 6.
25. Thomas Black, 'Cemex should have financed 'more conservatively': week ahead', *Bloomberg* (2 November 2009).
26. 'A Q&A with Cemex CEO Lorenzo Zambrano', *Bloomberg BusinessWeek* (29 October 2009).
27. *Ibid.*
28. Geri Smith, 'Hard times ease for Cemex, Mexico's cement giant', *Bloomberg BusinessWeek* (29 October 2009).
29. Thomas Black, 'Cemex says debt terms create "nightmares" of missing cement acquisitions', *Bloomberg* (14 June 2010).
30. *Ibid.*
31. *Ibid.*
32. 'Cemex supplies ready mix concrete for one of the tallest buildings in Asia', Cemex press release. www.cemex.com/MediaCenter/PressReleases/PressRelease20101021.aspx (21 October 2010).

33. Jose Fernandez, 'Cemex takes the high road', *NYSE Magazine* (2006).
34. Devidutta Tripathy, 'Mexico's Cemex close to $550 million India buy', *Reuters* (22 November 2010).
35. Adam Thomson, 'Cemex says it is ready for China', *Financial Times* (28 April 2006), 16.
36. This case was co-authored by Ms Denise Larsen and Professor Alain Verbeke.
37. www-03.ibm.com/ibm/history/history/decade_1980.html. Accessed 10 April 2012.
38. Kathrin Hille, 'Lenovo proves it is a somebody', *Financial Times* (4 January 2010).
39. Kevin Brown, 'Long road to recognition for Asia's brands', *Financial Times* (31 May 2010).
40. *Ibid.*
41. *Ibid.*
42. David Oakley, 'Emerging markets grow internally, expand internationally', *Financial Times* (7 June 2011).
43. *Ibid.*
44. Kathrin Hille, 'Innovation, Chinese stye', *Financial Times* (2 February 2012).
45. *Ibid.*
46. *Ibid.*
47. *Ibid.*
48. Chuck Salter, 'Protect and Attack: Lenovo's new strategy', *fastcompany.com* (18 November 2011).
49. *Ibid.*
50. *Ibid.*
51. http://en.wikipedia.org/wiki/Cultural_Revolution. Accessed 10 April 2012.
52. Chuck Salter, 'Protect and Attack: Lenovo's new strategy', *fastcompany.com* (18 November 2011).
53. *Ibid.*
54. *Ibid.*
55. *Ibid.*
56. Ravi Dhar and K. Sudhir with Deepak Advani, 'How do you take a brand global?', *Qn: A Publication of the Yale School of Management* (April 2009).
57. *Ibid.*
58. Ravi Dhar and K. Sudhir with Deepak Advani, 'How do you take a brand global?', *Qn: A Publication of the Yale School of Management* (April 2009).
59. Mure Dickie, 'Lenovo pact could help ease investor doubts', *Financial Times* (31 March 2005).
60. *Ibid.*
61. Ravi Dhar and K. Sudhir with Deepak Advani, 'How do you take a brand global?', *Qn: A Publication of the Yale School of Management* (April 2009).
62. *Ibid.*
63. *Ibid.*
64. *Ibid.*
65. Tom Kraait, '1,000 staff to go in Lenovo restructuring', *ZDNet UK* (17 March 2006); Darren Murph, 'Lenovo laying off 1,400 employees, looking overseas', *Engadget* (21 April 2007).
66. *Ibid.*
67. *Ibid.*
68. *Ibid.*
69. Kathrin Hille, 'Lenovo set to reboot from the top', *Financial Times* (5 January 2009).
70. Robin Kwong and Kathrin Hille, 'Revamped Lenovo takes battle back to Acer', *Financial Times* (17 February 2011).

71. Kathrin Hille, 'Lenovo to buy back handset unit', *Financial Times* (27 November 2009).

72. 2011/2012 Interim Report Lenovo Group, www.lenovo.com

73. *Ibid.*

74. *Ibid.*

75. *Ibid.*

76. Alexandra Stevenson, 'NEC and Lenovo link up', *Financial Times* (27 January 2011).

77. *Ibid.*

78. Kathrin Hille and Robin Kwong, 'Lenovo buys Medion to bolster Europe profile', *Financial Times* (1 June 2011).

79. Chloe Albanesius, 'HP Reverses Course, Opts Not to Sell PC Division', *PCMag.com* (27 October 2011).

80. *Ibid.*

81. *Ibid.*

82. Maija Palmer, 'Dell Shrugs off harbingers of PC doom', *Financial Times* (8 September 2011).

83. www.acer-group.com/public/The_Group/overview.htm Accessed April 13, 2012.

84. Sean Smith, 'Ultra-thin notebooks to take centre stage at CES', *Financial Times* (9 January 2012).

85. www.asus.com/About_ASUS/Winning_formula/. Accessed April 10, 2012.

86. Robin Kwong, 'Asus dodges industry gloom', *Financial Times* (24 February 2012).

87. Damon Poeter, 'IDC: Strong Q4 iPad, Android tablet sales push 2012 forecast upwards', *PCMag.com* (13 March 2012).

88. Paul Taylor, 'Lenovo chief lays down Apple challenge', *Financial Times* (21 August 2011).

14

The role of emerging economies

Five learning objectives

1. To describe the complexities facing MNEs when operating in emerging economies because of 'institutional voids'.
2. To explain how to create a map of an emerging economy's institutional context and its implications for strategy.
3. To outline the various marketing dimensions where the MNE should reconfigure its approach to cater to the emerging economy context.
4. To explain the need for a proper understanding of the prevailing consumer culture when entering an emerging economy.
5. To explain the emerging economy's specificities affecting bounded rationality and bounded reliability facing the MNE.

This chapter examines Khanna *et al.*'s idea that emerging economies are primarily characterized by important institutional voids (i.e., a lack of both local intermediary firms and broader macro-level institutions such as contract-enforcing governmental institutions), and that the primary challenge for MNEs operating in emerging economies is to understand and deal with these voids. According to these authors, an emerging economy's institutional voids are even more important than traditional metrics (e.g., GDP analysis). Building on their theory, the authors supply a list of institution-related questions that senior managers should ask in order to assess whether and how to penetrate an emerging economy. These ideas will be examined and then criticized using the framework presented in Chapter 1.

Significance

Emerging economies are playing an increasingly important role in both the world economy and MNE strategic activity. Since the early 1990s emerging economies have provided the world's fastest growing markets for most products and services.[1] MNEs are attracted to these countries as they offer potential cost and innovation advantages, and represent new output markets. First, the availability of relatively inexpensive skilled labour and trained managers in emerging economies offers MNEs lower manufacturing and service costs. Second, these economies can also give MNEs access to a different genre of innovation than can be found in mature markets. The foundation of such innovation often resides in the creativity of individuals driven to find original solutions to meet basic needs of large but poor segments of the emerging economy's population. Finally, from a purely sales-related perspective, MNEs from North America, Europe and Japan need to enter emerging economies as a counter-strategy to the increasing expansion of emerging economy MNEs into the world's developed markets.[2]

Historically, these countries were called 'less developed' countries, 'newly industrializing' countries or 'third world' countries, but the rising interest in – and belief in – their growth potential has shifted perceptions such that, in economic contexts, they are now generally called 'emerging markets' or 'emerging economies'.[3] While the importance of emerging economies is increasing, there is still no definitive definition as to what constitutes an emerging economy. There are, however, three common aspects of a country's economy that underlie various definitions of 'emerging economy': first, the absolute level of economic development (e.g., GDP per capita); second, the pace of economic development (e.g., GDP growth rate); and third, the extent and degree of stability of the 'free market' system features.[4]

In a 1997 *HBR* article, **Tarun Khanna** and **Krishna Palepu** took a different approach, arguing that the most important criterion in defining emerging economies is the presence of **institutional voids**.[5] Institutional voids are forms of market failure. For example, in the absence of efficient, external capital market institutions, large firms must finance themselves and establish internal capital markets for resource allocation.

In 2005, **Khanna** and **Palepu**, together with **Jayant Sinha**, wrote an *HBR* article that extended the analysis of institutional voids, elaborating on how these voids affect MNE strategic decisions.[6] The authors suggest that MNEs face difficulties in emerging economies due to the unavailability of two kinds of institutions that can facilitate business: efficient local intermediary firms, and certain broader macro-level institutions (e.g., contract-enforcing governmental institutions). In the (developed) home country, these would be considered generally available location advantages, and often taken for granted. In the emerging economy, they are absent, and MNEs would do well to notice their absence and adapt accordingly.

The authors propose that MNE success in emerging economies depends upon managers understanding the institutional context of the local economy, identifying the institutional voids and developing strategies to work around or fill such voids. Senior managers must not assume they can do business in emerging economies the same way they do in developed nations.

Consider the effects of the absence of intermediary firms. In advanced economies, intermediary firms provide a valuable source of location-bound, complementary resources allowing MNEs to deploy and successfully exploit their non-location-bound FSAs. For example, the strong retailing networks found in advanced economies offer MNEs some confidence that their products will be effectively and efficiently distributed, an assumption that typically cannot be made in emerging economies. Other examples of 'market inter-mediary' institutional voids include a lack of skilled market research firms to inform MNEs about customer preferences, few end-to-end logistics providers to assist in distribution and a lack of human resources management firms to help screen potential employees.[7]

The authors recommend that MNEs customize their approaches to fit each nation's specific institutional context (i.e., to reduce the institutional distance). Put another way: institutional voids in emerging economies require MNEs to engage in substantial investments to create compensating location-bound FSAs, instrumental to the successful exploitation of the MNE's extant, internationally transferable FSAs.

However, the difficulty of doing this makes many MNEs simply avoid such markets. For example, in 2002, American corporations had only 2.5 per cent of their US $6.9 trillion worth of assets in emerging economies such as Brazil, Russia, India and China.[8]

As described in Chapter 1 of this book, MNE cross-border expansion should have well-defined motives, such as natural resource seeking, market seeking, strategic resource seeking or efficiency seeking. Furthermore, the choice of a particular host country should take into account that host country's location advantages vis-à-vis potential alternative locations. Khanna *et al.* note that senior managers generally do try their best to assess the potential for successful FSA transfer and resource recombination in alternative locations, but the managers are usually subject to severe bounded rationality constraints. Therefore, senior man-agers' actual selection of a target country may be based on their personal ex-periences, family ties, gut feelings, anecdotal evidence, a rival's entry strategy or simple biases.[9]

Khanna *et al.* argue that, when choosing host countries, senior managers' priorities are almost completely backwards. The authors argue that understand-ing institutional distance should rule location decisions,[10] yet empirical evidence from a McKinsey Global Survey of business executives indicates that 61 per cent place market size as the priority in entering a new country, 17 per cent rank political and economic stability as the most important factor and only 13 per cent indicate that structural conditions, or the institutional context, is the most important factor.[11]

A key bounded rationality problem facing MNE managers is that many analyses of host country location advantages do not account for the unique institutional makeup of individual emerging economies. In fact, Khanna *et al.* argue that traditional analyses of emerging economies may conceal more than they reveal. These traditional approaches include country portfolio analysis, political risk assessment, GDP analysis, per capita income growth rates, population composition, exchange rate analysis, purchasing power parity, a nation's standing in the World Economic Forum's Global Competitiveness Index and Transparency International's corruption ratings.[12] Unfortunately, such tools often leave out information about the country's institutional characteristics, and therefore about the institutional distance to be overcome by MNEs.

To illustrate the difficulty with traditional rankings for emerging economies, the authors compare Russia, China, India and Brazil on six traditional indices.[13] These four emerging economies obtain rather similar scores on most indices, yet their location characteristics in terms of parameters relevant to MNEs – i.e., relevant to (a) the transfer, deployment and exploitation of extant, non-location-bound FSAs, and (b) the need to develop new, location-bound FSAs – varies widely. For example, while multinational retail chains have been able to penetrate China and Russia, Brazil only has a few global chains in key urban centres, and India prohibited FDI in retailing until February 2005.[14] Thus, MNEs considering entering any or all of these emerging economies must design a unique distribution strategy for each. In each case, the combination of extant non-location-bound FSAs with newly developed, location-bound FSAs will be idiosyncratic.

To facilitate the understanding of differences among emerging economies, the authors provide a conceptual device for mapping a country's institutional context. They isolate the five components of the institutional context they consider most relevant to MNEs: macro-level political and social context, macro-level openness of the economy, product markets, labour markets and capital markets.

So, in the case of Chile, for example, the authors look closely at that country's macro-level political and social context, capital markets and labour markets. Chile's political milieu has allowed for liberal economic policies that in turn have led to vibrant capital markets. At the same time, however, the political system has constrained trade unions, which in turn has left the country's labour markets underdeveloped and inefficient. Efficient labour markets require at least some level of power in the hands of the suppliers of labour. If this is not the case, and wages of unskilled and skilled labour alike can be suppressed at will by powerful employers, there is no incentive for upgrading the labour supply pool. In Chile, there is little such incentive. Similar effects can be observed in China, where workers also cannot form independent trade unions.

In the case of South Africa, the authors examine its macro-level political and social context and capital markets. In South Africa, institutional support for the transfer of assets to historically disenfranchised indigenous Africans has hindered the development of capital markets. For MNEs, the underdeveloped South African capital markets have made it difficult to value potential South African acquisitions or partners.[15]

Khanna *et al.* flesh out these five components of the institutional context they consider most relevant – macro-level political and social context, macro-level openness of the economy, product markets, labour markets and capital markets – by providing a series of questions for each component. These questions are tools for MNE senior managers to create a map of a country's institutional context and gauge the extent to which the MNE would need to invest in location-bound FSAs in each context. (The authors do not focus on conventional industry analysis, as they suggest this is useful only *after* understanding the country's institutional context.[16])

First, as regards the analysis of the macro-level political and social context, senior managers should identify a country's power centres and assess whether there are checks and balances in place. To understand this first of the five components, important questions to be answered include: what form of private property rights protection exists? How independent are the media? How accountable are the politicians? Can strangers be trusted to honour contracts?

As an illustration, the US and EU systems are characterized by vibrant democracies with checks and balances. MNEs can count on the rule of law. The media and NGOs within the US and EU also provide further checks on corporate activity. In contrast, while Brazil and India have vibrant democracies with a dynamic press, these countries also have rampant bureaucracy and moderate levels of corruption. The emerging economy of Russia is characterized by stifling bureaucracy and corruption at most levels of government, and the media is largely controlled by the government. Finally, in China the Communist Party has a monopoly on political power and the media and NGOs have little influence.

Second, senior managers should determine the country's openness. Openness refers to the extent that the country welcomes FDI, but it also includes openness to ideas and openness to travel (e.g., are MNE managers free to travel inside and outside the host country?).

The level of openness in a country affects the markets directly relevant to firms. For example, open economies are more likely to attract global intermediaries, thus supporting MNE operations by offering both local and global intermediary services. Khanna *et al.* also note, however, that highly open countries may also reduce the strength of the MNE's FSAs relative to host country firms. For example, local firms in open economies are as likely as foreign MNEs to have access to the international capital markets. To assist in assessing the openness of emerging economies, useful questions include: Are the government, media and the population at large receptive to foreign investment? Can a company make greenfield investments and acquire local companies? Are foreign intermediaries allowed (e.g., advertising firms, retailers, auditing firms)? Can executives leave and enter the country freely? Can citizens travel abroad?

For example, the developed economies of the US and EU are largely open to all forms of FDI except where monopoly or national security concerns prevail. The emerging economies of Russia and Brazil allow greenfield investments and acquisitions, but MNEs often partner with local firms to get access to needed local expertise in Brazil and access to government and local inputs in Russia. Joint ventures in India, on the other hand, are the only entry mode for MNEs in some sectors of the economy, as there are certain restrictions on greenfield investments. Finally, China appears open, allowing both greenfield investments and acquisitions, but MNEs must be aware that many acquisition targets used to be state-owned, and may have hidden liabilities. In addition, freedom of movement for employees and MNE managers can be somewhat restricted in China.

Third, as regards product markets in emerging economies, these are becoming increasingly attractive, but MNEs still struggle to get reliable information about the consumers in such markets. From the consumer's perspective, emerging economies tend to lack consumer courts or advocacy groups, thus creating consumer distrust of large MNEs. In assessing emerging economies' product markets, MNE managers should assess such areas as intellectual property rights, brand perceptions and brand management. Managers will also need to gauge the availability and quality of intermediaries such as suppliers, logistics providers and retail chains. Questions to facilitate such assessments include: What is the availability of data on customer tastes and purchasing behaviour? Are there cultural barriers to market research? Can consumers obtain unbiased information? Can companies access raw materials of good quality?

The product markets of the EU and US are characterized by sophisticated design capabilities, national and international suppliers, mature markets with a profusion of brands and governments that enforce and protect trademarks. The emerging economies vary on most of these aspects of the product market. For example, focusing on intellectual property rights (IPR) reveals that while Brazil and India have some IPR problems with the US, Russia exhibits an ambivalent attitude towards IPR and China struggles with severe problems of imitation and piracy.

Fourth, in the labour market sphere, emerging economies are often characterized by large labour pools, but these countries often lack both managerial and skilled workers. Part of the difficulty with emerging economy labour markets is the difficulty in assessing the quality of talent available. MNEs encounter this problem because of a lack of recruiting agencies to screen potential employees as well as a lack of organizations that rate the quality of the training provided by various training institutions and business schools in emerging economies.

In assessing emerging economy labour markets, MNE managers should gauge the education infrastructure, particularly technical and management training, as well as the availability of data to sort out the quality of the educational institutions. Other useful questions include: what is the language of business? Are there large post-recruitment training needs? Can employees move easily from one company to another?

Applying a labour market analysis suggests that the US and EU have a large and varied pool of management talent, and India also possesses a large pool of English-speaking management. Brazil and Russia have large pools of managers with varying degrees of English proficiency, while China has a small market for managers that shows no signs of growing.

Fifth, emerging economies' capital markets are largely inefficient and lack specialized intermediaries in areas such as credit rating, investment analysis, banking services, venture capital and auditing. Here, it may be difficult for the MNE to raise capital, evaluate the creditworthiness of other economic actors and enforce contracts.

MNE senior managers should therefore assess the capital market's inefficiencies in a wide variety of areas, including barriers to raising capital, weaknesses in corporate governance (especially as regards investor protection), absence of financial intermediaries, inefficiencies in regulating the financial services sector, poor accounting standards and inadequate procedures surrounding financial distress.

Whereas the US and EU financial markets are largely efficient, and do not suffer much from all the problems described above, the emerging economies' capital markets are not as advanced. The emerging economies of India and Brazil have reasonably developed banking and equity markets, while China is somewhat underdeveloped on this measure. Russia has a strong banking system, but it is largely dominated by state-owned banks.

Khanna *et al.* propose that, after determining these five components of an emerging economy's institutional context, MNE managers need to choose among three options. The first option is for the MNE to adapt its business model to the host country while keeping its core dominant logic constant. In its simplest form, this option was described in Chapter 1 of this book as Pattern III of FSA development, whereby the MNE melds non-location-bound FSAs from the home country with newly developed location-bound FSAs in the host emerging economy. The MNE adapts its business model to the unique context of each emerging economy, paying special attention to filling the key institutional voids that make 'business as usual' a non-starter.

A second option available to MNEs is to change the emerging economy's institutional context (e.g., to create more efficient markets). Obviously, this option is only available to a limited number of large MNEs. For example, when Japan's Suzuki entered India, it forced local suppliers to raise their quality standards, and this had significant positive spillover effects on quality management in a number of other industries.[17] Here, resource recombination not only benefits the MNE, but also has important societal spillovers.

A third option available to MNEs is simply to stay out of emerging economies where the requirements for new FSA development are too high. For example, Home Depot's business model builds upon the US transportation system and sophisticated logistical management systems to reduce inventory. The company also utilizes employee stock ownership to motivate employees. In emerging economies, however, a lack of transport infrastructure combined with certain institutional voids – namely, a lack of logistics intermediaries and a lack of sophisticated capital and labour markets – make it difficult for Home Depot to realize its value proposition of low prices, great service and good quality. This became apparent with Home Depot's unsuccessful attempt to enter Chile and Argentina, where operations had to be sold at a loss only a few years after being established.[18]

Context and complementary perspectives

The new framework for analysing emerging economies described above was published in *HBR* in 2005. As noted above, this piece extended Khanna and Palepu's earlier 1997 *HBR* article, which first discussed the important issue of institutional voids in emerging economies.[19] The 1997 article argued that focused strategies are usually appropriate in highly developed economies. Here, large firms limit their activities to where they have true FSAs compared to what is available in the external markets. In contrast, in emerging economies, highly diversified conglomerates may have more success because they can fill the institutional voids themselves. Conglomerates can control or produce internally all the inputs and intermediate goods not provided effectively and efficiently by external markets.

Building on the 1997 article, Khanna *et al.*'s 2005 piece focused much of its analysis on the emerging economies of Brazil, China, India and Russia. These countries illustrated how traditional tools of analysis fail to reveal many of the unique and critically important institutional features of emerging economies. Because understanding a particular country's institutional voids is so important to the MNE's success, senior managers need to use more than just these traditional tools of analysis. While the four large emerging economies provided much of the context for the article, the conclusions are applicable to emerging economies in general.

David Arnold and *John Quelch's* 1998 *SMR* article 'New strategies in emerging markets' usefully complements the 2005 Khanna *et al.* piece by offering another framework for assessing the market potential of emerging economies, and by giving practical advice for marketing strategy in emerging economies.

Much like the Khanna *et al.* piece, this article presents a compelling case that emerging economies are increasingly important to MNEs. For example, the article describes the case of Coca-Cola, which "predicts that its $2 billion dollar investment in China, India and Indonesia . . . can produce sales in those countries that double every three years for the indefinite future, compared with Coke's 4 to 5 per cent average annual growth in the US market in the past decade".[20]

Arnold and Quelch suggest two drivers for the possibility of increased sales in emerging economies. The first driver is the increase in disposable income and thus the creation of a potentially profitable market. The second driver is the growth of the Internet, which allows new markets to flourish by avoiding the high costs and difficulties associated with conventional channels.

The authors suggest that senior MNE managers interested in penetrating emerging economies should not assume that these are markets with a low level of sophistication where old strategies can be readily deployed, in the spirit of international projector archetypes. Instead, managers should seriously reconfigure their conventional marketing strategies. To assist managers in this endeavour, Arnold and Quelch suggest four areas where MNEs need to reconfigure their marketing approach: the timing of entry, market assessment, product policy and partner policy.

With regard to the *timing of entry*, conventional wisdom suggests that MNEs might want to postpone entry. Institutional voids make early entry riskier. The authors argue, however, that some types of first-mover advantages may be particularly high in emerging economies, especially the possibility of developing FSAs in government relations and the chance to enjoy high revenues quickly due to pent-up demand. Weak marketing levels overall also create the possibility of having a substantial marketing impact as a first mover in the market. Moreover, early movers have an opportunity to develop new FSAs in the form of pools of experienced managers and "innovative distribution processes or product packaging that is transferable to developed markets", the latter obviously referring to non-location-bound FSAs.[21] In other words, early entry facilitates the deployment and exploitation of extant non-location-bound FSAs and the easy development of new, location-bound FSAs, including personal relationships with key local players in both the public and private sectors. In addition, new FSAs with international exploitation potential may also arise as a result of creative resource recombination, such as innovative distribution processes that can be transferred from the host emerging economy to the developed markets. Finally, the pent-up demand in emerging economies can be viewed as a location advantage of these markets.

Like Khanna *et al.*, Arnold and Quelch suggest that traditional approaches to evaluate *market attractiveness* may not be appropriate in emerging economies. For example, traditional approaches may rely upon macro-economic and population data, but these data may simply be unavailable. This bounded rationality problem is compounded further by the need to choose from among a large number of emerging economies: "the number of countries to assess is so large it taxes even the most resourceful [MNEs]".[22] Arnold and Quelch propose an evaluation of the pool of candidate country markets in stages, with each stage allowing a further reduction of the candidate pool. First is the assessment of each country's long-term market potential. Second is the evaluation of present business prospects. Third is the prediction of potential profit levels.

The third area requiring a reconfiguration of the MNEs' marketing approach is *product policy*, especially in terms of required product adaptation in emerging economies. Traditionally, MNEs of the *centralized exporter* and *international projector* types have adopted an international product life cycle approach to emerging economies, serving these markets with mature products. The problem, however, is that "consumers in emerging economies see no need to use products that are now mature and obsolete in the developed world: they want the latest products now".[23] Consumers in emerging economies with substantial disposable income may actually be quite sophisticated in terms of product knowledge.

Sometimes, a firm's existing products are simply inappropriate for an emerging economy, and adaptation to local conditions is not feasible. For example, an automobile manufacturer cannot simply adapt its SUVs to the Chinese market. In these cases, the authors warn that MNE managers should not overestimate the profit potential of their existing products. Managers should instead try to build location-bound FSAs, as expressed by local brands.

The authors make the important point that infrastructural (and also institutional) voids provide an *opportunity* for technological leapfrogging, meaning the marketing of products that do not require conventional infrastructure (and institutions).

The final area where MNEs should reconfigure their marketing approach is in the area of *partner policy*. This is especially the case when government regulation imposes cooperation with local partners on the MNE and when distance vis-à-vis the host environment is large. While such partnering assists MNEs in overcoming bounded rationality constraints, these partnerships also open the MNE to greater bounded reliability hazards. Like Arnold in Chapter 11, the authors note that, "In many cases [MNEs] plan to switch to direct distribution soon after achieving a critical mass of sales in order to gain greater control over their business because distributors follow their own interests."[24] As discussed in Chapter 11, this can create a vicious cycle of increasing bounded reliability challenges. To avoid these problems, the authors suggest selecting partners on the basis of competence, meaning the longer-term complementarity of their FSAs with those of the MNE, rather than on a product-market familiarity basis. In order to curb bounded reliability problems, the authors also suggest that MNEs avoid delegating their entire marketing strategy to intermediaries and remain open to multiple partners. Finally, the authors note that emerging economies often necessitate direct selling because of the lack of distribution and communication infrastructure, or in Khanna *et al.*'s terms, because of institutional voids.

A second complementary perspective to Khanna *et al.*'s piece is provided in a 2003 *CMR* article by **Maria Flores Letelier**, **Fernando Flores** and **Charles Spinosa**.[25] Letelier *et al.* argue that, when penetrating an emerging economy, an MNE must have a deep understanding of the consumer's culture: "The key is to understand the particular value created for the end-user, which often can only be found through a deep cultural understanding of the issues faced by end-users in these markets."[26] Such understanding includes realizing that low-income consumers want to improve their economic status: the implication for the MNE may be that potential consumers should also be viewed as potential producers. In other words, the MNE should not only sell goods to meet consumer demand. It should also help its consumers to develop producer-type skills that will become more valuable over time.

Letelier *et al.* specifically warn against the common penetration strategy adopted by many MNEs to penetrate emerging economies, namely reducing costs and prices by simply eliminating desirable product features. This strategy, requiring only minimal adaptation and practically no cultural understanding, is typical for *centralized exporters* and *international projectors*.

In practical terms, Letelier *et al.* suggest MNEs develop a new FSA with three components. The first component is to identify culturally relevant opportunities that will improve customers' lives. The second component is to build relationships and move away from simple contracting by engaging customers. This will help offset bounded reliability tendencies: consumers in emerging economies typically view MNEs with suspicion. The third component is to craft new measures for assessing success; such success measures might include the growth in their customers' wealth.

Letelier *et al.* use the cases of the Grameen Bank and CEMEX as key examples to show how emerging economy customers can be treated as producers, building upon a deep cultural understanding of the challenges they face. CEMEX, the world's third largest cement company, responded to emerging economy needs by developing an FSA in the form of the 'Patrimonio Hoy' programme. This programme allows do-it-yourself homebuilders to form small groups that take joint responsibility for making weekly payments to build or add rooms to their own homes. This structure gives lower-income customers the ability to become producers by building their own home, while also providing a demand for CEMEX's products. By its very mandate, the well-known Grameen Bank treats emerging economy customers as producers instead of consumers. The founder of the bank, Nobel Peace Prize-winner Muhammad Yunus, had a vision that all human beings can be entrepreneurs, and thus he focused on loans to cater to customers' productive inclinations. The bank also developed FSAs based on a deep understanding of the cultural challenges faced by its customers. For example, having member ownership in the bank allowed Islamic customers to remain within the bounds of Islamic law by paying interest to an institution of which they were part owners.

Khanna *et al.* contend that emerging economies are characterized by institutional voids and that MNEs must understand and work around these voids to be successful in such markets. Further, the authors suggest that each emerging economy is likely to have its own unique set of institutional voids to be filled. Thus, the MNE's recombination capabilities are critical to success in emerging economies. Substantial bundles of location-bound FSAs will likely have to be developed for each country.

MNE adaptation to the local context of emerging economies can involve various FSA development patterns.

As Figure 14.1 illustrates, Pattern III and Pattern IX represent the most common FSA development patterns in the emerging economy context. With both patterns, extant, non-location-bound FSAs are combined with new, location-bound strengths developed in the emerging economy. The resulting recombination is specific to the unique emerging economy context. It should be noted that Pattern IX, a network-based source of FSAs, captures cases whereby MNEs source ideas from multiple, emerging economy operations to address common challenges posed by these various contexts.

Pattern VII and Pattern X are also included in Figure 14.1 to capture the possibility of FSAs developed in emerging economies being transferred to other emerging economy locations or even to developed economies. These two patterns will occur when adaptations to the unique emerging economy context create FSAs deployable in MNE operations in other locations and contexts. However, it is likely that any international transfer of FSAs will need to be associated with developing additional, location-bound FSAs in the various recipient countries.

Sustained FSA development in emerging economies may also enhance the location advantages of these host economies. The filling of similar institutional voids by several MNEs at the same time may lead to new intermediaries being set up by entrepreneurs sensing a business opportunity. For example, if several MNEs are forced to organize their own logistics operations in-house, even though they are not very good at this, this creates an incentive for new third-party logistics providers to enter the market, thereby allowing these activities to be outsourced. Also, having several MNEs address institutional voids may also drive a variety of stakeholders to push for changes in the existing institutional system (e.g., in terms of providing better property rights protection, training for workers, deregulation of capital markets – see Chapter 3). This impact of MNEs should not be under-estimated by readers familiar only with developed economies: MNEs will cause more institutional spillover effects in emerging economies than they would in developed economies, as suggested by the shaded bands in Figure 14.2A, whereby MNEs attempt to fill significant institutional voids. The enlarged LA areas in Figure 14.2B represent the enhancement of the host country's location advantages, associated with extensive investment in location-bound FSA development by MNEs in emerging economies.

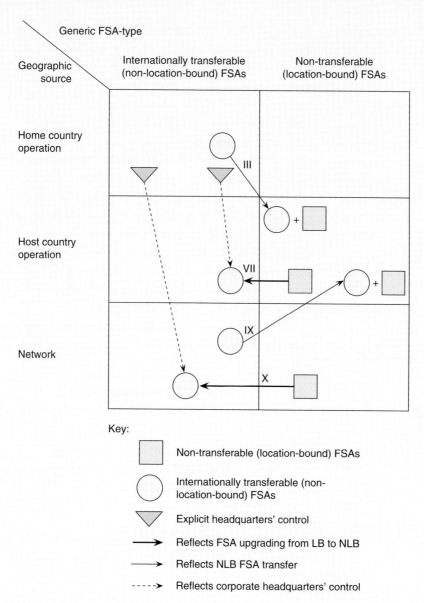

Figure 14.1
Patterns of FSA
development
in emerging
economy MNEs

Generic FSA-type

Geographic
source

Internationally transferable
(non-location-bound) FSAs

Non-transferable
(location-bound) FSAs

Home country
operation

III

Host country
operation

VII

Network

IX

X

Key:

Non-transferable (location-bound) FSAs

Internationally transferable (non-
location-bound) FSAs

Explicit headquarters' control

Reflects FSA upgrading from LB to NLB

Reflects NLB FSA transfer

Reflects corporate headquarters' control

Market seeking is not the only motivation that can cause MNEs to develop emerging economies and enhance their location advantages – natural resource seeking and strategic resource seeking can have similar effects. For example, upstream MNE activity in the realm of R&D, as discussed in Chapter 6, can play an important role in upgrading the location advantages of emerging economies through technology and capital transfers and formal human resources training. Furthermore, bringing in new activities such as JIT logistics and sophisticated internal accounting introduces best practices to emerging economies.

In spite of the business potential provided by emerging economies, senior MNE managers face important bounded rationality and bounded reliability challenges. For example, institutional voids in capital, labour and product markets make it difficult to assess potential partner firms, employees and customers. This lack of information exacerbates the bounded rationality challenges.

A similar challenge exists with respect to bounded reliability, in terms of both benevolent preference reversal and opportunism. The mix of high cultural, institutional, economic and spatial distances between the MNE's home base and most emerging economies increases the danger of benevolent preference reversal, i.e., subsidiary employees in the emerging economy foregoing the pursuit of corporate-wide goals in favour of local goals, in line with routines prevailing in host country firms. The lack of transparency in these economies (e.g., in terms of reputational assessment) also hinders the proper evaluation of business partners' efforts to fulfil commitments. Deficiencies in the rule of law and lax protection of intellectual property rights also increase the likelihood of opportunistic behaviour by limiting the MNE's recourse in the face of failed commitments.

These increased problems of bounded rationality and bounded reliability imply that operating in emerging economies requires investments of resources to both

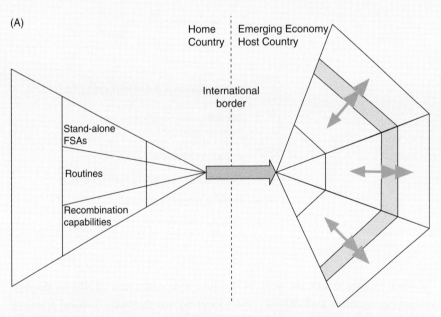

Figure 14.2
MNE operations
in emerging
economies

(A)

Home Country | Emerging Economy/Host Country

International border

Stand-alone FSAs

Routines

Recombination capabilities

The double-headed arrows on the emerging economy side reflect the close alignment the emerging economy operations must develop between the firm's LB FSAs and the host's LAs. The shaded band between the LB FSA and LA segments of the emerging economy's triangle represents an enhancement in progress of these LAs. Such enhancement becomes possible because of the MNE's investments in LB FSAs related to filling institutional voids. The extra arrowheads, pointing to the LA, reflect the positive spill-over effects on the emerging economy's LAs.

Figure 14.2
(cont.)

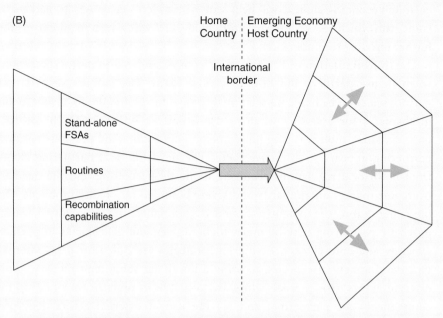

(B)

Home Country | Emerging Economy Host Country

International border

Stand-alone FSAs

Routines

Recombination capabilities

As a result of multiple MNE investments in the emerging economy, and the associated efforts to fill institutional voids, the emerging economy's LAs greatly improve as shown by their larger area in the figure.

prevent and remediate these problems. Khanna *et al.* do not discuss how to do this, which represents the first of three limitations of their article. Khanna *et al.* do identify the problems posed by institutional voids when MNEs work with partners to secure services normally associated with simple, arm's length contracting in developed economies (e.g., transportation services). Khanna *et al.* make the important observation that institutional voids reduce the MNE's access to critical information and its ability to enforce contracts. Limited analysis is provided, however, on what the MNE can actually do to prevent and remediate the hazards of bounded rationality and bounded reliability when working with partners. For example, there is limited analysis of how to obtain credible commitments from partners.

A second limitation of Khanna *et al.*'s study is the lack of analysis regarding the unique characteristics that the MNE brings to the MNE–emerging economy relationship. The institutional context of emerging economies is undoubtedly an important parameter in MNE strategy, but equally important are the MNE's administrative heritage (***centralized exporter, international projector, international coordinator or multi-centred MNE***) and motivation for international expansion (market seeking, natural resource seeking, strategic resource seeking or efficiency seeking). A thorough understanding of both the MNE and the emerging economy context will help senior managers decide which markets to enter, with which FSAs, with what entry mode, and with which requirements for further resource recombination.

The third limitation of Khanna *et al.*'s piece is related to partner selection: when to use partners and how to choose them. The authors suggest that partner selection be based on relational competencies, but do not elaborate on mechanisms for assessing when to use a partner and how to choose this partner. This problem is magnified in emerging economies, precisely because partnering appears so attractive there. The need for local partnering stems from both local regulations requiring domestic partnering and the need to overcome market unfamiliarity and severe bounded rationality problems. On the other hand, the potential bounded rationality and reliability hazards posed by partnering may be much higher, given the deficiencies in partner selection and enforcement. Partnering strategies are called for if (a) internal FSA development is expected to bring a lower net value than reliance upon external actors, (b) external actors are available in practice (not tied up by competitors) for partnering, and (c) the use of external actors does not jeopardize the specific expansion project considered (e.g., because of goal divergence). As regards this last point, MNEs may wish to internalize services provided by emerging economy partners when only one or a few local suppliers of these services exist and new service suppliers are prohibited from entering the market.

To conclude, emerging economies provide increasingly attractive locations for MNE expansion. The difficulties in selecting specific countries and operating in those countries, however, remain substantial. To meet these challenges, senior MNE managers should carefully scrutinize the institutional context of these markets and assess whether and how the MNE's FSAs can be augmented so as to allow successful operation in these idiosyncratic environments.

Five management takeaways

1. Reflect on the key institutional context dimensions of each newly entered emerging economy and create a 'map' of this institutional context to determine the required investments in location-bound FSAs.
2. Decide, when contemplating entry into an emerging economy, whether you are: (1) willing to adapt your business model to this host country, or (2) capable of changing this emerging economy's institutional context, or (3) ultimately unwilling to take the risk of investing in this emerging economy, therefore staying out because of the challenging institutional context.

3. Revisit your marketing strategy on four dimensions when entering an emerging economy: timing of entry, market assessment, product policy and partner policy.
4. Focus sufficiently on understanding the cultural specificities of the potential customer base in the emerging economy.
5. Carefully envision the various possible patterns of capability building specific to expansion in a particular emerging economy as compared to a more developed economy, including the impact of the 'relational component' of contracting.

Case 14.1 AIG: Filling the institutional voids in China

CASE

In 1992, US-based American International Group (AIG), one of the world's largest insurance companies, was given the first licence issued to any foreign company to operate in China's insurance market. Although other foreign companies started to receive licences in 1995, by 2001 AIG still held 8 out of the 12 licences granted to non-Chinese firms in the Chinese insurance industry. Moreover, the other foreign insurers had to set up joint ventures with local Chinese firms and were limited to either life or general insurance. In contrast, AIG was permitted to run wholly owned subsidiaries selling both life and general policies in Shanghai and Guangzhou.[27]

How did AIG gain this unique position? Why did AIG decide to enter China when the market was still small and highly regulated? How did AIG fill the institutional voids? And how should AIG address the new challenges of the increasingly competitive Chinese market?

AIG: Its origin and expansion strategies

AIG was founded in 1919 by a Californian World War I veteran named Cornelius Vander Starr. Partly because of his former experience with an insurance agency in San Francisco before joining the army, Starr founded property/casualty insurer American Asiatic Underwriters (AAU) in Shanghai, underwriting businesses for other insurers. In 1921, Starr began selling life insurance policies to the Chinese, at a time when other foreign insurers were unwilling to do so. Starr reasoned that many Chinese already lived long lives and that life expectancy would probably continue to rise due to improving living standards. Over the next ten years, his businesses expanded in the Far East. In 1926, Starr set up a New York office called American International Underwriters, specializing in foreign risks incurred by American companies.

The Japanese invasion during World War II, and later the Communist Party takeover, interrupted AAU's operation and finally forced AAU to cease its operations in China in 1950 and shift its focus to the US. Starr's businesses in other regions continued to grow, and AIG was established in 1960 as a holding company for Starr's insurance companies around the world. In 1962, Starr handed over the management of the company to Maurice Greenberg, who changed the business focus from personal insurance to high-margin corporate coverage. Moreover, Greenberg switched the distribution channel from using agents to working with independent brokers, so as to avoid paying agents' basic salaries when business was down. AIG went public in 1969.[28] In Asia, with the exception of mainland China, AIG also expanded with growing market shares. By 1975, AIG had become the largest foreign insurer in Asia.

During its long history, AIG developed the strategy of entering markets in their early stages of market development. According to then-CEO Greenberg, "AIG companies were the first foreign insurance companies to enter Japan, South Korea, and many Southeast Asian countries. Our joint ventures in Central and Eastern Europe were the first of their kind in those markets."[29] In Japan, AIG started to operate "almost the day after MacArthur landed there following World War II".[30]

Early entry brought AIG three major first-mover advantages. First, AIG could develop favourable government relations. When the markets were protected, AIG could nonetheless win approvals and new businesses by utilizing its government connections through unusual (often informal) channels.

Second, competition in these markets was less fierce than in the US or Europe, so AIG could dominate niche markets. Even if competitors did enter later, AIG had by then already established its brand and it could also apply so-called grandfathering provisions to protect its existing rights. For example, other foreign insurance companies were required by the Chinese government to set up joint ventures with local Chinese firms, but AIG was given permission to set up two new wholly owned branches.[31]

Third, AIG was able to reach a minimum efficient size quickly and then compete with latecomers from that low-cost position. With low overhead costs in these markets and low operating costs through a centralized command system, AIG was able to reach its minimum efficient size quickly. Because it then had lower costs than latecomers, it earned a high profit margin.

The Chinese insurance industry in the late 1970s and 1980s

After the communist takeover in 1949, the Chinese government created the People's Insurance Company of China (PICC), which became the only insurance company operating in China. Between 1959 and 1979, even PICC ceased most of its operations, with its activities largely confined to international business, such as aviation and marine cargo insurance. In these years, China basically had no domestic general insurance business or life insurance business. As recalled by Greenberg, "When I first met with PICC in 1975, it was tiny. There were probably about 200 people in the whole insurance industry in China. There was no need to insure anything because everything was government owned."[32]

Since the economic reforms initiated by Deng Xiaoping in 1978, both the macro-economic environment and the insurance industry gradually improved. First, the Chinese economy grew significantly. Economic growth typically leads to a strong expansion of life insurance premiums, after the GDP per capita passes the threshold of US $1,000–1,300. In the late 1980s and early 1990s, a few cities and several provinces in China had passed that threshold.

Second, the Chinese government started to introduce new laws to govern domestic economic activities, including insurance activities. Important milestones included the Economic Contract Law (1981) and the Provisional Ordinance of Insurance Enterprise (1985). However, in the 1980s such regulations were still rudimentary, and enforcement was patchy. Thus, 'good relationships' (guan'xi) with local and central governments remained crucial for doing business successfully in China.

Third, the Chinese government, lacking experienced personnel in the insurance industry, decided to open the insurance market gradually to both foreign and domestic companies. For example, China Pacific Insurance Company and Ping An Insurance Company entered the insurance market in the 1980s, resulting in some domestic competition.

Despite these slight improvements, the Chinese insurance industry in the late 1970s and 1980s did not look like a promising place to invest. According to Greenberg, "No other foreign insurance company was even paying attention to China at that time, and no one thought there was a chance to get a license in China."[33] However, Greenberg still decided to work on China, mainly because he believed that "one day China would join the world of open markets because 1.3 billion people cannot exist in isolation for long, and you cannot have a truly global trading system if China is not part of it".[34]

Opening the market in China, step one: Building relationships

Greenberg decided to put the company "at the leading edge of opening markets".[35] To get into markets early, he followed five rules: know what you want to do, develop a long-term view, understand the local culture, be persistent and "have the CEO out front".[36]

Greenberg made his first visit to China in 1975, only three years after Nixon's visit. Between then and the time that AIG's first licence was granted in 1992, Greenberg made between 40 and 50 trips to China. Greenberg's initial visits led AIG to establish a representative office in 1980 and a joint venture called the China-American Insurance Company between AIG and PICC in 1979. Focusing on insurance related to Sino–America trade and worldwide reinsurance, the China-American Insurance Company had only a niche market with modest commercial success. However, it transferred know-how from AIG to PICC and, for AIG, the joint venture helped develop relationships with State Council members and deputy prime ministers.

In the mid 1980s, AIG opened an infrastructure fund and soon started its first project in Shanghai, with an investment of US $195 million in the Shanghai Centre Office-Residential Complex. This large investment was viewed as a firm commitment and won AIG the support of Zhu Rongji, then mayor of Shanghai and later premier of China. Several years later, Zhu asked Greenberg to help create the International Business Advisory Council for Shanghai. The Council became so influential that almost every ministry in Beijing sent officials to attend the council's meetings. In the late 1980s and early 1990s, Greenberg's network expanded to the top echelons, including Jiang Zemin, General Secretary of the Chinese Communist Party Central Committee, and Rong Yiren, Vice Chairman of the National People's Congress Standing Committee.

Nonetheless, an application for a licence to sell insurance in Shanghai through Zhu Rongji was blocked by PICC. Zhu, then Deputy Prime Minister, suggested that Greenberg should personally try to convince every member of the State Council, especially Li Peng, then Premier. Greenberg recalled how hard it was to convince Li Peng, as it was difficult to see him and he did not want to discuss the issue at all. When Greenberg, at that time travelling in Europe, was finally offered a 10-minute meeting with Li Peng in New York, Greenberg flew back and the meeting actually lasted almost an hour and a half.

What Greenberg did to win licences went beyond the insurance industry. For example, AIG bought the bronze windows that had been stolen from the Summer Palace by foreign forces in 1900. These windows had been hidden until 1992, when they reappeared at a Paris gallery. AIG had the windows authenticated and sent back to China as a donation. This was viewed as a nice gesture by both Chinese officials and the public at large, as Chinese people have always desired to bring missing relics back home.[37]

Opening the market in China, step two: From relationships to business

In 1992, AIG was finally granted a licence. Greenberg said, "It had taken some seventeen years since my first visit to China to get our first insurance license . . . it was worth the wait."[38] By 2001, AIG was granted licences to sell life insurance in Shanghai, Guangzhou, Fushan and Shenzhen, and property and casualty insurance in Guangzhou. AIG had 12 wholly owned subsidiaries in these cities, even though, as noted above, all other foreign companies had to form joint ventures to enter China. In 2001, AIG was granted four new licenses, namely in Beijing, Suzhou, Dongguan and Jiangmen. The firm's insurance products were divided into two sections; life insurance versus property and casualty insurance, which are often referred to as general insurance. AIG's life insurance is sold under the subsidiary The American International Assurance Company Limited (AIA), while its general insurance is sold under the subsidiary Chartis Inc.

Gaining access to the market was only the first step towards profits. AIG still had to tailor its products and distribution channels to the Chinese market in three major ways.

First, because China had so few agents with expertise in insurance, AIG made substantial investments in training its agents. By the year 2000, according to Greenberg, "over 6,000 agents currently employed by the domestic insurance industry were trained by AIG".[39]

Second, AIG introduced the agency distribution system to China. AIG only paid commission to its agents – not a basic salary. In this way, AIG realized huge savings. At present, the agency distribution system is widely adopted by most insurance companies in China.

Third, as many Chinese customers view life insurance as bringing bad luck, AIG designed endowment policies for Chinese customers and marketed these policies as savings instruments rather than insurance products.

AIG's China's life insurance operations have been successful. In Shanghai and Guangzhou, AIG had a market share of respectively 13 per cent and 7 per cent in 2000, behind only the domestic firms China Life and Ping An. In 2003, AIG bought a 10 per cent stake in PICC, China's largest non-life insurer. In 2004, AIG sold policies worth US $580 million, accounting for 1.49 per cent of the life insurance market and positioning itself as the largest foreign life insurer in China.[40]

Prior to 2007, general insurance was sold in branches under AIU Insurance, a subsidiary of Chartis. In September 2007, AIG General Insurance Company China Limited (AIG General) was incorporated and became AIG's first wholly owned foreign enterprise in China.[41] In July 2009, it began operating under the name Chartis Insurance Company China Limited. Chartis has been able to expand the geographic coverage of its operations, establishing a branch in Beijing in 2008 and in Jiangsu in 2012.

AIG bailout

AIG put itself into a dangerous position when its subsidiary, AIG Financial Products, became heavily involved in the mortgage-backed securities markets in the United States. When the housing bubble burst in 2007, AIG faced an inevitable crisis. In August 2008, AIG reported losses of US \$5.36 billion and in September of that year the company had US \$14.5 billion in capital requirements from derivative contracts.[42] The US Treasury was faced with a vital decision on whether AIG should be bailed out or left to fail. On 16 September 2008, the US treasury offered an US \$85 billion emergency loan to AIG.[43] This loan was later renegotiated with the government as an extended five-year loan valued at US \$60 billion with the government taking an 80 per cent share in the company.[44] The US Treasury and the Federal Reserve expressed the importance of backing AIG due to the potentially devastating consequences of losing a firm with a swap portfolio valued at over US \$441 billion.[45] Over the next several years the government intervened and renegotiated the terms of the loan several times. By April 2012, US taxpayers had put approximately US \$182 billion into the AIG bailout.[46]

However, by 2012 AIG had realized a substantial turnaround from its bailout just four years earlier. The company reported net income of US \$3.1 billion for the first quarter of 2012. President and CEO, Robert H. Benmosche, also announced that AIG "achieved the milestone of reducing total outstanding or authorized U.S. government assistance by 75 percent".[47] Analysts were projecting that by April 2013, the US government would no longer own any part of the company.[48] The company's turnaround has been controversial as the government allowed AIG to claim prior losses against current income, which will provide years of tax breaks for the firm.[49]

Impact on AIG in China

The bailout of AIG created some uneasiness in the company's operations in Asia. AIG's subsidiaries aimed to reassure their clients that their financial situation was healthy and policy claims could be met.[50] The American International Assurance (AIA), the Asian life insurance arm of AIG, stated that "although AIG faces short-term liquidity pressures, we have strong, well-positioned businesses in diverse markets around the world and a deep asset base".[51] The China Insurance Regulatory Commission also closely monitored the situation after the bailout.

Given AIG's shaky financial situation, the company realized that selling off parts of its business was necessary to pay back the bailout loan. AIG looked to sell part of its stake in AIA to Prudential, a UK insurance company. The deal eventually fell through so AIG issued shares of AIA to the public in 2010, raising US \$20.5 billion.[52] AIG announced in March 2012 that it was again issuing shares in AIA for loan repayment purposes. By the end of this second round of financing, AIG would control only 19 per cent of AIA.[53]

Challenges and opportunities

Although AIG has successfully penetrated the Chinese market, both its market share and profits are modest. Its position as the largest foreign insurer in China was lost to Italy's Assicurazioni Generali in 2005.[54] In recent years, it has faced several major challenges.

Most importantly, on the domestic front, allegations by US regulators that AIG inflated its revenues forced Greenberg to step down as CEO, thereby leaving a void in AIG's political networks in China.[55] Although Greenberg was still warmly welcomed in China,[56] AIG had to find ways to replace Greenberg's networks and to convince Chinese officials that the new AIG was still committed to China. A number of analysts noted that both Edmund Tse, AIG's senior vice-Chairman of life insurance, and Donald Kanak, COO focusing on Asia, had good relationships with Chinese politicians,[57] while others commented that political connections were not as important as they had been five years before, as the insurance market in China had matured.

The second challenge was to design the right products. Although AIG had the opportunity to sell products through the 4,300 branches and 128,000 agents of PICC, it had to find the right balance between invading the turf of PICC and finding a sizeable niche market worthy of investment.

A third challenge is the changing role of banks in the Chinese insurance industry. Previously, banks were used only as a distribution channel for insurance; however they now design and market insurance products themselves. Large partnerships are beginning to form between local banks and large international insurance firms, which is drastically changing the insurance environment. In a study completed by PwC in 2011, it was found that the three key drivers in the Chinese insurance industry were regulatory changes, bank entry into the industry and competition among domestic insurers.[58]

Finally, foreign insurance companies continue to struggle in China, whereby only 11 of the 47 foreign companies posted profits in 2010.[59] Foreign market share continued to be low with non-Chinese companies holding 5 per cent of the life insurance market and a mere 1 per cent in general insurance.[60] Furthermore, investment opportunities available to insurance companies were still limited due to government regulations.

The market still holds opportunities for foreign insurers with foreign life insurance companies expecting 20–40 per cent growth in 2011. General insurance was expected to grow by 30–50 per cent between 2011 and 2014.[61]

Furthermore, an opportunity arose for AIG from the Chinese government's plan to lift its restrictions on foreign insurance companies covering mandatory third party liability automobile insurance. Prior to the announcement in 2011, foreign companies were restricted to providing only optional coverage, making insurance contracts unattractive to locals who desired full, comprehensive coverage.[62] Removing the regulatory restrictions was expected to allow foreign insurance companies to gain access to the lucrative 50 billion dollar market. Kevin Goulding, the head of Chartis China, sees large potential for business stating, "It's an extremely large market and will also allow us to offer other products to consumers."[63]

Given the above challenges, AIG's profits in China did not grow much during the past decade; however with government restrictions slowly being loosened and the market growing, the long-term future for AIG does not look too bad.

QUESTIONS

1. What, if any, were the relevant institutional voids in China?
2. Based on the framework developed by Khanna *et al.*, what types of strategies should foreign insurance companies pursue? What did AIG do to cope with the institutional voids?
3. What were AIG's FSAs developed in China? What non-location-bound FSAs had been transferred to China? What first-mover advantages did AIG reap in China?
4. How did AIG combine the use of its location-bound FSAs and non-location-bound FSAs in China?

Case 14.2 Just Google it: China and India

CASE

With offices in nearly 50 countries around the world and a network of over 150 Google domains available in multiple languages, Google Inc. is by all accounts a highly successful MNE. In 2011, 96 per cent of Google's US $ 38.6 billion in revenue was derived from advertising revenue from Google-owned sites and partner sites. Partner sites pay Google every time a client clicks on a text-based or graphics-based ad.

According to Netmarketshare, Google's worldwide share of the search engine market is approximately 85 per cent.[64] In fact, the term 'google it' has become synonymous with finding something on the Internet via a computer, laptop, mobile phone or tablet. Google continuously upgrades and enhances its best-in-class search technology and invests in new Internet or mobile technologies via acquisitions or through its own R&D.

Rapid international expansion was critical to Google's early domination of the Internet search market. Google's initial international expansion strategy was to provide core search capabilities to foreign markets in local languages. Google's portal was eventually made available in multiple foreign languages. Google recognized that a local market presence was required to grow its revenue producing service, AdWords. In 2012, Google had offices in nearly 45 countries. These offices range from AdWords sales and customer support units to full-fledged R&D offices. As Google opened local offices in countries that did not subscribe to democratic principles and viewed democracy on the Web as a threat to internal security, Google faced difficult decisions. Should it adhere strictly to its core principle of democracy on the Web and provide users with access to all information? Or should it adapt to local regulations and norms by complying with censorship requirements? Google's approach to this question was quite different in two emerging economies, China and India.

China and India have long been known as outsourcing destinations that provide access to skilled, inexpensive labour to perform lower-level jobs considered undesirable in Western countries. Today China and India are developing R&D centres with highly skilled human resources reservoirs. MNEs have opened R&D offices in India and China and assigned product development roles previously reserved for highly educated Western countries. Silicon Valleys have arisen in North Beijing, China and in Bangalore, India. It has even been proposed that increasingly 'reverse innovation' occurs, whereby products are designed and developed for emerging markets in a first stage, and sold to developed markets in a second stage.[65] If this were indeed correct, then MNEs that are not participating in reverse innovation will lose global market share as emerging market companies develop competitive products and become first movers. Google is an example of a company that operates R&D offices in China and India. However, the road has not been an easy one.

From dorm room to boardroom

In 1995, Larry Page and Sergey Brin met in Stanford University's computer science PhD program.[66] A year later, Page and Brin worked together on a new search engine called *Backrub*, which utilized their proprietary, sophisticated search technology. In 1997, the service was re-named *Google* . . . a play on the word googol, which is the number 10 followed by 100 zeros. Page and Brin thought the name represented their mission to "organize a seemingly infinite amount of information on the web".[67] Google's search engine technology utilizes "Googlebots"[68] to crawl the Web searching for new content. The content is indexed and copied, and a website's importance is analysed using an algorithm called PageRank™ as well as other secret criteria based on approximately 200 indicators. When a user enters a search query, Google searches for key words and returns results based on a website's importance. PageRank™ provides Google with an advantage over competitors that only return search results based on key words.

Google strives to deliver search results that are as neutral and relevant as possible; therefore it does not allow advertising customers to purchase better search placements. While many of Google's competitors allow advertising customers to pay for better search placement, advertisements on Google.com are placed separately from non-paid search results so that users can tell if a link is from a paid source. Google earns revenue each time a user clicks on a paid advertisement link.

After graduating from Stanford in 1998, Page and Brin opened up the first Google Inc. office in their friend's garage thanks to a US $100,000 investment from Sun Microsystems' co-founder, Andy Bechtolsheim. In December of the same year, Google received a huge break. *PC Magazine* singled out Google as the top search engine in 1998, praising Google for having "an uncanny knack for returning extremely relevant results"[69].

Google never looked back, moving out of the garage two months later with eight employees to an office in Mountain View, California, close to Stanford University. One year later, in June 2000, Google became the world's largest search engine, with one billion websites indexed.

Google continued to grow over the next four years, quadrupling its number of indexed images and Web pages, and moving to a new location with 800 employees in Mountain View, California, called the "Googleplex".[70] During this time, Google opened its first international office in Tokyo, Japan, followed by an office in Sidney, Australia.

Partnerships were forged with Yahoo Inc. and AOL to provide Google search and sponsored links. Google also partnered with Universo Online, which led to Google's leading market position in Latin America. In August 2004, Google went public, and in its Founders' IPO Letter, Page and Brin declared: "Don't be evil. We believe strongly that in the long term, we will be better served – as shareholders and in all other ways – by a company that does good things for the world even if we forgo some short-term gains. This is an important aspect of our culture and is broadly shared within the company."[71]

Google has become well known for continuous innovation through research and development, strategic acquisition or through partnerships. Google's senior management team credits its success to a highly innovative, laid-back corporate culture that enables Google to cultivate creative, talented and dedicated employees. Today, Google is more than a search engine. Google is also known for email (Gmail); maps (Google Maps); digital imaging (Google Earth); blogging (Blogger); Web browser (Google Chrome); video (YouTube); translation in over 50 languages (Google Translate); and a free, open source mobile platform (Google Android) to name a few. With multiple offices in over 40 countries around the world, Google has rapidly grown into an Internet powerhouse. If Google's US $12 billion purchase of Motorola Mobility in 2011 receives international regulatory approval, Google will have access to Motorola's 17,000 patents and 7,500 patent applications in the mobile telecommunications industry, as well as mobile phone manufacturing. Google has received regulatory approval from the United States, the European Union and China for this take-over. Speculation abounds that Google is preparing to take on Apple Inc. in the mobile category. Google now already sells branded phones, tablets, and other mobile devices. Will Google's entry into the hardware game incite competitive handset makers to stop installing Google's Android operating system? Google's strategy is to operate the handset business completely separately from the remainder of the Google businesses, but is the risk to Google's revenues worth any potential upswing from mobile phone sales?

Life as a "Googler"

Google is committed to maintaining the entrepreneurial, innovative culture first crafted in the founders' garage office near Stanford University. Google's informal hierarchy encourages open communication and a willingness to share ideas. Google cares about its employees' development, health and well-being, and in turn, asks for dedication and hard work.

Google's core principles, or "Ten Things we know to be true", are[72]:

1. Focus on the user and all else will follow.
2. It's best to do one thing really, really well.
3. Fast is better than slow.

4. Democracy on the Web works.

5. You don't need to be at your desk to need an answer.

6. You can make money without doing evil.

7. There's always more information out there.

8. The need for information crosses all borders.

9. You can be serious without a suit.

10. Great just isn't good enough.

In January 2012, *Fortune Magazine* ranked Google number one in its "100 Best Companies to Work For" survey.[73] In 2012, Google had over 18,500 employees in the United States and 10,000 employees in its international offices. Google is an employer of choice. Many engineers, computer developers and business graduates dream of becoming a Googler. *Fortune* reported that Google received over 1.1 million applications for only 7,000 jobs in 2011[74]; one might have better luck winning the lottery than landing a job at Google. This prestige gives Google access to the best and the brightest, and cultivates a sense of pride in its employees. *Fortune* noted that Google employees "rave about their mission, the culture, and the famous perks of the Plex"[75].

Google's physical work environment at the MountainView Googleplex and other international offices reflects its open communication policies. While not all offices are identical, they share many themes. There are very few enclosed offices; instead, Googlers work on laptops and share yurts, cubes or huddle rooms. Google provides complimentary shuttles to and from work, and offers no-charge, healthy gourmet food for breakfast, lunch and dinner in its cafes. Snacks and beverages are also available at no charge throughout the day.

It is not uncommon to see Lava lamps, bean bag chairs, foosball tables, video games, pool tables, wave pools and gyms with yoga and dance in Google offices. At Google's corporate headquarters in Mountain View, employees can bring their dog to work, a practice that began early in Google's life. If a Googler gets a sore back from sitting in front of a laptop computer for hours, he or she can get a free massage. If Googlers suddenly realize that their hair has become a mess, they can visit the hair salon.

Googlers are encouraged to dedicate 20 per cent of their time to personal, innovative Google initiatives. New projects can be presented to senior managers through weekly group discussions and are pursued if senior management sees merit in them. AdSense and Google News are examples of employees' "20% time" projects that were developed into products.[76]

Work life at Google may sound like a party; however, the firm's performance-driven culture rewards employees based on results. An underperformer is not likely to last long at Google.

Google in China: A core principle is challenged

The Chinese Internet market is one of the largest in the world, with over 500 million Internet users as of September 2011, more than double that in the United States.[77] Given its population of more than 1.3 billion people (as of 2011) and the country's continued economic growth, China represents an important market with enormous opportunity for many MNEs. Before China's entry into the World Trade Organization in 2001, the country was essentially a closed market, with high trade tariffs and many market impediments. In 2006, China opened its markets to the world with the goal of improving work prospects for its citizens.[79] While the economic reforms allowed China to achieve rapid economic expansion and provided its citizens with greater wealth and opportunities, the country is still characterized by a totalitarian regime that utilizes intimidation and brutality to enforce its rule. Journalists, online bloggers, religious leaders and other dissidents have been jailed indefinitely and/or tortured for speaking against the communist regime.

China has one of the world's most extensive Internet monitoring operations in the world.[80] The country has installed numerous routers and firewalls that attempt to keep banned information from entering the country's Internet system. Chinese government agencies control the Internet infrastructure, and also employ tens of thousands of people to police the Internet to look for banned content. Internet service providers are required to keep track of all websites visited by customers, and must turn this information over to officials. Officials also police Internet cyber cafes, and cyber cafes are required to obtain client photos and keep records of all Internet activity. The government also relies on individual citizens to provide information regarding offensive content.

Google maintains its principles in China

In 2000, Google began offering a Chinese language version of Google.com, but as a result of extensive filtering at China's Internet service providers, the portal was unreliable and slow in mainland China.[81] Over the next five years, Google refused to comply with Chinese censors, and the service vacillated between horrendously slow to inaccessible.

While Google was holding steadfast to its principle of democracy on the Web, Google's competitors did not have such reservations. Yahoo was the first US company to open an office in Beijing and offer a Chinese language search engine hosted within China's borders. Yahoo openly complied with censorship restrictions; however, the policy of cooperation tragically backfired in 2006 when Yahoo provided information to Chinese officials that led to the arrest and detention of a Chinese journalist.[82] Since 2006, Yahoo has worked to keep personal data out of the hands of repressive governments. Microsoft also opened an office in China during this time period, and openly cooperated with officials when required. In 2005, in response to criticism in the US after Microsoft shut down a Chinese dissident's blog, Microsoft's Chairman Bill Gates stated that it is required to operate under the laws of the country in which it does business, and that "the ability to withhold information really no longer exists".[83]

Google revisits its censorship policy

Mid 2005, Google hired Kai-Fu Lee, a former Microsoft executive, as global vice-president responsible for opening a research centre in China.[84] Lee grew up in Taiwan and received his PhD in computer science at Carnegie Mellon.[85] Lee was revered in China, admired as someone who used his success in America to assist in China's economic development.

The Chinese government informed Google it would have to censor search results if it was to be granted an operating licence. Google reluctantly agreed with the censorship terms for websites

443

operating in China, and launched Google.cn in January 2006. The Chinese language Google.com search engine remained available, uncensored, in spite of the problems described below. A few months later, Google opened an office in Beijing in an area known as China's Silicon Valley. Google's China office contained the usual perks, including exercise balls, foosball tables, a gym, massage room, a full-service cafeteria with free meals, and a karaoke room.[86] Lee's presence in China created a celebrity-like fervour. His recruiting events were attended by thousands of aspiring Chinese Googlers.

Google's decision to censor search results generated widespread criticism in the United States and other democratic nations. Critics claimed the move violated Google's core principle of democracy on the Web. Google advised critics that it would not maintain any servers containing personal or sensitive information in China, such as Gmail, Blogger, Picasa or YouTube. In 2008, Google, Microsoft and Yahoo drafted, in conjunction with human rights activists, a document which outlined operating guidelines designed to reduce the risk that the companies' actions would lead to human rights abuses in China and other countries.[87] One of the guidelines stated that the companies would only censor if required to do so via a formal, legal request.

From the outset, the relationship between the Chinese government and Google was strained. After agreeing to censor certain websites upon request, Google assumed it would be allowed to operate smoothly. This did not happen. Chinese officials revoked Google's licence in December 2005, just prior to the official launch of Google.cn, claiming they were unsure whether Google was operating a search engine or a news portal. News portals were not allowed in China. It took a year and a half for Google to convince Chinese authorities that it was, in fact, operating a search engine. Google continued to operate Google.cn while it attempted to have its licence reinstated, but the portal sustained numerous performance problems.[88] Google's licence was reinstated in June 2007. The terms of the agreement were never disclosed.

Meanwhile, Chinese Googlers were having a difficult time adjusting to Google's corporate culture. They could not get used to being allowed to dedicate 20 per cent of their time to pet projects without first obtaining permission. In addition, Chinese Googler engineers felt they were being disadvantaged as compared to their counterparts around the world, as they were not given access to the Google source code. Google encouraged its engineers to work with its source code for product improvements; however, this option was not offered to Chinese Googlers. A perceived lack of openness and transparency was deeply distressing to Chinese Googlers, who felt treated as "second-class citizens"[89].

Additional issues occurred on the government relations front. Google needed someone who could assist in maintaining a positive relationship with the Chinese government.[90] A Chinese former executive was hired, who had a great deal of experience with the Chinese government. Unfortunately, she did not speak English and was never formally educated about the constraints Google was operating under with respect to ethics related policies and the US Foreign Corrupt Practices Act. She was let go when she gave free iPods to Chinese officials and charged the expense to Google. In China, it is common practice for companies to provide gifts to other companies and to government officials; however, such behaviour violates the US Foreign Corrupt Practices Act.

Google complied with the minimum amount of censoring it thought it could get away with. In 2008, censorship requests intensified when China hosted the summer Olympics. The government asked Google to remove links to politically sensitive information on Google's Chinese language version of Google.com.[91] Extending censorship beyond Google.cn was unacceptable to Google as it would affect Chinese-speaking individuals (including former Chinese citizens) around the world. As such, Google refused to comply with the request.

Meanwhile, the Beijing Google search team observed that Chinese users entered shorter search queries due to difficulties with typing, and they developed a new search feature called Google Suggest.[92] Google Suggest returns a search based on logical suggestions to a few characters or words. The innovation was rolled out to all global Google users with great success. Unfortunately, Chinese officials insisted that users could be automatically directed to pornographic sites using Google Suggest. Google insisted that this was out of its control, and blamed illegitimate spamming of key words for directing users to pornographic sites. Google's strained relations with the Chinese government continued, and Kai-Fu Lee decided to leave Google China.

The proverbial last straw

Google's relationship with the Chinese government went from strained to the breaking point in December 2009. Google learned that someone had hacked into its main computer system and stolen sensitive intellectual property. Worse, Google learned that the hackers had also gained access to the Gmail accounts of Chinese dissidents and human rights activists. Even more troubling was the fact that the hackers were traced to China, and Google believed that the sophistication of the attack pointed to a government source, or at least government backing.[93]

For many of Google's senior executives, particularly Sergey Brin, the attack signalled the end of Google's cooperation with China. Brin, having grown up in the communist Soviet Union, was deeply upset by the notion that information obtained from Google's servers would be used to suppress Chinese activists. How many would be tortured, or jailed, as a result? Brin was able to convince other senior executives that Google should stop complying with censorship regulations. Eric Schmidt, then CEO, did not agree, but Larry Page eventually sided with Brin. In January 2010, Google stopped censoring Google.cn.[94]

Google issued the following statement on its blog: "These attacks and the surveillance they have uncovered – combined with the attempts over the past year to further limit free speech on the Web – have led us to conclude that we should review the feasibility of our business operations in China. We have decided we are no longer willing to continue censoring our results on Google. cn, and so over the next few weeks we will be discussing with the Chinese government the basis on which we could operate an unfiltered search engine within the law, if at all. We recognize this may well mean having to shut down Google.cn, and potentially our offices in China."[95]

By March 2010, all Google.cn searches were automatically redirected to Google's uncensored Hong Kong portal, Google.com.hk.[96] The Chinese government threatened to shut the service down completely, until Google agreed by June 2010 to stop automatically redirecting users to the uncensored Hong Kong site. Instead, visitors to Google.cn would have to click on a link to visit Google's Hong Kong portal. In July 2010, the Chinese government renewed the Google.cn operating licence. However, the service continued to be plagued with downtime and performance issues.[97] Google maintained a trimmed down Beijing office.

The price of principle

Nearly two years after Google announced it would no longer comply with Chinese censorship regulations, Google renewed its presence in China. In January 2012, it announced it was hiring additional engineers, salespeople and product managers to design and sell products for its Android operating system for mobile devices. Google also hired online advertising and web search employees.[98] The Android operating system for mobile devices is growing rapidly, and Google plans to introduce Google Play to Chinese users of Android-powered mobile devices. Google Play contains thousands of Android mobile applications that users can download. Google is also hoping to attract Chinese consumers with local-based searches that do not require official censorship, such as searches for Chinese store discounts and other online retailers.[99] Google is likely, once again, to encounter censorship issues with Google Play, as app. markets currently operating in China are required to remove apps that do not comply with government regulations.

According to Analysys International, a Beijing-based research firm, Google's share of the Chinese Web search market declined significantly over the last two years, from 36 per cent in the fourth quarter of 2009 to 16.7 per cent in the fourth quarter of 2011.[100] Competitors Baidu.com (78.3 per cent), Sogu (2.7 per cent), Tencent Soso (1.5 per cent) and Netease Youdao (0.4 per cent), and others (0.4 per cent) make up the balance of the Internet search market.[101]

Google has a lot of ground to cover in China, and there is no doubt that a rocky relationship exists between Google and the Chinese government. However, given the sheer size of the opportunity in the Chinese market, it appears Google has decided to swallow a bit of principle for a lot of payoff.

Google in India: Adaptation pays off

India, with 1.2 billion people, is one of the world's largest democracies.[102] Seventy per cent of its population lives in a rural setting. Although the number of Internet users continues to grow, at the end of 2010 there were only 100 million Internet users in India[103], which represents only about 8 per cent of the population. The vast majority of Internet users live in urban settings due to better access to infrastructure and higher disposable income and education levels.

There are over 800 million mobile phone users in India.[104] Of these mobile phone users, only 12 million subscribe to broadband services despite the fact that 90 per cent of India is covered by broadband.[105] Broadband service is required for Internet access over a mobile phone. The government plans to increase broadband subscribers to 175 million by 2014 through programmes designed to keep costs low for the end user.[106] The government also plans to connect India's village councils, numbering approximately 250,000, with broadband by 2014.[107]

There are several issues limiting Internet use in India. The first is a lack of wired telecommunications infrastructure, particularly in rural areas. Wired broadband Internet access is not available throughout the country, which limits accessibility to graphics-rich sites like YouTube. A second complicating factor is that only approximately 5 per cent of India's small and medium sized enterprises have an online presence.[108] The vast majority of businesses in India does not see value in the Internet, and thus it is difficult for Internet-based services to grow in these areas. With few local businesses online, the online community is limited. The final challenge is derived from India's multi-lingual society, whereby 22 officially recognized languages create barriers for local businesses to develop accessible online content.[109]

Google India

In 2004, Google opened its first R&D centre outside the United States in Bangalore, India.[110] Bangalore is India's Silicon Valley information technology hot spot. Foreign MNEs, such as Google, Yahoo, IBM, GE, etc. have opened offices in Bangalore to access a large pool of low-cost, educated information technology professionals and engineers. Most of India's educated workforce speaks English as the post-secondary education system is primarily taught in English. Google India not only operates an R&D centre in Bangalore, but also a customer support centre for AdWords (pay-per-click ads) in Hyderabad, and government relations and advertising offices in Mumbai and Delhi.[111] Google India's portal, Google.in, is available in seven languages including Hindi (30 per cent of the population), Urdu, Bengali, Gujarati, Kannada, Tamil and Telugu.[112]

Life as a Googler in India

Google is an employer of choice in India. Landing a job at Google increases one's marriage prospects, and in a country where arranged marriages are common, this is a big deal.[113] Google's appeal can be attributed to its higher salaries (up to three times higher than average for a similar job), stock options for higher-level employees, taxis to and from work and health insurance for employees and their parents. Google India's main office in Bangalore also has the usual Google perks, including bean bag chairs, video games, a gym, and free food and beverages. Although the perks and salaries are a huge draw, Google's appeal to Indian IT workers may in fact be more basic: it is considered a cool place to work.

Indian Googlers have developed some of Google's most innovative products, including Google Finance, which grew out of a 20 per cent project,[114] Google Mapmaker and mobile text messaging platforms.[115] Google India also developed its own "Indic translation technology", enabling users to type phonetic imitations of words in their own language using a regular Roman alphabet key-board.[116] The technology was originally developed to address the lack of available suitable Internet content in India's 22 official languages, but has since been extended to other languages.[117]

Google India is a success

Google's foray into India has been very successful, by all accounts. It is the number one search engine in the country, claiming 80 per cent of the share of the search engine market.[118] In the mobile market, Google's Android mobile platform has had tremendous growth. Neilsen Informate Mobile Insights found that smartphone users in India spent 25 per cent of their time using Google apps, including search, Gmail, Google Maps and Google Play (Android app store).[119] Google's social media platform, Orkut, was released in 2004. Orkut did not do well in

Western markets, including the United States, but it took off in India and Brazil. However, the tide seems to be turning as Facebook has overtaken the social networking market in India.

At US $5 billion, India's total advertising industry is quite small, given the size of the country's population base.[120] Indian businesses focus on the bottom-line and will only advertise if it is affordable and will achieve directly measurable results. As such, less than 100,000 businesses in India advertise.[121] Google believes that businesses will consider online and mobile advertising as a very affordable option compared to expensive print and television advertising, once India's wired and wireless Internet users climb from 100 million to 300 million and upward. Digital advertising expenditures in India represented US $291 million in 2011, as compared to "$7.4 billion in China and $32.2 billion in the U.S., according to media-buying company Group M".[122] Clearly, given the size of India's potential Internet consumer pool, there are a lot of growth prospects for digital advertising in India.

Democracy on the Web has limits

Censorship is well-entrenched in centrally controlled, authoritarian countries like China. In the United States, censorship is largely non-existent. However, the waters become a bit murky when it comes to democracies like India. Religious and ethnic tensions have historically created tension and violence within the country. India's constitution allows the State to impose "reasonable restrictions" on free speech when needed "in the interests of the sovereignty and integrity of India, the security of the State, friendly relations with foreign States, public order, decency or morality, or in relation to contempt of court, defamation or incitement to an offence".[123] India's Information Technology Act of 2000 allows the State to require Internet portals to block sites that it deems objectionable.[124] Corporate officers who do not comply with requests to remove offensive material may face fines and jail terms of up to seven years.[125] These regulations are remarkably similar to China's restrictive policies.

While Google maintains that it would prefer to follow its core principle of democracy on the Web, it has not been able to do so wholeheartedly in India. In 2009, after an Internet user alerted Google lawyers to offensive comments about a politician on the Orkut social networking site, Google removed the comments as it feared the comments would heighten tensions and incite violence. Nicole Wong, Google's deputy general counsel in 2010 stated, "In those gray areas it is really hard. On the one hand, we believe strongly in political speech and, on the other hand, in India they do riot and blow up buses."[126] Wong advised that Google already automatically bans materials like child pornography and hate speech on all sites around the world, but that it only blocks other content when it is brought to its attention by users or law enforcement authorities, and only when it considers the request valid or when it is legally compelled to do so.

The future of democracy on the Web in India is uncertain. In early 2012, Google India removed content from its Google.in and Google.in.co portals after it was ordered to do so by a New Delhi court in response to a civil lawsuit launched by Mufti Aijaz Arshad Quasmi, an Indian activist who requested material be removed that is offensive to Muslims.[127] Google is also defending itself against criminal charges filed by Indian journalist Vinay Rai, who claims that Facebook, Google's

YouTube and Orkut, and several other Indian websites contained material that "seeks to create enmity, hatred and communal violence . . . that will corrupt minds".[128] Google has maintained that India's Information Technology Act of 2000 only requires it to remove content if asked to do so by the State. Google stated that it is impossible for it to police all content on the Internet, and that to do so would curtail democracy on the Internet. Google and Facebook have both asked for the case to be dismissed, and a ruling was expected in the second half of 2012. Google has also removed most of the objectionable content cited by Rai.

If India's courts find Google and/or Facebook guilty of not policing the Internet for objectionable content, the future of India's potentially explosive Internet economy is uncertain. Billions of dollars and millions of jobs are at stake if Internet companies decide India is not a safe bet to do business.[129]

QUESTIONS

1. How did Google's market entry strategies differ in India and China?
2. What are Google's FSAs? Are Google's FSAs location-bound? Why or why not?
3. Should Google revisit its core values in light of the differences in foreign country policies towards free speech?
4. Should Google have complied with censorship requests in China? Why or why not?
5. Why did Google readily comply with censorship requirements in India, but not in China?
6. Should Google re-enter the Chinese search market? Why or why not? Should it continue to keep sensitive information outside of Chinese borders? Why or why not?

Notes

1. T. Khanna, K. G. Palepu and J. Sinha, 'Strategies that fit emerging markets', *Harvard Business Review* 83 (2005), 63–76.
2. *Ibid.*
3. D. J. Arnold and J. A. Quelch, 'New strategies in emerging markets', *Sloan Management Review* 40 (1998), 7–20.
4. *Ibid.*
5. T. Khanna and K. Palepu, 'Why focused strategies may be wrong for emerging markets', *Harvard Business Review* 75 (1997), 41–51.
6. Khanna, Palepu and Sinha, 'Strategies that fit emerging markets', 63–76.
7. *Ibid.*, 67.
8. *Ibid.*, 63–76.

9. An example of biases in market selection comes from the 1950s work of MIT political scientist Harold Isaacs. He proposed that American firms favoured China over India because of America's romance with China that developed from the work of missionaries and scholars in China during the 1800s (Khanna, Palepu and Sinha, 64).

10. Khanna, Palepu and Sinha, 'Strategies that fit emerging markets', 64.

11. *Ibid.*

12. *Ibid.*, 63–76.

13. The six indices used by the authors are: Growth Competitiveness Index ranking, Business Competitiveness Index ranking, Governance indicators, Corruption Perceptions Index ranking, Composite Country Risks Points and Per cent weight in Emerging markets index.

14. Khanna, Palepu and Sinha, 'Strategies that fit emerging markets', 65.

15. *Ibid.*, 66.

16. *Ibid.*, 67.

17. *Ibid.*, 74.

18. *Ibid.*

19. Khanna and Palepu, 'Why focused strategies may be wrong for emerging markets', 41–51.

20. Arnold and Quelch, 'New strategies in emerging markets', 7.

21. *Ibid.*, 11.

22. *Ibid.*, 12.

23. *Ibid.*, 16.

24. *Ibid.*, 19.

25. M. F. Letelier, F. Flores and C. Spinosa, 'Developing productive customers in emerging markets', *California Management Review* 45 (2003), 77–103.

26. *Ibid.*, 78.

27. Jean-Philippe Bonardi and Tony S. Frost, 'AIG and China's accession to the WTO', *IVEY case number 9B02M021* (2002).

28. Andrew Bolger, 'Putting down new roots on familiar soil', *Financial Times* (15 March 2000), 30.

29. Maurice R. Greenberg, 'Opening markets in a turbulent world', *Georgetown Journal of International Affairs* (Summer/Fall 2003), 149.

30. *Ibid.*, 153.

31. James Kynge, 'Beijing secures compromise on treatment of AIG', *Financial Times* (7 December 2001), 12.

32. Greenberg, 'Opening markets in a turbulent world', 150.

33. *Ibid.*, 151.

34. *Ibid.*, 150.

35. *Ibid.*

36. *Ibid.*

37. Xinhua News Agency, (2 December 1993).

38. Greenberg, 'Opening markets in a turbulent world', 152.

39. AIA refers to American International Assurance, AIG's subsidiary for life insurance in China. Maurice Greenberg, 'Statement submitted to the US House of Representatives' (16 February 2000).

40. Geoff Dyer and Andrea Felsted, 'AIG loses its edge in China', *Financial Times* (24 May 2005), 27.

41. 'American International Group, Inc; AIG General Insurance Company China Limited receives approval to establish branch in Beijing', *Business & Finance Week* (21 July 2008), 57.

42. Nanette Byrnes, 'Where AIG went wrong', *Bloomberg BusinessWeek* (18 September 2008).
43. Nanette Byrnes, 'AIG's uphill battle', *Bloomberg BusinessWeek* (26 February 2009).
44. *Ibid.*
45. Phil Mintz, 'Another handout for AIG', *Bloomberg BusinessWeek* (2 March 2009).
46. Roben Farzad, 'AIG may not be as healthy as it looks', *Bloomberg BusinessWeek* (26 April, 2012).
47. 'AIG reports first quarter 2012 net income of $3.2 Billion', AIG press release. http://ir.aigcorporate.com/phoenix.zhtml?c=76115&p=irol-newsArticle&ID=1691406&highlight= (3 May 2012).
48. Roben Farzad, 'AIG may not be as healthy as it looks', *Bloomberg BusinessWeek* (26 April, 2012).
49. *Ibid.*
50. Bruce Stanley, Jackie Cheung, James T. Areddy, Shai Oster, 'The financial crisis: AIG at risk AIG's Asian units seek to allay customers' fears; companies stress their independence, solid capital status' *Wall Street Journal (Eastern Edition)* (17 September 2008), A.10.
51. *Ibid.*
52. Denny Thomas and Clare Baldwin, 'AIG to sell $6 billion in AIA stock to repay bailout', *Reuters* (5 March 2012).
53. *Ibid.*
54. Geoff Dyer and Andrea Felsted, 'AIG loses its edge in China', *Financial Times* (24 May 2005), 27.
55. Francesco Guerrera, 'Departure will leave a void in Asian strategy', *Financial Times* (15 March 2005), 26.
56. Richard McGregor, 'Ousted AIG chief welcomed by Chinese', *Financial Times* (18 March 2006), 9.
57. Dyer and Felsted, 'AIG loses its edge in China', 27.
58. PwC, 'Foreign insurance companies in China' (2011), 18.
59. 'Growing pains', *The Economist* (3 December 2011).
60. PwC, 'Foreign insurance companies in China' (2011), 4.
61. PwC, 'Foreign insurance companies in China' (2011), 5.
62. Noah Buhayar, 'AIG targets China drivers in $50 billion insurance market', *Bloomberg* (3 April, 2012).
63. *Ibid.*
64. Marketshare, company information.
65. Jeffrey Immelt, Vijay Govindarajan and Chris Trimble, 'How GE is Disrupting Itself', *Harvard Business Review* (October 2009).
66. Google, company information.
67. *Ibid.*
68. *Ibid.*
69. *Ibid.*
70. *Ibid.*
71. Google, company information 2004.
72. Google, company information.
73. *Fortune Magazine*, The best companies, 2012.
74. *Ibid.*
75. *Ibid.*
76. Google, company information, 2004.

77. Amir Efrati and Loretta Chao, 'Google softens tone in China', *WSJ.com* (12 January 2012).
78. http://data.worldbank.org/country/china
79. Kristin Martin, 'Google Inc. in China', *Business Roundtable Institute for Corporate Ethics* (2006).
80. Robert McMahon, 'US Internet Providers and the Great Firewall of China', *Council on Foreign Relations* (23 February 2011). www.cfr.org/china/us-internet-providers-great-firewall-china/p9856
81. Justine Lau, 'A history of Google in China', *Financial Times* (9 July 2010).
82. Robert McMahon, 'US internet providers and the great firewall of China', *Council on Foreign Relations* (23 February 2011).
83. *Ibid.*
84. Justine Lau, 'A history of Google in China', *Financial Times* (9 July 2010).
85. Steven Levy, 'Inside Google China's misfortune', *Fortune Tech* (15 April 2011).
86. *Ibid.*
87. Justine Lau, 'A history of Google in China', *Financial Times* (9 July 2010).
88. Steven Levy, 'Inside Google China's Misfortune', *Fortune Tech* (15 April 2011).
89. *Ibid.*
90. *Ibid.*
91. *Ibid.*
92. *Ibid.*
93. *Ibid.*
94. Richard Waters, Chris Nuttall, Joseph Menn, Maija Palmer and Kathrin Hille, 'Google takes on China on censorship', *Financial Times* (13 January 2010).
95. *Ibid.*
96. Justine Lau, 'A history of Google in China', *Financial Times* (9 July 2010).
97. Amir Efrati and Loretta Chao, 'Google softens tone in China', *WSJ.com* (12 January 2012).
98. *Ibid.*
99. *Ibid.*
100. *Ibid.*
101. Analysys International, 'Baidu, Google China, Sogou hold top 3 in China internet search market 2011Q4' (23 February 2012).
102. Amy Yee, 'Challenges facing Indian broadband', *Financial Times* (23 June 2008).
103. Surabhi Agarwal, 'India will be an 'online and mobile first' ad market', *Livemint* (15 April 2011).
104. Hari Kumar, 'Increasing internet can raise GDP, study says', *NYTImes.com* (23 January 2012).
105. *Ibid.*
106. *Ibid.*
107. *Ibid.*
108. Neil Munshi, 'Google India's SME drive', *Financial Times* (3 November 2011).
109. Akanksha Awal, 'Google: Welcome to the Indic Web', *Financial Times* (22 June 2011).
110. Sheridan Prasso, 'Google goes to India', *Fortune* (23 October 2007).
111. *Ibid.*
112. *Ibid.*
113. Sheridan Prasso, 'Google goes to India', *Fortune* (23 October 2007).
114. *Ibid.*
115. Joe Leahy, 'India: A nation develops', *Financial Times* (10 January 2010).

116. *Ibid.*
117. *Ibid.*
118. Surabhi Agarwal, 'India will be an 'online and mobile first' ad market', *Livemint* (15 April 2011).
119. 'In India, Google leads the smartphone app race', *Nielsen Wire* (10 February 2012).
120. Surabhi Agarwal, 'India will be an "online and mobile first" ad market', *Livemint* (15 April 2011).
121. *Ibid.*
122. Amol Sharma, 'Facebook, Google to stand trial in India', *The Wall Street Journal* (13 March 2012).
123. Jillian York, 'India's downward spiral', *Electronic Frontier Foundation* (8 February 2012).
124. Ketaki Gokhale and Pratap Patnik, 'Google removes Search, YouTube content on Indian court order', *Businessweek* (8 February 2012).
125. Amol Sharma and Jessica E. Vascellaro, 'Google and India test the Limits of Liberty', *The Wall Street Journal* (4 January 2010).
126. *Ibid.*
127. Ketaki Gokhale and Pratap Patnik, 'Google removes Search, YouTube content on Indian court order', *Businessweek* (8 February 2012).
128. Amol Sharma, 'Facebook, Google to stand trial in India', *The Wall Street Journal* (13 March 2012).
129. *Ibid.*

15

Emerging economy multinational enterprises

Five learning objectives

1. To predict when developed economy MNEs versus emerging economy MNEs will end up as winners or losers in competitive battles in international markets.
2. To describe the growth and international expansion trajectories of MNEs from emerging economies.
3. To explain the specific challenges facing MNEs from emerging economies, given their particular location advantages and FSAs.
4. To highlight the significance of 'good-enough' market strategies in the emerging economy context.
5. To provide a classification of international expansion strategies pursued by MNEs as a function of their R&D and marketing FSAs.

This chapter builds on **Pankaj Ghemawat** and **Thomas Hout's** view expressed in the *HBR* that it is unclear at the outset whether developed economy versus emerging economy MNEs will end up as the future 'global giants', i.e., the undisputed international market leaders in their industry.[1] Much will depend on: (1) how these two sets of firms will react and flexibly adapt to the underlying FSAs and location advantages of their counterparts, and (2) how effectively each set of MNEs will be able to emulate and deploy FSAs similar or equivalent to those held by the counterpart companies in the various locations where they compete with each other. The authors focus primarily on firms operating in China and India, both foreign MNEs and the firms that are the subject of the present chapter, namely emerging economy MNEs (EMNEs). The authors describe the different parameters that will ultimately determine which firms will end up as the winners in the international market place. As is the case in the other chapters, the ideas presented by Ghemawat and Hout will be assessed in terms of their managerial relevance, using the framework presented in Chapter 1 as the frame of reference.

Significance

There has been a sharp rise in the number and relative importance of EMNEs in recent years. A general observation has been that companies from emerging economies are successful primarily in industries with a low level of technology and advertising intensity. In most cases, initial success comes from effectively using low-cost labour and materials in the context of large-scale manufacturing plants, and then combining these production efficiencies with equally efficient inbound and outbound logistics. Privileged network ties with local stakeholders, especially regulatory authorities that can make life difficult for foreign MNEs, further amplify and allow sustaining these production-cost driven advantages over longer periods of time. However, Ghemawat and Hout focus on several contemporary cases, whereby MNEs from the developed world have attempted to emulate the FSAs of their rivals in emerging economies, and on cases whereby firms from emerging economies have tried to develop or acquire technology-based or marketing-based FSAs. In other words, both sets of firms are de facto trying to disprove the idea that 'industry is destiny'. These firms attempt to engage in new forms of resource recombination. EMNE success appears to result largely from a mix of experimenting with 'upgrading' and a 'coopetition' mindset whereby these firms try to emulate the FSAs of rivals, and engage in various forms of cooperative behaviour (alliance formation, M&As) to access the desired knowledge if they cannot develop this internally at a reasonable cost and risk, and within an acceptable time frame.

For example, the authors discuss how Google and eBay started as industry leaders in China, but were then beaten at their own game by firms such as Baidu and Taobao respectively. These Chinese firms were perhaps not able to provide the same level of global content or quality assurance respectively, but were better equipped to understand local customer preferences and address regulatory requirements, e.g., in the realm of self-censoring content viewed as inappropriate by the government, thereby capturing dominant market shares in the Chinese market. As one example from India, the wind power firm Suzlon was better able than international rivals at providing one-stop shopping for wind energy solutions, addressing such issues as gaining government permits to establish wind farms, doing the maintenance thereof, and selling the power generated.

In the above cases, competitive success of local Chinese and Indian companies domestically against large, foreign MNEs resulted from FSAs in low-cost production, combined with a deep understanding of evolving local customer needs and stronger network ties with regulatory authorities.

However, initial FSA bundles are not static but evolve over time. This explains why Procter & Gamble (P&G) was able to gain a dominant position in China in multiple market segments (e.g., the high-end, economy ànd low-end segments) for many consumer products: it creatively combined its extant superior technology with access to low-cost products and factors in China and with knowledge about local customer preferences. Resource recombination was achieved in various ways. P&G sent local product developers from China to its international technical centres, where the developers would meet product specialists with extensive international expertise. Second, it learned how to adapt to social networks in emerging economies, thereby overcoming various instances of cultural and institutional distance. Alliances and acquisitions were critical here.

The EMNE can react in four different ways to developed economy MNE entry and resource recombination efforts in its home country. *First*, the EMNE can continue specializing in cost-efficient, mass-scale manufacturing at home, as an OEM supplier to large MNEs from developed economies, with the latter increasingly focused on two sets of FSAs, namely back-end platforms, i.e, routinized business processes, and customer-end strengths in marketing and sales. Here, learning by the emerging economy MNE may then still entail extending its value chain scope over time, but at an incremental pace.

Second, the EMNE can try to perpetuate its initial cost advantages by spreading its own value chain across borders, acknowledging that other countries may become more cost efficient as locations for various activities in the value chain, especially if home country labour costs are rising rapidly as has been the case in the Indian software development industry.

Third, the EMNE can attempt to increase its own value added by moving up the value chain in the form of technology development or creating brand names. However, internal FSA creation on the technology or branding side may take too much time or may simply not be feasible because of insufficient knowledge resources in these areas inside the firm. Both acquisitions and alliances may then speed up the knowledge accessing process. For example, Ghemawat and Hout describe the case of the Chinese company Wanxiang taking over poorly functioning US manufacturers of auto parts in the Midwest of the United States, restructuring these companies and gaining access to these companies' knowledge-based FSAs.

Fourth, the EMNE may decide to specialize in narrow segments of the value chain, namely those segments where it is most competitive and can command high value. The authors give the example of India-based Barthi Airtel, specialized in mobile telephone services. This company outsourced much of its value chain to companies such as IBM (for IT services) and Ericsson, Nokia and Siemens (for network management). Bharti Airtel itself decided to focus on developing FSAs in customer care and relationships with regulatory authorities.

The main challenges for EMNEs, as they grow and expand internationally, ultimately become very similar to those faced by incumbents from developed economies: managing an internationally dispersed network of operations is very difficult, and engaging in resource recombinations whereby initial FSAs are complemented with location-bound ones in new host countries can be very challenging, as explained throughout this book, especially if what binds the different parts of the firm together, i.e., what is non-location bound, is neither in the technology area, nor in the brand name sphere. As stated by Ghemawat and Hout: "[EMNEs'] biggest vulnerability ... is inexperience in coordination and conflict management across borders and a lack of depth in global customer and channel knowledge".[2] The likely outcome could then be that "as emerging players grow, they soon face the same problems established [MNEs] do: international coordination, diminishing usefulness of the [centre] for delivering products or services, loss of product uniqueness, and the need to tap more pools of talent around the world".[3]

The main point made in Ghemawat and Hout's paper is simply that EMNEs should not take for granted that their initial FSAs in low-cost, mass-scale production, deep knowledge of local customers and their privileged network ties (e.g., with home country regulatory authorities) will remain unchallenged. Foreign MNEs, including developed economy companies, will try to emulate these FSAs or engage in new resource recombinations to improve their own competitive position. Sustained competitive success of EMNEs requires continued resource recombination for new capability development. Here, expanded size and internal network development across borders quickly leads to new management challenges very similar to those faced by incumbents from the developed world.

Context and complementary perspectives

Ghemawat and Hout's 2008 article provides a welcome alternative perspective to the mainstream view that EMNEs will continue to dominate cost-driven manufacturing and services industries in the decades to come, whereas sectors and sector-segments characterized by advanced technology development as well as strong brand name recognition will remain largely out of reach. Ultimately, competitive success results from the ability to recombine resources in such a way that viable business opportunities are acted upon. Here, the appropriate strategy is often a hybrid of the conventional, discrete choices between (1) low-cost leadership in production and logistics versus (2) differentiation on the technology or marketing side.

Orit Gadiesh and *Till Vestring*, in their 2008 *SMR* piece 'The consequences of China's rising global heavyweights' provide a somewhat different perspective on the role of EMNEs, as compared to Ghemawat and Hout's view.[4] The authors focus on the rise of Chinese MNEs, and argue that their success can be largely attributed to their focus on products of sufficient quality and sufficiently low price to gain market share in segments of the middle class and the business-to-business market. One example is Huawei Technologies, which has become a major player in the Chinese market for telecommunications networks. Huawei is a firm for which not industry, but strategy is destiny. This strategy has been built on three main pillars. The *first* pillar has been that of government support, which allowed the firm to increase market share in China. The *second* pillar has been to augment the company's initial FSAs in cost leadership with advanced technologies and brand names by engaging in partnerships with firms such as 3Com, a computer network infrastructure specialist (acquired by HP in 2010; an earlier attempt by Huawei at gaining a minority equity share in 3Com through an acquisition formerly conducted by Bain Capital, was aborted due to resistance from US regulators). Huawei's *third pillar* has been to outsource some of the manufacturing to Chinese suppliers, while engaging itself in low-cost R&D and engineering. This approach is reminiscent of what developed economy MNEs have done with their own OEM suppliers.[5]

The outcome has been that in some industries such as TV sets and washing machines, the share of the *good-enough* products represents 80 per cent of the total market. One strategy of foreign MNEs to counter the efforts of Chinese firms to develop FSAs in technology and branding has been to engage in so-called *dual branding*, with products covering either the upscale portion of the market or the good-enough market. One example of dual branding is the one applied by the firm Gillette (a unit of P&G), which sells Duracell batteries in the (small) upscale segment of the market and Nanfu batteries in the much larger *good-enough* segment. The latter has been possible as the result of the 2003 acquisition of Fujian Nanping Nanfu Battery Co. by Gillette.[6]

In order to achieve success in the *good-enough* market, foreign MNEs have often been compelled to pursue joint ventures with – and acquisitions of – Chinese manufacturers. The outcome has been both broader product portfolios and newly acquired cost advantages. The longer-term result of acting on the opportunities provided by the Chinese *good-enough* market for both Chinese and foreign MNEs, has been an increase in exports and in other forms of market involvement in developing economies characterized by the rapid growth of their own domestic *good-enough* market.

As was the case in Ghemawat and Hout's paper, the focus of the analysis is on the dynamics of competing in an emergent economy. Here, many Chinese firms may benefit from an initial FSA in providing low-cost products to *good-enough* markets, but foreign MNEs may then engage in a two-pronged approach, whereby they try to complement their initial FSAs in upscale market segments with new FSAs to be deployed in the potentially much larger, *good enough* market.

A second complementary perspective to Ghemawat and Hout's paper was developed in a 2010 *CMR* article by **Huei-Ting Tsai** and **Andreas B. Eisingerich** on the internationalization strategies of emerging market firms[7].

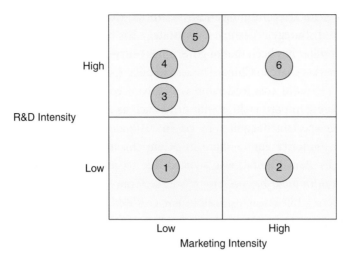

Figure 15.1
Six types of
EMNEs

The authors looked at the international expansion strategies of firms from four emerging markets, namely South Korea, Taiwan, Hong Kong and India. Given the conventional perspective discussed above that EMNEs are not supposed to have any particular initial strengths in R&D or branding, the authors investigated to what extent R&D and branding were actually present in EMNEs. They developed a simple framework that allows positioning any firm as a function of its relative focus on R&D and branding. This is represented in Figure 15.1, where the vertical axis reflects the presence of FSAs in R&D (low or high) and the horizontal axis represents FSAs in marketing (low or high).[8]

As could be expected, many EMNEs were found to have low R&D intensity and limited strengths in marketing. These *first* category firms can be positioned in quadrant two of Figure 15.1. The authors classified these firms as *regional exporters/importers*. At the output side, these firms engage primarily in sales and distribution of their products in neighbouring countries. These countries are usually other developing economies, where limited competition can be expected from large, developed economy MNEs. This category of MNEs builds upon cost-driven strengths in narrow product niches.

The *second* category of firms consists of *global exporters/importers*. These companies are positioned in quadrant four of Figure 15.1. These firms invest much more in sales and distribution than companies in the first category, but do not perform much R&D. Such companies focus on product quality and are supported by well-functioning, international supply chains and distribution arrangements.

Three more categories of firms can be found in quadrant one of Figure 15.1. The *third* category consists of *technology fast followers*, which are really contract manufacturers. These firms hardly invest in marketing but do attach importance to technology, so as to be able to pursue original equipment manufacturing (OEM) or original design manufacturing (ODM) contracts with other large MNEs. A distinct fourth group of firms consists of *technology leaders* in the OEM sphere. These firms rely much more than the previous category on their in-house technological innovation, but do not attach much importance to sales and marketing. The fifth category of firms is represented by the *global market niche players*, which typically have both high R&D expenditures but are also focused more on marketing than the two previous sets of companies. Their continued success depends on finding a narrow product niche where they can be successful in international markets.

Finally, the *sixth* category of firms is located in quadrant three of Figure 15.1. These *multinational challengers* are companies that invest heavily in R&D and in marketing, and as a result can engage in head-to-head competition with large MNEs from the developed world. Examples include South Korea-based LG and Samsung.

The dispersion of EMNEs across six categories, which can be positioned in the four quadrants of Figure 15.1, illustrates that MNEs from emerging economies are a very diverse set of companies, some of which are indeed attempting to move up the *smiling curve*, as shown in Figure 15.2. The smiling curve was first proposed by Stan Shih, the founder of Taiwanese computer manufacturer Acer, as a way to position his firm in industry. Ram Mudambi, a well-known international management scholar, extended the smiling curve concept to position firms in knowledge-intensive industries.[9] The point is that not each activity in the value chain leads to similar value creation per unit produced. Some activities, especially knowledge-intensive ones, lead to more value being created than 'commodity-type' activities, which in the extreme case could be simply outsourced to contract manufacturers.

In Figure 15.2, the horizontal axis describes all the value chain activities that can be performed by a company, with upstream activities such as R&D on the left-hand side, assembly and manufacturing of products according to pre-set specifications in the middle, and downstream activities such as market research and

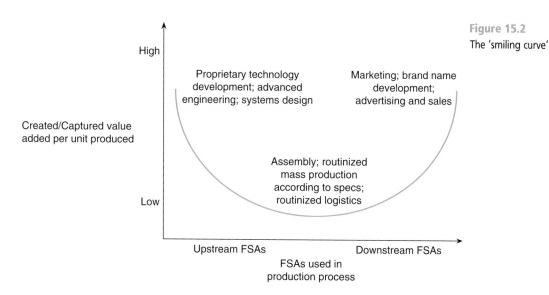

Figure 15.2
The 'smiling curve'

branding on the right-hand side. The vertical axis measures the degree to which each activity creates value added per unit produced for the company. The smiling curve assumes that most EMNEs start as producers of commodity-type products and services, often resulting from OEM/OED contracts with large MNEs from the developed world. In other words, these emerging economy firms tend in a first stage to assemble and manufacture according to the exact specifications of a powerful international client, who can request OEM contract bids from several suppliers, thereby making sure that supply costs are kept low. As time goes by, the OEM supplier from an emerging economy will typically attempt to perform more upstream activities in the form of technology development, and engage in marketing so as to increase revenue. If these strategic moves are successful, value will be added both at the upstream and downstream ends of the value chain, with the overall value added per unit produced increasing substantially, and the EMNE potentially becoming a rival of its original MNE client. The question obviously remains what party in international transactions will actually be able to capture the value and profits resulting from moves on the smiling curve.

Ghemawat and Hout's article complements Khanna *et al.*'s piece discussed in Chapter 14, which focused on the dynamics of filling institutional voids by creative resource recombination. The present paper focuses less on the MNE – host country linkages – and more on the dynamics of competition between EMNEs and their rivals from developed economies. The authors contend that industry is not destiny, but that both sets of MNEs face particular challenges in crafting resource recombinations leading to new FSAs.

For EMNEs the key challenge is really to upgrade their home-grown, location-bound FSAs into internationally transferable ones, somewhat as described by Pattern II in Figure 15.3. However, the unique feature of this pattern in the EMNE case is the proposed infusion of resources from *outside* the home country at the outset, whether in the form of upstream or downstream knowledge, to allow an upgrade of the firm's capabilities in the emerging economy to achieve non-location-bound FSA status. We have labelled this process as Pattern II-B in Figure 15.3.

In other words, the EMNE case is an excellent example of a situation whereby a multiple diamond approach to international competitiveness, as outlined in Chapter 3, is required to understand the resource upgrading process inside the firm. Here, foreign direct investment supporting the upgrading process will typically be of the asset-seeking type. When entering developed economy markets through FDI to support such asset seeking, entry will typically occur through alliances or acquisitions to allow rapid access to the desired knowledge and subsequent absorption in the home country. Pattern II-B does acknowledge that the EMNE must have some initial, internationally transferable FSAs to engage in international activities, even if mainly consisting of entrepreneurial acumen and the

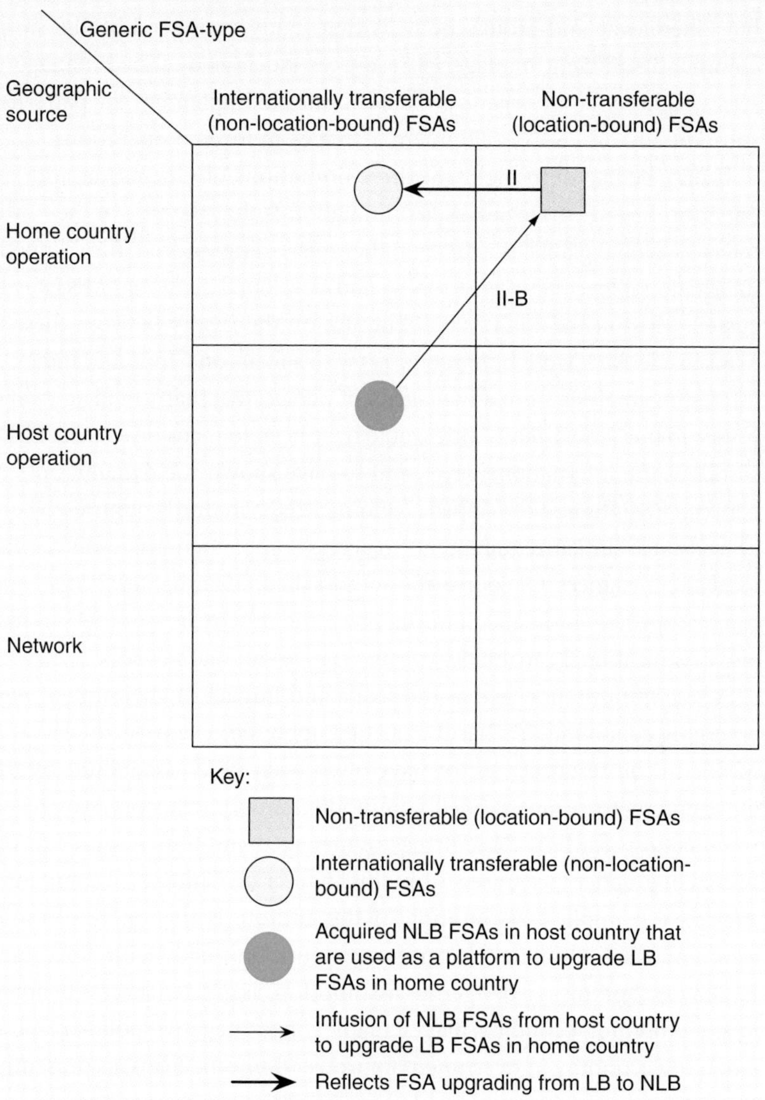

Figure 15.3
FSA development
in EMNEs

charismatic personality of company founders and senior managers, and internalized strengths in low-cost production based on location advantages. However, it is then the newly acquired FSAs in host country environments that allow further upgrading of extant, location-bound FSAs in the EMNE's home environment.

When penetrating other emerging or developing economies, Pattern III in Figure 1.7 is often a common scenario. Here, home-based cost advantages and extant market knowledge can often relatively easily be transferred, deployed and profitably exploited, e.g., through exports, with only a limited need to develop additional location-bound FSAs. Obviously, all other patterns of FSA development described in Figure 1.7 in Chapter 1, could in principle be found in EMNEs, but Ghemawat and Hout's point is that many younger EMNEs simply do not command sufficient managerial resources (such as qualified managers for overseas assignments) or organizational routines to implement the patterns that draw substantially on FSA development activities in foreign operations.

It may be useful to highlight three limitations of Ghemawat and Hout's *HBR* paper on EMNE strategies. A *first* limitation is that the title of their article, which refers to 'global giants' is actually rather misleading. Indeed, the competition at the international level between EMNEs and developed economy MNEs is hardly discussed. Most of the analysis concentrates on the rivalry between these two sets of firms inside the EMNE home country (with a focus on China and India). An equally interesting analysis from a management perspective that would actually have done justice to the 'global giants' title would have been to focus on specific EMNE success stories at the international level, and to have shown the dynamics of competition between EMNEs and developed economy MNEs in third countries, where both sets of firms face similar requirements to access complementary resources and adapt to local circumstances. Of course, the authors do predict that few EMNE success cases can be expected in the medium run given the relative lack of FSAs in management and organizational capabilities to run an international network.

A *second* limitation is that the scope and impact of government regulation in emerging economies are hardly touched upon. For example, the fact that Chinese MNEs in the resources sector have often been used as conduits by the Chinese government to secure needed commodity supply from overseas has enormous ramifications for how these firms are managed and how resource recombination occurs in practice (see Case 15.1 in this chapter on Chinese oil companies entering Africa). An implicit assumption of the authors is that MNEs from developed economies will ultimately learn how to work optimally with emerging economy regulators, but this is a dangerous assumption, as greater success by foreign MNEs in the emerging economy may actually trigger negative policy responses of the emerging economy's government to protect domestic firms, as presently observed in China.[10] In such cases, regulatory dynamics may actually work against successful FSA recombination engineered by foreign MNEs. Several foreign MNEs experienced this in Venezuela, when starting in 2007, President Hugo Chavez engaged in efforts to nationalize local operations of foreign MNEs in the energy, cement, steel, glass manufacturing and retail industries.

A *third* limitation is that Ghemawat and Hout do not distinguish between *value creation* and *value capture*, though this distinction should be at the heart of any discussion on the costs and benefits of moving away from OEM contractor status, and contemplating alternative strategies. The point is that there may actually be enormous economic value added created already by EMNEs supplying products to MNEs from developed countries, but without the possibility for these suppliers to command high prices for their products, because of weak property rights protection and low social embeddedness of the FSAs involved, and most importantly, a weak bargaining power vis-à-vis foreign MNE clients and other economic actors in the value chain. The real question therefore, when contemplating strategy alternatives for these firms, is not simply how to rearrange a supply chain, nor how to lower costs further, nor how to enter into alliances with other companies, nor even how to specialize, but rather how to capture value and retain profits inside the firm. Doing more R&D and having more advertising expenditures, i.e., moving up the smiling curve, sound like good ideas to escape from the 'industry as destiny' syndrome, but the reality is that both R&D and branding may require the allocation of large amounts of scarce resources without necessarily any guarantee of a positive return in terms of value capture at the level of the individual firm trying to move up the value chain, whether upstream or downstream. In other words, the real question is to know in which activities of the value chain FSAs can be developed and protected over the longer term, i.e., cannot be emulated by rivals or substituted by other companies, while being associated with a bargaining position sufficiently strong to allow value capture by the firm. As the example of Flextronics – founded in Silicon Valley in 1969 and presently headquartered in Singapore – demonstrates (see Chapter 7), an MNE can achieve extraordinary success building upon OEM status.

Five management takeaways

1. Understand that FSAs from EMNEs evolve over time, and there may be a natural tendency for these firms to try to capture more value through new FSA development, therefore making them more of a competitive threat than would be suggested by a static industry analysis.
2. Consider that the Achilles heel of many EMNEs remains their lack of managerial and organizational capabilities to govern a multinational network. Therefore, platform capabilities in the form of well-oiled routines/business systems may be the best tool to keep EMNEs at bay.
3. Remember that building a successful business in emerging economies while competing with EMNEs, may require a prime focus on the *good-enough* market. FSA development should therefore be carefully tailored to allow accessing that market.
4. Carefully classify EMNE rivals as a function of their relative strengths in R&D and branding. Each type of rival will require a different competitive response.
5. Keep the eye on *value capture* rather than on mere *value creation*. Moving up the *smiling curve* may be instrumental to value creation but it does not guarantee value capture.

Case 15.1 Chinese energy goes African[11]

Over the past decade, the many implications of the rise of the People's Republic of China have become a topic of intense debate, as many seek to understand the impact of Chinese economic growth on the functioning of international markets. Of particular interest have been Chinese efforts to secure various physical resources, notably oil and gas. Chinese analysts expect the projected energy mix to increase from 25 per cent to 27 per cent reliance on oil by 2030, thus implying this commodity will remain of vital interest for the country throughout the next two decades.[12] In an effort to ensure viable energy sources, the Chinese Ministry of Foreign Affairs has sought to strengthen relationships between China and various oil-producing countries in partnership with three key state-owned oil and gas companies. As Africa is increasingly being viewed as the 'final frontier' insofar as global energy supply is concerned,[13] it is not surprising that China has dramatically increased its footprint on the continent. This is illustrated by the exponential growth of trade between the People's Republic of China and Africa. According to the Forum on China-Africa Cooperation, trade volumes have soared from approximately US $12 billion in 2002 to just over US $91 billion in 2009.

China's primary oil and gas firms

In 2012, there were three major players within China's oil and gas sector: China National Petroleum Corporation (CNPC), China Petroleum and Chemical Corporation (Sinopec) and China National Offshore Oil Corporation (CNOOC). While integrated through the entire value chain of oil and gas development (which includes upstream, midstream and downstream activities), each firm maintains a specific focus in terms of production capabilities.

CNPC is the nation's largest oil and gas producer and supplier, and has great strengths in engineering construction. The firm currently has operations in over 30 countries. In June 2010, PetroChina, a subsidiary of CNPC, became the second highest valued company in the world in terms of market capitalization. The 2010 fiscal year saw the firm reporting just over RMB 124 billion.[14]

Sinopec is one of the largest integrated energy and chemical companies in the world, with a focus on the downstream end of production. Sinopec operates under a mission of "Enterprise development, contribution to the country, shareholder value creation, social responsibility and employee wellbeing".[15] Sinopec is China's second largest producer and supplier of crude oil, refined oil products and major petrochemical products. In 2009, Sinopec became the first Chinese firm to be listed on the *Fortune Global 500* list. In 2010, the firm's revenues were just under US $308 billion.[16]

CNOOC is the third largest of China's national oil companies. Its emphasis has long been on offshore oil and gas exploration. By focusing on exploitation, exploration and development of crude oil and natural gas offshore, the firm has become China's largest producer of crude oil. In 2010, CNOOC had total profits of almost RMB 98 billion.[17]

While all three oil and gas firms operate independently, they function under government control. As such, their initiatives and operations follow the directives of the State-owned Assets Supervision and Administration Commission of the State Council of China, making it almost impossible to separate the business dealings of the three firms from the ambitions of China as a nation.

Arguably the state-controlled nature of CNPC, Sinopec and CNOOC presents these firms with an increased latitude for risk taking, particularly when it comes to capitalizing on high-risk, high-reward ventures such as FDI in smaller and unstable economies. Furthermore, privileged access to capital allows Chinese firms to shift their planning from reaching short-term profitability targets towards long-run objectives,[18] increasing their competitiveness over time.

Additionally, Chinese oil and gas firms benefit from their experience in dealing with onerous government regulations. While other international firms, particularly MNEs from developed economies, may be less accustomed to dealing with the red tape commonly associated with a highly politicized bureaucracy, Chinese firms must navigate and circumvent ambiguous political constraints on a continuous basis.

A final benefit afforded by the state-owned nature of Chinese oil corporations is that the government frequently consults the industry on policy matters. This allows Chinese firms to advocate for offshore developments that not only enhance national energy security, but also allow them to gain the experience needed to compete effectively with the leading international oil companies.[19] As a result, the Chinese oil industry is better able to align overseas operations and company directives with state policies as they pertain to the nation's energy security strategy. Ultimately, this creates a situation of mutual benefit for the oil and gas industry and the Chinese government.

China's energy security strategy

While China still consumes less energy than North America, the pace of its industrial and social development already requires energy consumption levels that surpass those of western Europe.[20] With insufficient domestic reserves China has been forced to seek supply of natural resources in the international market and, as a means of circumventing oil price volatility and physical supply disruptions, China has elected to purchase oil and gas rights in Africa.[21] Guiding Chinese MNEs' entry decisions in the African continent and beyond has been the nation's energy security strategy. The key objective is to secure adequate and reliable sources of energy at a reasonable cost. Furthermore, it is critical to the nation that accessing energy supplies does not jeopardize internal values and objectives.[22] That is to say, China will only pursue energy opportunities that ensure continuity with its domestic programmes and strategies, namely the 'One China' policy. The 'One China' framework precludes China from engaging in relationships with other nation states that do not acknowledge there is only 'One China', of which Taiwan is a part. This policy also ensures that the Chinese government is viewed as the sole governmental voice for the People's Republic of China. As such, states seeking to establish diplomatic or commercial relationships with China must, at a minimum, acknowledge the policy.

In contrast to Western nations that have resisted a full acknowledgement of the 'One China' policy, the African continent has witnessed little controversy on the issue and has encountered almost no opposition to its acceptance and recognition. The reality is that many of the poor and conflict-ridden African nations are eager to attract Chinese investment, as these business ventures have very few covenants attached on issues beyond the narrow business case at hand and respect a non-interference policy.

Sino-African relations: A brief history

Despite prevalent Western media beliefs, China's relationships and interactions with African nations are not wholly centred on the regime's energy security needs. China has been involved on the continent from as early as the mid 1950s. During that era, when many African states sought to establish their freedom from colonial powers, China proved to be a vital ally both from a financial and a diplomatic perspective. The symbolic diplomacy offered by China through its Five Principles of Peaceful Coexistence: (1) mutual respect for sovereignty and territorial integrity; (2) non-aggression pacts; (3) non-interference in international affairs; (4) equality and mutual benefit; and (5) peaceful coexistence, allowed African states to assert their independence in an environment of non-interference and non-alignment. For the Chinese government, at the time led by Mao Zedong, the early support of African states provided an opportunity to differentiate itself from its ideological rival, the former USSR.[23]

China did not become an importer of African oil until 1993, and prior to this there was little outward FDI, with the exception of investments in Sudan.[24] Over the past decade this pattern of investment has changed significantly, as China is now the impetus for the current construction boom in Africa. In exchange for mining and oil rights, China has undertaken numerous construction projects on the continent, most notably in South Africa, Zambia and Sudan. One example of such investment was the more than US $70 million pledged to assist South Africa in completing the stadium in Ndola prior to the 2010 Football World Cup.[25] Further examples can be observed in Sudan where Chinese influence supports the nation's new infrastructure, including the Friendship Hall conference centre, the Chinese school, as well as a plethora of buildings that embody various elements of traditional Chinese architecture. In addition to gaining support for these types of infrastructure programmes, affiliation with China has allowed many African nations access to substantial loans, financial grants and technical support.[26]

There have been concerns raised that China only involves itself in African states that possess the raw materials needed for continued Chinese economic growth; however, in the Ethiopian capital of Addis Ababa, a country essentially devoid of the natural resources desired by China, the infrastructure now bears a visible footprint of Chinese influence as an increasing number of Chinese firms take root.[27] China likely seeks to establish and maintain its presence in Africa for reasons beyond its energy security strategy, including new markets for finished products, domestic support, development cooperation, alternatives to Western models of governance, as well as a means to emphasize China's status as a superpower.[28]

The Chinese perspective: Internationalization motives

When contemplating the establishment of a presence in Africa from a mere commodity availability perspective, West African oil is particularly appealing to China due to its high quality and low sulphur content,[29] which translates into lower refining costs. Through their investment in Africa, Chinese oil and gas firms have been able to secure low-cost and reliable energy sources for their nation. This valuable commodity was up for grabs for China due to the void left behind by Western oil companies. The early twenty-first century marked an era of high activist involvement and lobbying in Western nations against Western investment in nations with a poor human rights record, whether in the context of labour rights or broader human rights violations. Due in part to the visibility of the genocide in Darfur, international human rights standards and the abuse thereof were pushed to the forefront of the Western mindset. In response to public outcry and non-democratic political conditions in Africa's authoritarian countries, investment in Africa was no longer deemed acceptable, and many Western firms were forced to pull investments from countries at war or with allegedly repressive governments.[30] At this time, China was evaluating various expansion opportunities in line with its energy security strategy. In March of 2005, CNOOC offered to purchase the California-based petroleum exploration firm Unocal for a reported US $18.5 billion in cash. The issue became highly politicized by several Republican congressmen, and the Chinese offer was brought to the attention of former president George W. Bush on the grounds that such a merger would jeopardize national security. Coupled with the rejection by Unocal's board of directors and the harsh political reaction that ensued, CNOOC withdrew its bid and, in August of that same year, Chevron acquired Unocal at a lower price. The failed bid revealed to China the hostile political environment in North America and other Western markets. In response, China elected to pursue expansion opportunities available in the southern hemisphere.

Beyond China's energy security interests, investment in Africa also serves to create new markets for the country's own products. Further, as Chinese corporations embed themselves in African markets and build relationships with local governments, they secure access to future opportunities.[31] China has managed to essentially ingratiate itself to many African populations as a loyal and dependable ally. A platform has been created for many future investment opportunities.

There have, however, been numerous occasions where Chinese policies of non-interference have not led to the desired outcomes, e.g., when 29 Chinese employees were kidnapped in Sudan in January 2012. On several occasions, China's diplomatic errors have led to some degree of alienation by African governments.

The Chinese government cannot be said to have entirely removed itself from peacekeeping efforts in Africa. In 2007, China encouraged Khartoum to accept UN peacekeeping forces. By 2008, Chinese contributions to the UN peacekeeping force accounted for 3 per cent of the total amounts dedicated to the mission – more than many European states.[32]

Having entered the market for oil imports less than 20 years ago, China is essentially a novice in the industry, with the related level of inexperience. This knowledge deficit may have resulted in Chinese management's improper assessment of risks and costs associated with particular projects, and consequent purchasing of overpriced assets and shares, whether in Africa or elsewhere, e.g., Sinopec's 2008 US $2.8 billion takeover of Syrian-based Tanganyika Oil, which later turned out to have no proven reserves. However, such overpayment is often (wrongly) perceived in the West as a demonstration of cash flow usage to assert China's rise to superpower status with no need to respect the conventional rules of capitalism (whereby poor investments lead to market punishment of the firm involved, with ensuing bankruptcy as the worst case scenario).

The African perspective: The good and the bad of Chinese investments

Several African countries have clearly benefited from Chinese investments through the establishment of strong diplomatic ties with China and the construction boom associated with Chinese FDI. African nations have historically tended to engage in bilateral deals, due perhaps to the unwanted complexity associated with multilateral agreements.[33] This penchant makes African nations ideal trading partners for the People's Republic of China, which also favours bilateral agreements. A shared preference for bilateralism simplifies the political aspects of relationship building and reduces associated costs for participants.

Chinese investments have become instrumental to the recent economic development of the African continent. The construction industry has not witnessed such progress since the independence movements of the 1950s, and many nations out of favour with Western powers have been awarded business opportunities otherwise unavailable to them. Through interactions with Chinese oil and gas firms, African governments have been encouraged to reflect and adopt policies that best address the challenges associated with globalization.[34] For some states, notably Angola, Chinese interests have actually allowed more diversity in trading relationships. China's investment reduced Angola's reliance on Western European markets and increased competition, thereby allowing Angola to gain more equitable pricing of its imports.[35]

Despite the positive impact Chinese oil money has had on African development, one of the major drawbacks has been the lack of African, skilled labour associated with projects: most, if not all, positions are occupied by Chinese labour.[36]

It has been estimated that over 50,000 Chinese workers are responsible for the reconstruction of infrastructure in Angola.[37] Many of the Chinese-backed ventures also use materials imported from China – a strategy that is unlikely to encourage development of local manufacturing and agriculture.[38] In fact, Angola is perhaps the only African nation to currently have a positive trade balance with China. All other nations have import levels higher than the value of their exports.[39]

The above concerns notwithstanding, many African states continue to view Chinese investment as an opportunity among equals[40] and avidly encourage oil and gas ventures on the continent.

The Western perspective: China's legacy in Africa and its impact on international trade policies

Chinese oil and gas development in sub-Saharan Africa has been a source of growing concern in the West. The catalyst for this concern was the close ties established between China and the government in Khartoum (capital of Sudan).[41] Many Western states are concerned that China's continued investment in Sudan perpetuates the authoritarian regime and its flagrant human rights abuses. The continued source of income and support for infrastructure development coming from China has allowed states such as Sudan to ignore and even undermine Western sanctions and embargoes.[42] Chinese policies of non-intervention, coupled with this country's own record of human rights violations, are feared to condone silently the extensive abuse of vulnerable peoples on the African continent. China is seen in the West as a neo-colonial power that has become so desperate that it heedlessly invests billions of dollars in poor and war-torn nations, e.g., Mozambique.[43] China's environmental policies and their impact on the global environment also cause concerns. The resulting fear is that the Chinese legacy will be one of exploitation, corruption and pollution.

Western media have drawn attention to the trade deficits between Africa and China. There is now a perception in the West that Chinese firms are destroying local industrial capacity and are actively discouraging African nations from developing industries beyond natural resources exploitation. By not fully diversifying, many African countries are inherently increasing their level of risk as they rely solely on one industry and, most often, extensively on one trading partner.

The West's final and overarching concern is China's motivation to provide alternatives to Western economic models and to consolidate its status as a superpower. There are numerous examples of Chinese firms having eclipsed, and even impeded Western investors in the African market.[44] Many African nations would prefer to engage in business with Chinese firms, as these firms appear to worry little about domestic host country policies and practices beyond those affecting narrow business operations (a reflection of China's Five Principles for Peaceful Coexistence). There is also the potential for African nations to obtain substantial financial grants and loans from China – opportunities typically not available when these countries engage in trade with Western states.

The totality of the above concerns of Western nations has resulted in the demonization of Chinese investment as a means of destabilizing the current international economic and diplomatic system. Many Western states are concerned that, as China's influence mounts, theirs will decrease, resulting in a shift of the current 'global hierarchy of nations'.

The idiosyncratic characteristics of Chinese energy firms

The main idiosyncratic feature of Chinese oil and gas firms is that it is almost impossible to separate strategic decisions made by Sinopec, CNPC and CNOOC from the actions of the Chinese government. As agents of the state, these corporations have secured durable competitive advantages thanks to the funding and access to decision-making bodies in the national, political arena. If it were not for the continuous flow of capital provided by the Chinese government, the poor cost–benefit balance of overseas acquisitions could have led Chinese oil and gas MNEs into a process of economic decline at a minimum, and into bankruptcy in the worst-case scenario.

Even more pressing and controversial is the issue of public policy in relation to state-run enterprises. Western firms must adhere to stringent human rights codes and environmental policies. Those that ignore international conventions may face sanctions and penalties from their home countries, as well as intense public backlash, especially at the downstream end of operations. In the case of state-run firms, however, such sanctions may not exist. How does the business world effectively monitor and react to abuses conducted by state-owned organizations without violating international law? As Chinese firms continue to develop, this will become a fundamental issue to be addressed.

QUESTIONS

1. What are the FSAs of Chinese oil and gas firms?
2. What are the Chinese firms' administrative archetypes?
3. What are their motivations for expansion into Africa?
4. What location advantages exist in African countries where the Chinese firms seek expansion? Are these location advantages readily available to the Chinese firms? Were the Chinese firms able to successfully recombine their FSAs with the location advantages of African host countries?
5. Describe China's CSR issues in Africa. Would a proactive CSR strategy help alleviate concerns from the West regarding the Chinese investment in Africa?
6. Discuss the relationship between China's location advantages and the FSAs of Chinese state-owned firms. Can the two concepts be clearly unbundled in this case?

Case 15.2 Infosys: The rise of a leading IT giant from India[45]

Founded in 1981 with seed capital amounting to only US $250, Infosys Limited (hereafter Infosys) turned into an international consulting and technology services company with headquarters in Bangalore, India. Infosys was the first Indian information technology (IT) company to be listed on the NASDAQ (National Association of Securities Dealers Automated Quotations, established in 1971). In 2012, Infosys' workforce consisted of nearly 150,000 employees operating in 64 offices and 68 development centres around the world, and the firm generated sales of US $6.99 billion.[46] Infosys had also established several strategic alliances with leading technology providers in order to deliver innovative solutions to clients' business needs that promised high-value benefits, e.g., in terms of improved quality parameters. Infosys prides itself on trying to achieve value maximization for its clients. This attitude pays off: 97.4 per cent of the firm's sales are based on long-term strategic client relationships.[47]

Company background

Two years after N. R. Narayana Murthy and six engineers established Infosys in Pune, India, in 1981, the company decided to relocate its offices to Bangalore, the 'Silicon Valley' of India. This naming reflects the intended similarity with Silicon Valley, based in California, United States, the world's leading region for high-tech innovation and development, especially in the IT software sphere. Today Bangalore represents the major hub for India's IT industry.

Infosys' strategic relocation to Bangalore turned out to be the right choice. After strengthening its local business, Infosys opened its first international office in Boston, United States, in 1987.

Six years later, in 1993, Infosys was listed on the Bombay Stock Exchange in India. Despite the fact that Infosys' initial public offering (IPO) was undersubscribed, the stock leaped up 60 per cent on the first trading day. This injection of fresh capital helped accelerating Infosys' international expansion. At the same time, Infosys created an incentive programme for its workforce, namely the Employee Stock Options programme. In 1994, Infosys opened its first international development centre in Fremont, United States, that was followed by its first European office in the United Kingdom and two global development centres in Toronto, Canada, and Mangalore, India. In 1995, as one of the first companies worldwide, Infosys initiated electronic business, the so-called e-business, and started to apply information and communication technologies (ICT) in support of all operational activities. This approach has become the new standard in today's business world, as it supports routinized business processes and seeks efficiency gains along the entire value chain. The development and implementation of a global delivery model across all subsidiaries worldwide enabled Infosys "to produce where it is most cost-effective and sell services where it is most profitable".[48]

In 1998, Infosys started to offer its Enterprise Solutions applications. This software supports organizations in information management activities and business transactions, and covers subject areas ranging from enterprise resource planning, to customer relationship management, and business intelligence. The Enterprise Solutions practice achieved sustained success and in 1999, Infosys generated sales of US $100 million and was introduced on the American stock exchange NASDAQ.

Building upon its extensive internationalization programme into countries such as Germany, Sweden, Belgium, Australia, France and Hong Kong and further expansion into countries where it already had some presence, such as the United States and Canada, Infosys doubled its revenues to US $200 million within a 12-month time period. Revenues reached US $1 billion only four years later. Thanks to the sustained growth of its operations, development centres and foreign subsidiaries, Infosys has created a strong international presence. In 2005, Infosys succeeded in placing an international equity offering of US $1 billion from India. At the time of Infosys' 25th anniversary in 2006, the firm employed more than 50,000 people and had more than US $2 billion in revenues. During the same year, Infosys' founder N. R. Murthy retired. However, Infosys' continuous growth was not affected by this change of the guard. With the opening of subsidiaries in Latin America, the appointment of Kris Gopalakrishnan as the new CEO and the addition of 20,000 new employees, Infosys reached more than US $3 billion turnover in 2007. In the following years, Infosys grew at similar speed. In 2009, the Indian firm established its first Latin American development centre in Belo Horizonte, Brazil, and a second in Monterrey, Mexico. By 2010, revenues reached the US $5 billion mark. Since then, an extra US $1 billion in sales has been added on a yearly basis, leading to a sales volume close to US $7 billion in 2012. In addition, 30,000+ employees joined the company within the last three years and this has helped to extend Infosys' reach.

This impressive international development of an emerging economy MNE shows growth rates that are out of reach for many MNEs from developed countries. Infosys has become one of the fastest-growing IT companies in the world and the leading provider in business consulting and customized IT solutions in industries ranging from airlines to financial services and life sciences.

Alliances

Infosys aims to "accelerate innovation, increase productivity, reduce costs, and optimize asset utilization", but does not rely solely on its own strengths; it has joined forces with leading international technology partners.[49] By forming a strong network, Infosys and its partners generate business value, and reduce implementation risks and time-to-market.[50]

Infosys distinguishes among three different levels of partnership agreements. The Indian IT firm shares and combines its own Intellectual Property with the technology and services of its 'global alliance partners', in order to create and promote Infosys' business solutions for a wide spectrum of industries around the world. 'Global alliance partners' represent the *first level* of alliances, and include Microsoft for global systems integration, Oracle for customized special-ization services, and SAP for systems integration and implementation.

'Alliance partners' represent the *second level* of partnerships. Here, the focus is more on one particular industry or geographic region. In contrast to 'global alliance partners', the 'alliance partners' solely provide training sessions and technical support. Examples of 'alliance partners' are Siemens for Product Lifecycle Management, IBM for tailored software solutions, and Hewlett-Packard (HP) for global hardware systems integration.

'Teaming partners' represent the *third level* of partnerships, and these involve independent service providers in hardware, software, consulting, sales or distribution. Teaming partners collaborate with Infosys and provide customized solutions to their clients' needs. Teaming partners are mostly specialists, e.g., ATG, an expert in e-commerce; EMC, a global information infrastructure technologies developer and provider; and Netezza, a leader in data warehouse appliances.

Building tomorrow's enterprise

Infosys aims to create awareness of the need for IT as an instrument to drive corporate growth and improve the competitive position of its clients. Infosys measures the business value of IT investments, building upon three different approaches:

1. Business Transformation: In collaboration with both business consulting and IT services, Infosys provides an integrated approach that combines a general strategy as well as an execution perspective, and delivers customized IT solutions.[51]
2. Accelerating Innovation: By identifying "seven game changing trends", the Indian service provider assists clients in discovering new business prospects that accelerate innovation and growth.[52]
3. Efficient Operations: Through analysing the entire business and using benchmarks execution excellence is promoted.[53]

Through the above, three-pronged approach, Infosys challenges existing prejudices vis-à-vis IT investments that apparently cannot deliver actual results. At the same time, it provides solutions in form of business benefits frameworks, multi-layered benefit realization programmes, models and metrics for Return on Investment articulation, and integrated value chain approaches.[54]

Sustainability

In addition to focusing on research, innovation and knowledge co-creation, Infosys engages in a wide spectrum of sustainability related activities. The firm has implemented what it considers to be a "sustainable approach to business".[55] Senior management is exploring the linkages between the firm's contributions to its stakeholders (including employees, business partners and society at large) and corporate growth. With the objective of crafting sustainable solutions and ultimately sustainable growth, three sustainability pillars have been defined that serve as guidelines for managerial action, namely 'Social Contract', 'Resource Intensity' and 'Green Innovation'.

The agenda of the 'Social Contract' pillar covers multiple programmes targeting employees, local communities and the environment. In the realm of volunteering initiatives, employees are encouraged to work in Indian Non-Governmental Organizations (NGOs), while receiving an Infosys allowance for up to one year. Moreover, Infosys' employees and the Infosys Foundation donate to victims of natural disasters such as earthquakes, tornados etc. Furthermore, over a three-year period commencing in August 2008, the SPARK programme has enabled more than 350,000 children and teachers to gain insight into information technology and to learn about science and mathematics. Likewise, Infosys has been promoting education and research through various channels such as teaching children from underprivileged communities in the United States, and mentoring 2,500 Indian teachers to impart knowledge to local students. Thanks to the firm's excellent reputation and achievement in innovation, members of the board of directors of Infosys have been invited to serve on international associations in the sustainability sphere, such as the World Business Council for Sustainable Development, and are shaping policies in "corporate governance, education, healthcare, diversity, and the environment".[56]

The second sustainability management pillar, namely 'Resource Intensity', addresses Infosys' ecological footprint and focuses on the usage of natural resources. For example, in the context of 'green infrastructure', the new buildings of the Indian IT provider conform to the Leadership in Energy and Environmental Design platinum norms and thus, aim to respect the highest international standards. In addition, Infosys is one of the largest solar energy consumers in India, and targeted a 20 per cent green energy rate of the total energy consumption by the end of 2012. In the context of 'water sustainability', Infosys reuses rain and wastewater from indoor plants and recycles it for further usage, e.g., for toilet flushing. Moreover, Infosys strives towards a green environment and plants more trees than it has employees. As an additional green initiative, it promotes minimal paper usage and has implemented a waste management programme that generates energy from organic waste. In order to achieve preset goals, Infosys tries to involve its employees allowing them to measure their own carbon footprint and to obtain advice for improvement.

The third sustainability pillar, 'Green Innovation', focuses on green computing. For example, the iSustain program helps to monitor the consumption of water, energy, etc. and the generation of garbage as well as emissions, so that firms can assess progress and compile sustainability reports. Other initiatives, such as the Integrated Real Time Campus Management System, support the management of energy consumption and aim to optimize its use. However, Infosys does not only develop applications for clients, but has also crafted its own corporate programmes such as the Carbon Footprint Calculator and the InGreen Energy Management system. Through these programmes, Infosys' employees become more sensitive to their own individual footprint, and therefore often attempt to reduce the company's overall per capita energy consumption.[57] Some innovative approaches go even further and provide solutions to monitor and reduce energy consumption of mobile devices, personal computers and household devices. The iSmart Intelligent Power Strip measures the power usage of e.g., a smart phone and transfers the data to an application server. Thanks to this analysis, the user can monitor and regulate the power consumption as well as improve the energy efficiency and consumption of his cellphone. In 2012, this innovative energy management tool was selected as one of the most creative responses to the 'Grand Challenges' identified in the *Technology Review (India)*, the innovation magazine published by the Massachusetts Institute of Technology (MIT).

According to Newsweek's Green Ranking, Infosys has become one of the world's top 10 green companies. The rating is based on the environmental impact, management and disclosure of global companies.[58]

Human resources management

Due to Infosys' pursuit of rapid growth and the limited number of Indian graduates in computer science in the 1980s, Infosys had to recruit graduates from other programmes. These non-computer experts enabled Infosys to widen its talent pool and hence, created diversity among its employees.

However, as a consequence of Infosys' rapid expansion, human resources (HR) management turned out to be a great challenge and the hiring of new employees could barely keep up with the company's need for highly skilled people. Therefore, as of the early 1990s, Infosys had to improve its personnel recruitment and training approach by strengthening its HR department and implementing an education and research department. Thanks to the Internet and subsequent systems of online recruitment and Intranet development, Infosys has started to link HR practices to general corporate goals.

In 2007, Infosys received 1.3 million applications for 17,000 job positions in India alone. The screening of applicants requires a high degree of automation. Approximately 10 per cent of all applicants are invited to take an online test that can be administered simultaneously to 10,000 candidates across several cities in India. Ultimately, less than one per cent of the applicants is invited to join Infosys. The Indian IT firm is one of the most attractive employers in India, but until recently it had remained relatively unknown with international graduates. In order to respond to the increasing global demand for innovative and customized IT solutions, Infosys increased its focus on diversity and launched an international internship programme, namely InStep, as well as a corporate programme, Campus Connect, associating the firm with universities in India and abroad. The efforts in international recruitment were necessary in order to catch up with Infosys' international expansion trajectory. For example, in 2007 a total of 98 per cent of Infosys revenues were earned overseas, but the firm employed only 3 per cent non-Indian employees. Infosys therefore also introduced the Global Talent Program, a recruitment initiative that focuses on international young graduates. In 2006, the first year of the programme, a class of 126 new recruits from US universities was sent to India.[59]

International new recruits as well as Indian ones, with a non-computer science related background, follow a 16-week training programme at Infosys' education centre in Mysore, India, in order to acquire technical knowledge and improve social competences. *Fortune Magazine* has dubbed this facility the "Taj Mahal of training centers" as it can accommodate up to 14,000 employees per day for professional education and training purposes.[60] At the end of the training period, an online system matches the new recruits' individual job preferences with the open positions. In a first stage, new employees can exercise selectivity in terms of desired job characteristics, but not regarding the location of their work. However, they can change their initial job position through usage of a 'swap portal', which is also open to more senior employees wishing to apply for internal job openings. To keep track of its approximately 150,000 employees worldwide, Infosys has set up a personal master data management system called Career Central that saves information about individual skills, education and certifications.

The Indian IT company is acutely aware of the importance of employee satisfaction, and hence organizes several monthly activities to integrate new recruits in the company and in the (typically) new location where they will reside. Further, Infosys started programmes such as HALE (Health Assessment and Lifestyle Enrichment Plan) and HEAR (Hearing Employees and Resolving), two employee-focused initiatives that provide services for the general well-being of each individual.

Infosys enjoys high corporate growth rates, but at the same time faces a constant demand for skilled employees. The reason is the company's high turnover rate, as the average tenure of an Infosys employee is only about two years.[61] To reduce turnover and build a bond between employees and the company, Infosys is attempting to engage its workers in loyalty programmes and to promote a strong corporate culture. The acronym C-LIFE (Customer delight, Leadership by example, Integrity and transparency, Fairness, pursuit of Excellence) represents the values of Infosys that are communicated in form of case studies, discussions, 'awards for excellence' events, etc.

Infosys' new recruits are mostly young, high potentials from India with great ambition to climb the ladder of professional success. Unfortunately, they sometimes overestimate their own potential and may be overly ambitious in terms of the time needed to rise in the Infosys hierarchy. To avoid possible conflicts and later disappointments, Infosys has initiated Career Clarity, a matching programme between the new recruits' expectations on the one hand, and the corporate opportunities on the other.

Infosys introduced an Employees Stock Offer Plan in 1994 as an incentive mechanism and means to increase employee retention and satisfaction. However, in 2003, the Indian IT services provider changed its compensation scheme to a more variable system that links pay with performance of (a) the individual employee; (b) the business unit he/she works in; (c) the corporation as a whole. Along with a 360-degree benchmarking approach whereby employees assess each other's performance, Infosys has created a compensation system that relies on both performance measurement and employee engagement.

India's location advantages

As noted above, Infosys attracts thousands of young graduates each year and has access to a huge talent pool of 'high potentials' because India has a youthful population and an increasing number of graduates. The country has the world's second largest labour force, with almost 500 million workers, of whom 34 per cent are employed in the services sector.[62] Thus, India offers great advantages as a location, vis-à-vis Western countries. Compared to other emerging economies, Indian labour is not only inexpensive, but the workforce consists of many, well-educated university graduates with good English language skills. This makes India a favourite location among MNEs, to offshore and sometimes also outsource, their business operations. In addition, India has become the leading provider in software development and software enabled services. India's successful growth has been driven by the government's efforts towards economic liberalization in the 1990s. With the implementation of economic reforms and thus the opening of the Indian market, foreign direct investment has increased from US $165 million in 1991–92 to US $28.4 billion in 2011–12.[63]

However, local companies such as Infosys benefit at least as much as foreign investors from India's location advantages. For example, Infosys sends its Indian employees to clients abroad in order to work on site. Opponents of India's cheap labour claim this amounts to employee exploitation and the violation of local labour laws. Whether employee exploitation and disrespect for local labour laws actually occur is a highly controversial issue; a trial about visa fraud at Infosys in 2012, called this business practice once more into question: "According to [the] complaint, the company has been illegally using B1 visas in lieu of H1B visas. Unlike H1B visas, which allow employees to work in the US, B1 visas are only meant for visiting for conferences or business negotiations."[64]

India was ranked 132nd out of 183 economies in the annual study 'Doing Business' published by the World Bank in 2012.[65] This study measures the ease of doing business by evaluating key indicators covering ten subject areas (e.g., starting a business, paying taxes and enforcing contracts). The study also benchmarks the results against the other 182 economies. In terms of the Global Competitiveness Index (GCI 2011–12) of the World Economic Forum, India was ranked 56 out of 142 countries included, five places lower than the previous year.[66] The GCI comprises three sub-indices, namely 'basic requirements', 'efficiency enhancers', and 'innovation and sophistication' factors, that measure key drivers of competitiveness and allow a comparison between emerging economies such as India and developed countries such as the United States. Despite India's deteriorated position in the overall ranking, the country improved its result in absolute terms. Together with other emerging economies such as China and Brazil, it is closing the gap with the United States, thereby becoming even more attractive to foreign investors.

The future

After years of extraordinary growth, Indian IT services providers are bound to face more complex market conditions in the future. Rivalry exists among the six major Indian IT companies that are best described by the acronym SWITCH, referring to Satyam (acquired in 2009 by the Mahindra group), Wipro, Infosys, Tata Consultancy Services, Cognizant and HCL. However, there is also competition from established service providers in the United States (e.g., Accenture) and smaller companies from other emerging economies such as Pakistan. Infosys therefore has to continue to invest heavily in human capital, in order to make a difference through shared value creation and green innovation.

QUESTIONS

1. What are Infosys' home country location and firm-specific advantages?
2. How does Infosys exploit these advantages in favour of its international expansion?
3. Select one of Infosys' international alliance partners and analyse its role as a partner for Infosys. You can use materials available on the Web.
4. What is the administrative heritage of Infosys? What roles do (Indian and international) employees play in Infosys' organization?
5. Studies such as the 'Doing Business' ranking of the World Bank give important signals to foreign direct investors. Please analyse one additional emerging economy and compare its results with the scores of developed countries. What are the location advantages of that emerging economy? Based on the results of 'Doing Business', is it recommendable to exploit these location advantages as a developed economy MNE?

Notes

1. Pankaj Ghemawat and Thomas Hout, 'Tomorrow's global giants? Not the usual suspects', *Harvard Business Review* (2008).
2. *Ibid.*
3. *Ibid.*
4. Orit Gadiesh and Till Vestring, 'The consequences of China's rising global heavyweights', *Sloan Management Review* 49 (3) (2008).
5. *Ibid.*
6. *Ibid.*
7. Huei-Ting Tsai and Andreas B. Eisingerich, 'Internationalization strategies of emerging markets firms', *California Management Review* 53 (1) (2010), 114–35.
8. *Ibid.*
9. Mudambi, Ram, 'Location, control and innovation in knowledge-intensive industries', *Journal of Economic Geography* 8 (2008), 699–725.
10. See for example: www.businessweek.com/magazine/chinas-new-protectionism-10272011.html
11. This case was co-authored by Ms Miranda Spensley and Professor Alain Verbeke.
12. E. Downs, 'The Chinese energy security debate', *The China Quarterly* 177 (2004), 21–41.
13. M. Klare and D. Volman, 'America, China and the scramble for Africa's oil', *Review of African Political Economy* 108 (2006), 297–309.
14. CNPC website: www.cnpc.com.cnlenlaboutcnpcldefault.htm.
15. Sinopec Annual report (2010).
16. Sinopec website: http://english.sinopec.com/about sinopec/our company/20l00328/8532.shtml.
17. CNOOC website: http://en.cnooc.com.cnldatalhtmllenglishlchannel 110.html.
18. L. Caniglia, 'Western ostracism and China's presence in Africa', *China Information* 165 (2011), 165–84.

19. E. Downs, 'The Chinese energy security debate', *The China Quarterly* 177 (2004), 21–41.
20. L. Caniglia, 'Western ostracism and China's presence in Africa', *China Information* 165 (2011), 165–84.
21. E. Downs, 'The Chinese energy security debate', *The China Quarterly* 177 (2004), 21–41.
22. *Ibid.*
23. M. Klare and D. Volman, 'America, China and the scramble for Africa's oil', *Review of African Political Economy* 108 (2006), 297–309.
24. L. Caniglia, 'Western ostracism and China's presence in Africa', *China Information* 165 (2011), 165–84.
25. N. Ford, 'Boom time for African construction', *African Business* 344 (2008), 38–50.
26. L. Caniglia, 'Western ostracism and China's presence in Africa', *China Information* 165 (2011), 165–84.
27. N. Ford, 'Boom time for African construction', *African Business* 344 (2008), 38–50.
28. L. Caniglia, 'Western ostracism and China's presence in Africa', *China Information* 165 (2011), 165–84.
29. S. Naidu and D. Mbazima, 'China-African relations: A new impulse in a changing landscape', *Futures* 40 (2008), 748–61.
30. L. Caniglia, 'Western ostracism and China's presence in Africa', *China Information* 165 (2011), 165–184.
31. S. Naidu and D. Mbazima, 'China-African relations: A new impulse in a changing landscape', *Futures* 40 (2008), 748–61.
32. L. Caniglia, 'Western ostracism and China's presence in Africa', *China Information* 165 (2011), 165–84.
33. *Ibid.*
34. S. Naidu and D. Mbazima, 'China-African relations: A new impulse in a changing landscape', *Futures* 40 (2008), 748–61.
35. R. Aguilar and A. Goldstein, 'The Chinisation of Africa: The case of Angola', *The World Economy* 11 (2009), 1543–62.
36. N. Ford, 'Boom time for African construction', *African Business* 344 (2008), 38–50.
37. R. Aguilar and A. Goldstein, 'The Chinisation of Africa: The case of Angola', *The World Economy* 11 (2009), 1543–62.
38. M. Klare and D. Volman, 'America, China and the scramble for Africa's oil', *Review of African Political Economy* 108 (2006), 297–309.
39. L. Caniglia, 'Western ostracism and China's presence in Africa', *China Information* 165 (2011), 165–84.
40. *Ibid.*
41. *Ibid.*
42. L. Caniglia, 'Western ostracism and China's presence in Africa', *China Information* 165 (2011), 165–84.
43. 'A ravenous dragon', *Economist* 386 (2008), 3–6.
44. L. Caniglia, 'Western ostracism and China's presence in Africa', *China Information* 165 (2011), 165–84.
45. This case was co-authored by Ms. Jenny Hillemann and Professor Alain Verbeke.
46. Infosys Homepage, What we do, retrieved on 28 March 2012: www.infosys.com/about/what-we-do/pages/index.aspx
47. Infosys Homepage, What we do, retrieved on 28 March 2012: www.infosys.com/about/what-we-do/pages/index.aspx
48. Infosys company information, 2008.

49. Infosys Homepage, Industry, retrieved on 3 April 2012: www.infosys.com/industries/pages/index.aspx

50. Infosys Homepage, Alliances, retrieved 3 April 2012: www.infosys.com/about/alliances/Pages/index.aspx

51. Infosys (2011), Case Study: Business Technology Investments, 3.

52. Infosys (2011), Case Study: Business Technology Investments, 4.

53. Infosys (2011), Case Study: Business Technology Investments, 5.

54. Infosys (2011), Case Study: Business Technology Investments, 2, retrieved on 3 April 2012: http://www.infosys.com/building-tomorrows-enterprise/Documents/business-technology-investments.pdf

55. Infosys Homepage, Sustainability, retrieved on 3 April 2012: http://www.infosys.com/sustainability/Pages/index.aspx

56. Infosys Homepage, Social Contract, retrieved on 3 April 2012: www.infosys.com/sustainability/social-contract/Pages/index.aspx

57. Infosys Homepage, Green Innovation, retrieved on 4 April 2012: www.infosys.com/sustainability/green-innovation/Pages/index.aspx

58. 'The world's greenest companies', *Newsweek* (16 October 2011), retrieved on 4 April 2012: www.thedailybeast.com/newsweek/2011/10/16/green-rankings-2011-world-s-greenest-companies-photos.infosys.html

59. Ram Subramanian, 'Infosys Technologies Limited: The Global Talent Program', *Asian Case Research Journal* 12, (2008), 249–73.

60. Infosys company Information, 2011.

61. Julian Birkinshaw, 'Infosys: Computing the power of people', *Business Strategy Review* (1 December 2008).

62. CIA, The World Factbook India, retrieved on 4 April 2012: www.cia.gov/library/publications/the-world-factbook/geos/in.html

63. Kulwindar Singh, 'Foreign direct investment in India: a critical analysis of FDI from 1991–2005', Centre for Civil Society; (http://unpan1.un.org/intradoc/groups/public/documents/apcity/unpan024036.pdf) Ernst & Young, 2012 India Attractiveness Survey.

64. 'Infosys – Jack Palmer visa case trial to start from August 20', *The Economic Times* (3 December 2011).

65. World Bank 2012.

66. World Economic Forum, The Global Competitiveness Report 2011–2012.

16A

International strategies of corporate social responsibility

Five learning objectives

1. To explain the significance of corporate social responsibility (CSR) in the MNE context.
2. To illustrate the linkages between strategy and CSR in contemporary MNE business practice.
3. To examine how CSR applied by MNEs can improve labour standards.
4. To develop an understanding of the trade-off between maximizing MNE profits in the short run and fulfilling obligations to society.
5. To clarify that there is no 'one size fits all' CSR approach across all types of economies (developed, emerging and least-developed) and all types of MNE administrative heritage, and that there can be various patterns of CSR capability building.

This chapter examines Dunn and Yamashita's idea that MNEs truly can 'do well' and 'do good' at the same time. In other words, MNEs can engage in initiatives that not only benefit their stakeholders but also fulfil the firms' 'corporate citizenship' obligations to society. Dunn and Yamashita detail the benefits that can accrue to the MNE from 'corporate citizenship' initiatives, including market growth, knowledge, contacts and the development of international leaders. These ideas will be examined and then criticized using the framework presented in Chapter 1.

Significance

CSR refers to good citizenship by the firm – i.e., its obligations to society, particularly when society is affected by the firm's strategies and practices.[1] When expanding abroad, MNEs are expected to act as good local citizens in all the locations where they are active. Once considered merely a philanthropic option, good corporate citizenship is now increasingly imposed by the new economic reality of powerful NGOs, grassroots consumer networks and rapid international information dissemination. While good citizenship can be viewed as the equivalent of a cost increase, it can also be an opportunity to develop FSAs and to improve performance.

In a 2003 *HBR* article, **Debra Dunn** and **Keith Yamashita** suggest that it is often possible for firms to **do well** and to **do good** simultaneously.[2] That is, profitable business models can go hand-in-hand with good citizenship and produce positive CSR outcomes. The authors focus on Hewlett-Packard's (HP) CSR efforts, particularly its i-community initiative in the Kuppam region of India.

According to HP, its international citizenship efforts are based on a simple framework: "strong ethics and appropriately transparent governance form the platform of integrity on which all our policies and decisions must be based".[3]

In practice, HP focuses its CSR in three areas. First is privacy, as demonstrated by HP advocating international data protection for consumers. Second is the environment, as demonstrated by HP designing products to minimize their ecological impact. Third is e-inclusion, in which HP uses technology to improve people's access to both social and economic opportunities.[4]

HP's citizenship efforts are closely aligned with its business strategy. HP establishes clear strategic objectives for each social issue that is addressed, and attempts to apply sound business practices to each project. Dunn and Yamashita detail seven such practices utilized by HP in its i-community initiative in Kuppam.

The first business practice applied in Kuppam is unearthing customer needs. HP's technology business operations demand the ability to "divine the needs of their customers by probing at underlying problems and transferring that understanding to the innovation process".[5] In the technology industry, products are rarely developed simply by asking customers what they want. Instead, customer problems must be uncovered (often with some effort) and technological solutions then developed to solve those problems. HP reports that most community development initiatives do not approach the problem with this type of underlying needs analysis.

In addressing social challenges, HP invests in a needs-finding process that takes the form of an iterative cycle. This resource recombination process, which HP refers to as its 'living lab methodology', involves uncovering a need and quickly developing a prototype solution. The prototype solution is then deployed on a limited basis, which allows for observation and solution modification. After modification, the cycle is started over again.

A second business practice applied to citizenship efforts is fielding a diversely talented team. MNEs often entrust community development initiatives to individuals with a background in philanthropy or development. Drawing on its business experience, HP sees the benefit of complementing those philanthropic and development skills with a broader range of knowledge, including line-management knowledge, expertise in government affairs, and a rich understanding of culture. In other words, citizenship efforts cannot be effective and perhaps even translate into FSAs without involvement of (human and other) resources that are the core of the firm's more conventional FSAs.

A third business practice is adopting a systems approach. A systems approach does not attempt to optimize individual parts, but instead views these parts in a broader context and aims to optimize the whole. In HP's case, this approach suggests that development initiatives should do much more than provide technology. "Community leaders must advocate for the solution, trusted individuals within the community must lend their reputations to the effort, Kuppam businesses must get involved, and other technology companies must integrate their technology into the solution."[6] This third business practice shows the complexity involved in HP's efforts to combine its extant FSAs in technology with resources in the local environment.

Related to the above is the adoption of a fourth business practice, namely the creation of a leading platform. In the ICT industry, the concept of leading platform refers to a standardized, generally accepted configuration of hardware as well as a specific operating system and other software, which allows the functioning of computers and computerized devices (e.g., personal digital assistants and cell phones), and which can be linked to other hardware or software. Working with all the partners involved, HP provides the main ICT infrastructure (both hardware and software), to which each partner can then add its own technologies and applications. HP's partners can thus add value by building upon their own distinctive strengths.

In conjunction with creating a leading platform, a fifth business practice is building an ecosystem of partners. HP recognizes that most sustainable communities have many different stakeholders with a vested interest in a long-term solution. Thus, HP brings together government, local leadership, business people, health care professionals, NGOs, informal networks within the community and local and international technology partners. While it is not easy to align these interests in the short term, HP believes that the long-term alignment of strong interests from all these parties is the best path to sustainable solutions. The alignment of interests offers protection from hazards associated with each partner's bounded reliability. In short, HP does not attempt to drive all the value creation itself, but instead tries to create a healthy ecosystem of partners, all dedicated to solving problems and bringing their complementary resources to the initiative.

A sixth business practice that HP applies to community development initiatives is simply to set a deadline for the project. HP has found that deadlines create a sense of urgency, which keeps all participants in the partnership focused. Deadlines move the initiative to the action phase and encourage participants to find common ground quickly. Setting a deadline indicating the end of the MNE's active involvement also focuses the project on becoming self-sustaining after the MNE's direct involvement has ceased.

The seventh business practice used by HP in its community development initiatives is what the firm calls 'solving, stitching and scaling'. This practice, derived from HP's experience in taking new products to market, initially customizes a solution for a single customer. This focus eliminates the bounded rationality challenge of trying to figure out all the possible forms the solution will eventually take. The single customer solution is also known as the lighthouse account because of its ability to point other customers towards the firm. Building upon such experiences with single customers, managers can then begin to stitch a collection of solutions into a total solution that can be scaled.[7]

Dunn and Yamashita illustrate how HP has applied these seven business practices to its community development programme in Kuppam, India. Kuppam can be viewed as HP's first community development customer. The lessons learned and solutions developed in this region are scaleable and transferable to other regions in need of community development.

Kuppam makes for a tough testing ground as nearly half of its population lives below the poverty line. One third of the population is illiterate, half has no electricity and there is a high rate of HIV. HP sees value in this region, however, as regions that are very different from established markets and 'conventional customer thinking' may offer new potential for innovation.[8]

Within its three CSR areas noted above (privacy, the environment and e-inclusion), HP centred its efforts in Kuppam on e-inclusion. E-inclusion means using technology to reduce economic and social divides. In this programme "the company creates public–private partnerships to accelerate economic development through the application of technology while simultaneously opening new markets and developing new products and services".[9] One tangible expression of this community initiative is the Kuppam information centre, which allows people to make phone calls, photocopies and faxes, and offers computers with access to the HP-built i-community portal. The centre not only offers the infrastructure for micro-enterprise development but it is also itself owned by locals selected by an NGO. This ownership structure fits well with HP's 'ecosystem of partners' approach to community development. Kuppam's i-community now includes five community information centres where students, teachers and parents can develop skills to access information via the Internet.

For the MNE manager the business value of the project is the template or routine from which the project was developed. In this case, the template consists of four key phases of project development. The first phase, lasting approximately five months, is the 'quick start'. This phase attempts to establish credibility and momentum by achieving a few quick successes. Other elements in this phase include visioning exercises and the gaining of high-level alignment with partners in the public and private sectors. The second phase, lasting approximately eight months, is the 'ramp up'. This phase is characterized by gathering resources for prototyping, evaluating solutions and training stakeholders so they can take ownership of the initiative. Key to the ramp up phase is bringing the ecosystem of international and local partners into a true coalition. Third, running from the beginning of the second to the middle of the third year of the initiative is the 'consolidation' phase. In this phase, HP evaluates the intellectual property generated to date, helps local partners decide which solutions to deploy and stops sub-projects unlikely to reach their goals. Fourth, overlapping with the consolidation phase is the 'transition' phase, which runs from the beginning of the second year to the end of the third year. Here, community leaders are identified, and power and knowledge are transferred to local participants.[10]

The benefits of the Kuppam initiative have extended to other communities. For example, HP transferred the lessons learned from the Kuppam i-community project and applied these to a project that tested new technology by providing portable solar-powered digital photography hardware to women entrepreneurs. These women were able to utilize the technological infrastructure to develop a solid business model. This approach gave them the confidence to seek a line of credit from a co-op bank, and the extra income offered the means to provide education for their children.

HP realized that its earlier philanthropic donations, though generating results, were actually suboptimal, and that much more could be accomplished if doing good and doing well could be made mutually reinforcing.[11] The benefits of the Kuppam initiative for HP have included market growth, leadership training and technological development. HP emphasizes that projects such as Kuppam are not about short-term profits but about the opportunity to achieve long-term growth and, in the process, improve the human condition in regions where the firm does business. Through the process, HP has also gained knowledge and contacts within new markets and these benefits have made HP a stronger competitor in those markets. These citizenship initiatives also help HP develop international leaders. In fact, the firm reports that more can be learned from living labs like Kuppam in three years than from virtually any leadership development programme or graduate course: "Indeed, though it wasn't among the primary goals of the i-community, teaching leaders new ways to lead may be one of the largest competitive benefits of the initiative. Ultimately, it's the knowledge that these leaders and their teams gain in places like Kuppam that will allow HP to become a stronger competitor."[12]

Context and complementary perspectives

In the years since Dunn and Yamashita's 2003 article, the pressure on MNEs to pursue good citizenship initiatives has intensified. Recent movements such as the *Make Poverty History* campaign have put pressure on governments, banking institutions and MNEs to help eradicate global poverty.[13] Thus, community development efforts such as HP's Kuppam project fit well with the current global context that demands CSR initiatives for less-developed communities.

Dunn and Yamashita's article focuses on efforts in India, an emerging economy. Dunn and Yamashita suggest that HP's i-communities initiative is scaleable and transferable to other emerging economies. What about countries that are not emerging economies, such as the poorest regions of Africa? The question arises whether HP-type initiatives are transferable to these regions of extreme poverty and institutional voids. Unfortunately, it is unlikely that ***doing well*** and ***doing good*** could in fact mutually reinforce each other in the world's extremely poor regions. MNE activity cannot replace the role of a government in terms of providing public goods such as basic education, general infrastructure and enforcement of the rule of law, which are really preconditions to be fulfilled for any HP-type initiative to come to fruition. Being forced to provide such public goods on a large scale might not only make many foreign investment opportunities prohibitively costly, but would also force the MNE into a role it is not meant to fulfil, and is unlikely to fulfil effectively and efficiently; enforcing the rule of law is the most obvious type of activity that should be performed primarily by government.

Good citizenship efforts in the least-developed countries may therefore still need to take the form of pure philanthropy until a minimum baseline of institutional infrastructure is developed. As the authors state in their *HBR* article: "change is not possible until there is a capable network to support it".[14] In other words, MNEs filling institutional voids may be instrumental to new FSA development and to the upgrading of a poor emerging economy (or region within that country), as discussed in Chapter 14, but MNEs cannot substitute for the lack of a baseline institutional infrastructure.

Beyond a renewed focus on poverty eradication, another movement since the publication of Dunn and Yamashita's article has been the heightened concern over climate change. This environmental concern has increased the pressure on MNEs to include environmental policies in their CSR initiatives. The role of the environment in MNE citizenship is not the focus of Dunn and Yamashita's article, and we cover this topic in Chapter 16B.

Richard Locke and Monica Romis provide a first complementary perspective to Dunn and Yamashita's *HBR* piece.[15] Their 2007 *SMR* article focuses on MNE CSR efforts to improve labour standards. The authors argue that MNEs need to go beyond monitoring suppliers for compliance with labour codes of conduct and should instead collaborate closely with suppliers to attack problems of poor working conditions at their source.[16]

The extension of supply chains to developing countries, particularly by efficiency-seeking MNEs, has heightened the need for MNE senior managers to incorporate labour standards into their CSR policies, including their interactions with suppliers. Hazardous working conditions, poor wages and child labour are problems that MNEs must address in sourcing from suppliers in countries where governments have a limited capacity or desire to introduce or enforce labour laws providing baseline protection to workers. Many MNEs and NGOs now monitor whether suppliers comply with codes of conduct in the realm of working conditions, but "[i]nformation is central to this model of private, voluntary regulation".[17] The main problem in developing countries, however, is a bounded rationality challenge: does monitoring actually measure real workplace conditions, given the possibility for suppliers to hide relevant information from those performing the monitoring?

To further explore the utility of monitoring codes of conduct, Locke and Romis conducted a structured comparison of two Mexican firms that manufactured products for US-based Nike, the largest athletic shoe company in the world. Both factories had earned similar scores on Nike's principal monitoring tool, yet the two factories differed significantly in the type of working conditions found on the shop floor. For example, one supplier paid higher wages, capped overtime hours and offered more worker empowerment than the other supplier.

Nike's monitoring of suppliers' compliance with codes of conduct began in 1992, when the MNE realized that substandard labour conditions in its suppliers' shops were damaging Nike's international brand image. It has even developed an FSA in this area: Nike now trains its suppliers to follow the code of conduct and has a team of 90 compliance staff based in 21 countries to monitor these suppliers. In 2002, Nike developed the management and working conditions audit ('M-Audit'), a tool that consolidates into a single score the performance on more than 80 items related to hiring practices, worker treatment, worker–management communications, and compensation.[18]

Such compliance tools represent the MNE's effort to reduce the problem of suppliers' bounded reliability by aligning these suppliers' interests with those of the MNE, particularly the MNE's CSR interests. Composite indices such as the M-Audit are also an attempt to overcome the bounded rationality problem associated with having to measure multidimensional labour conditions adopted by multiple suppliers in multiple countries. This bounded rationality problem is compounded by the difference between the management practices found in supplier firms and those prevailing within the MNE.

Locke and Romis found that composite measures of compliance with codes of conduct do not, however, lead to a complete understanding of the difference in working conditions among supplier factories, as illustrated by the case of the two Mexican suppliers. The authors found that the key variable influencing the working conditions in these facilities was the differing systems of work organization and human resource management.[19] The Mexican facility characterized by better working conditions provided greater worker autonomy, invested heavily in training and organized workers into production cells. This facility also had more frequent visits with Nike management and participated in joint problem solving with the MNE. Such interactions reduced both the bounded rationality and bounded reliability problems associated with the MNE–supplier relationship.

Locke and Romis' "findings suggest that interventions aimed at reorganizing work and empowering labour on the shop floor in global supply chain factories can lead to significant improvements in working conditions".[20] These interventions should flow from increased communication and interaction between the supplier and the MNE in the context of a collaborative and transparent relationship. In alignment with these findings Nike has created the 'Generation 3' compliance strategy. This strategy acknowledges that mere monitoring of suppliers should be supplemented with collaborative initiatives to transfer workplace and human resources management best practices among suppliers.[21] This development of supplier human resource practices under the guidance of the MNE is somewhat similar to Pattern VI of FSA development, described in Chapter 1. In this case, however, the MNE is supporting FSA development inside a supplier firm rather than inside a subsidiary. Ideally, this support enables the supplier to serve Nike in a sustained fashion with its key complementary resources (manufacturing excellence at very low cost), without this relationship being disturbed by external stakeholders. A possible positive spillover effect is that the supplier firm itself may in turn diffuse this FSA further through its global or local network.

Sushil Vachani and *N. Craig Smith's* 2004 *CMR* article provides a second complementary perspective to Dunn and Yamashita's *HBR* piece. This article explores the MNE's CSR in the context of drug pricing in developing countries – a very timely topic, given civil society's focus on eradicating poverty and fighting AIDS in Africa. The article concludes that in order to make drugs affordable for customers in developing countries, the MNE must mobilize and recombine complementary resources provided by governments, multilateral institutions and NGOs. Echoing Dunn and Yamashita on the necessity of an 'ecosystem of partners', Vachani and Smith conclude that all of these stakeholders must be involved in order for the initiative to be successful.[22]

Vachani and Smith suggest that pricing decisions are an interesting type of CSR because they typically present the MNE with a stark trade-off between maximizing profits in the short run and fulfilling obligations to society. In other words, socially responsible pricing affects the bottom line immediately and directly. The idea of socially responsible pricing can involve agreeing to pay higher prices for inputs, as seen with fair trade coffee. The concept of fair trade means that vulnerable producers are given prices for their production that will allow them a minimum level of economic security and sustained self-sufficiency, and will empower them as legitimate economic participants in international supply chains. Fair trade is particularly important in countries that lack sufficient institutional infrastructure to make markets work effectively and efficiently. In the absence of a fair trade approach adopted by MNEs from developed countries, vulnerable producers with virtually non-existent mobility to deploy their knowledge in other sectors or geographic locations, and lacking organizational competencies to counter power imbalances in multilayered logistics chains, often cannot even satisfy their families' most basic needs as human beings. The great benefit of a fair trade approach is that it recognizes the comparative, overall efficiency of international supply chains orchestrated by MNEs vis-à-vis alternative supply options. MNE-managed fair trade chains are characterized by the continued, productivity-enhancing recombination of resources by chain participants, but also by the presence of respect and related monetary compensation granted to the most vulnerable chain participants, mostly in the world's poorest countries. CSR expressed by support for fair trade can be viewed as a reputational resource for MNEs, often indicative of an FSA in stakeholder management.

On the output market side, most CSR pricing involves the MNE lowering prices, often by adopting differential pricing benefiting poorer customers less able to pay.[23]

Vachani and Smith highlight the case of AIDS drugs in developing countries to illustrate how drug pricing policies can affect both the MNE and societal welfare. As much as 95 per cent of people with AIDS live in developing countries, yet despite price reductions on antiretroviral AIDS treatments, the annual cost for these medications remains above the annual per capita GDP of many of the least-developed countries.[24] Arguments can be made that local governments should pay for increased access to AIDS drugs, particularly when contrasts are made with health expenditures and spending on defence for some of these countries. Nonetheless, pharmaceutical MNEs face considerable pressure to increase access and affordability for these drugs. These companies are often viewed as insensitive and 'profit hungry' in their pricing policies in developing countries. However, pharmaceutical MNEs are often limited in their ability to drop prices without jeopardizing profits from developed countries. Vachani and Smith review three main approaches used by MNEs to improve access to drugs in developing countries: drug donation, out-licensing and differential pricing.

First, the **_drug donation_** approach, as the name suggests, increases access to drugs in developing countries by offering the drugs free of charge. An example of this approach is Merck's development of a treatment for river blindness. Merck invested several million dollars to develop drugs to prevent this disease that are now administered to 25 million people annually through a free distribution programme. Drug donation gives the MNE tax benefits and gives the developing country social welfare benefits. One problem with this approach, however, is that host countries are often burdened with hidden costs such as drug distribution costs. In addition, this approach is not sustainable for diseases requiring extensive and long-term treatments, such as AIDS, because the MNE's ability to fund donation programmes depends upon its own financial health, which may be highly uncertain over the long term.

Second, the **_out-licensing_** approach is consistent with an international projector strategy of licensing. A host country manufacturer produces the drugs under licence, though the MNE usually forgoes profits in the form of royalties. This approach has the advantage of offering the MNE distance from the lower price offered in the developing country. Distance from lower prices reduces the potential for **price referencing**, in which downward pressure on prices in developed markets is caused by reference to the lower price charged in developing economies. Out-licensing has the further advantages of leading to favourable media attention for the MNE (a form of FSA development in the reputational sphere) and providing a commercially appealing response to competition from generic manufacturers.[25] A problem with this approach, however, is the limited complementary resource availability, as developing country manufacturers may not possess adequate quality control systems. In addition, drug access may still be limited as the price may not be low enough for a large portion of the population. Finally, the price referencing problem is unlikely to disappear completely.

Third, the most common approach to increasing drug accessibility is **differential pricing**, which entails selling the same product at different prices in different markets. In conventional economics, price discrimination follows the consumer's willingness-to-pay, with the monopolistic producer reaping the consumer surplus.[26] Differential pricing is easily applicable in the drug industry, where non-location-bound FSAs, often in the form of patents, result from large and risky investments in R&D. These (usually stand-alone) FSAs can mostly be transferred easily as they are fully codified in the form of the products' patented formulas, and manufacturing costs are often a small fraction of total costs. Thus, MNEs can use their monopolistic position, as sole owners of patented knowledge, to sell in developing countries while covering only their manufacturing costs.[27]

While differential pricing arguably provides the flexibility to balance pharmaceutical MNE revenues and social welfare, this approach also has risks. As with drug donation and out-licensing, differential pricing has the risk of diversion. For example, if intermediaries such as wholesale distributors are unreliable, they may divert the product to other destinations. One example of such bounded reliability is the illegal resale in Germany and the Netherlands of low-priced drugs meant for African consumers. Such practices can only be stopped by government regulation in both developing and developed countries against product diversion.

As with out-licensing, differential pricing also has the risk of price referencing. Recent actions by Brazilian authorities illustrate the risk of price referencing when differential pricing is employed. In 2007, the president of Brazil authorized the country to bypass the patent on Efavirenz, an AIDS drug manufactured by Merck. The country will instead import a cheaper, generic Indian-made version of the drug. The decision came after talks between Brazil and the US MNE broke down. Merck offered Brazil almost a third off the cost – pricing the pills at US $1.10 instead of US $1.59. However, Brazil wanted its discount pegged at the same level as Thailand, which pays just US $0.65 per pill.[28] As shown in this example, price referencing develops in a context of bounded rationality, where governments (in this case from an emerging economy) are not interested in understanding the importance of recouping total R&D costs and have little patience for CSR-inspired MNE pricing structures. Governments simply want the lowest price charged elsewhere, and use this as a reference for an appropriate price in their country. From the MNE senior management's perspective, governments engaged in pricing negotiations are therefore unreliable (and in some cases opportunistic) actors who may have little respect for the protection of proprietary knowledge.

Beyond price referencing and product diversion risks, MNEs also encounter high administrative overhead costs from setting up, managing, policing and fine-tuning differential price systems. These costs, while necessary to achieve CSR goals, may be difficult to justify in all countries. Setting a price correctly becomes particularly complicated if a country lacks infrastructure for drug delivery, or complementary resources from intermediaries and other contracting parties.

A further risk stemming from the lack of infrastructure is that the drugs may not be taken as prescribed, thus potentially leading to drug-resistant strains of the disease, strains which may spread to developed markets, thus reducing the value of the drug in those profitable markets. Vachani and Smith suggest that NGOs and governments must play a key role in developing the infrastructure necessary for efficient drug distribution.

Finally, differential pricing may have an unintended bounded reliability effect: MNE price reductions can reduce, *ex post*, host government (and donor) efforts to provide appropriate financial support for drug access.[29]

Vachani and Smith supplement their discussion of CSR and pricing with an analysis of AIDS drug pricing from 1999 to 2003. The authors found that "having lost the support of developed country governments in the intellectual property rights battle, facing severe competition from generics, and with donors showing signs of substantially increasing assistance, multinationals cut prices significantly".[30] While these price reductions have increased access substantially, it could be argued that such reductions should have occurred much earlier. Vachani and Smith's analysis suggests that MNEs could have accepted suboptimal earnings in developing countries that would have reduced their total profits by less than 1 per cent. The authors admit, however, that their analysis is made with the benefit of hindsight, a benefit that suppresses the a priori bounded rationality problem surrounding the potential risks of dropping prices.

In this context, Vachani and Smith make the normative claim that pharmaceutical firms are in a social contract, which gives the firms special treatment with regard to intellectual property. "In return, society expects the profits from these activities to provide the incentive to develop new drugs, many of which may be life enhancing if not life saving."[31] Arguably, this is another example where firms can do well by doing good: CSR initiatives by pharmaceutical firms support the social contract, thereby providing a normative rationale to retain a highly profitable business model.

Dunn and Yamashita's *HBR* piece highlights the crucial point that CSR initiatives should be aligned with MNE strategy and build upon the company's FSAs if these initiatives are to be sustained in the longer run. The authors' description of doing well by doing good emphasizes that MNEs should apply their current FSAs to CSR initiatives. This was illustrated by HP's application of the living lab to the Kuppam community development initiative. The doing well by doing good approach also increases MNE competitiveness by allowing the firm to develop new FSAs through participating in CSR initiatives. This was illustrated by HP's ability to develop leaders and foster innovation through participation in community development projects. HP benefits by being able to transfer newly trained leaders and innovations to other international operations. This development of non-location-bound FSAs through participation in host country development programmes is captured by Pattern VII of FSA development, described in Chapter 1.

One important theme shared by all three articles is the importance of engaging and partnering with multiple stakeholders when pursuing CSR projects. Dunn and Yamashita described HP's use of an ecosystem of partners, in which many different players share a common interest in building a long-term solution. Locke and Romis argued for close partnering between MNEs and their local suppliers to improve working conditions. Vachani and Smith emphasized the importance of partnering with NGOs and governments to develop conditions conducive to lowering drug prices in developing countries. In each case, partnering with appropriate stakeholders may help reduce bounded rationality and bounded reliability challenges. Increased familiarity with each other and relationship building may help align the interests of the various stakeholders involved. Partnering also provides potential access to complementary resources instrumental to effectively deploying the MNE's FSAs in these high-distance host environments.

A first limitation of all three pieces reviewed in this chapter is their focus on CSR solely within the developing/emerging economy context. The *HBR* piece focused on community development in an emerging economy, the *SMR* piece centred on the working conditions in developing country manufacturing facilities and the *CMR* piece explored MNE policies towards drug access in poor developing countries. A focus on developing/emerging economies for MNE CSR is appropriate given the particularly sensitive nature and importance of CSR issues in those countries. These countries suffer from substantial institutional voids (as discussed in Chapter 14) and extreme poverty. This focus is limited, however, as it neglects the role of CSR and CSR initiatives in developed economies.

It is worthwhile to widen the analysis and, with the help of Figure 16A.1, examine the potential of different forms of CSR in different country types.

In developed countries, CSR efforts can largely take the form of mandated CSR, as the institutional context in these countries usually establishes appropriate guidelines for good corporate citizenship. This institutional context is strongly affected by influential NGOs and the media, as well as the legal, tax and educational

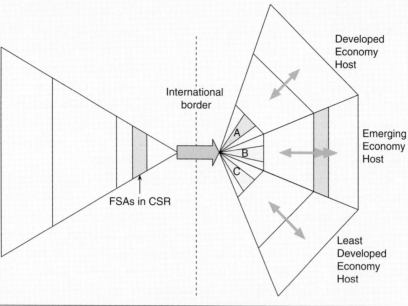

Developed
Economy
Host

International
border

Emerging
Economy
Host

A
B
C

FSAs in CSR

Least
Developed
Economy
Host

In the Home Country triangle the bold vertical lines highlight the subset of the MNE's NLB FSAs that are in CSR. In the Emerging Economy Host triangle the double head on the right end of the arrow reflects the need for extra effort to access LAs through LB-FSA development using CSR initiatives due to institutional voids. The shaded area on the right represents the strengthening in Host Country LAs due to these CSR initiatives.

systems. This institutional context provides fertile ground for pursuing CSR initiatives that may be very different from those pursued in countries lacking such context. MNE citizenship in developed economies is likely to centre on following the rule of law, paying taxes (including environmental taxes and multiple other taxes imposed on business based on externality or deep pocket arguments), supporting the existing social and political system and engaging in some targeted philanthropic initiatives. Building upon stakeholder-mandated CSR initiatives, firms may be able to develop internationally transferable FSAs, as suggested in Figure 16A.1.

In contrast, institutional voids – but also potentially lucrative markets – characterize emerging economies. The location advantages of emerging economies suggest the pursuit of CSR initiatives that are strategic (meaning here long-term performance driven) from the outset. Here, increasing social welfare is aligned with the MNE's performance objectives: the firm can do well by doing good. As discussed in Chapter 14, and as indicated by the double arrow in Figure 16A.1, a CSR initiative may substantively improve the location advantages of an emerging economy (much more than it would improve the location advantages of a developed economy), but this also requires substantial investment by the MNE. Here, CSR initiatives and the development of more traditional business operations go hand in hand.

In the least-developed countries, and with the exception of fair trade pricing, CSR initiatives usually focus on philanthropy. The least-developed countries possess neither the baseline institutional infrastructure to impose mandated CSR initiatives comparable to those prevailing in developed economies, nor the market potential of emerging economies to trigger strategic ('doing well by doing good') CSR initiatives. Examples of this form of CSR include the drug donation programmes described above. Philanthropic CSR initiatives may help the least-developed countries move towards an institutional and market baseline, at which point other forms of CSR initiatives could be implemented.

A further benefit of reflecting on the importance of location for MNE CSR initiatives is that MNEs need to select the best locations to pursue their CSR initiatives. In most cases CSR initiatives will simply be deployed in countries where the MNE also wants to grow its business. However, sometimes the optimal location for business and the optimal location for CSR initiatives do not necessarily coincide. This is largely an issue of the time horizon adopted: CSR initiatives, and possibly the deployment of the MNE's internationally transferable FSAs in CSR (represented by the bold vertical lines in Figure 16A.2), in specific emerging economies may lead to substantial societal spillover effects in the form of institutional voids being filled. However, the business opportunities in those countries may take a long time to materialize.

Figure 16A.2
Location advantages
and MNE CSR

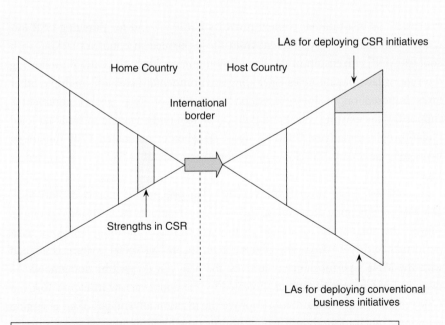

The small size of the shaded area representing LAs for deploying CSR initiatives reflects the potential discrepancy between the LAs for CSR initiatives and those for traditional business initiatives: the host country may not be the optimal environment in which to apply the firm's CSR strengths.

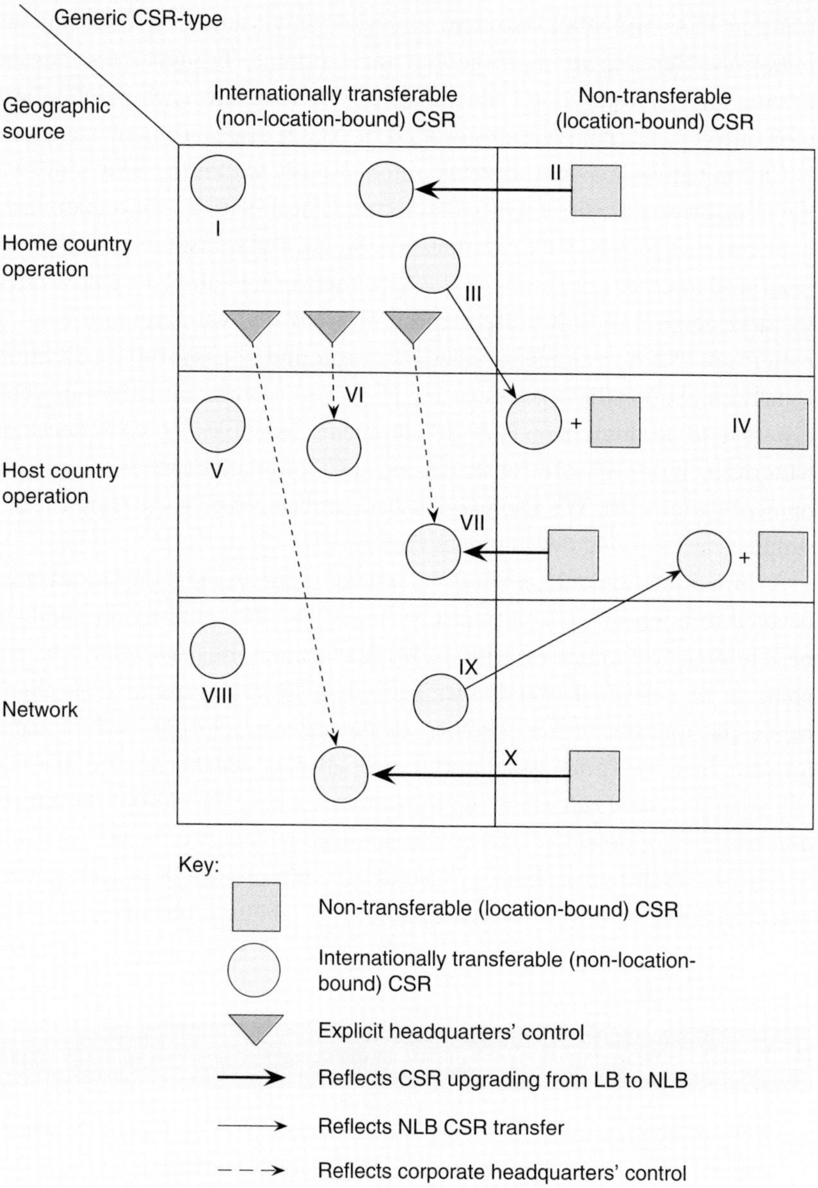

Generic CSR-type

Geographic source

Internationally transferable (non-location-bound) CSR

Non-transferable (location-bound) CSR

Home country operation

Host country operation

Network

Key:

▢   Non-transferable (location-bound) CSR

◯   Internationally transferable (non-location-bound) CSR

▽   Explicit headquarters' control

⟶   Reflects CSR upgrading from LB to NLB

⟶   Reflects NLB CSR transfer

⇢   Reflects corporate headquarters' control

Figure 16A.3
Patterns of CSR development in MNEs

The vertical line through the host location advantage component of Figure 16A.2 illustrates this potential discrepancy between the location advantages for CSR initiatives versus those for traditional business initiatives. The two types of initiatives focus on different elements within the spectrum of a host country's location characteristics.

A second limitation of Dunn and Yamashita's piece is the lack of attention devoted to the different ways CSR initiatives can develop within the MNE. Figure 16A.1 and Figure 16A.2 illustrate the simple case whereby the MNE transfers FSAs and other resources to the host environment so as to pursue CSR initiatives. Here, senior managers at the corporate headquarters may be the driving force behind these CSR initiatives. Alternatively, such practices may be motivated by external pressures exerted by NGOs or government agencies.

CSR initiatives may also develop autonomously within the host country, with the same drivers as above. Once developed, CSR initiatives can remain location-bound or they may become non-location-bound and transferred as best practices (routines) to other operations in the MNE network. Figure 16A.3 illustrates that the development of CSR initiatives can be associated with any of the ten major patterns of FSA development. Indeed, strategic and philanthropic CSR initiatives usually build upon the MNE's existing FSAs, and strategic initiatives are generally expected to lead to new FSA development. Examples of CSR development patterns include HP's previously described CSR initiative, which followed development Pattern VII. We also previously described Nike's partnering efforts with suppliers as following development Pattern VI.

A third limitation of Dunn and Yamashita's *HBR* article is the lack of attention devoted to bounded reliability in CSR initiatives. The authors do highlight the need to align CSR initiatives with the MNE's business interests if the initiatives are going to be sustained over longer periods of time. Assuming such alignment exists, the question arises whether all the external partners will actually put forward their best efforts to support the initiative, or whether some of these actors will attempt to *free ride* (i.e., reap the initiative's benefits without exerting the *ex ante* expected or promised effort). The bounded reliability of Nike's suppliers and African AIDS drug distributors illustrates the importance of proper governance mechanisms to prevent or mitigate bounded reliability problems.

Five management takeaways

1. Determine the meaning of 'corporate citizenship' in each country where you operate and across all of the firm's international operations.
2. Assess each CSR initiative in terms of its joint contribution to 'doing well' and 'doing good', and evaluate the longer-term business opportunities that CSR activities can create for the firm in host countries.
3. Improve working conditions and labour standards at your factories and your suppliers' by effectively implementing CSR activities.
4. Rethink your pricing decisions by trading off profit maximization against fulfilling obligations to society.
5. Align your CSR activities to your host country business objectives and the host country socio-economic and institutional context.

Case 16A.1 Talisman: An unexpected war?

CASE

When Talisman Energy, a Canada-based oil and gas company, bought 25 per cent of the shares in the Greater Nile Petroleum Operating Company (GNPOC) by acquiring Arakis in August 1998, Jim Buckee, Talisman's CEO at the time, was full of enthusiasm about the 'spectacular potential' of the deal.[32] Although Talisman foresaw political risks involved in the project, it never expected itself to become caught in an international storm of protest from shareholders, non-governmental organizations (NGOs) and human rights groups both abroad and at home. Frustrated by the negative impact of the Sudan project on Talisman's share price, the enormous managerial energy required to deal with the protests, and the danger of being de-listed from the New York Stock Exchange, Talisman sold its Sudanese oil assets in October 2002 to Oil and Natural Gas Corp, India's national oil company.

However, Talisman's retreat from Sudan has been a hollow victory for the campaigners. Even in 2012, people in South Sudan have yet to benefit from oil revenues and are facing severe food shortages, which affect over half of the population.[33] What happened during the whole process? Why did so many stakeholders want Talisman to get out of Sudan? Who actually benefited from Talisman's departure?

Sudan, the war and human rights

Sudan declared independence in 1956, before which Great Britain controlled Sudan as two separate colonies, the South and the North. Civil wars between Northern Sudan and Southern Sudan have ravaged the country for most of the time since the country's independence.

Historically, Southern Sudan was predominantly black and Christian, while Northern Sudan was mainly Arab and Muslim. Great Britain further worsened these divisions during the colonial period by forbidding people from the south to go north or vice versa. The increased isolation laid the seeds for further conflict between Southern Sudan and Northern Sudan. The year 1983 saw the start of the most recent round of fighting between the South and the North, when President Nimeiry revoked the autonomy granted to the South in 1972 and imposed Islamic law on the Christian South. This intensified the anger of the South, which had always felt it was given an unfair share of national resources. The South organized the Sudanese People's Liberation Movement (SPLM) to fight against the government. However, by the late 1990s, the fighting only led to a more disintegrated South, with the government controlling garrison towns, and SPLM and many other factions controlling the rest. The war has resulted in at least two million fatalities, as well as the large-scale abduction of women and children, and the displacement of families.[34]

While the conflict in Sudan had been ongoing more or less continually since independence, it was the emergence of two regional conflicts in the early 1990s that elevated human rights violations and genocide to the world stage. From 1992 to 1995, some 200,000 Muslims were killed in Bosnia by forces allied to Serbia, while in Rwanda during 1994 some 800,000 Tutsi tribesmen were put to death by the Hutu majority.[35] Intervention by the world community seemed muted while the atrocities were happening, though condemnation did follow when it became increasingly clear what was taking place.

Several perpetrators of the atrocities were eventually brought to justice, but not before much soul searching, including the deliberation of the Bosnian genocide case at the International Court of Justice.[36] In 1993, a landmark court case was introduced: for the first time in the 60-year history of the International Court of Justice (ICJ), one state, Bosnia and Herzegovina, accused another state, Serbia and Montenegro, of genocide. Clearly the world community was waking up to the challenges posed by ethnic conflicts.

By the late 1990s, the ongoing conflict in Sudan, pitting a largely Arab and Muslim regime in the North against a largely black and Christian population in the South, had found a resonating chord with human rights activists. Mounting pressure from human rights and religious groups made Sudan into one of the Bush Administration's priorities.[37] Nina Shea, the director of the Center of Religious Freedom in Washington, DC, commented on the significance of this case: "Sudan is the litmus test for human rights policy under the Bush administration."[38]

Oil, Sudan and Talisman

The production of oil in Sudan came well after Sudan's independence, and was driven by a rapid rise in the price of oil, first in the early 1970s and then again in the early 1980s. An oil embargo by members of OPEC during the Arab–Israeli conflict in the 1970s, and then consequences of the Iranian revolution in the early 1980s, caused several countries to increase their efforts to find oil from non-OPEC sources. Sudan, as a non-OPEC oil country, was perceived as a location where oil might be found and profitably exploited.

Chevron was the first foreign oil company to explore oil in Sudan, with a concession granted by Sudan in 1975. In 1980, Chevron discovered the Unity and Heglig oilfields in Southern Sudan. However, armed attacks against Chevron's facilities forced the company to withdraw from Sudan by selling its concession to Vancouver-based Arakis in 1993. Arakis continued to drill for new oil and announced in 1997 that it had identified 1.2 billion barrels in the Heglig and Unity oilfields.[39]

In 1996, Arakis formed a consortium called GNPOC, with China National Petroleum Company (CNPC) holding a 40 per cent interest, Malaysia's Petronas 30 per cent and Sudan's Sudapet 5 per cent. However, Arakis was unable to finance its share, and it finally was acquired by Talisman in 1998.

Sudan, the Nile and water

Oil is not the only resource that attracts attention and is essential to modern societal functioning. Water and its uninterrupted supply in sufficient quantities and quality is a major objective underpinning sustainability and sustainable development of human communities. Its absence or potential absence has often been raised to explain emerging and continuing conflicts among different nations and even different stakeholders within one nation.[40] This is certainly the case of the Nile region, whose drainage incorporates Egypt, Sudan, Ethiopia and parts of central Africa.

Egypt has consistently been able to dominate the use of the Nile's water resource, even though virtually all of the water flowing through it originates outside its territorial boundaries. Mindful of the Nile's importance, Egyptian regimes have consistently tried to limit the ability of upstream stakeholders to interfere with its flow, while also increasing its own buffer capacity useable during periods of abnormally low rainfall. The Aswan dam was completed in 1971, and has provided a significant reserve of water to sustain consumption during periods of otherwise low water flow. Furthermore, Egypt has sought to influence the development of the Nile's water resource in upstream countries, particularly Sudan, by discouraging projects that could lead to increased water usage there. While diplomacy and economic means have been the preferred tools Egypt has employed, use of force has never been far beneath the surface considering its clear military advantage vis-à-vis upstream countries.[41]

The aspirations of some of the countries in the Nile region to wield regional power were constrained by the Cold War superpowers, even as local, low-grade conflicts continued. Internal ethnic and political strife in upstream countries discouraged development projects, thus indirectly supporting Egypt's objectives. Ethiopia was waging a low-grade conflict, first with separatist forces in Eritrea and later with an independent Eritrea, as well as with Somalia. Sudan was embroiled in a separatist war with stakeholders in its south.

The end of the Cold War and the decline in the constraining influences of the US and the former USSR changed this situation. Egypt recognized that instability in the other Nile-region nations could be useful to its long-term objectives, and therefore fostered instability, so as to maintain its regional hegemony. It sponsored anti-governmental forces, including the rebel Sudanese People's Liberation Army in Southern Sudan during the 1990s.[42]

Thus, Egypt bears at least some responsibility for the conflict in Sudan. The conflict is not solely rooted in ethnicity, religion and domestic politics.

Talisman and its initial involvement in Sudan – "This is a world-scale, highly-visible project"[43]

Headquartered in Calgary, Canada, Talisman Energy was initially established in 1953 as the Canadian subsidiary of British Petroleum (BP). After BP sold its Canadian interests in 1991, Talisman became an independent energy company and was later listed on both the TSX and NYSE. Its main business activities include the exploration, development, production, transportation and marketing of crude oil, natural gas and natural gas liquids.[44]

Since its establishment, Talisman has focused on both exploration and acquisitions to deal with the depletion of its Canadian oil reserves. For example, Talisman acquired Encor in 1993, Bow Valley Energy in 1994 and Arakis Energy in 1998.

This expansion path also took Talisman to the international market. The 1993 Encor acquisition brought Talisman its first international assets (in Algeria and Indonesia). By late 2001, Talisman's exploration and operations areas had expanded from North America (the US and Canada) to the North Sea, South East Asia (Indonesia, Malaysia and Vietnam), the Caribbean and Latin America (Columbia and Trinidad) and Africa and the Middle East (Algeria, Sudan and Qatar).

The opportunity provided by Arakis came to Talisman at a time when Talisman was actively pursuing offshore acquisition opportunities. Commenting on the 1998 Arakis acquisition, President and CEO Jim Buckee said, "We have looked at lots and lots of acquisitions and this one is by far the most exciting we see. It's a good time to be making this sort of move."[45] By 2001, this move was supplying Talisman with one-tenth of its oil.[46]

The economics made good sense for Talisman. Talisman estimated that the GNPOC concession could hold between 8.5 and 12.5 billion barrels of oil, with the prospect for new discoveries in the region. Oil production increased from an initial 120,000 barrels/day in the mid 1990s to 200,000 barrels/day in 2000. In 1999, Talisman estimated that GNPOC's upstream revenues would amount to US $10.45/barrel, with net revenue of US $7.28/barrel.[47]

Moreover, oil in Sudan was of high quality, with low sulphur content. Therefore, the oil was relatively easy to refine, resulting in low extraction costs and high revenues.

Finally, Talisman was also welcomed by the other three partners. Talisman's financing and technological expertise would complement both the inexpensive labour provided by the other three parties and the political power provided by CNPC.[48]

Although the Sudan project involved dangers because of the civil war, Buckee considered the security risk 'very acceptable',[49] especially given the support from his three state-owned partners. Moreover, Talisman interpreted the civil war as mainly a domestic conflict involving 300 tribes – a situation much less dramatic than that described in the international press. Finally, the risk of bad publicity was expected not to hurt Talisman much either, given Talisman's position as an upstream producer, rather than a company selling directly to consumers. Petrol station boycotts would not affect Talisman.[50]

In early 1999, Buckee expressed Talisman's perspective on human rights issues in Sudan in a letter to shareholders, stating that "Because Sudan presents significant challenges, we realized that this project would attract questions from varied sources. However, careful study last summer [1998] persuaded management that this is a sound business investment and our involvement could be carried out in a responsible, ethical manner. Experience to date confirms that judgment . . . We recognize Sudan's chronic troubles, including poverty and conflict."[51]

The Sudan project never failed to meet Talisman's economic expectations. It was the social issues that finally led the company to abandon the project.

Public pressure and the divestment campaign

Soon after its investment in Sudan, Talisman found itself under attack by some NGOs, shareholders, government-based entities and other stakeholders. In 1999, the list of critics even included US Secretary of State Madeleine K. Albright, US Congressman Donald M. Payne, a New York-based church coalition called the Interfaith Center on Corporate Responsibility, the Task Force of Churches for Corporate Responsibility in Canada, the Canadian Department of Foreign Affairs and International Trade, Africa Watch and Human Rights Watch, among many others. They all spoke out against Talisman because of the firm's alleged involvement in human rights abuses, its support of the Sudanese government by providing oil revenues, and its role in displacing civilian populations.

For example, the Christian church leadership in Sudan condemned Talisman and other multinational oil companies for providing revenues to the government to purchase weapons and for allowing the government to use their airstrips and all-weather roads for military purposes.[52]

Such international criticism damaged Talisman's reputation, but what really hurt the company were actions taken by stakeholders in Canada and the US.

Talisman's involvement in Sudan became a major story in Canada. Media coverage in North America about Talisman's Sudan project increased substantially during the course of 1999. In 1998, only 14 stories about Talisman's involvement in human rights in Sudan were published in regional/local newspapers in Canada, such as the *Calgary Herald*, *Toronto Star*, *Ottawa Citizen* and *Alberta Report*.[53] In contrast, in 1999, around 292 articles were published, many of them in major publications such as the *Financial Times*, the *Globe and Mail* and the *National Post*.[54] Most of the articles focused on the NGOs' opposition to the project, further tainting Talisman's image.

Many stakeholders protested against Talisman's Sudan project, while some shareholders proposed initiatives to address this issue during Talisman's annual meetings. For example, during Talisman's annual meeting on 3 May 2000, several hundred shareholders protested against the company, carrying placards, distributing leaflets and shouting 'shame on Talisman' outside the hotel where the annual meeting was held. At the same time, 15 institutional investors proposed an initiative that would require Talisman to compile and publish within six months a report on its compliance with internationally accepted standards for human rights. The initiative was rejected by the shareholders, with an alternative resolution passed, giving Talisman more time to audit its Sudan project.[55] The 2001 annual meeting experienced similar protests.[56]

Some pension funds started to sell their holdings, partly because of mounting concerns over Talisman's Sudanese operations. For example, in 1999, the Texas Teachers Retirement Fund sold its 100,000-share stake in Talisman; a US investment house, Manning and Napier, sold 1.2 million shares; and TIAA-CREF, a New York-based college teachers' fund, also reduced its holdings of more than 260,000 shares.[57] As a result, Talisman's share price fell to three times its cash flow, much lower than a typical price of roughly five times cash flow.[58] Put in other words, the controversy reduced Talisman's share price by somewhere between a few dollars per share to as much as CAN $15 per share, as estimated by oil analysts in 2000, a time when the stock traded at around CAN $35.

Furthermore, the Canadian government became involved, sending a mission to Sudan in 1999 to investigate human rights violations and Talisman's operations. John Harker led the mission, with the report released in mid February 2000. The Harker report concluded that there had indeed been a major displacement of civilian populations related to oil extraction; airfields and roads built for Talisman had been used in a few cases by the Sudanese government for military purposes; non-Arabs were seldom hired by GNPOC; and oil was exacerbating conflict in Sudan.

The Harker report also made a few recommendations: Talisman should firmly advocate a cease-fire in South Sudan, Talisman should try to arrange a trust fund to set oil revenues aside for use after peace is restored and Talisman should make sure its Sudanese operations comply with human rights and humanitarian law. While acknowledging that many Canadians expected Talisman to pull out of Sudan or halt production, the report nonetheless predicted that Talisman would be able to pursue an engagement strategy rather than leave Sudan.

Although Talisman had concerns about interfering with issues pertaining to the actions of a sovereign state, and cited its limited influence on the Sudanese government, the Harker report concluded that "if the company is either unwilling or unable to constructively influence the government of Sudan (GOS), perhaps it should not be in the Sudan at this time".[59]

Talisman's defence

Talisman tried very hard to justify its Sudan operations. For example, in 1999, Talisman flew 20 analysts and reporters from Canada and the US to Sudan to investigate the situation there. Some of them wrote "glowing investment reports on Talisman".[60] In the same year, Talisman hired several senior lobbyists from Hill & Knowlton to lobby the departments of natural resources, foreign affairs and industry to influence Canada's policy on Sudan issues.

First, Talisman argued that many of the claims about human rights issues and forced removal were false. In 1998, Buckee called media reports of the dangers in Sudan "lurid and exaggerated".[61] In 1999, Buckee stated that "the Sudanese government was losing a propaganda war because it was doing a 'very poor job of presenting a better face'".[62]

Second, Talisman argued that it benefited the people of Sudan through its CSR. In its Corporate Social Responsibility Report 2000 Sudan Operations, Talisman described its approach to promoting ethical business activities in Sudan in the areas of human rights, community practice, employee rights, business conduct, and health, safety and environment.[63] For example, Talisman engaged in an extensive dialogue with the Sudanese government to promote a peace process; it completed 15 independent community development projects; and it implemented an Ethical Business Conduct Management System while GNPOC adopted a Code of Ethics.

Third, Talisman argued that peacemaking was beyond its expertise.

Fourth, Talisman asserted that the GNPOC project would have been developed with or without Talisman. Talisman argued that its involvement had made things better, and its withdrawal would make things worse. According to Buckee in November 1999, "The Chinese and Malaysians both wanted 100 per cent of the project and they're going to do it with or without us, so our view is having a Western presence, and the fact that we keep reporting back to our shareholders, actually ventilates the situation."[64]

Finally, Talisman argued that the firm had limited influence on either GNPOC or the Sudanese government. Talisman held only 25 per cent of GNPOC, and pushing human rights in GNPOC could be overruled by Petronas and CNPC, as decisions within GNPOC required "an affirmative vote of at least two consortium members holding at least 60 per cent interest".[65] However, Human Rights Watch argued that Talisman actually controlled the ground operations of GNPOC and that it was the lead partner.[66]

Mounting frustration and the final withdrawal

Despite Talisman's actions, it was relentlessly criticized for its Sudanese operations. The continuous vehement debate with NGOs occupied management's attention and hurt employees' morale. Buckee, after spending most of the 2000 annual meeting answering questions about the firm's Sudan operations, said that "We're not getting recognition for the things we do . . . People who say we should get out will certainly not help the people of Sudan. We think, directionally, our presence helps. If we withdraw . . . it will be taken up by somebody else who, I promise you, cares less than we do."[67]

More pressure came from the US. In 1997, President Bill Clinton signed an executive order barring American companies from operating in Sudan, but non-US companies did not fall under this restriction. However, in June 2001, the US House of Representatives passed the Sudan Peace Act barring companies operating in Sudan from raising capital in the US. If the Act became law, Talisman faced the real possibility of being de-listed from the New York Stock Exchange. Although the bill without the capital sanctions was signed by the President in late 2002, the initial bill and the following policy debate put even more pressure on both Talisman and its shareholders. Buckee admitted that access to US capital was ultimately much more important than the firm's operations in Sudan. Talisman would certainly abide by US laws, even if it had to sell its interest in the Sudan project.[68]

For Talisman, the threat from the Sudan Peace Act seemed to force it to rethink the political risk involved in its international operations. In June 2001, when Talisman acquired Sweden-based Lundin Petroleum, it excluded from the purchase Lundin assets in Sudan, Libya, Russia and Somalia. In October 2002, Talisman announced it would sell its interests in GNPOC for CAN $1.2 billion to ONGC Videsh, a subsidiary of India's national oil company Oil and Natural Gas Corp. The Sudanese government reported that it actually preferred to have ONGC as a partner as "it is state owned and the pressures of non-government organisations on it are less than they are on privately owned companies".[69]

In 2003, Talisman still suffered from its tainted image. As of mid June 2003, Talisman's shares traded at slightly more than three times its forecast 2003 cash flow, far below the ratio of 4.4 for rival EnCana. Moreover, protesters still met to protest against Talisman during its annual meeting in May 2003, even though Talisman had already sold its Sudanese operations.[70] Buckee later remarked that, "we were in Sudan for a brief period. Now we're out. We make a convenient whipping boy."[71] Finally, the American Anti-Slavery Group, the Presbyterian Church of Sudan, and other plaintiffs launched a lawsuit against Talisman in November 2001. The lawsuit claimed that Talisman was not only aware but also supportive of the Sudanese government clearing out civilians in areas with potential for oil exploration.[72] This lawsuit was dismissed in September 2006, as the court found no evidence provided by the plaintiffs for their claims of Talisman's involvement in rights abuses in Sudan.[73] The case was later filed under the US Court of Appeals due to the government passing of the US Alien Tort Claims Act, which allows cases involving international law to be brought to a US court, regardless of where the case originated. The case was finally dismissed in 2010, after two further attempts by the Presbyterian Church of Sudan to appeal the ruling.

Paradoxically, the Sudan issue may have supported Talisman's international operations. For example, some analysts felt that the Sudan affair "actually earned Talisman goodwill in the Middle East, because of Buckee's unapologetic manner and hard-line against the opposition".[74] In 2012, Talisman had operations or interests in Algeria, Indonesia, Iraq, Malaysia, Papua New Guinea, Peru, Poland, Sierra Leone and Vietnam.

Since 2004, Southern Sudan has been more or less at peace, but Western Sudan has become the new killing field. The international pressure on Sudan's government to put an end to violence in Darfur has been ongoing.[75] Under pressure from the US and other countries, the Sudanese government signed a power-sharing accord with Southern Sudan in May 2004. According to the resulting formal peace settlement in 2005, oil revenues would be divided between the Sudanese government and Southern Sudan. However, the peace agreement accomplished very little, and the division of Sudan's oil revenues remained a major hurdle because of disputes over whether some functioning oil wells lay in the north or the south.[76]

South Sudan

After years of civil unrest, South Sudan became an independent state on 9 July 2011, following a referendum on the matter. The division of the country placed roughly 75 per cent of the oil reserves in South Sudan yet left the majority of the infrastructure, including vital pipelines, in Sudan.[77] This has created an unusual situation whereby oil collected in South Sudan needs to be transported via pipelines through Sudan to reach markets in the Middle East. Tension between the two countries mounted when reports surfaced that Sudan had illegally siphoned crude oil from the pipelines. Sudan claimed that the actions were taken to collect on pipeline transfer payments that were unfulfilled by South Sudan. In January of 2012, South Sudan responded by shutting off oil exports to Sudan. Sudanese President Omar al-Bashir subsequently refused to transport any oil through Sudan until disputes over border security were settled.[78]

The impact of blocking exports has had a dramatic effect on South Sudan, which receives 98 per cent of its revenue from oil.[79] The UN World Food Programme report estimated that nearly 4.7 million South Sudanese, more than half of the population, would face food shortages in 2012.[80] The issue had become so severe that the United Nations threatened to impose sanctions against the two countries if they did not work towards finding a solution to their conflict.[81] In May 2012, negotiations had yet to develop a solution and the health of both South Sudan and its citizens were in jeopardy.

Lessons learned

After its alarming experience in Sudan, Talisman has re-evaluated its processes for selecting foreign investment locations. Working with the Canadian and American governments has become an important step for Talisman when considering new opportunities. Working with various branches of government helps in getting a better picture of the possible alignment between the Canadian company and a potential investment location. Talisman also works with local NGOs to get opinions on what social issues are affecting each country. This helps Talisman gain a more local perspective and gauge the complexity of the issues it may face. In-depth analysis is performed of potential technical, economic, commercial, legal, political, regulatory, environmental, security and human rights challenges.[82]

For example, before entering Iraq in 2009, Talisman completed an extensive assessment to ensure itself that its operations would be supported by local stakeholders. Consulting with the US Government was also a crucial step, as it is a key stakeholder in both Talisman's operations and in Iraqi affairs.[83] The decision to invest in Kurdistan, Iraq did raise some public concern, but Talisman spokesman David Mann stated that "It's [Kurdistan] not a war zone like the rest of the country. We recognize there are issues, but we've done our due diligence. We think it's manageable."[84]

Talisman has worked hard to change the perception of its corporate responsibility practices, and the effort is starting to pay off. Maclean's magazine rated Talisman's CSR in 2007 as 'B+', stating that: "In the years since its exposure to significant human rights issues while in Sudan, Talisman has emerged as a leading company in terms of human rights policies and management."[85] As of 2010, the firm was selected as a 'Top 50 socially responsible company' by the same magazine. Talisman is now a part of several initiatives including the Extractive Industries Transparency Initiative, which follows standards to report and present information regarding payments from its operations. The company also participates in the United Nations Global Compact, which focuses on human rights, and labour and environmental practices.

In 2008, indigenous tribes began voicing concerns over potential exploration areas in Talisman's operations in Peru. Learning from its past experience, Talisman reacted by ensuring that no production would begin unless the firm reached an agreement with local tribes. CEO Mazoni affirmed "I think the lessons (of Sudan) have been learned deeply inside the company."[86]

QUESTIONS

1. What were Talisman's motivations to invest in Sudan? Was it a sound decision to do so at the very beginning, from an economic perspective? From a social perspective?
2. What were Talisman's FSAs and Sudan's LAs? Did the FSAs and LAs complement each other?
3. Did Talisman foresee pressures? What were the major elements cited by NGOs against Talisman? How did Talisman try to defend itself and was its reasoning convincing?
4. What led to the final withdrawal of Talisman? Did the withdrawal help improve the social welfare in Sudan?
5. Would a proactive community engagement strategy on the part of Talisman have reduced the pressure to do something about human rights abuses?
6. What options were open to Talisman to shape the behaviour of the combatants?
7. Were CNPC and Petronas subject to the same stakeholder pressures that Talisman was subjected to?
8. Has Talisman changed because of its experience in Sudan?

Case 16A.2 Sweatshop wars: Nike and its opponents in the 1990s[87]

In the 1990s, US-based Nike Inc., the largest athletic shoe company in the world, was accused by labour and human rights activists of operating sweatshops in Indonesia, Vietnam and China. Nike initially viewed such accusations as public relations problems, but finally changed its defensive tactics to a more proactive approach after serious damage was inflicted to its reputation in the late 1990s.

In the new millennium, Nike has tried to distance itself from its tainted image associated with worker exploitation, by monitoring its contractors more closely, integrating its supply chain through lean manufacturing and pushing for consistent global standards in the apparel industry. Ultimately, Nike had to learn the lesson of corporate social responsibility in a very hard way.

History and Nike's business model

Nike started as a venture in 1964 between Phil Knight, an undergraduate and athlete at the University of Oregon, and Bill Bowerman, his track coach at the same university. They identified a need for high-quality running shoes at a time when Adidas and Puma dominated the American market. Phil Knight went on to do his MBA at Stanford, where he realized that he could combine inexpensive Japanese labour and American distributors to sell cheap but high-quality track shoes in the US, thereby ending the European dominance of the market. In 1964, Knight and Bowerman founded the Blue Ribbon Sports Company, which was re-named Nike in 1971.

Nike's business model had three major components. First, Nike would outsource all manufacturing to low-cost areas in the world. The money thus saved would be invested in the two other components of the business model: research and development of innovative new products on the upstream side, and marketing to promote these products on the downstream side. In its marketing, Nike went beyond conventional celebrity endorsements and actually named Nike shoes after famous athletes such as Michael Jordan and Tiger Woods. These celebrities further strengthened Nike's image.

This business model worked very well. In the early 1980s, Nike became the leading athletic shoe company in the US. In 1991, Nike became the first sports company to surpass yearly sales of US $3 billion. During this time, Nike shifted its contract manufacturing locations, first from Japan to South Korea and Taiwan, and then later to Indonesia, Vietnam and China, always taking advantage of the cheapest labour in the new emerging economies.

Labour rights in Indonesia and Nike's initial response to criticisms

By 1990, Indonesia had become a key location for Nike. Labour costs in Indonesia were only 4 per cent of those prevailing in the US. Moreover, Indonesia had a population of 180 million, with a high unemployment rate and weak employment legislation. To Nike, that meant millions of people willing to work for low wages. Six of Nike's contract manufacturers were located in Indonesia, together employing around 24,000 workers and producing 8 per cent of Nike's global output.

In the late 1980s and early 1990s, Indonesia started to experience labour unrest. The number of strikes reported by the Indonesian government rose from 19 in 1989 to 122 in 1991, and Indonesian newspapers also documented some labour abuses by Indonesian factories. An NGO called the Asian-American Free Labor Institute (AAFLI) produced a report on working conditions at Indonesian factories in 1991, based on research by Jeff Ballinger, a labour activist assigned to be the Indonesian branch leader of the AAFLI in 1988.

Ballinger found that his criticism of Indonesia in general did not draw worldwide attention to labour rights abuses in Indonesia. The criticism lacked focus, and it was unclear what sympathetic people in developed countries could do to help the situation. Then Nike emerged as the perfect target for Ballinger: Nike contractors paid their workers less than US $1 a day; Nike contractors hired children in Indonesia; and moral outrage could be capitalized upon to tarnish Nike's brand names and image. Applying the more focused 'one country-one company' strategy, Ballinger started to publish reports and distribute newsletters specifically about labour issues at Nike's contractors in Indonesia.

In January 1992, as a result of criticism from activists like Ballinger, the Indonesian government increased the minimum daily wage to 2500 rupiah (US $1.24). Nike was aware of the labour conditions at its Indonesian contractors, but it believed that such issues were its contractors' responsibility, as Nike did not own any manufacturing facilities itself. Firm in its stance, Nike did draft a Code of Conduct in 1992, addressing issues of child labour, forced labour, compensation, benefits, hours of work/overtime, environment, safety and health.

Until that point, criticism of Nike's Indonesian operations came almost exclusively from Indonesia itself.

Criticism spreads to the US: Nike's hot seat

However, it didn't take long before Nike was criticized in the US media too. In 1992, *Harper's Magazine* published an article by Ballinger, famously demonstrating that it would take an Indonesian factory worker 44,492 years to earn Michael Jordan's endorsement fee at Nike.[88] In the same year, a prominent newspaper in Oregon (Nike's home state) also published articles criticizing Nike's Indonesian operations. In 1993, a CBS report revealed that Indonesian workers at a Nike contractor's factory were paid only 19 cents an hour, and that women employees could only leave their on-site dormitory on Sundays and with written management permission.

Such criticism drew national attention, but Nike's stance was still firm. Nike argued that it had provided job opportunities and contributed to local economic development. Phil Knight, Nike's CEO, dismissed any criticism, stating "I'm proud of our activities."[89] He argued that, taken in context, Nike was benefiting Indonesia: "A country like Indonesia is converting from farm labour to semiskilled – an industrial transition that has occurred throughout history. There's no question in my mind that we're giving these people hope."[90]

Further, Nike responded to the above criticism by hiring Ernst & Young, the accounting and consulting firm, to audit Nike's foreign factories, but the objectivity of the auditing was questioned by activists.

In the next several years, criticism directed towards Nike continued to rise. In April 1996, Kathie Lee Gifford, a popular daytime talk show host at CBS, had learnt from human rights activists that a line of Wal-Mart clothing endorsed by her had been manufactured by child labour in Honduras. She soon apologized on national television, spurring a wave of media coverage on labour issues in developing countries associated with other Western companies. In July 1996, *Life* magazine published an article about child labour at Nike's contractors in Pakistan. Then, on 17 October 1996, CBS News ran a *48 Hours* programme focusing on Nike's shoe manufacturing plants in Vietnam, reporting low wages, physical violence inflicted on employees and sexual abuses of several women workers. The programme informed US viewers that temporary workers were paid only 20 cents an hour. On 14 March 1997, Reuters reported physical abuses of workers at Nike contractors' factories in Vietnam. As a result of such widespread negative news coverage, Nike gradually emerged as a symbol of worker exploitation.

Such news coverage also drew the attention of political leaders to look for legislative solutions. In 1996, Robert Reich, the US labour secretary, launched a campaign to "eradicate sweatshops from the American garment industry and erase the word entirely from the American lexicon".[91] Even President Clinton convened a presidential task force on sweatshops and called for industry leaders to develop acceptable labour standards in foreign factories.[92]

To quell the above criticisms, Nike tried to build credibility in two main ways. First, Nike established a Labour Practices Department in October 1996 and a Corporate Responsibility Department in 1998, to deal formally with worker issues in its supply chain. Second, in 1997, Nike hired Andrew Young, a former UN ambassador and civil rights leader, to review Nike's Far Eastern factories. However, Andrew Young's conclusion from his 10-day visit to China, Vietnam and Indonesia that Nike was doing a good job was publicly challenged at the time and later shown to be flawed.[93]

Changing to managing responsibility

Pressures continued to rise. In May 1997, Doonesbury, the popular comic strip, focused several times on Nike's labour issues. Millions of readers read the strip, making hurling stones at Nike so popular that a media critic commented, "It's sort of like getting in Jay Leno's monologue. It means your perceived flaws have reached a critical mass, and everyone feels free to pick on you."[94] Later in 1997, an internal report prepared for Nike by Ernst & Young was made public by the Transnational Resource and Action Center. The report found that workers at a Nike factory in Vietnam worked in unsafe conditions, were forced to work 65 hours a week and were paid only US $10 a week.

Around this time, Nike realized that it had made a big mistake. Phil Knight noted in 1998 that "The Nike product has become synonymous with slave wages, forced overtime and arbitrary abuse."[95] Nike's sales, financial performance and stock prices slumped in 1998 as a result of its tarnished image, its failure to follow shifting consumer preferences and the Asian financial crisis.

On 13 May 1998, Nike finally bowed to "pressure from critics who have tried to turn its famous shoe brand into a synonym for exploitation".[96] Nike, Inc. promised to allow human rights activists and independent auditors to investigate the working conditions in Nike contractors' factories in Asia, and to increase the minimum age for new hires at shoe factories to 18 and the minimum age for new hires at other factories to 16.

Nike did not address the below-subsistence wage issue, one of the key human rights problems in Nike's overseas factories. Nike paid workers in China and Vietnam less than US $2 a day and workers in Indonesia less than US $1 a day, much lower than the US $3 a day required to reach adequate living standards. However, Nike's promises did elicit positive comments from several organizations.

By 2000, the anti-sweatshop movement's efforts had forced several Western firms to improve working conditions. Knight noted that the movement's efforts "probably speeded up some things that we might have done anyway . . . Basically, the workers in footwear factories, not just our factories, are better off today than two years ago."[97] In 2001, Nike released its first Corporate Responsibility Report, with one section dealing with its labour practices to explain how it monitored child labour and legal minimum wages at contractor factories.[98]

Hard to be responsible: Adjusting Nike's business model

Although Nike started to audit its approximately 900 suppliers in the late 1990s, the suppliers' failure to respect Nike's labour codes continued to be reported by the media. For example, the NGO Global Alliance uncovered a string of problems including verbal abuse and forced overtime after the Alliance surveyed 4,450 workers at nine Indonesian Nike factories.[99] In May 2001, a BBC documentary revealed that Nike and GAP contractors in Cambodia had broken their own strict anti-sweatshop codes of conduct.[100]

The frustrated Nike CEO convened a team to figure out why Nike was not able to implement its own codes of conduct. The team, led by Nike's vice president for corporate responsibility, Maria Eitel, concluded that it was partially Nike's business model that counteracted its efforts to improve working conditions at its suppliers.

The problematic component of Nike's business model was the effort to minimize costs in its supply chain through outsourcing. Nike's procurement teams chose suppliers based on price, quality and delivery times, and the core goal was to search for lower prices. Such a business model both encouraged Nike to switch to low-cost suppliers whenever possible, and pushed Nike's contractors to push costs down to extremely low levels in order to win Nike's orders. Moreover, the prevailing trade agreement in the apparel industry, the Multifiber Arrangement (MFA), set country-based import quotas for the US market. Thus, Nike had to search for spare quotas, hindering efforts to establish long-term relationships with suppliers. Finally, Nike managed inventory tightly. Whenever forecasting errors occurred, suppliers were pushed to meet delivery deadlines, thereby increasing the use of overtime in their factories.[101]

Nike's analysis suggested that it would have to change its business model to accommodate the new goal of improving worker conditions. After the MFA expired on 1 January 2005, Nike started to move towards lean manufacturing (i.e., a seamless supply chain, from purchasing inputs to serving the customer, with a focus on waste reduction, consistent quality and reliability), and towards establishing more stable relationships with its suppliers. Nike hoped that these changes would help its suppliers implement its code of conduct.

In its corporate responsibility report in 2004, Nike used a full section to explain its approach to labour conditions in contract factories.[102] As compared with the narrow first report from 2001, this second report in 2004 described a more detailed monitoring process, with Compliance Rating Criteria to assess a factory's compliance on a wide variety of issues. Moreover, Nike started to build strategic relationships with manufacturers for a more integrated supply chain. Nike realized that its influence on suppliers was dependent on the relationships it had with each subcontractor. These relationships varied substantially between shoe and apparel suppliers. The company's contracts with shoe suppliers were typically long term and allowed Nike to have more influence on processes. Contracts with apparel suppliers were shorter term, which made it more difficult for Nike to influence behaviour. Finally, in 2005, a group of Nike factories opened their doors to research teams from MIT's Sloan School to identify the root causes of problems, as Nike had found that monitoring could identify only problems – not underlying causes, much less solutions. The report stated that in spite of "significant efforts and investments by Nike ... workplace conditions in almost 80% of its suppliers have either remained the same or worsened over time".[103] The solution for Nike was to implement lean manufacturing in an attempt to provide more on the job training and organization. Nike hoped that the additional training would make suppliers more concerned about keeping their skilled employees and ultimately motivate managers to provide better work environments for their employees.

Collective responsibility: Nike won't go it alone

Nike was afraid that adopting responsible practices could bring competitive disadvantage, if its competitors in the industry did not act accordingly. Therefore, since the late 1990s, Nike had been involved in creating mandatory global standards in the industry. It joined multi-stakeholder organizations such as the Fair Labor Association (FLA) and the Global Compact (an initiative by UN Secretary-General Kofi Annan) to harmonize global compliance standards. Nike substantially improved its corporate social responsibility practices, but it made sure it did not have to do so alone.

What happened in Indonesia?

In the new millennium, the shoe business has partially moved out of Indonesia to China and Vietnam. After Nike terminated its relationship with the Doson factory (a 7,000 employee factory where most of the workers were unionized), Indonesia accounted for only 24 per cent of Nike footwear production in 2011, a big drop from 38 per cent in 1996. However, Nike still employed, through its suppliers, 120,000 people in Indonesia, and it made the (disputed) claim that it had decided to terminate its business with the Doson factory not because of unionization, government regulations or wages in Indonesia, but because of the factory's overall unsatisfactory performance as compared with other factories.[104]

Nike continues to manufacture shoes in 43 other Indonesian factories but still struggles to maintain optimal labour practices.[105] A lawsuit was settled in January 2012 on overtime pay that was not distributed to employees in a factory over a two-year period. Nike agreed to pay US $1 million to cover payments and set up stronger grievance procedures to avoid repetition.

In 2011, contract plants in Vietnam, China, Indonesia and India produced 39 per cent, 33 per cent, 24 per cent and 2 per cent of Nike brand footwear, respectively.[106] Some commentators claim that labour leaders misread competitive conditions faced by Indonesian companies, and that these leaders actually jeopardized jobs in Indonesia.[107] Opinions differ as to whether the new labour environment – fewer jobs, but with better working conditions – is better for Indonesians.

Public movement pressures Nike

Although Nike is now strongly focused on corporate social responsibility, it continues to face pressure from the public. In 2009, Nike ended a contract with a factory in Honduras. Unfortunately, severance pay and unemployment benefits were not provided by the subcontractor. It did not take long for university students in the United States to pressure Nike to accept responsibility in this matter. The University of Wisconsin-Madison ended its contract with Nike and Cornell University threatened to follow suit if something wasn't done. Although Nike reaffirmed that this was not the firm's responsibility, the company adopted a different approach than before and provided support to the subcontractor's employees. By July of 2009, Nike had set up a US $1.54 million worker relief fund for the affected employees, a measure reinforcing the suggestion that Nike had learned from its mistakes.[108]

"Never-ending challenge"[109]

More than a decade after Nike decided to change its CSR practices, the public's perception of the company has also changed, but the firm continues to face challenges.

Shifting the majority of its production to China and Vietnam has created a new environment of labour conditions for Nike to manage. With the added attention from the 2008 Beijing Summer Olympics, Nike was keen to exhibit transparent supply chain management in China. China is now one of Nike's largest supplier countries, which has made the evolution of corporate social responsibility compliance statistics in that country very important in determining the progress of Nike's initiatives. The results so far have been somewhat disappointing, though not unexpected. Nike stated in this context that "corporate responsibility is a relatively new, rapidly evolving business practice in China. Adoption and understanding vary widely."[110] Noncompliance occurs mainly due to false documentation, unpaid wages, lack of grievance processes and usage of underage workers.

To combat noncompliance, Nike has developed two methods to monitor Chinese factories. The first method, 'management audit verification', involves verifying the conditions associated with the individual employee, including hours worked, wage, benefits and complaints. The second method, 'environment, safety and health audits', monitors the conditions within the given factory.[111] Results from these tests revealed that Chinese factories, when compared to other international factories, often had poorer grievance systems, overtime tracking, and fire safety and health. Nike has suggested that improving the labour conditions in China is a priority, but government laws and regulations create obstacles. It has been argued that discrepancies between Chinese labour laws and guidelines set by the International Labour Organization create unfavourable conditions for Chinese workers.[112]

Nike's companywide corporate social responsibility team consists of 140 people aiming to implement better practices in all aspects of Nike's businesses.[113] Nike's 2011 corporate responsibility report outlined the progress and challenges the firm continues to face. Unfortunately, Nike saw a decrease in the percentage of factories given an 'A' rating, down from 6 per cent in 2010 to just 4 per cent in 2011. Additionally, 'B' factories increased from 33 per cent in 2010 to 45 per cent in 2011. This prompted a strong message to all suppliers from Hannah Jones, VP of sustainable business and innovation, stating: "We will be moving away from companies that are not committed to putting workers and sustainability at the heart of their growth agendas."[114] The report outlined the goal that all suppliers must meet Nike's standards by 2020.

CEO Mark Parker is proud of how far Nike has come, but realizes that CSR is "a never-ending challenge".[115]

QUESTIONS

1. What are Nike's FSAs? What is Nike's business model?
2. What were Nike's FDI motivations in Japan, Taiwan, Indonesia and Vietnam? What are the LAs of these countries in the context of Nike's business?
3. Nike tried to revise its business model to integrate its supply chain. How did Nike's earlier business model affect its contractors' behaviour? To what extent do you think the changes to Nike's business model will improve contractors' compliance with Nike's codes of conduct? Could there be any drawback as a result of such business model changes?
4. Why did Nike push for a global labour standard in the apparel industry?
5. Nike was afraid of competitive disadvantage as a result of its own socially responsible behaviour. Would competitive disadvantage be likely?
6. Can you provide an update on Nike's responses to human rights complaints, using materials available on the Web?

Notes

1. S. Vachani and N. C. Smith, 'Socially responsible pricing: lessons from the pricing of AIDS drugs in developing countries', *California Management Review* 47 (2004), 118.
2. D. Dunn and K. Yamashita, 'Microcapitalism and the megacorporation', *Harvard Business Review* 81 (2003), 47–54.

3. *Ibid.*, 53.
4. *Ibid.*
5. *Ibid.*, 50.
6. *Ibid.*, 51.
7. *Ibid.*, 52.
8. *Ibid.*
9. *Ibid.*, 48.
10. *Ibid.*, 50.
11. *Ibid.*, 54.
12. *Ibid.*, 53.
13. For a description of the Make Poverty History campaign, see www.makepovertyhistory.org.
14. Dunn and Yamashita, 'Microcapitalism and the megacorporation', 53.
15. R. M. Locke and M. Romis, 'Improving work conditions in a global supply chain', *Sloan Management Review* 48 (2007), 54–62.
16. *Ibid.*, 54.
17. *Ibid.*
18. *Ibid.*, 57.
19. *Ibid.*, 59.
20. *Ibid.*, 55.
21. *Ibid.*, 60.
22. *Ibid.*, 118.
23. *Ibid.*
24. *Ibid.*, 120.
25. *Ibid.*, 121.
26. *Ibid.*, 119.
27. *Ibid.*
28. BBC, http://news.bbc.co.uk/2/hi/americas/6626073.stm, accessed on 4 May 2007.
29. Vachani and Smith, 'Socially responsible pricing', 127.
30. *Ibid.*, 131.
31. *Ibid.*, 133.
32. 'Fuelling a fire', *The Economist* 356 (2 September 2000), 62–3.
33. 'Half of South Sudan facing food shortages, warns UN', *BBC* (16 May 2012).
34. Randolph Martin, 'Sudan's perfect war', *Foreign Affairs* (March/April 2002), www.foreign affairs.org/20020301faessay7976/randolph-martin/sudan-s-perfect-war.html, accessed on 11 April 2007.
35. www.unitedhumanrights.org/, accessed on 7 October 2007.
36. www.ppu.org.uk/genocide/g_genocide_intro.html, accessed on 7 October 2007.
37. Jemera Rone, 'Rebels, religion and oil – Sudan', *World Today* (1 December 2003), Volume 59, Issue 12.
38. Edward Alden, 'Bush poised to head off oil sanctions in Sudan bill', *Financial Times* (8 August 2001), 7.
39. 'Sudan pipeline operational', *Petroleum Economist* 66 (August 1999), 15–16.
40. Michael Klare, *Resource Wars: The New Landscape of Global Conflict* (New York: Henry Holt and Company, 2001).
41. *Ibid.*
42. *Ibid.*
43. W. J. Simpson, 'The human factor', *Petroleum Economist* 66 (December 1999), 48.
44. Talisman company information, www.talisman-energy.com/, accessed on 11 April 2007.

45. W. J. Simpson, 'Accelerating move abroad', *Petroleum Economist* 65 (October 1998), 33.
46. David Buchan, 'Oil company defends Sudan operation', *Financial Times* (17 October 2001), 14.
47. 'Sudan: Talisman ups Muglad basin reserves estimate', *Petroleum Economist* 66 (February 1999).
48. While CNPC is a business corporation, it is also closely linked to the Chinese government. The motivations of CNPC, Petronas and later ONGC for entering Sudan were driven by strategic factors linked to security of energy for their respective governments. Indeed, Sudan has come to dominate China's foreign oil reserves, accounting for more than one-half of them (Carola Hoyos, 'China and India fill void left by rights campaigners', *Financial Times* (1 March 2006), 3).
49. Simpson, 'The human factor', 48.
50. Graham Bowley, 'Talisman may not find good fortune from Sudan oil', *Financial Times* (19 November 1999), 14.
51. James W. Buckee, Talisman CEO, 'President's letter to shareholders', 10 March 1999, www.Talismanenergy.com/ar98pres.html, accessed on 3 February 2001.
52. New Sudan Council of Churches (NSCC), *Statement of the Sudanese Churches on the oil factor in the conflict in the Sudan*, press release (12 April 2000). The statement was signed by the chairmen and other officers of the Sudan Council of Churches (SCC) based in Khartoum and the NSCC based in Nairobi, 14 April 2000, the temporary branch of the SCC. Cited by Human Rights Watch, 'Sudan, oil, and human rights' (2003), www.hrw.org/reports/2003/sudan1103/23.htm#_ftn1183, accessed on 11 April 2007.
53. Search on ABI, based on human rights, Sudan, and Talisman in document texts in the year 1998, accessed on 7 April 2007.
54. Search on ABI, based on human rights, Sudan, and Talisman in document texts in the year 1999, accessed on 7 April 2007.
55. Ian McKinnon and Carol Howes, 'Talisman unfazed by Sudan protests. Annual meeting; shareholders reject proposed timeline for operations report', *National Post* (4 May 2000), C.7.
56. James Stevenson, 'Sudan overhangs Talisman annual meeting despite record profit, new dividend [First quarter results]', *Canadian Press NewsWire* (1 May 2001), n/a.
57. Charles Frank, 'U.S. teacher fund sells Talisman shares', *Calgary Herald* (10 December 1999), C.1.FRO.
58. Paul Waldie and Charlie Gillis, 'Talisman to embark on share buyback: Buckee admits Sudanese operations have hurt stock price', *National Post* (15 December 1999), C.1.FRO.
59. John Harker, 'Human security in Sudan: the report of a Canadian assessment mission' (January 2000), prepared for the Minister of Foreign Affairs, 17–18.
60. Timothy Pritchard, 'Talisman Energy criticized over its holdings in Sudan', *New York Times* (26 November 1999), 10.
61. Simpson, 'Accelerating move abroad', 33.
62. Simpson, 'The human factor', 48.
63. Talisman Energy, 'Corporate Social Responsibility Report 2000: Sudan operations' (2001).
64. Elizabeth Wine, 'Paying a heavy price for a partnership', *Financial Times* (31 March 2000), 04.
65. Talisman Energy, 'Corporate Social Responsibility Report 2001' (2001), 13.
66. Human Rights Watch, 'Sudan, oil, and human rights' (2003), www.hrw.org/reports/2003/sudan1103/23.htm#_ftn1183, accessed on 11 April 2007.
67. Ian McKinnon and Carol Howes, 'Talisman unfazed by Sudan protests. Annual meeting; shareholders reject proposed timeline for operations report', *National Post* (4 May 2000), C.7.
68. Claudia Cattaneo, 'Talisman raises (ps)250M: Denies it went to Europe to avoid Sudan controversy', *National Post* (6 April 2002), FP.3.

69. 'Redrawing the map', *Petroleum Economist* (May 2005), 1.

70. George Koch, 'Stuck in the sand', *National Post* (1 July 2003), 46.

71. 'Canadian values at the international table', *Petroleum Economist* (January 2005), 1.

72. David Glovin, 'Talisma court upholds Sudan genocide suit dismissal', *Bloomberg* (2 October 2009).

73. Shaun Polczer, 'Talisman cleared of Sudan charges: judge rejects suit alleging rights abuses', *Calgary Herald* (13 September 2006), A.1.Fro.

74. Petroleum Economist, 'Canadian values', 1.

75. 'Turning the screw Darfur', *Economist.com/Global Agenda* (4 January 2007), 1.

76. BBC News Online, http://news.bbc.co.uk/1/hi/world/africa/4594242.stm, accessed on 10 April 2007.

77. Jared Ferrie, 'South Sudan says it will no longer export oil through Sudan', *Bloomberg Businessweek* (23 April, 2012).

78. 'Sudan's Bashir says no to S.Sudan oil exports without security', *Reuters* (16 May 2012).

79. Jared Ferrie, 'South Sudan says it will no longer export oil through Sudan', *Bloomberg Businessweek* (23 April, 2012).

80. 'Half of South Sudan facing food shortages, warns UN', *BBC* (16 May 2012).

81. Jared Ferrie, 'South Sudan says its ready to negotiate deal on oil at talks', *Bloomberg Businessweek* (10 May 2012).

82. Talisman company information, 'Human rights', 2012.

83. Darren Campbell, 'Lessons from Talisman Energy Inc's Sudanese foray', *Alberta Oil* (1 June 2011).

84. 'Talisman heads into Iraq with $300 million stake', *Calgary Herald* (24 June 2008).

85. 'The company rankings', *Maclean's 120* (48) (10 December 2007), 68.

86. 'Talisman's learned lessons from Sudan', *Calgary Herald* (1 May 2008).

87. Donna Everatt and Kathleen Slaughter, 'Nike Inc.: developing an effective public relations strategy', *Richard Ivey School of Business Case 9A99C034* (1999); John Hendry and Toshiaki Fujikawa, 'Nike in Asia – Just do it', *The University of Cambridge Case 300–069–1* (2000); Debora L. Spar, 'Hitting the wall: Nike and international labor practices', *Harvard Business School case 9–700–047* (2002); Debora L. Spar and Lane T. La Mure, 'The power of activism: assessing the impact of NGOs on global business', *California Management Review* 45 (2003), 78–101; Simon Zadek, 'The path to corporate responsibility', *Harvard Business Review* 82 (2004), 125–32.

88. Jeffrey Ballinger, 'The new free-trade heel', *Harper's Magazine* 285 (August 1992), 46–7.

89. Nena Baker, 'The hidden hand of Nike series: Nike's world power & profits', *Portland Oregonian* (9 August 1992), A1.

90. Donald Katz, 'Triumph of the Swoosh', *Sports Illustrated* (16 August 1993), 64.

91. Olessia Smotrova, 'US takes up arms against sweatshops', *Financial Times* (15 July 1996), 4.

92. Aaron Bernstein, 'A floor under foreign factories?', *Business Week* (2 November 1998), 126–30.

93. Bob Herbert, 'Mr. Young gets it wrong', *New York Times* (27 June 1997), A.29; Thuyen Nguyen, 'Report on Nike work force glossed over issues', *New York Times* (30 June 1997), A.10.

94. Jeff Mannings, 'Doonesbury could put legs on Nike controversy', *The Oregonian* (25 May 1997), Do1.

95. John H. Cushman Jr, 'Nike pledges to end child labor and apply U.S. rules abroad', *New York Times* (13 May 1998), 5.

96. *Ibid.*

97. Steven Greenhouse, 'Anti-sweatshop movement is achieving gains overseas', *New York Times* (26 January 2000), A.10.

98. Nike, 'Corporate responsibility report 2001' (2001).

99. Daniel Akst, 'Nike in Indonesia, through a different lens', *New York Times* (4 March 2001), 3.4.

100. Paul Kenyon, 'Gap and Nike: no sweat?' *BBC* (15 October 2000), http://news.bbc.co.uk/2/hi/programmes/panorama/archive/970385.stm.

101. Zadek, 'The path to corporate responsibility', 125–32.

102. Nike, 'Corporate responsibility report 2004' (2004).

103. *Ibid.*

104. Sadanand Dhume and Maureen Tkacik, 'Footwear is fleeing Indonesia – output drop by Nike, others has implications for key export model', *Wall Street Journal (Eastern Edition)* (9 September 2002), A.12.

105. 'Nike contractor to pay workers for overtime', *Wall Street Journal (Online)* (12 January 2012),.

106. Nike, '2011 Annual report' (2012), 5.

107. Timothy Mapes, 'Newly aggressive labor groups pressure companies in Indonesia', *Wall Street Journal (Eastern Edition)* (14 August 2002), A.1.

108. Elizabeth Murphy, 'Nike finally just does it', *Dollars and Sense* 290 (September/October 2010), 3–4.

109. Eugenia Levenson, 'Citizen Nike', *Fortune* 158 (10) (24 November 2008), 165–170.

110. 'Nike report cites continuing problems in China', *Wall Street Journal (Eastern Edition)* (15 March 2008), A.7.

111. The Economist Intelligence Unit Limited, 'Just doing it', *Business China* (31 March 2008).

112. Tom Mitchell, 'Nike sees 'gaps' in China labour law', *Financial Times* (10 March 2008), 3.

113. 'When the job inspector calls, working conditions in factories', *The Economist* 402 (8778) (31 March 2012), 73.

114. Matt Townsend, 'Nike raises factory labor and sustainability standards', *Bloomberg* (3 May 2012).

115. Eugenia Levenson, 'Citizen Nike', *Fortune* 158 (10) (24 November 2008), 165–170.

16B

International strategies of corporate environmental sustainability

Five learning objectives

1. To assess the impact of environmental regulations as a created location advantage (or disadvantage) in the international business context.
2. To explain the impact of environmental regulations on firm-level innovation by MNEs.
3. To highlight the possibilities for new FSA development as a result of environmental innovation.
4. To develop a classification scheme of alternative MNE environmental strategies.
5. To clarify that not all firms should try to develop environmental FSAs, since this may be a resource intensive undertaking with uncertain outcomes.

This chapter examines Porter and van der Linde's idea that government-imposed environmental regulations can enhance competitiveness by pushing companies to come up with innovative ways to use resources more productively and potentially develop green FSAs. In this way, environmental regulations can actually benefit the firms being regulated. Porter and van der Linde recommend that senior managers respond to environmental regulations by adopting a resource productivity approach (embedding new environmental initiatives into the production system), rather than a pollution control approach (just dealing in new ways with whatever waste the production system generates). The authors note that raising resource productivity is good for both the firm and the environment. These ideas will be examined and then criticized using the framework presented in Chapter 1.

Significance

In a classic 1995 *HBR* article, **Michael Porter** and ***Claas van der Linde*** argue that government-imposed environmental regulations can trigger innovative solutions to environmental problems, which may in turn lead to cost efficiencies or value enhancement. These positive effects at the firm or industry level are often sufficiently high to offset any costs associated with these regulations for the companies involved.[1] The authors thus suggest that stringent environmental standards may lead to new FSAs.[2]

If environmental regulations can indeed benefit firms, then senior managers should stop reflexively opposing new environmental regulations or attempting to delay their implementation, as such behaviour benefits mainly lawyers and consultants thriving under an adversarial regulatory regime with a strong litigation orientation, while doing nothing to solve the environmental problems at hand.

Porter and van der Linde suggest a shift away from end-of-pipe and waste disposal solutions to a dynamic, *resource productivity* model of environmental regulation: "The concept of resource productivity opens up a new way of looking at both the full systems costs and the value associated with any products. Resource inefficiencies are most obvious within a company in the form of incomplete material utilization and poor process controls, which result in unnecessary waste, defects, and stored materials."[3] The authors point out that resource inefficiencies occur not only in the firm's production system, but also at the customer end of the value chain. Such inefficiencies include discarded packaging that has to be disposed of, pollution created when actually using the product (as is the case with automobiles) and costs of product disposal after its use by the customer has ended. Here, senior managers should adopt a systems approach to environmental strategy that takes into account all the above resource costs over the products' life cycle, as well as the benefits from environmental innovation in the various value chain activities.

The systemic, resource productivity approach suggests that environmental initiatives should be embedded in the production system. This approach is very different from the more conventional pollution control approach whereby equipment is simply placed at the end of the production process, and attempts are made to dispose effectively of the waste that has been created. As a starting point, Porter and van der Linde suggest that companies inventory all their unused, emitted or discarded resources. This waste requires solutions, not at the end-of-pipe, but at the source, through materials or equipment substitution and more generally through process innovations.

In conjunction with advocating a resource productivity approach, Porter and van der Linde also note the importance for companies to be proactive in redefining relationships with stakeholders such as environmentalists and regulators: "How can companies argue shrilly that regulations harm competitiveness and then expect regulators and environmentalists to be flexible and trusting as those same companies request time to pursue innovative solutions?"[4] Stakeholder engagement offers MNEs an opportunity to seek innovative solutions to environmental problems – solutions that may lead to FSA development.

According to Porter and van der Linde, environmental regulation can trigger two broad forms of innovation. The first form of innovation involves technologies that reduce the costs of dealing with pollution. Some of the most creative innovations actually convert physical pollution into something of value. To illustrate this type of innovation, Porter and van der Linde describe the case of the French MNE Rhône-Poulenc's plant that made a large investment to install new equipment for the recovery of previously discarded diacids (a by-product of making nylon). The recovered diacids were subsequently sold as additives for dyes and generate substantial annual revenues.[5]

The second form of innovation addresses the root cause of pollution by improving resource productivity. Innovations of this second form lead to better utilization of inputs, better product yields or simply better products. To illustrate this innovation type, Porter and van der Linde describe the case of US-based Dow Chemical's move to reduce its use of caustic soda. Dow traditionally used caustic soda to scrub hydrochloric gas in order to produce a variety of chemical products. The wastewater from this process was then stored in evaporation ponds. The company redesigned the process for creating these chemicals, substantially reducing the use of caustic soda. This US $250,000 process improvement not only reduced the need for caustic soda and subsequent wastewater storage, but also saved Dow US $2.4 million a year.[6]

The above examples illustrate how managers can turn environmental improvements into productive opportunities. The early adoption of advanced environmental management approaches may also produce a first-mover advantage for companies, and herein lies the article's relevance for international business strategy. The authors note that "world demand is putting a higher value on resource efficient products. Many companies are using innovations to command price premiums for 'green' products and to open up new market segments."[7] Porter and van der Linde illustrate this point by describing the case of German companies that have benefited from an international first-mover advantage by reducing the packaging intensity of their products. This advantage resulted directly from Germany's early adoption of recycling standards. In this case, environmental regulation conferred a location advantage on the firms subject to the regulation, which in turn led to FSA development.

This case highlights the fact that location advantages can be created by government regulation. Environmental regulation motivates, alerts and educates companies to adopt environmental innovations and thus helps overcome bounded rationality challenges, especially the often-observed senior management's relative lack of knowledge about – and limited attention devoted to – environmental issues.

Porter and van der Linde describe five major features that, in their opinion, make for good environmental regulations. First, good environmental regulations "create maximum opportunity for innovation by letting industries discover how to solve their own problems".[8] The regulations should require that specific results be achieved, but should not specify the means. For example, the regulations should not force the adoption of specific so-called 'best practice' technologies. Second, in order for environmental regulations to encourage real behavioural change in industry through innovations, the regulations should be stringent rather than modest. Third, to reflect the realities of researching, developing and adopting new technologies, the regulations should allow for a phasing-in period. Fourth, regulations should encourage environmental improvements as close as possible to the source of the pollution, i.e., early in the value chain. In other words, the regulations should encourage a resource productivity approach rather than a conventional pollution control approach. Fifth, countries should ideally develop regulations before other countries, thereby allowing domestic industry to gain first-mover advantages on the international stage. This last recommendation is obviously subject to the condition that the general movement of environmental regulation on the international stage is correctly anticipated. Otherwise, a competitive disadvantage may result.

Porter and van der Linde offer some examples of regulations spurring environmental innovations that have been instrumental to success in the international marketplace. The US and Scandinavian pulp and paper industries are an illuminating example. In the 1970s, the US imposed strict regulations with insufficient phase-in periods to allow the best technologies to surface. These regulations led US firms to adopt costly end-of-pipe solutions to meet the new regulations. In contrast, strict Scandinavian regulations were announced but not immediately imposed. As a result, firms could act in anticipation of new regulations without being subject to impossible time limits. Given the extra time, firms could comply with the regulations by improving their production processes rather than adopting end-of-pipe solutions. The firms were able to incorporate environmental innovations into their normal capital replacement programmes. As a result, Scandinavian firms simultaneously met tough new emission requirements and lowered their operating costs. With the rise of the environmental movement worldwide, the superior Scandinavian technology resulted in price premiums for environmentally friendly products well into the 1990s.

The authors also point to the example of the Dutch flower industry. In response to concerns over pesticide, herbicide and fertilizer contamination of soil and groundwater, the Dutch flower industry was forced to innovate. These innovations included developing a closed loop system, which used greenhouses to avoid soil and groundwater contamination. The industry also "innovated at every step in the value chain, creating technology and highly specialized inputs that enhance resource productivity and offset the country's natural disadvantages".[9] These responses to environmental concerns led to improved product quality and lower handling costs, and resulted in the Dutch flower industry commanding 65 per cent of cut flower exports in the world.

Context and complementary perspectives

Environmental management is playing an increasingly important role in broader MNE corporate social responsibility (CSR) approaches. Recent concerns over global warming have put the environment at the forefront of consumer and non-governmental organization (NGO) advocacy efforts. MNEs are particularly scrutinized for their environmental footprint by a variety of stakeholders, as these firms tend to dominate pollution-intensive sectors such as the oil and gas, chemical, energy utility and automotive industries.

Porter and van der Linde's article was published in 1995, before the development of the Kyoto protocol and the general rise of public concern over global warming. While the article does not speak specifically to climate change issues, the arguments in favour of environmental regulations that improve resource productivity – and potentially lead to FSAs – nonetheless apply. For example, carbon emissions can be reduced by using energy resources more efficiently (an example of increased resource productivity). These efforts will also reduce energy input costs, thus resulting in a more competitive firm. The company that makes this sort of change first may develop FSAs stemming from first-mover advantages.

Porter and van der Linde's arguments against end-of-pipe solutions also apply to the climate change context. Their arguments call into question many of the current climate change proposals involving carbon dioxide storage and sequestration, as well as many of the carbon trading schemes.

As an illustration of the article's current relevance, one can think of General Electric's (GE) adoption of 'ecomagination' initiatives. GE's CEO Jeff Immelt, who launched the company's large-scale investment in environmentally friendly technology and processes, dubbed it 'ecomagination' after GE's slogan, 'imagination at work'. The strategy assumes that governments will, sooner or later, move to constrain the emissions of greenhouse gases. Immelt argues that GE can either be a victim of new and forthcoming regulation by merely reacting to it, or else turn the regulation into a business opportunity and use the changed scenario to its advantage by getting in front of it. GE's environmental approach is a large-scale, international test case for the proposition that environmental sustainability can mean economic opportunity, not just financial burden. If Immelt succeeds in substantially lowering operating costs and increasing value for customers by mitigating negative environmental effects and becoming a world leader in the adoption of green technologies, he may help redefine the corporate world's attitude towards capital investment in greening. Success looks probable for GE's initiative, as revenues from GE's eco-products and services already reached US $85 billion in 2010, seven times higher than in 2006 and more than four times as high than expected back then. Immelt believes in the growth perspectives of

'ecomagination' and announced positive forecasts for the next five years. For example, the market for energy-efficient home-improvement is expected to increase from US $38.3 billion in 2009 to US $50.2 billion by 2014.[10]

Stuart Hart and *Mark Milstein's* 1999 *SMR* piece provides a social activist perspective[11] complementing Porter and van der Linde's article. Hart and Milstein advocate international business strategies that align with the goal of global sustainability. Firms must develop radically new FSAs through environmental innovation, not only to satisfy present consumer demand, but also to increase the probability that future generations will be able to satisfy their needs. Such innovation is becoming increasingly important because, according to the authors, the present world economic system is unsustainable, in the sense that it would require the resources of three Earths to cater to the world's demand, if the whole world's demand were to reach present North American per capita levels. The authors describe the rapid demise of the very ecological systems that feed the expansion of many sectors, including mining, energy, agriculture, forestry and chemicals. Here, resource waste and inattention to product life cycle costs place an enormous burden on the environment and on future generations.

Furthermore, the authors argue, resource waste and inattention to product life cycle costs also sow the seeds for the future destruction of the firms creating this waste and ignoring life cycle costs. Thus, even purely self-interested MNEs have an interest in using resources efficiently.

Unfortunately, most incumbent firms in the above industries often fail to recognize either the necessity or the opportunity of radical environmental innovation, and as a result may be overtaken by new entrepreneurial companies. Hart and Milstein frame their analysis in terms of the economist Joseph Schumpeter's idea of creative destruction. Schumpeter took a dynamic view of the economy, one characterized by continual churn of innovative upstarts unseating established firms through creative destruction. While overcoming bounded rationality problems is an obvious challenge for managers in incumbent firms when contemplating highly disruptive, sustainable development initiatives, Hart and Milstein contend that "armed with proper tools and frame of mind, managers of incumbents can be as foresighted as the CEO of the hottest new IPO".[12]

MNEs in particular can drive creative destruction by transferring radical environmental technologies and related FSAs across national borders. Here, Hart and Milstein offer senior MNE managers guidance in approaching the sustainability opportunity in a heterogeneous international marketplace by distinguishing among three types of economies: developed, emerging and surviving, each with its own sustainability challenges.[13]

First, the **developed** or consumer markets represent an economy of one billion wealthy customers, and are characterized by advanced infrastructure for rapid manufacturing and distribution. In these markets, managers should seek to reduce the firm's ecological footprint by reinventing products and processes.

Developed markets at present contain many mature technologies and product systems that tend to leave a very large environmental footprint, associated with enormous resource waste and environmental spillovers. These mature systems and technologies also provide diminishing performance gains from large investments in technology, and thus are ripe for replacement by radical new technologies. For example, the automobile industry shows signs of a mature technology reaching its limits, as such components as metalworking and the internal combustion engine are, according to the authors, inherently inefficient. The industry is susceptible to creative destruction via radical technologies that will greatly improve resource use. These radical technologies may include fuel cells, ultralight bodies and new drive trains.[14]

The authors also point to the chemical industry as another example of a mature industry susceptible to radical innovations. According to the authors, even the generalized adoption of so-called best practices such as the 'responsible care' programme, an expression of self-regulation by industry, made mandatory by the Chemical Manufacturers Association, does not cut it: simply having the entire industry adopt prevailing best practices (including principles and codes related to preventing pollution, engaging in proactive environmental behaviour and involving the firm in the community) ultimately does not serve global sustainability goals at the societal level. The latter would require drastic reductions in the levels of resources used and negative impacts on the environment. However, the good news is that some firms such as DuPont are trying to move away from being large-volume producers of chemicals with a large ecological footprint, towards becoming high value-added producers of information services and 'green' products, thereby shedding their most resource and pollution-intensive activities.

Second, the **emerging** economies, with roughly two billion people, have mainly customers who can meet their basic needs but have minimal purchasing power. Here, MNE managers must avoid a major imbalance between the expanding demand for products, fuelled by population growth, urbanization and industrialization, and the limited physical capacity of these countries to provide the necessary infrastructure and institutional context for efficient supply and disposal. MNEs should avoid simply transferring conventional practices or technologies from rich economies to emerging ones, because these markets' ecological, infrastructural and institutional systems simply cannot sustain these practices and technologies. This book, in Chapters 14 and 16A, already addressed extensively the issue of MNE activity in emerging economies with a focus on the voids to be filled by the MNEs themselves. In the environmental sphere, Hart and Milstein suggest that managers should explicitly assess the sustainability of perceived opportunities, because the presence of fragile ecosystems, combined with infrastructural and institutional voids (e.g., in the area of health and safety regulations) could otherwise lead to particularly negative outcomes. Here, key issues are whether the existing ecosystems can sustain rapid industry growth and whether leapfrog technologies (e.g., the generalized use of mobile telephone systems, without the presence of conventional, fixed line infrastructure) can be deployed to avoid nonsustainability.[15] Essentially, managers operating in emerging economies must develop the ability to meet rapidly growing demand without repeating the wasteful and outdated practices prevailing in developed markets.

Third and finally, *survival* economies, with three billion potential customers, are largely rural. Most individuals have unmet basic needs. These markets have minimal or non-existent infrastructure. MNE managers should recognize the opportunity presented by this massive consumer group. In line with the idea of recombining resources and deploying FSA bundles to match the location advantages of a given market, Hart and Milstein suggest that managers should apply state-of-the-art technology in fundamentally new ways to meet the basic needs of customers in survival economies. More specifically, conventional infrastructure that meets basic needs in developed economies, such as a large, grid-based energy supply system, may well be infeasible to develop, thus providing unparalleled opportunities for deploying more decentralized systems, building upon solar power, wind and hydro energy as credible and economically viable alternatives.

Managers must be aware of which industries and products are vulnerable to creative destruction. As noted above, these are the industries and products for which large investments in technical development yield only small gains in performance. Entrepreneurs who can introduce radical new technologies that generate significant performance gains will sow creative destruction and experience tremendous success.

The authors recommend that managers shift their performance metrics to include such factors as pounds of materials consumed per monetary unit of sales, or shareholder value created per pound of materials consumed. The adoption of such metrics should lead to divesting large-footprint, low knowledge-intensity activities in favour of information-intensive businesses providing value-added services. Hart and Milstein recommend in-depth managerial reflection, especially in developed economies, and much in line with Porter and van der Linde's perspective, on issues such as product life cycle costs as compared to product price, the opportunity to recycle waste products, the opportunity to improve resource productivity, the opportunity to add valuable services with low natural resource intensity and more generally the possibility of radical as opposed to incremental innovation.[16]

Overall, Hart and Milstein suggest that senior managers in large companies, including MNEs, do not have to accept the role of their firm as an incumbent, engaged in incremental innovation but generally sticking with the status quo until the firm is destroyed in the future by upstart entrepreneurs with radical technologies: "To capture sustainable opportunities, managers must fundamentally rethink their prevailing views about strategy, technology, and markets. Focused attention through the three lenses – consumer, emerging and survival economies – will enable them to see new business opportunities."[17] In this case, ***doing good*** (i.e., radical environmental innovation) would appear to be a strict precondition for ***doing well*** in the long run.

As a second complement to Porter and van der Linde's piece, **Ans Kolk** and **Jonathan Pinkse's** 2005 *CMR* article on climate change classifies and analyses the strategies that firms can use to mitigate their climate change impact.[18]

Kolk and Pinkse suggest that flexible public policies in the climate change sphere are more prevalent now than in earlier years. This flexibility implies that managers have more choices available to them in adopting climate change impact mitigation strategies. Kolk and Pinkse focus on two strategic goals at the firm level: innovation and compensation. Innovation means, in line with Porter and van der Linde, that firms can improve their business performance through new FSA development, driving emissions reductions. Managers can pursue an innovation approach focusing either internally on their own production processes or on the firms they interact with in their supply chain, or outside their supply chain by exploring new product/market combinations. Alternatively, firms can use compensation approaches to essentially transfer/trade, often internationally, emissions or emission-generating activities.

In practice, Kolk and Pinkse observe that managers who perceive climate change as a business risk tend towards the compensation approach. In contrast, managers who see the potential business opportunities of climate change policy are more likely to adopt an innovation-based approach. To test the potential configurations of climate change impact mitigation strategies in practice, the authors analysed data from 139 companies included in the *Financial Times Global 500* that had participated in the Carbon Disclosure Project, an initiative pushed by 35 institutional investors. The results of this analysis suggest that, including two types of inaction, firms fall into six broad types: cautious planners, emergent planners, internal explorers, vertical explorers, horizontal explorers and emissions traders.

Cautious planners are firms preparing for action but showing little activity related to any of the potential climate change strategic options presented above. As would be expected, these firms mention measures to reduce greenhouse emissions as a future possibility but cannot provide any specific details on what mechanisms might be utilized to achieve this goal. The US-based electric utility FirstEnergy was a typical cautious planner. Up to recently, the firm reported efforts to reduce emissions; however, it was unclear about the results of these efforts, or the firm's current position and targets. In part, this position stemmed from FirstEnergy's view that there were only limited possibilities for process improvements in its operations. Today, the firm strongly promotes the idea of environmental sustainability and implements a variety of sustainable initiatives and policies.

Like cautious planners, ***emergent planners*** have not yet implemented climate change measures. Unlike cautious planners, however, emergent planners have set targets for greenhouse gas reduction. US-based Bristol-Myers Squibb, a pharmaceutical firm, was an example of an emergent planner, as in the past the firm had well-developed targets but lacked long-term plans to reach those goals. "The opportunities it identifies are not in the redesign of products or processes, but in the stakeholder recognition that the company receives for its environmental initiatives."[19] Emergent planner firms like Bristol-Myers Squibb not only have targets to reduce their own greenhouse gas emissions, but they may also extend these targets to suppliers. Recently, Bristol-Myers Squibb developed to a market leader in sustainability and intensified its stakeholder management in order to meet long-term goals.

Internal explorers are firms with a strong internal focus entailing a combination of targets and improvements in their production process. Firms in this category usually try to improve their energy efficiency in an effort to reduce CO_2 emissions. Nippon Steel is one example of an internal explorer, as this firm set a goal of 20 per cent energy savings in reaction to the 1970s oil shocks and has followed this target with an additional 10 per cent savings in reaction to climate change concerns to be achieved by 2010. In this particular example, however, the early efficiency gains have made subsequent energy reduction and emission targets more difficult to obtain. This has pushed the firm to modify its supply chain for further efficiency gains and to acquire certified emission credits by transferring emission-reducing technology (one of its FSAs) to other countries in Asia that do not have targets for emission reductions. (Hence, Nippon Steel has evolved, and is now a hybrid vertical explorer/emissions trader.) For an MNE such as Nippon Steel, the very ability to transfer its environmental FSAs is an FSA in and of itself. This FSA means the firm gains access to Kyoto-related certified emission credits, thus increasing its strategic options to mitigate its climate change impact.

Vertical explorers are firms with a strong focus on environmental measures within their supply chains. "The reason for a company to concentrate on upstream and downstream activities can be twofold: it relies on natural resources that are vulnerable to extreme weather conditions and/or its manufacturing process has relatively low climatic impact compared to the consumption of its products (for instance, the automotive industry)."[20] Unilever is an example of a vertical explorer because the firm's reliance on agricultural supplies exposes Unilever's production to risks from natural disasters such as floods and long-term drought. At the same time, the climate change impact of some of Unilever's products depends strongly on household consumer behaviour, for example the water temperature used in consumers' washing machines.[21] These conditions are pushing Unilever to look for emission savings within its own supply chain by encouraging environmental standards among its suppliers and on the downstream side by utilizing life cycle analysis in its product design.

The final two configurations, **horizontal explorers** and **emissions traders**, were the least common forms found in Kolk and Pinkse's sample (at 5 per cent and 4 per cent respectively). Horizontal explorers seek opportunities to mitigate their climate change impact in markets outside their current business scope. For example, Stora Enso, the Finnish forest products company, entered the green electricity market by developing biofuels from sawmill and logging residues. Emissions traders, on the other hand, trade on emission markets and participate in offset projects. "This group of companies directly focuses on the opportunities of emissions trading and combines this option with an internal reduction target that has a global reach and with a favourable position towards new products and markets."[22] Mitsubishi's involvement in establishing a Japanese greenhouse gas market and its participation in emission reduction trading schemes in the UK makes it a typical emissions trader.

Kolk and Pinkse note that of the six climate change profiles presented above, most companies fall into either the cautious planner or emergent planner category. This distribution indicates that most firms are still in the preliminary phase of planning their climate change impact mitigation strategies, which is probably because of the enormous bounded rationality challenges confronting senior MNE managers. Because it is highly uncertain what many countries' climate change policies will be, many managers understandably adopt cautious and non-committal approaches. Firms become less likely to pursue radical innovations, because policy uncertainty increases the risk that new FSAs will not be effectively deployable at home and abroad, and will not gain them first-mover advantage internationally.

Finally, although Kolk and Pinkse examine both the innovation and compensation approaches, it is important to realize that the innovation approach to addressing the climate change challenge is more likely to lead to the dual benefits of meeting emission targets and developing FSAs. In contrast, the compensation approach to climate change, while offering strategic flexibility that is important in high bounded rationality contexts, will not lead to direct FSA development, except for the firms that specialize in the compensation business, i.e., the emission traders.

MANAGEMENT INSIGHTS

All three articles emphasize that environmental innovation can lead to the development of new FSAs. Implicit in linking environmental management with competitive strategies is the alignment of firm-level and societal interests, as also discussed more broadly in Chapter 16A. Porter and van der Linde have the important insight that environmental stewardship can be achieved through higher resource productivity, which in turn increases the competitiveness of the firm. Thus, the concept of resource productivity brings the profit-seeking interests of the firm into alignment with society's interest in environmental sustainability.

Porter and van der Linde also attempt to capture the role of bounded rationality in environmental strategies. For example, the authors address the following question: if efficiency gains from environmental initiatives are so prevalent, why would regulations ever be needed to encourage companies to adopt such initiatives? Wouldn't firms adopt the initiatives out of their own self-interest? Porter and van der Linde offer the following answer to this question: "the belief that companies will pick up on profitable opportunities without a regulatory push makes a false assumption about competitive reality – namely, that all profitable opportunities for innovation have already been discovered, that all managers have perfect information about them, and that organizational incentives are aligned with innovating".[23] Thus, environmental regulation is needed, not only to align interests, but also to push companies towards reaching efficiency frontiers that they themselves cannot identify due to bounded rationality constraints.

The bounded rationality problem surrounding environmental issues is further illustrated by the difficulties of predicting the direction of environmental policies. For example, the idea that CO_2 would be considered a pollutant was not on most managers' radar screens 15 to 20 years ago. The difficulty in predicting environmental trends is also illustrated by Monsanto's environmentally motivated shift from a chemical to a life sciences company. As a life sciences company, the US-based MNE has developed genetically modified crops that have reduced the need for pesticides and herbicides, thus producing what the firm thought was an environmentally friendly product. Unfortunately, bounded rationality constraints obscured the firm's ability to foresee the consumer, NGO and government backlash against genetically modified crops. This backlash resulted in governments imposing strict regulations against the company's products, a one-third drop in Monsanto's market capitalization, and the dismissal of Robert Shapiro as the MNE's CEO. Both the Porter and van der Linde and the Hart and Milstein articles correctly identify that regulatory flexibility will minimize such firm-level risks; strict, inflexible regulations are unlikely to lead to resource productivity and innovation gains.

While Porter and van der Linde's piece captures the role of bounded rationality in firm-level decision making, the article has three important limitations. First, it does not address fully the impact of environmental regulations on location advantages in an international context. To address this limitation, Figure 16B.1 illustrates the role of environmental regulations as a potential source of location advantages.

The top part of Figure 16B.1 shows Porter and van der Linde's 'single diamond' perspective on environmental regulation. They suggest that strict environmental regulations should be viewed as a location advantage, which can then translate into new location-bound FSAs for the firms encouraged to lower costs, innovate and improve resource productivity. Ultimately, this may lead to domestic firms earning a first-mover advantage internationally when compared to firms from countries that lag behind in establishing stringent environmental regulations. Here, environmental regulation is the source of new, internationally transferable FSAs, thereby making domestic firms more competitive abroad.

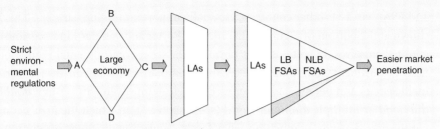

Figure 16B.1
The Porter and multiple diamond model perspectives on environmental strategy

The light-blue-shaded areas on the left represent the new LAs resulting from environmental regulation in the single diamond, large economy case. These new LAs give rise to new LB and NLB FSAs, represented by the shaded wedge along the bottom of the triangle, and should facilitate the MNE's international expansion.

A. Factor conditions
B. Related and supporting industries
C. Demand conditions
D. Firm strategy, industry
   structure, and rivalry

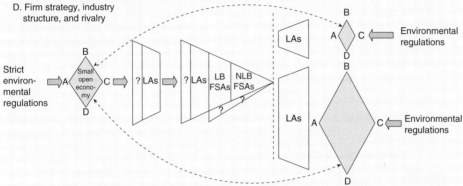

The question marks at the bottom indicate it is highly uncertain whether environmental regulations in small open economies will give rise to LAs, LB or NLB FSAs. The long dotted arrows indicate changes in relative strength of domestic and foreign diamonds, when environmental regulations are different in each country.

Porter and van der Linde's perspective is appealing for governments and firms in large, technologically advanced economies that can play a leadership role in setting the agenda for international negotiations on environmental regulation, or can otherwise influence the scope and substance of environmental regulation in a large number of other countries. If the domestic market is particularly large and attractive to foreign firms, it makes sense to set high environmental standards, thereby encouraging domestic firms to conform as quickly as possible, and providing incentives to foreign firms to follow these examples. In other words, this advice appears to be particularly appropriate for a country such as the US, whose MNEs are largely home-market oriented, but also operate in host countries with less stringent environmental regulation.

However, the advice to enact stringent environmental regulation is dangerous for governments in small open economies that lack a large domestic market and do not wield any power, whether formal or informal, in setting international environmental standards. Here, it is an open question what the impact might be of stringent domestic regulations on business, both in terms of location advantages and FSAs, vis-à-vis other countries, especially important trading partners. This is shown at the bottom of Figure 16B.1. Indeed, Porter and van der Linde curiously admit themselves, in spite of their pleading for strict environmental regulation, that "government cannot know better than companies how to address [resource inefficiencies and potential areas for technological improvement]".[24] In a ***double diamond*** or ***multiple diamond*** world (see Chapter 3), in which the firm's competitiveness depends as much on what foreign governments do as on domestic regulation, unilateral imposition of strict environmental regulation by the home government would appear unwise. For example, in the case of Canada, the US represents close to 80 per cent of the smaller country's two-way trade. In this case, it is critical for the Canadian government and Canadian-based firms to understand US environmental regulations and to benchmark Canadian regulations against the US ones. This does not imply a loss of national sovereignty, nor an obligation to copy US standards. However, it does suggest that imposing stringent environmental regulations domestically, without understanding the equivalent regulations in the US, might seriously hurt the competitiveness of Canadian-based firms when doing business in their largest host market. In other words, the actual development of FSAs by Canadian-based companies is highly uncertain, and the creation of first-mover advantages internationally is particularly doubtful.

The above does not imply that governments of small open economies should pursue the opposite strategy, namely lax regulations, often associated with earning the status of a ***pollution haven***. In fact, the pollution haven approach, aiming to attract foreign MNEs using lax regulations, is not currently supported by conceptual or empirical analysis, both of which suggest that environmental regulations have little effect on MNE location decisions.[25] One reason why is that many MNEs from highly developed economies have some national responsiveness but generally attempt to transfer their best practices across borders in the form of routines, so as to facilitate the operation, coordination and control of their internal networks (i.e., to reduce bounded rationality and bounded reliability challenges). These MNEs require only that environmental regulations are within the substantial bandwidth that their routines require. Environmental regulations are not critical to these MNEs' location choices.

In fact, having environmental regulations far below what is considered appropriate internationally may lead to a negative country effect for domestic firms attempting to do business internationally, as experienced by Chinese firms in 2007. In that year, Chinese exports of contaminated food supplies and toxic or otherwise dangerous toys led some US politicians to use, perhaps exaggeratedly, the concept of 'Chinese roulette' to indicate the alleged dangers faced by US consumers when buying Chinese products.

A second limitation of Porter and van der Linde's article is the relative lack of focus on possible patterns of environmental FSA development. As discussed in

Chapter 16A, in the broader context of corporate social responsibility, each of the ten patterns discussed throughout this book can be observed in a variety of MNE contexts. However, whereas the case for developing at least some FSAs in good corporate citizenship is compelling, this is less evident in the environmental sphere. Figure 16B.2 illustrates the patterns of developing transferable environmental FSAs. These non-location-bound, green FSAs may form through development Patterns I, II, V, VI, VII, VIII or X. In all cases, the resulting FSAs are internationally transferable, though it may often be necessary also to develop location-bound FSAs in specific host country environments, as depicted by

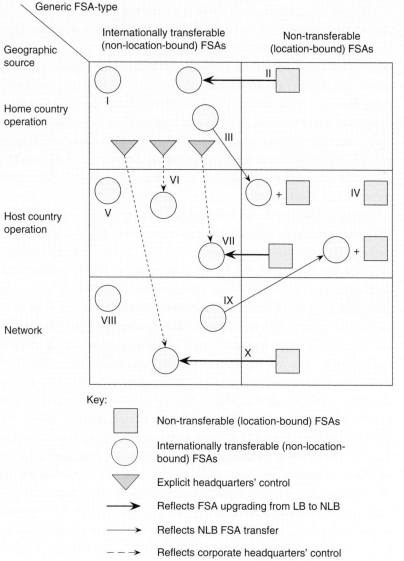

Figure 16B.2
Patterns of environmental FSA development in MNEs

Patterns III, IV, VII, IX and X. The importance of internationally transferring and deploying environmental FSAs, in the sense of imposing routines on the entire MNE network, is suggested by findings that a higher degree of multinationality is often associated with superior environmental performance. One explanation for such findings is that external pressures from international environmental regulations increase more rapidly than the firm's bargaining power.[26] However, an alternative, and perhaps more credible explanation is that a higher degree of deploying routinized environmental practices across borders actually expresses the MNE's general superiority in institutionalizing its routines across borders, thereby leading to stronger performance, both in the economic and environmental sphere.

There is a third limitation to Porter and van der Linde's work, related to the actual substance of environmental management in practice. Here, a distinction should be made among three categories of firms. The first category consists of firms in industries with distinctive, high-profile environmental issues (oil, electricity, automobiles). In these industries, environmental impact mitigation can be a source of competitive advantage. The second category consists of firms that specialize in goods or services instrumental to mitigating environmental impacts or anticipating, influencing or responding to public policy/regulation. These two categories of firms must continually develop FSAs through *internal* investment, using the various FSA development patterns discussed above.

However, most firms fall into the third category: firms that can essentially *outsource* their environmental impact mitigation. MNEs faced with multiple national and regional regulatory regimes may do best to simply adopt the best available practices accessible in external markets. For example, if the MNE's legitimacy in a particular home country, from the perspective of the firm's stakeholders, arises from perceived purposeful action towards environmental impact mitigation and from measurable/measured improvements, this does not necessarily imply conventional FSA development: visible environmental commitment does not require the internal creation of new FSAs. In fact, the only FSA of MNEs in this category may be their proximity and easy access to multiple external markets providing best available practices. For example, improvement of environmental impacts in the production sphere may result from purchasing greener and productivity-enhancing technologies. Employees can be made more environmentally conscious by investing in externally provided employee training programmes (e.g., at the industry level). In order to develop organizational competencies in the environmental sphere that stretch across functional areas, the firm may purchase new tools in the market to facilitate internal communication (e.g., software and related support to measure impacts of virtual teamwork, leading to reductions in pollution costs). In the context of formal management systems and procedures, the firm may adopt externally developed tools where possible (e.g., the climate change impact measurement tools, developed by reputable audit companies, or the standardized trading processes introduced by intermediaries as in the case of carbon emission trading schemes). Finally, in the realm of strategic planning, senior management may monitor external developments on environmental mitigation policies and competitor strategies, but outsource all non-crisis environmental stakeholder management where possible (e.g., lobbying with industry associations).

Especially given the sometimes high country and regional specificity of government environmental policies, the above strategy of outsourcing, while not a conventional FSA, will give the MNE flexibility, thereby reducing bounded rationality and bounded reliability challenges in the environmental strategy sphere. It is indeed sometimes difficult to anticipate correctly when and how vote-needing politicians in several countries around the world will introduce specific, new environmental regulations, and what these regulations might entail substantively. In the face of this high political uncertainty, environmental complexity, and the substantial risk associated with making non-redeployable resource investments in the environmental sphere, reliance on external markets may be a wise strategy to pursue.

Five management takeaways

1. Keep track of expected, new environmental regulations and assess not only their likely cost, but also their potential contribution to green FSA development.
2. Fight ill-conceived messages from external stakeholders that more stringent environmental regulations at home will lead to first-mover advantages abroad, since this is usually not true for firms based in small open economies.
3. Develop new FSAs through environmental innovation by considering the different consumer groups in developed, emerging and survival economies that might benefit from such innovation.
4. Analyse the scope of the MNE's environmental strategy (inside focus; vertical value chain focus; broader industry focus) to identify relevant environmental initiatives.
5. Beware of exaggerating the economic potential of environmental innovation initiatives, especially if the firm is unlikely to build unique expertise in this area and may be better off 'purchasing best practice solutions' in the external market.

CASE

Case 16B.1 Shell's environmental management strategy

Since the early 1990s, Shell's reputation has been battered by corporate social responsibility problems such as the Brent Spar controversy and the Ken Saro-Wiwa trial in Nigeria. (Ken Saro-Wiwa was the environmentalist who was hanged and whose death some attributed in part to Shell.) Shell gradually realized that dismissing environmental and social issues could seriously hurt its business. It started to develop a company-wide environmental policy in the late 1990s, in spite of its heritage of being a rather decentralized firm with highly autonomous operating companies. As a result of this autonomy, environmental management approaches at Shell's international subsidiaries varied substantially and depended on the direction chosen by subsidiary managers. Subsidiary discretion led to inconsistencies, especially between operations in developed and developing countries.

As a multinational energy firm with 90,000 people operating in more than 80 countries, Shell had traditionally been viewed as being at the forefront of modern, corporate environmental management, but this record did not prevent the firm from becoming subject to substantial criticism in the 1990s.[27]

Decentralized management

Shell's history can be traced back to a small, London-based business established by Marcus Samuel in 1833 to import seashells for collectors. Marcus Samuel Jr, the son of Marcus Samuel, when searching for seashells in the Caspian Sea, identified an opportunity to deliver oil to the Far East in the early 1890s. This led to the construction of a fleet of dedicated tankers. During the same period, August Kessler established Royal Dutch in the Netherlands, to develop oil fields in Asia and to deliver oil. In the late 1890s and early 1900s, the fierce competition with Standard Oil ultimately forced Shell and Royal Dutch to merge into the Royal Dutch/Shell Group Companies in 1907, with Royal Dutch controlling 60 per cent of the shares and Shell Transport and Trading Company 40 per cent.

By the late 1990s, Shell consisted of two parent companies, nine servicing companies and around 450 operating companies around the world. The two parent companies, Royal Dutch and Shell Transport and Trading Company, never engaged in operations directly, although they appointed the five members of the Committee of Managing Directors (CMD). The Chairmanship of the CMD rotated with a fixed single term. The CMD identified key issues, set strategies and exercised managerial control within the corporation. However, the operating companies had the operating authority and financial responsibility. With its unique structure directed by multiple executives, and with responsibilities largely allocated to operating companies, Shell was widely viewed as one of the most decentralized companies in the world.

This decentralization was reflected in Shell's approach to environmental management. Until the late 1990s, Shell maintained that a decentralized structure would allow operating companies to tailor corporate environmental standards/objectives to local needs. Although the firm reviewed environmental performance annually, Shell's national companies were allowed to focus their environmental efforts according to the requirements of local environmental regulations, even if some of those were not particularly stringent. According to James McArdle, safety and environment coordinator for Shell UK, "While policy guidelines for Shell as a whole are laid down by the committee of managing directors ... we have the freedom to adapt these guidelines to suit local needs."[28]

Shell argued that such decentralization benefited innovation. One commentator noted: 'Shell refused to set overall objectives for its subsidiaries. Instead, it allows individual companies to decide their own strategy, "reflecting the national and cultural background in which they work". Shell portrays this as a strength, arguing that by putting the responsibility on local managers' shoulders, it encourages a sense of ownership, which in turn provides the most fertile ground for innovation. "Striving for consistency", said one Shell manager, "would be the kiss of death for continuous improvement."[29]

At the corporate level, Shell developed Policy Guidelines on Health, Safety and the Environment as early as 1977. In 1991, Shell had a policy of continuous improvement towards the goal of having no emissions of environmentally harmful substances. Also in 1991, Shell developed a few policies to ensure that products would be recycled or disposed of safely. However, implementation of these guidelines was still made subject to decision making by subsidiary managers.

Environmental management practices at Shell's operating companies

In the late 1980s and early 1990s, environmental management practices varied strongly across Shell's international operations, depending on local regulations and institutional requirements. Moreover, environmental activities at Shell were largely passive responses to external pressures, rather than proactive initiatives.

For example, by the late 1980s, Shell Canada had consciously incorporated environmental management into its operations, mainly through prevention of potentially negative environmental impacts. J. M. MacLeod, Shell Canada President and CEO, stated in an interview in 1991, "For 20 years, we've been consciously managing and minimizing our emissions and our effluents from gas-processing plants and we've been reclaiming our drilling sites."[30]

However, many of Shell's environmental strategy actions were primarily a response to exogenous circumstances, rather than a proactive search for environmental improvements. One example of this occurred at Shell's major gas processing plant in Waterton, Alberta, Canada. Here, Shell had to manage a very difficult relationship with the local community in the early 1970s, as the prevailing view in the community was that the plant emitted excess amounts of sulphur dioxide. Shell Canada spent CAN $25 million to install a new process to increase sulphur recovery, even though "there was no economic return in the way one would normally perceive it; that is, the additional sulphur recovered would not pay for the process".[31] Except when forced by strong stakeholder pressures, MacLeod's view was that Shell Canada did not "go beyond regulations to any significant extent, no more than other companies do".[32]

In the Netherlands, Shell introduced sulphur emission controls at its Rotterdam factory, supposedly signalling Shell's commitment to the environment. However, critics viewed such environmentally friendly changes as, again, merely a response to external pressures (governments and environmental NGOs had been pressing for the controls for years), rather than a reflection of a proactive environmental stance. One Greenpeace campaigner, complained that "It (the Rotterdam factory) used to be the number one source of acid rain in the Netherlands. We had to work very hard to get Shell to improve environmental standards there. Finally, they agreed, and then, of course, they claim all the credit."[33]

During the same period, Shell's environmental management in the developing world was less than impressive, as can be seen by its oil spills in Nigeria. According to research by Greenpeace, in the ten years between 1982 and 1992, Shell's spills in Nigeria accounted for around 40 per cent of Shell's total spills in the world, releasing 7.3 million litres of oil in the Nigerian Delta Region. Environmental Rights Action, Friends of the Earth and others have estimated that Shell and its partners have spilled around 13 million barrels in the Niger Delta in the past 50 years. This volume is 50 times higher than the spill caused by the Exxon Valdez tanker accident off Alaska. In 2002, Shell admitted that there had been 262 oil spill incidents in Nigeria in that year and that around 548 sites needed actions to avoid contamination.[34] However, Shell claimed that most of the spills in Nigeria were caused by sabotage to make compensation claims.

Besides spills, Shell also engaged in the controversial practice of flaring off excess natural gas at its oil fields, until a Nigerian court demanded in 2006 that it stop within 12 months.

With their diverse environmental practices around the world, Shell's companies did bring to the market innovations that benefited the firm both environmentally and financially. One of these innovations was the Shell Coal Gasification Process (SCGP),[35] which converts coal into syngas and steam. Syngas is a mixture of carbon monoxide and hydrogen. During gasification, the energy loss is only 5 per cent, with 80 per cent of the coal's energy contained in the syngas and 15 per cent contained in the steam. Byproducts in the process, including sulphur and ash, can be recovered and sold to the chemical industry and the construction industry, respectively. Shell started to develop this technology in 1972.[36] After three pilots in the Netherlands, Germany and the US, and its full-scale adoption in the Buggenum plant in the Netherlands, Shell started to capitalize on the technology with several ongoing projects in China, where SCGP would replace the naphtha-based feedstock at the Sinopec fertilizer plant, thereby reducing feedstock costs.

Shell weathers a media storm in the mid 1990s

Shell's commitment to environmental issues was actually increasing in the early 1990s, but that progress – however small – was overwhelmed by two events in the mid 1990s that received enormous negative media coverage: the Brent Spar controversy and the Ken Saro-Wiwa affair.

The Brent Spar controversy was a major confrontation between Shell UK and Greenpeace in 1995 over the decommissioning and disposal of a giant oil storage platform called the Brent Spar. While it was one of more than 400 offshore rigs, which belonged to a number of different owners including Shell, it was the first of many to be decommissioned over the next two to three decades. Greenpeace felt that the decision to decommission the platform by sinking it offshore in the

North Atlantic would significantly pollute the ocean. It thus decided to oppose the decision using a combination of direct action and savvy manipulation of the media.

The Brent Spar was an oil storage platform used by Shell to help develop one of its concessions in the huge oil fields lying beneath the North Sea.[37] Oil extracted from the Brent field was stored in it and later transported by tanker for processing in the United Kingdom. Completed in 1976, it was installed in the Brent field in June 1976.

The Brent field was one of many fields located in the oil bearing geologic formation that straddled the offshore jurisdiction of the United Kingdom, Norway, Denmark, the Netherlands and Germany. While the German, Dutch and Danish sectors contained some oil, the bulk of the oil production came from the Norwegian and British sectors. Although oil was first produced in 1971, it was not until the 1980s, with rising oil prices and more sophisticated technology, that the North Sea became a significant source of non-OPEC oil.

As production increased, the infrastructure to collect and transport the oil to onshore processing facilities became more sophisticated. By the early 1990s the Brent Spar had become redundant as the oil field was connected to the mainland by underwater pipelines and collecting systems. The Brent Spar ceased operating in September 1991.

Shell then considered its options for disposing of the Brent Spar. Between 1991 and 1993, the company embarked on a series of internal and external studies centred on finding the best method for the Spar's disposal. More than 15 separate independent studies on the engineering and environmental dimension were commissioned, detailing a number of options. Two of the options – horizontal onshore dismantling and deep sea disposal – were examined in detail.

Extensive consultation with scientific and technical communities and ongoing discussions with various government departments suggested that the deep sea disposal alternative had significantly lower safety risks and costs, while having a minimal environmental impact. An independent study conducted by Aberdeen University subsequently condoned the deep sea option in February 1994.

By the end of 1994 Shell had prepared and submitted its final Abandonment Plan to the UK Government Department of Trade and Industry. In December 1994 Shell received formal approval. Thus, at this point, the disposal plan had followed the procedures, principles and standards of the UK regulatory regime. All options had been reviewed both internally and externally, taking into account environmental, safety and economic factors. The unique characteristics of the Brent Spar suggested that deep sea disposal was the best option and was in fact the option that the US government had been pursuing in the Gulf of Mexico to create artificial sea reefs for marine life.

While Shell had cleared hurdles linked to regulatory approval by the UK government, the disposal option still needed to be vetted by the so-called OSPAR commissions (see below). Increasing interest in the North Sea by oil and gas interests led to the creation of two conventions covering the protection of the marine environment in the early 1970s: the 1972 Oslo Convention on Waste Dumping at Sea and the 1974 Paris Convention on Pollution of the North Sea and Adjacent Areas from Land-Based Sources. These conventions established an international framework through which to manage industrial activity that could have a negative impact on the marine environment, including the North Sea. These conventions provided guidance to governments concerning disposal of waste in the vicinity of the North Sea. Key features included public disclosure of information regarding activities affecting the state of the North Sea and measures to prevent pollution, and advising member states to the convention regarding compliance.

The conventions were administered through a permanent bureaucracy referred to as the OSPAR commissions. The commissions handled the day-to-day activities generated by the Conventions, including any significant input coming from the political sphere. One such input, which could have far-reaching consequences for policy formation, was the Conferences of Environmental Ministers from countries bordering the North Sea. By 1995 three conferences had been held, while a fourth was scheduled for June 1995 in Esjberg, Denmark.

The UK government announced its decision to the signatories to the Oslo convention in February 1995. It did not receive any objections, thus opening the door for Shell to publicly announce the deep sea disposal plan. Thus, not only was the plan authorized by the British government, but it also conformed to international rules and agreements dealing with ocean pollution.

By April 1995, however, Greenpeace had become actively involved in attempting to reverse the decision. Greenpeace is an international environmental organization with regional and national offices around the world. The regional and national offices are guided by a governing council based in Amsterdam, which sets overall priorities for the organization and identifies issues that will guide the behaviour of the regional and national offices. These offices are largely autonomous in selecting activities on which to focus, though they agree to let global issues determined by the council guide the local level.

While Greenpeace has since expanded the range of issues it gets involved in beyond ocean-related matters, in the 1980s and early 1990s it was very much focused on marine issues. It had elevated the disposal of man-made waste in the oceans to a key campaigning issue. Although Greenpeace was known to use lobbying and conference attendance in its repertoire of influencing tactics, its preferred method in the 1990s was direct action and media savvy to put pressure on key decision makers. This it elected to do beginning on 30 April 1995 with Brent Spar's occupation by Greenpeace activists.

Greenpeace relied on the strong environmental ethos in continental Europe that had been on the rise since the environmental activist Green Party won seats in Germany's national parliament in the mid 1980s. By the mid 1990s, the party had emerged as a significant player on the German political scene, becoming Germany's third political force in a country that traditionally relied on coalition governments. "Political parties that don't acknowledge [green policies] will face great difficulties", said Guenter Albrecht, chief economist at the Association of German Chambers of Commerce.[38] Thus, the Green Party in Germany was an important mechanism that Greenpeace could use to affect important decision makers.

In May 1995, the German Ministry of the Environment protested against the disposal plan while Greenpeace called for a continental boycott of Shell products. At the fourth North Sea Conference of Environment Ministers in early June, several European countries called for onshore disposal of all oil installations, while Britain and Norway argued for a case-by-case approach. Public opinion in northern Europe grew increasingly opposed to the ocean disposal, leading

Chancellor Kohl of Germany to protest to British Prime Minister John Major at the G7 summit in Canada. Prior to leaving for the meeting he told German television: "My urgent advice is not to do it."[39] During the third week in June, German protesters threatened to damage some of Shell's 1,700 service stations, with some 50 subsequently damaged, including two that were fire bombed and one that was sprayed with bullets. Dutch consumers boycotted Shell service stations.

Most telling was the reaction of some Shell service station managers themselves: five Shell stations shut their doors for 24 hours in the German town of Koblenz. A confused news conference was convened in Hamburg at which the company's surprise over the public uproar was evident. At first, Peter Duncan, head of Shell's German subsidiary, Deutsche Shell AG, announced that the company would defer its decision. However, he was quickly contradicted by officials from Shell's headquarters in Rotterdam. The collegiate decentralized management structure that Shell had so assiduously cultivated was beginning to fracture, with many Shell managers criticizing the handling of the Brent Spar affair by Shell UK and its failing to recognize the pro-environmental leanings of many of the countries in continental Europe.

After a protracted battle, Shell eventually backed down. The platform was subsequently moved to Norway, where it was moored waiting for the eventual outcome. Following an extensive public consultation programme, and a request for proposals, the platform was decommissioned and became part of a ferry quay in Norway.

Ken Saro-Wiwa, Nigeria and Shell

Ken Saro-Wiwa was the leader of a Nigeria-based group, The Movement for the Survival of the Ogoni People, created in 1990 as the vehicle through which to channel grievances of the Ogoni people. The movement protested the environmental damage inflicted by Shell and other oil companies in the Niger Delta, as well as the human rights abuses committed by the Nigerian military on the Ogoni people and other ethnic minorities. Following the murder of moderate elements of the movement by more radical members allied with Saro-Wiwa, the Nigerian military arrested Saro-Wiwa and eight followers. After a trial that was widely regarded as a sham, Saro-Wiwa and eight of his colleagues were executed on 10 November 1995. Shell was widely criticized in the press for contributing to the tragedy and failing to use its influence to obtain clemency.

Shell Petroleum Development Company (SPDC) of Nigeria was the operating company of a joint venture with the Nigerian National Petroleum Corporation, which held a 55 per cent stake, followed by Shell with 30 per cent. The remaining 15 per cent was held by Elf and Agip. SPDC operated in the Niger Delta, in which the Ogoni lands accounted for some 4 per cent of the operating area. Shell began operations on Ogoni land in 1958, and by the time it was forced to leave in 1993 due to the civil unrest, its cumulative production on Ogoni land had amounted to 634 million barrels valued at US $5.2 billion. Of this revenue, 15 per cent went to cover production costs, 79 per cent went to the federal government and 6 per cent went to the private partners, including Shell.[40]

Very little of the money allocated to the Nigerian government ever trickled down to Ogoniland. By all accounts, the Ogoni people lived in conditions of extreme poverty. Most villages lacked electricity and piped water. Frequent oil spills had destroyed croplands and polluted streams, severely damaging the Ogoni people's subsistence lifestyle. In addition to oil spills, flaring of natural gas from the five large pumping stations and 96 wells located in Ogoni ancestral lands created a sooty, eery landscape with uncertain environmental impacts.

Shell's view on these events could be characterized as distant. While the environmental standards Shell upheld for Nigeria were lower than in Europe or North America, Dick van den Broek, Shell's Coordinator, Western Hemisphere & Africa, defended that difference, arguing that "It's a question of priorities. Nigeria is a poor country. How much should it spend on environmental protection? . . . Shell is a minority partner [in SPDC] and any expenditures must be absorbed on a prorate basis [by all partners]."[41] Even though social conditions in Ogoni communities could be regarded as primitive, Shell's policy of limited involvement was defended by Alan Detheridge, Shell's West African Coordinator, who stated that "We can offer advice and we can point out the consequences of an action. But we do not lecture or try to give orders because we do not interfere in politics or government."[42]

While Shell saw only a small role it performed in the past or could potentially perform in the future regarding the abject poverty in the region, others painted a different picture. Napoleon Agbedetse, a London barrister who returned to Nigeria, observed that Shell's treatment of one community in the Niger Delta over the previous 27 years had left 3,000 or so villagers in a state of "depression, neglect and poverty".[43]

The campaign against Shell started in 1990 when the Movement for the Survival of the Ogoni People was formed. The objectives of the Movement included gaining more control over local government, better protection of the environment and a greater share of the wealth flowing from the petroleum resources. The movement was originally led by conservative traditional leaders, with the first president being Garrick B. Leton, a former federal minister. Ken Saro-Wiwa, a successful writer and TV producer, became its spokesman.

While the movement initially succeeded in gaining a commitment from the Nigerian federal government for 3 per cent of the total annual oil revenue for Ogoniland, this commitment was never honoured. The social and environmental conditions of the Ogoni people remained brutal and oppressive.

While traditional leaders continued to favour negotiation and dialogue, Saro-Wiwa advocated a more confrontational approach. The rift between the traditional leadership and Saro-Wiwa grew as he organized additional branches of the movement including the National Youth Council of the Ogoni People. As his influence increased, he allied the movement with the Unrepresented Nations and Peoples Organization in the Hague and carried his story of oppression and abuse, including Shell's Nigerian environmental legacy, to the United Nations, Europe and the US.

Several respected sources disagreed with Saro-Wiwa's portrayal of the Niger Delta's environmental problems, however. For example, a 1995 World Bank study called "Defining an environmental strategy for the Niger Delta", while agreeing that oil pollution had unquestionably caused environmental damage, indicated that "oil pollution is of moderate priority when compared to the spectrum of environmental problems in the Niger Delta".[44] The report went to conclude that, in fact, most of the region's problems could be linked to a fourfold increase in the local population since 1958.

Nonetheless, vandalism against Shell facilities continued to increase to such an extent that in late 1992 the firm asked the government to send in troops to protect its operations. When the local conditions continued to deteriorate, Shell eventually left, asking that federal forces continue to protect the installations it had left behind. Detheridge, Shell's West African Coordinator, said that the company would not return until it had the local community's support.[45]

Soon after Shell left, the five pumping stations on Ogoni land were either damaged or destroyed, though it was unclear who was culpable – the military or the Ogoni leaders. In June 1993, in a disagreement over strategic direction and tactics, the conservative wing of the Ogoni movement resigned. In early 1994, Shell reportedly requested that the government deploy its mobile police to protect its assets.

The response by the authorities was quick and ruthless. An internal memo written in May 1994 by the commander of the internal security force called for "wasting targets cutting across communities and leadership cadres, especially vocal individuals" and suggested "putting pressure on oil companies" to help pay for the costs of the operation.[46]

On 21 May 1994, Saro-Wiwa was detained by federal forces while campaigning in Ogoniland and taken to Port Harcourt. Meanwhile, conservative elements of the movement were meeting elsewhere in Ogoniland. Members of the more radical youth movement set upon the small gathering of elders and chiefs, brutally killing four. Saro-Wiwa and eight other MOSOP leaders were arrested, charged with incitement to murder, and subsequently convicted in what was widely regarded as a sham of justice.

Shell was only one of a number of actors that were asked to seek clemency for Ken Saro-Wiwa. President Clinton's special envoy to Nigeria, Ambassador Donald T. McHenry, met with American companies, including Exxon and Mobil, to mobilize their support for clemency, but to no avail.

Widespread pleas for a stay of execution from the international community fell on deaf ears. Saro-Wiwa and his eight alleged co-conspirators were executed on 10 November 1996.

Outrage was nearly universal. Nigeria was expelled from the Commonwealth, while the EU instigated an embargo on arms and aid. Calls for tough economic sanctions, though, went unheeded. Britain was the largest exporter to Nigeria, enjoying a significant trade surplus based on machinery and machine tools. Furthermore, British companies including Guinness, Glaxo and Cadbury-Schweppes had non-oil investments of GBP 1.4 billion. With oil accounting for nearly 80 per cent of Nigeria's revenues, the oil sector was seen as the most effective way to apply sanctions. Shell, accounting for nearly 50 per cent of the Nigerian oil industry, seemed to have the ability to give teeth to an embargo.

However, the Nigerian operations had been strategically important to Shell, which lacked sufficient high-quality crude elsewhere to meet the requirements of its refineries and gasoline stations. Of the nearly one million barrels of oil the company had pumped daily, it took a quarter for its own use. The rest was given to Nigeria. Furthermore, according to Nick Antill, an analyst with the London securities firm Barclay, de Zoete, Wedd, Shell's Nigerian operations accounted for 10 per cent of Shell's worldwide production and exploration profits, or US $170–190 million a year. Despite calls for Shell to stop its massive GBP 2.6 billion Niger Liquid Natural Gas project, the project planning continued even though the International Finance Corporation (part of the World Bank group) declined to participate.

Withdrawing from Nigeria would not promote a shift to democracy, according to Mark Moody-Stewart, one of the four managing directors of Royal Dutch/Shell at the time. "All we can pull out are our 270 expatriate staff. The Nigerians can run the oil industry on their own and buy help on the market", in which case "the French would replace us in a flash".[47]

While the EU stopped short of banning Nigerian oil sales, it reaffirmed measures adopted in 1993, including suspension of military cooperation following the military coup, which brought General Abacha to power in 1993.

Nigeria remains a dangerous place for Shell to conduct its operations. Attacks, kidnappings and theft occur on a consistent basis as the Movement for the Emancipation of the Niger Delta continues its actions.[48] Spills continue to be frequent, but Shell is working with local governments, businesses and communities to develop online tools to track problems and assist in response procedures. Unfortunately, two spills in 2008 affected the rural settlement of Bodo and some 11,000 residents, who were dependent on farming and fishing in the community.[49] Shell has accepted responsibility but claims that the majority of spills are the result of outside foul play. It was estimated that in 2010, 98 per cent of the spills that Shell reported were the result of theft attempts or intentional attacks.[50]

Shell still has plans to continue operations in the Niger Delta; however, it divested its stake in several onshore assets in 2010 and 2011. With violence still prevalent in Nigeria, Shell is aiming to ease tensions and leave exploration to local companies. CEO Peter Voser has stated that "Nigeria is still a heartland for Shell, but we no longer depend on it for our growth aspirations."[51]

Although Shell never accepted responsibility for the death of Ken Saro-Wiwa, it offered to set up a US $15.5 million trust fund for the Ogoni people in 2009, 15 years after his death.[52] Although this positive gesture has eased some pains, the Ogoni people continue to suffer from – and fight against – the damage from oil spills they are still experiencing today.[53]

Shell's responses

Continuous stakeholder pressures as well as events such as the Brent Spar controversy and the Ken Saro-Wiwa affair drove Shell to respond by hiring new environmental scientists, developing new environmental policies and auditing the environmental performance of Shell's operations. Shell also launched innovative and environmentally friendly products (e.g., cleaner diesel) and technologies (e.g., capturing and using surplus sulphur).

By 1997, Shell set corporate standards for the environmental management systems for all its companies. Each company wrote its own policies based on the corporate standard.[54] Since 1998, Shell has published an annual Shell Sustainability Report, covering details from renewable energies to disputes with local communities. In the next ten years, Shell will continue to add guidance and policies. For example, in 2006, Shell launched the first Shell-wide Code of Conduct, and revised the guidance for new upstream projects to integrate environmental considerations into major decisions.[55]

However, Shell's environmental approach is still widely challenged, especially its operations in environmentally sensitive and complex areas. In the Arctic, Shell has been forced to halt exploratory drilling by a US court as the result of a court challenge from green groups and indigenous Alaskans who maintained that Shell's drilling would threaten western grey whales and polar bears;[56] Shell has also been criticized for its decision to build a production pipeline at Corrib, Ireland; and it has been continuously criticized over its pollution in Nigeria.[57] In the North Sea, Shell has been warned repeatedly by the British Health and Safety Executive about the poor state of its platforms.[58] In addition, after a spill in 2011, Shell was criticized for being slow to release information to the public. However, the company eventually apologized and released daily feeds on the progress of the spill.[59]

There seem to be two major challenges that Shell has to face internationally. First, Shell has to deal with accusations of using a double standard, "one that often provides cleaner facilities in areas around the world with predominantly Caucasian populations as compared to dirtier and more hazardous facilities located in places where people of color live".[60] Shell has responded as follows: "We apply the same Shell standards worldwide and all our assets in Nigeria are certified to ISO 14001 standard by external assessors."[61] Shell did admit that its operation in Nigeria had "a substantial backlog of asset integrity work to reduce spills and flaring",[62] but then quickly explained that the delay was due to "under-funding by partners over many years, operational problems and, more recently, the lack of safe access to facilities".[63] Shell also argued that it had invested over US $3 billion to reduce continuous flaring in Nigeria since 2000, and that Shell's flaring had been reduced by 30 per cent as of 2005.

An often-cited example suggesting Shell's double standard is the comparison between the South African Petroleum Refinery (SAPREF) in Durban, South Africa, and Shell's refinery in Denmark. Friends of the Earth maintains that SAPREF emits 19 tons of sulphur dioxide into the air every day, six times more than that released by the Danish refinery.[64] Shell replies that it has taken steps to improve its environmental performance at the South African refinery.

Activities from Friends of the Earth have pushed the British government to "reform company law so overseas communities can seek redress and compensation in the UK for human rights and environmental abuses carried out by British companies and their subsidiaries".[65]

Second, Shell has to deal with criticisms that its commitment to renewable energy projects has been limited. Interestingly, while Shell has estimated that by 2050, 20 per cent of energy will be derived from alternative sources only 1 per cent per year of spending is invested back into developing these alternative energy sources.[66] Jeroen van der Veer, Shell's former CEO, suggested "that the investment in renewable was small, saying it would be 'throwing money away' to invest in alternative energy projects that were uncommercial and people could not buy".[67] In 2009, Shell announced that it would no longer be investing in solar, wind and hydropower as it saw stronger potential in biofuels. This has raised criticism from environmentalists who claim that biofuels often have high emission levels. However, current CEO, Peter Voser agrees that alternative energy sources are not one of Shell's priorities and has indicated that in 2012, Shell is dedicated to discovering energy efficient technology.[68] With the potential for energy demand to triple by 2050, Voser believes that it will be more important for people to focus on becoming more energy efficient.[69] The company plans to invest in carbon capture and sequestration technologies to help reduce the amount of carbon dioxide that is released when burning fossil fuels.

In 2004, Shell merged Royal Dutch and Shell Transport and Trading into a single company called Royal Dutch Shell plc with one board, one chairman and one chief executive. The new structure should lead to better accountability for shareholders, but it has not been easy to shake off the criticisms of its environmental approach. Moreover, getting the necessary consistency in environmental strategy implementation across Shell's operations has not been easy, though Shell expects that more training and reinforcement will help.[70]

Shell is not alone in terms of having a less than favourable reputation in environmental performance, as most other large energy firms, including ExxonMobil, Chevron, Total and PetroChina, have similar, tainted reputations.[71] Even BP, which before the Deep Horizon oil spill in 2010, was often considered in the developed world as one of the cleaner players in the energy industry, does not have a clean reputation everywhere. As one example, as early as 1998, it was accused of water contamination, illegal deforestation and the dumping of untreated toxic waste in Colombia, according to an investigation by the Colombian government's independent ombudsman into BP's environmental record.[72]

Impacts of the Deep Horizon oil spill

On 20 April 2010, the Deep Horizon oil rig operated for BP suffered a severe explosion. The damage from the explosion and ensuing fire caused an acute leak, which released millions of gallons of crude oil into the Gulf of Mexico. It took almost three months and numerous attempts before BP was finally able to cap the leak and control the spill. The disaster caused severe environmental damage, which is still noticeable two years later. It is now considered the largest oil spill in history and has inexorably tarnished BP's reputation.[73] Numerous investigations were conducted to analyse the cause and handling of the spill by BP. One report stated that "[the] disaster was preventable if existing progressive guidelines and practices had been followed".[74] Public outcry was inevitable given the stature of BP and the severity of the damage.

The impact of the spill has brought much needed attention to oil companies and their environmental practices. Firms now face intense scrutiny from the public, which is pressuring governments to enforce stricter environmental controls. Shell has responded to the spill by signing the UN Global Compact LEAD, to signify its commitment to leadership in sustainable practices. In Nigeria, Shell's Chairman has described the impact as follows: "As soon as the BP thing happened, of course we had to go back to reassess our entire well-management processes, procedures and techniques."[75] In the Netherlands, Shell was required to go through hearings to discuss the impact the company had in Nigeria. The purpose of the hearings was to gain a better understanding of the situation in the Niger Delta, and to help implement potential courses of action. It is estimated that nine million barrels of oil have spilled in the Niger Delta from all oil exploration, which is more than what was released from the Deep Horizon spill in the Gulf of Mexico.[76]

A year after the disaster, Shell gained approval from the American government to be the first company to continue deepwater exploration. A statement released by the Bureau of Ocean Energy Management, Regulation and Enforcement argued: "Shell's submission has satisfied the heightened environmental standards that we are now applying and I am confident that other operators can satisfy the same standards."[77]

QUESTIONS

1. What has been Shell's traditional managerial style? How did Shell manage environmental issues across different countries?
2. Did regulation/lack of regulation drive environmental initiatives? Did Shell improve economic and environmental performance simultaneously in some cases? How did Shell achieve this?
3. Did Shell develop any FSAs in environmental management? Did it try to transfer any practices or technologies across borders?
4. Use the information in the case as the background for assessing the latest Shell Sustainability Report, available on the Web.
5. Should MNEs apply a globally consistent standard for environmental management or adapt to local regulations?
6. Could a proactive environmental strategy on the part of Shell have prevented the tragedy of Ken Saro-Wiwa?
7. How did Shell's administrative heritage contribute to the Brent Spar debacle?
8. How is the social licence to operate linked to the court of public opinion?
9. Could a proactive environmental strategy on the part of Shell UK have prevented the Brent Spar debacle?
10. How did Ken Saro-Wiwa and the Brent Spar contribute to the greening of Shell?
11. Can you provide an update on Shell's recent responses to environmental criticism and activism? For the most recent updates, please use materials available on the Web.

Notes

1. M. E. Porter and C. van der Linde, 'Green and competitive', *Harvard Business Review* 73 (1995), 120.
2. *Ibid.*, 128.
3. *Ibid.*, 122.
4. *Ibid.*, 133.
5. *Ibid.*, 125.
6. *Ibid.*
7. *Ibid.*, 127.
8. *Ibid.*, 124.
9. *Ibid.*, 130.
10. GE Ecomagination, Annual report 2010.
11. S. L. Hart and M. B. Milstein, 'Global sustainability and the creative destruction of industries', *Sloan Management Review* 41 (1999), 23–33.

12. *Ibid.*, 24.
13. *Ibid.*, 26.
14. *Ibid.*, 27.
15. *Ibid.*, 28.
16. *Ibid.*, 27.
17. *Ibid.*, 32.
18. Ans Kolk and Jonathan Pinkse, 'Business responses to climate change: identifying emergent strategies', *California Management Review* 47 (2005), 6–20.
19. *Ibid.*, 13.
20. *Ibid.*, 14.
21. *Ibid.*
22. *Ibid.*, 15.
23. Porter and van der Linde, 'Green and competitive', 127.
24. *Ibid.*, 128.
25. A. M. Rugman and A. Verbeke, 'Corporate strategies and environmental regulations: an organizing framework', *Strategic Management Journal* 19 (1998), 363–75.
26. *Ibid.*, 372.
27. Shell company information (2007), www.shell.com.
28. Anne Ferguson, 'Good to be green', *Management Today* (February 1989), 46–51.
29. Wright (1995), cited in Peter Thayer Robbins, *Greening the Corporation* (London: Earthscan Publication Ltd, 2001), 84.
30. 'Environmental stewardship at Shell', *Canadian Business Review* 18 (1991), 7–13.
31. *Ibid.*
32. *Ibid.*
33. Wright (1995), cited in Peter Thayer Robbins, *Greening the Corporation* (London: Earthscan Publication Ltd, 2001), 83.
34. 'Shell hit by $1.5bn Nigeria spill claim: senate action on pollution adds to damage from reserves scandal', *The Guardian* (26 August 2004), 26
35. Shell company information, www.shell.com/home/content/shellgasandpower-en/products_and_services/coal_gasification/coalgasification_1106_1655.html, accessed on 31 August 2007.
36. Shell company information, www.shell.com/static/globalsolutions-en/downloads/industries/gas_and_lng/brochures/coal_gasification_brochure.pdf, accessed on 31 August 2007.
37. www.shell.com/home/content/uk-en/about_shell/brentspardossier/brentsparstory/history_09101005.html, accessed on 29 September 2007.
38. Cacilie Rohwedder and Peter Gumbel, 'Shell bows to German Greens' muscle – reversal of plan to sink rig shows growing clout of environmentalists', *The Wall Street Journal* (21 June 1995), A15.
39. Nathaniel Nash, 'Oil companies face boycott over sinking of rig', *The New York Times* (17 June 1995), A3.
40. www.shell.com/home/content/nigeria/news_and_library/press_releases/2001/2001_2301_01031504.html, accessed 29 September 2007.
41. Paul Lewis, 'Blood and oil: after Nigeria represses, Shell defends its record', *The New York Times* (13 February 1996), A1.
42. *Ibid.*
43. Robert Corzine, 'Shell faces distrust in the Delta', *The Financial Times* (6 July 1996), 18.
44. Paul Lewis, 'Blood and oil', A1.
45. *Ibid.*
46. *Ibid.*

47. *Ibid.*
48. 'Will Shell pull out of Nigeria?', *African Business* 362 (March 2010), 42.
49. Guy Chazan and Jane Croft, 'Shell sued in UK over Nigeria spills', *Financial Times* (23 March 2012), 22.
50. Tom Burgis and William Wallis, 'Shell faces tougher scrutiny of Nigeria drilling', *Financial Times* (18 June 2008), 3.
51. 'Will Shell pull out of Nigeria?', *African Business* 362 (March 2010), 42.
52. Guy Chazan, 'World news: Shell faces query on Nigeria – Dutch parliament hearing expected to touch on corruption in oil-rich delta, as spills spur concerns', *Wall Street Journal (Eastern Edition)* (4 January 2011), A.10.
53. International: Spilling over; Shell in Nigeria', *The Economist* 319 (13 June 2009), 8635–51.
54. Malcolm Brown, 'Shell environmental policy', *Business Date* 5 (July 1997), 1–4.
55. Shell, 'Meeting the energy challenge: the Shell Sustainability Report 2006' (2007), 5, www.shell.com/static/investor-en/downloads/publications/2007/shell_sustainability_report_2006.pdf, accessed on 31 August 2007.
56. Terry Macalister, 'Wildlife claims stop Shell drilling in Arctic', *The Guardian* (24 July 2007), 21.
57. Terry Macalister, 'Shell faces ecological assault on three fronts at general meeting', *The Guardian* (15 May 2006), 26.
58. Terry Macalister, 'Shell safety record in North Sea takes a hammering', *The Guardian* (5 March 2007), 23.
59. 'Oil and trouble: North Sea spill', *The Economist (Online)* (17 August 2011).
60. Friends of the Earth *et al.*, 'Behind the shine: the other Shell report 2003' (2004), 8, www.foe.co.uk/resource/reports/behind_shine.pdf, accessed on 31 August 2007.
61. Shell, 'The Shell Sustainability Report 2006 – Nigeria' (2007), http://sustainabilityreport.shell.com/workinginchallenginglocations/nigeria.html, accessed on 28 August 2007.
62. *Ibid.*
63. *Ibid.*
64. Friends of the Earth *et al.*, 'The other Shell report 2003' (2004), 8.
65. David Cow, 'Flare-up over Shell's "double standards": FoE report questions oil group's green credentials', *The Guardian* (24 June 2004), 26.
66. Tim Webb, 'Shell dumps wind, solar and hydro power in favour of biofuels', *The Guardian* (17 March 2009).
67. Terry Macalister, 'Renewables: profits up a fifth but Shell emits more CO_2 than most countries', *The Guardian* (2 Feburary 2007), 28.
68. Ucilia Wang, 'Shell CEO: Energy efficiency, not clean power is key', *GigaOM* (22 March 2012).
69. *Ibid.*
70. Shell, 'Meeting the energy challenge: the Shell Sustainability Report 2006' (2007), 5, www.shell.com/static/investor-en/downloads/publications/2007/shell_sustainability_report_2006.pdf, accessed on 31 August 2007.
71. Mandy Turner, 'Environment: scramble for Africa', *The Guardian* (2 May 2007), 9.
72. Michael Sean Gillard, Melissa Jones, Andrew Rowell and John Vidal, 'BP in Colombia: a tale of death, pollution and deforestation', *The Guardian* (15 August 1998), 4.
73. Campbell Robertson and Clifford Krauss, 'Gulf spill is the largest of its kind', *The New York Times* (2 August 2010), A.14.

74. Deepwater Horizon Study Group, 'The final report on the investigation of the Macondo well blowout' (1 March 2011).

75. Tom Burgis and William Wallis, 'Shell faces tougher scrutiny of Nigeria drilling', *Financial Times* (18 June 2008), 3.

76. Guy Chazan, 'World news: Shell faces query on Nigeria – Dutch parliament hearing expected to touch on corruption in oil-rich delta, as spills spur concerns', *Wall Street Journal (Eastern Edition)* (4 January 2011), A.10.

77. 'First deepwater oil drilling plan approved since BP spill', *Environment News Service* (22 March 2011).

Conclusion: The true foundations of global corporate success

This book has tried to identify the limits of many insightful, but oversimplified, normative models of how to conduct international business strategy. As a general rule, those models do not spell out correctly the requirements for achieving international, let alone global, corporate success. The problem with most prevailing models is that they attempt to apply to all international business situations a set of prescriptions that are valid only for solving a narrow set of problems. Each MNE has a particular history, a unique resource base, a specific competitive position in its industry, and its own vision of what constitutes desirable international expansion. With international business strategy, one size does not fit all.

What all MNEs do have in common, however, is that they all face opportunities and challenges inviting serious analysis, building upon a small set of conceptual building blocks. These key building blocks are: *firm-specific advantages*, or *FSAs* (both *location-bound* and *non-location-bound*), *location advantages*, *value creation through resource recombination*, *complementary resources of other economic actors*, *bounded rationality* and *bounded reliability*. These building blocks permit us to recognize and understand most international business opportunities and challenges facing senior MNE managers. Importantly, this small set of building blocks also allows us to identify the limitations of normative messages and models that prescribe how to conduct international business strategy.

Drawing upon these conceptual building blocks, and their application throughout the book, I conclude by briefly touching upon *five themes*, each consistent with the observation that the world of international business strategy is far from flat, and unlikely to become much flatter in the foreseeable future. These *five themes* are the observed *dominance of regional over global strategies, the 'new forms' of international expansion, the tension between radical international innovation and internal coherence, the problem faced by MNEs to link effectively their back office activities with the front office* and finally, *the rising importance of recombination capabilities*. This last issue is of particular importance for the era to come, in which gross global production will be unlikely to grow at more than 2 to 3 per cent per year, and MNEs will no longer have the option to expand into large emerging markets with double-digit macro-economic growth, i.e., a growth level that represents 'requisite luxury' in times of international economic crises such as the one that started in 2008.

Dominance of regional over global strategies[1]

Much international business strategy is conducted regionally, rather than on national or global levels. Past research suggests there are only a handful of truly global firms (i.e., firms with a balanced distribution of sales and assets worldwide). One study, looking at the *Fortune Global 500* identified only nine truly 'global' firms (i.e., firms having at least 20 per cent of their sales in each of three key regions of the world, namely Asia, the European Union and North America) based on data from 1999. These nine firms were, in descending order of total sales: IBM, Sony, Philips, Nokia, Intel, Canon, Coca-Cola, Flextronics and LVMH. A few other MNEs were close – such as Bayer, Alstom, Sun Microsystems and 3M – but the vast majority of firms had a strong home region orientation, though many senior managers, as well as company directors and owners, wanted their firms to achieve a more balanced distribution of sales. A balanced geographical distribution of sales would signal worldwide customer acceptance of the firm's products and services.

A more recent study,[2] again looking at the *Fortune Global 500* companies, but using 2008 data, concluded that many MNEs had become more international, but not more global since 1999: Foreign sales rose from 33% to 41%, but intra-regional sales remained very high at 74.6% as compared with 76.4% in 1999. In spite of the rise of asset-seeking FDI, and the increased dispersion of MNE value chains across borders (with foreign assets increasing from 28.4% to 36% in 2008), there was little change in the share of intra-regional assets. These assets still represented 75.5% of total assets, as compared with 78.7% in 1999.

The observed dominance of the home region in sales and assets has important implications for strategy. When engaging in strategic decision making, senior management committees of geographically diversified firms focus first on the geographic area that represents more than 50 per cent of sales and assets. The '50%+' (in most cases actually '75%+') geographic area is usually the main source of the firm's cash flows, its knowledge generation capabilities and its employees, and it typically is the cash cow allowing expansion into other geographic areas. Any senior executive at the corporate level, accountable to a varied set of stakeholders, will devote prime attention to the business or set of businesses that represent the majority of sales and assets. This observation reflects simple managerial effectiveness. A lack of focus on the firm's largest markets would imply a governance problem, with top management committees paying insufficient attention to what really matters, and paying excessive attention to 'pet projects' in 'pet destinations', at least if such pet projects have only limited proven growth potential.

In the above context of largely home region-oriented sales (the precise definition of what constitutes the home region is obviously firm-specific), senior MNE managers then often adopt a regional, rather than a national, approach to international strategy, particularly if the firm wants to expand into another key region of the world. When Asian or North American firms contemplate expansion to Europe, the main concern in boardrooms and top management committees is increasingly 'How do we crack the EU market?' rather than 'How do we penetrate Germany?' When European firms venture outside of Europe, the key question is systematically 'How do we gain market share in Asia, and where should we set up a regional office (or regional offices) for this geographic area?' Only in the North American context is it correct that Asian and European MNEs still think primarily about the national US market rather than about the NAFTA region, because of the relative size of the US market, though even that prime focus on the United States has become much less attractive to many foreign firms after the 2008–2012 economic crisis.

The observation that most large MNEs have more than 50 per cent of their sales in their home region is likely to remain relevant in the future. Especially in the EU and North America, but increasingly in Asia, ***intra-regional distance*** is decreasing, driven by a reduction of trade and investment barriers, and other attempts towards institutional convergence. Thus, further sales and asset expansion within the home region will often continue to be easier than equivalent sales and asset growth elsewhere in the world.

The question arises whether the present internationalization patterns of emerging economy MNEs will change the above observations, especially as these firms often enter foreign markets to source knowledge that may be unavailable in their home region and can only be accessed through M&As or alliances in host regions. The correct answer may be that these MNEs from emerging economies will typically also have the bulk of their foreign sales and assets in their home region, especially if these firms have rather weak FSAs in managing an international, internal network.

The message for senior MNE managers, whether from highly developed nations or emerging economies, is simply not to overestimate the non-location-bound nature of their company's FSAs, and to be very selective in their international expansion programmes. These managers must determine the correct geographical reach of their extant bundles of FSAs, as well as the requirements for investing in additional strengths when entering foreign environments. Too much adaptation will lead to excessive costs. Too much attention to scale and scope will prevent access to location advantages in host environments. Too much focus on exploiting national differences will lead to vulnerable supply chains and severe coordination problems.

A continued strong focus on selling in a carefully selected geographic space, in accordance with the firm's limited resource base, may therefore be a wise path of action for the present majority of MNEs. This majority lacks the required levels of internationally transferable FSAs to reproduce globally whatever past success has been achieved in a restricted geographic area.

The 'new forms' of international expansion

The MNE's history, the environmental context within which it developed and the resulting firm-level routines all play a key role in determining what constitutes desirable strategy for the future: no one formula can guarantee success. The increasing diversity of the MNE population provides ample evidence of this. While many MNEs continue to originate in the most highly developed economies and base their competitiveness on traditional FSAs such as advanced technology, an increasing number now comes from emerging economies such as China, Russia and India. In many cases these firms are reaching out to exploit the strengths they have developed based on the location advantages of their home countries whereas in the past MNEs from Europe, Japan or North America might have reached inside these countries to access those same location advantages (low labour costs, abundant natural resources, large pools of highly skilled but inexpensive ICT specialists, etc.).

Chinese companies have reached out to undertake large-scale investments in politically volatile environments, so as to secure the supply of raw materials. Chinese MNEs are taking advantage of their governmental owners' ability to influence these foreign environments through aid and diplomacy, as well as their relative insulation from the type of protests that might deter Western firms.[3] Russian firms have begun developing international, strategic asset seeking links that will bring in much needed technology. These firms typically take advantage of their leaders'/owners' domestic political connections and resultant ability to navigate through domestic – and former Soviet Union-related – waters many non-Russian investors may fear to enter. Indian ICT entrepreneurs have cast off the role of passive recipients of outsourcing/offshoring contracts. Their firms have established operations in America's high-tech centres, thereby developing their own direct customer linkages to improve service and capture a larger slice of the economic value created in the supply chain, i.e., these firms are now moving up on the *smiling curve*. While ICT tools such as the Internet may have increased the scope for developing long-distance, arm's-length relationships, the international expansion of MNEs from emerging economies shows the continuing need for feet on the ground and face-to-face contact.

For many firms in emerging economies it is not proprietary R&D outcomes or brand names that count the most, but rather the personalities, skill sets and drive of their entrepreneurs, whether senior managers or owners. These individuals give emerging economy firms the ability to succeed abroad in direct competition with long-established MNEs from Europe, Japan and North America. Perhaps in time they will develop the more traditional types of advantages in the same way that Korean firms such as Samsung and LG, have emerged with brand names and technology that are now well known around the world.

Developed-economy MNEs will need to carefully identify and nurture their own FSAs, if they are to avoid being displaced by the newcomers now engaged in sustainable patterns of value creation ànd value capture. The new forms of outsourcing/offshoring, going far beyond conventional cost-reduction purposes, are one expression of novel resource recombination by established MNEs.[4] This book's framework is entirely compatible with these 'new', unconventional types of FDI and other international activity by both established firms and newcomers, even if such expansion patterns cannot be accommodated within the simplistic rules of thumb that have emerged from much existing prescriptive research. In fact, this book has argued implicitly that most prescriptive models of the MNE are too 'MNE centric', meaning that success abroad always results from new forms of 'resources bundling', or 'recombination'.[5] Analysis of what will likely constitute a pattern of successful international expansion must therefore always consider the MNE's extant stock of FSAs, as well as the generic location advantages of the host countries entered and the particular complementary resources required from other economic actors and non-market actors such as governments and NGOs.

The tension between radical innovation and internal coherence

Sustained international success will also require that senior MNE managers resolve the ongoing tension between the desire to take advantage of the vast array of opportunities offered in today's international marketplace, and the need to retain an appropriate level of control over the firm's geographically dispersed operations. Economic and political changes in the last two decades have raised hundreds of millions of people from subsistence and isolation to the point where their energy and creativity can begin to be harnessed for the advancement of material and social conditions around the world. On the one hand, there are good reasons for the firm to give its overseas operations the scope to engage creatively in unanticipated resource recombination to take advantage of these new opportunities. On the other hand, there are good reasons for the firm to craft and deploy routines to manage 'distance' and the 'liability of foreignness'. Striking this balance is a key challenge, and unfortunately senior managers cannot simply adhere to a single guideline given the diversity and rapidly shifting nature of individual parent–subsidiary relationships.

Final decisions on what to do and what not to do, what to internalize and what not, may need to be taken centrally, but subsidiary managers can and must be allowed to play a vital role in ensuring these decisions fully reflect locally available knowledge. This can best be accomplished through the promotion of **process** characteristics such as **respect** and **procedural justice** for subsidiary managers: these individuals should not be viewed primarily as a source of bounded reliability (or as an 'agency problem'), but rather as a critical resource for effective and efficient international business strategy development and execution. The fast-growing and highly profitable MNEs of the present and future will be those that are flexible enough to constantly reevaluate and adjust this delicate balance between the dual need for both entrepreneurial freedom and internal coherence. In recent work published elsewhere, I have argued that the MNE's innovation process performance (and, more fundamentally, its resource recombination capability) must be looked at *in its entirety*, meaning from the initial appearance of creative ideas to the profitable delivery of new products to customers.[6] Here, senior managers should be careful not to place too much faith in the 'periphery', neglecting the businesses that are now providing the cash flows needed for future expansion, and experimenting on a grand scale with new governance models. Most large MNEs work with a mix of product and geographic divisions in a multidivisional governance system, with individual divisions usually responsible for the bulk of resource recombination activities. There are solid reasons for this, namely the needs for:

- specialization in decision making by corporate headquarters and the divisions
- selectivity in inter-divisional interactions
- standardized, quantitative monitoring and incentive systems
- specific roles for corporate headquarters and the divisions in general innovation strategy
- careful and informed management of the tensions that may arise between incremental and breakthrough innovations.

The tension between the MNE's 'back office' activities and its 'front office' needs

The tension between the 'back office' and the 'front office' in large organizations such as MNEs has sometimes been naïvely described as resulting from the difference between what the firm can reasonably deliver in an economic environment where cost discipline is critical and what the customer would ideally like to experience without paying for the real cost of superior quality.

The reality is more complex. The front office in large MNEs consists of individuals supposed to understand – and cater to – customer needs in local environments. In contrast, the back office is populated by individuals supposed to support the front office by providing rigorous, routinized data analysis (e.g., regarding which products and markets are the most profitable versus the least profitable), as well as a variety of services that make the supply chain run smoothly.

Unfortunately, many large firms, and especially MNEs in the services sector, are now characterized by the *tyranny of the back office*. This concept implies that individuals and groups in the organization (including most people working at the corporate head office) have become so divorced from the customer and from customer needs, that they become a cancer, negatively affecting the front office. The tyranny of the back office means killing all superior quality delivery in the MNE, especially in foreign subsidiaries. This point is different from the discussion of the previous theme, where internal coherence and *entrepreneurial discipline* were advocated so as to avoid diversifying into undesirable product areas or geographic markets.

Here, the problem is the rise of dysfunctional routines, often supported by sophisticated ICT systems, which ultimately do not allow front office employees to deliver customer service in a fashion that would deviate from standard protocol but would at the same time optimize customer service quality. All readers of this book will have undoubtedly experienced this many times when using the services of an international airline or hotel chain, or engaging in international financial transactions. Individuals responsible for service delivery in foreign locations are forced to respect standard protocols, often at the expense of customer needs and without creating any real cost advantage or satisfying a legitimate quality require-ment. The customers affected cannot interact directly with the individuals in the organization at the source of the front office dysfunction. The ultimate impacts on a firm's reputation can be disastrous, as exemplified by the song written by a disgruntled United Airlines passenger. His song, 'United [Airlines] Breaks Guitars' has had more than twelve million YouTube viewings.[7]

A vicious cycle of bureaucratization results, whereby especially front office managers become demotivated to communicate to the head office and to the more broadly dispersed back office what is going wrong in interactions with customers, or how customer experience can be improved. In other words, bounded reliability at the MNE's back office has strong negative effects. These negative effects result from senior managers in the back office giving priority to: (a) expedient internal network monitoring; (b) outputs that can be easily codified and are particularly visible (such as results from cost-cutting programmes, quar-terly profit reports, or the evolution of the number of formal customer com-plaints); and (c) the pursuit of empire building goals and the benefits of a rich social life commensurate with that of a large-company leader. Such goals typically go hand-in-hand with a systemic, substantive neglect of the front office. Customer service quality is the first victim. Front office managers experiencing a lack of respect from the back office, and often confronted with ill-informed cost cutting routines and more centralization, become demotivated and transform into bureaucrats themselves, as if they had been 'body snatched' by their new back-office masters.

Interestingly, we observe here that bounded rationality in the back office ('let us focus only on information that really matters') resulting from 'distance' vis-à-vis the front office, leads the back office to lose its reliability in terms of delivering what the front office needs. In turn the front office becomes unreliable in the sense of not delivering the best service that could be delivered to customers at a particular level of costs.

How to escape from the tyranny of the back office? A two-pronged approach should be pursued. *First*, the CEO should be the voice of the consumer. In other words, the CEO should educate both the back office and the front office on what matters most in the organization as a precondition for continued shareholder value creation. This requires a lot of 'wandering around', both at home and internationally, and a diminished focus on looking at quantitative data in an executive suite filled with back office suits. Remember the famous words of Jack Nasser, the former Ford CEO, who started his career with Ford as a financial analyst in the Australian subsidiary? He testified before a US House Subcommittee and explained as follows the absence of action by Ford in the United States (in contrast to action in several developing countries), when faced with roll-overs of Explorer vehicles equipped with Firestone tyres: "We are a data driven company."[8] Or to put it in the words of Suresh Sethi (a manager from Modi, an Indian tyre equipment company): "Makers of autos and tires around the world were overly concerned about price and market share. Not enough thought had been given to safety . . . You buy a $30,000 vehicle . . . and what does the tire cost? The companies were trying to save $1 per tire because $1 per tire adds up to a lot. That is responsible for this."[9] It is certainly a pity for any company to focus on short-term profit outcomes at the expense of data related to customer service quality, since the latter will ultimately determine the prospects of long-run survival and financial sustainability.

Second, proper communication channels should be established between the back office and the front office. More is required than procedural justice when having a 'back office–front office' dialogue on a variety of routines shared across the MNE (whether in the accounting, financial, customer service, ICT, etc. . . . spheres). The back office employees must understand that their role is to support the front office subject to a number of constraints (in the realm of cost discipline and long-term strategy options). However, their role is not that of a mere road-block to effective front office functioning, with deviations from back-office-crafted routines made impossible or being punished indiscriminately. All large business organizations, and especially the world's largest MNEs, need a 'serving' back office rather than a 'self-serving' one. Fortunately, only MNEs with a properly aligned 'back office–front office' organization are likely to survive in the long run, in line with the last theme below.

The rising importance of recombination capabilities

Almost every significant challenge facing the world today, such as human over-population, shortages of natural resources and climate change, requires us to reconcile global necessities and pressures with action taken at the local or individual level. Local and individual actions, which often lead to imperfect outcomes, create the need for scapegoats. As visible and strong evidence of the growing international interdependence among countries, the large MNE unwittingly and often undeservedly plays this scapegoat role, and thus becomes the subject of unjustified criticism and fear.[10]

Yet MNEs may actually offer society an array of governance models for addressing difficult global–local trade-offs, and might also perform a direct and constructive role in the resolution of the underlying problems. Large, internationally successful MNEs represent the only governance mechanisms specifically designed both to facilitate resource recombination across product and geographic space simultaneously, and to reconcile international and local pressures and priorities, thereby increasing world economic welfare.[11] MNE governance models could therefore, subject to necessary qualification, serve as best practices for the future, public institutions of international and global governance that will become increasingly important, as pressure mounts from the type of problems described by the 'tragedy of the commons'.[12]

MNE managers often do play a direct role in improving, not only economic efficiency, but also intercultural understanding, social justice and environmental sustainability around the world. The principal reason they play this positive role is that when MNEs and their managers enter a foreign country, especially outside their home region, they are usually in a position of vulnerability, in spite of their non-location-bound FSAs. MNEs and their managers have five main types of vulnerability:

- to breakthrough, resource recombination efforts from existing or new international rivals
- to the problems posed by running dispersed internal affiliate networks
- to the actors providing complementary resources in a wide array of international cooperative business arrangements
- to the decisions of sovereign governments, and a multitude of other stakeholders, including host country customers and employees

- to the scrutiny of the international media and internationally operating pressure groups.

The persistent vulnerability and contestable position of even the world's largest MNEs and their senior managers paradoxically guarantee that these firms make and will continue making positive contributions to improving human conditions globally. Vulnerability engenders humility, and humility creates openness to new ideas and new approaches; such humility can, in short, strongly encourage the firm's resource recombination efforts. Vulnerability-driven resource recombination invariably leads to change inside the MNE. This change may be resisted by the corporate immune system, but the internal dynamic of the process is usually to identify and respect the values that people in host environments treasure most. The change process thus ensures that some core values from the host environment are preserved, and possibly even spread internationally. Here, accountability to all relevant stakeholders in any host environment, is much in line with the thinking of the late Elinor Ostrom, recipient of the 2009 Nobel prize in economics, who advocated a system of *polycentric care for the commons.*[13]

Thus senior MNE managers, especially those with extensive expatriate experience, function – perhaps unexpectedly – as agents of change in an imperfectly governed world. Often, they are willing to engage in a constructive dialogue with a multitude of stakeholders, including external pressure groups. Therefore, they can contribute immensely to the improvement of general, societal conditions while simultaneously pursuing their firms' interests. The possibility that MNEs can create a win-win situation for themselves and for the host nation should not be underestimated.

As the twenty-first century advances, the capability of resource recombination will become increasingly important. Brazil, China, India and Russia will develop to become mature markets with macro-economic growth rates similar to the ones now characterizing most of the developed world. In this environment of low macro-economic growth, MNEs can meet the capital markets' expectations of double-digit levels of revenue and earnings growth only by continuously recombining resources across product and geographic space. In other words, MNEs must move continuously to new, fast-growing businesses that are related to their extant resource base. At present, few MNEs in the world have mastered the General Electric-type ability to reinvent themselves as a matter of routine. In the past, General Electric might not always have brought good things to life,[14] but it certainly provides an exceptional example of a truly superior resource recombination capability. General Electric has developed routines – FSAs, in fact – for firm-level recombination and reinvention. By contrast, in most traditional MNEs, routines and recombination capabilities unfortunately operate to some extent as opposites, with the former being instrumental to efficient usage of existing resources and the latter conducive to effective transformation of these resources into new strengths.

The need for firm-level routines to reinvent the MNE organization at regular intervals is the great challenge facing tomorrow's generation of senior MNE managers: such reinvention routines imply continuous reflection on which existing activities to shed (or de-internalize) and which new activities to add (or internalize). Importantly, a strong resource recombination capability held by MNEs is also the key precondition for survival of the present market system: only if established firms, most of these being MNEs, can recombine resources effectively and efficiently can low macro-economic growth rates on a global scale be reconciled with high growth in revenues and earnings of individual firms, as expected by capital markets.

However, continuous resource recombination and the related innovation processes usually create losing parties (for example, the economic actors operating in the activities that are de-internalized and left behind by the MNE, as well as the groups dependent on such activities in specific locations). We are already witnessing today how senior MNE management is increasingly pressured by society to respect social justice objectives. One perspective that is gaining momentum across the planet is that employees should enjoy the same treatment as equity capital. Senior MNE managers consider it legitimate to shed economic activities in order to secure the firm's long-term survival, profitability and growth, thereby showing appropriate accountability towards holders of equity capital. Arguably, these managers should demonstrate the same accountability towards their employees, who – just like capital owners dedicate equity capital – have dedicated themselves to the firm for prolonged periods of time. Just as senior managers must avoid capital destruction, they must also avoid the destruction of the lives of the very individuals who have put forward their best efforts to serve the firm's goals. The most effective way to protect employees is usually to ensure their mobility – to foster their ability to move easily to other jobs in the economy. In practice, this implies continuous investment in training, retooling and new skills development.

I believe that an increasing number of MNE senior managers will prove to society at large, especially in host environments, that resource recombination can indeed be a benevolent process. MNE managers from around the world must now rise to this challenge. **Benevolent resource recombination** legitimates the claim that the MNE is both a superior governance mechanism to achieve efficiency, and an institution whose leadership can confidently be relied upon as having the heart and compassion needed to improve the human condition. Benevolent resource recombination is the key to both global corporate success and the further peaceful economic integration of nations.

Notes

1. See Alan M. Rugman and Alain Verbeke, 'A perspective on regional and global strategies of multinational enterprises', *Journal of International Business Studies* 35 (1) (2004), 3–18, as well as Alan M. Rugman and Alain Verbeke, 'Liabilities of regional foreignness and the use of firm-level versus country-level data: a response to Dunning *et al.*', *Journal of International Business Studies* 38 (1) no. 1 (2007), 200–5.

2. Alan M. Rugman, Chang Hoon Oh and Dominic S. K. Lim, 'The regional and global competitiveness of multinational firms', *Journal of the Academy of Marketing Science* 40 (2012), 218–35.

3. See, for example, Randall Morck, Bernard Yeung and Minyuan Zhao, 'Perspectives on China's outward foreign direct investment', *Journal of International Business Studies* 39 (2008), 337–50.

4. See A. Y. Lewin, S. Massini and C. Peeters, 'Why are firms offshoring innovation? The emerging global race for talent', *Journal of International Business Studies* 40 (2009), 901–25.

5. This same point was made explicitly in two brilliant papers, see Jean-François Hennart, 'Down with MNE centric theories! Market entry and expansion as the bundling of MNE and local assets', *Journal of International Business Studies* 40 (2009), 1432–54 and Shih-Fen Chen, 'A general TCE model of international business institutions: Market failure and reciprocity', *Journal of International Business Studies* 41 (2010), 935–59.

6. I have explored in more depth this challenge of reconciling the quest for new international opportunities with the requirement of internal coherence; see Alain Verbeke and Thomas Kenworthy, 'Multidivisional versus metanational governance of the multinational enterprise', *Journal of International Business Studies* 39 (2008), 940–56.

7. See www.forbes.com/sites/bruceupbin/2011/05/11/seven-signs-of-a-customer-focused-ceo/

8. See www.stern.nyu.edu/om/faculty/zemel/ford_firestone.pdf

9. *Ibid.*

10. Alan M. Rugman and Alain Verbeke, 'The world trade organization, multinational enterprise, and civil society', in Michele Fratianni, Paolo Svona and John J. Kirton (eds.), *Sustaining Global Growth and Development*, 5 (Aldershot, Hants., and Burlington, Vermont: Ashgate, 2003), 81–97.

11. See the insightful piece by Kasra Ferdows, 'Made in the world: the global spread of production', *Production and Operations Management* 6 (2) (1997), 102–9.

12. The *tragedy of the commons* concept was popularized in a highly influential piece by Garrett Hardin, 'The tragedy of the commons', *Science* 162 (3859) (13 December 1968), 1243–8.

13. Elinor Ostrom, 'Beyond markets and states: Polycentric governance of complex economic systems', *American Economic Review*, 100 (2010), 1–33.

14. See, for example, the extraordinary movie *Deadly Deception: General Electric, Nuclear Weapons, and Our Environment*, produced and directed by Debra Chasnoff, winner of the 1992 Academy Award for best short documentary, as well as the winner of the 1992 American Film & Video Festival Red Ribbon, the 1992 National Educational Film & Video Festival Silver Apple award, the 1991 CINE Golden Eagle and the 1991 Chicago International Film Festival Gold Hugo.

Appendix: Suggested additional readings

Below, I have selected one substantive additional reading for each chapter in the book. I based my selection on the criterion that each reading should convey a truly important message (or series of messages) complementing the chapter's storyline. The readings provide understanding critical to managerial practice in the international business strategy sphere. I have tried to be eclectic in my selection. In some cases the additional reading is more academically grounded; in other cases it is more immediately practice oriented. But the reading's main purpose is always the same: allowing the student of international business strategy to learn beyond the present book, thereby further sharpening the mind about the topic she or he is passionate about.

Chapter 1: Dunning, J. H. and Lundan, S. (2008). *Multinational Enterprises and the Global Economy* (2nd edition), Cheltenham: Edward Elgar

Dunning and Lundan's volume complements the present book in two important ways. First, it provides an overview of the environment of multinational enterprises, with much attention devoted to the worldwide picture of foreign direct investment and business–government interactions. Second, it addresses in great detail the wide variety of impacts MNEs have on society. Dunning and Lundan's volume is by far the most detailed account of multinational enterprise activity ever written.

Chapter 2: Teece, D. J. (2009). *Dynamic Capabilities & Strategic Management: Organizing for Innovation and Growth*, Oxford: Oxford University Press

Teece's book brilliantly addresses the problems of creating, transferring, exploiting and rejuvenating FSAs. He demonstrates that the proprietary ownership of assets that are difficult to transfer is insufficient to sustain firm-level competitive advantage over the long term. Teece focuses on the importance of entrepreneurial judgement, and on the linkages between firm-level routines and resource recombination processes as preconditions for achieving competitive advantage. He focuses especially on the capability transfer problems facing MNEs. He also shows how FSAs can ultimately affect location advantages and the wealth of nations.

Chapter 3: Sassen, S. (2001). *The Global City: New York, London, Tokyo*, Princeton: Princeton University Press

Sassen explores the linkages between the expansion of multinational activity and the growth of cities such as New York, London and Tokyo. One of the key points demonstrated is that large, internationally diversified firms de-internalize many activities formerly conducted by headquarters to a variety of specialized companies (e.g. accounting, legal, public relations, etc.), which benefit from agglomeration economies, and therefore concentrate in large economic centres. Paradoxically, the de-internalization of activities that benefit from agglomeration economies makes the activities remaining in large MNEs more footloose, i.e., more mobile across geographic space. When the specialized services firms operating out of large cities expand internationally themselves, they usually locate in other centres where agglomeration benefits can be earned. This leads to complex economic linkages among some of the world's leading cities. The formation of international networks by the world's leading business cities has several negative spillover effects: reduced connections between the evolution of the large city and that of its hinterland; high inequality between those working in the specialized, knowledge-intensive sectors and those that do not; transformation of the economic activities that are not part of the specialized services, and cannot compete for resources with those specialized services.

Chapter 4: Ghemawat, P. (2011). *World 3.0: Global Prosperity and How to Achieve It*, Boston, Massachusetts: Harvard Business Review Press

Ghemawat's volume synthesizes much of his prior work on international strategy and its linkages with the firm's international environment that has been published in the form of cases, academic articles and practice-oriented pieces. He focuses on the various forms of distance (cultural, administrative, geographic, institutional) and the ways to overcome these. This is a simple, well-written introduction to the challenges of semi-globalization faced by senior MNE management and public policy makers.

Chapter 5: Forsgren, M. (2008). *Theories of the Multinational Firm: A Multidimensional Creature in the Global Economy*, Cheltenham, UK: Edward Elgar

Forsgren's book provides a useful synthesis of six strands of thinking on the MNE, which he calls the 'dominating', 'coordinating', 'knowing', 'designing', 'networking' and 'politicizing' views of the firm. Importantly for MNE managers, Forsgren's analysis shows how many scholars and observers may develop completely diverging views on the MNE in terms of what constitutes the firm's key capabilities, its organizational features, the role of the head office, the role of the environment and the firm's expected spill-over effects.

Chapter 6: Murmann, J. P. (2003). *Knowledge and Competitive Advantage: The Coevolution of Firms, Technology, and National Institutions*, Cambridge: Cambridge University Press

Murmann provides a historical account of the evolution of the synthetic dye industry in France, Great Britain, Germany and the United States. Murmann carefully uncovers why some German firms ended up as the dominant players in the industry. Several factors, including a favourable patent system, a special educational system and close linkages with public knowledge institutions in organic chemistry, led to these German firms' international success. It was a mix of managerial adaptation and environmental selection that led to successful innovation and international growth. The absence of a similar co-evolution among firms, technology and national institutions in the other countries explains their lesser innovative and economic performance.

Chapter 7: Saxenian, A. L. (2006). *The New Argonauts: Regional Advantage in a Global Economy*, Cambridge, Massachusetts: Harvard University Press

Saxenian describes how foreign-born individuals, educated and trained in the United States, move back to their country of origin and engage in entrepreneurial activity, thereby setting up new production in these countries, improving these countries' location advantages and acting as a bridge with economic activity in the United States. Extensive analysis of case studies from Israel, Taiwan, China and India demonstrates how this new breed of entrepreneurs engages in cross-fertilization between Silicon Valley and new technology development and exploitation centres located in what was until recently viewed as the periphery.

Chapter 8: Rugman, A. M. and Li, J. (eds.) (2005). *Real Options and International Investment (International Library of Critical Writings in Economics)*, Cheltenham: Edward Elgar

Rugman and Li have put together a comprehensive collection of the best published papers addressing the use of real options in international investment analysis. Real options reflect the possibility to vary elements such as location, size, timing, governance and usage of a project after the initial investment phase is over. In other words, risk is reduced because the firm can adjust to new information (e.g., in the technology or marketing sphere) as it becomes available. Real options have major implications for international investment decisions, including the timing of international investment, the choice of entry mode, the design of the MNE's international network, etc.

Chapter 9: Quelch, J. A. and Jocz, K. E. (2012). *Global Brands: All Business is Local, Why Place Matters More Than Ever in the Global Virtual World*, New York: Penguin Books

Quelch and Jocz's book convincingly demonstrates that MNEs must carefully tailor their marketing management to locational specificities, i.e., their message is the opposite of Levitt's views on the need for global marketing. Such specificities have various dimensions: psychological, physical, virtual and geographic. The point is that locational elements should profoundly affect MNE branding efforts and general marketing strategy, at least if international marketing management is to be successful.

Chapter 10: Dowling, P. J., Festing M. and Engle A. D. (2013). *International Human Resource Management: Managing People in a Multinational Context* (6th edition), Singapore: Cengage

This is a simple but comprehensive textbook on the various dimensions of international human resource management, including *inter alia*, chapters on staffing, recruiting and selection for international assignments, international training and development, international compensation, performance management, the host country perspective on HRM, and industrial relations in an international context.

Chapter 11: Welch, L. S., Benito, G. R. G. and Petersen P. (eds.) (2007). *Foreign Operation Methods: Theory, Analysis, Strategy*, Cheltenham, UK: Edward Elgar

This book provides an in-depth analysis of MNE entry mode choices, namely exporting (including the role of distributors), international subcontracting, franchising, licensing, management contracts, large project operations, alliances and FDI, with a focus on mixed mode approaches and mode switching in order to be successful in international markets. According to the authors, each individual mode should be assessed in terms of parameters such as the risk incurred, the firm's ability to monitor the resulting operations, the expected revenues/profits, etc. By choosing a particular mode package, MNE management can eliminate the deficiencies of the individual modes and establish a highly effective foreign market penetration regime.

Chapter 12: Contractor, F. J. and Lorange, P. (eds.) (2002). *Cooperative Strategies and Alliances in International Business*, Oxford: Elsevier Science

This is a comprehensive, scholarly collection on alliances in international business, mostly written by leading scholars in the field. It has sections, *inter alia*, on alliance governance and performance, learning, cooperative knowledge creation, network building, process issues, etc. In short, it covers just about any type of challenge and opportunity that can arise when developing international cooperative strategies.

Chapter 13: Rosenbloom, A. H. (ed.) (2002). *Due Diligence for Global Deal Making: The Definitive Guide to Cross-Border Mergers and Acquisitions, Joint Ventures, Financings, and Strategic Alliances*, New York: Bloomberg Press

This is a useful, hands-on collection of papers for senior MNE managers. It attempts to prepare these individuals for complex international transactions. The book does not only address the strategic and operational problems that need to be anticipated properly, but it also covers issues in the realm of finance and accounting, legal and taxation issues, organizational issues and intellectual property related challenges. The book's main point is that many problems surfacing in international expansion programmes involving other partners may haunt the firm for long periods of time, but could probably have been avoided if due diligence had been applied before a deal was struck.

Chapter 14: Prahalad, C. K. (2010). *The Fortune at the Bottom of the Pyramid: Eradicating Poverty Through Profits* (revised and updated 5th anniversary edition), Upper Saddle River, New Jersey: Wharton School Publishing

This is the best book written on how MNEs can reinvent themselves by serving the several billion poor people (mainly) in emerging economies, i.e., the so-called Bottom of the Pyramid, or BOP. These individuals need to be viewed not as poor people but as potential entrepreneurs and valued customers. By creating new markets, MNEs can alleviate poverty and social injustice. The great contribution of this book, in spite of its somewhat exaggerated enthusiasm, is the view that capitalism and economic development are not necessarily mutually exclusive, but on the contrary can reinforce each other, thereby creating a win-win situation for all actors involved. Prahalad also describes the managerial and organizational challenges firms must overcome in order to make BOP strategies successful.

Chapter 15: Van Agtmael, A. (2007). *The Emerging Markets Century.* New York: Free Press

In this informative, albeit somewhat overly optimistic book on the future of emerging markets and their home-grown companies, Van Agtmael, discusses 25 MNEs from emerging economies. The author describes these firms as 'world leading' or on their way to earn such status. Readers learn about these firms' historical trajectories, strategic objectives and main sources of competitive advantage. Suggestions are made to managers of developed economy MNEs on ways to counter the rise of these new giants such as Lenovo, Infosys, Tata, Haier, Samsung, Embraer, Petrobras, Cemex, Tenaris and Concha Y Toro.

Chapter 16a: Hart, S. L. (2010). *Capitalism at the Crossroads: The Unlimited Business Opportunities in Solving the World's Most Difficult Problems* (3rd edition), Upper Saddle River, New Jersey: Wharton School Publishing

Hart is one of the world's most visionary management scholars (in a non-superficial-guru sense). This book discusses how capitalism in general and individual firms (especially large multinational enterprises) in particular can support a quantum leap towards a more sustainable economic system. Here, firms grow profitably, but at the same time contribute to alleviating poverty and protecting the environment. Hart's view is that large firms are well positioned to steer the planet towards more sustainability, given the observed lack of effective global, public governance, the divisiveness of religious fundamentalism and the limited resources and organizational capabilities of civil society.

Chapter 16b: Stern, N. (2007). *The Economics of Climate Change*, Cambridge: Cambridge University Press, and Arrow, K. J. (2007). 'Global climate change: a challenge to policy', *The Economists' Voice* 4:3, Article 2

The report on global climate change by Sir Nicholas Stern demonstrates unequivocally that carbon emissions do increase temperatures globally, and will continue to do so in the foreseeable future. Climate change will have large-scale detrimental effects on human society, including the possibility of a significant drop in wealth per capita worldwide. It could cost 1 per cent of the gross world product to stabilize emissions during the next twenty years and to make those emissions drop afterwards. Major economic and policy changes are required, most notably cleaner energy and transport technology, reductions in consumer demand for products that are heavy in pollution, a global market for carbon pricing and an emissions trading system that would have a geographic scope far beyond the European Union and would be linked to stringent emission reduction targets. In a short paper discussing the Stern report, Nobel Prize winner Arrow credibly argues that he was personally made aware of human-activity-induced climate change during his training as a weather officer in 1942 at New York University. There was no controversy about this scientific fact more than 65 years before writing his 2007 article. The Stern report and Arrow's paper are useful reading for senior managers whose firms are directly affected by climate change and the regulation meant to mitigate it, or by the possibility of business opportunities arising from climate change challenges.

Index